Criminal Justice in Hong Kong

How were Hong Kong's criminal justice institutions and practices formed? What has been its experience of law and order? How has Hong Kong's status as between 'East' and 'West' affected its social, political and legal institutions?

Hong Kong in the twenty-first century is known as a world city, a global financial centre and, for some, the epitome of free market capitalism. Despite its phenomenal economic success and rapid 'modernisation' it has nevertheless been associated with social stability, political tranquillity and one of the lowest crime rates in the world. A clean, safe, modern metropolis, it defies theories of the relationship between crime and 'development'. A liberal capitalist society, it also defied the supposed trajectory of modernity by reverting, in 1997, to Chinese Communist sovereignty.

According to the classic narrative of colonialism, Hong Kong – city of crime, vice, corruption, drugs and lawlessness – was made safe and successful by British rule of law and criminal justice. Drawing on original documents as well as academic commentary, this book attempts to deconstruct this story. It challenges the orientalist and orthodox versions of Hong Kong's past, and seeks to place crime and criminal justice in their wider socio-political context. It argues that, in both the colonial and post-colonial periods, it is politics, rather than crime rates, that have been the main driver of criminal justice.

This careful examination of the criminal justice system in Hong Kong suggests that any understanding of the current system requires dialogue with, and an understanding of, rich and complex narratives of history. It contains a wealth of archival material, statistical data on crime and criminal justice, as well as an analysis of how perceptions of the 'crime problem' have altered over time.

Carol Jones is Professor of Law at the University of Wolverhampton. She previously worked in Hong Kong, is currently engaged in an empirical socio-legal study of crime and justice in China, and remains a Visiting Fellow of the Centre for Asian Studies, University of Hong Kong.

Jon Vagg previously taught at the University of Hong Kong. He has written widely on crime and criminal justice in Hong Kong, as well as crime in the UK, Europe and the Asian region.

Criminal Justice in Hong Kong

Carol Jones
with
Jon Vagg

Routledge
Taylor & Francis Group
LONDON AND NEW YORK

First published 2007
by Routledge-Cavendish

Published 2016 by Routledge

2 Park Square, Milton Park, Abingdon, Oxon OX14 4RN
711 Third Avenue, New York, NY 10017

Routledge is an imprint of the Taylor & Francis Group, an informa business

Typeset in Times by
RefineCatch Limited, Bungay, Suffolk

British Library Cataloguing in Publication Data
A catalogue record for this book is available from the British Library

Library of Congress Cataloging-in-Publication Data
Jones, Carol A.G.
Criminal Justice in Hong Kong/Carol Jones and Jon Vagg.
p. cm.
Simultaneously published in the USA and Canada.
Includes bibliographical references.
ISBN 978–1–84568–038–1 (pbk.: alk. paper) 1. Criminal justice, Administration – of – China – Hong Kong – History – Sources. 2. Juvenile – delinquency – China – Hong Kong – History – Sources.
I Vagg, Jon. II. Title.
KNQ9392.4.J66 2008
364.95125 – dc22 2007015693

ISBN10: 1–84568–038–3 (pbk)
ISBN13: 978–1–84568–038–1 (pbk)

For mater

Contents

Acknowledgements

A number of people have contributed to the production of this book.

I should particularly like to thank Sonny Leong and Madeleine Langford at Routledge-Cavendish, for their faith in this project and their assistance in bringing it to fruition. Jon Vagg performed miracles with the many statistical tables, rendering order out of my chaos, and often doing so under great pressure. His painstaking help with organising and editing the text considerably improved the final product. Austin Kerrigan generously assisted with the colonial and police archives.

In Hong Kong, the Centre of Asian Studies, the University of Hong Kong provided me with an institutional base, whilst Bernard Hui and staff at the Hong Kong Public Records Office made the task of researching the colonial archives a (relatively) painless experience.

My work in Hong Kong was eased by the friendship and help of many people, but particular thanks must go to Linda Chan, Samson Chan, Pinky Choy, Jill Cotterrell, Yash Ghai, Toby and Josephine Ho, Gloria Kwok, Bill and Ina Kyle, Laurie Lau, Alice Lee, Francis Lee, Mike McConville, Paul and Esther Morris, Tom Stanley, Christopher Wong and Eddie Wong.

In the UK friends, family and colleagues provided sustenance and support one of kind or another. Special thanks are owed to Kate and Mike Bradley, Rachel Cryer, Claire Lewis, Helen Power, Richard Owen, Becky and Sam Radford, Carl and Emma Steventon and Michael Stuckey.

Finally, I owe a huge debt to those students of criminal justice and public order in Hong Kong, whose questions, observations and curiosity first prompted the writing of this book.

Table of Ordinances

Chapter 1

Introduction

Crime and the institutions of criminal justice are interesting not simply for their own sake, but for what they tell us about society at any given time, how it defines and responds to 'deviant' conduct, and what social, economic, political and cultural factors shape these definitions and responses. This book looks not only at how crime is related to social change in colonial and post-colonial Hong Kong, but also at the forces that have shaped the formation of its criminal justice institutions and practices over time.

Most of the literature on criminal justice is written against a background of broadly Western-style state structures in which governments develop policies and pass laws designed to allow those policies to be implemented, but at the same time broadly accept basic legal principles of human rights and the rule of law. Matters in Hong Kong have been rather differently structured. The kinds of assumptions that lie behind many of the ways we try to understand criminal justice simply do not hold up in discussions of crime and criminal justice in colonial and post-colonial Hong Kong.[1] Consequently, the kinds of theoretical models used in mainstream criminological literature to characterise criminal justice systems cannot be uncritically applied to the territory. The history of colonialism and imperialism also mean that its experience of crime and criminal justice is not simply a replay of the 'West'.

The official record

The story told here of crime and criminal justice in Hong Kong draws on the official record, the internal correspondence of colonial officials, as well as other articles, documents and sources.[2] They include the official account of crime, recorded in the crime statistics. Though in recent years criminologists have recovered them as useful tools of crime-trend analysis,[3] official crime statistics are fraught with well-established problems. But their gaps and silences are as significant as the activities they record, revealing much about official attitudes of the time and indicating the ways in which discretion in official decision-making operates.[4] Official statistics and internally produced documents tell us much about the assumptions underpinning official thinking in any given period. They are useful sources of information about the stories governments told about themselves, about the Chinese they colonised, and the world they inhabited.[5]

Criminal justice institutions are partly shaped by how societies see themselves.[6] The official documents and archives of colonialism are places where historians can examine the ways in which European communities 'produced themselves through ideas of colonialism and colonial ideologies including race, class and gender' (Coleborne 2005: 93). Colonial archives reflect and reproduce colonial ways of seeing and thinking, producing colonial populations and identities. They were (and are) themselves sites of contest, where historians 'make sense' of how the British exercised their authority (ibid.).[7] The records of crime and criminal justice are sites of knowledge production about crime and colonised peoples, a 'monument to particular configurations of power' (Ritchie and Hermanus 2004).[8] What official accounts tell us cannot be counted as 'objective' or 'true' or the complete story, but it does help us understand what drove the past so that we might, as Coleborne puts it, question the accepted versions of that past (Coleborne 2005: 94).

In Hong Kong's case, orthodox versions of its history present this as a story of a society marked by low crime, ever-increasing integration, orderliness and stability. Writing of England, what Emsley calls the traditional view of police, law and penal reform characterises them as progressive, driven by 'far-sighted reformers' seeking to control crime and disorder, motivated by humanitarianism and rationality towards modern forms.[9] This (the Whig interpretation of history) suggests that:

> With the advance of rationality, humanitarian sentiment and social scientific research, modern society would leave in the past penal brutalities and excesses . . . and move steadily down a long, unending path of penal reform, culminating . . . in the post-war emphasis on the scientific treatment and rehabilitation of criminals. In this way, the past and the present seemed to mutually confirm the inexorable course of history towards a planned, rational and humane penal system (Pratt 2005: 27).

Yet the way in which Hong Kong's criminal justice institutions were formed, changed and developed was never a matter of linear evolution in the direction of progressive civilization. An alternative view, championed by Foucault, is that penality in modern society is more 'regulated and finely tuned', 'more secretive, extensive and systematic', a strategy 'designed to control entire populations' (Pratt 2005: 32).

Though it is the traditional view that characterises the official story of crime and criminal justice in Hong Kong, it would be an error to mistake rhetoric for reality. In practice, at any given time numerous local and international factors have shaped the direction and tenor of criminal justice. Many of these – such an international relations and geopolitics – had nothing directly to do with crime. Even within the Colonial Office itself, visions of colonialism and penality were inconsistent. Homogeneity of outlook was rarely achieved, partly because conflicts with the Foreign Office subordinated Hong Kong issues to wider foreign policy concerns, and partly because different British administrations had different ideas about how the colonies should be governed. Dissident fractions of the Hong Kong elite were also sometimes able to mobilise to mitigate penal policies that offended their sensibilities, or undercut the mission of colonialism. As we shall see, for the colonial government – and indeed for its post-colonial successor – criminal justice was always a matter of governance more broadly conceived and, equally important, the focus of competing views of governance.

Hong Kong's past

A British colony since the 1840s, Hong Kong was, for many years, regarded as a rather quiet *entrepot* on the South China Sea, less profitable than many of Britain's other colonies but also less problematic. After the Second World War, it was even mooted that the territory be handed back to China, in line with Britain's general policy of decolonisation. But with the Communist victory in the Chinese Civil War in 1949, the colony acquired a new value, as part of the 'Bamboo Curtain', the West's defence against communism in the Far East. In the 1960s, it assumed a new identity as the 'miracle economy', whose cheap manufactured plastic goods and textiles ruled world markets. In the 1980s, it changed again to become an international financial centre and, in the 1990s, a 'world city'. Hong Kong was also a colony that reversed orthodox understandings of colonialism, not least by overtaking the 'motherland' in terms of economic prosperity. For advocates of minimal government and the free market, Hong Kong was also the exemplar; it remains hailed as the classic expression of *laissez-faire* economics. In 1997, it was again reincarnated as an astounding political experiment, the first liberal capitalist society to be handed back to an authoritarian communist state, throwing the supposed trajectory of modernity into total confusion.

The widely accepted orthodox view of Hong Kong's past is that all this sprang from a 'barren rock', ceded to the British in 1841.[10] It is a view that Chan and other historians rightly dispute, but it has powerfully shaped public perceptions of the territory's development. The dominant narrative is of a 'barren rock' transformed into a sparkling diamond by dint of British institutions and Chinese industry. In general terms, the key institutions and principles of English law were introduced and applied, but the introduction of the rule of law probably owed as much to the *realpolitik* of colonial rule as the 'civilising mission' – experience elsewhere had taught the Colonial Office that the best means of establishing the *pax britannica* was by attaching the native population to colonial rule through rule of law and associated institutions.[11] Its extension to the colonies supposedly made 'all of the Crown's subjects, whether coloniser or colonised . . . equally amenable to its force and protection' but, as we shall see, in Hong Kong as elsewhere:

> Certain sections of the population . . . were deemed to fall outside its full protection . . . the rule of law represent[ed] the interests of a demographically narrow group of people posited universally [it was] massively attenuated when viewed in relation to colonised populations . . . [it] appealed rhetorically to impartial justice and equality [but] its material interests were comprehensively colonial (Evans 2005: 58).[12]

As other histories of colonialism have shown, the transition to the hegemony of colonial state law was generally 'a slow and often incomplete process in the many and varied contexts of the British Empire'.[13] In theory, the British government retained overall control but, typically, it allowed its colonial governors considerable latitude in addressing local problems.[14] It was, therefore, not unusual for the substance of the law and the organisation of criminal justice in British colonies to differ from arrangements in Britain, and there were many instances in which law and criminal justice in Hong Kong diverged from that in England and Wales.

In common with many other colonies, the initial role of government was to establish law and order so that trade could flourish. From the earliest days, however, there were those amongst Hong Kong's elite who regarded it as more than a trading outpost of Empire, seeing it as the fulcrum of civilisation in the East and themselves as settlers with a responsibility to bring to the East the fruits of this civilisation. The story they wished to tell about themselves (and about criminal justice) was, as we shall see, quite often at odds with that told by the government and other sections of the ruling elite.

Hong Kong criminology

Orthodox accounts of Hong Kong's past are matched by the orthodoxy of Hong Kong criminology. Chan argues that globalisation and 'reflexive modernisation' have facilitated a 'free trade' in criminological knowledge, 'accelerated the deterritorialisation of culture and politics' and increased challenges to criminology as a discipline (Chan 2005: 337).[15] As yet, there has been little evidence of this in Hong Kong. Hong Kong criminology has a decidedly administrative character. It has a close association with social and public policy, pursuing solutions to officially defined problems, such as juvenile delinquency. For administrative criminologists, explanations and theories of crime are always secondary to the 'practical goal of prevention' (Jefferson 2005: 147).[16] Like Singapore, Hong Kong academics have yet to produce any particularly distinctive local theory, and the framework they use 'does not differ in any marked degree from those in Western democracies'

(Ganapathy 2005: 167).[17] This is despite the fact that Hong Kong's experience of crime has never simply been a 'replay' of the West.

The stories Hong Kong criminologists tell of crime and criminal justice have, therefore, proved a rather weak corrective to those told by the state itself. It has tended to shy away from critical theory and has, instead, acquired a marked preference for American social control theories of crime.[18] The result has been a conservative approach to deviance that emphasises the family as the key source of moral values, the key aid to conformity and social discipline (ibid). As in Singapore, this tends to:

> . . . arrest the development of any alternative discourse . . . the state has been very successful in ideologically propagating a criminology that seeks to individualise the problem of criminality . . . a consequence of this is the neutralisation of alternative explanations of crime that seek to focus on macro-level social and economic institutions. Whatever potential the explanatory power of social control theory has, the reduction of criminological theory in this way has forced a general abdication of intellectual responsibility to look at equally important structural factors such as those of class, race and gender . . . (Ganapathy 2005: 171).

The end result has been what Barton describes as a somewhat unimaginative and individualised discourse that has displaced criminal actors from their broader structural, economic and political contexts (Barton et al. 2007: 3). Crime is conceived as a problem to be solved so that social stability can be maintained, and Hong Kong's economic prosperity preserved.

This correctionalist emphasis focuses study on ways in which deviant individuals can be 're-adjusted' to re-join the ranks of consensual and contented society.[19] As Young says, positivism is 'the handmaiden of social engineering' (Young 2005: 71). Administrative criminology assumes that the social order 'is underscored by consensus, that its policing is unproblematic and the legal definition of crime uncontested' (Carrington and Hogg 2002: 3), whilst the subject presumed by administrative criminology is 'purely rational/voluntaristic' (ibid.). This view chimes well with the dominant discourse of *laissez-faire* capitalism in Hong Kong, with its emphasis on minimal state intervention in social and economic affairs, hard work, rational choice, self-help and the 'just deserts' theory of social inequality.[20] It also dovetails with the government's monopoly on what counts as consensus. Hong Kong is not and never has been a democracy. It has, instead, a vast network of consultative channels, established in the 1970s. The government:

> . . . is able to maintain its position by interpreting what it says is the consensus. This has been rationalised in the past as the outcome of the process of consultation and consent. In practice, government has rarely been required to take action contrary to the direction in which it wishes

> to move. The interpretation of consensus is an enormously important aid to legitimising its decisions . . . The inference might be drawn that government thought it [had] a monopoly on the judgement of public opinion. It has certainly often acted on that premise. In times of stability, when there has been consensus or at least acquiescence, this has not caused major problems. At a time of division and uncertainty, however, a claim to interpret a consensus, which is not a consensus, may simply lead to cynicism about the way in which decisions are made (Scott 1989: 329).

The absence of a loyal opposition in the territory's legislative assembly (LEGCO) has also made it possible for government to claim a monopoly on interpreting consensus on crime issues. In addition, and for a variety of reasons, the Hong Kong academy has seldom been in a position to challenge the government's account. Instead, it has tended to go along with the widely accepted modernisation theory of crime and development, which sees crime as a regrettable but inevitable side effect of Hong Kong's economic success. Modernisation theory holds that societies follow an evolutionary path from tradition to modernity. Crime and social disturbances are seen as the side effects of economic growth, urbanisation and industrialisation, to be contained and controlled through measures reinforcing social and cultural consensus (Harrison 1983: 25). On this view, as societies 'modernise' not only do they become more prosperous but their old institutions of social control break down; new conflicts and social problems occur, and they experience rises in crime. Hong Kong fascinates comparative criminologists because, in common with the other 'little dragons' (Taiwan, South Korea, Singapore) it is a 'modern' capitalist society which has not replayed this experience of crime and development.[21] Its recorded crime rate is significantly lower than much of Europe, the USA, Australasia, other newly developed countries, or 'developing' countries.

Successive Hong Kong governments have regarded the territory's low crime rate and social stability as proof that their explanations for, and solutions to, crime are broadly correct. One consequence of this has been a lack of interest in the social, economic and political contexts that produce and reproduce both crime and the state's response to crime (see Barton et al. 2007: 4).[22] A general antipathy towards politically sensitive issues has also tended to depress social structural interpretations of crime. Hong Kong's economic success since the 1960s has, moreover, also generated a rather unfortunate tendency to value knowledge principally for utilitarian purposes, reinforcing the currency of administrative criminology and insulating the study of crime from more critical disciplines, such as politics, sociology, anthropology and history. One result has been a lack of the kind of inter-disciplinary studies of crime and criminal justice found elsewhere. It is difficult, however, to see how one can understand the story of crime and criminal justice in Hong Kong without an appreciation of the periodic political upheavals in China, Hong Kong's own geopolitical position during the Cold War, the tremors which Indian and Malaysian Independence provoked throughout the British Empire, the problems of legitimacy in a post-colonial world, the events of 4 June 1989 or Hong Kong's retrocession to China in 1997.

In government circles, criminal justice has long been conceived of in terms of such wider socio-political drivers, and particularly regime legitimacy. The state's response to crime was seldom simply seen in narrow terms, such as solving particular crime problems or responding to rising crime rates. Yet in the academy, theories which hold that definitions of crime owe much to the social constructions of the powerful, ask questions about the 'cultural and institutional contexts in which certain acts become defined as criminal',[23] or discuss the class and power dimensions of law and order have (with very few exceptions) failed to secure serious attention. Research on crime has focussed, for example, on juveniles and youth, but has generally glossed over the fact that the youths processed by the Hong Kong criminal justice system are typically working-class (principally males from urban areas).[24] There is also remarkably little data on the socio-economic composition of Hong Kong's 'underclass' (Thomas 1999: 31).

This 'blind spot' in Hong Kong criminology reflects the state of sociology more generally. It has significant implications for how authoritative sources of knowledge on the nature and extent of crime and crime control are constructed in any given socio-historical period (Hardie-Bick et al. 2005: 8).

The dominant discourse of Hong Kong represents it as an economic city of politically apathetic seekers after wealth. On this view, 'delinquent' acts do not, on the whole, require a class or political interpretation. Theories that explain crime and criminal justice in terms of the fundamental conflicts and inequities underlying capitalism are ignored, as is the coercive role of the state in maintaining capitalist interests and/or the possibility that states govern *through* crime and its control (ibid.).[25]

Hong Kong: colony and capitalist society

Another narrative that has powerfully influenced accounts of crime and criminal justice holds that Hong Kong is an essentially stable, peaceful and safe place. Moments of resistance, protest, riots and demonstrations are here reduced to mere 'blips' on a supposedly tranquil past. However, as recent academic studies have revealed, Hong Kong has a long if 'little tradition' of political activism and resistance. Equally, recent studies have been critical of the fact that the territory's social, political, legal and economic orders have long been designed to protect the interests of the business and commercial elite. Successive administrations have been very open about this. The colony was conceived as a capitalist society, first as a merchant city and *entrepot*, then a centre for manufacturing, and more recently as a global financial centre. Throughout, it has been governed by an undemocratic elite which (though its composition has altered) has unswervingly pursued the interests of capital. In the early years, the clear and explicit role of the police and the criminal justice system was to protect the private and commercial property of the elite – the police, courts and prisons were from the start intended to maintain the status quo. Law, order and stability were seen as necessary prerequisites for enterprise to flourish. This remains the view of the post-1997 government as much as for the early colonists. Hong Kong has acquired a reputation at home and abroad not only as a hugely successful economy, but also one of the safest cities in the world. The maintenance of this reputation for stability and low crime permeates its institutions of criminal justice, and underpins much of the ruling regime's legitimacy.

It is by no means the case that the economically powerful always order society and define crime in their own interests. In Hong Kong, cross-cutting alliances between members of the colonial and colonised populations always made for a more complex story than this. Within the ruling elite, for example, there was never complete support for repression. Local cross-cutting alliances, as well as links with London, enabled disparate groups to oppose authoritarian measures. In the colonial period, London's policy towards Hong Kong was also variously influenced by changing views of colonialism, and by the utilitarian ideas of Bentham and the liberal theories of Mill, as well as leading penal administrators such as du Cane. Dissenters were often able to draw support from evangelical, humanitarian and liberal voices within Britain itself, and the Empire more broadly. In this way they occasionally managed to restrain the more illiberal tendencies of the British – and later the Chinese – ruling elite.

The shared capitalist interests of these elites also meant that the Chinese elite sometimes had more in common with the Europeans than with the native population. Between the 1880s and 1930s, for example, they made common cause against Hong Kong's nascent working-class movement. Since 1997, common cause has again been joined between the pro-China conservative fractions of this elite and the post-colonial administration, producing an oligarchy that once more rules in elite interests. The use of law and order, and criminal justice measures during these periods of conflict suggests that on occasion the colonial and post-colonial state has, indeed, been the managing committee of the bourgeoisie, though in contemporary Hong Kong it faces new challenges from below.

The good citizen and the civilised society

The pervasive narrative of Hong Kong (as a meritocratic, economic city, a free and open economy based on the rule of law and *laissez-faire* principles) has as its hero the 'bootstrap capitalist', who came to Hong Kong as a refugee with nothing but, by virtue of hard work, thrift and self-reliance rose to become a millionaire. This, the Hong Kong version of the American Dream, holds that anyone can 'make it' in Hong Kong. The way in which wealth is accumulated is less important than the fact that it is acquired at all. The exclusion of the majority of the Chinese from the political process has also meant that it is in the economic sphere that they have been able to pursue this dream by improving the wealth, prestige and status of themselves and their families.

Such narratives[26] convey to the public at large what kind of conduct is required of the successful, well-adjusted citizen. Lam argues that successive Hong Kong governments have cultivated a passive and somewhat shallow sense of citizenship, stressing qualities such as self-reliance, hard work, economic usefulness and contribution to society, affirming 'the historic vision of Hong Kong people as economic animals' (Lam 2005: 310). Ideal citizens are co-operative, responsible, active, and public-minded. They work hard and make an economic contribution to society; they are self-reliant, diligent, obedient, subservient to government and elites, and (since 1997) they 'love China'.

This discourse has long dominated the institutions of Hong Kong criminal justice, which deal with the unacceptable flip-side of this stereotype – the criminal, the vagrant, and the deviant, the 'misfit,' accused of 'just wanting excitement, lacking self-control, behaving in an ill-mannered way' (Lam 2005).[27]

A consistent theme throughout the territory's criminal justice history has also been the need to 'civilise' the local population by eliminating hazards and minor incivilities (such as spitting, littering), which 'purportedly escalate the tendencies of real crime' (Ganapathy 2005: 165). From the earliest days of the colony, one of the main preoccupations of government was with regulations to intervene in what they regarded as unsanitary, unwholesome, disorderly places, impressing upon the native population the need to observe geographical as well as social boundaries so that order and authority on the streets was not transgressed (see Walton 2002).[28]

As the crime statistics indicate, the authorities never quite succeeded in this mission, but they also never abandoned it – the drive for a clean orderly and morally hygienic environment continues to this day, and has on occasion provided a useful vehicle for the mass mobilisation of the population around common enemies.

As Ganapathy says, such an agenda echoes the right realist approach to crime. Like Singapore, the Hong Kong government in the 1970s engaged in a state-orchestrated project to 'engineer a collective 'public minded strategy', with numerous mass campaigns to 'Keep Hong Kong Clean', as well as a plethora of regulations affecting people's lifestyles and etiquette (ibid.). This focus upon the underemployed, non-productive, 'untidy' members of society, 'failed citizens', 'anti-citizens', 'those who are incapable of exercising responsible self-government' (Rose 2000: 331)[29] reinforces their social marginalisation.[30] The crime surveys, which began in Hong Kong in 1979, confirm the existence of this marginalisation. Being a good citizen, by contrast,

> . . . means at least partly, satisfying the economic demands of the government. Good citizens should not constitute an economic burden. Instead, they should be able to contribute to the economic growth of the city. Worthy of note, such demands from the governments would intensify when Hong Kong's economic situation deteriorates . . . The instrumental overtone of the official stories on citizenship is also revealed by government emphasis on social control. Good social control leads to good citizenry, which is potentially beneficial to economic growth. If citizens were all politically cooperative and socially responsible, they would pose no threat to stability. And social stability is a prerequisite for economic growth according to the governments (Lam 2005: 313–14).

This, too, dominates thinking about crime, rehabilitation and the goals of criminal justice.

Crime and legitimacy

Citizens' beliefs about public safety are crucial to social stability, and are closely related to their perceptions of (and satisfaction with) government performance. Elsewhere, in Africa and Latin America for example, it has been suggested that individuals' experiences with crime and insecurity:

> . . . reduce support for democratic government and increase support for non-democratic alternatives . . . The presence of personal insecurity as a result of crime influences (negatively) citizens' attitudes regarding liberal democracy . . . perceptions of personal insecurity due to crime may give rise to non-democratic responses . . . Those who have recently had experience with crime will be less supportive of democracy than those who have not; those who have favourable assessments of public safety will be more supportive of democracy than those who do not (Fernandez and Kuenzi 2006: 1).[31]

Perceptions of (and stories about) crime are thus central (rather than peripheral) to politics, since public safety is regarded as one of the 'public goods' governments should supply. The perception that crime is out of control may stimulate calls for regime change and support for authoritarian (as opposed to liberal) measures to deal with it. It may also be in the interests of the ruling elite, from time to time, to play up the 'crime problem' since in the presence of high crime, the public may prefer stability over democratic competition and elite turnover (Fernandez and Kuenzi 2006: 3).

In order to endure, however, any regime that adopts this strategy must also be seen, for at least some of the time, to be successful in reducing crime and improving citizens' sense of personal security. This may help explain why, given its comparatively low crime rate, Hong Kong pays so much attention to the politics of crime and its control, and why successive governments have felt the need to maintain the territory's status as one of the safest cities in the world.[32] Like all hegemonic projects, maintaining public confidence in a regime requires constant and ongoing work. This book is concerned with Hong Kong's stories about 'crime and justice' and 'law and order', and their place within this wider hegemonic project.

Notes

1 The term 'post-colonial' is used here but there is a body of thought which holds that the end of British rule in 1997 resulted not in independence, as usually understood, but only in 're-colonisation' by the PRC.

2 The history of Hong Kong criminal justice remains understudied. For sections on the early police and courts two works have been particularly helpful. These are Munn's (2001) book, *Anglo-China*, and Kerrigan's (2001) unpublished PhD thesis on the early colonial police.

3 See, for example, Young, P. 2005.

4 There are numerous studies relevant here. Two of the best classical studies are A.K. Bottomley's 1973 study, *Decisions in the Penal Process*; and A.V. Cicourel's 1968 book, *The Social Organisation of Juvenile Justice*. See also, for example, Goldstein 1960.

5 Such documents can be found, for example, amongst the colonial correspondence between Hong Kong and London, and in internal government memoranda. The problems of using such documents in historical research are discussed in Coleborne (2005).

6 In Hong Kong, the tenor and nature of criminal justice has partly been shaped by the need to impress upon the public that the colony was not 'like China', where the system in both Imperial and Maoist times handed down more summary justice and harsher penalties. In England, Peel's plan for policing was similarly designed to distinguish it from France, where the state impinged too closely on civil liberties and the gendarmerie kept civilians under close surveillance. Godfrey et al. also note William's argument that the post World War police force in the UK was designed in opposition to the German Gestapo, 'a peaceable kingdom watched over by kindly police father figures rather than "jack-booted" bullies'. See Godfrey et al. 2002: 14; and Williams 2002.

7 For further reading on this topic see, for example, Benton 2002; Emsley and Knafla (eds) 1996; Stoler 2002; Withers 2002: 303–11.

8 Ritchie and Hermanus 2004.

9 Emsley 1991.

10 Chan, W.K. 1991. It was, he notes, a moderately prosperous, if out-of-the-way, corner of Xinan county with a population of probably about 7,500.

11 See for example, Munn 2001 and Jones 2007.

12 Evans, J. 2005.

13 Dunstall and Godfrey (eds) 2005 *Crime and Empire*. See also Benton 2002; Mommsen and De Moor (eds) 1992; Mann and Roberts (eds) 1991.

14 It is worth bearing in mind that Britain itself has three separate legal jurisdictions; England and Wales, Scotland and Northern Ireland.

15 Chan, J. 2005. Chan is correct, however, to note that certain theories, such as restorative justice, have enjoyed a favourable reception in East Asia, but the domestic forces driving this reception remain unexplored.

16 See Jefferson 2005.

17 Ganapathy 2005.
18 The dominance of British and US theories in Hong Kong may also owe something to (1) a reliance, in the colonial periods, upon overseas lecturers in the field, since in keeping with other colonial institutions, the universities were slow to localise; and (2) the prestige which attaches to UK and US degrees. This not only leads local students to pursue their studies overseas but also to an undue, uncritical, reverence for dominant theories in the field.
19 See Young, J. 2002.
20 Carrington and Hogg. 2002.
21 See Smelser 1969: 43–68; Harrison 1988: 42. European studies from the latter part of the 1800s suggested *inter alia* links between patterns of urbanization and industrialization, business cycles, unemployment, variations in the prices of staple foods, migration and mendacity, and crime. 'Developing' countries, it was suggested, would experience a 'replay' of the West's experience. Clinard and Abbott (1973) and Lopez-Rey (1970) both suggested that high crime rates in 'developing' countries emerged as a gap opened up between growing affluence and more quickly rising material aspirations, and that the gap decreased and crime rates thus fell as the economy matured and growth slowed. The bulk of the literature on the global transformation of capital since the 1970s (Castells 1989, Castells and Henderson 1987, Harvey 1989) focuses on the economic impact of these changes in the Western countries, but there are a few traces in the literature of one of the more serious effects of restructuring, namely the extent to which it generates crime.
22 Traver (1991) has used the theories proposed by Clinard and Abbott (1973) and Lopez-Rey (1970) to suggest that throughout the 1970s in Hong Kong, a gap developed between growing affluence and more quickly rising material aspirations, which decreased as the economy matured and growth slowed.
23 Sheptycki 2005.
24 This blindness to class as a significant dimension is as striking as the gender-blindness identified by 1980s feminists in 'Western' criminological theory. Moreover, the kind of legitimacy crisis which Hall et al. argue marked a rupture in the political and economic life of British society in the 1970s also occurred in Hong Kong in the 1960s, when young people – mainly young working class males – participated in mass rioting. This triggered not 'authoritarian populism' in Hong Kong but a top-down re-engineering of civil society. See Scott 1989 and Jones 2007.
25 Hardie-Bick et al. 2005. For conflict theories see, for example, Quinney 1970, 1974; Chambliss 1975: 149–70; Box. 1983; Sutherland 1949; Swaaningen 1997.
26 See Lam, Wai-man 2005: 309–22.
27 Lam discusses riots and skirmishes with the police in 1966, 1981, and 2002–3 to illustrate her point that official discourse surrounding 'problem' youth depicted them as undereducated, underemployed, or unemployed in contrast to 'good, responsible citizens'.
28 Over the years, the policing of traditional street festivals has also sanitised what were once more noisy, rowdy congregations of people.
29 See Brown 2005; and Rose 2000: 321–39.
30 Barton et al. (eds) 2007.
31 Fernandez and Kuenzi 2006.
32 This has remained true even though the crime rate in Hong Kong (like many other countries) did rise sharply during the 1960s and early 1970s. Crime rates in Hong Kong rose rather quickly throughout the 1970s, a period marked by massive economic restructuring, fast growth, the absorption of large-scale immigration, and attempts to limit further immigration. The incidence of reported crime roughly

doubled from 704 per 100,000 persons in 1970 to 1,472 in 1980. Property crimes increased from 367 per 100,000 persons in 1970/71 to 812 in 1980/81, while over the same period violent crimes increased from 134 per 100,000 persons to 317 (Traver 1991). The largest single annual increase in crime took place in 1974, which showed, on a per capita basis, an increase of 38 per cent in reported crime over the previous year. This figure, however, has a somewhat different story behind it, again one reserved for later chapters. It was almost certainly the result of major initiatives to deal with political problems and police corruption, which had until that point depressed crime figures for a variety of reasons, including the necessity to bribe officers in order to report crimes. Crime rates continued to rise throughout the 1970s. Both reported crime figures and victim surveys indicate that crime levels peaked in 1982–4 at a total reported crime rate of about 1,600 per 100,000 population, and have hovered since that time in a range of about 1,400 to 1,500.

Part I

Colonial Rule, 1841 to Second World War

Chapter 2

Hong Kong: the early years

In 1841, Captain Elliot laid claim to Hong Kong Island on behalf of the British Crown. Following two years of negotiations with the Chinese, it was ceded to Britain in 1843. Unlike other trading colonies, Hong Kong was not placed under the control of the East India Company. Experienced in exercising power in many of Britain's other colonies, its vested interests in the opium trade led London to doubt that it would deal impartially with China (Pottinger 1997: 118). Instead, Britain made Hong Kong a Crown Colony, answerable directly to London.

Governing colonial territories was always a complex matter involving a number of different parties and interests, including the Colonial Office and individual Governors, who mainly wished to establish order in the colonies at minimum cost. A second was the evangelical missionaries, who carried their Christian mission across the Empire but also influenced public opinion at home. Along with philanthropic and humanitarian groups, they had their own visions of how best to assimilate indigenous peoples. Lester also notes the role of capitalist interests, with their 'targeted visions of capital accumulation' (Lester 2001: 4). Later, in the late 1800s and early 1900s, trades unions also raised concerns about matters including working conditions in the colonies and the impact of colonial trade. The task of the Colonial Office was to mediate (and sometimes restrain) these competing interests, whilst itself ensuring that individual Governors operated with the general terms of government policy and the rule of law.

Some of those involved in colonial governance (including criminal justice) travelled widely across the colonies, transmitting views, values, expectations and experiences about the nature of the colonial enterprise from one territory to another, as well as from the territories to the 'home country'. Both meant that certain ideas and practices became the subject of widespread debate about British colonial rule. Like the campaign against slavery, these debates sometimes forced both the home government and the British public to address uncomfortable questions about the ways in which the business of empire was conducted.

One consequence of this process was that colonial rule in each colony was often the product of a different 'mix' of influences, factions within the ruling elite of each colony holding different ideas about how best to govern. The newer histories of Hong Kong chart the play of these influences, showing how they altered as Hong Kong ceased to be a 'frontier society' of European and Chinese sojourners in the 1840s and 1850s, and became organised around specific communities and institutions (see for example Chan 1991, Tsai 1993). As the composition of Hong Kong's population began to change, and first the Chinese elite, and then the Chinese labour guilds and unions, gained in prominence, so the European 'cultural hegemony over the populace' began to unravel (Tsai 1993: 289). These challenges brought new problems of governance for the colonial authorities, to which they responded, in part, by bringing the criminal justice system to bear on their troublesome subjects.

Some issues – such as crime, public order and internal security – were manifestly shaped by trends in Britain and Mainland China. In Britain, different shades of opinion came and went in the Colonial Office, the Foreign Office, and the Board of Trade, the main departments dealing with colonial affairs. At any given time, various factions of Hong Kong society might (or might not) be able to count on support from like-minded individuals at 'home'. Equally, although Hong Kong was a British colony, its Chinese elite had links with the gentry and merchant classes of China. Likewise, the vast majority of Hong Kong's labouring class retained links with their Mainland compatriots. On occasion, they too turned to like-minded groups in China for help and support. Equally, these Mainland groups sometimes sought to exert direct influence on events in Hong Kong. This 'China factor' played a significant part in shaping the character of Hong Kong society.

What also becomes clear from the recent histories of Hong Kong is that the power of Hong Kong's European elite was, like colonial power everywhere, tempered by competing factions within the elite itself, as well as by relations between the colonisers and the colonised. Just as Hong Kong society became more heterogeneous as a result of population growth and economic expansion, so too did nineteenth-century British society undergo massive political and economic shifts. Bodies hitherto excluded from colonial policy-making – such as the trade unions – made their voices heard on issues such as the treatment of workers. New voices also emerged from China, where the nationalist and communist movements also challenged prevailing ideas of political authority. Being so closely related to the socioeconomic and political conditions of China, and Sino-foreign relations,

> Hong Kong cannot be studied in isolation. Constantly subject to the repercussions from the changing political and socioeconomic conditions outside the colony, all major events in Hong Kong have been the results of interactions between local and external forces . . . (Tsai 1993: 8).

Tsai's account of events between 1895 and the First World War clearly demonstrates how Hong Kong's proximity to Mainland China was 'a decisive factor' in shaping the colony's history. Its close social, economic and political connections with China 'made its Chinese residents liable to the political influence and control of Chinese officialdom. Canton and Hong Kong authorities claimed the Chinese residents' allegiance, putting them in an ambivalent relationship with both' (Tsai 1993: 36).

As Tsai says, under British colonial rule, Hong Kong had its own path of historical development: 'peculiar socio-political experience made it different from China in some ways, although its society remained distinctly Chinese' (Tsai 1993: 288). Before – and perhaps more so after – the border was erected in 1950, the Hong Kong Chinese held to common traditional Chinese values, dialect groups, native places, kinship groups and associations (ibid). Between the 1860s and World War I, the Chinese community in Hong Kong also coalesced around its own elite leadership, provided by the Committees of the Man Mo Temple, the Tung Wah Hospital and the Po Leung Kuk (Sinn 1989; Smith 1985; Chan 1991; Tsai 1993; Lethbridge 1978a).

This elite became, in many ways, an alternative parallel government. Liaising with the colonial authorities, it was allowed to manage the affairs of the Chinese community. As merchants and traders, its members shared the interest of the European elite in maintaining stability and trade. Its control over the Chinese population recommended it to government as a device for mediating with the lower classes during times of conflict. Essentially conservative and Confucianist in outlook, it mimicked the role of gentry as a mediating force in Mainland China. Yet like the labouring Chinese (the 'coolie class') it too had ties with family and officials in southern China. From time to time, this meant that the elite was subject to competing loyalties: it could not always be relied on to support the colonial government.

Moreover, the fact that it operated as a parallel government eventually made this elite a threat to the reach of the colonial authorities: it suggested that there were parts of the colony where the government's writ did not run. There were also those within the European elite who steadfastly refused to share power with the Chinese under any circumstances. Calling upon the Chinese elite for help in crisis situations (such as public order situations which pitched the police and the army against the Chinese 'coolie class') was thus a double-edged sword.

As one of the principal means of governing native peoples, the criminal law and criminal justice system were often a focus of these conflicts between rulers and ruled, colonisers and colonised. But equally, within the European elite itself, they were also the subject of competing ideas about the proper mode of colonial governance. The history of criminal law, criminal justice and public order legislation in Hong Kong is marked by contests between these ideas. It is a story of false starts and experiments, of liberal reforms as well as conservative retrenchments, of humane and evangelical influences as well as of repression, reaction and racial discrimination. It is not a story of a colonial elite with a unified vision of how to govern, nor is it a story of outright and unmitigated repression. Neither is it simply a story of the state of crime and how the colonial authorities responded to it. It is a story that tells us something about crime but, perhaps, more about how the colonists saw the Chinese they governed, how the Europeans saw themselves and their mission in Hong Kong, and how these views were challenged and changed both by fellow colonists, the colonised themselves, events in China and British politics.

Competing visions

The accepted or 'standard' story of Hong Kong's past, as Tsai reminds us, is one of continuous growth and stability, with a politically apathetic Chinese population governed by benevolent British colonial rulers. This is the story told by what were, until recently, the standard texts on Hong Kong history, as told by British and Europeans, but it is a story which omits the complexities of colonised/coloniser relations. These were not always antagonistic – Tsai characterises them, rather, as ambivalent, sometimes hostile and sometimes collaborative. Hong Kong's historical development, he argues, was punctuated by a long series of social crises in which both the Chinese elite and the 'coolie' class expressed their dissatisfaction with British rule (Tsai 1993: 292). This 'long tradition' of Chinese resistance, the anti-colonial protests, civil disobedience, popular unrest and disorder has, until recently, been absent from the dominant narrative of Hong Kong history.

Also absent has been any analysis of class relations – most accounts present the fundamental division in Hong society as a racial division. Tsai and Chan, however, insist that we must also take account of class. Chan in particular looks at class formation in colonial Hong Kong, whilst Tsai reveals the role played by the Chinese working class (the 'coolie class') in shaping colonial and capitalist relations. He also highlights the manner in which, between 1895 and the First World War, nationalist and patriotic sentiments combined with class concerns to produce a series of protests, demonstrations, strikes and boycotts – the biggest challenges to colonial rule in the history of Hong Kong. These events remain under-recorded in Hong Kong history. This absence, or silence, has allowed a particular narrative of Hong Kong and its people to remain dominant. This is a narrative in which Hong was founded as a trading colony, whose *raison d'être* has remained trade and commerce, whose people are hard-working, politically apathetic seekers after wealth. On this view, Hong Kong is, and has always been, an economy rather than a society, whose success has been built on the principles of *laissez-faire* or free trade.

This dovetails with an older view of colonisation, propounded by British political economists such as Ricardo, who saw it as essentially as a commercial affair: Britain could 'wield informal dominion' through free trade (Hall 2002: 30). Trade between the colonies and the motherland would contribute to their mutual benefit and prosperity; colonies should not become a burden; governing them should not result in costs to the home country. Some amongst the colonial elite clearly felt that Hong Kong was so 'rocky and barren' that it could not be expected 'under any circumstances to afford to pay any considerable revenue towards the payment of its own expenses' (Martin 1846: 30). Because of its geographical position and the surrounding poverty and piracy of the natives 'it could never be a colony [nor] be viewed as a commercial Emporium' (ibid). Equally, it was impractical as a fortress, 'politically injurious' because of its proximity to the Mainland, and 'ineffective for the dissemination of Christian Civilisation' because of the 'dissolute, marauding, unsettled character of the inhabitants' (ibid). Others begged to differ, seeing in China's system of waterways easy access for missionaries to South China's major centres of population (Lovett 1899: 451). For Lovett, the Southern Chinese were drawn to Hong Kong because, as industrious people with an energetic capacity for enterprise and business (ibid), they saw in it an opportunity for commerce:

> Hong Kong is unlike every other place in which the Society is carrying on missionary operations . . . [It] has the advantage of being a British colony, and the population feels the presence of a large European element. The life of the natives under these circumstances if more free [than in the Chinese Empire] and, owing to European influence, their ideas are liberalized; and British rule affords security for life and work which is of very great value (Lovett 1899: 453).

Lovett's views chimed with those advocated by Wakefield and his converts in the Colonial Office (including Bentham and Mill). This held that colonies were about more than trade. As the nineteenth century progressed, British colonialism acquired a more distinct evangelical flavour that saw colonies as outposts of British civilization, places where emigrants from England ('white settlers') could establish farms and families, and lead a British way of life. The purpose of empire (the 'white man's burden') was to provide, by example and education, a morally uplifting way of life to those hitherto excluded from the 'civilised world'. Bringing Christianity to the natives was one part of a mission to improve the lot of indigenous peoples, a duty owed by the rich and civilised to others in the world less fortunate than themselves. In its way, the philanthropy of nineteenth-century colonialism reflected older British aristocratic notions of *noblesse oblige*. The anti-slavery movement had already established a more humanitarian conception of indigenous peoples, albeit one that was still heavily paternal.

These different strands of colonial thought were present in early Hong Kong, where the view was expressed that its 'native people' could aspire to equality with European civilisations by adopting the values, institutions, and habits of the British way of life. As Hall argues, family and class, duty, diligence, hard work and domestic life were all central to this new conception of colonisation, first implemented in South Australia. Free men in the settler colonies would enjoy all the civil, social, economic and religious liberties of England. They would go there to make their fortunes, but also to settle, work hard and build a better world; their cities, laws, moral influence and institutions would mirror the best of British society (Hall 2002: 29–32).

Although Hong Kong was not a settler colony (see Munn 2001: 57) this did not stop some colonists seeing themselves as a distinctive society of permanent settlers. Nor did it prevent them from hoping that British institutions – such as their way of life and their adherence to the rule of law – would secure the hearts, minds and souls of the local population, as well as their allegiance to the British crown. Theirs was a world in which distinctions of class and status, of divisions between gentry, professional and bourgeois and well as connections between family, church and voluntary associations, reflected society at home. Munn describes a community that did its best to recreate bourgeois English life through its bungalows, clubs, gardens, churches, fashion, amateur theatre, food and clothing, and in which:

> Minute social distinctions, gossip, scandal and ostracism served important regulatory functions, isolating and trapping Europeans within their own universe, and demarcating them clearly from other communities. Mass Chinese immigration, racial, cultural and linguistic barriers, crime and war accentuated these demarcations and bound Europeans of all classes and nationalities more tightly together (Munn 2001: 58).

Hong Kong's colonists numbered amongst themselves some who still saw colonisation as purely a matter of trade. But even these traders and merchants brought with them the attitudes and beliefs of the newly enfranchised English bourgeoisie at home, including a readiness to challenge existing social and political institutions where these impeded their interests. These captains of trade and industry exerted considerable influence in the colony, where there was no established aristocracy to block their path.

The colonists also included a fair sprinkling of humanitarians, liberals, and evangelical missionaries, whose influence was brought to bear on criminal justice policy from time to time. Their writings depict a mostly poor Chinese population, scattered amongst coastal villages, welcoming, hospitable and – as far as the missionary enterprise was concerned – 'biddable'. However, on visiting the outlying districts in the mid-1840s, the Bishop of Victoria, George Smith, did lament the fact that missionaries seemed able only to make contact with Chinese of the 'lowest' character, 'the lowest dregs of native society' who flocked to Hong Kong in the 'hope of gain or plunder' (ibid). Smith echoed European sentiment of the day when he described the colony as:

> ... the resort of pirates and thieves, so protected by secret compact as to defy the ordinary regulations of police for detection or prevention ... The temerity and dexterity of Chinese robbers is proverbial and the greatest proficients appear to favour Hong Kong with their visits. Sometimes they will surround a house, attack and plunder it, even continuing their work of depredation under the fire of our troops (Smith 1847: 60).

Though secret societies (triads) flourished in China, the discovery of their 'secret papers' in Hong Kong itself was recent. Here, their secrecy, 'mutual connivance' and 'predatory character' hampered the prevention and detection of crime (ibid). As a domestic problem, this occasioned the first Anti-Triad Ordinance but, as Smith notes, because their potential for rebellion so alarmed the Chinese authorities, Hong Kong's own anti-triad measures were mirrored by even more severe proclamations in Canton (Smith 1847: 81).

Despite the presence of such issues, for one writer of the time, Hong Kong was:

> ... a place of rising importance ... I hope many who go there will embody the British character; settling down, not as a mere group of money-getters, tea-buyers, and opium-sellers, but, as men with hearts in their bosoms, that beat for the real good of all mankind. Too often do Englishmen, when abroad, bring dishonour on England. May the residents of Hong Kong be of a different character; open-hearted, hospitable, and generous, spreading around them knowledge, humanity, and justice, kindness, virtue and piety (Old Humphrey 1844: 12–17).

Those amongst Hong Kong's colonists who did set a less than virtuous example were generally regarded as the 'degraded underclasses' of Britain (Lester 2001: 114). Their number included the 'footsoldiers' of Empire – the working class of manual workers, tradesmen, sailors, merchant seamen, soldiers, and adventurers whose gambling, drunkenness and disorderly behaviour was regarded with disdain at home and in the colonies, where they faced fewer social restraints. In their study of colonial policing, Anderson and Killingray suggest that:

> ... the study of the exercise of power and the establishment and maintenance of authority lie(s) at the very heart of the historiography of empire: as the most visible public symbol of colonial rule, in daily contact with the population and enforcing the codes of law that upheld colonial authority, the colonial policeman – be he a European officer or a local native – stood at the cutting edge of colonial rule (Anderson and Killingray 1991a).

Often in the 'front line' of the colonisation process, these soldiers and sailors – recruits into Hong Kong's early police force – often had more frequent and immediate contact with the natives than any other group. Their treatment of the indigenous peoples in other colonies (such as Australia, New Zealand, Africa and America) had also shown them to often be the most brutal:

> As the most degraded representatives of the metropole, they had the greatest potential to introduce the indigenes to 'knowledge of depraved acts and licentious gratification of the most debased inhabitants of our great cities', leading inevitably to both the decline and corruption of the local population . . . (Lester 2001: 14)

As police officers, these 'dregs of our countrymen' enjoyed considerable opportunity to inflict physical and moral damage on the local population, undercutting the loftier claims of British justice. Their behaviour led to frequent criticism and calls for their replacement (see below). It also focused the colonisers' mind on the question of what to do when fellow Europeans were accused of committing a crime. In theory, it was the mission of Hong Kong's judiciary to apply justice equally to all. The 'civilising' view of colonialism held that all colonial subjects, irrespective of race, deserved the protections, rights and liberties of English law. However, the judges found themselves fiercely criticised by members of the elite when they sentenced fellow Europeans to the kinds of punishments meted out to the local Chinese. In particular, the elite objected to any punishment (such as flogging or the *cangue*) that subjected fellow members of the colonising race to public humiliation before an audience of the colonised. Differential punishments for the two principal races were supported on a number of grounds. English punishments were said, for example, to hold no fear for a Chinese population more used to the 'barbaric' laws of China. For punishment to deter Chinese criminals, it was therefore justifiable to subject Chinese to public floggings and execution. Traditional paternalists also argued that native peoples were less 'mature' or 'developed' than Europeans – it was therefore unfair and inappropriate to extend to the Chinese laws they were as yet unable to appreciate. English law, instead of treating all men equally, needed to be adjusted to take account of the 'less advanced' Chinese.

Meanwhile, humanitarians within the elite, influenced by new ideas of penal reform at home and the decline of public punishments throughout Europe (Spierenburg 1984) made the case for the abolition of all 'barbaric' punishments, whilst evangelical missionaries argued for types of punishment that held out the possibility of redemption for all, regardless of race. Another, *laissez-faire*, view was that the British authorities should stay out of the affairs of the Chinese community rather as government should stay out of trade. It should, instead, be seen to respect Chinese laws and customs, allowing the Chinese to live freely *as Chinese* in an otherwise British Hong Kong (Endacott 1964: 29). The Chinese should, on this view, be left to their own devices on matters affecting the regulation of their own communities. This equal respect for European and Chinese ways of life extended to respecting their different penalities.

Later, these different perspectives would again be brought to bear on debates in Hong Kong and London about the regulation of prostitution, the reservation of specific areas for European occupation, as well as the toleration of *mui tsai*, concubinage, and corruption (see Jones 1994; Miners 1987). The flip side of the respect-for-Chinese-custom argument was, of course, that the Europeans be allowed to live freely *as Europeans*, equally 'unpolluted' by Chinese ideas and practices. It allowed a line to be drawn between the two races, limiting their living spaces and their daily intercourse. As Endacott points out, in other treaty ports, such as Canton, it was already established practice for the British and Chinese communities to live apart, each respecting the other's customs and punishing its own criminals in accordance with its own laws (Endacott 1964: 28). In Hong Kong, this philosophy of 'difference' later contributed Chinese distrust of a legal system that applied the law more diligently to some than to others. Thus, though the British in Hong Kong promised a legal system that would treat all men equally, benign intentions coupled with competing ideas about race and culture led to the differential – and discriminatory – treatment of Chinese offenders.

The 'crime problem'

The perceived vulnerability of the colonial minority, exacerbated by the incidence of crime and disorder, meant that, from time to time, fear united the colonists to favour stringent punishment and control of the Chinese. The view that the vast majority of the Hong Kong Chinese were lower class, dangerous, prone to violence, depravity, and criminality was widely shared but, as Munn points out, the suspicions and fears of the colonists often magnified the significance of events, turning non-existent problems and minor acts of resistance into colonial emergencies (Munn 2001: 85). Dominant narratives paint a picture of early Hong Kong as a sort of 'Wild West' frontier town inhabited by 'riff raff' from the Mainland. Its Chinese population was regarded by the Europeans as mainly criminal, backward, dirty and dangerous.

Some of the Chinese population had fled to Hong Kong seeking to evade the Mainland authorities; others sought to exploit new opportunities for gain, including piracy and banditry. The *Times* of 17 November 1844 described Hong Kong to the British reading public as a migratory community where:

> . . . property is most insecure, and life often in danger, from the bands of piratical robbers that infest this and neighbouring islands . . . Many of

> the worst description of Chinese resort there, and I have seen during one evening at Victoria more open scenes of vice and debauchery than I had observed during my three years stay in the north of China. So much for the boasted march of civilization (Kerrigan 2001: 61; CO129/18: 470).

In similar vein, the missionary James Legge described early Hong Kong as a place of frequent disorders in the day, coupled with burglaries at night (Kerrigan 2001; Legge 1872: 177). Eitel also spoke of 'a continuous influx of criminals from the neighbouring mainland of China' (Kerrigan 2001: Eitel 1983: 237). Writing of the 1840s, Milne claimed that, before the British arrived, the 'native population on the island [were] chiefly a set of low, poor, and degraded quarrymen, smugglers, fishermen and pirates' (Milne 1861: 17–19). Munn argues that, so extensive did piracy become in the waters around Hong Kong that the colony, instead of being seen as a haven of stability and order, rapidly acquired a reputation as the headquarters of piracy and other organised crime (Munn 2001: 73).

Interestingly, few historians have attributed to the Chinese the same eagerness displayed by European sojourners to re-invent their homeland in Hong Kong. Similarly, whilst the 'European' histories of Hong Kong play up the degenerate nature of Hong Kong's early migrants, few refer to the presence of European 'outcasts', criminals and 'riff raff'. Lethbridge is an exception (Lethbridge 1978b: 189). Equally, whilst the European fortune seekers are generally presented as entrepreneurial merchants, the Chinese are depicted as pirates, adventurers and criminals. Lethbridge probably provides the most measured account:

> The majority of immigrant Chinese in Hong Kong came from the Canton delta region of the neighbouring Kwantung Province, from the counties . . . bordering on the Pearl River and including the large urban complex of Canton – from such counties as Hsinan, Hsiangshan, Shunte, Tungkuan, Fanyu, Sanshui, Nanhai, and other riverine districts. Immigrants from such localities soon established types of clan or territorial associations. The pattern was little different from that in Singapore or any place where a large overseas Chinese community was to be found. Such associations – those recruiting members from among people sharing the same surname or among people from the same area of China – helped the Chinese adapt to Hong Kong by putting them in touch with potential employers or by offering some sort of temporary support, such as lodgings or medicine if sick (Lethbridge 1978b: 3).

Instead of a disorganised society ridden with criminals, thugs and ruffians, this account suggests an early Chinese community characterised by a degree of social organisation, as well as welfare provision and mutual aid. These forces, Lethbridge argues, helped maintain the stability of early Hong Kong society for, although it was a highly transient place, they helped the new immigrant adjust to unfamiliar conditions (ibid). Though Tsai argues that the new immigrants lacked the traditional forms of social control with which they would have been familiar on the Chinese mainland, this did not mean that no forms of social control were present. As he says, people speaking the same dialect clung together for protection and mutual assistance; craft and trade guilds were formed and, like the disparate Europeans, they brought with them their own religion, customs, concepts and experiences of social organisation (Tsai 1993: 37). Like the Europeans too, they attempted to re-create a version of their home society, adapted to Hong Kong conditions. This was eventually to include, as Lethbridge points out, the creation of a Chinese leadership that looked after their fellow clansmen and villagers (Lethbridge 1978b: 3).

Spatially as well as socially, the two populations became segregated. Certain areas of early Hong Kong were quickly labelled areas of 'Chinese criminality' or 'European respectability' (later, the Chinese elite would graduate towards these same 'respectable areas'). The Lower Bazaar (Jervois Street to Bonham Strand), Upper Bazaar (Queen's Road) and Tai Ping Shan, at the western edge of Victoria, was regarded by the Europeans as a 'notorious district', associated with 'undesirable elements', thieves and squatters (Kerrigan 2001; Smith 1971: 30). When the Chinese began to spill over into Middle Bazaar, the authorities thought it advisable, 'for the interests of the community', to remove them back to Tai Ping Shan, so as to prevent as far as possible 'their being mixed up with the Europeans'.[1] The only Europeans allowed to reside in the Chinese area were members of Hong Kong's rudimentary police force.[2]

This absence of the colonial authorities in places such as the Lower Bazaar left a vacuum in which Chinese gangs and secret societies flourished. Some of their leaders achieved wealth, power and status whilst acting as sources of intelligence or as go-betweens for the colonial authorities (Munn 2001). They were able, through their corrupt relationship with colonial officials, to acquire rights to land, property, and revenue collection, which in turn gave them power over fellow Chinese. As slum landlords, they controlled housing and workplaces; as crime bosses, they demanded protection money; and as go-betweens, they colluded with officials in the running of illegal businesses. In 1845, for example, whilst walking through the 'native part of the town', Smith observed the home of . . .

> . . . a wealthy Chinese named A-quei. He possesses about fifty houses in the bazaar, and lives on the rent, in a style much above the generality of Chinese settlers, who are commonly composed of the refuse of the population of the neighbouring Mainland. During the war, A-quei acted as a purveyor of provisions to the British armament, and acquired some wealth. After the war . . . he settled at Hong Kong, where he is said to encourage disreputable characters by the loan of money, and in various

> ways to reap the proceeds of profligacy and crime . . . he introduced us to a partner, named A-tai . . . A-tai had just purchased, as the highest bidder, from Government, the exclusive right of selling opium by retail, in any quantity less than a chest . . . A-quei conducted us into a room where he was sitting, with his two wives, handsomely attired, looking from a window on the crowd assembled in the street to witness the performance of a native juggler (Smith 1847: 83).

The Lower Bazaar became, Munn argues, a place of gambling dens, brothels, amusement halls, restaurants, as well as opium and pawn-broking shops. It was an 'affront to colonial rule and colonial morality', a place both impenetrable to the police, and 'a symbol of the crime, clannishness and sleaze that colonists came to identify with the colony's early Chinese community' (Munn 2001: 76).

Though the Lower Bazaar later became more 'respectable' after its rebuilding following a fire in 1851, and the subsequent influx of Chinese traders, similar power-bases continued to operate elsewhere on Hong Kong Island, in the Bazaar at East Point, and in the southern towns of Stanley (Chek Chu) and Aberdeen (Shek Pai Wan). Local bullies and crime bosses became entrenched here, partly because they were cultivated by successive colonial governments as informants and intermediaries with the Chinese community (Munn 2001: 78). The linguistic and cultural barriers that kept the colonial authorities at a distance made such intermediaries indispensable. Throughout Hong Kong's colonial history, the authorities were to rely heavily upon go-betweens and compradors as a means of penetrating the Chinese communities under their rule. In later years, with the emergence of a Chinese elite, the government found more respectable go-betweens; it was also able to draw on the cadet system, which took a small number of colonial officials from Britain to Canton for training in Chinese language, history and culture prior to their secondment to Hong Kong. These new intermediaries were to become central to the government's communication with the Hong Kong Chinese, albeit communication at a distance. Until their emergence, however, the Hong Kong government had only one English intermediary, Daniel Caldwell. Like other go-betweens, however, the very fact that he was so familiar with Chinese subaltern groups meant that questions would be raised about his character.

Places such as the Lower Bazaar, and incidents such as raids on godowns and ships, prompted fear and anxiety amongst the colonists, who already felt themselves surrounded by a strange and potentially dangerous race. Their alarm prompted calls for repressive measures to keep the Chinese in check. These were, however, at odds with London's longer-term goal of easing colonial governance. One of the most effective ways of gaining native support for colonial rule was said to be through moral example and education, rather than repression.[3] Thus, when Hong Kong's traders and merchants complained loudly about Chinese thieves and robbers – regarding all

Chinese as essentially untrustworthy, 'insubordinate and semi-barbarous people', heathens whose sworn oaths could not be trusted and for whom the civilized laws of England were unsuitable (Munn 1995) – it fell to London to remind the Hong Kong government that, in order to attach the Chinese to colonial rule, it needed to act in an even-handed and respectful manner. The rule of law was central to this 'even-handed' approach. English law, with its rhetoric of justice, equality and liberty, would demonstrate to the locals the superiority of British values.

Officials in the Colonial Office were also concerned to 'bring to colonial policy a humanitarian sense of the duty to safeguard the interests of the indigenous peoples' (Endacott 1964: 28). This often meant checking the more rapacious tendencies of colonial elites, which were inclined to favour repression whenever their properties and liberties were threatened.

Even within Hong Kong there was, as Munn notes, never complete consensus amongst the colonial elite on the use of repression: at the very same time as some of its members demanded harsh measures, others used the leading newspapers of the colony to express vehement criticism of the authorities (see Munn 2001). Meanwhile, those rare occasions on which Europeans *were* dealt with severely and Chinese *were* treated mercifully by the courts provided opportunities to convince both the natives and fellow colonists that the rhetoric of British rule of law was not 'mere' rhetoric (see Thompson 1975).

There was, however, a good degree of consensus amongst the European elite about where the 'crime problem' lay. Crime, in their view, was something committed almost entirely by the Chinese. This was partly because many of the day-to-day activities of the Chinese, as well as their movements about the colony, had been recently criminalised by new colonial laws. Crime was constantly related to vagrancy, to 'dangerous characters' coming to Hong Kong from the Mainland, to the hawkers cluttering the streets, and the struggle to impose order on a highly transient population. As Lethbridge says, most of the new immigrants came to Hong Kong to seek work, especially when conditions were bad in China; most also returned to China when conditions improved in their home villages, or when conditions worsened in Hong Kong (Lethbridge 1978b: 2). Meantime, they wandered Hong Kong's streets looking for work, which brought them to the attention of the largely Indian police as 'vagrants'. Tsai explains that this 'coolie class' usually congregated in 'coolie houses' with people who spoke the same dialect or came from the same area. Low wages resulted in overcrowded living conditions, since rents could only be kept low by sharing a room with a large number of people. Such conditions came to be associated with dirt and disease. To curb both, new sanitary laws were introduced by the colonial authorities, with the result that those dwelling in areas such as Tai Ping Shan again found themselves disproportionately policed and criminalised.

Their social and physical distance from the Chinese led the Europeans to dub *all* Chinese as 'the same': they were all potentially 'dangerous strangers'; their presence and proximity was fearful and unsettling. In the context of early colonial Hong Kong, stereotypes of the Chinese meant that crime came to be routinely expected – or suspected – of them. In the second half of the 1800s, as crime statistics became available and the police force expanded (and this in itself presented a variety of problems), there were periodic 'moral panics' about crime, and about the ineffectiveness of measures used to control various segments of the population. These are discussed later.

The colonised

The European elite viewed the Chinese with 'indifference, distrust and occasional hostility' (Chan 1991: 49). It was an elite made anxious by being the vast numbers of Chinese surrounding them, and whose numbers swelled whenever there was domestic turmoil in China. Whilst certain 'pull' factors, such as the demand for labour and opportunities for trade in the new colony, may have drawn some Mainland Chinese to Hong Kong, others were 'pushed' there by poverty, upheaval and disorder within the Chinese Empire, much of which had been exacerbated by the war with Britain over opium. Banditry, civil unrest, inter-ethnic fighting, natural disasters and rebellion all added to the strife and hardship of life Mainland China (Munn 2001: 70). For many, therefore, Hong Kong seems to have been something of a refuge though, as in later decades, they seem to have seen the colony more as a temporary than as a permanent home.

Hong Kong's Chinese population was, therefore, directly (and regularly) affected by events in Mainland China. It was, Munn says, a socially complex community, relatively few of whom were the traders and merchants whom the British had hoped to attract. Some acted as compradors, translators and teachers, but most were artisans, boatmen, labourers, porters, and shopmen, organised primarily around native-place and kinship associations. They were also quick to demonstrate an ability to unite along class lines in opposition to government and capital (Munn 2001: 71). Tsai argues that this was partly because, whilst community organisations were still generally undeveloped in early Hong Kong, the labouring classes faced certain common problems that required collective solutions (Tsai 1993: 38). Very often, the common problem was the Hong Kong government, and/or the European elite, who together owned most of the trades and industries in which the Chinese working class were employed, and determined the conditions under which they lived (Tsai 1993: 37–8).

As a number of commentators have noted, early immigrants to Hong Kong were often the poorest sections of Mainland society. Tsai lists the outcast Tanka boat people, Punti and Hakka labourers, artisans and adventurers who profited by trade with the foreigners, defying Mainland orders not to do so. Colonial histories have tended to paint all early immigrants as vagabonds, pirates, triads and criminals fleeing Mainland justice. As Munn says, some reports come close to depicting the early population as a 'criminal caste', with the first Registrar General, Samuel Fearon, describing the Hakkas as:

> . . . people whose habits, character and language mark them as a distinct race. Careless of the ties of home and those moral obligations, the observance of which is deemed absolutely necessary to the preservation of the national integrity; uneasy under the restraint of law and unscrupulous of the means by which they live they abandon without hesitation their hearths and household gods, their birthright and their fathers' tombs, to wander, unrespected, whither gain may fall. The unsettled state of the Colony, and the vast amount of crime during its infancy afford abundant proof of the demoralising effects of their presence (cited in Munn 2001: 68).

Recounting what was to become a familiar narrative of British rule, in 1849, Sirr charted Hong Kong's transformation from 'a mere fishing village, populated scantily by the most depraved and poor of the Chinese nation' to 'a British colony inhabited by many of Great Britain's merchant princes of the East' (Sirr 1849: 1). Those who prospered did so against the odds: the climate was 'pestilential', hot, rainy, and 'fatally injurious' to the Europeans, who fell victim to fever, cholera, and malaria; the Chinese were 'an unhealthy people' afflicted by scrofula, leprosy, and cutaneous diseases (Sirr 1849: 11). When the Chief Justice, Hulme, died of fever the authorities were, Sirr says, anxious to keep it out of the papers lest it deter others from settling in the colony (Sirr 1849: 13).

Hong Kong was equally regarded by Mainland Chinese as an island of ill repute, 'the resort of pirates, thieves, and depraved characters of every description' (Sirr 1849: 4). Munn confirms that the Mainland Chinese authorities also saw Hong Kong under British rule as a refuge for criminals and subversives, triads and 'Chinese traitors'. However, though some of the early immigrants were indeed outlaws, triads, opium smugglers, prostitutes, and gamblers, most were simply lower-class coolies and small traders driven to Hong Kong in search of a living (Tsai 1993: 39). This mix of people, together with the absence of traditional social controls, is usually said to have made Hong Kong a sort of 'Wild West' frontier society, with the authorities battling against the odds to impose some semblance of law and order. Even the more recent correctives to colonial history, such as those written by Tsai and Munn, still argue that crime was 'rampant' and that pirates were 'numerous and daring'. Welsh quotes reports from 1843 which talk of 'a continual shifting of a Bedouin sort of population, whose migratory, predatory, gambling and dissolute habits utterly unfit them for continuous industry, and render them not only useless but injurious subjects in the attempt to form a new colony' (cited in Welsh 1993: 163). Like Munn, he notes that government officials such as Fearon blamed the Hakkas for the colony's crimes, and spoke of Hong Kong as being 'invested by numbers of the Triad Society' (ibid). A report to a House of Commons Select Committee spoke of situations in which ' "thirty, forty, or even fifty men come armed; I have seen two men shot at our own premises [Mathesons]. We shot two men one night there", and of a lady who awoke to find "fifty Chinamen in her bedroom" ' (Welsh 1993: 162).

In the absence of an alternative narrative, these (mainly European) writings and anecdotes have provided us with the dominant representation of the colony as an unsettled, criminal sort of place to which the colonial power brought peace, stability and order. Insight into the reaction of the Chinese to these government controls has to be read in other ways, principally by looking at what the Chinese in Hong Kong did as opposed to what the colonists said about them. For example, shortly after taking over the governorship from Pottinger, Davis sought to enforce a system of compulsory registration, using powers available to him under an 1844 Ordinance. Initially, this required all inhabitants of the colony to register. However, following protests from the European community, registration was limited to the Chinese population alone. We know something of their response to this new imposition from the fact that they immediately went on strike. Three thousand of them left Hong Kong for the Mainland, bringing the colony to a halt.

The same labourers who downed tools and left Hong Kong were also the most likely to find themselves criminalised by the colony's new laws and regulations – including those relating to public behaviour and sanitation. Looking for work, for example, they fell foul of laws that made loitering on the streets a crime, rendering them liable to arrest for vagrancy as well as nuisance and other offences (Munn 2001: 84). To keep rents low, the poor shared their accommodation with many others. The rudimentary nature of their lodgings necessitated washing and urinating outdoors, but this made them liable to arrest for indecent exposure, or punishment under new sanitary and hygiene regulations (ibid). The Europeans who lived above Tai Ping Shan repeatedly demanded that the authorities take action to prevent men, women and children from the area relieving themselves on the hillside. In multiple ways, therefore, the Chinese 'coolie class' attracted official intervention.

Ordinance No. 5 of 1844 and Ordinance No. 14 of 1845, providing for 'Good Order and Cleanliness' in the colony, responded partly to such demands, and partly to concerns about the spread of disease. Other ordinances were designed to police the daily lives, leisure time and general conduct of the colony's Chinese subjects. They did this by prohibiting gambling, riotous, disorderly or noisy conduct, assembling together at night time without a lawful excuse, as well as the licensing of alcohol (Kerrigan 2001). Specific offences ranged from everything including the erecting houses of matting or other inflammable material, to the exposure of offensive substances such as dirt and dung (ibid).

Governing a transient population: law

For Pottinger, Hong Kong's first Governor, and his successor, Davis, the problem of crime was inextricably linked to the problem of governing this constantly fluctuating population. It was a problem made more difficult by competing views about whether the Chinese should be punished according to English or Chinese law. Numerous Europeans, Indians and other nationalities – as well as Chinese from Mainland China – passed through Hong Kong on an almost daily basis. Relatively few stayed for any length of time. A small number of indigenous Chinese had been living on the island when the British arrived – it was argued that they should now become British subjects, governed by British law. These few were, however, quickly outnumbered by new immigrants from Mainland China. Between 1843 and 1845, the population of the colony rose from around 7,500 to 23,000; between May 1841 and March 1842 alone, it increased from 5,650 to 12,361 (Tsai 1993: 19). By 1849 the population stood at 28,297, and by 1853 at 37,536. As Tsai points out, it grew rapidly after 1854, when many Chinese fled the Triad and Taiping unrest in the Mainland. By 1854 alone, it had risen to 55,715, and by 1865 it had reached 121,497 (Tsai 1993: 22). Most of these Chinese travelled to and from the Mainland at frequent intervals, coming to Hong Kong for work and returning home to visit family and friends, and perhaps to trade between the two places.

When, in 1844, Pottinger gave Caine the power to apply the laws and customs of China to Chinese offenders within the colony, it was therefore unclear whether this rule applied to *all* the Chinese – exactly who counted as a 'resident' of Hong Kong became central to the operation of Hong Kong's rudimentary system of criminal justice. During the 1841–3 negotiations between Britain and China the Chinese side argued that, since the British in China's treaty ports insisted on being exempt from Chinese law and subject only to English law, it followed that the Chinese in Hong Kong should be exempt from English law, and subject only to the laws and institutions of China. This was not simply an argument about sovereignty – the Chinese authorities were anxious that Hong Kong did not become a safe haven for subversives and fugitives fleeing Mainland justice. The British wished to exert control over those who lived within the territory of Hong Kong island, but were also worried that the more liberal laws of England – which they hoped would appeal to 'respectable' Chinese traders – would instead draw the 'dregs' of Chinese society, those trying to evade Mainland justice. Unless Hong Kong's population was governed by laws as harsh as China's, the island would become a refuge for these fugitives from Mainland justice. This view was to be aired at several points in Hong Kong's history.

Some in early Hong Kong also believed that Chinese officials were, in fact, deliberately promoting the exodus of pirates, vagabonds, and thieves to Hong Kong, in an attempt to undermine the colony and discourage respectable Chinese from living there (Munn 2001: 45; Sinn 1986). (Similarly, the flood of refugees released by China into Hong Kong in the 1950s and 1960s was seen by some as an attempt by Communist China to destabilise the colony.) In the 1840s, no satisfactory arrangements had been formulated to allow criminal suspects to be handed over between the two sides. Moreover, the suggestion that the British should hand Mainland offenders back to China was opposed by those who regarded Chinese punishments as barbaric, and who saw the mission of the British as being to abjure, rather than to collude in, such barbarity. Similar arguments resurface throughout the colony's history, (most recently in opposition to calls to hand over to China suspects who would face the death penalty, or suffer unduly harsh punishments for acts not considered criminal under English law). Indeed, the question of who should have jurisdiction over those suspected of committing crime on either side of the border was to become something of a *leitmotif* in later Hong Kong/China relations, particularly in the 1990s.

On the question of which law should apply to the Chinese in the 1840s, a compromise position was originally arrived at. This was to apply English law to the Europeans and Chinese law to the Chinese. Though it had its opponents, there was also a feeling that the British were forced into this position by the logic of their insistence, in the Treaty Ports, that British subjects be governed by the laws of England. In the face of this, it was difficult to argue against a similar rule for the Chinese inhabitants of Hong Kong. The compromise was, however, short-lived. Arguments in London revolved about the issue of whether Hong Kong should be likened to the Treaty Ports, since the British had acquired Hong Kong by conquest and operated there as a sovereign power. Her Hong Kong subjects should, therefore, now become British subjects governed by British laws. Lord Stanley, at the Colonial Office, opposed the idea of handing over serious offenders to the Chinese authorities precisely because 'The same crime might have to be defined differently to satisfy British and Chinese legal usages, and there might be discrimination where English and Chinese were jointly accused of the same crime' (Endacott 1964: 30). Lord Aberdeen, at the Foreign Office, on the other hand, favoured the idea and supported the notion of having Chinese magistrates based in Hong Kong exercising jurisdiction over Chinese offenders according to Chinese law. The Law Officers of the Crown, meanwhile, advised that the Hong Kong Chinese were British subjects and should be governed by English law, but 'this legal opinion was disregarded' (ibid). From the very start, then, what happened in Hong Kong was subject to the differing views of officials in Hong Kong as well as the Colonial Office. Moreover, officials in the Foreign Office saw Hong Kong affairs through the lens of international diplomacy and imperial politicking with China, whilst the Department of Trade saw its task as that of making colonialism profitable. Hong Kong affairs – and especially the treatment of the Chinese – were also influenced by the different political views of members of the British parliament, and by a British public alerted to colonial injustices by the networks of evangelical missionaries across the Empire who aired their views through the pages of the British press (see Lester 2001).

In Hong Kong, Pottinger quickly changed his mind on the question of handing over transient Chinese offenders to a Chinese magistracy based in the Kowloon Walled City (in the 1840s, still a part of Mainland China), where they would be punished according to the laws of China. The idea was, Munn says, to be one of the many false starts that characterised the early years of British rule. Pottinger now argued that full British sovereignty should be asserted over the island and all who dwelt there (Munn 2001: 54). English law would apply to everyone; the police would have powers to question and detain anyone; and those Chinese who did not like this arrangement should be allowed to leave the colony.[4] Just as the large Chinese communities in the Straits Settlement and in Mauritius all 'happily lived under British law' (Endacott 1964: 30), so Pottinger imagined all would all live happily under British law in Hong Kong.

When, in 1844, Pottinger was replaced as Governor by Davis, the new Governor also refused to adopt the principle that the Chinese in Hong Kong should be exempt from English law. He insisted that if any of the Chinese inhabitants committed an offence under English law, they would receive the same treatment as members of the British community. However, when in 1844 an ordinance to establish the Supreme Court was drawn up, 'the principle was that the law of England as at 5 April 1843 was to prevail . . . except where inapplicable, but on the side of criminal jurisdiction the ordinance gave power to punish Chinese criminals according to the law of China'.[5]

Administrative policing: the registration system

The debate about which law to apply to Hong Kong's inhabitants was, until 1844, largely theoretical for there was in Hong Kong no legal professional capable of applying English law to anyone. Traders relied partly upon arbitration to settle their disputes, whilst Pottinger and Caine, the chief magistrate, applied a mixture of military law, 'common sense', and what Caine (mis)understood to be Chinese penal law. In the first years of the colony, Hong Kong had no professional police, lawyers, judges or courts. In the early 1840s, justice was dispensed by Her Majesty's Plenipotentiary, Henry Pottinger. All legislative, executive and judicial power was vested in his person. What would have been deemed a despotic concentration of power in settler colonies was regarded as necessary in Hong Kong, where these powers were to be used to establish the basic infrastructure of the colony, securing order so that trade could flourish. Pottinger's role was to both dispense justice to the European and native populations, as well as apply the *lex mercatoria* to trade disputes arising amongst the British in China's treaty ports.

In the interim period between 1841 and 1843, Pottinger proposed that no one be allowed to settle in Hong Kong without first being registered. Between 1842 and 1844 Caine imposed a series of controls – the 'light and pass' laws – on the movements of the Chinese in the colony. The first of these, introduced in 1842, imposed a night curfew on the Chinese, deemed necessary in order to prevent robberies at night. The curfew prohibited Chinese residents from being out of their houses between the hours of eight and ten at night without a large lantern or light (in 1844 this was extended to eleven at night); after ten at night no Chinese were to be out on the streets unless they possessed a pass specifying their purpose in being out at such an hour. Passes could be issued by European employers (Proclamation of Caine, Chief Magistrate of Police, 8 November 1844).

The system of census and registration was seen by what Munn calls the early military-bureaucratic authorities as essential for the control and management of the Chinese population. Davis's Ordinance No. 16 of 1844[6] for Establishing a Registry of the Inhabitants of the Island of Hong Kong and its Dependencies established a Registry Office and the post of Registrar General (Protector of the Chinese). It marked the beginning of what Munn describes as the colonial government's obsession with getting to know the identity, habits and beliefs of its Hong Kong subjects. Such knowledge may, perhaps, have helped fight crime but it was also used to monitor political agitation and to measure Hong Kong's success in attracting the more 'respectable' Chinese to the colony. However, when Davis levied a poll tax on all persons of Chinese origin, it foundered in the face of unanticipated protests from the European community, who feared it would cause these much-needed Chinese merchants to depart the colony. Nevertheless, from 1844 onwards, the annual census and system of registration mapped the identity and whereabouts of all Chinese in the colony. It functioned to keep the Chinese 'in their place' – literally away from those areas of the city occupied by Europeans. This informal spatial segregation reflected the idea, expressed in early reports, that the Chinese 'riff-raff' had a deleterious and demoralising effect on the colony (Munn 2001: 68). Spatial segregation mirrored the social distance between the 'respectable' and 'unrespectable', the law-abiding and the criminal, European and Chinese, coloniser and colonised. The Europeans protested their inclusion in the Registration Ordinance and won an exemption. Registration thus applied only to the non-European population of Hong Kong, principally the Chinese.

This swathe of 'anti-Chinese' legislation provided the authorities with what were essentially administrative powers of control and surveillance over the Chinese population. 'Light and Pass' laws placed the Chinese under curfew – Hennessy was later to denounce them as 'a monstrous piece of class [race] legislation' (Lowe and McLaughlin 1993: 66), whilst Munn describes them as 'the most universal, most visible and most durable form of anti-Chinese discrimination' (Munn 2001: 132). He comments that, more than any other law, the curfew singled out the Chinese for special treatment, causing resentment and leaving European troublemakers free to cause mischief.

The curfew had to be suspended in 1847, when the Colonial office questioned its legality, but it was revived again in the late 1850s and remained in force until almost the end of the nineteenth century (Munn 2001: 131). Since obtaining a ticket of registration involved paying an annual fee, the ordinance effectively imposed a discriminatory tax upon the Chinese population, to which they took exception. The second series of controls, which required all boats arriving in Hong Kong to be registered, also required their owners to report to the police; anyone unable to establish their credentials was required to leave the colony.

Further stringent rules on the registration of households and inhabitants were enacted in 1846 (Wesley-Smith 1994). Under these provisions, all Chinese males over 21 were required to register annually, submitting details of their occupation, family, marital status, size of family, and date of arrival in the colony. *Tepos* (headmen) were required to provide the names and occupations of all persons resident in their villages (see Kerrigan 2001). Davis's hard line on the enforcement of this registration system found support in London, where it was felt that 'effective restraint and a government not to be trifled with are objects of such primary importance that it is worth while to secure it even at the expense of adopting a policy the most opposed to our feelings' (ibid). (Davis's further attempt to reserve the right of appeal in the courts to Europeans only was, however, thwarted by London.)

The Chinese reaction to this discriminatory legislation was, as Munn says, a series of boycotts, minor riots, trade stoppages and strikes, all of which demonstrated how easily Chinese resistance to colonial rule could be organised (Munn 2001: 129). The experience, Munn argues, helps explain why the government later responded so harshly to attempts by labour to organise against the Europeans, and why colonial opinion 'increasingly opposed conciliation with the Chinese community' (Munn 2001: 130).

As a crime-fighting tool, the Registration Ordinance was a failure. It was, Munn argues, a reflection of the extremes to which the government was prepared to go in order to pin down the shifting Chinese population. Compulsory registration 'sought to provide both an apparatus of surveillance and a tool for weeding out the economically unproductive and the untrustworthy . . . (and) . . . a means of fathoming the covert political organization of the Chinese communities' (Munn 2001: 127). It reflected what Munn describes as the 'desperation' of a government convinced that it was surrounded by triads, pirates and secret societies, predators and parasites (Munn 2001: 130). The fears of the colonists were such that, in 1844, Davis had gone so far as to enact an ordinance allowing the government to declare martial law in any district of the colony (Munn 2001: 125). The ordinance was put up for disallowance by the Colonial Office but, Munn says, at the same time, two stark official proclamations were issued in Chinese. These suggested:

> . . . a readiness by the government to circumvent legal formalities. One, by Chief Magistrate Caine in July 1844, threatened the inhabitants of the troubled village of Stanley with a collective fine of $50 if any robbery should occur in their neighbourhood. The other . . . offered a reward of $25 to any policeman who killed a robber in the act of committing robbery, and a lesser reward of $20 for the arrest of any robber who was later convicted (Munn 2001: 125).

Such illegal use of collective punishments was followed by other legislation, in 1845, providing for three years' imprisonment, branding on the right cheek, and banishment for any Chinese found to belong to a triad society (ibid). This ordinance, was, Munn suggests, less a response to the true extent of triad activity in Hong Kong than a political gesture, designed to show support for, and cooperation with, Mainland officials' attempts to quell anti-Qing resistance in their own counties. Handing over anti-Qing triads was, of course, also in the interests of Hong Kong's peace and security, since agitators could easily find supporters amongst disaffected Chinese in the colony.

Nevertheless, the legislation provoked an outcry amongst the European elite, who likened it to the persecution of the Jews in Spain (Munn 2001: 126). The Colonial Office, worried that exiled offenders would be executed in China, and concerned about the pain caused by branding on the right cheek, forced Davis to water down his proposals (ibid). Banishment remained one of the penalties for triad membership, along with transportation from Hong Kong and branding (with a black arrow) under the left arm.

Criticism of the legislation persisted, however, the elite referring to it as 'the notorious branding and mutilating act' (ibid). Realising that no jury would convict using this legislation, David 'quietly instructed the Magistracy to deal with triad members by punishing and expelling them under the Registration Ordinance' (Munn 2001: 126).

Policing through native institutions

Schemes to map and track Hong Kong's Chinese population were a constant preoccupation of the colonial authorities (Munn 2001: 127). On the surface, such schemes looked like a natural way of tackling crime, poor policing and uncontrolled immigration (ibid). In this, they proved singularly unsuccessful, as crime – and the fear of crime – continued to rise in the colony. But such schemes remained useful if they provided the colonial authorities with intelligence about the organisation of the Chinese community, their popular leaders, and any attempts at organised political resistance (Munn 2001: 127). Registration would allow the government to track down not only criminal suspects but also political agitators. This point was well understood by Fearon, the first registrar general (ibid). Lack of resources to enforce the scheme meant, however, that dubious characters escaped detection whilst others, who had unintentionally failed to register in time, fell foul of the law's heavy penalties (ibid).

One of Davis's schemes sought to marry this policy with an existing Chinese system of surveillance known as the *baojia*. In 1844, he enacted an Ordinance that experimented with the institution of native peace officers (Ordinance No. 13 of 1844, Appointment of Native Peace Officers (the *paouchong* and *paoukea*)). This aimed to adapt a traditional Chinese institution to the colonial authorities' needs to maintain order. The peace officers were to possess all the power of an ordinary police constable except the power to punish (see Kerrigan 2001). Each officer would be rewarded or fined according to his performance (Munn 2001: 123). The *pao chia* system of registration, familiar to Chinese imperial rule, was a system of mutual surveillance. It required each household to keep a register of its inhabitants and report the existence of any strangers or crimes to the head of every ten households. The ten-household head maintained the register and forwarded reports of crimes and suspicious characters to the head of every 100 households, who then passed this information to government officials. Davis apparently explained the system of Chinese peace officers to London by drawing an analogy to parish constables (Munn 2001: 123). In a dispatch to London he wrote:

> I have been led seriously to reflect in consequence of the appalling amount of robbery and other crimes of violence which have hitherto existed . . . The attempt to regulate and restrain the Chinese population by a European police is attended with difficulties. The ignorance of their language, their customs and their persons gives an insuperable advantage to the vicious part of the population and it becomes moreover a sort of patriotic combination against the rule of the foreigner. I was accordingly led to the conclusion that the Chinese in towns and villages would be best locally governed by their own system consisting precisely of tithings and hundreds superintendents. This species of self government will be the most efficient in its results and at the same time entail no charge on the colonial funds as the officers are elective and honorary.[7]

Davis explained that, in China, these native institutions assisted the police in apprehending 'malefactors' as well as alerting them to the presence of robbers, fugitives, smugglers, and unlawful meetings. They kept a record of everyone in their 'ward' and noted anyone who could not furnish an account of themselves. They were also 'answerable for the preservation of the peace, preventing riots, drunkenness, noisy assemblies, and other nuisances'.[8] However, according to Munn, as early as 1844 the government had abandoned this complex system, and turned instead to using the *tepo* (headman), elected by the villagers and approved by government, to keep a register of village inhabitants, assist the police in investigating cases, help with the apprehension of offenders, keep the peace, vouch for land claims, manage burial grounds, help collect land rent, and resolve civil disputes (Munn 2001: 123). They also produced alibis, acted as character witnesses, petitioned for pardons, and lobbied government on other local concerns (ibid). Paid for by voluntary local subscription and the treasury, their main privilege lay in direct access to government officials (Davis cited in Munn 2001: 123). Whilst failure to do one's duty or obey orders could result in punishment, being an approved *tepo* elevated the headmen . . .

> . . . well above the lowly level they traditionally possessed in China . . . The high official salaries, the staff and official premises that some *tepos* maintained, the many duties successively heaped don them, their prominence in the ceremonial addresses presented to departing officials, and the tendency of some rising families or individuals to acquire the position, suggest that some *tepos* at least commanded respect from both the government and the communities they served (Munn 2001: 124).

The *tepos'* powers were confirmed in 1853, following a petition to Bonham from Chinese leaders. By 1858, when the system was at its height, Hong Kong had 16 *tepos* in five urban areas, two towns and nine villages; they were paid up to three times as much as a Chinese police constable (ibid). By 1861, however, the system seems to have disappeared – Munn suggests that the work of Daniel Caldwell and his Chinese detective squad may explain its decline (ibid). However, the *tepo* system also suffered from a drawback, which the government gradually attributed to most native institutions. Ruling the Chinese *through* the Chinese may have improved the government's ability to fight crime and identify suspicious characters but, equally, it placed a good deal of power in the hands of those elected as *tepos*. The *tepo* system also indicated the limits of European influence and the extent to which they were forced to rely upon the Chinese to govern themselves: colonial officials were simply unable to penetrate Chinese communities. Moreover, *tepos*' loyalty to their communities was always in tension with their loyalty to government – for example, in 1857, at the height of unrest in the Mainland and in the colony, a *tepo* in Stanley was discovered to have been at the centre of plots against the colonial government (Munn 2001: 124).

In general, however, the strategy of using native institutions to govern and police the Chinese chimed with London's view that the *pax britannica* was sometimes best achieved by working *through*, rather than by eliminating, indigenous institutions. This notion of 'indirect rule' would later be elaborated by Lugard as a distinct mode of colonial governance, but even in the 1840s, it was already understood by Pottinger and Davis. Colonialism in these early years thus never entailed the total eclipse of indigenous institutions. Indeed, it is clear that the colonial authorities sought to co-opt such institutions in an attempt to reach into communities from which they were otherwise excluded. As Munn notes, the police concentrated on Victoria, the principal European district; policing seldom extended to the Chinese areas. As a result, those living in those areas were left both unprotected and susceptible to recruitment by local criminal bosses (Munn 2001). In the mid-1850s, there were plans to demarcate the European and Chinese districts not only by police patrols, but by erecting actual physical barriers to separate the two populations.[9]

Davis himself argued that the use of *tepos* had improved public order (see Kerrigan 2001). For Lethbridge, this makes sense – prior to the arrival of the British, some of the local communities would have been governed by exactly this kind of native institution (Lethbridge 1975: 105). Its use in Hong Kong would hence have been familiar to the Chinese population. However, the immigrants from Mainland China formed new urban communities that lacked these traditional forms of control. Though many migrants came from the same areas of China and shared dialect groups (Tsai 1993), life in Hong Kong placed new strains on existing forms of mutual assistance. Here, as in China, the migrants remained on the margins of society.[10] Their situation was made worse by the fact that the government was unable – and unwilling – to appoint senior Chinese police officers to help protect them.

By the late 1850s, Hong Kong had, however, begun to attract more 'respectable' Chinese inhabitants. These were both concerned about crime and disorder and capable of establishing some sort of 'native policing' within their own communities. By the 1860s, a shifting commercial balance had taken place between the races, as Chinese merchants began to overtake their European counterparts in terms of wealth. They 'constituted the largest body of ratepayers' (Lowe and McLaughlin 1993: 66). It was this new Chinese merchant elite that eventually set up the district watchman scheme in 1866. Required to contribute towards the rates, they felt the police were deployed mainly to protect European properties, leaving their own poorly protected.

As Lethbridge argues, it was not simply the merchants' intention to establish a force that could help the police – the district watch was, rather, intended to act as an entirely separate Chinese police force (Lethbridge 1971). On 1 February 1866, the merchants met with other members of the Chinese community to request permission from the government to establish a force of Chinese watchmen. Having had their proposal accepted, they met again to discuss how best to organise and control such a force. One option was for the entire force of five chief watchmen and 40 ordinary watchmen to be appointed by a Central Committee of Chinese Merchants, themselves appointed from within the Chinese community. Another was to operate separate Councils in each district, to which the watchmen would be accountable. The compromise solution was for a community of five districts to elect and control the watchmen. The five stations they rented, as well as uniforms and salaries, were paid for out of voluntary contributions.[11]

The district watch quickly became the principal means of policing Hong Kong's suburban Chinese communities. It proved a much more effective detective force than the European or Indian police and the decision of the 1872 Police Commission to experiment with a more Anglo-Chinese force was probably influenced by its success, as well as by arguments in favour of local Chinese recruitment forwarded by a local 'China expert', James Legge (see Kerrigan 2001: 213). However, the establishment of the district watch created a third force in Hong Kong, and created tensions with both the official police and the detective force of the registrar (protector) of the Chinese (Kerrigan 2001). In 1868, however, the then-registrar general, Smith, attributed the colony's fall in crime to the effectiveness of the district watch. Kerrigan notes that the discipline of the district watch was also reported to be good, in stark contrast to that of the official police force. The chief watchmen attended the offices of the registrar and superintendent of police every day to report events over the previous 24 hours contributing to a unity of action between all three forces of law and order. In 1869, crime in the colony fell for the fourth year in succession. Though Creagh, MacDonnell and Deane, the new captain superintendent of the police, all credited this to the police reforms of MacDonnell's regime, the contribution of the district watch was also a factor.[12] By 1870, the success of the district watch was such that its duties extended to settling disputes within the Chinese community, including wages and family matters, as well as conveying government policy down the colony's hierarchy to the native population.[13]

Despite this success, however, there were those who disliked the new system intensely. Charles May was one of these, as was the chief justice, Smale. Part of their argument to the 1872 Police Commission was that the district watch prevented some crimes from being reported to the police. Leaving the Chinese to police themselves was also highly problematic. Crucially, it left the colonial authorities highly dependent upon intermediaries for intelligence about crime in the Chinese community, and about the activities of subversives within such communities. If this chain of intelligence failed, as it did, for instance, a century later, prior to the riots of the 1950s and 1960s, the authorities could find themselves without a presence in the Chinese communities.

By the 1870s, however, the Governor of the day, Hennessy, had concluded that, to survive in Hong Kong, the colonial government must accept the emergent Chinese elite as its main link with the 'coolie class', and begin to take the interests of the Chinese into account. In his own criminal justice policies he promoted the recruitment and training of Chinese police and prison officers. He also sought to restrain European demands for harsher law and order measures, though this brought him into direct conflict with powerful members of Hong Kong European elite (see Lowe and McLaughlin 1992).

Though, as we shall see, the hierarchy of the Hong Kong Police force itself only fully embraced Chinese police officers very late in its history, reliance on some form of 'native policing' was to continue in tandem with the official police force. This was especially so in the rural areas of Hong Kong, where traditional forms of Chinese authority remained essential to the reach of the colonial state. Up until the 1950s and 1960s, headmen and their native patrols were still provided with arms and training by the Hong Kong police, whilst rural District Officers sat as magistrates alongside native leaders to dispense 'palm tree' justice. The colonial authorities promoted local leaders to elite positions, increasing their status and effectively making them the official spokesmen for their communities. Thus, Sinn, for example, has demonstrated the importance of the Man Mo Temple and, later, the Tung Wah and Po Leung Kuk as institutions around which the Chinese community organised itself (Sinn 1989). In return for their limited autonomy, they became an invaluable adjunct of colonial governance. As traders and merchants themselves, the interests of the Chinese elite often coincided with those of the Europeans – both were, for example, equally concerned to limit the disruption to commerce caused by crime and the activities of workers' organisations.

As we shall see, from the 1880s onwards, the Chinese elite was crucial to colonial governance. Equally, however its identity of interests with the European merchant elite conflicted with its role as leader of the Chinese community. Ultimately, this was to weaken its standing as a moderating influence during civil unrest.

Notes

1 Davis to Stanley No 44 Financial 26 July 1844 CO129/6: 435.
2 Caine, Gutzlaff and Gordon to Woosnam, Lands Office 2 April 1844.
3 Martin (1846) *Reports, Minutes and Dispatches on the British Position and Prospects in China* CO129/18: 462.
4 Pottinger to Aberdeen 13 June 1843, No 59 CO129/3: 359.
5 Endacott 1964: 36; Davis to Stanley 21 October 1844, CO 129/7.
6 *Hong Kong Gazette* 27 July 1842, 2 (71).
7 Davis to Stanley 27 February 1844 CO129/6.
8 Davis to Stanley No 25, 8 March 1845, CO129/11: 160–61 cited in Kerrigan 2001.
9 Ordinance No. 7 of 1866 'The Victorian Registration Ordinance' allowed the Governor in Council to enclose parts of the Town and that 'all ingress or egress in or out of the same shall be prohibited'. Kerrigan 2001: 149.
10 Sinn 1986: 84; Kerrigan 2001.
11 Registrar General's report 1867; *Hong Kong Gazette* 14 March 1868; Kerrigan 2001. See also Lethbridge 1971, and Smith 1971.
12 *Hong Kong Government Gazette* 17 April 1869; Kerrigan 2001.
13 For further discussion of the role of the district watch see Kerrigan 2001.

Chapter 3

The Hong Kong police

The ethnicity of the police

In the first years of their rule, the British colonists had few resources and fewer set plans for the government of Hong Kong. The years 1841–3, before the formal establishment of Hong Kong as a colony and the appointment of a Governor, were particularly years of 'make do and see', but also years when order superseded law as the administration's priority. Munn (2001) notes that the earliest Hong Kong police force relied mainly on Chinese 'picked up from the refuse' of early immigrants. In the first few years, both Pottinger and Davis employed Native Chinese Peace Officers to extend control into the villages where there were no government police:

> Their duties under the Chinese Government consist in giving timely notice of robbers, gamblers, fugitives, smugglers of salt, distillers of spirits, sellers of saltpetre and sulphur, persons that obtain money under false pretences, hold unlawful meetings, – They assist the police in apprehending malefactors – They furnish the census of the inhabitants in their respective wards and mark everyone who cannot give an account of himself. They are answerable for the preservation of the peace, preventing riots, drunkenness, noisy assemblies, and other nuisances.[1]

Early press reports of a native police refer to them as 'constables' and 'subconstables'.[2] However, this force was disbanded in 1842, its members thought to be more interested in concocting false accusations than fighting crime (Munn 2001: 120). Press reports also indicate the existence of another, municipal, force maintained by the residents of Tai Ping Shan, in which 15 officers were paid out of a tax levied on prostitutes to protect their houses at night.[3] In addition, European merchants maintained their own small, private police to guard their wharves and godowns. The European merchants constantly complained about the lack of policing of their homes and warehouses. Pottinger's first solution had been to arrange for soldiers to be seconded from the military, along with Indians and Malays who had served elsewhere in the

Empire. In 1844, Captain J. Bruce of the Royal Irish Rangers (Kerrigan 2001: 80) replaced Captain Haley of the 1st Madras Native Infantry as Superintendent of Police There was soon general agreement, however, that the English and Irish soldiers were of 'poor quality'. Many had simply agreed to undertake police duties to escape the army; they regularly engaged in public drunkenness, street fighting, and assaults upon the population they were supposed to police. Their effectiveness was also hampered by the fact that they could not speak Chinese. The authorities were thus dependent upon a variety of 'truculent' interpreters (Eitel 1895 [1983]: 237, cited in Kerrigan 2001: 63).[4]

The poor behaviour of the 90 constables from the Irish and English regiments, and their lack of success in fighting crime, eventually prompted Pottinger to petition London for 50 expatriate police inspectors and constables, to form a professional police force. The Colonial Office, however, concerned with costs, agreed to give him only one superintendent and two inspectors. The low cost of deploying native police made this the Colonial Office's preferred option. There was, however, never any possibility of persuading the European elite to accept Chinese police in their districts.

On 3 September 1844, a Superintendent of Police, Charles May, was appointed, recruited from the London Metropolitan Police where he had served since joining the police in 1835. The Commissioners of the Metropolitan Police recommended him, along with his inspectors, Thomas Smithers and Hugh McGregor. They left London for Hong Kong in October 1844, confident that an effective police force could be established.[5] On 25 March 1845, May presented his 'Plan for the Improvement of the Hong Kong Police' to Davis.[6] Some of this called for London-style policing, though unlike London (where the idea of police as a *gendarmerie* was strongly opposed) some of May's police were to carry arms.

The presence of some armed police within the early Hong Kong Police Force has led some to conclude that the Hong Kong force was based on a 'blueprint' devised by the British for policing throughout the Empire. In many countries that have a colonial history, police forces were established soon after they became colonies. Brogden (1987a: 4ff) for example, argues that policing was one of the institutions the British transplanted to its colonies to impose centralised control and 'incorporate local society as a branch of imperial society'. Policing, like law, was a means of colonisation. The police had, Brogden argues, 'a major reserve function: available in emergency to be rushed to squash distant disorder'. Local policing practices were de-legitimatised and imperial policing was imposed.

But the English colonies on the whole did not follow a particular pattern, and it was to be the 1950s before anything like a Colonial Police Force emerged across the Empire. Moreover, it is clear that the original plans of the government and the Colonial Office were for Hong Kong to establish a municipal police force paid for, and answerable to, the ratepayers – quite the opposite of a paramilitary force answerable only to government. In addition,

Hong Kong in the 1840s was a very different place from colonial Ireland, which Brogden takes as his template for colonial policing. In the 1800s, Ireland was an English colony, but with a popular anti-English nationalist movement. The Royal Irish Constabulary (RIC) had the task of the military pacification of the country. It operated in a quasi-military fashion: patrols were conducted by groups rather than by individual officers; and officers were armed, lived together in barracks, and had a larger and more overtly political 'public order' role in dealing with protest and dissent. This 'Irish model' had three distinct features: police were: (1) organised more or less along military lines (which also meant they were armed); (2) housed in barracks rather than living amongst the community they served; and (3) centrally controlled. But in fact, the 'new police' established by Peel in London in 1829 also shared these features (unsurprising, since Peel himself established the IRC).

May would have been familiar with these 'models' but, at the same time, his position in Hong Kong called for a very different approach. By the mid-nineteenth century, British colonial practice emphasised that British rule should, as far as possible, be conducted with the consent of the local population, with some administrative powers devolved to local chieftains, clan heads, and other 'responsible' or 'reliable' local elites. Whilst Ireland was heavily policed, in the colonies one European officer 'frequently presided over huge tracts of territory and large, if scattered, populations, with only a handful of locally recruited and often untrained constables under their charge' (Anderson and Killingray 1991a: 53). The use of the police as a quasi-military force only became visible in periods of disorder or uprising.[7]

As Anderson and Killingray point out, in fact no colonial police force really replicated the Irish practice. More recent work on colonial policing by Hawkins has also questioned whether the use of such 'models' as the 'Irish model' and 'English model' helps our understanding of colonial policing (Hawkins 1991: 52). The character of Hong Kong's police seems, indeed, to have been driven less by 'blueprints' for colonial rule than by local circumstances and the colony's geopolitical position (see below).

The force that May inherited was, however, largely composed of former military (rather than civilian) recruits, and a military-style ranking structure had already been transposed the from the military 'mess', encouraging a certain *espirit de corps* between the European officers, and reinforcing status differences between this group and the Indian and Chinese rank and file. May, aware that Peel's Royal Irish Constabulary and his 'new police' in London carried arms, also initially proposed to arm the entire police force with pistols and cutlasses ordered from England. However, he specifically excluded the Chinese.

Provision was made in 1844 for two police stations to be built on the north side of the island, whilst another two smaller stations were to be built Chek Choo, and two more at Sai Wan and Pokfulam. The police headquarters was to remain at Victoria. A station was built in 1853 on Caine Road, adjacent to the complex housing the magistracy and Victoria prison. Visitors passing through Hong Kong at the time described these as imposing white buildings, elevated on a hill above the main thoroughfares of the colony. Between 1845 and 1859, two more stations were built in the European districts of Stanley and one in Stanley's Chinese sector; two were built in the Chinese areas of Victoria, and one at Aberdeen. In the 1860s, with the acquisition of Kowloon up to Boundary Street at the conclusion of the Second Opium War, further stations were constructed on the Kowloon peninsula. However, most of these outlying police stations were little more than huts or mat sheds (see Kerrigan 2001).

May's plan envisaged day and night time policing, beat policing, and the use of police patrols (Kerrigan 2001: 101ff) The police were to be housed in 'section houses' or barracks similar to the 'section houses' used for single male officers in the Metropolitan Police until the 1970s. They were to be uniformed (with different uniforms for different ethnic groups) and identifiable; they were to wear police buttons bearing the impression of the Crown and the words, 'Hong Kong Police', as well as legible numbers on the coat and jacket.[8] Inspectors and superintendents were to wear a uniform similar to those worn in England.

May's plans were forwarded to Whitehall, where the Metropolitan Police Commissioners reviewed them and confirmed that the rules and regulations proposed resembled those of the London police.[9]

However, unlike the London (and New York police) the early Hong Kong police made no attempt to infiltrate the local communities in order to prevent crime, and indeed for many years did not even maintain a force of detectives. They did, however, engage in large-scale operations to suppress gambling and prostitution, and to demolish or disinfect whole districts affected by the bouts of plague and disease that hit the colony with some regularity. In this, the Hong Kong police were agents of what is generally called the 'civilising mission' of British colonialism. As Anderson and Killingray (1991a: 60) argue, 'The urban social ills of vice, vagrancy and liquor were as much the enemy of the ruling classes of the colonial world as they were of their . . . counterparts in England'. This 'public service' use of police forces is not a feature solely of colonial states.[10] However, the colonial government in Hong Kong used the police and the military to do any and every administrative or practical task required at the time. Later, this use of the police to deal with practical problems was to turn into a positive policy of 'Concord', 'community service, an effective means of winning the hearts and minds of the local community' for what Anderson and Killingray describe as the 'rather uncertain legitimacy of the colonial state' (Anderson and Killingray 1991b: 61). In the Cold War, using the police and army to deliver electricity generators to remote areas and outlying islands, monitor the water supply, and so on helped to off-set the threat of communism by pacifying the locals (see below).

In the 1840s, however, it was local interests and domestic forces – as well as costs – that shaped the character of the police. Since European recruits were expensive, Pottinger was advised to fill all the rank and file positions locally. This was not an option that recommended itself to the colonial elite, for whom all Chinese constituted potential criminals with loyalties to their own kind rather than to their colonial masters. Thus, the colonists remained 'consistent opponents of giving the administration of the law into Chinese hands' (Norton Kyshe 1971: 228–9). Davis himself argued that the Chinese police 'can never be trusted in this Colony. If not actually collusive with their countrymen, they have not the resolution to do their duty in case of emergency, and it therefore follows that either a European or a Sepoy Police or a number of both will always be necessary'.[11]

For these reasons, the numbers of Chinese recruited into the police remained low, the authorities preferring to rely upon Europeans recruited locally,[12] as well as men brought from India, where British colonialism had already cultivated a native population loyal to the Crown. Because they could speak no Chinese, and because a certain animosity prevailed between the two groups, the 'Hindustanis' were thought less likely to connive with the Chinese population they policed. Any Chinese police were to be recruited from outside Hong Kong and always subject to the supervision of a European officer:

> There are many reasons for believing that a Chinese police, with European officers, will be more efficient and economical than any other. The obstacles thrown in the way of a European in his attempts to ferret out the haunts of the lawless men who are numerous and insurmountable; ignorance of the language, feelings and habits of the people. From China itself there is no difficulty in procuring good steady men, either secured by a Mandarin or by a contract.[13]

May himself opposed employing Chinese constables and his policing plan ensured that they were never trusted with night duty. This was, instead, to be carried out by Hindu and European officers. Whilst during the day Chinese and European officers were deployed together on the streets of Victoria together, greater use was to be made of the European and Hindu police for all duties. At night time, armed Indian police were to patrol the European business and residential districts.

Rather than patrolling their beats, police constables were stationed at conspicuous points in the town, where they were readily visible to the population. Apart from crime, they were to tackle street hawkers, public nuisance, the indiscriminate dumping of rubbish, and the existence of open sewers and drains (Kerrigan 2001: 93 ff). As Munn has argued, this policing of public cleanliness particularly criminalised the Chinese population in the Tai ping Shan district.

May also re-organised the water police to patrol at night for pirates. The waters around Hong Kong were sub-divided into specific beats, but here too, the Chinese police were to be outnumbered by Europeans and Indians (Kerrigan 2001: 93ff). This official reluctance to allow local Chinese to patrol without European supervision was to remain a feature of the police force until well into the twentieth century. Compared to the British, the Chinese were said to have a 'corrupt notion of justice' and were 'not to be entrusted with the administration of the law' (Norton Kyshe 1971: 127). There were 'no more corrupt people on earth than the Chinese' (Norton Kyshe 1971: 338). Similarly, they were not trusted to carry arms.

Davis regarded both the Chinese and Hindu contingents as unreliable and remained convinced that it was the Europeans who were indispensable to the police.[14] However, the European police in fact proved highly unsatisfactory. They lacked discipline, were often seen drunk in public, frequently suffered from ill health, and absconded in numbers when a better paid job came along. Davis was forced to recognise the need to appoint someone (he suggested a 'trustworthy Chinese' with a 'knowledge of the haunts of suspicious persons' and able to provide 'timely information') to join the secret service.[15] The only European officer capable of communicating with the Chinese, Daniel Caldwell, was duly appointed as assistant to the superintendent of police in 1846, along with his Chinese informant (Munn 2001: 121). He replaced one of May's English Inspectors, McGregor, who retired that year (Kerrigan 2001). Though European, Caldwell's marriage to a Chinese woman, his knowledge of the language and his contacts within the Chinese 'coolie class' made him central to the force's detective capability and to the government's understanding of the local 'crime problem'. However, Caldwell's close association with this criminal underworld also made him a somewhat liminal character, leading to some serious doubts about his integrity. He resigned from the police in 1847, fleeing his creditors, but re-emerged in the 1850s to play a pivotal role in policing. Despite a major scandal in which he was associated with one of Hong Kong's most notorious pirates and criminals (see below) he survived. By the 1870s, he had proved so useful that powerful figures within the government were unwilling to lose his services. As a result, he rose to become the Registrar (or Protector) of the Chinese, the government's key interface with the Chinese community, charged with protecting the Chinese and with the discovery and apprehension of criminals within the Chinese community.[16]

As Table 3.1 shows, though the need for a Chinese detective force was well understood by the 1870s, local Chinese did not begin to form a substantial part of the police force in the 1920s. Despite Caldwell's assistance, this pattern of recruitment resulted, as Munn points out, in the lack of an effective detective force capable of gathering intelligence from, and detecting crime amongst, the Chinese community. Even when Chinese were recruited, they were excluded from the higher ranks of the force. It was not until 1936, almost 100 years after the colony began, that the first ten Chinese probationary sub-inspectors were appointed, followed by a further ten in 1937 and 14 in 1938 (Cartwright 1996: 99).

Table 3.1 Ethnic composition of the Hong Kong police 1848–1946

	1847	*1848*	*1861*	*1867*	*1872*	*1891*	*1900*	*1911*	*1926*	*1946*
European	57	43	71	89	146	124	150	130	246	353
N. American			10							
S. American			1							
Indian	93	114	195	377	365	210	350	360	572	325
Singhalese			1							
West Indian			2							
Arabian			3							
Malay			2							
Macanese			11							
Weihaiwei/ Shantung									370	305
HK Chinese	24	23	80	132	206	181	249	314	576	1,630
Grand total	**142**	**180**	**376**	**598**	**717**	**515**	**749**	**804**	**1,764**	**2,613**

Sources: Report of Police Commissioner 1872 CO/129/164; CO/129/389 Enclosure 2; CO/129/81 and CO/129/47 cited in Cartwright 1996:5; CO129/120; CO129/33 May to Hillier, 31 December 1847, cited in Kerrigan 2001. Also see HKPARs 1926 and 1946.

Whilst local Chinese police were cheaper to employ, the colonial elite's entrenched view of them as 'untrustworthy' made their recruitment impossible. The elite's preference was for a force composed entirely of more expensive Europeans and Sikhs. Throughout the nineteenth century, this preference was periodically challenged by the need to keep costs down and improve the force's detective capability. Between 1852 and 1854, for example, Bonham revisited the idea of recruiting more Chinese police partly because, as he wrote to the Duke of Newcastle, their knowledge of the language, habits and customs of their countrymen would make them more efficient than the Indian police.[17] However, an attack by Tai Ping rebels on the Kowloon Walled City in 1854 re-fuelled European fears of a larger Chinese uprising, and prompted a review of how well the police were placed to cope both with possible unrest and with the influx of refugees from Mainland China. The authorities, always afraid that many of its Chinese police might belong to triads, wondered how many secretly sympathised with the Tai Ping rebels. Despite his previous arguments, Bonham thus reduced their numbers, increased the Indian police, and created an auxiliary police force as a temporary measure. By 1854, the establishment of the police stood at 131 police officers, 27 of whom were European, 66 Indian and 38 Chinese.[18] As May acknowledged, since almost all the Chinese were restricted to constable rank, this left the force with no detective capacity. Meanwhile, the local press continually criticised the European police as 'debauched', the Indians as 'lazy', and the Chinese as 'rascally', their collective incompetence leaving Hong Kong dependent upon the military for its safety.[19]

Bonham's successor, Bowring, faced further pressure to reduce the costs of policing. Seeking an increase in overall strength to 166, he was compelled to recruit some Chinese constables but managed to raise the number of Europeans to 31, Indians to 107, and reduce the overall Chinese contingent from 38 to 29 (the Indian police thus comprised 64 per cent of the entire force). He also ensured that command remained with European officers. Chinese constables were used to police the locals, under the strict supervision of the European officers. European districts were patrolled exclusively by the European and Indian police. However, this deployment meant that, in addition to the centres of Chinese population around Tai Ping Shan and Lower Bazaar, areas now occupied by respectable Chinese merchants were left unpoliced.

The 1850s saw the recruitment of some American sailors into the police. A report in the *Friend of China* disapproved, it being felt that 'by habit and custom', if they were allowed to carry deadly weapons they were more likely to use them, turning Hong Kong into the 'Wild West'.[20] The Portuguese, Indians, Malays and 'Manila men' recruited were also unsatisfactory, since none could speak Chinese, were said to be hated by the locals, and thought to be corrupt. Bowring, trying to recruit reliable men cheaply but not trusting the local Chinese, continued to appoint more Europeans, despite being dismayed by their drunkenness and bad character. The general pattern of recruiting expatriates to officer and junior ranks thus continued, generally unchecked and unquestioned, until 1952, when recruitment to junior rank ceased. (Direct recruitment from English civilian life into the inspectorate ranks continued, however, into the 1990s).

Thus, for most of Hong Kong's colonial history, the command and control of the Hong Kong Police remained firmly in the hands of expatriate officers. The Second World War – often regarded as bringing colonial thinking to an end – failed to shift the established mindset. India's refusal to allow Indian officers to return to the force (following Indian independence) forced some localisation, but the process was extremely slow. Expatriates retained their position in the hierarchy well into the 1990s, even though corruption amongst the expatriate members of the force in the 1960s and 1970s finally stripped away any sense that the British were more morally fitted for the task of policing. Anti-government riots in 1966 and 1967 persuaded the authorities of the need to rebuild the legitimacy of the force, partly by recruiting and promoting more locals, and the prospect of Hong Kong's return to China in 1997 also acted as a further catalyst for the cessation of expatriate recruitment and the promotion of local Chinese officers to senior positions. These changes are discussed later.

Corruption

The colonial state's capacity to deal with crime and domestic instability was permanently undermined by the corrupt and ill-disciplined character of its officialdom, especially as regards law and order. In the midst of the emergency that beset Hong Kong in the 1850s, for example, Bowring[21] was faced with a major scandal involving Daniel Caldwell. The Attorney General, Anstey, accused Caldwell (whom Bowring had appointed Registrar of the Chinese) of corruption and involvement with prostitution, piracy and organised crime. Caldwell's closeness to the Chinese community, coupled with his remit as Registrar, placed him in a position of some power and certainly provided opportunities for corruption. (The revised Registration Ordinance of 1857 had shifted powers originally vested in Caine and May in the 1840s to the Registrar).

According to Norton-Kyshe, Caldwell was notorious across Asia as someone with 'too many irons in the fire' (Norton Kyshe 1971: 647). The emergency measures adopted in the 1850s also made the authorities heavily dependent on him for intelligence, resulting in a concentration of his powers, and resentment amongst some of the more powerful members of the elite. But, as Sayer points out, the elite itself was riddled with scandal: the Chief Justice had been dismissed for 'excessive indulgence in intoxicating liquor', the Attorney General (Anstey) for accusing the Registrar General (Caldwell) of 'associating with pirates', whilst the Registrar General 'hinted that the Captain Superintendent of Police (May) had 'a financial interest in brothels'. The Colonial Secretary had been accused by a local editor of 'receiving a bribe in connexion with the opium monopoly'; the Lieutenant Governor (Caine), accused of 'taking commission on the stall-rents at the Central market', and the Governor (Bowring) himself 'pilloried in another newspaper for giving privileged treatment in the matter of Government contracts to a certain eminent firm' (Sayer 1980: 186).[22]

Anstey's accusations eventually led to the appointment of a Commission of Inquiry. This found no evidence on eight charges brought against Caldwell, but four others were proved. However, the Commission was not persuaded that Caldwell deserved to be dismissed. The 'best colloquial linguist Hong Kong ever possessed' (Eitel 1983: 271) he acted as interpreter, assistant superintendent of police, Registrar General, interpreter to the Supreme Court and Chief Magistrate, and head of the Chinese detective force (Sayer 1980: 193). He was, therefore, regarded as indispensable, one of the few civil servants who could penetrate the Chinese community. Papers that came to light after Anstey's own suspension from office nevertheless further implicated Caldwell in dealings with a particularly notorious pirate, Ma Chow Wong, prompting a second Inquiry (ibid).[23]

At the beginning of the 1860s, such scandals meant that the sanitary, social and moral reputation of Hong Kong at home was so bad, that 'the governorship of Hong Kong afforded no encouragement' to the kind of person required to 'clear out this redoubtable Augean stable in China' (Eitel 1983: 23). In 1859, the new Governor (Robinson) instituted both a Commission of Inquiry into Civil Service abuses and a Cadet scheme requiring candidates for appointment to be trained in Chinese language, customs and culture. This enabled his administration to appoint someone other than Caldwell (C.C. Smith[24]) to the position of Registrar General. These new Cadets were to convey to the Chinese population the 'nature, purport and details' of every government measure affecting them, whilst also informing the government of what the Chinese 'really needed or wanted to say' (Eitel 1983: 364).

As a result of the Commission of Inquiry, Caldwell resigned. A local newspaper editor made repeated calls for further enquiries, but these were refused by the Colonial Office. In an attempt to eradicate police corruption, a new head of police (Quin) was appointed from the Bombay Police, and recruits for the force were sought in Bombay and Madras (Eitel 1983: 379).

Despite these efforts to clean up the civil service and the police force, however, when MacDonnell succeed Robinson as Governor in 1866 he commented that:

> I have no doubt that on my arrival more than half of the Inspectors were in receipt of monthly allowances higher than their salaries, from the Keepers of Brothels and gaming establishments. In fact, every new Police Law was a new source of profit to them, and the Chinese had been early so habituated to similar practices on the part of the petty Mandarins and officials in their own country, that such proceedings seemed to them quite natural.[25]

In MacDonnell's view, the Chinese had become either terrified of, or 'squeezed' by, the police. All sections of the force enjoyed the opportunity to be 'bought off from doing their duty' because all took turns to police the gaming areas and vice establishments. As far as the colonist were concerned, crime was 'rampant' throughout the 1860s, and gambling 'a national vice . . . rooted in an eradicable, because congenital, disease of the Chinese social organism' (Eitel 1983: 428). Chinese gambling habits, they held, were 'filling the streets with riot and honeycombing the Police Force with corruption' (Eitel 1983: 411). With an economic depression looming and property depreciating,

> . . . the cry of the colonists now was for a strong and resolute Governor, one who would give his undivided attention to the needs and interests of the Colony and govern it accordingly, undeterred by what the foreign community of Hong Kong now called the 'vicious system of colonial administration in vogue at home' . . . The sort of man the colonist now desired . . . was a dictator rather, with a strong mind and will, than a weak faddist or an obsequious henchman of the machine public. The cry was for a Caesar. As Providence would have it, it so happened it was just such a man . . . that the Colonial Office . . . selected (Eitel 1983: 411).

Corruption – especially that associated with turning blind eye to gambling – was seen as the biggest obstacle to effective policing. Bowring had taken the view that it was impossible to find constables who would not 'wink at and profit by existing abuses rooted in the inveterate Chinese habit of gambling', particularly rife in the Taipingshan area (Eitel 1983: 337). One way of ending police corruption was thus to end the force's responsibility for enforcement of the gambling regulations; another was to licence it completely, as had been tried in Macau. MacDonnell first tried stamping out police corruption before embarking on these two options.

For a time, MacDonnell's 'terror of determination' to weed out corrupt police meant that corrupt members of the force 'dared not take bribes' and the keepers of gambling houses 'curtailed their operations and redoubled their precautions' (Eitel 1983: 429). But by mid-1867, corruption within the police remained as entrenched as ever. Consequently, MacDonnell proposed instead to license it. Licensing and regulation would, he hoped, eradicate corruption in the police – Robinson had previously reached the same view, arguing that the best hope of containing gambling was to control it.[26] MacDonnell applied the same strategy to the regulation of prostitution, which was also linked to police corruption.[27]

Those who disapproved of the policy saw it as the government's positive encouragement of vice. MacDonnell blamed 'local clerics' – nicknamed the 'moral six' – for this view, but they were supported by other Europeans, including the Social Science Association, which, in turn, protested to Parliament; the Colonial Office itself strongly disapproved (Eitel 1983: 435). Licensed gambling, it was said, 'lower[ed] the prestige of the British Government in China'. Members of the Chinese community also petitioned against licensed gambling,[28] claiming that it not only led to crimes (such as embezzlement, cheating, and robbery) but also to people losing their businesses, selling their children, committing suicide, and eating opium. Eventually, MacDonnell was obliged to end the licensing system but, since the Registrar's office now became charged with gambling suppression, the link between gambling, corruption and the police force was substantially weakened.[29] Existing licenses were revoked and gambling houses closed down. Whilst the poor took to gambling in the streets, the rich moved their activities into private clubs or secret venues in Kowloon.[30]

Twenty years after MacDonnell's campaign, however, gambling and police corruption resurfaced. In 1886, 53 constables were arrested for accepting bribes from an illegal gambling establishment in Tai Ping Shan Street (Kerrigan 2001). According to the *China Mail*:

> The revelation of the corruption in the Chinese branch of the police force is enough to make the authorities despair of ever being able to train up a body of men free from the venality which characterizes the Chinese when placed in an official position. Whether it would be well to continue the

> experiment of employing Chinese for ordinary police duties is a question which will admit of some argument. One thing however is certain. If Chinese are to be engaged, they must be recruited from a different class of men, a superior class, men whose reputation for reliability (we will not say honesty) is undeniable and from whom with careful looking after, as honest work as it is possible to extract from Chinese as may be expected. (cited in Crisswell and Watson 1982: 67; also Kerrigan 2001).

Amongst the evidence discovered in police gambling house raids was a list of government officers receiving bribes. They included Inspectors Stanton, Witchell, Baker and Quincy, as well as a Sergeant Holt (Kerrigan 2001). Though European officers were the main culprits, the Chinese constables were principally blamed, May himself arguing that their complicity made the suppression of gambling and corruption 'a Herculean ask quite beyond the reach of the most upright and powerful Government' (ibid). Such views confirmed the colonists' worst prejudices about the character of the Chinese, halting their greater incorporation into the police force.

Policing by strangers and the control and finance of the police

As the foregoing implies, in the first century of colonial rule, the composition of the police force reflected a tension between the need to keep the costs of the colony down and the elite's distrust of the local population. Chinese police were cheaper to employ than Europeans[31] but the elite found the idea of a cadre of senior Chinese police officers unthinkable. It was not until 1878, during Hennessy's governorship, that any Chinese police officer was given training in the use of firearms; 20 to 30 were then allowed to carry rifles, and there was also some talk of allowing Chinese officers on night patrol to carry revolvers (Cartwright 1996: 53). Elite resistance to Hennessey's policy of 'equality for the Chinese'[32] meant, however, that as soon as he left the colony, such practices were abandoned and, once again, only non-local police officers were allowed to carry arms (Miners 1990: 312). Until the 1940s, Sikhs were preferred to Chinese for most rank and file positions though, from time to time, they were supplemented by Chinese from Shantung province in northern China and from Britain's other Chinese colony, Weihaiwei, as well as by men from the West Indies.

This practice of 'policing by strangers' was a tried and tested strategy of British policing at home and abroad. Throughout the empire, foreigners were drafted in to police the local population. English police constables, for example, held posts outside their home areas, in case their loyalty to the Crown was weakened by loyalties to local kin and friends. 'Policing by strangers' inhibited the formation of such local ties. The British employed it in the American colonies, where they used native American Indians from one tribe to police those from another. They also used it in Ireland, as well as in London where, in the 1830s, the Metropolitan Police specifically recruited its constables from outlying areas. Like London's 'new police', the Hong Kong police were also uniformed, lived in barracks which isolated them from the community, and patrolled given areas (beats) of the city.

Though May brought this style of policing to Hong Kong, local circumstances as well as the emergency of the 1850s significantly altered his plans. The character of the Hong Kong police force thus came to owe much to the political and social organisation of Hong Kong society, as well as the colony's geopolitical position on the edge of China. The British already had experience of policing Shanghai as well as other colonies. Though they certainly borrowed men and practices from elsewhere, this was done on a somewhat *ad hoc* basis, often because a particular Governor wished to transplant to Hong Kong some notion of policing with which he had experimented in another outpost of Empire.

The intersection of various concerns – costs, crime, political exigencies, and local events – meant that the character of policing was never settled but was constantly under review. Along with the administration of justice and colonial penality, policing acted as a lightning rod for competing views of colonial governance, so that whatever path the authorities followed they found themselves subject to criticism from some fraction of the colonial elite.

It was precisely these relations between government and elite which, almost incidentally, determined that Hong Kong police constables would not become accountable to their local communities, as they had in England. The independent constabulary power of the English police owes much to the peculiar history of British policing. As Lustgarten notes, when the first English police forces were formed in the 1830s, the office of constable was grafted on to 'the ancient and honourable office' of constable in common law (Lustgarten 1986: 25). Originally, the constable was part of English village life, a public official elected by the local community and 'a self-directed decision-maker answerable only to the law' (Lustgarten 1986: 30). However, the formation of municipal police committees in England meant that all 45 police forces were each partly paid for, and accountable to, their local committees. Local people were thus able to exert a degree of control over local policing policy, and could call senior officers to account if they disagreed with this policy.

In Hong Kong too, the original intention was to hand policing over to a municipal authority, reducing the costs to government but also reducing central government control of the force. Officials in London had suggested that the inhabitants of Hong Kong might wish to have some control over their own affairs by means of municipal self-government (Endacott 1964: 73), and to this end, Pottinger was instructed to levy a rate on all town buildings to pay for municipal services, including a police force. His successor, Davis, was urged by London to consider such matters as the location of police stations, whether there should be a night police, whether the force would obviate the need for watchmen, what 'class of men would do for the street Police', and how the expense of a force could be met. Davis drew up a plan to divide Hong Kong into three districts (eastern, central and western) and to appoint commissioners for police, lighting, roads and sewerage, with the power to levy rates (ibid). Since they were to be involved in meeting the expense of the force, Davis consulted the colony's leading trading houses on the extent of the police required.

The plan resembled England's organisation of such services. In Hong Kong, however,

> . . . The police rates ordinance was delayed until August, and though the assessments were low, it aroused the greatest opposition amongst the merchants, who regarded the new rate as exorbitant and unconstitutional . . . they vaguely demanded some form of self-government but . . . were much more interested in opposing taxation than in the municipal issue, since this would have shifted to them the burden of finding the money (Endacott 1964: 75).

The plan for a municipal force was therefore scuppered when the local ratepayers – European merchants, traders and property owners – refused to meet the cost of the rate that needed to be raised to maintain a force. They argued that the Governor's raising of public funds by levying rates was unconstitutional, raising the whole issue of self-government. However, as London understood, a government elected by the ratepayers would (as the elite knew) automatically exclude most Chinese. The prospect of a self-interested European elite governing the local population made the Colonial Office nervous, for it was felt that 'The English minority can hardly be trusted with the powers which it would give them over the Chinese and other alien and ignorant ratepayers'.[33]

These well-intentioned concerns for the indigenous population meant that London resisted the elite's calls for self-government. But the elite's refusal to contribute towards the police rate meant that the police force remained dependent upon the colonial authorities, with no democratic accountability to the communities it policed. The merchants' refusal to accept responsibility for policing left Davis with little option but to '. . . take the police directly under government control . . .' (ibid). Had the plan to hand policing over to a municipal authority been agreed, the character of the police force would have been very different. As it was, the police remained an arm of government. For some, this was as it should be: municipal control of the police was incompatible with 'the decisiveness and energy of proceeding which are almost necessary for the very existence of a European government surrounded by millions of Asiatics' (ibid).

Merchant hostility to Davis was apparently so intense that nothing much else could be achieved under his governorship. However, in 1849 a new

Governor, Bonham, again offered the justices of the peace (none of whom were Chinese) control of the police, provided they met the gap between the true cost of the police force and the amount raised by the police rate. They again refused. Since the superintendent of police, Charles May, and his two assistants were funded by London, their appointment was to remain in the hands of the colonial secretary, though they were directly responsible to the Governor for the proper administration and operation of the force. Bonham's offer was reiterated in 1851, but again the justices refused, arguing that the force was inefficient and that, if they took control of it, raising its efficiency would entail more spending on the police than the Governor had indicated. They were happy to assume control of the police provided the government met all the costs, and argued that policing should have first call on public funds because it was a vital service to the community (Endacott 1964: 78). Bonham disagreed: the police force was adequate, crime was not rising, and there was, therefore, no need for increased spending. But the Hong Kong merchant class wanted, Endacott says, 'maximum freedom at minimum administrative cost' (Endacott 1964: 79). Having recently secured representation in the Legislative Council, the justices and the merchant class were now less inclined to support a municipal government for whose services they would partly have to pay (Endacott 1964: 78).

The initiative of municipal self-government was thus abandoned. Autonomy for Hong Kong residents had been pursued by London both as a matter of principle, and as a means of reducing the financial burden on the home government. When it failed, the Hong Kong police became a *de facto* arm of central government.

Later, this arrangement was to contribute to the stereotypical image of the Hong Kong police as a repressive arm of colonial power, contrasted with the English constable, who traditionally had the autonomy to decide how the law should be enforced in local circumstances, was independent of any political control from government or Crown, and subject only to the law, via the courts. But as this episode reveals, the Hong Kong police became an arm of government virtually by default – it had never been the colonial authorities' intention to retain control. The result, however, was that Hong Kong police as a whole never became responsible or accountable to the public under any legislative enactment.[34]

The 1850s saw policing shaped by a number of cross-border disturbances, as well as these domestic demands and criticisms. There were three Commissions of Inquiry into the police, two of which were abandoned in 1855.[35] The third, in 1856, considered the capacity of the police to respond to agitation and unrest, as well as their ability to tackle crime. One of the many victims of robbery was the chief police magistrate himself, somewhat denting attempts to convince the elite that they could rely on the police force for protection. In October 1856, at a public meeting held to discuss the inefficiencies of the police force, sections of the Chinese population complained that the Indian police treated them cruelly, spent their most of time in brothels, taverns, and routinely slept on the beat (Norton Kyshe 1971: 407). Several cases in the late 1840s and 1850s suggested that these complaints had merit. In 1856, two Indian police were convicted of extortion, and another, English, constable was also convicted of extortion and demanding money with menaces; in 1851, two Chinese constables stood trial for taking protection money from illegal brothels (Kerrigan 2001: 140). Some Chinese shopkeepers, meanwhile, complained of thefts by the Indian police.

These activities led the local press to call for 'a searching and unsparing investigation' into the police, which it described as 'a refuge for the discontented'.[36] The 1856 Commission, having heard evidence from the public, concluded that whilst some of the problems might be addressed by closer supervision of members of the police force, others required a radical overhaul of the entire force. There was to be new legislation, stricter rules and regulations, and more recruitment of soldiers (Kerrigan 2001: 145). The Commission concurred with Bowring, however, that the force should consist of fewer Chinese and more Europeans, Malays 'or other coloured men'. There were to be new pension entitlements and salary scales, designed to attract and retain good men; the presence of the rural police was to be stepped up, as was that of the water police (ibid).

Defraying the cost of the colony's police was, as ever, a pressing issue for London. One suggestion from the Commission was that one third of the costs be met by London, one third by local taxation and one third by local Crown revenue. As Kerrigan notes, neither the Commission nor Bowring was convinced that there was any point reviving the idea of merchants paying for the police through raising a municipal rate, something favoured by Hillier (now chief magistrate and member of the Commission). In a dispatch to Labouchere in London, Bowring complained that the European merchant community rarely participated in public affairs, and only did so when their private interests were concerned.[37] He was also opposed to using revenue gained from the colony's trading activities to pay for the police. This, for Bowring, undercut the very principle of free trade that had contributed to the colony's success.[38]

Having taken evidence of the Chinese 'Watch and Ward' system, the 1856 Police Commission rejected its adoption but accepted an offer from the Chinese merchants to act as a sort of auxiliary police force to assist the official police. Bowring had noticed that:

> . . . a somewhat better class of Chinese (had) been rising to some amount of opulence and influence with the progressive prosperity of the Colony and that through these (with Mr Caldwell's invaluable assistance) we may introduce a portion of the machinery by which, on the Chinese Continent, localities are made responsible for the misdeeds committed on them.[39]

Bowring now sought to build upon the co-operation of this section of the Chinese community. Writing to Labouchere in 1856, he said he 'attached the greatest importance to the co-operation of the Chinese for introducing any really valuable police reform' (Kerrigan 2001: 151). In the short-term, that reform failed to transpire. The police retained their image as a raggle-taggle force, poorly equipped, poorly clothed, and poorly behaved. Ten years later, Chinese leaders were disappointed that the force they had helped to support was still failing to police Chinese districts effectively. Instead, they decided to pay for their own police and were permitted, by the Registration Ordinance of 1866, to form their own District Watch, in effect a Chinese police force which ran in parallel with the official Hong Kong Police (see Lethbridge 1978; Kerrigan 2001).

Problematically, however, the creation of the District Watch now meant that there were three organisations policing the Chinese – apart from the official police and the District Watch, the Registrar (or Protector) of the Chinese also retained a responsibility for detecting crime within the Chinese community, to which end Caldwell maintained his own detective force. A lack of co-ordination between these three forces itself came to be seen as an explanation for the authorities' failure to cut crime. As the Chief Justice, Smale, argued, it was becoming uncertain whose job it was to detect offenders.[40] His view, which he expressed in the Legislative Council, was that this division of authority between the police, the registrar and the District Watch was one of the main causes of police inefficiency (ibid).

When, in 1859, Bowring was replaced by Robinson, the new Governor arrived with his own plans for the police force. Within a year, he was faced with the task of policing Kowloon, ceded to the British under the Convention of Peking at the conclusion of the Second Opium War. This task he handed to May, appointed as Civil Commissioner of Kowloon in 1861; a detached force was stationed there consisting of nine Europeans, nine Indians and ten Chinese.[41] In the rest of the colony, the force was still heavily dependent upon the Indian police (12 members of whom were recruited from the Bengal Native Light Infantry). Robinson planned more recruitment from India and moved to replace the southern Indians with Sikh police (Kerrigan 2001:166ff). He was prepared to trawl the Indian army, as well as the West Indian colonies and 'the Malays' for possible recruits, having himself been seconded from the army and formerly stationed as Governor in the West Indies. Overtures were made to recruit volunteers from the Indian army, with a view to recruiting more later:

> I am satisfied . . . that the bulk of the Police Force here must always be Indian, and that the best chance of improvement will be by endeavouring to obtain from India, or from Indian regiments serving in China, really good men. In filling up the present increase to be able to make a move in this direction, I obtained the sanction of the Major General

> Commanding in China to the employment in the Police, as a temporary and experimental measure, of half a company of the 5th Bombay Native Infantry at present in the colony.[42]

Another 150 men were to be recruited by a Captain Grant in India from the 3rd Bombay Regiment in Bombay and Bangalore (ibid). Favourable terms of service were offered in order to recruit and retain men 'of good character' who were 'young and healthy'; some married men were allowed to bring their families; the term of enlistment was for five years in the first instance, and a return passage to India was included (ibid). Whilst the Europeans were to remain in overall command, their numbers were to be kept low as they had proved themselves unsuitable for the task in hand (ibid). He suggested, however, that the Cadet system be extended to Hong Kong, so that there would be some Europeans within the government capable of communicating in Chinese, translating where necessary and, as Lethbridge puts it, 'assisting with control over a Chinese lumpenproletariat without a stake in the colony'.[43]

Robinson also subscribed to the view that there was no mileage to be had by increasing the Chinese membership of the police:

> The native character . . . is unsuitable for either a preventative or detective police, as the office of Constable would assuredly be used as a means for affecting fraud, injustice and speculation, and the main employment of the Chinese in the force must always therefore be mainly confined to services, such as rowers of police boats, and such like occupations, which carry with them no positive possession of power.[44]

However, in 1864, Robinson's new superintendent of police requested the appointment of a small detective force consisting of 12 Chinese constables (Kerrigan 2001: 161ff). Robinson had also begun to replace May's regime. In 1861, he appointed an acquaintance, Quin, as superintendent of police. He had served with Quin in St Kitts and Quin, by now an accountant with the Treasury in Antigua, had been involved in the suppression of disturbances in St John's in 1859.[45] Following a great deal of criticism, however, by 1867 Quin had been replaced by Rice, a former inspector of police in Mauritius, who brought with him a good deal of experience of policing other colonies.

Robinson's overhaul of the police force included a new Police Ordinance, introduced in 1862. This specified, in great detail, the duties and conduct required of a police officer (Ordinance No 9 of 1862). It not only set out a revised structure of the force but also a hierarchy of wages for the different nationalities (Europeans earned the highest salaries, followed by the Indian police, then the Chinese). All police officers were required to be sober, civil and ready for duty at all times; they were not to enter taverns or gambling houses, not to accept gratuities, and always to wear their uniform when on duty (Kerrigan 2001: 161ff).

Despite these reforms, however, criticisms of the police persisted, principally concerning their inability to reduce crime. Thus when Robinson's successor, MacDonnell, arrived in the colony in 1866, he too arrived determined to shake up the police force and crack down on offending. Shortly after his arrival, he described the police force to London as a body of corrupt men, ineffective, with no policing experience, willing to connive with others in breaking the law, and eager to be bribed.[46] He regarded Quin as completely unsuitable to command the police force,[47] claiming that Quin spent too much time in his office and had neglected to supervise personnel under his command. As a consequence, police laws were not being enforced. Quin left in 1867. Deane, whom MacDonnell regarded as energetic and who spoke Chinese,[48] assumed temporary command of the police force (he had been appointed Captain Superintendent of Police in July 1868). He was eventually succeeded by Rice. At the same time, MacDonnell embarked on a programme of 'exceptional legislation', which was, he believed, required if the colony was to survive 'the permanent state of siege by the criminal population, which is ever surging around it and threatening it with invasion' (Kerrigan 2001: 161ff).

Inefficiency, reform – and more issues of ethnicity

Under MacDonnell's governorship, the last years of the 1860s witnessed a swathe of legislation, much of it highly punitive and aimed at the Chinese immigrant community. Informers were offered rewards for information on crime, laws were passed enabling male offenders over the age of 16 to be whipped, and those convicted of child stealing to be whipped and/or kept in solitary confinement. In addition to his attempts to suppress gambling and control prostitution and disease, MacDonnell introduced new laws to suppress piracy, limit public meetings, reinforce the 'pass laws', and permit trial without jury. Magistrates' powers of punishment were increased to enable imprisonment for up to two years, and to enable them to punish offenders arrested but not convicted. In addition to public flogging, the practice of branding, prohibited by London in 1845, was reintroduced under doubtful legislative authority.

As part of his reforms of the police, MacDonnell reversed Robinson's recruitment of police from Bengal, preferring instead to attract Sikh recruits into the force. To this end he sought assistance from the Governor General of India, requesting that:

> The Sikh contingent in question should have at its head some person who is a gentleman by birth and education, it being my belief that in no other way can the government be secured against corrupt practices.[49]

MacDonnell also took advice from an old family friend, Creagh, an assistant superintendent of police in the Punjab who possessed some competency in Oriental languages (Kerrigan 2001: 161ff). Creagh suggested recruiting 100 Sikhs already trained in police duties, each on five-year contracts. MacDonnell then sought permission from India to have Creagh transferred to Hong Kong.[50]

By 1869, the authorised strength of the force stood at 634, but it was still overwhelmingly a non-Chinese force, with 182 Sikhs, 126 Indians, 123 Europeans and only 72 Chinese land police and a few Chinese amongst the 131 water police (Kerrigan 2001: 161ff). Few could communicate with – or gather criminal intelligence from – the local Chinese population. Blind to the effects of their own prejudices, however, the authorities continued put most of the blame for the failings of the entire force on the Chinese section, the smallest group in the police. They were blamed for being less 'efficient' than their counterparts – statistics compiled for the captain superintendent's annual report of 1870 claimed that the Chinese police made fewer arrests per constable. (However, they reported more cases and secured an equal number of convictions).[51] The figures took little account of the fact that the Chinese police, unlike their European and Indian counterparts, were not allowed to carry arms, nor participate in certain types of investigation, nor were trusted to patrol the European districts around Victoria. Since the Chinese were not allowed to bear arms, and since Creagh took the view that patrolling at night, guarding prisons, and protecting government buildings all required an armed presence, he increased the Indian component of the police (Kerrigan 2001: 161). The Chinese were also still restricted to the lowest ranks and wages.

Little, then, had changed since the 1840s. The same diagnosis of the 'problem' within the police engendered the same solution: more non-Chinese recruits. This in turn repeatedly meant that the force was fundamentally hampered in its attempts to cut crime because it could neither communicate with, nor detect crimes among, the majority of the population. Officials constantly assumed that no 'men of quality' could be recruited from within Hong Kong's own Chinese community. According to Deane, the lower ranks were 'lethargic' and performed their work 'strictly according to regulations, thus shielding themselves from the possibility of a severe reprimand' (see Kerrigan 2001: 161ff). A 'want of energy and interest' was, he claimed, a 'characteristic' of the Chinese, whilst those recruited from India were blamed for their supposed racial 'characteristics'. The Europeans, too, fell far short of what was required, with their 'natural love of change' and their excessive drinking. Hong Kong's 'intemperate climate' also made them problematic and hard to retain.[52] Deane thus concluded that:

> The present plan of enlisting men from all quarters of the world throws great obstacles in the way of efficiently employing the Force. So many prejudices of colour, caste, and nationality have to be overcome, so great

> difficulties arise with reference to quarters and cooking arrangements, and so many petty internal jealousies are nurtured, that all spirit of mutual co-operation for the good of the Public is lost . . . With reference to the several nationalities in the Force, Europeans appear to be unable to refrain from excessive drinking; the West Indians, with four or five exceptions, are found to be almost worthless owing to their stupidity and other bad qualities. These men, however, having previously lived in the Colony, without employment, are not fair specimens of their race. The Sikhs continue to be most useful in cases of assault and arrests for drunkenness, but their want of knowledge of English continues to be a drawback. The same to a lesser degree applies to the Indians, but amongst both are those who have made great progress in English and in Chinese.[53]

Deane had, however, understood that, as far as detecting crime was concerned, the 'Chinese portion' of the police probably 'knew what was going on' in the Colony, whereas their European colleagues did not. For this reason, he argued, 'I should prefer a European and Chinese Force only' (ibid). He was not, however, a supporter of native organisations like the District Watch, arguing that 'Chinese police men among a Chinese population' could only be trusted if placed under the strict supervision of the police department.[54] The same applied to Caldwell's detectives or 'runners', whom he alone commanded and who had come to constitute an essentially 'private' police force.

In 1870, Whitfield (Acting Governor during MacDonnell's absence) was forced to deal with European complaints about rising crime. Serious crime had, it was said, risen by 78 per cent, and minor crime by 20 per cent. All crimes had risen by 32.4 per cent compared with 1869, whilst robberies with violence, burglaries and assault with intent to rob were said to have risen by an astonishing 400 per cent.[55]

These increases were initially blamed on the release of several long-term prisoners, the influx of '100 dangerous characters from the Mainland' fleeing the Mainland authorities, and the presence of 49 Chinese criminals, deported by the French from Saigon to Canton, who had clearly sneaked back into Hong Kong (Kerrigan 2001: 192). Keeping track of these 'habitual criminals' became an obsession. A number of legal and administrative measures were tried (see below). Deane proposed that they be dealt with under vagrancy laws, with deportees branded on the body with letters which would correspond to an official register containing details of a person's prior criminal history. They would also be photographed.[56]

The elite, however, blamed the startling rise in crime in 1869/70 on attempts by liberally inclined officials (such as the Chief Justice, Smale) to reverse MacDonnell's punitive policies during his absence.[57] In August 1870, one of the (European) justices of the peace declared that he intended to call for an inquiry into the state of the force (Kerrigan 2001: 193). In 1871, the unofficial JPs held a meeting to discuss the 'alarming increase in crime in the colony and the apparent powerlessness of the police to prevent it . . .' (Norton Kyshe 1971: 189; *Daily Press*, 31 October 1871; Kerrigan 2001: 193).

Whitefield had been warned by London not to implement any major changes whilst MacDonnell was on leave. The unofficial JPs thus took their complaints directly to the Secretary of State for the Colonies, presenting him with a letter signed by over 400 European residents.[58] In it, they claimed that there had been an alarming rise in crimes of violence and against property, that serious criminal cases remained unsolved, and the whole situation had been made worse by the cessation of flogging and branding. That the police were 'hopeless faulty in composition', numerically weak, morally worthless, open to corruption, 'without discipline' and 'utterly wanting in discretion' had, they argued, been made known to the authorities by the captain superintendent's own report of 1870 (ibid).

Responding to their complaints, Whitefield argued that the crime statistics misrepresented the true situation: the level of crime had not increased overall since 1868. He also argued that Hong Kong's location – 'within a rifle shot of mainland China' and easily accessible by criminals from Macau and Canton – made it a particularly difficult place to police (Kerrigan 2001: 188). Deane, (also on leave) was already under fire for having mismanaged the force. He now argued that the crime records were not a reliable guide to the level of crime in the colony – some crimes, for example, might have been entered twice (ibid). This response did not impress the complainers, who continued to cite evidence of increased attacks by pirates, murder, 'wholesale robbery, kidnapping, [and] highway robbery of various kinds, and burglary'.[59] Secret societies were said to be committing crimes faster than the police could catch them; it was dangerous to go out after dark; the police were powerless to help.

Whitefield blamed both Deane and Creagh for the problems within the police force itself. When they went on leave, he appointed Rice as acting superintendent of police, and conducted his own inquiries into the state of the force (Kerrigan 2001). In a dispatch to the Secretary of State for the Colonies (Kimberley) in 1870, Whitefield complained of poor organisation within the police, of their inability to communicate, of an inadequate supply of arms, and of the poor order and hygiene of their stations and barracks. The force, he argued, was:

> . . . composed of various nationalities: English, Chinese, Sikhs and Indians, whose languages being very different render them almost useless in combined action. The European public of Hong Kong cannot understand either the Sikh, Indian or Chinese constables, and the Sikhs and Indians cannot communicate with the Chinese constables, or with each other.[60]

Like others before him, Whitefield took the view that the Sikhs could not be 'made fit to perform police duties', the Bengalese were 'not to be trusted', that he had little confidence in 'the Madrasses', that the integrity of the Chinese was 'questionable', and the conduct of the Europeans 'unsatisfactory'.[61] His preference was to recruit West Indians who could read and write and 'upon whose pluck we could depend in an emergency' (ibid).

Meanwhile, Rice drew parallels between the situation in Hong Kong and that in Mauritius, which had a large Chinese population and which he knew well. Unlike Hong Kong, the police in Mauritius had managed to incorporate the Chinese into the force, and to form an effective detective wing (Kerrigan 2001: 195). Since he arrived in Hong Kong in 1867, Rice had been able to bring his experience to bear, forming his own conclusions about the deficits of the police. Put in charge of the force, albeit temporarily, he was in a position to influence matters. One practice of which he disapproved was the secondment of constables to heads of other departments (such as the colonial surgeon's office, when they were required to carry out inspections of brothels or enforce sanitary laws). Whilst carrying out such tasks might be a necessary part of their job, placing them under the control of another department weakened their police discipline. He argued for a clearer definition of police duties and responsibilities as well as a system of discipline and management.

It was Rice's considered view that, although the Commissioners of the Metropolitan Police had men available to join the Hong Kong police, the costs would deter London from agreeing to their appointment. Instead, he proposed recruiting West Indian police, whom he thought better disciplined. He also recommended following the example of Singapore, Penang, and Malacca where the police forces had recently been organised along the lines of the force in Mauritius – if the system could operate efficiently in Mauritius, with its large Chinese population, so too could it operate in Hong Kong (ibid).

Rice identified seven other main failings. The first was the impact on the police of 'outside interference' (including pressure from heads of other departments); the superintendent of police must, he argued, be independent. Secondly, he identified the fact that the police had a high proportion of officers to constables – there were too many superior officers in the force. Thirdly, the deployment of the police was such that too few were used for policing at night, the time regarded as most dangerous. In his experience elsewhere, at least two-thirds of the force should patrol at night time. The system of maintaining crime statistics was, moreover, so defective that it was unlikely the authorities had any clear idea of the state of crime. He was also critical of the division of responsibility between the police, District Watch and the Registrar's Office (Caldwell's detective force). While both had proved aides to detection, they consisted of 'irregular agents' who were

> too liable to abuse their power, and by means of intimidation, to become rather a scourge than a protection to the natives, and hush up crimes when paid to do so, while the information given to the Government on

> some points is the price of withholding it on others . . . [they were] too liable to be influenced by their countrymen, and to lean at times more to criminals than to the authorities; and hence the danger of employing them excepting the strictest surveillance.[62]

Rice sought to amalgamate both bodies, bringing them under the single authority and supervision of the police force. Creagh remained completely unconvinced that it was possible to form any sort of detective force in Hong Kong, principally because of 'the dishonesty of the natives upon whom we have to depend for information' (Kerrigan 2001: 200). However, Rice's experience of Mauritius persuaded him that it was both possible and necessary to have a 'properly organised . . . properly supervised Detective force, under the direct control of a responsible and competent head' (ibid). It would, he argued, be 'the eye of the police force'. Without this, the police would remain forever inefficient.

Having identified the lack of training amongst the police as a problem, Rice further argued for compulsory instruction and attendance at a police training school. Finally, he held, it was not the size of Hong Kong's population that should determine its size of its police force, but rather the nature of the place and its population, as well as the area to be covered – since 1860, the authorities had acquired responsibility for Kowloon which, by the 1870s, was both under-policed and a haven for dangerous criminals.[63] In fact, compared to other cities at home and abroad, the ratio of police per head of population in Hong Kong made it one of the most intensively policed places in the British Empire (Munn 1996).[64]

On his return to the colony in December 1871, MacDonnell sought to pacify the elite by re-establishing his regime of punitive and deterrent punishments. A firm believer in their efficacy, he attributed the increase in crime in 1870/71 to their cessation whilst he was on leave. At the same time, however, he agreed to establish a police commission in 1872, to 'set the record straight'. That commission consisted entirely of members of the European elite, including the attorney general (Hayllar), F.W. Mitchell, William Lemann, William Keswick, Frederick Stewart, George Falconer, and Henry Lowcock, all representatives of merchant and trading interests; no members of the Chinese elite were involved. Moreover, despite their vociferous complaints about the state of crime (and calls for the reintroduction of harsh penalties), very few of the European elite responded to the commission's invitation to give evidence (Kerrigan 2001: 202ff). The Commission did, however, take notice of the fact that crime in the Chinese residential and trading districts had apparently been brought under control by the District Watch, the force set up by the Chinese merchant elite to provide security to their own communities.

A police inquiry report handed to MacDonnell's successor, Hennessy, in 1879 demonstrated that the increase in crime in the 1870s had been due not to lenient penalties but to poor night policing in the town of Victoria. MacDonnell's assertion that Chinese criminals were only deterred by severe punishments was thus seen more as a justification for his punitive policies than a creditable response to crime. As Hennessy put it, it was the 'wretched state of the Police Force at the time' which was 'the real fact of the year 1871'. Crime fell when the means of detection and prevention – not the method of punishment – were improved.[65]

MacDonnell had, however, instigated the 1872 Police Commission, which was in many ways rather more reformist and progressive in character, recommending changes to the police both in terms of composition and duties. However, as Hennessy discovered when he took over as Governor in 1877, no attention had been paid to Rice's claim that the police needed to be deployed in a more effective fashion, principally by increasing night policing around the city of Victoria. Indeed, Hennessy discovered that the number of police deployed in this district and on other regular beats had actually been reduced, whilst some beats had been left completely unmanned; despite this shortage, between 1874 and 1877, no one had approached the Governor for an increase in police numbers. Hennessy accordingly instructed Deane to restore and increase night patrols in Victoria, and not to alter the number of police patrols without first reporting it.[66] One apparent effect was a fall in crime. By 1878, Hennessy felt able to compliment the police on their performance:

> In the whole of Her Majesty's Colonial Empire there is no Police Force of equal strength, and perhaps I can add with truth, of greater efficiency, as compared with the size and requirements of the Colony. The Government of this Colony has spent money, not lavishly but wisely, in providing for the preservation of order, a body of men that can compare with the police force in any part of the Colonial Empire.[67]

At the same time, on a trip to Macau, Hennessy discovered that the Governor had armed the Chinese members of the Macau force. He subsequently informed the Colonial Office of his plan to arm the entire Hong Kong force:

> I have proceeded slowly and with due caution, in entrusting arms to the Chinese police, and up to this (moment), not more than thirty or forty have been given rifles by Mr Creagh and Mr Deane. It may be possible, however, before long to have all the night patrols of the Chinese Police armed with revolvers (Norton Kyshe 1971: 274; Kerrigan 2001:202).[68]

Creagh conducted firearms training with the Chinese police, but only with those deemed 'trustworthy' by their European officers (Kerrigan 2001: 202). A bilingual instruction book for Chinese constables was also prepared, containing the rules and regulations of the police department as well as local laws (a similar book was proposed for the Indian section of the police). All contingents were also to receive more systematic training, based on that delivered to the Metropolitan Police (ibid).

Like Hennessey's penal reforms (discussed later) these changes were designed to win the support of the Chinese elite by removing some of the colony's more discriminatory measures. At once, however, he faced the ire of the conservative section of the European elite, who blamed a rise in crime in the mid-1870s on his abolition of branding and flogging. In October 1878, a public meeting was held 'to consider and discuss the existing state of insecurity of Life and Property in the Colony'.[69] At this meeting, Kerrigan notes, several resolutions were put forward:

(1) That during the past 18 months, life and property in this colony have been seriously jeopardised and a feeling of insecurity, the result of recent events, has been engendered, which in the opinion of this meeting has been mainly caused by a policy of undue leniency towards the criminal classes.
(2) That in the opinion of this meeting there is no necessity for any change in the laws and police regulations of the colony, but that the remedy for the existing statute of affairs is in a firm and unfettered administration of the laws as they stand, especially those . . . That flogging in public has found to be the only really deterring punishment for the class of criminals frequenting the colony, and to its suspension and the suspension of other necessarily stern modes of treatment enforced during previous Governments is attributable the daring boldness which has lately characterised crime in Hongkong.
(3) This meeting views with great apprehension the opinion of the Colonial Surgeon, with regard to the effect of the use of cat-o'-tails on the backs of criminals and the action of His Excellency the Governor in respect thereto, and proposes that a commission of medical men be appointed to inquire into the matter.
(4) That in the opinion of the meeting the almost total abolition of the system of deporting habitual criminals, which in most cases simply means returning the deported to the place from which they came to violate the laws of the colony, is injudicious and will result in gaol accommodation having to be provided for an undue proportion of the criminal population of the south of China at an expense the colony should not be called upon to bear.
(5) That this meeting is strongly of opinion that it is desirable that Her Majesty's Government should appoint a commission from England or from some colony other than Hongkong, with full powers to inquire into the present administration of the Government of this colony, especially as regards the application of the criminal laws, the carrying out of the sentences of the courts, and the relations existing

between the head of the Government and the other officials in every department.

(6) That His Excellency the Governor is hereby requested to direct that a watch committee be formed consisting of the three non-official members of the Legislative Council, with three bankers, one American, one German, and one Indian merchant, of which three members, consisting of one Member of Council, one merchant, and one banker form a sub committee. That the duties of the watch committee be the general supervision of police matters in Hongkong and its dependencies, for which purpose the Governor be requested to clothe them with substantial powers.

(7) That the Chairman of the meeting do forward these resolutions to the Honourable Colonial Secretary, requesting that His Excellency the Governor will forward a copy of the same to the Right Honourable the Secretary of State for the Colonies by the first opportunity.

Unpersuaded by these protestations, Hennessy ordered his own officials to compile reports both on the state of crime and the state of the police force. He reiterated that crime flourished because of inadequate policing:

> . . . the theory that the Hong Kong criminals are individuals who flock into the Colony from the adjacent provinces of China does not bear careful examination. It was a convenient theory in one respect, for it covered up defects in the Police system[70]

Whilst Deane and Creagh argued for an increase in police numbers, Hennessy insisted that the remedy lay, not with the revival of branding and flogging nor with more police, but with the enhancement of beat policing, especially at night, and especially around the residential and commercial properties of the Europeans: '87.5% (141) of the police force were to be available between 6 pm and 6 am leaving only 12.5% (20) for policing by day' (Kerrigan 2001: 236). Hennessy's other proposals included incorporating the district watch into the official policing system, using mounted police and employing Europeans as detectives (ibid).[71] Many of these ideas had been discussed by the 1872 Police Commission, when influential liberals in the colony (missionaries and educationalists like Eitel and Legge) had argued for greater localisation of the police.[72] The fact that the district watch was proving so successful had also recommended greater Chinese incorporation to the Commission.

It is said that when Hennessy departed Hong Kong in 1882, members of the colonial elite declined to see him off, so unpopular with them were his 'pro-Chinese' policies. His departure also saw the reversal of many of his reforms so that, by the 1890s, very little progress had been made either in integrating the Chinese into the police, or improving the force's detective capability. He left at a point in the 1880s when a Sino-French conflict was just erupting over the border. In1884, this spilled over into Hong Kong as local Chinese heeded Mainland China's call for a boycott of French goods and services. Anticipating trouble in the colony, Hennessy's successor, Bowen, prepared to deploy both armed police and the military, though rather than have to suppress disturbances, Bowen hoped to prevent them by letting the Chinese populace 'see that the Police is well armed, and well disciplined' (Kerrigan 2001: 242).[73] To achieve this, it was suggested that a Military Adjutant be seconded to the police to provide instruction in drill, musketry and maintenance of weapons; an Indian military man was also to be appointed to provide the same instruction to the Indian contingent of the police (the Chinese were still not to be armed).

Both Deane, the Captain Superintendent of Police, and Dempster, (a soldier) Acting Captain Superintendent of Police, also advocated the development of a paramilitary capability (ibid) as did the merchant elite, who feared that riots in Canton would spill over into Hong Kong, to the detriment of their trade and security. Bowen, however, apparently resisted the wholesale transformation of the force along these lines:

> I desire it to be understood that nothing can be further from my wish or intention than to invest a Civil Police Corps with too military a character. But, seeing that the English and Sikh portion of the Police Force at Hong Kong is regularly armed with rifles and sword bayonets, and that it is analogous, in many respects, to the French Gendarmerie, and to the Royal Irish Constabulary, and that it is expected to give efficient support to our weak garrison in the event of foreign attack, or of serious internal disturbance, it is obvious that it should have the advantage of being drilled by a military officer, either as Superintendent or as Adjutant. All experience shows that nothing is more useless, and that nothing may become more dangerous, than an armed Force under imperfect discipline.[74]

Clearly, though Bowen was aware of the need for a quasi-military force to suppress disorder, he was at the same time keen to ensure that such a force remain both disciplined and under civilian control. His concerns were justified: few of the officers equipped with arms had ever been trained to load and fire them (Kerrigan 2001: 244), whilst many of the colony's police stations were incapable of being defended – Bowen argued for police stations modelled on those in Ireland, defensive buildings with loop-holes for muskets (ibid).[75]

In 1884, the Sino–French conflict reached Hong Kong as the Mainland authorities issued a proclamation banning workmen from assisting in the repair of French boats; it also affected the loading and unloading of French cargo ships. Those who defied the order were liable to severe punishment. In Hong Kong, two boat operators who obeyed the proclamation (for fear, it was said, of bringing harm to their relatives on the Mainland) found themselves hauled before the Police Magistrate, convicted and fined. The legality of the fines was a contested issue, later debated in EXCO. However, the immediate response of the boat handlers' guild to this heavy-handed treatment was to call a strike. Caught as they were between the Mainland authority's threat to punish anyone who handled French boats, and criminalisation by the Hong Kong courts if they did not do so, on 30 September 1884, the cargo boat handlers withdrew their labour en masse.

During the strike that followed, the police opened fire on the crowds (see below). Forced to retreat under a hail of stones thrown by rowdy crowds, one officer lost a revolver and another an ammunition pouch; five had to be sent to hospital. The Riot Act was read and the military called out. At an Extraordinary meeting of the Executive Council it was decided that:

> (1) That an order be given to the police to bring up the rioters taken by them, that afternoon, if possible, and that the Police Magistrates be requested to deal with the cases at once.
> (2) That the sentences passed on the rioters be placarded in Tai Ping Shan and the Chinese portion of the town.
> (3) That His Excellency the Major General Commanding be requested to send a picket of one hundred men to be available for the assistance of the police and to remain until the police report that they are no longer required.
> (4) That the Police Magistrate be warned that one of them must remain on the spot with the picket who cannot act without his orders.
> (5) That Messrs. Thousett, Coxon, McEvan and Tripp be warned that they may be required to act as Magistrates with the picket.
> (6) That the Police be directed to report the number and disposition of their men and whether they have an adequate force, and to report immediately if any addition is necessary.
> (7) That special constables be enlisted and sworn in, if, in the opinion of the Acting Superintendent of Police, it is necessary.
> (8) That, if it clearly appears to the police that an attack in force is commencing on any house or building with a view to its sacking or destruction, and that the police are unable without assistance to repel the attack, the Military are to be called upon to assist: the moment the Military are called on to assist, the Riot Act shall be read by a Magistrate in English, and also, if possible, in Chinese.[76]

As Tsai observes, the strike and riots were mainly a working people's reaction to colonial government's suppression of anti-French sentiment, anti-foreignism being interpreted as a sign of patriotism in the China of the times:

> The strike and riots were led by occupational guild associations . . . as

> well as the Triad societies. The Triads, who permeated the working population of all occupational and dialect groups, engaged in a wide variety of acts, ranging from petty crimes to patriotic actions against foreign imperialism. Triads permeated the guild associations of the cargo coolies, boatmen, hawkers and chair coolies and often became politically active in times of strike and popular disturbances. The Guangzhou Mandarin authorities sought to enlist the Triads to fight against France by promising them material rewards and by appealing to their anti-imperialist patriotism. But not all actions of the Triad activists were sanctioned by the Guangzhou authorities. Just as in many strikes in other places and times, the activists attempted to enforce strike solidarity and concerted action by using coercion and intimidation against refractory elements among the working people who, compelled by the necessity to earn a living, wanted to return to work (Tsai 1984: 7; Kerrigan 2001: 252).

The involvement of the triads is, however, unclear. Sinn notes that the rioters were armed with only stones and bricks and points out that if the riot were organised, they would surely have been better armed.[77] Moreover, none of those arrested were identified as triads.[78]

That the authorities suspected a 'black hand' behind the disturbances partly explains why they responded with such force. Dempster, Acting Captain Superintendent of Police, 'bore testimony to the forbearance and firmness exhibited by the whole force . . . [and] further noted, with satisfaction, the loyalty that had been displayed by the Chinese contingent of the police force' (Kerrigan 2001: 253).

The government adopted a hard line. In October 1884, it enacted a highly repressive piece of legislation, the 1884 Peace Preservation Ordinance, which allowed it to banish 'undesirables' from the colony, prohibit the posting of Chinese notices and forbid any Chinese to possess firearms. The police were granted the power to call upon bystanders to help them suppress riots, as well as immunity from prosecution if they maimed or killed persons who had previously been warned to disperse.[79] Other laws followed in 1887, akin to the 'light and pass' laws employed in the earliest days of colonial rule to regulate the movement of the Chinese population. Whilst the workers remained on strike, the government also refused negotiate with the strikers or quash the punishment handed out by the Police Magistrate. The result was an impasse that brought trade in the colony to a halt. The punitive response of the Hong Kong authorities turned, Chan argues, what had started as an expression of Chinese patriotism into 'a popular mobilization against the local British establishment' (Chan 1990: 282).

Between 1884 and 1925, Hong Kong experienced repeated episodes of labour unrest and patriotic disturbances (see below). In March 1895, for example, coolie housekeepers led hundreds of workers in a strike against new government regulations. By May 1895, 20,000 people were on strike and workers in Canton jointly mobilised.

Kerrigan argues, however, that these strikes and disturbances were not the sole justification for the turn towards armed para-military policing. He notes that in 1894, the Captain Superintendent of police reported that clan disturbances (which he described as guerrilla warfare) were only halted by armed police (Kerrigan 2001: 259).

At the same time, the police were still being used to assist the civil authorities. For example, 'Between 1 May to 30 September 1894, between 5 to 10 per cent of the Force was engaged on plague work. Both the police and the military assisted the Sanitary Board with disinfecting and cleansing operations.[80] The police were required to bury, demolish, disinfect, burn and evacuate residents' (ibid). A rise in crime of over 50 per cent between 1894 and 1895 was attributed by the police to the existence of properties abandoned during the outbreak (ibid).

By the 1890s, then, Hong Kong policing was developing a mix of para-military and civilian approaches, driven both by the character of domestic politics and crime, as well as by Mainland Chinese issues and wider international conflicts. The fragility of the colonial government's position made retaining the loyalty of the police essential, and in 1887, it took steps to improve the pay and terms of service of serving police officers, as well as crackdown on corruption and indiscipline within the force.[81] A new Superintendent of Police, F.H. May, was appointed in 1893 to continue this 'professionalisation' of the force. However, turnover of personnel remained high, and in 1897, large numbers of Chinese police officers resigned following a reduction in their pay (Kerrigan 2001: 262). This came partly in response to a scheme, introduced in 1894 and 1898 by May, to promote good conduct amongst the Chinese police by replacing periodic bonuses with good conduct awards (ibid). This and other changes came at a time when the cost of living for the Chinese population had increased by about 10 per cent; rents had also undergone a 100 per cent increase between 1879 and 1889 (ibid).

May had, in any event, never been convinced by the argument for making the majority of the police Chinese. In his view, they were illiterate, idle, and corrupt. There was something to the corruption allegation – in 1887, 51 Chinese constables were prosecuted for receiving bribes for protecting gambling houses. But corruption was not confined to the Chinese section of the force. In 1897, for example, when May personally carried out a raid on a gambling house:

> Amongst the exhibits seized was a list of officers in the government service who had been accepting bribes. The keeper of the gambling house was charged and convicted for his role. Following his conviction, he provided information that led to the identification of police officers that appeared on the list found by May. Based on this information, Governor

> Robinson . . . interdicted police Inspectors Stanton and Quincy and Sergeant Holt, the principal officers of the detective department and Inspector Baker, the officer in charge of the district in which the gambling house was located. The majority of the 22 Chinese detectives whose names had appeared on the list were, in addition to being dismissed, banished from the colony. Criminal charges were laid against Inspector Witchell [sentenced to six months' imprisonment and dismissed from the police force] the only police officer against whom sufficient evidence existed. It was not possible to obtain sufficient evidence against the remaining police officers to justify criminal charges. Notwithstanding, there was no doubt that they had been conniving with the operators of the Gambling Houses. Police Inspectors W. Stanton, W. Quincy and W. Baker and Police Sergeant Holt were later dismissed from the police force on the ground of gross neglect of duty. It was hoped taking such a firm approach would act as a deterrent to others in the police and government service. May also believed that Corcoran, Chief Inspector, had heard of the gambling house and that others were receiving bribes and like Witchell, he had wanted a share (Kerrigan 2001: 291).[82]

A local newspaper asked whether, in the light of these revelations, Chinese police should continue to be employed at all:

> One thing however is certain. If Chinese are to be engaged, they must be recruited from a different class of men, a superior class, men whose reputation for reliability (we will not say honesty) is undeniable and from whom with careful looking after, as honest work as it is possible to extract from Chinese as may be expected.[83]

However, no such question was asked of the European contingent, though it was equally inclined towards venality. Instead, in 1899, May requested more European officers, informing the Colonial Secretary that shortages left him without enough European officers to man the launches of the Water Police and the additional stations to be built the next year.[84] For May, 'the backbone of this Force is the European contingent, and on the efficiency of that contingent depends the efficiency of the entire Force . . .'.[85] Thus, even when it became apparent that European officers were by no means necessarily more trustworthy, the view persisted that they were better fitted for police positions than the locals. Only in the 1970s, when the Independent Commission Against Corruption (ICAC) exposed the full extent of corruption amongst senior European officers did this view finally unravel.

In any event, it was in fact the Indian police who formed the 'backbone' of the force both in numerical terms and in terms of their paramilitary capability. In1898, they became crucial to the policing of the New Territories (NT) ceded to Britain by China and extending the colony beyond the boundary established in 1860 after the second Opium War. The New Territories were ceded for a period of 99 years, the lease to end in 1997. Its utility lay in the distance it placed between the city of Victoria and the Mainland, though the aggrandisement of the colony was also part of the wider European 'scramble for China'.[86] A rural area comprising scattered villages, the NT possessed its own local leadership, settled customs and established clans, some of whom were to prove highly resistant to colonial rule. In 1898, the authorities believed that there were 'preconcerted plans of invasion into the New Territory by large numbers of rowdies' from the Mainland, bent on fighting the British as soon as they set foot in the NT. They thus anticipated deploying armed force to subdue this 'native resistance'.[87] According to Kerrigan, the Governor (Blake) had received a copy of a placard that called on the villagers to resist the British. This read as follows:

> We hate the English barbarians who are about to enter our boundaries and take over land, and will cause us endless evil. Day and night we fear the approaching danger. Certainly people are dissatisfied at this and have determined to resist the barbarians. If our firearms are not good, we shall be unable to oppose the enemy. So we have appointed an exercise ground and gathered all together as patriots to drill with fire arms. To encourage proficiency rewards will be given. On the one hand we shall be helping the Government; on the other we shall be saving ourselves from future trouble. Let all our friends and relatives bring their firearms to the ground and do what they can to extirpate the traitors. Our ancestors will be pleased, and so will our neighbours. This is our sincere wish. Practice takes place every day. First prize: One gauze coat. A packet of 1,000 crackers. Second prize: One pair of brown gauze trousers. A packet Third prize: One straw hat.[88]

The NT was, it was said, an anarchical place beset by piracy, robbery and clan feuds. As in the 1840s, the British saw their mission as bringing law and order to an otherwise lawless land.[89] They planned to build several police stations and establish regular patrols in the area (Kerrigan 2001: 270). Unlike the 1840s, however, in the NT they met with such violent armed resistance that they were forced to call upon the Viceroy of Kwantung for assistance in quelling the opposition. He issued proclamations advising residents against any further disturbances, and ordering the Chinese contingent in the Kowloon Walled City to provide the British with armed support if required (Kerrigan 2001: 276). Further attacks on the police continued, however. No building work or patrols could be undertaken without military protection. A major confrontation took place at Tai Po in 1899,[90] culminating in eventual victory for the British, but sporadic resistance continued to characterise policing of the area for years to come, suggesting that the NT was never fully subdued.

However, having immediately succeeded in suppressing local resistance, in 1899 the British sought to administer the NT by employing 'Indirect Rule'. This method, simultaneously being developed in colonial Africa, was offered up in 1906 by Lugard (colonial administrator in Africa and soon to be Governor of Hong Kong) as a template for colonial rule.[91] Lugard's view was that British administrators of colonial territories should always establish their superiority (by, for example, living in a house equal, if not superior to, that of the local leader). At the same time, however, the compliance of the native population could be more readily gained by 'Indirect Rule'. His 'blueprint for colonial administration' was based on ideas, current in the 1890s, that colonised states might more readily governed if they continued to make some decisions of their own, preserving some traditions and participating in decisions about the pace of 'modernisation' (Flint: 1978). Ruling through 'native institutions' involved co-opting local leaders as 'middle men' (political 'go-betweens') through whom British administrator would exercise control whilst retaining the respect of the native population. To this end, whilst some British laws outlawed 'barbaric' native customs, much would remain unaltered and useful indigenous institutions preserved.

In the NT, a District Officer (a Cadet who could speak Chinese) would act as the intermediary between the locals and the government. Village elders were to regulate village life and be held responsible for any rioting (Kerrigan 2001: 285).[92] Village tribunals were to be retained and village constables made responsible to a Watch Committee for good order within the villages. The Resident Commissioner 'was to be the final court of appeal in all matters civil or criminal cognisable by native tribunals' (ibid). All criminal cases punishable by death were to be heard by the Hong Kong Police Magistrate (ibid).

Stewart Lockhart, as a Cadet, was deemed best placed to liaise with the native population. In his initial report on the NT he recommended that:

> A European should be appointed as head of the police . . . A force of at least 30 Chinese and 20 Indians should be enrolled and stationed at headquarters or other convenient places, from when they could patrol the territory . . . in order to maintain peace and good order, and to protect the lives and property of the inhabitants. This force should be properly drilled and partially mounted. A detective force of 15 men will also be required. The existing system of village constables should be maintained, the Tepo or head constable, being held responsible to the Watch Committee of the village for the good order of the village. The number of these village constables in the Tung Lon, or eastern section, must be over 1,000. Their pay, which is at present defrayed by the villages, is very small, and will, no doubt, have to be increased in order to secure efficiency. It is hoped that this large force may be gradually improved and converted into a well-disciplined force of military force. To begin with, however, it will be necessary to take them as they are, and make the best possible use of their services. The village council should, for the purposes

> of police, act as a watch committee, and control the village constables, the Tepo being in the first instance responsible to them.[93]

A number of 'traditions', established at this point, were to remain part of NT governance and criminal justice for a century to come. For example, when acting as Magistrate, Lockhart sat alongside local village leaders to dispense justice, much as his successors were still doing in the 1950s.[94] Police in the NT consulted its District Officers and, when the District Officer system was adopted in the urban areas in the 1970s, such 'indirect rule' continued both as a mode of policing and as a mode of governance more generally. The Indian police, who formed the majority of officers in the NT in the 1890s, were also to remain a feature of NT life. In the 1950s, they would be detailed to staff the emergency units, located in the NT (see below). NT villager guards, employed by the government to maintain order, were also paid and supplied with arms right up until the 1970s. Because the NT villages remained unpredictable and potentially volatile, police tactics would always require great tact and diplomacy. Even so, the NT's walled villages would continue to present a challenge, suspected of harbouring illegal gambling dens, pirates, gangs of robbers, smugglers and, in the 1960s, political subversives.

The need to police the NT prompted the Governor, Blake, to seek an increase in police establishment from London, and the appointment of a Police Cadet as Assistant Superintendent of Police. The present incumbent (Halifax) was needed as Police Magistrate in the NT. Since he could not speak Hindustani, he could not communicate with the Indian police, nor could he easily access those parts of the NT around Tai Po. May, acting as Colonial Secretary wrote to London arguing that the police force was now 'under-officered':

> . . . in other words, there is not and there has not been, sufficient supervision of the subordinate ranks. One of the contributing causes of the grave scandals in connection with the bribery and corruption which occurred in 1897 was this very want of supervision. In a memorandum which I wrote in 1897 on the subject of the prevention of corruption in the Police Force, and which I observe was not sent to the Secretary of State, I pointed out that the defects in the administration of the European contingent which had probably tended to favour the growth of corruption were (a) laxness of discipline (and I may say that when I took charge of the Force, discipline was very slack). (b) want of knowledge of Chinese on the part of the officers. (c) the promotion of subordinate officers to the rank of executive officers. (d) the placing of much responsibility in the hands of the Detective Branch. And I recommend . . . that the Detective staff should always be under the supervision and control of one of the Executive Officers . . . The Force has been increased to a total of 848 men . . . distributed in 32 stations scattered over a very

> large area . . . For the appointment [of Assistant Superintendent] I would recommend Mr P.J. Wodehouse. There is no Cadet at present in the Colony who has any inclination for police work nor can I think of one who would be suitable for it. I have never advocated the appointment of Cadets to junior posts in the police . . . in my opinion it would be far better to appoint a young man like Mr Wodehouse, who is willing to devote his career to police work without looking for appointments . . . in other Departments, which Cadets invariably do. Mr Wodehouse is a Volunteer, has a knowledge of drill, is making extremely good progress in Chinese, is of fine physique and active habits and above all is a gentleman, and in my opinion it would be difficult to find a better candidate.[95]

Not all Cadets, it was argued, would make good policemen. However, London saw May's letter as a 'determined effort to job in young Mr Wodehouse', who had been given an appointment in the Registrar Generals' office on the understanding that he should not expect promotion.[96] The Governor, Blake, took the view that:

> Personally, I have no doubt that Mr Wodehouse would make an excellent officer, and speaking Chinese as he does, it is a question whether an exception should be made in his case. But as a general principle I am of the opinion that the gentlemen appointed to the Force should be Passed Cadets. Otherwise the officers would probably be of inferior standing. As to the inclinations of the Cadets, they must accept the appointment that may be available to them, and the Police appointments, besides somewhat better pay, offer advantages to men who prefer an active to a sedentary life.[97]

However, since there were no other Cadets in the colony fitted for police work, Blake's Irish background led him to suggest that an otherwise suitable Cadet might be trained up in police work with the RIC; alternatively, the appointment might be filled by someone from the Indian Police in the Punjab. A compromise was reached with the Colonial Office. Blake suggested sending Halifax to India to learn Hindustani; London agreed 'that an appointment should be given to a Cadet and not to Mr Wodehouse'.

Plans to bring the district watch (under the control of the Registrar General) into closer association with the main police force finally took shape in 1900, when watchmen were placed on police beats under police supervision. In September 1900, the Registrar General and the District Watch Committee approved the building of a District Watchmen's house in Central, on resumed land in Taiping-shan; two European officers were also to lodge in the quarters to 'effect an improvement in the discipline of the watchmen'[98] Such measures combined the twin aims of keeping policing costs down by employing locals, and effecting control though native institutions. Lockhart, appointed Registrar General in the 1890s, also advocated institutionalising the government's links with the Chinese elite, many of whose members now ran the District Watch. In 1891, legal status had been granted to the district watch, and a Committee of Management appointed by the Governor consisting of 'twelve Chinese gentlemen' (Chan 1991: 112). This Committee now became an adviser to the government on Chinese affairs, through the office of the Registrar General and Protector of the Chinese. Very soon, this Committee superseded that of the Tung Wah as the most powerful body:

> In reality, the Committee is the Chinese Executive Council of Hong Kong and is consulted on all matters affecting them. Candidates are suggested by the Chinese from among the most influential and wealthy men in the Colony, but are appointed by the Governor. Usually, though not invariably, the members have had a long period of service upon less important Chinese semi-official committees, such as that which controls the Tung Wah Hospital. Appointment is very eagerly sought after because of the great prestige attached to the office, and of certain marks of distinction to which members are entitled . . . Moreover, the Chinese representatives upon the Executive and Legislative Councils are often selected from the District Watch Committee . . . the members have wide influence among their compatriots and give important assistance to the Government in guiding and directing the mass of the population (Mills 1942: 398–9 cited in Chan 1991: 112).

Absorbing the district watch into the main body of policing was, thus, part of the broader strategy of 'indirect rule' practised since the 1840s but, at the same time, it removed a possible rival centre of power and made policing cheaper and more effective.

In the NT, too, policing assumed a more local character once the main thrust of resistance subsided. Police numbers were being reduced after a fall in incursions by 'criminal gangs' and pirates who had taken part in a rebellion in neighbouring Kwai Sin in the autumn of 1900.[99] By August 1901, the NT had a force of 22 Europeans, 97 Indian and 39 Chinese rank and file, the Indian contingent being the largest section of the force.

In 1902, however, the Indian police fell victim to British anxieties about their loyalty, specifically their possible recruitment by enemy states. The Secretary of State for the Colonies (Chamberlain) raised the question of what steps were taken to repatriate Sikh police at the conclusion of their contracts, so as to prevent them 'falling into the hands of Foreign Powers'. The Governor replied that Sikh police were usually recruited locally, though 'at times it is necessary to send to India for recruits'. In the Colony as a whole, there were 189 Sikhs and 173 'Mohammedans'. Another 150 Sikhs were employed as private watchmen 'over whom the Government exercises no direct control'; a further 200 Indian police could be found in Shanghai and Hankow, and there were also 'a large number of Sikhs in military service in the Colony, not under the control of the Government'.[100] The government did not arrange the repatriation of retired officers at the end of their duties, though most appeared to return home 'to live there in the enjoyment of their pensions. Their return however is not compulsory' (ibid). Blake was prepared to shoulder the cost and responsibility for repatriating Indian officers dismissed from the force 'generally bad characters . . . and it is hardly expected that the British Minister at Pekin would care to utilise their services in China as suggested [by] the Foreign Office' (ibid). In Blake's view, the most effective way to prevent Sikhs 'entering the service of Foreign Powers' would be for the Indian government to 'exercise some control over all Sikhs leaving India and, if possible, to ensure that they only do so to take up some recognised employment acceptable to the Government' (ibid).

The question of Indian police was addressed again by May in 1914 when it was suggested that sepoys from the Indian army might be recruited into the police, and as private watchmen. May was in principle keen to agree.[101] At the same time, however, he recognised that the number of Indians employed in Hong Kong was already large, and that there was a danger that Hong Kong could 'become a centre for spreading sedition and anti-British sentiments' (ibid). There were

> . . . grounds for supposing that a great number of Indians here are at present 'anti-British' but, to anyone who has experience of Indians it is obvious that one reason why the Indians here get out of hand – so to speak – is that there is no British official here who understands them, their ways, their language, sufficiently well, who is in any way their representative (ibid).

In solving this problem, May did not see the need to attach a senior British officer from the Indian army to Hong Kong Force. Instead, he preferred to send one of the three Hindustani-speaking European officers to India to improve their knowledge of its language and customs. In addition, it was proposed that new recruits be drawn from men who had served three years in the Indian army, ensuring 'a better class of men' who 'in view of their military training' would be more useful than the present police (ibid).

In the middle of the decade, following May's promotion and his replacement as head of the police force by Badeley, problems began to surface in the police force more generally.[102] Commenting on a report on the police force written by May (now Colonial Secretary) Blake observed that it was 'a very important report, but not pleasant reading'. Badeley did not possess 'the qualities necessary for the successful command and guidance of the mixed police force in this Colony'.[103] He was 'deficient in energy' and incapable of securing discipline, with the result that a force brought to a high level of efficiency by May, had deteriorated in both morale and efficiency'. There was 'a slackness in the men, on whose conduct in the performance of street duty very unfavourable comments are made by the general public, by foreign officers and by our own Naval officers' (ibid).

Badeley's deputy, Captain Lyons, was also said by May to be unfit to command the detective force, since he spoke no Chinese and seemed to 'have learnt his police work in a novel school' (ibid). Wodehouse was 'so tied to his office' that he had no time for patrolling: This is not satisfactory' (ibid). The system of paid spies in Canton had also fallen into disuse, partly because of the 'low character' of the men employed. May recommended sending detectives on the ferries to and from Canton and Macau, whilst also seeking the help of the Consul-General in Canton to engage the services of a spy who would inform the Hong Kong Police of the movement of 'bad characters' between Canton and Hong Kong (ibid).

Blake recommended Badeley's transfer to another branch of the Cadet service or to the Straits Settlement. This was to be accompanied by his replacement by a specially selected man, and an inquiry into the condition of the police force. Because, in his view, 'strict discipline is absolutely essential if the police force is to be efficient' (particularly given the 'indifferent quality of the material'), Blake also rebuked several other senior European officers for failing to ensure that discipline was enforced, and for 'rubber stamping' summonses without scrutinising them. The large number of marines recruited into the force since 1899 had caused him constant trouble. They were 'inclined to insubordination', had a 'want of respect for their superior officers', were of 'a lower educational standard and on a lower moral plane' than the class of men that used to be obtained for the European contingent (ibid). May recommended the dismissal of those found to be thoroughly unsatisfactory; others might be retained until the end of their five years' contract but then let go, otherwise, 'the day will come when the ranks of Sergeants and Inspectors will by weight of seniority be filled . . . by ex-Marines. I consider that would be one of the worst misfortunes that could overtake the Hong Kong Police' (ibid) 'Men of a better stamp than Marines' were needed for the European section of the force (ibid).

Appointments appeared to have been made on no rational basis: May complained, for example, that the only qualification of the man put in charge of enforcing the Women's and Girls' Protection Ordinance was that 'he is married and steady . . . He is a notoriously stupid man' (ibid).

Blake's response was to bring Halifax back from the NT to take command of the Detective force, whilst May recommended trawling British police forces for trained and 'well-educated' recruits.[104] As ever, this had cost implications, for attracting good men from Britain necessitated improvements in pension levels and terms of service (ibid). Lyons suggested a better uniform and status for European constables: 'I do not like seeing them fall in for inspection and drill with Indians and Chinese . . . I have made endeavour to keep them separate' (ibid). He also banished 81 triad 'headmen' and put more police on patrol but, in a familiar refrain, blamed much on the poor quality of local recruits: '[they] have always been the trouble and always will be, just as is the case with Malays. They will smoke, sit down and sleep while on duty . . . go home and elsewhere to see their friends . . . but they are necessary'.[105]

Demonstrations and disturbances in the first decade of the new century also underlined this emphasis on Force discipline and its paramilitary capabilities. Wodehouse and Lyons survived May's report long enough to help tackle the disturbances which erupted in November 1911 throughout the Colony, following reports that Peking had fallen to Sun-Yat-sen's forces. But Wodehouse, under a new Governor (Lugard) complained that:

> We are having rather a strenuous time here – especially the police. The Governor is very irritable and peevish nowadays! Last Monday night, the whole of Hong Kong turned out to celebrate the fall of Peking . . . Enormous crowds paraded the streets, cheering and waving the Republican flag. They were most orderly, except in one instance when an attack was made on a newspaper office, which was supposed to have Imperialist leanings. I spent about 3 hours on the telephone and had to run all the special Police arrangements, as Lyons couldn't be found. The unfortunate man has been jumped upon for not leaving word where he was dining. The Governor sent a message to me that Lyons was to report to him at once if military assistance was required. This message could not be got to him . . . so . . . I telephoned [the Adjutant] . . . privately [to warn him that troops might possibly be required] so as to avoid taking him entirely by surprise. This apparently innocent action has called down a regular storm upon my devoted head. It was construed by the Governor into being a 'request for troops'! I was also jumped upon for issuing an order, on my own responsibility, which probably saved a serious riot . . .[106]

The order that Wodehouse had issued was designed to stop 'overzealous' constables from enforcing the law against firecrackers, lest such interference with the celebrations sparked off a riot. Misconstrued, it looked like an order to call the troops out, fuelling rather than cooling a potentially explosive situation. Internal memoranda[107] show that the Governor did indeed blame Wodehouse for the mistake and this, together with other matters, prejudiced his chances of succeeding Badeley.

In December, when things had returned to normal, Wodehouse went on to complain that they had had 'the usual spasmodic increase in the Police Force, which I object to so strongly', and that Badeley and Lyons could not be prevailed upon to ask for a steady year-on-year increase in establishment for fear of making themselves unpopular with the Governor, who 'has been worrying the Police tremendously during the last month'.[108] Lugard had taken the matter of May's report to EXCO, which had subsequently passed a resolution expressing misgivings with the way senior officers were running the police, and recommended that an outside officer be appointed to head the force. Wodehouse now worried that he would lose his job because of the shortcomings of Badeley and Lyons: 'Naturally, the result of having had officers like this at the head of the Force has been to bring all of us into discredit' (ibid).

By 10 December, Lyons had left the colony prior to retirement. Arguing for the appointment of Halifax as his successor, Lugard faced resistance from London. In support of his case, he argued that the disturbances provoked by unrest and turbulence in China, and associated attacks on the police and 'European ladies', meant that a man of special qualities, as well as repressive measures, were needed. There was 'only one man (Halifax) who has special qualifications both in police experience and training and in character and ability' (ibid). Lugard opposed Wodehouse's promotion to the post, holding him partly responsible for an increase in crime in 1910, when he had deputised for Lyons, who was on leave.[109] The police had blamed this rise in crime on 'the spasmodic energy of Chinese officials', said to be 'driving great numbers of criminals from China into this colony', and to a raid on pirates in Macau, which had driven 'sea-robbers' to Hong Kong.[110] Badeley also blamed the suppression of opium divans for the drop in arrests. This made it more difficult for the police to locate the 'criminal classes' who were 'apt to congregate in the lowest class or dross divans' (ibid). They had taken instead to raiding gambling houses 'not merely in order to suppress gambling but because among the gamblers there are very many of the criminal classes who can thus be got rid of by deportation' (ibid).

To tackle this crime situation, Lugard drew up a list of measures, including the 'more drastic enforcement of the Banishment Ordinance to rid the colony of criminal aliens'; an increase in the deployment of the District Watch, the acquisition by the Registrar-General of information from Street Committees and from other Chinese sources; an increase in police strength; the introduction of deterrent punishments; increased co-operation with the Mainland authorities; a prohibition on light craft moving about the harbour after dark; making a senior Chinese detective responsible for knowledge of the inhabitants of his district; and secreting armed police on junks in waters known to be frequented by pirates.[111]

As this list of measures implies, the increase in crime in 1910 seemed to reflect a number of different forces. Wodehouse alone could not be blamed, and in Lugard's opinion, his faults were mainly due to lack of training and experience. He was prepared to retain him as a deputy to Halifax since the emergency situation which prevailed made it imperative to strengthen, rather than weaken, the European section of the force, and to retain officers who could speak Chinese.

In the years following 1911, anti-foreign feeling intensified. It manifested itself in small ways, in jeering and stone throwing at police and soldiers called upon maintain order and break the boycotts. With regard to the policing of boycotts and strikes, the Chinese elite generally supported the government's use of repressive tactics, since stoppages of work and trade harmed their economic interests as much as those of the European merchant elite. With respect to the 1911 Revolution in China, however, their loyalties were more mixed.

The years between 1911 and the First World War were characterised by a series of further strikes, boycotts and 'anti-foreignism', spurred by political events in what was now Republican China (see below). At the end of the war, the May 4th Movement in 1919 revived nationalistic feelings on the Mainland and in the Colony, whilst throughout the 1920s, organised labour in Hong Kong tested the resolve of the government and the capabilities of the police (see below). Two incidents in particular (the 1912/13 Tramways Boycott and the 1922 Seamen's Strike) developed into full-scale confrontations between the 'coolie class' and Hong Kong ruling elite; throughout the period, small-scale skirmishes occurred on a regular, if sporadic, basis. In 1922, the Governor, Stubbs, agreed to Emergency Regulations which allowed him to deport, arrest, detain, and exclude 'undesirables' from the Colony, as well as suppress publications. To prevent local strikers leaving for Canton, where a Chinese 'comfort mission' was providing succour and support, the Governor issued a proclamation preventing any Chinese from leaving the Colony without official permission.[112] The result was clashes with the police, as strikers moved en masse towards the border. In one incident, at the Kowloon Water Works, police and troops opened fire on the crowd after warning them to disperse; five people were killed. A judicial enquiry, set up to investigate the incident, reached a verdict of justifiable homicide, thereby exonerating the police (ibid).

Indian and European officers continued to be trained in firearms skills, but it was not until 1925 that Cantonese police received revolver training in numbers. Chinese criminal gangs, on the other hand, gained access to firearms amongst ordnance left over from the First World War, and smuggled into China from Europe and America.[113] As was to occur after a mass demobilisation of the People's Liberation Army (PLA) in the 1980s, the easy availability of discarded uniforms and weapons meant that civilians found themselves 'at the mercy of so-called troops, often bandits in disguise' (ibid).

Throughout 1922, the government in Canton continually changed leaders and in these unsettled circumstances, 'crime flourished' (ibid). Political instability in China also had other repercussions for Hong Kong. The British government supported the Nationalist regime. Both suspected that Communists from Mainland China living in Hong Kong were engaged in subversive activities – a police report of 1930 specifically alleged that they were directing industrial disturbances, but local cells were in fact too disorganised to capitalise on the discontents of the local population (Chan 1999: 182–4). As far as the authorities were concerned, however, as a civil war unfolded in China, there now arose the possibility that the loyalties of some Chinese members of the police might become divided, and that the force would be infiltrated by Communist or Nationalist sympathisers. The Indian police were said to be loyal to the government and had received regular firearms training since 1911, when Lyons had decided to issue them with revolvers during the disturbances following Sun Yat-sen's victory.[114] An Emergency Unit was set up in Kowloon in 1927 to match the one already in existence on Hong Kong island, and an Anti-Communist Squad formed within the Political Bureau (which became, in 1933, the Special Branch).[115] The Emergency Unit, headed by three European officers, undertook training in riot drill and firearms. Its officers, seconded from normal duties for three months, were held in readiness for emergencies and minor disturbances.

When an increase in police strength was sought in the 1920s, of the 32 additional European officers recruited, a large number were ex-RIC men with experience of suppressing political turmoil in Ireland, whose services, it was said, 'should prove most valuable'.[116] Stubbs asked London to facilitate the recruitment of a 'number of European Police', specifically recruits from the RIC; 28 ex-RIC men were subsequently identified (Stubbs had wanted 32 trained and unmarried men).

Throughout the 1920s and 1930s, this recruitment of experienced Europeans (mostly from British police forces, though some 'White Russians' were also enlisted) continued. In 1919, May also furthered his agenda for a more professional police force by arguing that the Captain Superintendent of Police cease to be also the Superintendent of Gaol.[117] Instead, a complete separation of functions was proposed, along with the establishment of a new prisons department, and the building of a new prison to replace the 'already overcrowded' Victoria Gaol.[118]

In 1922, an investigation into the operation of the detective Branch resulted in the creation of a Criminal Investigation Division (CID) and the appointment of a Superintendent in charge of Criminal Intelligence. In 1924, CID recruited its first Chinese inspector (ibid), and in 1936, the first (ten) Chinese were recruited as Probationary-Inspectors, following an instruction to that effect from the government, with a view to their later relieving the European officers of some of their responsibilities.[119] Ten more were recruited in 1937 and 1938, and a further 12 in 1939.[120]

At the same time, however, the principle of 'policing by strangers' remained intact, driven by internal security concerns. During the 1922 Seamen's Strike, the Indian police were reckoned to have performed 'splendidly', in contrast to the Chinese who were 'apparently paralysed.'[121] In its aftermath, a pay increase for the Indian police was proposed but the Governor (Stubbs) called for a drastic overhaul of the Police and Secretariat for Chinese Affairs to weed out 'the useless members of the Chinese Police Force.'[122] However, reorganisation of the District Watch was postponed on the basis that the government did not wish to antagonise the Chinese elite, upon whose support it had relied on during the series of strikes and boycotts since the late 1880s.

Stubbs also asked for '... a number of Northern Chinese from the Weihaiwei' in the hope that they would provide a 'non-local backbone', being less amenable to political influence and intimidation from Canton than the Hong Kong police (ibid). In addition to taking over any European officers from Weihaiwei, Stubbs sought the transfer of at least 50 Northern Chinese police from that colony. This was also seen as an alternative source of recruits, should recruitment from India dry up as a result of political events unfolding in that country.[123] Recruiting in India had re-opened in 1919, after the end of the First World War, and although said to be good, the 'type of recruit has fallen off in a very marked degree' (ibid). The increase in pay in 1922 was partly aimed at stopping those Indian Police already in Hong Kong from becoming 'discontented and possibly disloyal, a state of things which, at all times highly undesirable, is particularly so at the present time'[124]

The 16-month Canton–Hong Kong General Strike and Boycott in 1925 presented the police with 'probably the most difficult situation that had arisen during the history of the Force'.[125] According to official reports, however, the Chinese section of the force performed better than it had in 1922 – there were fewer desertions, and 'good and energetic work was done, especially by the Chinese Detective Staff' (ibid). Stubbs forwarded to London a report mentioning the names of officers who had performed especially well. Whilst most of those singled out for special mention were European, one Chinese – Detective Inspector Chu Haung, head of the Chinese Detectives – was said to have done 'extremely well', setting 'an excellent example to his men, and constantly obtaining most valuable and reliable information'.[126] Another, Ng Ping-wa, an interpreter, was also described as 'exceptionally zealous, and useful ... and quite fearless in the discharge of his duties' (ibid). Chinese Detectives at Frontier Stations were also mentioned for the long hours they worked and the risks they had taken, but also because they 'shewed no signs of defection, although constantly exposed to enemy influences' (ibid). Though the Secretary of State's expression of satisfaction with their loyalty was delayed, London felt it important 'not to let slip any chance of stiffening the backbones of the HK Chinese', and proposed that Clementi (who succeeded Stubbs as Governor in November 1925) issue a despatch noting their loyalty.[127]

Because the boycott had brought the Colony to a standstill, the police were also able to 'exercise much closer supervision than is normally possible' over all arrivals, break up criminal gangs, and arrest intimidators.[128] By 1930, however, even though crime was said to be rising and causing some alarm in the territory,[129] political policing had become the focus of the police force. Local Communists tried to organise demonstrations on nine occasions during the year. Twenty-nine leading Communists were banished and one local newspaper proscribed, the editor and manager being banished.[130]

Police also broke up a meeting at the Nah Yang Tobacco Co's premises, where 600 female workers were, it was thought, being encouraged by Communists to go on strike – the leaders were arrested, convicted and deported (ibid).

Despite this general climate of spies, suspicion and subversion, in the mid-1930s, a scheme was proposed whereby more 'Asiatic' police 'of good education and culture' would be recruited and promoted to replace some of the European officers, this being deemed more economic and efficient.[131] To recruit suitable men, the Inspector General of Police:

> . . . has been in communication with headmasters of schools of standing in the Colony, from whom he will obtain lists of boys recommended for engagement . . . on the score of their proficiency in English and Chinese . . . This method of selection has been adopted on the basis of past experience, which has shown that, in appointments of this kind and in view of local conditions, character is of more importance to the success of the scheme than intellect or scholarship.[132]

The Governor (Caldecott) proposed that 'exceptionally able' Chinese might become eligible for promotion to the commissioned ranks of assistant superintendents, but, at the same time he argued that 'it is not considered desirable at present to hold out such prospects, or necessary at this stage to make recommendations as to the salary of an officer who will not in any case be appointed for at least twenty-one years to come' (ibid). The scheme having been approved by EXCO, he proposed to begin recruiting ten Chinese sub-inspectors in September 1936.

By 1939 and 1940, the prospect of losing Indian recruits made greater localisation imperative. Unrest amongst Sikh members of the police prompted inquiries into the source of 'subversive influences' as well as a request to India that Indian Police interrogators 'experienced in Sikh trouble' to be sent to Hong Kong.[133] Growing concern about Sikh unrest eventually caused the Governor (Northcote) to contact MI5 about the number of desertions amongst Hong Kong police and military units'. One police officer was found in possession of anti-British literature 'apparently emanating from Shanghai: 'It is suspected that some unidentified organisation is subverting Indians in Hong Kong and Governor is anxious for an Indian Police Officer to be placed at his disposal in near future to protect Indian troops from subversive influences . . . Colonial Office concur'.[134] These two issues – of localisation and the role of the Indian police – were to re-surface as key questions during the period of reconstruction following the Japanese occupation of Hong Kong during the Second World War.

Notes

1 Davis to Stanley, No. 25, 8 March 1845, CO129/11 pp 160–61 cited in Kerrigan 2001: 83.
2 *Friend of China* 24 April 1844 cited in Kerrigan 2001. Little reliable scholarship exists on the early police. Much of this section relies on Kerrigan's excellent research on the Hong Kong police 1844–99.
3 *China Mail* 22. May 1844.
4 As one of the few Europeans who could speak Chinese Eitel found himself seconded to government as interpreter, detracting from his missionary work.
5 CO129/9:317, Kerrigan 2001: 93.
6 Davis to Stanley 21 May 1845, CO129/12: 108 cited in Kerrigan 2001: 93ff.
7 See also Palmer 1975.
8 CO129/14: 26 in Kerrigan 2001.
9 May to Philips and Sir James Graham, Metropolitan Police 11 October 1845, CO129/14: 200 in Kerrigan 2001.
10 In other colonial police forces too, officers were required to undertake a wide variety of non-policing duties; in many European countries, they administered licensing, market trading, individual registration and many similar tasks, and police in China under Mao were also required to undertake a vast array of non-policing tasks.
11 Davis to Stanley No. 26, 21 June 1844, CO129/6: 282–3 in Kerrigan 2001.
12 These Europeans were often destitute 'beachcombers'. See Lethbridge 'The Condition of the European Working Class in 19th Century Hong Kong', in Lethbridge 1978b.
13 *Friend of China & Hong Kong Gazette* 3 (150) 17 April 1844: 436; see also Davis to Gladstone No. 47 Financial, 4 May 1846, CO129/6: 293; Bowring to Grey No. 73 Financial, 25 September 1854, CO129/47: 85 in Kerrigan 2001.
14 Davis to Stanley No. 64 Civil, 21 May 1845, CO129/12: 97–8 in Kerrigan 2001.
15 Davis to Earl Grey No. 142 Civil, 16 December 1846, CO129/17: 436–7 in Kerrigan 2001.
16 For further details about Caldwell see Munn 2000.
17 Bonham to Newcastle No. 2 Financial, 2 January 1854, CO129/45; Kerrigan 2001.
18 May's report to Bowring, forwarded to Grey No. 73, 26 September 1854, CO129/47: 85–103.
19 *Friend of China and Hong Kong Gazette* 22 August 1849; Kerrigan 2001: 139.
20 *Friend of China & Hong Kong Gazette* 1 March 1856, cited in Kerrigan 2001: 140.
21 Bowring became Governor in 1854; he was succeeded by Robinson in 1859.
22 Bowring's son, Sayer tells us, was a director in Jardine Matheson and was thus 'connected by the closest ties with the 'princely hong'. The newspaper editor who suggested this link might have been abused found himself 'incarcerated in the local jail for libel' Sayer 1980: 187. In May 1859, Bowring left Hong Kong, his administration being described as 'wicked and corrupt'.
23 See Munn 2000.
24 Later to become Sir Cecil Clementi Smith. See Sayer 1980: 194
25 MacDonnell to Earl of Carnarvon No. 783, 7 January 1867, CO129/120: 43; Kerrigan 2001.
26 Robinson to Chamberlain No. 173, 13 August 1897, CO129/276: 317–18; Kerrigan 2001.
27 MacDonnell's proposals stipulated that no foreigners would be allowed to play in government gaming houses; later, this was refined so that only Chinese and Malays

were allowed to play, though Chinese servants, cashiers, schroffs and bill collectors were excluded. See Eitel 1983: 433.

28 CO129/149: 208; Kerrigan 2001.

29 Proclamation of January 1872, CO129/156; Kerrigan 2001.

30 Report from Captain Superintendent of Police, September 1873; Kerrigan 2001.

31 In 1872, the cost of employing 146 Europeans was $65,592 compared to $22,569 for 206 Chinese and $61,326 for 365 Indians.

32 According to Lethbridge, as an Irish Catholic Hennessy prided himself on supporting 'oppressed nationalities' and took sides with the Chinese against the European community. See Lethbridge 183: viii.

33 Davis to Stanley No. 114, 20 August 1845, CO129/13; cited in Endacott 1964: 75.

34 Lomas, 'Policing in Hong Kong', paper to 18th senior Command Course, Police Staff College, Bramshill: 16.

35 See Kerrigan 2001 Chapters 4 and 5 for details of these Commissions.

36 *Friend of China & Hong Kong Gazette* 1 March 1856, cited in Kerrigan 2001: 140.

37 Bowring to Labouchere, No.203 Executive, 10 December 1856, CO129/59 p 239 in Kerrigan 2001: 142.

38 Ibid.

39 Bowring to Labouchere No. 203 Executive, 10 December 1856, CO129/59 in Kerrigan 2001: 151.

40 CO129/152: 178–83 in Kerrigan 2001.

41 CO129/18 1861: 166; Robinson to Newcastle No. 7 Executive, 25 January 1860, CO129/80: 50 in Kerrigan 2001: 166ff.

42 Robinson to Newcastle No. 198, 30 October 1861, CO129/82 in Kerrigan 2001.

43 Lethbridge 1970: 38; G.N. No. 115, *Hong Kong Gazette* 12 October 1861; Kerrigan 2001.

44 Robinson to Newcastle No. 86, 6 May 1862, CO129/86: 45; Kerrigan 2001.

45 Kerrigan 2001; Robinson to Newcastle No. 73, 26 April 1861, CO129/81.

46 MacDonnell to the Duke of Buckingham and Chandos No. 52, 10 June 1866, CO129/131: 96.

47 Although MacDonnell considered Quin to be a worthy and honest public servant, as head of the police force he concluded that:

> 'he is eminently unfitted for the superintendence of such a body as the Police force of Hong Kong, and for the discharge of the extremely novel and peculiarly difficult duties of that post, – duties more difficult, I venture to affirm, than devolve on any one Police Officer in any British Colony' (MacDonnell to Carnarvon, No. 184, 7 January 1867, CO129/120 in Kerrigan 2001: 193).

48 MacDonnell to Carnarvon No. 184, 7 January 1867, CO129/120 pp 80–83 in Kerrigan 2001.

49 MacDonnell to Lawrence, Governor General of India No. 654, 30 November 1866, CO129/120: 70–75.

50 Creagh to MacDonnell 7 October 1866, CO129/120: 56–60; Mercer, Colonial Secretary, to Creagh, CO129/120: 74 in Kerrigan 2001: 193.

51 Captain Superintendent's Report for 1870, *Hong Kong Government Gazette* 24 June 1871, Vol XVII; Kerrigan 2001. Interestingly, however, a brief downturn in the official crime figures in 1868/9 had elsewhere been taken as evidence of the success of the (Chinese staffed) district watch.

52 Whitfield to Kimberley No. 157, 16 October 1871, including Deane to Colonial Secretary No. 199, 23 September 1871, CO129/152: 210–11 in Kerrigan 2001.

53 Report on the Police Force 1871, *Hong Kong Government Gazette* 24 June 1871 in Kerrigan 2001.
54 CO129/152: 313 in Kerrigan 2001.
55 Report on the Police for 1870, Deane Captain Superintendent of Police, *Hong Kong Government Gazette* No. 25, 24 June 1871 Vol XVII; see Kerrigan 2001: Chapter 9.
56 Deane, Captain Superintendent of Police CO129/152: 206–21 in Kerrigan 2001.
57 This was not, however, a unanimous view among the European elite. While some blamed what they saw as a rise in crime on the suspension of some of the punishments during MacDonnell's absence, others welcomed their cessation, arguing that not only had they failed to have any effect upon crime but were, in any case, uncivilised.
58 Memorialists to Austin, 27 September 1871, CO129/152; see also Kerrigan 2001.
59 Report of the 1872 Police Commission Para 9; for details see Kerrigan 2001.
60 Whitefield to Kimberley No. 102, 9 September 1870, CO129/113–46; Kerrigan 2001.
61 Endacott 1964; Whitefield to Kimberley No. 157, 16 October 1871, CO129/152: 312 in Kerrigan 2001.
62 Rice to Austin 21 September 1871, CO129/152: 268 in Kerrigan 2001.
63 Rice to Austin 21 September 1871, CO129/152: 222–8 in Kerrigan 2001.
64 See also Rice to Austin CO129/152 and Kerrigan 2001: 194 for table of comparison.
65 Report of the Committee on the Police Force and Crime in Hong Kong 7 March 1879, CO129/184: 108–17.
66 Hennessy to Hicks-Beech No. 94, 19 March 1879 in Kerrigan 2001: 241.
67 *Hong Kong Government Gazette* 9 March 1878, Vol. XXIV in Kerrigan 2001: 240.
68 Hennessy to Carnarvon, No. 23, 27 February 1878, CO129/181: 188 cited in Kerrigan 2001.
69 See Kerrigan 2001: 230; *Supplement to the Hongkong Daily Press* 10 October 1878, CO129/182: 210.
70 Hennessy to Hicks-Beach, No. 26, 7 March 1879, CO129/184 in Kerrigan 2001: 235.
71 Ibid.
72 For a full discussion of the 1872 Commission, see Kerrigan 2001, Chapter 9.
73 Bowen to Derby, No. 334, 10 December 1883, CO129/213: 93 in Kerrigan 2001: 242.
74 Bowen to Derby, No. 334, 10 December 1883, CO129/213: 87–90 in Kerrigan 2001: 244.
75 Such stations are still found in modern Hong Kong, but were made redundant in the 1960s by the advent of high-rise blocks from which assailants could fire over a station's defensive walls.
76 Special and Extraordinary Meeting, 3 October 1884, CO129/217 in Kerrigan 2001: 250.
77 Sinn 1982: 81; Kerrigan 2001: 253.
78 Kerrigan 2001: 253.
79 A temporary measure, the Ordinance became part of Hong Kong's permanent law in 1886 and was to influence the policing of riots well into the 1950s and 1960s.
80 Kerrigan notes: 'The residents of Tai Ping-shan took the full force of the plague a situation that resulted in panic and the estimated departure of about 80,000 of the native population . . . Police search parties began with house-to-house searches . . . Gangs of coolies were also hired to clean houses discovered to have been

infected with the plague and special flushing of the sewers, drains, and streets was also undertaken. Cleansing and disinfecting gangs also flushed streets and drains ... Chinese police were used to warn inhabitants of the intention of cleaning certain properties, which was done to avoid complications. The daily work practices of those involved included: (a) the house to house searchers, (b) the collectors of bedding and clothing from the rooms or cubicles from which plague patients had been removed to hospital, (c) the fumigating parties, (d) the cleansing parties, and (e) the parties in charge of the fires in which the infected clothing, bedding, and rubbish were burned. The cleansing parties were required to sprinkle the floors of houses with a disinfecting fluid and chlorinated lime. The walls were then lime-washed and floors washed down with disinfectant ... Eviction parties were stationed in the area to prevent people from wandering off and also to prevent the unauthorised removal of articles which may have been infected. Once houses were vacated a party would then nail up the house to prevent any unauthorised entry ... Simultaneously, with the evictions at Tai Ping-Shan, police and the military (sworn in as special constables) implemented and maintained a cordon sanitaire. Report of Messrs F. May and J.R. Crook on the work carried out by them in connection with the plague. 28 September 1894, CO129/270.' 'The Permanent Committee & The Plague Workers', *Hong Kong Daily Press* 27 September 1894 cited in Kerrigan 2001: 259.

81 See Kerrigan 2001: 261 for details of the Police Ordinance 1887.

82 Robinson to Chamberlain, No. 173, 13 August 1897, CO129/276: 328.

83 Crisswell and Watson 1982, cited in Kerrigan 2001: 292.

84 Blake to Chamberlain, 13 July 1899 enclosing May's report on the state of the police.

85 F.H. May, Captain Superintendent of Police, to Colonial Secretary, 3 July 1899, CO129/292 pp 300–306 cited in Kerrigan 2001: 292.

86 The nineteenth century saw a similar competition amongst European powers to carve up Africa, usually described as the 'scramble for Africa'.

87 Encl 142 Telegram from Mr Bax-Ironside, Peking 7 May 1899 in Kerrigan 2001: 273.

88 17th Day 2nd Moon. 25th Year of Kwong Sui (28 March 1899). A placard issued by the Yuk on Hin (Wish for Peace library) of Ping-shan. Translated by A.W. Brewin; No. 82, Governor Blake to Chamberlain, Secretary of State, No. 82. 1 April 1899; *Hong Kong Government Gazette* 26 August 1899 p 1,352 cited in Kerrigan 2001: 274 n. 21

89 For a full account of the resistance put up by local inhabitants, see Kerrigan 2001, Chapter 10 and Blake to Chamberlain, No. 155, 24 April 1899, CO129/292.

90 For a summary of the 'battle of Tai Po' see Kerrigan 2001: Chapter 10.

91 See Lugard, Frederick D. (Lord) (1922, reprinted 1965); Perham (1956 and 1960). The doctrine of 'Indirect Rule' was contained in Lugard's 1906 Political Memoranda, a series of notices and pamphlets based on his experience in Nigeria and circulated amongst colonial administrators.

92 Endacott, 1964; CO129/130 cited in Kerrigan 2001.

93 Report by Mr Stewart Lockhart, Colonial Secretary, on the Extension of the Colony of Hong Kong, 8 October 1898, CO129/289 p 206 cited in Kerrigan 2001: 286.

94 See, for example, Coates 1968.

95 May to Blake, 26 July 1900, enclosure to Colonial Office CO129/300: 207ff.

96 Despatch from Blake, 18 August 1899, CO129/300.

97 Blake to Chamberlain 27 July 1900, CO129/300: 205.

98 Blake to Chamberlain 20 September 1900, CO129/301: 31.

99 Captain Superintendent of Police to Colonial Secretary 19 August 1901, CO129/306: 266.
100 Blake to Chamberlain 9 December 1902, CO129/313: 420.
101 See May to Harcourt 1 December 1914, CO129/415: 20 and the enclosed minutes of May's meeting with Moberley.
102 Between 1903 and 1904 May was appointed to administer the colony until Blake's successor (Nathan) was appointed; from 1912 to 1919, he became Governor.
103 Blake to Lyttelton, Secretary of State for the Colonies, 7 November 1903, CO129/319: 565.
104 For May's Report see Enclosure No. 1 to Governor's Confidential Despatch 7 November 1903, CO129/319: 570.
105 Ibid. May also complained that he had seen one constable 'stood with both his hands on his hips while an Inspector passed him'.
106 Letter from Wodehouse to Stubbs, Colonial Office 15 November 1911, CO129/381: 315/6.
107 Lugard to Harcourt 10 December 1911, CO129/381: 320ff.
108 Wodehouse to Stubbs 4 December 1911, CO129/381: 317. In fact, Lugard had pressed for increases in establishment and pay. London agreed: 'A colonial force is not the same as a Home force, requiring a much larger reserve of strength': see CO129/377: 193.
109 Lugard to Harcourt 10 December 1911, CO129/381: 320. Serious recorded crime had increased by 7.86 per cent over 1909 to 263. There were only four convictions out of 19 murder cases, and one conviction out of five manslaughter cases, whilst 56 gang robberies were reported against 36 in 1909, of which no arrest was made in 34; against nine cases of piracy in 1909, there were 22 in 1910, although the police had agreed to act as hired guards for the shipping companies, who faced difficulty finding recruits. Overall, of the five most serious categories of crime, convictions had been obtained in only 20 out of 124 cases. Petty larcenies formed the largest category of all crimes.
110 Lugard to Harcourt 17 May 1911, CO129/377: 196/6.
111 Ibid. Hong Kong's Police Museum contains a number of the files and photographs of the large number of people banished in 1911 and subsequent years, mainly for minor offences, such as vagrancy.
112 HKPAR 1922: 12.
113 HKPAR 1922: 14.
114 Despatch to Harcourt, Secretary of State for the Colonies 10 December 1891, CO129/381: 323. Lyons had taken this step without consulting his superiors.
115 HKPAR 1925.
116 HKPAR 1922: 15.
117 Memoranda 11 December 1919, CO129/456.
118 Ibid. 'It is, I think, clear that we must arrange for a separate prison, preferably on the mainland, where long sentence convicts can be properly instructed in handicrafts, for there is no space in Victoria Gaol. It will be necessary to retain Victoria Gaol as a prison for short sentence prisoners and I hope to make arrangements for a separate institution, more on Borstal lines, for juveniles'.
119 HKPAR 1936.
120 HKPARs 1937–9.
121 Severn (officer administering the Hong Kong government) to Winston Churchill, Secretary of State for the Colonies 4 July 1922, CO129/475.
122 Severn to Winston Churchill 22 August 1922, CO29/476.
123 Wei Hei Wei was a British colony on the Mainland to which Lockhart had been

appointed Governor after his tour of duty in the NT. In the early 1920s, Britain was considering its retrocession to China. Its police force was therefore to be disbanded, providing a supply of potential recruits for Hong Kong.

124 Severn to Churchill 4 July 1922, CO129/475.

125 HKPAR 1925: 14.

126 Stubbs to Amery, Secretary of State for the Colonies, enclosing Report of Captain Superintendent of Police on work done by the Hong Kong Police Force during the 1925 strike 15 September 1925, CO129/489.

127 Memo dated 15 September 1925, CO129/489.

128 HKPAR 1925: 15

129 There were 22 cases of murder, including that of a European woman and a police constable (shot by a police constable who ran amok and then killed himself) and of a Chinese detective, shot in a Yau Ma Tei restaurant, where he was trapped with two detectives from Canton (see below). Minor crime had increased to 3,500 cases, mostly involving hawkers, mendicants, nuisance and traffic cases, the latter showing an increase following the introduction of road traffic legislation in 1912. Anti-gambling legislation passed in 1930 also led to a crackdown on lotteries connected to local race meetings. See HKPAR 1930: 13–15.

130 HKPAR 1930: 14.

131 Memo of 22 April 1936 and Despatch from the Governor (Caldecott) to Ormsby-Gore, Secretary of State for the Colonies CO129/559.

132 Caldecott to Ormsby-Gore 22 July 1936, CO129/559: 2.

133 Secret Telegram No. 816 Hong Kong via India Office to Government of India 30 September 1940, CO129/587.

134 Telegram from Secretary of State to Government of India 4 November 1940, CO129/587.

Chapter 4

Hong Kong's internal security

From its very inception until the 1870s, the Hong Kong police force was frequently criticised from all sides for its inefficiency. Some of this criticism was directed against all members of the force, regardless of race but the ever-present colonial anxiety about the loyalty and reliability of local members of the force gave rise to particular criticism of the Chinese, reflecting entrenched discriminatory attitudes and producing some deeply discriminatory practices. The 1872 Police Commission represented something of a break with both, but its attempts to encourage a more 'local' police force were periodically undermined by a pervasive distrust of the Chinese, which intensified during periods of local unrest and turmoil on the Mainland. For a colonial regime lacking popular legitimacy, internal security concerns were always present, fuelled partly by the fear that, if domestic and Mainland discontents ever united, they could challenge British rule in Hong Kong. This realisation informed questions of internal security, as well as police loyalty and reliability.

Given that academia has frequently represented the Hong Kong Chinese as politically apathetic, it might be thought that internal security was seldom a problem for the colonial regime. But recent histories of Hong Kong have dented this narrative, revealing a long tradition of resistance.[1] The territory and many segments of its population were far more politically animated than is often realised. The years between the1880s and the 1920s, for example, were characterised by numerous strikes, boycotts and demonstrations, some arising over working conditions and wider economic trends, some out of events in Mainland China, and some out of measures imposed by the Hong Kong government. During this period, the colonial authorities were forced to face their worst fears when workers in Canton mobilised in support of Hong Kong workers, forming the biggest challenge yet to both the colony's merchant class (Chinese and English) and the government. The victories scored by organised labour against the mighty colonial state in these years became part of the institutional memory of the regime. For many years to come, they would shape its determination to suppress the labour unions. Coups against the Mainland government were also fomented in Hong Kong by revolutionaries (both Nationalist and Communist) who found temporary shelter in the colony. Such activities sparked periodic anxiety about the regime's ability to contain unrest and manage Hong Kong's internal security situation, anxieties that always militated against greater political liberalisation and, indeed, against the localisation of the police force.

The colonial state was, however, never monolithic. Within it (and within the European elite more generally) there were liberally inclined fractions who wished to see the colony evolve along more humane lines, and who were repulsed by the more repressive tendencies of the administration. Throughout the nineteenth century there were also recurrent concerns within the European elite about corruption within government agencies, and its corrosive effect on their reliability and efficiency. Most of this concern related to the police and, because the police force was so central to the maintenance of law and order, the government did not shrink from enquiring into, and charging and prosecuting, its own officers – even senior European officers – in such cases. The more enlightened sections of Hong Kong society realised the damage inflicted by corruption on the image of the British as bringers of law, justice, order and good government which, in turn, undercut their efforts to 'attach' the Chinese to British rule through the rule of law. Yet, despite their attempts to root out corruption, the cases brought to court represented only a small fraction of the most serious instances of corrupt behaviour and, for many decades, government officials and police officers continued to exploit their power and position to generate and maintain unofficial incomes based on bribes.

Internal security

For most of the nineteenth century – and at intervals up to and after the Second World War – its 'crime fighting' capability was only one aspect of the Hong Kong police force. Charged with civil affairs duties as well as maintaining internal security, it frequently found itself required to perform a wide variety of tasks with poor resources. It ineffectiveness as a crime-fighting tool stemmed partly from the inability of its officers to communicate with the local population. Caldwell, being one of the few Europeans able to speak Chinese, was an exception and quickly became indispensable as head of the detective force. As the 'eyes and ears' of the administration, he and his men were also invaluable as gatherers of local intelligence, collecting information on subversion as well as crime. The regime also employed a series of paid spies in Mainland China, principally in cities such as Canton and Shanghai, whose job it was to alert the Hong Kong authorities whenever known criminals or agitators planned to travel to the colony. 'Internal security' was, however, not simply directed at preventing the 'enemy without' (Mainland Chinese rebels and troublemakers) from undermining the colony, but also at preventing the 'enemy within' from breaching the *cordon sanitaire* of peace and stability that the Europeans wished to secure for themselves.

Internal security was thus the constant backdrop against which all other government policies proceeded. Intrusions from within and without the colony frequently interrupted the administration's best-laid plans and intentions. Unrest in the colony had briefly surfaced in the 1840s, provoked by a swathe of anti-Chinese legislation. It simmered throughout the 1850s, fuelled partly by the Tai Ping rebellion in China, and partly by the Second Opium War between Britain and China. The population of the colony swelled to 94,000, mostly immigrants fleeing turmoil on the Mainland but also said to include 'the vilest outcasts' and 'scum' of the Chinese empire. The comparative prosperity of the colony was thought to have attracted the Mainland's 'criminal classes', prompting fears of an increase in crime, as well as renewed concern amongst the elite about their 'health, security and general well-being' (Munn 2001: 263). Alarmed by these new threats to their security, the Europeans also felt threatened on a daily basis by the basic, unsanitary dwellings thrown up by new immigrants in Taipingshan. In 1856, the area became the site of a minor epidemic, confirming their worst fears.

The situation in the mid-1850s was likened to the 'anarchy' of Hong Kong's early years (Munn 2001: 264). European fears for their own safety grew to such a point that the 1856 Police Commission was even presented with a submission to erect physical barriers between the European and Chinese areas, restricting the movement of the Chinese (Kerrigan 2001: 149). In 1866, the Victorian Registration Ordinance did empower the Governor-in-Council to close off certain sections of the town of Victoria by means of gates 'or otherwise', and to prohibit all ingress and egress 'at such times and for such period and in such manner as . . . shall seem fit'.[2] The police force was increased by 20 more Europeans and 50 Indian constables, to provide greater supervision.[3]

This general climate of insecurity was exacerbated by hostilities in the Crimea which raised British fears about Russian ambitions in the Far East. Soldiers sent from Britain to shore up the Hong Kong garrison were also diverted instead to India, where Britain was facing the Indian Mutiny (2001: 138). Other colonies in the region were also beset by unrest. In Hong Kong, the 'incendiarism, assassination plots and premiums placed on European heads threatened to destabilize the colony' (Munn 2001: 275). The 'war against foreigners' in China prompted officials to call for the extermination of the British. Spies were sent to Hong Kong to engage in subversive activities, such as plots to blow up the Cathedral, attack government offices and the premises of Jardine Matheson, poison the Europeans, and firebomb property (ibid). In 1858, trade stoppages and the desertion of 25,000 servants and tradesmen paralysed the colony. Lacking faith in the ability of the police force to protect them, Europeans took to carrying revolvers, locking up their Chinese servants at night, and erecting barricades at the end of certain streets (Munn 2001: 284).

More soldiers were secured to guard the colony, a commercial steamer was deployed to patrol the harbour and neighbouring waters, and a curfew was imposed on the Chinese. Vagrants were encouraged to leave the colony by the intensive enforcement of existing anti-vagrancy laws (ibid). The 'emergency' thus bound a frightened European community more closely together by turning all Chinese into potential enemies.

In 1857, Bowring introduced a Peace Preservation Ordinance, an attempt to maintain a tight rein on public order by requiring 'fit persons' to carry a night pass when out between the hours of eight in the evening and sunrise. The definition of a 'fit person' lay with the authorities; any Chinese found without a pass was liable to imprisonment with hard labour, public whipping or exposure in the *cangue*; they could also be deported. The provisions of the early Registration Ordinance were also re-enacted. Amongst other things, these specified that no Chinese could be present at a public meeting without a written licence signed by the Governor (Kerrigan 2001). 'Pass vigilantes' were encouraged to police these provisions. They were permitted to fire upon, and kill, any Chinaman whom they reasonably suspected of being abroad for unlawful purposes[4] (ibid). These 'respectable' and 'faithful' inhabitants of the colony were encouraged by Caine to form a 'Special Constabulary' or Corps of Volunteers to protect their own families and properties. The Chinese merchants erected their own watchtowers and provided assistance in fire-prevention (Munn 2001: 284).

A new version of the Registration Ordinance, published in 1857,[5] was designed to help the authorities monitor the 'large number of suspicious characters' flooding into Hong Kong from the Mainland, and to control the 'seditious and treasonable demonstrations' on the streets, organised by 'secret emissaries' from the rebels in China.[6] The Registrar General's office (established in 1856 as a separate entity under Caldwell) was granted extensive powers and controls over the Chinese community, Caldwell himself being used to detect spies, track down wanted criminals, advise on Chinese sentiment, and cultivate support amongst the Chinese population (Munn 2001: 284ff).[7]

These emergency measures, Munn says, were designed not only to assuage European fears of an immediate Chinese uprising, but longer-lived European anxieties about crime and the Chinese in their midst (Munn 2001: 284). The usefulness of these 'emergency powers' meant that they remained on the statute books long after the emergency itself had subsided. Thus, the curfew remained on the books, despite occasional criticism by leading Chinese, because it was a cheap and effective means of controlling the Chinese population. It was not suspended until 1897, 'as a gesture of goodwill on the occasion of Queen Victoria's Diamond Jubilee' (ibid). The tendency to resort to emergency powers, particularly evident during periods of crisis was, Munn argues, matched by a reluctance to rescind these powers once the emergency had subsided. These 'dormant' laws were re-deployed whenever the colonists felt under threat and their accretion over time left a residue that became naturalised into the colonial way of life (ibid).

One of the principal fears of the colonial authorities was that triads – instigators of anti-Qing unrest on the Mainland – would use Hong Kong both as a base for subverting China and to recruit sympathisers for their cause. Alarmed by the potential for pan-Chinese alliances with anti-foreign forces in neighbouring provinces, the colonial authorities had introduced Ordinance 1 of 1845 to suppress triad and other secret societies. Triads were deemed 'inconsistent with the maintenance of good rule and constituted authority, and with the security of life and property'. Opposed to 'unpatriotic' political forces within China they were, by extension, likely to provide a rallying point for organised resistance to colonial rule in Hong Kong. Governments elsewhere in the British Empire had used triads as intermediaries to assist in the management of their Chinese communities. Arguably, however, Hong Kong's proximity to Mainland China, and the possibilities this offered for cross-border mobilisation on a grand scale, made triads more problematic. According to Munn, early anti-triad legislation in Hong Kong was aimed at placating the Chinese authorities by co-operating with them to suppress rebellion on the Mainland. But what Munn calls the 'quiet deportation' of triad members in the late 1840s provoked sharp criticism of the government, as deportation to China almost certainly meant that triad members would be executed. Co-operation with China's harsh regime was seen by many amongst the European elite as an abrogation of the benevolent and humane basis of colonial authority.[8]

The real power of triads in early Hong Kong remains, in any case, very unclear. Even during the 1850s, at the height of rebellion and unrest in China, the Superintendent of Police (Charles May) told the Caldwell Inquiry that 'at one time there was a notion that triads were very much to be feared, and to be driven out of the Colony; but the triads never did us any harm, and the feeling against them died away' (cited in Munn 2001: 126). By the 1880s, however, the old fears would return and the police would argue that all 'the lower criminal classes' and most of the Hakka population were triads (ibid).

Steps taken during periods of peace to reduce the exclusion of the Chinese were, therefore, always likely to be brushed aside in periods of anxiety, giving rise to a continuing sense of the fragility of Hong Kong's peace and stability. Thus, for example, the attempt made by Hennessey in the 1870s to give the Hong Kong police force a more Anglo-Chinese face, and to incorporate the more 'respectable' Chinese into the community were reversed when the colonists' latent distrust of the Chinese resurfaced during the Sino–French conflict of the 1880s. From the 1880s onwards, as strikes and boycotts became more frequent, so the resort to repressive measures became more routine.

The wave of anti-foreignism that swept China in the 1880s reached a peak during the Sino–French conflict of 1884, when the Chinese authorities in Canton issued a proclamation prohibiting any Chinese from providing the French with services, provisions and repairs (Tsai 1993: 124). Located only 80 miles from Canton, Hong Kong 'lay middle way between the war theatres of Hanoi to the south and Foochow and Keelung to the north'; its harbour would have provided the perfect shelter for French ships. Their arrival in September 1884 in Hong Kong led to serious popular insurrection (Tsai 1993: 125). Hong Kong boat workers refused to load or unload, or to service the ships, whilst merchants refused to sell them provisions. For these acts, some were fined by the magistrates, an act which brought all the cargo boat workers out on strike and brought the harbour to a halt (Tsai 1993: 126). On 30 September, a crowd of almost a thousand began to stone and drive away the remaining cargo and passenger boats; a notice threatening to blow up the premises of a French merchant, and warning its Chinese employees to leave, was posted on the door of the store (ibid).

The strike continued into October, marked by sporadic clashes with the police during which the Sikh police opened fire on the crowds, provoking further violence:

> . . . until the whole district from Central Street to East Street was in a state of turmoil. . All shops were closed, and coolies from all points flocked together to join the revolutionary movement . . . Strong police reinforcements were sent to the scene, including Sikh and Chinese police and some mounted Indian troopers. The huge mass of people that gathered on the Chinese Recreation ground threw stones at the police, who fired revolvers into the crowd . . . Meanwhile, the British military authorities had sent two companies of troops to the scene of the disturbance. With fixed bayonets, their presence did much to disperse the crowd . . . A hundred troops marched to the Tung Wah Hospital, to be quartered in its buildings . . . situated in a district densely inhabited by the Chinese . . . The streets were patrolled by police and troops at night, and the harbour by the launches and water police (Tsai 1993: 127–8).

Despite interventions by the Chinese elite, the strike and riots continued until 6 October, accompanied by sporadic pelting of Europeans and animosity towards the police. Though there was a strong anti-French feeling at work, this was transformed into anti-British feeling when the colonial authorities intervened to stop the initial boycott.

According to Tsai, two things thus cut across the parochialism of the workers.[9] The first was the mobilisation around anti-French, nationalistic feelings, which produced a patriotic solidarity. The second was the 'high-handed official provocations' of the British'. This turned what had started as an expression of Chinese patriotism into 'a popular mobilization against the local British establishment' (Ming Chan 1990: 282).

Organisational leadership was provided by the guilds as well as the triad societies, whose allegiance the Canton authorities had sought by promising them material rewards and appealing to their anti-foreign patriotism (Tsai 1983: 130). There were thousands of triads in the colony by 1884, and, according to Hong Kong police intelligence, 'about a hundred more triads were recruited to Canton . . . Some triad leaders became directors of the disturbances . . . the triads wished to stir up trouble, hoping to profit from it' (ibid). According to Tsai, the Hong Kong police received intelligence that the Canton government plotted to use three thousand dollars to employ some triads to blow up a French ship in Hong Kong harbour. This made it highly likely that the names of those who failed to support the strike would filter back through triad societies to the Mainland, where retaliation could be exacted against their families. At the same time, however, those who did strike faced repressive action by the Hong Kong government. Those who wished to avoid this, and return to work, had to be coerced by their fellow coolies into supporting the strike.

However, there were some Chinese officials, Tsai says, who were anxious not to antagonise the British, relying heavily upon Hong Kong's banking institutions to finance the war against France, and shipping weapons and munitions for the war through the colony. It was in the interests of these mandarins to discourage anything that would irritate the British and disturb trade. Chang Chih-tung, Governor General in Canton, apparently argued that:

> Canton and Hong Kong are co-terminous; they share each other's peace and peril. If coal, rice and flour from Hong Kong do not arrive for ten days, Canton suffers. If cattle, pig and vegetable supplies from the province do not go to Hong Kong for a day, people in Hong Kong become restless. When Hong Kong is in turmoil, the trade routes in the province are blocked. When the province is in disorder, bandits in Hong Kong rise up from all sides . . . When Hong Kong is in trouble, we [in Canton] become anxious. If we have problems, neither can Hong Kong rest in peace (cited in Tsai 1993: 134).

As in later decades, officials in China thus had good reason to call upon the Chinese in Hong Kong to halt disorder once it had served its purpose. Moreover, Tsai argues, whilst they were willing to encourage some triad activity, such officials were anxious to avoid a domestic triad uprising – problematically, once the triads became engaged, Canton could not always control them.

As Tsai says, the causes of the 1884 disturbances were due to more than the activities of some patriotic triads. They were much more complex, the strike acquiring a class dimension as hitherto disparate sections of the Chinese coolie class became united against a common enemy. Labour–management conflicts were readily transformed into confrontations between Chinese workers and British establishment partly because the few modern, large-scale enterprises and public utilities were mostly owned by British interests. In addition, the administration itself, when not silent on industrial issues, intervened on the side of capital against labour (see Ming Chan 1990). Thus, although the British sought to blame the triads for the unrest, there was already a 'solid social basis of popular animosity to the colonial authorities' that they could build upon:

> Another major source of popular discontent was the poverty and misery of the coolie class. As the Hong Kong English press admitted, coolies were forced by poverty to live 'in place where you would not stable horses in England . . . cathedrals, Churches, Chapels, Missions are a mockery in the midst of the squalid, filthy, crowded houses and narrow streets of this Colony; it was 'a disgrace to humanity'. Poverty and misery spawned social discontent and provided a general social context conducive to unrest (Tsai 1993: 135).

This pervasive social discontent stemmed, Chan argues, from the colonial state's failure to intervene in Hong Kong's economy and society on behalf of its most disadvantaged subjects. In this respect, the state's insistence upon a laissez faire policy meant that it never provided social welfare for the grass roots, never promoted social justice, and thus lost any claims it might have to moral legitimacy amongst the grass-roots Chinese (Chan 1990: 583). Moreover, its claims to fair-minded, even-handed administration and non-intervention were hollow, for when the interests of the state and the elite were threatened, it clearly was prepared to intervene, on the side of state and capital. The criminal justice system in particular was employed to suppress the labour movement – the official response to the 1884 strike was a highly repressive Peace Preservation Ordinance of 1884 which made it an offence to be a member of any society by whatever name known or formed for an unlawful purpose, or having among their objects purposes incompatible with the peace and good order of the Colony (Chan 1990: 583).[10]

The 1884 strike also demonstrated the diminishing influence of the Chinese elite as a check on the Chinese working class. In this instance, as Tsai points out, their interests were quite different, the merchant elite (like the European elite) favouring the continuation of trade and shipping within the harbour. Moreover, though the authorities sought the Chinese elite's help to end the strike, ambivalence had crept into in the British position:

> The British elite desired the advice and cooperation of the elite in restoring law and order, yet . . . they were also apprehensive of the elite's pretensions to political power and influence over the Chinese community . . . But the British authorities were sure of one thing – it was the British, and not the Chinese, who ruled the colony (Tsai 1993: 137).

The British, it seemed, were becoming more circumspect about allowing the Chinese elite a free hand in Chinese affairs, lest this create a 'state within the state' (see Chan 1990: 583). They still relied heavily upon the office of the Registrar General for advice on all things relating to the Chinese community (in 1884 the post-holder was made an ex officio member of LEGCO). Such channels were still seen as both sufficient and preferable as a means of absorbing the growing Chinese interests. But the events of 1884 meant that, where previously it had been content to allow the Chinese elite to govern the Chinese community, the government now became more determined to impose more direct control, and 'accelerate political integration' of the Chinese by bringing them more within the reach of the colonial policy, thereby reducing the role of the Chinese elite as mediators in government/Chinese relations.

The events of 1884 also indicated that the Chinese elite harboured divided loyalties. The Chinese elite's ties to Western capitalism led it to side with the British and discount coolie class strikes as 'valid' expressions of Chinese patriotism (Tsai 1993: 145). What Tsai calls a 'collaborative patriotism' now emerged. Though its commercial interests led it to favour collaboration with the government, the elite's patriotic sentiments, and its need for legitimacy with the Chinese population at large, also led many of its members to side with the Chinese cause against the French. Although many had by this time been co-opted by the administration and given positions of status, a question thus arose about their loyalty to the Crown.

Like earlier clashes, 1884 also brought home the fact that the stability of both Canton and Hong Kong was vulnerable to mass mobilisations when their Chinese populations made joint cause. The border between them was highly permeable; people and goods moved easily between the Mainland and the colony. At one level, this was how the authorities on both sides saw the Hong Kong–China relationship. However, the events of 1884 also revealed its drawbacks. 'Subversives' in Canton or Hong Kong had a capacity not only to disturb order in their own locale but in both places at the same time. This possibility made a lasting impression on the authorities. For the Mainland, one danger was that Hong Kong would become a base for subversives attempting to overthrow the Chinese government; for the British in Hong Kong, there was the prospect of Mainland groups suborning the local population to attack colonial rule.

Labour unrest and national movements between the 1880s and the Second World War heightened these fears, prompting increased repression, partly through the criminal law. From the 1880s onwards, a series of events were to arouse the collective consciousness of Hong Kong's Chinese workers and, as a consequence, heighten the colonists' sense of insecurity. In 1888, for example, a cargo boatmen's strike united workers against government legislation that required them to obtain a licence with a photograph, at the cost of 25 cents annually. The main use of the photograph was to enable the police to check for thefts of cargo and prevent cargo boatmen from impersonating each other (Tsai 1993: 171). A strike by the 4,000 boatmen in Hong Kong in

April 1888 lasted for 11 days, brought the port to a virtual standstill, and cost the merchant community thousands of dollars in losses. Both the merchants and the workers lobbied to have the new licence rescinded, but the government was unwilling to be seen to back down. As a result, the boatmen sought the support of other labourers in the colony:

> . . . a great mob collected on two of the principal streets was stopping all traffic, and was by threat, and in one or two cases by actual violence, preventing the jinricksha coolies and other labourers from following their occupations . . . The concerted cessation from work . . . of thousands of labourers . . . constituted a direct coercive measure and a menace to the Government (Des Voeux, cited in Tsai 1993: 171).

The Governor (Des Voeux) proclaimed the Peace Preservation Ordinance, stationed a gunboat off the Harbour Office, and sent troops into the Western District (ibid). Economic hardship eventually forced the boatmen back to work and, some time later, the government rescinded the license fee and made photographs compulsory only for those in charge of each boat (Tsai 1993: 172).

Despite the government's intransigence, then, concessions were gained. This was a lesson for workers, who learnt that 'by combination they could achieve their common purpose and defend their common interests' (ibid). But this unity of labour was episodic and conflicts occurred between feuding coolie groups. In 1894, for example, a three-day procession to mark the restoration of the Man Mo Temple was marred by a confrontation between coolies of different dialect groups. Some of these groups were involved in boxing – Tsai notes their connection to the numerous boxing clubs in the colony, places the police regarded as where 'low characters', as well as ordinary workers, congregated. Extra police were brought in to deal with the street fighting, which erupted when rival groups met on the Praya West equipped with revolvers, swords and iron bars; this apparently resulted in two deaths and several injuries.

Those originally involved found that their dispute had given rise to another sort of fight, between the 'low class ruffians' of the boxing clubs (Tsai 1993: 174). The Superintendent of Police (May) was determined to break up these clubs, organising raids at night and in the early hours of the morning to arrest and deport those involved. In this he was supported by a Chinese elite anxious to see public order restored to business as usual. Here, Tsai argues, is evidence of how difficult the elite was finding it, by the 1890s, to control the Chinese labouring class, and of how willing that elite was to call upon the government to suppress it (Tsai 1993: 175).[11]

By the 1880s, the 'coolie class' had grown suspicious of the colonial authorities and 'hated government regulation of their lives and work' (Tsai 1993: 176). Thus further attempts to regulate them provoked more anti-government feeling and disturbances. Apparently well-meaning legislation, passed in 1895 in the wake of the outbreak of plague, was introduced to improve the sanitation, safety and 'moral' character of coolie lodging houses. This prevented housekeepers from cramming as many coolies as possible into one place, but fewer lodgers meant increased rents for those who remained. Indirectly, then the new law meant an effective rent rise for the coolie class. A strike followed in March 1895, in which coolie housekeepers led hundreds of workers in a protest against the new regulations. Their action quickly attracted the support of other occupational workers, and by May 1895 20,000 people were on strike. The harm to trade led the European and Chinese elites to intervene. At a public meeting of the Europeans, Grenville Sharpe[12] lamented the passing of 'coolie' deference:

> When I first came to Hong Kong every Chinese coolie doffed his cap and stood on one side to allow you to pass. When do you see a coolie do that now? We do not exercise our undoubted superiority. We must rule by power . . . [The present position] is one of rebellion; it is war. The existence of a body of 20,000 coolies – lusty coolies – in Hong Kong, disaffected and armed with their formidable bamboo poles . . . is a direct menace to the Colony . . . I think we must . . . stand shoulder to shoulder and present an uncompromising front (Welsh, 1993: 381).[13]

In Sharpe's view, strikes ought to be outlawed and the disobedient coolie 'caned without his clothes, and then . . . sent into the street showing his blue and red back' (Tsai 1993: 178).

By 1895, these discontents of the labouring classes began to coalesce with growing patriotism amongst the Hong Kong Chinese more generally, and what Tsai calls Hong Kong's 'elite nationalists'. Some of this patriotism found expression in the 1895 Hsing-Chung-hui movement, based on a society founded in Hong Kong by a dozen revolutionaries, including Sun Yat-sen (Tsai 1993: 164–5). The group plotted to seize power in Canton but was discovered by Hong Kong officials and reported to the Canton authorities. Most of the society's members were banished from the colony (ibid). However, as Governor, Blake had some sympathy for the republican revolutionaries and allowed many to take asylum in Hong Kong. He seems to have been reluctant to help suppress revolutionary upheaval in Canton, even though instructed to do so by London. When, in later years, he was sent a list of those suspected of revolutionary activities in Hong Kong by the Canton authorities 'he protested that none of those named had been implicated in any way. The ring leader, Li Chi-t'ang, was even given extensive police protection against any . . . attempts at revenge on the part of the Canton government' (Welsh 1993: 342).

According to recent histories of Hong Kong, political events alone prompted few disturbances in the colony, even during the Boxer Rising, the

Hundred Days Reform movement, and the British occupation of the New Territories in 1898 (Tsai 1993: 168). The Boxer Rising and the Hundred Days Reform took place in the north of China. They did not affect the day-to-day lives of people in the colony, and thus provoked little response (ibid).[14]

However, unrest did continue. In 1905–6, a general boycott of American goods in China spread to Hong Kong, where coolies went on strike and US cigarettes were publicly destroyed (Welsh 1993: 345). Consumption of Chinese products became a sign of patriotism as well as protest. Labour participation in Hong Kong was sporadic and unorganised, targeting American-owned firms but never developing into an all-out strike against Americans in the colony. This was partly because the commercial elite saw law and order as essential for business[15] but also because the Canton authorities wished to avoid anti-foreign disturbances amongst the 'lower classes' (Tsai 1993: 197). The colonial government banned public meetings and banished for five years staff of a Hong Kong newspaper from Hong Kong who had published a 'low' and 'uncivilised' cartoon of Alice Roosevelt being carried by four turtles (intended to persuade sedan chair coolies to boycott Americans) (Tsai 1993: 200).

But this attempt by the Chinese bourgeoisie in Hong Kong and the gentry in Canton to control the boycott activists backfired:

> . . . the great commotion in 1905–6 vividly revealed how much more complex and heterogeneous the Hong Kong Chinese community had become . . . in a crisis situation the elite in the commercial union could no longer pretend to represent the consensus of the Chinese community in the colony . . . (Tsai 1993: 206).

The 1908 anti-Japanese boycott again joined issues of patriotism to the social and economic concerns of Chinese labour. In 1908, Hong Kong was suffering something of a trade depression, partly blamed on the loss of Hong Kong's China trade to Japan. A certain degree of anti-Japanese feeling thus already existed in the colony – during the 1894–5 Sino–Japanese War, a few patriotic Hong Kong Chinese had attacked the offices of a newspaper that published details of Chinese defeats (Tsai 1993: 168). Against this background a Japanese ship was detained by the Chinese authorities, who suspected it of smuggling. What Tsai calls the 'overbearing manner of Japan' in dealing with these events, and the Chinese authorities 'humiliating capitulation' to Japanese demands, led to a boycott of Japanese goods amongst the Chinese in Mainland China and in Hong Kong (Tsai 1993: 214). On the Mainland, the boycott partly stemmed from the desire of Chinese merchants to establish a market for their goods – boycotting foreign goods dovetailed with their interests, though apparently the Chinese gentry in China disparaged this use of patriotism (ibid). In Hong Kong, rumours spread of Japanese goods being poisoned; some Chinese importers of Japanese goods demanded that the police protect Japanese stores; boycott activists attacked and injured those breaking the boycott, and intimidated Japanese storeholders. In November, over two hundred and fifty rioters attacked Japanese stores and warehouses holding Japanese goods (ibid). Most of the rioting – which lasted for two days – took place around Western and Central districts. On 2 November:

> Around 11.00 am 'large mobs' congregated in several principal streets of the Central District. A large crowd made an attack on a shop in Wing Kat Street but the police charged them and drove them into Des Voeux Road (Tsai 1993: 229).

Though there was some looting, the attacks were generally disciplined, organised, and targeted, their main focus being shops suspected of selling Japanese goods. Rioting only broke out when the police intervened to arrest some of the crowd. At this point, the colonial authorities became the enemy:

> Around 1.30 pm a riot started near the International Hotel; the police drove the crowd toward the Land We Live In Hotel in Queen's Road West. Here the rioters were strengthened by 'mobs' that poured in from the East Street (Taipingshan). The riotous crowd now numbered between five hundred and one thousand men. They hurled bricks, stones, bamboos, flower pots and other things at the police. Some among the crowd were armed with bill hooks and boat hooks. Revolvers were discharged from the crowd firing at the police ... About a score of policemen received wounds in their struggle with the rioting crowds. The police fired into the crowd. A bullet hit a coolie named Chu Loi ... he died early the next morning ... In a subsequent court inquiry into the coolie's death, the jury (which consisted of Europeans) considered the shooting justified. ...
>
> ... Around 3.00 pm British troops numbering one hundred and fifty strong arrived at the junction of Bonham Strand and Queen's Road West. There they were met by Registrar General E.A. Irving and Ho Kam Tong, a prominent Chinese comprador, who continually advised the great crowd to disperse. The crowd took no heed of his words. The police scattered the crowd in all directions and soldiers paraded every street in the vicinity ... The following day ... the Hong Kong police court was 'crowded with unwashed [Chinese] coolies' in custody. In all, 119 arrests were made in the riots ... most of them were coolies (Tsai 1993: 230–31).

Between six and seven other Chinese were reportedly killed or wounded during the riots. The government's attempts to have the Chinese elite and

District Watch mediate were to no avail, 'again revealing the co-opted Chinese elite's alienation from the populace in the 1900s and their readiness to use coercion for social control' (ibid). As Munn puts it, the old patriarchal elite now held less sway over the young, modernising Chinese 'who sought change in China [as well as] integration into Hong Kong's political system' (Munn 2001: 377).

One of the coercive measures adopted was the banishment of the boycott activists – according to Tsai, the government took this opportunity to banish a number of 'undesirables', not all of whom were involved in the riots. Some were prominent merchants and newspaper editors, some ringleaders identified by the Chinese Vice-Consul. Although he lacked the powers to do so, in 1903 May also apparently deported a number of Chinese-language newspaper editors who had attacked the Qing government (Welsh 1993: 343). The Hong Kong police also tapped into other intelligence about the rioters from sources in Canton (Tsai 1993: 232). As in the 1840s (and in the future) governments on either side of the border thus cooperated in policing groups deemed troublesome in both places.

One activist, who denied the charges against him, refused to leave Hong Kong. Arrested and sent for trial, 'his defiance of the colonial authorities and his decision to test the validity of the legal proceedings against him aroused great interest and concern amongst the Chinese community in Hong Kong. On the day of his trial . . . several hundred Chinese thronged the court' (Tsai 1993: 234). Perhaps in a last-minute attempt to avoid further trouble, the authorities dropped the case and set him free (ibid).

The fear that leading merchants might be deported without trial and without warning apparently affected trade badly, and drew further protests from the merchant sector, which withdrew large sums from the Hong Kong Shanghai Bank, suspended business, and refused to accept Hong Kong Bank paper currency (Tsai 1993: 235). This in turn caused panic in the foreign business community, leading to pressure on the government to proclaim that no further action would be taken against anyone as long as they obeyed the law (ibid). This it did, followed later by withdrawing four of the banishment orders (ibid).

As this boycott and riot came to an end, in December 1908 a new campaign began. Triggered by a Chinese passenger being kicked to death by a ticket collector on a Butterfield and Swire steamer, this time the enemy was the British. However, anti-Japanese feeling rumbled on beneath the surface, resurfacing from time to time, sometimes associated with anti-foreignism and sometimes as a vehicle for expressing loyalty to China.

Patriotism and labour discontent became more expressly linked when Sun Yat-sen established a regime in Canton. For the Republican revolutionaries, their base in Hong Kong was pivotal – between 1895 and 1911, at least eight attempts to overthrow Imperial China were organised from Hong Kong (Tsai 1993: 238). Equally, once Sun Yat-sen had established his 'Canton regime' this began to demonstrate 'clear sympathy for labour and other mass movements', adding a 'new dimension conducive to Hong Kong labour mobilization' (Chan 1990: 584). Strikes and boycotts from 1911 onwards (some associated with the 1919 May 4th movement in China, others with the inflation spiral triggered by the First World War and the industrial boom of the 1920s) thus proved a heady mix of patriotism and worker grievances. Canton not only supported the Hong Kong workers in their actions against their employers, it also provided a sanctuary for Hong Kong strikers, allowing them to escape the repressive strike-breaking measures applied by the colonial regime (ibid).

The revolution of 1911 stimulated Chinese nationalism in Hong Kong, rousing concern with Chinese politics amongst all classes (ibid). Tsai notes that feelings favouring revolution became widespread. On 10 October and 18 October (Confucius's birthday), protests began against the symbols of Manchu power (Tsai 1993: 243). The establishment of a Republican regime in Canton inspired Hong Kong Chinese, Tsai says, to dream of a better political status for themselves, challenging the colonial authorities (Tsai 1993: 249).

Support for the revolution proved widespread in the colony, with crowds gathering to cheer, wave flags and stop the traffic (Tsai 1993: 225). Many men had their queues (long pigtails) cut off as a symbolic gesture; royalist newspapers and symbols were attacked; firecrackers set off, and stones thrown at the police when they intervened to curb the disturbances (ibid). Rumours that the Qing government had fallen swept through the colony's Chinese population, prompting what the governor, Lugard, described as 'the occasion of the most amazing outburst which has ever been seen of heard in the history of this Colony . . . The entire Chinese population appeared to become temporarily demented with joy' (ibid). It was in this context that Wodehouse had raised the possibility of using the troops to maintain order, incurring Lugard's disapproval.

For several months during 1911, Hong Kong witnessed sporadic outbreaks of 'popular civil disobedience' (Tsai 1993: 256). These 'expressions of displeasure with colonialism' took the form of crowds throwing stones at the colony's policemen, jeering them and attempting to rescue offenders arrested by them. The crowds were also rumoured to be threatening to 'kill the foreigners' and poison all the troops (ibid). Instances of policemen being mobbed by crowds were frequent, and a prominent member of the Legislative Council complained of being 'elbowed off the pavement in Queen's Road and into the gutter by a half-naked Chinese coolie'; another leading European spoke of the 'truculently insolent attitude' of the lower-class Chinese towards Europeans (ibid).

Lugard attributed these incidents to the 'lower class riff-raff' from Canton whose 'heads have become swollen by the contemplation at a safe distance of the exploits of others in the 'emancipation of China from the foreign (Manchu) yoke' (Tsai 1993: 258). Insecurity in China had pushed thousands of Chinese to seek refuge in Hong Kong – in 1911 alone, over 30,000 refugees arrived; by 1914, the total was over half a million (Tsai 1993: 244).

The link between anti-Manchu feeling in China and anti-imperialist feeling in Hong Kong highlights what Tsai calls a 'Sino-British synarchy'. Certainly the anti-Manchu sentiments of 1911 'let loose a flood of anti-imperialist sentiment and activities' in Hong Kong – once the Manchus had gone, there was a feeling that other foreigners should also be ousted, the Hong Kong Chinese being resentful at 'being treated as a subject people' (ibid). However, the government responded with further repression as, urged by the elite to curb the incidence of 'rowdyism' and 'hooliganism', Lugard reintroduced flogging by enacting provisions under the 1886 Peace Preservation Ordinance. Chinese leaders also supported the implementation of corporal punishment. In addition, the District Watch Committee led lectures against law breaking and public disturbances (ibid). Between December 1911 and February 1912, 51 prisoners were flogged for offences such as theft, police assault and resisting arrest. A new Societies Ordinance was introduced which, although ostensibly aimed at suppressing triads, 'reversed the usual methods of defining crime and drew a line between the respectable and unrespectable by requiring all societies to subject themselves to government monitoring' (Munn 2001: 376). Two battalions of infantry and one of artillery were also sent from India (Tsai 1993: 257). The Canton authorities, eager to cultivate friendly relations with Britain, also discouraged the Hong Kong disturbances, even though they had been inspired by events in Canton (Tsai 1993: 261). The Chinese elite sought to curb the agitation by promoting conservative Confucian values, such as the subordination of the individual, loyalty and filial piety, as well as obedience to one's superiors. As a tool of social control, however, it proved ineffective: Hong Kong's Chinese society had changed markedly since the elite's ascendancy in the 1870s, and the elite could no longer be sure of support among the 'coolie class' (Tsai 1993: 256).

That such measures failed to curb the unrest was due, Tsai argues, to the fact that the disturbances of 1911 were different in character to those of 1884, 1888, 1895 and 1908. In 1911, the crowds were provoked not by a specific grievance (such as wages) but by a more generalised discontent about colonial rule. Politicised by events in China, they were engaging in anti-colonial civil disobedience of a new kind. This seems to have been recognised by the colonial government which became deeply concerned about 'the peculiar and distorted views of "independence" and "freedom" . . . bred by the Revolution and interpreted to his own liking by every coolie . . . [This] will have a permanent effect on the traditional submission to regulation which has hitherto simplified the duties of officials.'[16]

The general mood of anti-colonial unrest continued to surface in a series of further strikes and disturbances. In the compositors' strike of 1912, workers not only demanded higher wages but also better treatment by European and Chinese employers. According to Tsai, the authorities were convinced that the strike was organised by revolutionary agitators from the Mainland. However, the Canton authorities again discouraged the strike. Though this attitude should have pleased the Hong Kong government (which could rely on Canton to co-operate in its efforts to detain agitators) Lugard was apparently anxious not to involve the Canton authorities too much, lest this encourage the notion that it was they, and not the British, who controlled the Hong Kong Chinese (Tsai 1993: 263).

In the climate of the times, what started as a dispute about a Chinese worker being struck by his European employer again turned into a more general strike by Chinese workers against their European employers (Tsai 1993: 260–61). In 1912 and 1913, nationalist feeling also prompted the Hong Kong Chinese to boycott Russians in the colony, provoked by Russian incursions into Mongolia. What Tsai calls 'war fever' hit Hong Kong; police tore down anti-Russian posters and arrested an agitator (Tsai 1993: 254).

The strikes that broke out between 1911 and 1912 were, by comparison, sporadic and small-scale, posing no serious threat to public order in Hong Kong. Though they had shown themselves capable of some collective action, workers in Hong Kong did not enjoy the same legal protections as British workers, who had won various rights to representation and to taking industrial action under Trades Union Acts of 1871, 1876 and 1906. These Acts did not apply to Hong Kong (Tsai 1993: 265), making the act of workers combining to promote better wages illegal, and the workers were liable to prosecution and imprisonment (ibid). Their precarious situation, coupled with the tendency to organise in guilds rather than in larger trades unions, meant that collective action was infrequent.

Instead, workers developed a strong sense of animosity towards the government, expressed partly as regular assaults on the police officials (ibid), including Sir F.H. May, former head of the police force and the gaol, and soon to succeed Lugard as Governor. Known as a disciplinarian and an 'old China hand', May spoke both Cantonese and Mandarin, having served in Hong Kong for 28 years between 1881 and 1911; he had then been sent to Fiji as governor (Tsai 1993: 266). Apparently well-respected by the European elite, he was known to the Chinese for suppressing the 1895 coolie strike and the resistance to the take-over of the New Territories in 1898 and 1899 (ibid). When he arrived to take up the post of Governor in 1912, firecrackers and other missiles were thrown into his car, and a shot was fired at him whilst he was being carried in a sedan chair (see Tsai 1993: 267). (The assailant was later sentenced to life imprisonment with hard labour.) Though the Chinese elite rallied round to express their support, May was left in no doubt, as he informed London, that 'the real feelings of the mass of the population towards Englishmen in this Colony [is one of] . . . animosity' (Tsai 1993: 268).

Generalised discontent amongst the 'coolie class' continued to find expression in a series of patriotic and anti-foreign protests. Between 1912 and 1913, for example, there was a boycott of the European-operated Hong Kong

Electric Tramway, prompted by its refusal to take Chinese coins from Canton, part of a more general colonial prohibition against the circulation of Canton currency (see Tsai 1993: 273). The ban, interpreted as a slur on Chinese dignity, provoked protests,[17] marches and demonstrations. A crowd of about a thousand people gathered at Shaukiwan tramway terminal. When the police arrested one of the protesters, they began to throw stones at the police: 'Inspector Gourlay had to threaten the crowd with his revolver before the arrested men could be removed to the police station' (Tsai 1993: 274). Another crowd later gathered at Des Voeux Road Central; when:

> . . . [a] large force of police proceeded to the scene from the Central Police Station . . . the crowd threw stones and missiles at the police. The police made four arrests, after which police pickets patrolled the tram route night and day. On November 28 fifty soldiers were sworn in as special constables to ride in the trams and as night pickets (ibid).

The authorities resorted to a Boycott Prevention Ordinance and an appeal to the Chinese elite to encourage their employees to end the boycott (Tsai 1993: 275). However, the elite's influence again proved weak. People in the street were directly affected by the tram company's refusal to take Chinese coins, since their employers insisted on paying them in Chinese currency minted in Canton. The refusal to take Chinese coins therefore directly impacted on their everyday lives, already marked by a struggle to make ends meet. Turned away when they attempted to use Chinese coins, they now refused to take the trams at all. Instead, they put up posters and intimidated the boycott-breakers. When the government sided with the tram company, the boycotters shifted their anger on to the government, at which point, both the colonial authorities and the Chinese elite called for strong action to be taken against the 'unruly and rowdy lower classes' (Tsai 1993: 281).

The tramway boycott lasted for more than two months, ending in 1913 when the government threatened to use the Boycott Prevention Ordinance to declare ten districts 'boycott areas' and impose a special tax on those living and trading in these areas to make up for the losses incurred. Merchants in these areas tried to pre-empt this tax by intervening directly with the lower classes. Some leading Chinese were rumoured to have bought books of tram tickets to give away to their employees to encourage them to ride on the trams (Tsai 1993: 285).

Though individually these disputes flared up and subsided with or without elite intervention, the government's 'high-handed measures' (ibid) tended to provoke even more anti-colonial feeling. Small-scale episodic skirmishing, attacks on the police, and sporadic boycotts kept discontent simmering in the colony up to the First World War. After the war ended, Hong Kong suffered an economic depression and inflation. Labour disputes and public protests now altered significantly in scale and character. Strikes became large-scale, organised affairs, more along the lines of 'Western' trade unionism (ibid). The rise of communism in China also meant that organised labour came to see its disputes with Hong Kong employers as class issues, i.e. disputes between capital and labour. The 1920s were, therefore, turbulent times.

Chinese secret societies had been supporting Hong Kong workers for some years before the 1920s, partly in the hope of recruiting them to the revolutionary cause (Tsai 1993: 240). Some of these activists had close ties with the Hong Kong Chinese Mechanics Association (founded in 1909). Their meetings were monitored by the colonial government – three mechanic activists were arrested by the police after giving speeches at a rally of five or six hundred members in 1909 (ibid). Similar societies, ostensibly set up for educational or occupational purposes, were also clandestine revolutionary associations operating under false names in order to escape police attention (ibid). Some of those recruited by the revolutionaries were triads; some were motivated by patriotism; others joined as paid mercenaries. Ties of localism helped link recruits together (ibid).

In 1920, a mechanics strike in Hong Kong saw over 9,000 workers from 26 industries leave the colony for Canton, where they received welfare and support. The existence of such a bolt-hole strengthened the workers' leverage – with Hong Kong paralysed, they could afford to wait for a satisfactory settlement. Following mediation by the Registrar (now the Secretary for the Chinese) the strikers eventually negotiated a 32.5 per cent pay rise (ibid).

The 'Canton asylum system' was crucial to this and similar labour victories (Chan 1990: 585). During the 1922 Seamen's Strike, for example, more than 10,000 strikers left Hong Kong for Canton; within a month, over 30,000 workers had gone on strike (ibid). The response of the governor (Stubbs) was to ban the newly-formed Seamen's Union as an 'unlawful society threatening the peace and order of the Colony', close down its headquarters and have the police remove its signboard (Chan 1990: 586). He also banned other striking 'coolie' guilds. This had the effect of escalating and intensifying the strike, transforming it from an economic matter into 'a confrontation between British colonial might and Chinese patriotic pride and national interests' (ibid). Consequently, more than 120,000 Hong Kong workers went on strike and Hong Kong once again came to a standstill.

The police force – which since 1884 had become a more militarised arm of government – was now required to operate against the strikers. When the government issued a proclamation prohibiting any Chinese from departing the colony the strikers, unable to travel by train, began to walk. On 3 March 1922, the army and police opened fire on the exodus, killing five workers; many others were wounded. Two days after this episode, popularly known as the 'Shatin Massacre' (Chan 1991: 173), an agreement was reached and the strike ended with the complete capitulation of the British as Stubbs rescinded his ban on the Seamen's Union. This result:

> Broken and dispelled . . . the myth of British imperial omnipotence . . . The real colonial casualty [was] an indispensable public sense of impartial fairness and liberal non-interference in the natural working of economic forces underlining any genuine claim to be laissez faire . . . In abdicating from its undeniable task of an impartial arbiter-mediator of inter-sector conflicts within the society and economy, the colonial state . . . diminished its own management capacity as well as effectiveness in societal conflict resolution . . . (Chan 1990: 587).

The 1922 strike was the most extensive labour strike in the history of modern China at the time (Chan, L.K. 1999: 21). At the height of the strike, more than 20 per cent of the colony's entire population downed tools (Chan 1991: 180). Though both the Nationalists and Communist claimed credit for it, the Communists were in fact too weak to take advantage of it (Chan 1999: 25).

Stubbs seems not to have immediately appreciated that his tactics had escalated the strike, for in 1925 he repeated the same mistake, prompting a 16-month Canton-Hong Kong general strike and boycott (Chan 1990: 588). The 1927 Illegal Strike and Lockout Ordinance continued what Chan describes as 'stern legal administrative measures' against organised labour and radical Chinese political activities. The Ordinance made strikes illegal if they were 'designed to coerce the government or had any objectives other than the dispute within a given industry'. It also prohibited the use of union funds for political purposes outside Hong Kong and the formation in Hong Kong of a branch of any union in China (Chan 1990: 589). The Seamen's Union – the main force behind the 1922 and 1925 strikes – was declared illegal, its offices razed, its leaders arrested, and its organisation banned (ibid). These prohibitions curtailed the ability of Hong Kong workers to engage in collective action against their employers. In the UK, employees and employers stood in a more equal relation (England 1989: 160) but the laws in Hong Kong placed labour at a distinct disadvantage, leaving capital in a dominant position, and producing an atomised labour force (ibid).

At the height of the 1922 strike, the Governor (Stubbs) had informed London that, in his opinion, 'we should hold Hong Kong for twenty years at the most' (Welsh 1993: 371). The government's ability to survive, and crush this nascent labour movement, owed much to the fact that an attempted communist coup in Guangdong province had simultaneously provoked a 'ruthless suppression' of the labour movement on the Mainland (Chan 1990: 589). The 'Canton sanctuary' ceased to be available to Hong Kong strikers, and the suppression of the labour movement in China depressed their activism in Hong Kong (ibid).[18]

After 1925, the new Governor (Clementi) attempted some 'friendly' gestures of social grace, cultural respect and political sensitivity' by making some concessions towards the Chinese (Chan 1990: 591). In 1926, for example, the first Chinese member of the Executive Council was appointed, and in 1927 the Department of Chinese at the University of Hong Kong was opened (ibid). In 1938, a Labour Officer (H.R. Butters) was added to the Secretary of Chinese Affairs office, to deal with trade unions, wages and conditions of work (Endacott 1964: 164; England 1989: 163). Other offices of government were 'modernised' – the Colonial Treasurer became the Financial Secretary, the Superintendent of Prisons became the Commissioner of Prisons, and an Inland Revenue Department was established (ibid). In the budget of 1935, the acting Colonial Secretary also committed the government to a policy of replacing European employees by 'Asiatics' wherever possible, and in 1936, the principle was established that, before any vacancy was advertised in the UK, local candidates with suitable qualifications were to be considered (ibid). Though this led to more opportunities for the non-European graduates being produced by the University of Hong Kong since 1911, the change was driven by a desire to save money (Endacott 1964: 169).

The years following the 1925 strike marked the beginning of a new phase of Communist development. Between 1927 and 1936, anti-communist purges on the Mainland forced the Communists to make Hong Kong the nerve centre of their activities (Chan 1999: 4). Hong Kong's Governor, Sir Cecil Clementi, was blatantly anti-communist and was inclined to co-operate with the Guangdong authorities to suppress communist activities (Chan 1999: 5). Fears of communist incursions and nationalist agitation now made secret policing indispensable to colonial rule (see Fu and Cullen 2003: 2). Police reports of 1928 and 1929 talked of anti-foreign agitation in China, anti-Japanese agitation in Hong Kong, the suppression of 'undesirable labour activities' by the Canton authorities, and continued police surveillance of communist agitators in Hong Kong:

> Communists have failed to obtain any serious hold in Hong Kong, but frequent raids by Police reveal that the Communist Party still maintains, or seeks to maintain, ells in Hong Kong. Their Agents are forced to conduct their activities with great secrecy . . . It is significant that most of the Party's Agents who have passed through the hands of the Police have been young student types, and appear to have been controlled from Shanghai. Their efforts had been directed to cause trouble among the labouring classes of society (cited in Fu and Cullen 2003: 3).

The Seamen's Union had by now been labelled a 'hotbed of Communists' by British intelligence. Stubbs's successor, Clementi, became extremely 'anti-red' and proscribed not only the Seamen's Union but also the Hong Kong Federation of Unions (Chan 1999: 80). Communists arrested by the Hong Kong police were returned to Guangdong, where they faced torture and execution. Undercover police mounted operations to detect suspects at Hong Kong/Guangdong entry points (Chan 1999: 95). The police arrested over 300 persons suspected of being involved in uprisings in Guangzhou; 246 people were detained and interrogated of whom 30 were released and the rest were deported (Chan 1999: 177). Once back in China, Communists were usually detained in a special prison (*Nanshitou*) operated by the Special Detective Squad of the Guangdong Public Security Bureau, before being interrogated and executed (Chan 1999: 186).

Despite the 'severe dislocation and disruption' caused to their activities by police suppression, the Communists still found Hong Kong less threatening than Guangdong; the CCP Guangdong Provincial Committee was even able to maintain an office on Hee Wong Terrace in Western District (ibid). Other hideouts (mainly in Western District) were set up so that they could be easily dismantled and removed. Vietnamese revolutionaries also came to Hong Kong at this time, to train and prepare for activities against their own country (Chan 1999: 189). Nevertheless, the police mounted several successful raids and in 1928, a 'traumatic swoop' captured several important leaders (Chan 1999: 119). They were released after several months' detention, partly because they had been able to secure expensive legal advice, and partly because corruption was so rife within the police (ibid).[19]

Plans to organise a large-scale, anti-Japanese demonstration in Hong Kong in 1928 eventually amounted to no more 'a few isolated cases of window smashing, which were promptly dealt with and checked' (Chan 1999: 122). Workers' distrust of the communists meant that Hong Kong people kept their distance from agitators; police were also offered an incentive – $50 per arrest – to arrest those distributing their pamphlets (ibid). There were also grand plans to organise an uprising in Hong Kong in 1930, strikes at the Swire Dockyard, Kowloon Wharf, the Taikoo Refinery, and walkouts at other major workplaces. A demonstration of five to six thousand people outside the Queen's Theatre in Queen's Road Central (parading via Pottinger Street, on to Des Voeux Road and ending at Central Market) was the most successful of those planned – others enjoyed far less support, including one anti-imperialist demonstration in support of the revolution in India:

> The whole incident appeared to be marked by a good deal of pomp and publicity. It began to the sound of firecrackers, and was accompanied by the shouting of slogans and the distribution of pamphlets. The CCP Guangdong Provincial Committee estimated that there were about 20–30,000 spectators en route (Chan 1999: 157).

In 1930, the new Governor, Sir William Peel, continued Clementi's anti-communist policy, and it was during his governorship that a number of leading Communists were executed in Guangzhou, following their deportation from Hong Kong (Chan 1999: 177). How it happened that Communists arrested in Hong Kong came to be imprisoned and executed in Guangzhou is a question which, Chan says, merits consideration. She points to clear evidence that the

Hong Kong government played a 'pivotal role in the final elimination of a considerable number of Communists in Guangzhou' (Chan 1999: 185).[20] They did this by (1) allowing Guangzhou undercover detectives to work secretly in Hong Kong, tracking down Communist agitators; (2) clandestinely handing over arrested Communists to Guangzhou agents in the colony; (3) banishing arrested Communists to China, with or without trial and (4) informing the Guangzhou authorities beforehand of the details of banishment orders (Chan 1999: 185).[21]

By this time, an Anti-Communist Squad had been established within the Hong Kong police, charged with monitoring left-wing agitators and gathering intelligence (Fu and Cullen 2003: 4). One member of the Squad was killed by communists whilst trying to obtain information about a communist anniversary, intensifying anti-communist operations (ibid). A report from the Guangdong Security Bureau indicates, however, that the Communists had no knowledge of the dead man's true identity as an undercover detective; he was shot because he was thought to be a defector (Chan 1999: 180). The Hong Kong Police were aware of his identity, referring to him as a Guangzhou anti-communist agent. They took his death in Jubilee Street to be a 'serious event marking the intensity of the efforts made by Communist agitators' (ibid).

The Hong Kong police received many of its leads from the Guangzhou authorities. On a request for assistance from Hong Kong, for example, the Guangdong Security Bureau sent two men to the colony to draw up an agreement that would permit Guangzhou detectives to be stationed in Hong Kong, to assist in operations against the Communists. Agreements were also put in place to facilitate the extradition of Communists from Hong Kong to Guangzhou (Chan 1999: 158–9). Chan argues that these Chinese special agents or detectives (estimated to number between three and four hundred men in Guangdong) were instrumental in the successful police action against the Communists. Irrefutable documentary evidence of this co-operation comes from a report filed by the Director of the Guangdong Security Bureau to the National Government in Guangzhou in July 1931, indicating that a Special Detective Squad from Guangzhou had been operating in Hong Kong since 1929, and probably since 1927 (Chan 1999: 179). Other evidence indicates that there was an informal agreement between the Hong Kong and Guangdong governments to extradite political criminals under cover as ordinary criminals (Chan 1999: 187).

In 1932, the Hong Kong Anti-Communist Squad changed its Chinese name to the *Zhengzhibu* (or Political Department); in 1933, its English name was changed to the Special Branch (Fu and Cullen 2003), a change that reflected the need to institutionalise intelligence gathering on communist organisations (ibid). In 1932, raids were carried out prior to some important communist anniversaries, and 'inflammatory documents' were seized. Many of the police raids on these hideouts were triggered by information provided by the Guangdong authorities (Chan 1999: 6). Those arrested were detained in Victoria Gaol, and occasionally in Lai Chi Kok Gaol in Kowloon. The most common form of torture applied to extract confessions seems to have been suspension by ropes, commonly known as the 'hanging aeroplane' (Chan 1999: 182).

The repression seems to have been partially effective – between 1935 and 1938 few incidents arose. For example, Chan says that the 1931 police raids on CCP hideouts hit the Communists particularly hard. Between 50 and 60 people were arrested, including most of key leaders then in Hong Kong (Chan 1999: 161–5). The Communists were further weakened when, in 1932, a Communist defector was killed and more raids took place from which they never recovered (ibid). By March 1932, the Hong Kong Communist cell was reduced to a bare skeleton; further raids in December allowed the police to claim that 1932 had been 'a very lean year for the Communists' (Chan 1999: 134). Popular distrust of Communists, coupled with their inability to organise, meant that the Communists were forced to watch helplessly 'as a golden opportunity to bolster their position [the Great Depression] slipped through their fingers' (Chan 1999: 167). By the end of 1932, the police had succeeded in containing the Communist threat (Chan 1999: 189).

More resources were ploughed into the Special Branch in the early 1930s – the 'rapid influx of staff' even necessitated its being re-housed in a new building (Fu and Cullen 2003: 4). Despite this, it seems that by 1941, it still lacked an adequate 'underground' system of intelligence gathering, obtaining most of its information from raids and arrests (ibid). It became more involved in using immigration and passport controls as adjuncts to the criminal justice system. On the outbreak of war with Germany in 1939, its remit extended to monitoring enemy aliens as well as liaising with the military authorities (ibid). However, with the victory of the Communists in Mainland China in 1949, and the outbreak of the Korean War, anti-communist surveillance again became a priority. The Special Branch came under 'intense pressure', its resources stretched to cover a variety of tasks including anti-subversion, security checks, the enforcement of the Societies Ordinance and, when the border was erected in 1950, the monitoring of immigration from Mainland China (Fu and Cullen 2003: 5).

After 1938, the communists found it easier to organise in Guangdong, though Hong Kong remained a major nerve centre. They continued to operate throughout the Japanese Occupation between 1941 and 1945, sabotaging the Japanese position and rescuing prisoners of war from the concentration camps (Chan 1999: 9). After the war, they were tasked to recruit supporters amongst local workers and students, organise in factories and set up leftist schools (Chan 1999: 11). According to Chan, communist work in the labour and educational sectors represented 'perhaps one of the most serious causes of friction between the Communists and the British Hong Kong administration during this period' (Chan 1999: 12).

Despite some conciliatory measures in the aftermath of the 1925 strike, therefore, the British administration remained generally nervous of the Chinese working class, whilst also 'arrogant, insensitive, often unfair and discriminatory as well as seemingly aloof, uncaring and unwilling to fulfil the basic responsibility of a conscientious modern state' (Chan 1990: 592). In the clash between a 'might is right' administrative-legality and the 'popular pursuit of social justice' (ibid) the criminal justice system was, by the Second World War, very much at the heart of the 'power-based' colonial state.

Notes

1 See, for example, Tsai (1993).
2 Section XVI Ordinance No. 7 1866.
3 Bowring to Labouchere, Foreign Secretary 21 May 1857, CO129/63: 154; Proclamation by Bowring 4 December 1856, CO129/59; Kerrigan 2001.
4 This 'shoot on sight' policy was rescinded later in 1857 and replaced by new regulations that allowed for the deportation of any non-British person from the colony, for any reason, for up to five years. Fines, added for failing to co-operate with the fire brigade, could be replaced by beatings with the rattan if the justices thought fit and the offender was Chinese. See Munn 2001: 286.
5 This placed a duty on every head of Chinese boats and households to issue identification tickets stamped by the Registrar General to every inmate of their property; the head of every ten households was to report any crime or stranger to the authorities and made answerable for the good conduct of residents; he was also to assist the police in searches of the premises and with making arrests (see Munn 2001: 287). The Registrar General was empowered to enter any Chinese dwelling to discover and prevent crime.
6 Kerrigan 2001; Proclamation No 123, issued by Caine in Chinese, 21 November 1856, *Hong Kong Gazette* 22 November1856, 2 (73); Ordinance No 2 1857.
7 However, Munn says, this reliance upon Caldwell meant that Bowring had travelled a long way from his original ideals about bringing clean, enlightened, and effective administration to the colony. See Munn 2001: 289.
8 Tellingly, what began life as anti-triad legislation was gradually transformed into legislation for the control or suppression of trade unions. The habit of using emergency legislation to deal with the problems of government became, Munn says, a habit of the colonial government that was brought under control only in the final years of British rule (Munn 2001: 17).
9 I.e. their particularistic ties to their clan lineages, native places in Canton and local dialect groups as well as 'guild mentality' associated with their occupations. See Chan 1990: 578.
10 According to Munn, the Peace Preservation Ordinance provided the basis for harsh, excessive anti-trade union measures until at least the Second World War. See Munn 2001: 376.
11 But the government of the day, whilst amenable to using the Chinese elite to help put down lower-class disorder, was still not inclined to regard it as an equal partner. Leading British members of the colony lobbied London, in June 1894, for constitutional reforms that would give them a louder voice in government affairs but entirely exclude the Chinese. Their petition was rejected by London, not happy to allow a small British oligarchy to govern what was effectively a Chinese city – 211,000 out of its 221,400 population were Chinese by 1891, and Chinese commerce dominated the economy (Endacott 1964: 122). London was prepared to

allow changes to the membership of the Executive Council, but suggested that a Chinese might be appointed rather than a European. London wished to see changes that, as Joseph Chamberlain put it, would attach the Chinese more closely to the British connection and increase their practical interest in public affairs (cited in Endacott 1964: 125). Though their co-operation in suppressing the 1894 disturbances indicated the shared interests of the British and Chinese trading elites, exclusionary attitudes still prevailed within government. Indeed, Endacott notes, one effect of the 1894 petition was to convince Colonial Office officials that Hong Kong could not be trusted to uphold the interests of the Chinese, and that London must therefore continue with its moral obligation to protect them (Endacott 1964: 135). This remained the view when, at the end of World War One, the elite again petitioned London for reform. According to Endacott, Bonar Law 'decisively rejected' the petition, unconvinced by arguments that reform would not simply enable a minority British administration to over-rule the Chinese (Endacott 1964: 140). Another demand for reform in 1921, from the Kowloon Residents association, argued for developments in Kowloon such as roads, a hospital for Europeans, and an area reserved for the Europeans, similar to that provided by the Peak Reservation Ordinance. Whilst the European merchant class was happy to co-opt the Chinese elite, it clearly did not wish to live alongside it.

12 Founder of the Matilda hospital, named after his wife and which refused to admit Chinese patients.

13 See also Chan, W.K. 1991.

14 In London, the reaction to the 'unsettled conditions of the Far East' in the 1880s and 1890s was strengthen the Hong Kong garrison, step-up the military element of the police force, improve fortifications, and provide for the senior military officer in the colony to deputize as Lieutenant Governor, administering the government in the absence of the Governor (Endacott 1964: 170). Once the threat from the Boxer Rebellion of 1900 ended, defence needs became less prominent. The Colonial Secretary was restored to the post of Lieutenant Governor (Endacott 1964: 175). However, the danger to the government from internal factors remained.

15 Welsh notes, however, that the Chinese Chamber of Commerce did organise a protest meeting but this was banned by the Governor, Nathan. See Welsh 1993: 345.

16 Administrative Reports for 1911, cited in Tsai 1993: 259.

17 According to Tsai sections of the Chinese elite deliberately invoked patriotic sentiments to protect their own economic interests in Cantonese currency.

18 See also England and Rear 1981; England 1990.

19 Useful legal contacts had been established by the Communists, and were employed whenever activists were held in police custody. One of these, a Hong Kong Chinese lawyer called Mo Yinggui, had studied law at Cambridge; another was a prominent British lawyer, Frank Loseby (see Chan 1999: 183–4).

20 Tsang argues that, although the Hong Kong government did, as a matter of policy, handover detained Communists to the authorities in China, and whilst a number of them were subsequently tortured or executed, this does not constitute 'clear evidence' that the Hong Kong government played a pivotal role in the elimination of Communists in Canton. See Tsang, S. 2004: 104.

21 Chan cites as an example the case of Lu Gengfu who in 1932 was released from arrest and allowed to leave Hong Kong, but not before the details of his itinerary had been handed over to secret agents from Guangzhou. He was arrested as soon as his boat docked in Shanghai.

Chapter 5

Civilising the natives: crimes, courts and punishments

That Hong Kong needed law as much as religion, science and the other 'fruits of civilisation' seemed clear to Hong Kong's early colonists. They saw the new colony as a crime-ridden place and remarked on the degenerate nature of the first Chinese migrants.[1] Rule of law was part of Britain's 'civilising mission'. One traveller, writing in 1849, noted that the Portuguese called Hong Kong 'the Ladrones, or Piratical Island . . . being . . . the resort of pirates, thieves and depraved characters of every description' (Sirr 1849: 2). Orthodox views of early Hong Kong were principally based on such anecdotes by European officials, missionaries and travellers. They described a place of rowydism, street fights, full-scale riots, piracy, and attacks on Europeans by Chinese robbers (see Munn 2001: 137–8).

The pronouncements of the Superintendent of Police on the level of crime, type of crime, and sources of criminality might be thought to command greater credence, but these too were a reflection of predominantly European anxieties. The colonists never felt completely safe or 'at home', and constantly scanned the criminal justice system to see if they were achieving order, stability, and 'civilisation'. A good deal of what we know about the criminal justice system in these early years stems from their complaints, loudly expressed in the pages of newspapers, in protest meetings, in letters home, and in official memoranda to the Colonial Office.

By contrast, we know very little about the experience of crime and criminal justice amongst the Chinese communities. The lack of police in the Chinese areas of town generally meant that their experience never found its way into the official record. The system itself (such as it was) regarded them as offenders rather than victims, feckless transients as opposed to the more industrious and settled Europeans.

It is this orthodoxy which has allowed the story to be told of how British officials wrought law and order out of a den of Chinese criminality. Almost universally, the Europeans depicted early colonial Hong Kong as a disorganised society with a shiftless population of criminals, thugs and ruffians. For Davis (who assumed the governorship in 1844) the Chinese could not fail to be impressed by 'the protection of equal laws, and, in a word, all the best fruits of science and civilisation transplanted direct from the European headquarters'.[2] But, as Chan says, whilst it might be true that:

> . . . most of the early immigrants were the 'lumpenproletariat' of Canton, and while it might even be true that most had criminal pasts, it does not follow that they had come to Hong Kong with intent to bring disorder. While there probably was a high incidence of robbery, deviant behaviour was surely not confined to the Chinese . . . Deviance and disorder were part of both communities . . . But British observers . . . (tended) to exaggerate the state of disorder, reflecting their own sense of insecurity . . . the image of a mass of 'the scum of Canton' filling the streets of Hong Kong simply does not square with the fact that it was thanks to the labour of this mass that a highly prosperous town was built. There must have been a lot of 'order' among this mass that the Europeans failed to see (Chan 1991: 3).

Downplaying the role of the Chinese in maintaining the social stability of colonial society left the impression that what stability did exist was due to the British – and order having been brought out of chaos, 'the credit naturally went to the administrators' (Chan 1991: 2). However, Chan, Tsai and Lethbridge describe a society already marked by emergent Chinese social organisations, welfare and mutual aid. They write of a place where fledging institutions helped new immigrants adjust to unfamiliar conditions and maintained social stability – much more effectively than British law and order which was, in any event, largely absent from Chinese lives.

The interaction between Chinese migrants, Chinese elites and European colonists meant that the society they jointly shaped and constructed was never completely 'like home'. Each changed the other and each other's institutions so that, in the end, hybrids were formed which reflected the conditions of Hong Kong as much as they reflected the influence of either China or Europe.

Adapting native institutions

In terms of criminal justice, early on Pottinger and Davis co-opted traditional native institutions – such as the Native Peace Officer (*baojia*) and the headman (*tepo*) system – and adapted them to colonial purposes. 'Respectable' Chinese shopkeepers and traders were likewise delegated the authority to settle disputes in the Chinese community (Chan 1991: 72).[3] Following a petition to Bonham from Chinese leaders in 1853, legislation was passed in which it was explained that:

> Whereas disputes occasionally arise among the Chinese of this colony

> which might be more conveniently and amicably settled by the Tepo, aided by the respectable Chinese inhabitants, than before an English tribunal; and whereas with a view to make the Tepos of the several districts of the colony more efficient, and to extend their usefulness, it is desirable that the voluntary fees now paid by the Chinese householders for the support of the said Tepos be made rateable and compulsory (cited in Chan 1991: 71).

Ratepayers in each district were to select from five to 12 'assessors' who would choose one *tepo* from among them, and fix his salary (ibid). The *tepo*, together with three or more assessors, would hear civil (but not criminal) complaints against any Chinese in the district; unresolved matters could be referred on to the English courts (ibid). Abolished in 1861 by the then-Governor, Robinson, little information remains about the working of this system. Eitel implies that it worked 'too well' and observes that, even after abolition, the Chinese still secretly stuck to it, preferring it over the English courts of law (Chan 1991: 71).

By the 1870s, Chinese local institutions were an increasingly significant element of colonial rule. In the 1900s, Chinese customary law and traditions were co-opted in the New Territories (NT), where local village leaders assisted in the governance of their villages, village men formed a semi-official militia, and a system of administration was established to provide a more 'personal' form of government that the one administered in the urban areas (Endacott 1964: 129). The Local Communities Ordinance of April 1899 divided the NT into eight administrative districts closely aligned to traditional settlement patterns. Villages were allowed to elect a committee man to represent them on local committees. In classic 'indirect rule' style, he was to be a person of some influence 'whose advice is listened to, and whose lead is generally followed. The wisdom of affecting with responsibility those to whom the people have been accustomed to look for leadership and of using them to elucidate the objects of government is evident'[4]. The Ordinance empowered village elders to sit as a tribunal to decide petty cases. However, the system never really functioned satisfactorily as the elders proved reluctant to participate (Endacott 1964: 131). In 1903, the Governor (Blake) observed that the villagers seemed more willing to take their disputes to Lockhart, who had become the government's adviser on all NT matters, and who was acting as the police magistrate. This did not quite fit Blake's plan to use traditional methods of Chinese administration, but it is likely that villagers regarded it as futile to use local leaders when there was a judicial authority available to which appeal could be made (ibid).

The way in which the NT was governed was later to provide the template for urban Hong Kong. By 1913, the NT had been divided into North and South Districts,[5] the former overseen by a District officer and the latter by an Assistant District officer, each acting as magistrates. In 1920, the officer in charge of the Southern District was made a full District Officer. The main duties of these officers revolved around the settlement of civil cases, land disputes, and the appointment of trustees. In these matters, as Endacott says, there had wide discretion. Adhering to the original intention to keep NT governance as traditional and personal as possible, no lawyers were allowed in the tribunals without permission.

The formal machinery of British justice ran in tandem with these local institutions. Each shaped – and was shaped by – the other. In 1926, a number of *tsz-yi* were appointed to assist the District Officers with disputes or other local issues. Appointment was intended to be for one year, in recognition of the long and faithful service of village elders (Endacott 1964: 134). However, this evolved into the Heung Yee Kuk, which became something of a closed body, appointing other elders at its discretion (ibid). Over time, the Kuk claimed to represent the voice of all NT indigenous residents, and wielded considerable influence over government policy in the NT. Paradoxically, given that it was an institution created by the British to ease their governance, the Kuk came to be regarded as an 'authentic' Chinese institution.

Lawyers, courts and judges: the Supreme Court

In the first two years of colonial rule, the authorities operated in something of a hiatus, awaiting the outcome of negotiations between Britain and China. Until these were finalised, few resources could be committed to law and order.[6] In the absence of a proper police force, most of the large trading houses, such as Jardine, Matheson & Co., employed armed watchmen to protect their warehouses; Jardine's had their own police force at East Point (Chan 1991: 82). To demonstrate that they were awake and alert between the hours of 8 pm and 5 am these watchmen were instructed to strike together two hollow pieces of bamboo as they made their rounds (tattooing). Chinese traders also employed private watchmen to guard their homes but only Europeans were allowed to keep pistols in their homes and on their person. The European community complained constantly that robberies and burglaries were rife, committed by 'impertinent gangs' and 'Chinese vagrants' whom, it was said, the floggings ordered by the Chief Magistrate, William Caine, failed to discourage.

The Royal Charter issued in 1843 established English law. Though the Justices of the Peace were drawn from 'the leading inhabitants of the colony' (Norton Kyshe 1971: 25) they played no role in the administration of criminal justice. When the Criminal Court opened in March 1844, Pottinger (Governor) and the Lieutenant Governor, Major-General D'Aguilar, presided as judges.[7] In his address to the jury, Pottinger, uneasy at having serious criminal matters decided by unqualified persons like himself, was at pains to impress upon the jury that:

> ... in all cases where you have doubts, it is a wise and humane principle of the law to give the advantage of those doubts to the accused, and our observance of this rule is more especially necessary when it is remembered that he can have no counsel to plead for him. I wish to God my share of the investigations on which we are about to enter had fallen into more qualified hands, but I least promise that I sit here to exercise the most rigid impartiality as well as to temper justice with mercy.[8]

By the mid-1840s, Hong Kong was held by the European elite to have arrived at that point 'when that great adjunct of civilization, a Supreme Court, needed to be established'.[9] The Supreme Court held its first sessions in October 1844, under Chief Justice John Hulme. The Attorney General, Paul Sterling, took the opportunity to explain to the assembled audience that 'English laws were not the laws of vengeance, but were intended to protect the innocent by the punishment of guilt not to punish guilt by mere vindictive feelings.'[10] Hulme added that, 'As inhabitants of a British colony, one of the greatest privileges you enjoy is the right to a due and even-handed administration of the English laws, and I am satisfied that the more you become acquainted with these Laws, the more you will learn to love and respect them'.[11]

The first criminal prosecution before the court was against Laong-awa and his wife, for having kidnapped two boatwomen (Munn 2001: 160). Laong-awa was sentenced to 18 months with hard labour, his wife 18 months' imprisonment without hard labour but with exposure once a month in the cangue, in the marketplace, a placard announcing her crime hung about her neck (ibid). The case was Hong Kong's first jury trial. It seemed, Munn says, exactly the kind of straightforward case needed to convey the benefits of British justice:

> In opening the case against the Laongs, the Attorney General explained to the prisoners that, 'the Queen does not prosecute them for the sake of vengeance but in order by the example set to protect the innocent and save the good'. The judge . . . urged the jury that 'if they had any doubts, they would give the prisoners the benefit of them' . . . The government proclaimed the punishment in Chinese 'for the information of the common people of Hong Kong, as a warning to criminals and to eradicate evils . . . The records of the early Supreme Court supply no better illustration of the principles of justice and punishment that the colonial government . . . wished to promote' (Munn 2001: 161).

However, despite the high ideals that accompanied its establishment, within a very short time the Supreme Court acquired a reputation for injustice. Though Sirr, writing in 1849, praised the Chief Justice, Hulme, for the 'masterly manner' in which he prepared the rules of the Supreme Court, for the 'urbanity of his manners, the soundness of his judgment, legal knowledge and impartiality upon the Bench',[12] Hulme showed himself not, in fact, to be impartial (ibid). He refused to increase the Supreme Court's two- or three-monthly criminal sessions, leaving remand prisoners in gaol awaiting trial. He quashed a fine imposed on a European merchant in Canton for kicking down a Chinese fruit stall and causing a riot, and denied justice to a Chinese merchant whose ship had been accidentally sunk by a British steamer, thereby undermining British claims to dispense even-handed justice (ibid). In 1847, during a bitter feud with the Governor, he was also suspended following allegations of drunkenness.[13] In other respects, too, the court failed to live up to its rhetoric: the all-European juries were prejudiced and inclined to convict regardless of the facts; procedures were confusing and poorly executed; defendants were often bemused by poor interpreters and legal representation; lawyers and judges were poorly qualified.[14] The Court was also criticised for failing to ensure that the oath sworn in court had any meaning for the Chinese. There were additional problems enforcing its sentences of transportation, leaving prisoners in the overcrowded gaol awaiting removal (Munn 2001: 208ff). The judicial personnel who served the Court were mainly second and third-rate lawyers and barristers with limited prospects in England (ibid). Hulme himself had no judicial experience before arriving in Hong Kong in 1848. The Attorney General (Sterling) had 15 years' experience as a barrister before coming to Hong Kong, but made a 'poor prosecutor'. McSwyney, the Registrar General of the Supreme Court, was accused of receiving money under false pretences, though he continued to practice, became Coroner and took up trading in opium. Campbell, the Attorney General in Sterling's absence and acting Chief Justice when Hulme was away, was appointed after a recommendation from his uncle, the Governor of Ceylon. Nepotism and connections, rather than professional expertise, often provided the basis for legal appointments. For example, the Governor's legal adviser, Burgess, was a crony of Pottinger's in Ireland and India.

Hong Kong's reputation as a place of sickness also militated against the recruitment of legal talent with the result, Munn agues, that most of Hong Kong's early lawyers had minimal legal qualifications, engaged in sharp practices such as charging excessive fees, touting for business, accepting a percentage of financial settlements as fees, practices which (in theory at least) were frowned upon in England. Standards improved with the arrival of barristers from England in the 1850s, but other imported practices (such as allowing the Attorney General to maintain a private practice, and of private practice barristers acting as Attorney General or Colonial Secretary) all ensured that the reputation of the law, and the integrity of lawyers, remained low (ibid).

The Supreme Court, established with high ideals, had by the 1850s proved incapable of fulfilling them. Instead it had become:

> . . . notorious as a tool for extortion and malicious prosecutions, as a dispenser of unsafe verdicts and unjust sentences. Its mystifying procedures, mediated through inadequate interpretation, smothered many cases in confusion and allowed well-prepared defendants to get off by exploiting technicalities or tampering with witnesses. At the same time, the unwillingness of juries to presume innocence in Chinese defendants produced injustices that often had to be corrected by executive intervention . . . Troubled by its inefficiency, colonial officials began to regret the Hong Kong Supreme Court almost as soon as it had opened. They set about narrowing its scope, circumventing its jurisdiction, and loosening its procedures to that by the late 1850s a tiny and declining proportion of defendants appeared before it under conditions that promised easier convictions than the purer forms of English justice of the time would normally have allowed (Munn 2001: 162).

The crime rate continued to rise. The government responded by ditching due process for crime control. It progressively dismantled the few due process protections introduced with the founding of the legal system, instead 'using the blunter, more violent instruments at their disposal to protect an increasingly frightened colonial community from an unassimilated Chinese population' (Munn 2001: 203). Bowring, eventually forced in the 1850s to concede that he had no means of ensuring a fair trial for the most serious offenders (ibid), allowed more cases to be diverted to the magistrates' court, which were granted extended powers and jurisdiction. Many difficult cases were handed over to the Chinese authorities in Kowloon. The rights of defendants were restricted, and the use of extra-judicial measures such as surveillance and deportation were intensified (ibid). The rise in the number of magistracy cases, and its increased powers, was accompanied by an abandoning of those rules of evidence that hindered conviction. The use of corporal punishment was also expanded.[15]

Conviction was made easier. Trial by jury – one the cornerstones of British justice – was amended to achieve easier conviction. Originally the jury itself consisted of six people (all male). This was extended in 1864 to seven people.[16] But within a few years of it being established, in 1851, the need to reach a unanimous verdict was abandoned. It could now convict by a majority (four out of six) verdict (Munn 2001: 242). Unanimity was only required in capital cases. Moreover, the jury was seldom made up of 'peers' of the accused. Elsewhere in the Empire, the authorities had managed to provide for half the jury to consist of the same nationality as the accused, thus going some way to ensure that trial by jury was a trial by one's peers (Munn 2001: 169). In Hong Kong, however, the juror was 'a male person between the ages of 21 and 60 . . . who is a good and sufficient person resident within the Colony and is not ignorant of the English language'.[17] From 1851, jury membership was based on property ownership and proficiency in English. Though there was nothing in the law specifically prohibiting Asian or Chinese jury members, these provisions effectively meant that none was qualified – indeed, for many years, only about a hundred people in the colony ever qualified for jury service.

Jury members were, therefore, invariably European. Few (if any) understood Chinese. It was a moot point as to whether they understood evidence given (as it usually was) in Chinese or some other Asian language. The same applied to the judges, solicitors and barristers conducting the trial proceedings in English.

Most of those brought before the early courts were accused of property offences, piracy and offences against the person (Munn 2001: 174). On conviction, they faced a range of punishments, including death, transportation (from seven years to life), imprisonment with hard labour, public flogging, and fines (ibid). Between them and their fate stood a mix of poor-quality translators, often unfamiliar with the variety of Chinese dialects of the defendants and likely to embellish or curtail the responses of the accused to fit prescribed legal formulae. Norton Kyshe writes of an occasion, in 1844, when 'Sentence of death was passed upon [a] Manila seaman who neither understood the proceedings of the court, presumably through there being no interpreter present, nor had had the benefit of counsel' (Norton Kyshe 1971: 3). A newspaper editorial of 1845 also argued that 'Great care should be taken, in giving testimony, especially where life is concerned, that every word be faithfully translated; otherwise how can judge and jury decide rightly' (Norton Kyshe 1971: 81). A high turnover meant that few ever acquired any expertise as court interpreters.

There were those who advocated the introduction of Chinese lawyers and Chinese in the courts but, for most colonists, the idea of appointing a Chinese to serve on a jury was an anathema. When, in 1858, the first Chinese name appeared on the jury list, members of the LEGCO expressed disbelief and astonishment. The Chief Justice voted against his inclusion (Munn 2001: 215) and it was not until 1888 (and again in 1891) that the names of 30 Chinese appeared on the jury list (Endacott 1964: 153).

The jury thus remained the province of the elite, albeit that some members were later drawn from the Chinese elite. Most saw it not as a civic duty but a waste of time (Munn 2001: 213). Trial by jury was, therefore, very far from being a fair trial or the practical embodiment of British ideals of justice. However, the British continued to regard Hong Kong as a haven of justice in the midst of barbarity, and constantly affirmed this by comparing justice in the colony with that meted out by Mainland officials. Numerous commentators of the time held that the Chinese came to Hong Kong not simply to escape Mainland unrest and poverty, but because the colony provided them with stability, security and protection. This motif of Hong Kong as a city of law in a lawless land was to remain part of the dominant discourse of colonial rule, even after it ended in 1997.

The magistracy

The version of British justice that most Chinese knew was a much abbreviated version, performed every day in the magistrates' court. By the 1850s, Munn argues, the magistracy – not the Supreme Court – occupied the central position in the criminal justice system, dealing with the bulk of cases and exercising wide powers of punishment. Caine, Chief Magistrate, was aided by Hillier, his assistant magistrate. The magistracy itself was housed in a building at Central, adjacent to the prison at Victoria and the Central Police Station[18] and it was on this site that public executions and floggings took place. Along with Government House, it came to represent the seat of British authority. The magistrates were among the busiest of colonial officials (Munn 2001: 114). Between 1841 and 1870, more than 175,000 men, women and children appeared before the courts on criminal charges, almost 8 per cent of the colony's population per year, as compared to 2 per cent in England and Wales (Munn 2001: 111). The Chief Magistrate, Caine, came into contact with the Chinese more often than all other officers of government except the police. For the majority of the Chinese, he *was* the face of British authority – they commonly mistook him for the head of the government (Munn 2001: 114). Lamenting what he saw as the weakness of the colonial authorities generally, Sirr observed in 1849 that:

> [Caine] is one of the few in authority perfectly qualified in every respect to govern, command and enforce respect . . . Experience has taught him the true character of the Chinese; the *unflinching firmness* which he invariably exhibits, combined with his *just and impartial conduct* on the bench, has produced so salutary an effect on the minds of the natives of China, that one word from him is sufficient to secure their respect and attention . . . When our vessel dropped anchor . . . the estimation in which this gentleman was held by the Chinese was exhibited; we inquired of some natives who came on board the ship to traffic, 'Who is the great man here?'. 'Major Caine'. 'Who is Governor?' 'Don't know *he*; but Major Caine number one mandarin: very great *big* man he.' They knew nothing of Sir Henry Pottinger or Sir John Davis . . . and on many subsequent occasions, when resident in the Colony, we have questioned the Chinese . . . they knew nothing of either, whilst the name of Major Caine was universally known and respected (Sirr 1849: 26).

Caine was a figure most familiar to the colonised population. His regime at the magistracy was infamous. The magistracy building, 'the most imposing, most substantial early pubic building', came to dominate the colony's early skyline (Munn 2001: 114). By the mid-1850s, it had become the clearest and most dramatic symbol of colonial power, of its 'capriciousness and brutality', and of Caine's reign there:

> . . . an overture in which many of the themes that dominated the succeeding few decades were played out: of a society systematically divided by race; of rule by selective collaboration rather than broad co-operation; of executive action supplanting due process of law; of a regime that spoke of inclusion and civilization but used the methods of a government of occupation.[19]

Appointments to the positions of Chief Magistrate, Attorney General, Acting Governor and Chief Justice were made from within a very small group of men drawn from the European elite, which in 1841 was dominated by military men.[20] The small size of this (male) elite meant that post-holders were obliged to alternate between positions to such a degree that the line between executive and judiciary was continuously blurred.[21] The expatriate politico-legal elite moved, in peripatetic fashion, from one colony to another, with the result that both the higher and lower the judiciary were late in developing any local character or identity with Hong Kong. Even in early Hong Kong, however, the overlap between the magistracy and the Executive was held by some to be undesirable:

> The Magistracy was not independent. The duties were performed by two paid servants of the Colony, from whose decisions there was no appeal. An unpaid Magistracy might not be an undesirable thing (Norton Kyshe 1971: 106).

The magistrate was also responsible for the police force, prisons and licensing. A good deal of power therefore resided in one person and, given the lack of checks and balances in the system, this power went largely unchecked. The close relationship between Caine and the ruling elite also meant that, on occasion, people were punished for slights committed against his friends, or small infringements of colonial etiquette (Norton Kyshe 1971: 96). This said, there were others amongst the elite who regarded Caine and his assistants as 'ignorant, incompetent, far from impartial [and] far too subservient to their superiors' (ibid). This, they realised, undermined the image of impartial justice they wished to convey to the native population. Though he had extensive experience in the judge-advocate's department of the army, Caine was 'totally unacquainted with the law',[22] as was his assistant, Hillier. If British rule of law was to be seen as merciful and fair, instead of capricious and brutal, professionally qualified lawyers were needed replace these 'needy soldiers and obscure adventurers' (Norton Kyshe 1971: 14).

Pottinger himself recognised that the exercise of 'military law'[23] by men like Caine generated public disquiet. In 1844, for example, Caine was censured for dispensing law 'which was not English law but Pottinger law which was not legalized'.[24] He was, it was said:

> ... [not] the kind of man to place in such a position as Police Magistrate over a people whom we are desirous of impressing with the purity of our institutions and the honour and high-mindedness which characterizes our general rule.[25]

For the elite (and the Colonial Office at home) the repressive, anti-Chinese practices of the magistracy also represented a failure to 'attach' the Chinese to British legal institutions. In 1847 a select Committee of the House of Commons received allegations that Caine had in fact received 'contributions' made by prostitutes admitted by the police to the Lock Hospital.[26] Combined with ongoing complaints about the excesses of his reign at the magistracy, this prompted demands for the appointment of a properly qualified magistrate and an independent head of police.[27] As Munn argues, the opening of the Supreme Court had symbolised the arrival of legality, the end of the military-bureaucratic state. It generated an expectation that the colony's legal system would be staffed by professional men of law.[28] Caine was promoted to Lieutenant Governor. His influence in the administration of justice persisted, however, and shaped the punitive tenor of criminal justice in this period.

Regulating the Chinese

The rhetoric of Hong Kong's 'equal laws' came, Munn says, to camouflage an ever more repressive legal regime, and one that was increasingly anti-Chinese. Laws against vagabonds targeted the Chinese but not unemployed Europeans or 'distressed seamen' stranded in Hong Kong (Munn 2001: 146). In the late 1850s, a special room was provided in Central Police Station for European vagrants, and some were even offered jobs in the police force (ibid).[29] Instead of being flogged or banished, European prisoners were sentenced to short periods of imprisonment. (Destitute Chinese, it was said, were not deterred by prison, since they regarded its provision of food and shelter a boon).

As elsewhere in the British Empire, the law was also employed to 'regulate the habits' of the colonised Chinese. Their strange festivities so alarmed members of the European elite that they pushed for the regulation of such 'nuisances', making the behaviour more acceptable to bourgeois European values (Munn 2001: 147). Traditional festivals, with their large gatherings, were always regarded by the authorities with particular nervousness.

Gradually, these were rendered more orderly, their more 'exciting' aspects curtailed by the colonial police.[30] Other 'nuisances' which the colonial authorities regulated included the obstruction of public highways by unlicensed hawking, unsanitary behaviour, street gambling, letting off fireworks, washing out of doors (lewdly exposing the person by bathing), using indecent or profane language, allowing ferocious dogs to roam at large, playing games, assembling together at night without a lawful reason, making bonfires, wantonly throwing stones, furious driving, defiling streams, being drunk in a road or passage, begging, exposing any sore or infirmity to excite compassion, behaving in a riotous, noisy or disorderly manner, insulting a female in public, herb gathering, tree-cutting, and carrying out burials on the hillsides (ibid). Between a third and half of all the offences from the 1850s onwards were, Munn says, these sorts of regulatory, ecological, and behavioural crimes that fell under the vague heading of 'offences under Ordinance No. 15 of 1845', enacted for the preservation of good order and cleanliness in the colony (ibid).[31] Such laws and regulations gave wide discretion to the police and made the Chinese 'coolie' class universally suspect. Numerous persons caught in possession of 'any thing which might reasonably be suspected of having been stolen or unlawfully obtained' without being able to give a satisfactory account to a (English-speaking) magistrate were imprisoned, not on proof or evidence but on mere suspicion:

> The profusion of regulatory offences, the powers of arrest under suspicion, the linguistic barriers and general ignorance among both police and population all combined to produce a climate of insecurity among the Chinese population. Liable to interference by the police for any number of daily activities, or simply for being in the wrong place at the wrong time, it was little wonder that complaints arose about the proliferation of laws and the insensitivity of the police . . . (Munn 2001: 150).

By the mid-1850s, the promise of equal, fair and even-handed justice was in shreds. It was replaced, Munn argues, by the sight of 'severed queues on display outside the Magistracy Building in Central', chain gangs 'at work on government projects', and 'frequent public floggings in Queen's Road or in the Land Office timber yard', where labourers gathered in search of work (Munn 1995: 216).

Despite the harsh nature of criminal justice, crime continued to rise. Although no reliable figures exist of the level of crime in the colony, four main categories of crime saw consistently high rates of prosecution. These were assault and violence against the person, theft, vagrancy, and miscellaneous offences.[32] The extremely high rate of crimes of violence reflected, Munn argues, the very volatile nature of early Hong Kong society, a place where simple grievances could flare up into dangerous confrontations (Munn 2001: 134). Most crimes of violence occurred during attempted robberies, disputes over debt, extortion, resisting the police, and/or the abuse of the Chinese by drunken Europeans (ibid).

What started as a legal system intended to assimilate Chinese people to British rule thus 'gradually became an instrument for reinforcing racial differences and for increasing the distance between rulers and ruled'.[33] This distance was made all the greater by the exclusion of the local Chinese from judicial office. This applied, as in the police, to all positions of responsibility. When Norton Kyshe refers to the appointment of one Chinese magistrate in 1845,[34] he is referring not to a magistrate but to the lesser appointment of JP, not magistrates exercising judicial power. Legally qualified magistrates were exclusively European, recruited from amongst the barristers and solicitors who traversed the Empire. They wielded considerable judicial power, and they did so with no understanding of the Chinese, their language, custom or culture.[35]

This situation obtained well into the twentieth century. Magistrates sent out from the UK to exercise power in the colonies were typically inexperienced young men who had to learn 'on the job'.[36] Arriving in the colony, they were assisted by a local Chinese clerk with knowledge of local customs rather than law. In rural areas, the government was heavily reliant on native leaders, aided by expatriate District Officers. Billed as the 'father and mother' of the native people, throughout the empire the District Officer was typically a cadet who came equipped with language skills. His task was to develop local knowledge and relationships with native leaders, becoming the eyes and ears of colonial governments on the ground, and the conduit by which local level grievances could be channelled up to government officials.

Magistrates were supposed to be legally qualified but, as Coates admits in his autobiography, 'I knew nothing about the law. I had never been inside a court in any country. I found it difficult to grasp a legal point, or understand the implications of a law. Furthermore, it would be useless to give me instruction . . . I would never be able to understand [the subject] and would certainly never succeed in passing an examination' (Coates 1968: 4). Fortunately for him, few of Coates's decisions involved the application of English law. In any case, with the emergence of a Chinese elite, British interference with Chinese norms and social customs faded somewhat, as Chinese leaders claimed for themselves the right to mediate local disputes.[37] At the same time, the establishment of formal legal institutions and a legal profession signalled the end for men who, like Caine and Hillier, lacked legal qualifications.[38]

The higher judiciary proved equally disappointing. Judges were generally second-rate and their personal conduct did not always live up to the expectations of public office. They were, however, hard to remove. The principle of judicial independence obtained; judicial appointments were permanent. With a few notable exceptions, however, the judiciary seldom gave the political establishment any reason to seek their dismissal. The judiciary was quiescent and did little, for example, to check the highly repressive anti-Chinese legislation of the period, leaving this task to others, such as missionaries and humanitarians, some of them in London. After the 1860s, the introduction of the Cadet system saw a new breed of officials arrive in the territory, trained in Chinese language and culture. Some were more sympathetic to the locals, but this was by no means always the case – in the 1890s, for example, Lockhart was to prove as unrelenting as Caine in his suppression of Chinese resistance in the New Territories.

Individual Governors did sometimes act to mitigate the worst excesses of the criminal justice system. Bowring, for example, was a radical who in 1846 brought the excessive flogging of Caine's regime to the attention of Parliament. A close friend of Jeremy Bentham, and editor of the *Westminster Review*, he enjoyed the support of powerful liberal figures in Britain.[39] Thwarted in other attempts to make Hong Kong a more liberal and inclusive society, Bowring nevertheless secured permission from the Secretary of State for the Colonies to allow members of the local Chinese population to enter the legal profession, with a view to their being appointed as magistrates (Welsh 1993: 218). He also attempted to ameliorate the worst aspects of the trade in 'coolie' emigration to the Californian gold fields 'but was not helped by the verdict of a Hong Kong court which, having found an Englishman and five Chinese guilty of imprisoning emigrants, sentenced the Chinese to prison but only fined the Englishman $5 . . . Whitehall commented that the sentences did not do "credit to British authority or increase respect for British justice" '(ibid). In 1857, at the height of concerns about internal security, Bowring also managed to secure a fair trial for the Chinese accused of the attempted mass poisoning of Europeans (including Lady Bowring). Although the defendants were initially dealt with in a highly summary manner, at trial they were acquitted by the jury due to lack of evidence about who actually poisoned the bread (Welsh 1993: 214). This said, Bowring felt it necessary to calm European fears about the Tai Ping rebels by imposing certain anti-Chinese emergency measures:

> Any Chinaman found at large . . . elsewhere than in his own Habitation . . . not having a Pass . . . shall be summarily punished by any Justice of the Peace by [Fine or Imprisonment] or by public Whipping and Public Exposure in the Stocks . . . Every Person lawfully acting as Sentry or Patrol is hereby authorized . . . to fire upon with intent or effect to kill . . . No Act done or attempted in pursuance of this Ordinance shall be questioned in any Court (cited in Welsh 1993: 215).

As was to be the pattern with other Governors who put Chinese interests above those of the colonial elite, Bowring made enemies amongst his fellow colonists. When he departed Hong Kong, for example, Chinese representatives presented him with 'the most magnificent testimonials'. The European elite, by contrast, hurled 'venomous epistles and libellous accusations' at him (Welsh 1993: 222).

The elite itself was, however, far from a unified whole. In the 1850s, for example, a bitter feud erupted between Anstey, appointed in 1854 as Attorney General, and other members of the legal establishment. This culminated in a lengthy letter from Anstey to *The Times* in which he criticised the

Chief Justice (Hulme), the Chief Magistrate (Hillier), the Governor and the Registrar General (Daniel Caldwell). This prompted an official enquiry into serious charges against Caldwell.[40] Bowring's successor, Robinson, presided over the Commission of Inquiry. Caldwell, a favourite of the establishment, was subsequently dismissed in 1862, but survived to return to office at a later date. Anstey, on the other hand, found himself with few friends, having offended his fellow Europeans and provoked the ire of the Colonial Office. Caine and Hulme retired in 1859, leaving the way open for the appointment of 'safer men' (such as Pauncefote, Attorney General) though for the most part not 'men of distinction' (Welsh 1993: 232–3).

Between the 1880s and the Second World War, when Hong Kong saw some its worst civil unrest, the courts and the legal profession invariably associated themselves with the status quo. The exception was Smale, Chief Justice in the 1860s and 1870s, MacDonnell's reign as Governor. Smale fought MacDonnell on a number of issues, especially the licensing of gambling houses, the use of branding and flogging, and the custom of *mui tsai*.[41] Reflecting contemporary British moral sentiments, Smale attacked the system of *mui tsai* as being akin to slavery. On licensed gambling, he found support in London but was undermined locally by Pauncefote, the Attorney General, who countered Smale's correspondence with the Colonial Office with his own, arguing that:

> Since the establishment of the licensed gaming houses, there has been a vast decrease in crime . . . I venture to express a hope that the Chief Justice [will] abstain from attacking the policy of the government from the bench, as there can be no doubt that he thereby encourages . . . every kind of falsehood which can bring odium on this Colony in relation to the system of licensing gaming house (cited in Welsh 1993: 240).

However, Smale remained a thorn in MacDonnell's side. He survived his clashes with MacDonnell in the early 1870s to find an ally in his successor, Hennessy. Like Smale, Hennessy regarded the practice of *mui tsai* as a form of slavery. This struck a nerve with the home government, which regarded slavery as 'incompatible with British jurisdiction and with the extension of civilisation that the British brought to the world' (Howell and Lambert 2006: 248). London readily recognised the discourse of anti-slavery and humanitarianism (ibid) and was thus predisposed to listen when both Smale and Hennessy described slavery in a British colony. Their views were not shared, however, by Hennessy's right-hand man in Hong Kong, Eitel, who saw *mui tsai* in entirely different terms. Eitel had long experience of Hong Kong Chinese language, customs and culture. He took issue with what he saw as Smale's legalistic definition of *mui tsai* as 'slavery' (Howell and Lambert 2006: 251). Though influential within the colonial bureaucracy, he failed to dissuade Smale of his view but did persuade Hennessy to listen to the Chinese elite and to leading Chinese such as Ng Choy,[42] whom Hennessy had recently appointed as the first Chinese police magistrate, part of his scheme for greater localisation (ibid). Ultimately, Hennessy rejected calls for the outright repression of *mui tsai*, though the issue was to rumble on until the 1930s.

In the 1880s, the elite was to face greater challenges than that of liberal dissidents within its own ranks. Between the 1880s and 1930s, the interests of the Chinese working class increasingly brought it into direct conflict with the European and Chinese elites. In these years, the law and the criminal justice system became a principal means of suppressing trade unionism, deporting and detaining political activists, and subduing organised labour[43] (see below).

Crime and punishment

One of the first official buildings erected by the colonists was a jail, built by Pottinger in 1845 on the site of Victoria Jail, adjacent to the Central magistracy.[44] It comprised eleven cells and housed prisoners awaiting execution (cited in Pottinger 1997: 130). Convicts sentenced to imprisonment were held here in what the Colonial Surgeon of the time, Dr Dempster, described as 'a filthy, disgusting place, badly ventilated and altogether unfit for occupation by any human being . . . It is a sink of iniquity.'[45] By the 1860s, Victoria prison had become so overcrowded that plans were drawn up for a new prison on Stonecutters Island. An old ship (a 'Prison Hulk') was to be refitted to detain prisoners off-shore in Victoria Harbour.[46] In 1863, *The Royal Saxon* was purchased and fitted in England as a Convict Hulk to be anchored off Stonecutters Island.[47] The building of a new prison at Stonecutters Island seems, however, to have met with resistance from an elite reluctant to spend their taxes on convicts. The building was used, instead, as smallpox hospital and a leper colony.

As is clear from the foregoing, in the early days of the colony, the Chief Magistrate, Caine, decided most legal cases and acquired a 'scandalous reputation for rough justice'.[48] In 1841, he was authorised by Pottinger to 'exercise authority according to the laws, customs and usages of China . . . over all the native inhabitants'.[49] Where a case would, according to Chinese law, 'involve punishments and penalties' such as 'more than three months' imprisonment, corporal punishment of more than 100 lashes, or capital punishment', Caine was instructed to remit judgment to the head of the government.[50] Section 25 of Ordinance 10 of 1844 also stated that Chinese defendants appearing before a Justice of the Peace were to be punished according to Chinese native law.[51]

Caine was both a judge and the head of the prison service.[52] The reputation he acquired on the bench applied equally to his penal practice. He was 'strong enough to carry a drum but ignorant of all law except martial law, and . . . had boldly asserted that all flogging and branding were punishments then inflicted upon soldiers so they ought to be inflicted upon the natives of the Colony . . . for the most trivial offences men had been sentenced to the lash'.[53]

A former military man, he held strong views on law and order, as well as trenchant views on the Chinese and their punishment:

> If it were ever my misfortune to be similarly situated, I should most probably adhere to the same determined and stringent measures which I consider to have protected the lives and property of the British public here . . . nine-tenths of our Chinese subjects, and about one half of our low European inhabitants, have been in a most depraved condition, so regardless of truth that circumstantial evidence has been preferred to their direct evidence on oath, and it is painful to add that these difficulties still exist, and must continue, as long as the people remain in their present state of immorality and total absence of principle (Munn 1995: 218).

Caine's 'stringent measures' meant that his regime 'came to personify all the brutality, corruption, and extravagance of the old colonial system'.[54] He applied what he thought were 'Chinese' punishments (such as the cutting of the queue, banishment, flogging, branding, and exposure in the *cangue*) all of which he apparently gleaned from a partial translation of the Qing penal code. Many colonists were familiar with tales of Chinese punishments, such as execution by striking the head from the body, strangulation, and death by a thousand cuts (Sayer 1980: 103). Most supported Caine, arguing that by comparison with these, English punishments were too soft to deter crime. Others, however, found the spectacle of regular public floggings in the centre of Hong Kong highly offensive. In Britain, Bowring complained to the House of Commons of the 'almost incredible' extent to which the lash was used in Hong Kong:

> Disgusting exhibitions of flogging were reported to be of almost daily occurrence in the town: in one case about an hour before sunset one afternoon, in the Queen's Road, between the foot of Pottinger and Cochrane Streets, one poor wretch being tied up to the door post of a public house next to the then temporary Police Station there, and afterwards stripped and his back 'lacerated with the rattan'. No pretension was made to an over-refinement of feeling, but the wholesale system of flogging inflicted by the Magistrates was objected to . . . the records of the Police Court, on examination, would show that there was more flogging in Hong Kong than probably in any country in the world according to the population . . . On Saturday, the 25th of April 1846, no less than 54 men were flogged and had their tails cut off – for no other reason than being on the island without registration tickets.[55]

Pottinger's replacement, Davis, shared the view that English penalties would not deter a Chinese population more used to the severity of the Qing penal code. The Chinese, he argued, saw English law as too lenient, and ridiculed it. Since their standard of living was very low, moreover, a spell in prison was not considered a punishment, as it provided them with free shelter and food. Defending the 'chastisements' handed down by Caine, he argued that they were hedged about with the 'requisite limitations and safeguards', but also they were necessary because of 'the preconceived habits and inveterate character of the Chinese'.[56]

The conduct of criminal justice in these early courts drew criticism from Hulme, Chief Justice. In one case, where nine Chinese suspects had been flogged after a highly irregular trial, Hulme observed that 'This mode of trial . . . might have answered very well when the black Douglases rode borders at the head of 1,500 men, executing "Jeddart" justice upon outlaws and other offenders, but in the nineteenth century it was hoped more regard was paid to form and to the impartial administration of justice'.[57]

The magistracy's methods also occasionally provoked an unexpected backlash. In 1866, for example, 150 police officers ('one quarter of the entire police force') were needed to control a crowd of spectators attending the execution of three pirates.[58] In 1857, Bowring avoided this kind of situation by handing over 73 pirates seized by the Royal Navy to the Chinese magistracy in Kowloon – two 1844 ordinances allowing the Supreme Court and magistracy to punish the Chinese in accordance with the laws of China[59] permitted him to hand over the pirates for execution to the Chinese authorities. Bowring, himself a liberal and reformer, was said to have 'shrank from the prospect of a mass execution'. A reprimand from the Colonial Office in London reminded him, however, that, 'the Supreme Court had been set up for the very purpose of dealing with such criminals'.[60] Nevertheless, whilst public executions demonstrated Britain's power to punish, they also provided opportunities for a show of anti-British sentiment. For the European elite, the executions themselves were also occasions that aroused conflicting opinions as to how best to govern by administering colonial criminal justice.

In England, the rise of imprisonment as the main form of punishment was gradually leading to the disappearance of public executions. The colonial state, however, felt the need to resort to public punishments for some time to come. Indeed, instead of declining as Britain 'civilised' her Chinese subjects, public displays of punishment increased. This was particularly so in the 1850s, when the summary jurisdiction of the magistracy was extended to relieve the caseload of the Supreme Court. Caine now was able to apply his particular style of justice to a far wider range of offences. Under his direction, imprisonment with hard labour became common – in 1853, the Surveyor General commented that 'a greater number of men have been confined for hard labour, I believe, than ever before'.[61] The law allowed a felon to be sentenced to indefinite imprisonment on the order of the Governor; prisoners were put to work as convict labour, building roads and other infrastructure projects necessary to establish life and commerce in the colony.[62] Those who were not imprisoned were fined, transported, banished, flogged, exposed in the *cangue* or executed. Chinese and Malay convicts were exiled to Canton, Shanghai, Kowloon, Singapore, Macao, Labuan, and Penang; European convicts were sent to England, Australia and Africa, colonies that needed cheap convict labour (but resisted taking Hong Kong's rejects).

Though there were interludes in which Hong Kong's courts handed down more humane forms of punishment, colonial fears meant that the punitive impulse was always liable to resurface. After his arrival in 1866, for example, MacDonnell responded to a moral panic about crime amongst the European elite by reintroducing flogging, branding, banishment, and a range of other harsh penalties for Chinese offenders. When, during his absence in 1870–71, these measures were temporarily suspended, fellow colonists blamed this for an apparent subsequent increase in crime.

Those, like Smale, who opposed MacDonnell's penal regime were in line with changing European ideas about punishment. Branding had been abolished in England in 1834, though flogging still remained part of the penal system (Foucault 1979: 10). By the mid-nineteenth century throughout Europe, public flogging, shaming in the stocks and public execution (part of what Spierenburg and Foucault call the great spectacle of physical punishment) were disappearing.[63] In Hong Kong, however, they remained part of the repertoire of colonial justice. Where capital and corporal punishment remained in Europe, they had moved inside the prison walls; in Hong Kong, MacDonnell and his supporters felt the need to retain public displays of punishment, believing them to act as a deterrent and symbol of colonial authority.

In Britain itself, penal practice was shifting towards more humanitarian themes and the rational reform of the criminal's soul and mind. This was reflected in the Colonial Office's plans for Hong Kong's prison establishments. In 1853, London pushed for a draft Ordinance regulating the colony's prisons. For the first time, this spelt out in great detail the duties and limits of prison officers, as well as the rights of prisoners. It stressed the need for an organised gaol consisting of orderly gaolers as well as inmates.[64] Gaolers were to exercise their authority 'with firmness, humanity, and good temper, on no account striking any prisoner without due authority'; they were not to put prisoners in chains or irons unless strictly necessary; punishments were not to exceed those specified by the Medical Officer and some punishments, such as corporal punishment, required the authorisation of the Colonial Surgeon. Prisoners were to be given the opportunity to wash every day, supplied with clothing and bedding, provided with useful employment, and allowed to see friends and relatives at specified intervals. Male and female offenders were to be separated, convicted prisoners held away from prisoners detained for re-examination, felons kept apart from those convicted of misdemeanours, and debtors and death sentence prisoners to be held separate from all other inmates. Chinese prisoners were to be allowed a Chinese diet. They were to be given 'at least two hot meals a day; 'other prisoners shall have three meals a day two at least of them hot meals'.[65] No Jewish prisoner was to be compelled to work on the Sabbath and no work was to be done on Sundays; the Medical Officer and the Chaplain were to liaise with each other when concerned about a prisoner's state of mind, and the Chaplain was to conduct religious services in the prison and visit prisoners in their cells to discuss spiritual matters. There were to be weekly visits by Justices of the Peace, and a weekly inspection of the gaol visitation book by the Governor.[66]

In intention if not in practice, these rules reflected the thinking of reformers such as Howard, Pinel, and Bentham. But although Bentham (creator of the 'Panopticon') was influential at the Colonial Office and across the empire, Hong Kong prisons never followed the model penitentiaries built at Freemantle, Melbourne, and Stateville, Illinois. And although Hong Kong's penal regimes bore some of the characteristics of what Garland (1985) has termed 'Victorian penality'[67] – such as hard labour and a spare diet – plans to erect a treadmill at Victoria Gaol were abandoned in favour of meeting other administrative goals, such as making the colony pay its way by putting convicts to work on infrastructure projects. Thus, whilst Hong Kong adopted some of England's methods for 'grinding rogues honest', it did not relinquish its physically harsh and spectacular public forms of punishment.

The scientific, reformist and humane approaches to punishment did find favour with some members of the European elite (such as the missionaries, liberals and evangelicals) as well as Colonial Office officials in London. During the debate about Caine's methods in the 1840s London had, for example, insisted that branding cease to be applied. But most of the colonial elite felt that the humane system of English prison discipline 'fell far short of the kind of 'cruel and oppressive character of Chinese gaol management' needed to deter Chinese criminals. They argued that whilst these English ideas were appropriate for English offenders, Chinese criminals required harsher treatment. Crime would continue to be a problem until more severe penalties were applied. They also resisted the new-fangled ideas on the basis that they involved increased expenditure from colonial revenues. 'Local conditions' meant, in any event, that magistracy punishments:

> . . . tended to suffer from the process of inflation. The poverty of most of those punished by the Magistracy meant that a large proportion of fines were quickly converted into sentences of imprisonment or flogging. Overcrowding in the gaol, especially in the mid–1840s and late–1850s, and the notion that imprisonment had no effect on Chinese offenders, encouraged magistrates to inflict corporal punishment wherever they could. Secondly, corporal punishment served both penal and policing functions. Marks from flogging or missing queues were . . . important measures of character for officials by whom 'the features of the Chinese were found . . . to be very difficult to recognize'. Thirdly,

> punishments varied according to race. This is most obvious in the corporal punishments, which were not applied to European civilians ... (Munn 2001: 151).

When he replaced Caine, Hillier continued the punitive policies of his predecessor (ibid). Chinese offenders were subjected to queue-cutting, banishment, flogging or beating with the rattan. The rattan cane, about twice the thickness of a pencil, was applied (usually by a non-Chinese employee) to the breech or back of the offender:

> The rattaning was usually carried out at the site of the crime or in a prominent place, such as the entrance to one of the markets ... [one observer wrote that the practice was] ... 'to stick the crime of the guilty party on his back on a piece of white paper written in Chinese characters and parade him from the police station to the place where he committed the theft and then flog him, first of all fastening him by the hands and feet to a triangle. I only saw him get two or three strokes by a black man with a rattan. There was an immense mob of his countrymen looking on with a mixture of riff-raff of most nations. The punishment is not severe' (cited in Munn 2001: 151).

During his term of office, MacDonnell replaced the rattan cane with the cat o' nine tails, increasing the pain and suffering inflicted. Such punishments undercut Britain's avowed aim of bringing to its colonies the fruits of civilisation and enlightened thinking, and stood in clear defiance of London's shift towards more evangelical and humane forms of punishment. This was nowhere more clear than in his deployment of flogging and branding as forms of punishment for Chinese offenders.

When first proposed in Hong Kong in 1845, branding had been successfully opposed by powerful figures in Britain on the basis that it left an indelible mark impressed on the cheek, marking the offender for life and consigning him to 'permanent infamy'. Its usage would obstruct his 'return to virtue', prevent his reintegration into 'reputable society', and prove an obstacle to employment.[68] However, MacDonnell took the view, shared the majority of Europeans, that the arguments of evangelical England did not apply to Hong Kong. Though a branded British thief might indeed experience difficulties finding employment in his own country, 'the Chinese reprobate is known to be of generally migratory habits. He comes and goes to or from any district ... Being what he is a conspicuous mark would not interfere prejudicially with his career any where out of the Colony'. [69]

Careless of London's view, MacDonnell proposed to banish branded offenders, as well as flog and imprison any who returned to the colony after deportation. According to Chan, 'triads, when caught, were branded on the cheek and deported to Canton, where they were promptly beheaded . . . later . . . they were branded under the arm before being deported'.[70]

These flogging and branding measures divided elite opinion and, for a time, the punishment of Chinese offenders became the focus of public meetings and the correspondence pages of local newspapers. In MacDonnell's absence in the early 1870s, Smale and the Attorney General took the opportunity to advise the Lieutenant Governor that MacDonnell had no legislative authority for branding. As a consequence, the practice ceased. Their victory was, however, short-lived. On his return to the colony, MacDonnell re-instated it, blaming abolition for an apparently dramatic rise in crime by 'desperado' Chinese, 'cunning and daring' former convicts who now 'collected in gangs' to perform violent burglaries and highway robberies, throwing the 'whole general community into alarm'.[71] Restricted by an instruction from London which specified that no legislation could be passed in the colony without the consent of Whitehall 'whereby persons of Africa or Asiatic birth may be subjected . . . to any liabilities to which persons of European birth or descent are not also subjected' (Welsh 1993: 246) MacDonnell also set about persuading the Secretary of the State for the Colonies (Kimberley) to sponsor legislation on branding and flogging. The official crime figures presented to Kimberley were deliberately massaged to demonstrate the effectiveness of branding as a deterrent.

MacDonnell had, meanwhile, reinstated branding on the cheek (or ear). Despite criticisms, he remained convinced that his approach was correct:

> I would prefer to see every criminal who has shown an inveterate habit of crime branded in some conspicuous place, and deported from the colony . . . Tenderness of any kind shown to these semi-brutalized beings is not only misplaced, but is construed by them into a sign of weakness, inducing them to resume their courses upon their release with more

Table 5.1 Conviction and punishment for serious crime in the Supreme Court 1868–73

	Convicted	*Acquitted*	*Death*	*Penal servitude*	*Hard labour over 1 year*	*Hard labour 1 year and under*	*Publicly flogged*	*Solitary confinement*
1868	81	47						
1869	75	21						
1870	80	12						
1871	106	26	–	18	30	32	12	2
1872	106	26						
1873	50	21						

Source: Blue Books 1868–74. 'Blue books' were the annual reports of the departments of the colonial government (so-called because they were collated and bound into blue volumes).

> audacity than before . . . The theory, would I think be speedily dispelled by a glance at a few of the dogged, evil and sullen countenances which belong to the ruffians to be found at any time within the walls of our prison. It is mere assertion, unsupported by evidence to say that such men may take to honest callings . . .[72]

A public meeting attended by leading European interests in the colony supported MacDonnell's stance, calling for the re-introduction of flogging and branding as a means of cutting crime. The complaints led to the establishment of a Commission of Inquiry into the effectiveness of the police in 1872.[73] During its deliberations, the Commission argued that:

> The punishments of our criminals cannot be passed without remark. It is a thing universally known that crime is expiated in China by sufferings terrible in their degree, and that shocking tortures are resorted to obtain evidence or confessions. The greater and lesser bamboo, the *cangue*, the executioner's sword or set of delicate knives, the rack, the fetid swarming dungeon, the cross, the cage of exposure, with a host of cruel expedients devised by magisterial rigour on the spur of the moment and only nominally illegal from the armoury of the Chinese officer, and to one or other of them the criminal has to look forward upon his conviction. Compare this state of things with the prospect before him when he crosses the harbour. Let him then but be shrewd enough to keep clear of detection in any of those crimes of violence which subject him to the wholesome influence of the cat, and conviction is followed by a life of luxury and ease greater than he has probably ever known before. Except for the mere restraint of confinement, which to most Chinamen is not very irksome, he finds himself surrounded with every comfort – roomy clean quarters, congenial society, the kindest of treatment, wholesome and plentiful food, work about sufficient to give him and appetite to enjoy it, medical attendance and comforts, a prospect of release amidst ample booty, and all the attractions of the brothels, theatres, shows and opium shops so dear to every Chinaman's heart, and with nothing worse behind it than a return to his present comfortable mode of life when he may happen to be caught again.[74]

The Commission, consisting of leading members of the colony (including its trading houses) agreed to cautious reforms of the police, but on punishment it shared MacDonnell's view. This now brought MacDonnell and his successor, Kennedy, into direct conflict with the Colonial Secretary, Lord Kimberley, who remained highly doubtful about the desirability and efficacy of branding. MacDonnell argued that the 'extraordinary rise in crime' in 1871 was a direct result of the cessation of branding in his absence. As Hennessy later revealed, however, this assertion was 'unaccompanied by any statistical evidence whatever'.[75] The 'authentic facts' and figures about crime in 1871 (which were contained in the Annual Reports or 'Blue Books') did not support the claim. MacDonnell 'not only asserted (incorrectly) that the more serious class of crimes had increased, but it was also assumed that they were committed entirely by Chinese, and that it was in fact Chinese criminals that filled the gaol'.[76] When MacDonnell's measures were repealed and policing was improved, crime fell.

MacDonnell delayed sending the Blue Books to the Colonial Office for several months. Kimberley thus had no reason to doubt the accuracy of the figures upon which he based his advice to the Queen to assent to the Branding Ordinance (No 4 of 1872). For the time being, then, MacDonnell prevailed. He managed to steer the Branding Ordinance through LEGCO partly by concealing Kimberley's reservations from its members, a device continued by his successor as Governor, Sir Arthur Kennedy.[77]

The real crime figures, later revealed by Hennessy, did not support MacDonnell's assumptions about the effectiveness of his penal regime, nor the view 'that the Chinese are an especially criminal race'.[78]

That policing – and not punishment – lay at the heart of Hong Kong's crime problem was also the conclusion of the 1872 Police Commission, set up to investigate problems within the police force. MacDonnell had constantly complained about corruption and inefficiency in the police force. It had 'been allowed to sink into a state of inefficiency'.[79] The courts' insistence on sticking to the rule of law when dealing with Chinese criminals, he argued, was also having a deleterious effect on the police:

> . . . during the course of my administration of this Government I have become daily more convinced of the unfitness of much of our criminal procedure to the circumstances in which we find ourselves. The hands of the police are tied and their utility often impaired by the necessary adherence of our courts to rules which, however well fitted to the place which gave them birth, have little practical value here. Their result often is that cases of importance fall through where had a little more discretion been placed in the hands of the Judge, convictions must have been inevitable.[80]

MacDonnell's administration encouraged the courts to set aside legal procedures in favour of conviction. However, abbreviated modes of trial, harsh punishments and repression only served to undermine the goal of attaching the local population to colonial legal and political institutions more generally (see Munn 2001).

James Pope Hennessy arrived in Hong Kong with a mandate to bring the colony's penal system more into line with the reformist policies of England. Like Bowring, whose reformist sentiments he shared, he met with fierce opposition from conservative sections of the European elite, not only because

Table 5.2 Reports of crime to police 1874–89

Serious crime	*1874*	*1875*	*1876*	*1877*	*1878*	*1879*	*1880*	*1881*	*1882*	*1883*	*1884*	*1885*	*1886*	*1887*	*1888*	*1889*
Murder	3	3	4	5	7	4	1	2	2	2	4	3	3	1	2	2
Robbery with violence	15	13	24	21	35	39	25	19	30	30	52	96	64	31	45	66
Burglary/Larceny	69	107	90	79	131	101	53	60	91	81	47	67	68	60	76	98
Assault with intent to rob	–	3	1	1	–	1	2	–	1	1	2	3	4	–	4	1
Kidnapping	51	63	55	73	53	51	65	59	55	30	32	53	78	90	91	75
Piracy	7	5	5	9	8	7	11	7	5	13	9	17	10	8	12	4
Unlawful possession	203	251	239	309	470	333	226	303	275	254	298	229	291	327	254	313
Larcenies	804	938	1,059	1,437	1,888	1,850	1,662	1,879	2,104	1,980	2,153	1,927	1,898	1,985	1,878	2,236
Other felonies	16	13	8	32	19	11	6	9	33	32	55	45	84	76	74	98
Total serious crime	1,166	1,396	1,485	1,966	2,611	2,397	2,051	2,329	2,596	2,423	2,652	2,466	2,500	2,577	2,436	2,893
Minor crime	*1874*	*1875*	*1876*	*1877*	*1878*	*1879*	*1880*	*1881*	*1882*	*1883*	*1884*	*1885*	*1886*	*1887*	*1888*	*1889*
Assault	866	796	786	841	875	838	746	904	730	1,118	753	1,031	1,101	958	1,212	
Gambling	200	255	159	282	353	157	358	397	261	86	104	255	248	99	62	69
Miscellaneous	1,507	1,505	2,438	2,073	1,794	1,442	1,815	1,879	1,750	2,629	2,441	1,901	3,735	3,941	3,905	2,807
Drunkenness	442	549	523	464	512	301	276	337	276	158	202	323	373	231	229	165
Nuisance	622	317	306	611	355	232	329	284	263	527	790	690	470	340	399	252
No pass or light	960	664	849	1,151	335	762	840	566	424	1,135	2,896	387	479	192	125	63
Total minor crime	4,597	4,086	5,061	5,422	4,224	3,732	4,364	4,367	3,728	5,265	7,551	4,309	6,336	5,904	5,678	4,568
Total crime	**5,763**	**5,482**	**6,546**	**7,388**	**6,385**	**6,129**	**6,415**	**6,696**	**6,324**	**7,688**	**10,203**	**6,775**	**8,836**	**8,481**	**8,114**	**7,461**

Source: Blue Books 1874–89.

Table 5.3 Punishment for summary offences 1871–1900

	Fine	Imprisonment in lieu of fine	Peremptory imprisonment	Whipping	Bound over	Reformatory	House of detention	Exposed in stocks	Total
1871	2,631	1,467	783	29	76				4,977
1872	7,066	110	1,204	42	196				8,708
1873	6,605	85	1,019	10	147				7,866
1874	5,676	101	633	72	136				6,618
1875	5,518	111	795	63	224				6,711
1876	6,236	110	816	53	137				7,352
1877	5,638	1,283	1,016	25	195				8,157
1878	5,010	1,496	1,279	22	120				7,927
1879	3,426	1,420	1,289	5	262				6,402
1880	3,474	1,616	1,104	2	252				6,448
1881	4,269	1,737	1,416	–	434				7,856
1882	3,590	1,360	1,481	–	363				6,794
1883	6,074	1,221	1,446	42	216				8,999
1884	9,973	1,560	1,276	35	281				13,125
1885	6,383	1,181	1,222	20	456				9,262
1886	9,533	2,205	1,185	35	969				13,927
1887	7,713	1,926	1,014	31	463				11,157
1888	7,521	1,397	956	36	192	4			10,106
1889	4,343	1,163	1,351	49	337	2			7,245
1890	5,035	1,366	1,258	82	318	2			8,061
1891	9,688	2,841	1,323	120	172	–			14,145
1892	7,967	2,560	1,456	101	211	–	18		12,316
1893	7,099	2,027	1,133	102	278	–	11		10,650
1894	6,466	2,057	1,139	70	278	–	44		10,054
1895	11,718	2,681	1,309	56	309	–	31		16,104
1896	12,945	2,782	1,697	38	304	–	20	7	17,793
1897	7,171	2,119	1,476	30	271	7	10	–	11,085
1898	9,251	2,034	2,125	96	252	–	24	–	13,784
1899	6,460	349	1,564 [1]	101	102	–	48	2	9,640
1900	10,366	1,500	1,604	84	213	–	54	1	13,824

Source: Blue Books 1871–1900.

[1] In addition, a number of offenders were sentenced to solitary confinement – 1899: 13; 1900: 1; 1901: 1; 1902: 8; 1903: 35; 1909: 2; 1910: 7.

he rejected outright the view that the Chinese were a 'criminal race', but also because, as an Irishman, he was thought to be more inclined to support the underdog. Though he arrived with all the credentials of a British Governor he was, then, seen as something of an unknown (and possibly untrustworthy) quantity.

Not long after his arrival, in 1877 Hennessy made a Statement in Council to the effect that branding would no longer be permitted, describing it as a practice 'opposed to all sound principles of dealing with criminals'.[81] He also told the Colonial Office that neither the Acting Chief Justice, the senior Police Magistrate, the Executive Council, nor others concerned with the administration of justice, supported MacDonnell's argument that branding deterred crime.[82] However, May, the first Police Magistrate, remained in favour of corporal punishment and of a return to the kinds of powers associated with Caine's early reign in the Magistracy. In his view, the 'humane system of English imprisonment' was 'so opposite to the cruel and oppressive character of Chinese Gaol management' that it rendered necessary something harsher if punishment was to deter crime. Imprisonment in the Victoria Jail, he argued, simply left Chinese prisoners better fed, better clothed and cleaner than the ordinary Chinese, and carried no stigma for the Chinese community generally. May was also broadly supportive of MacDonnell's implementation of a 'silent and separate' regime, and keeping inmates to a spare diet.[83]

The European elite's response to Hennessy's abolition of branding was unremittingly hostile. At a public meeting in March 1878, leading members of this elite called for the restoration of flogging, branding and deportation. They took the view that:

> The majority of Chinese residents in this colony are incapable of judging on the policy of a government on the principles of Western nations, and when the question of the good or bad administration of this, a British colony, is in question, they may very well leave the matter to be decided by the foreign residents.[84]

A newspaper campaign was launched against Hennessy and war was waged on his ideas through public meetings. Leading Europeans argued that the colony had been more secure before his arrival, and had since been overtaken by a 'crime wave', caused directly by Hennessy's 'soft' criminal justice policies.[85] 'Namby-pamby' English punishments were of no effect:

> There are poor but honest Chinese, though doubtless they are rarer than among Europeans, owing to their poverty and paganism. The dreary superstition which passes among them for religion exercises no elevating or purifying influence on their minds; it neither imparts joy in life or sheds a gleam of hope upon the grave. The fear of detection and consequent punishment alone operates as deterrent to evil; to abstain from

> crime through a sense of duty seldom occurs to them . . . The Chinaman is not a man to be caressed. He has never been used to it and does not understand it. Those best acquainted with the characteristics of the Chinese criminal class have no manner of doubt that a namby-pamby system of dealing with them would result in their encouragement to even greater acts of rascality.[86]

At the October meeting these Europeans demanded that magistrates,

> . . . instead of inflicting a paltry fine of ten cents or short terms of imprisonment, have the power to inflict summary chastisement on all rogues and vagabonds. Let them be taken from the magistracy and publicly flogged at the whipping post. By public flogging crime would rapidly decrease and the hordes of thieves at present hiding here would quickly disperse.[87]

Attempts by leading Chinese merchants to voice their opinions were deliberately stymied by the Europeans. At a further meeting in October 1878, they refused to have the resolutions translated into Chinese, at which point the Chinese left.[88] Hennessy dismissed the Europeans as a group of gentlemen 'who would wish to flog, brand and deport all Chinese prisoners'.[89] Despite being urged by the Colonial Office to proceed cautiously,[90] he forged ahead with his programme of reform. This included rehabilitating Chinese criminals through useful labour and training, and appointing two Chinese prison wardens who could speak Cantonese and therefore communicate with the prisoners. He paid close attention to prison conditions,[91] condemned the flogging laws (especially public flogging), and condemned outright the branding and deportation law as a 'penal enactment of exceptional severity, directed against one race in the colony only, the Chinese'.[92] In Britain itself, his actions were seen as those of 'a noble hearted and courageous man'.[93]

The European elite's response to Hennessy's measures had more to do with politics than crime. His reforms were upsetting 'the delicate balance of race relations in Hong Kong' (Lowe and McLaughlin 1993: 46). The elite feared 'that the Chinese were increasingly encroaching into the respectable European areas of the city, thus leading to "contagion" and a breakdown in the racial ordering of the colony's residential areas'.[94] When, in 1878, about 80 armed Chinese attacked a gold shop in central, injuring six police officers,[95] this prompted elite demands that the Colonial Office to set up an independent inquiry into the effectiveness of Hennessy's law and order policies.[96] It also reiterated its claims that branding and flogging were more effective and rational, because they cost the taxpayer less than imprisonment. The sparse conditions and spare diet of Hong Kong's existing prison regime were also said to make more economic sense than the expense of reform (the principle of 'less eligibility' determining that the prison diet remained below the level required by Chinese 'coolies' outside prison).

Hennessy's amendments to Hong Kong's penal laws were equally driven by political rather than crime control concerns. They formed part of his wider goal of co-opting the Chinese into colonial society, and ending the more glaring abuses of power, such as public flogging (Howell and Lambert 2006: 244). He laid his reforms before LEGCO in June 1881, by which point a committee headed by May had already proved highly critical of flogging. It also concluded that excessive punishments, such as branding and flogging, had little deterrent effect on crime, and that the increase in crime since 1870 bore no relation to the cessation of branding or relaxation in deportation.[97]

After 1877, reports of crime began to fall. This Hennessy attributed to better night policing of the colony.

The apparent success of Hennessy's policies meant there was no reason to suppose that severe punishment prevented crime (or that a more humane regime encouraged it). In February 1878, therefore, the Executive Council unanimously resolved to abolish public flogging and branding.[98] Though fully supported by the Secretary of the State for the Colonies, the move was resolutely opposed by most of the European elite. It regarded 'such leniency' as wholly misplaced in view of the 'notorious criminality of the lower elements of society', 'jeopardiz[ing] life and property' (Sayer 1980: 41–42). Nevertheless, in 1882, the year of Hennessy's departure, the Ordinance was finally passed, repealing branding as well as all ordinances imposing flogging exclusively on the Chinese, public flogging and 'the flogging of the Chinese on the back'.[99]

The elite's opposition to Hennessy's criminal justice reforms indicated that it understood – correctly – his attention to Chinese interests as a clear threat to its own privileged position. As with Bowring, it expressed its displeasure by pointedly avoiding his leaving ceremony. His pursuit of more equitable criminal justice policies had struck at the heart of European beliefs that Hong Kong existed solely for their purpose and pleasure. He was not however, driven by especially radical or democratic motives, nor was he 'anti-imperialist' (Howell and Lambert 2006: 235). Nor were his policies entirely driven by pro-native or philanthropic motives.[100] He was, however, 'convinced that imperial ambitions should allow for the political incorporation of colonial subjects' (Howell and Lambert 2006: 235). By the 1870s, those 'respectable' merchants the British wished to attract had begun to settle in the colony. Through his support for the Tung Wah Hospital and the Po Leung Kuk,[101] Hennessy encouraged their incorporation into colonial society. His criminal justice policies likewise reflected these attempts to obtain:

> . . . at the very least, the active consent of native populations in order to secure the legitimacy of imperial governance. Hence his determination to make clear that it was the duty of government to 'hold the balance evenly

Table 5.4 Offences reported to Police [1] or Magistrates [2] 1868–1900

REPORTS		*CONVICTIONS*						
Year	*Total cases*	*Against the person*	*Gambling*	*Offences against property*	*Other*	*Convictions*	*Acquittals*	*Total persons*
1868	5,705	586		540	3,589	4,715	2,730	12,247
1869	4,601	502		461	2,650	3,613	2,268	8,038
1870	5,530	693		531	3,388	4,612	2,477	9,793
1871	6,616	851		748	3,837	4,977	2,820	10,656
1872	10,350	783	511	927	6,457	8,708	2,892	16,199
1873	9,137	579	258	902	6,127	7,054	2,143	13,015
1874	8,079	627	206	990	6,256	6,618	1,920	10,101
1875	8,055	562	273	1,152	6,068	6,611	1,913	9,930
1876	9,103	604	260	1,401	6,838	7,352	2,044	10,426
1877	9,283	589	315	1,712	6,667	8,134	2,330	10,717
1878	9,100	754	476	1,868	6,002	7,927	2,377	10,552
1879	7,009	808	329	1,644	4,238	6,402	2,089	8,705
1880	7,098	726	540	1,391	4,441	6,448	1,962	8,657
1881	8,208	863	558	1,548	5,234	7,856	1,851	10,009
1882	7,567	728	425	1,567	4,847	6,823	2,177	9,402
1883	10,653	803	504	1,427	7,919	8,999	2,747	12,104
1884	14,065	754	640	1,697	10,974	13,125	2,562	15,935
1885	10,281	688	515	1,714	7,364	9,262	2,446	11,901
1886	14,611	926	909	1,865	10,911	12,958	2,388	16,647
1887	12,015	951	938	1,746	8,380	10,693	2,779	14,182
1888	11,647	1,087	608	1,887	8,065	10,125	2,849	13,309
1889	8,670	1,038	380	2,179	5,073	6,908	2,497	10,033
1890	9,739	896	168	2,021	6,654	8,061	2,557	10,772
1891	16,382	1,523	1,815	2,603	10,441	14,145	2,040	16,382
1892	11,920	1,151	677	2,167	7,925	12,316	2,078	14,471
1893	10,727	1,045	330	1,649	7,703	10,650	1,607	12,392
1894	10,447	811	222	1,604	7,810	9,778	1,811	11,953
1895	17,016	872	181	2,579	13,384	15,795	2,541	18,898
1896	17,767	831	133	1,695	15,108	17,489	1,574	19,568
1897	11,185	941	160	1,890	8,194	10,814	1,632	12,886
1898	13,341	1,181	369	1,844	9,947	13,530	1,289	15,289
1899	11,446	–	–	–	–	–	1,641	– [3]
1900	14,041	1,169	392	6,210	6,306	10,054	2,651	– [4]

Source: Blue Books 1868–1900.

[1] From 1881, the compilation of the crime figures changes. The Blue Book Annual Report for 1881 contains tables summarising the crime figures for the years from 1872, revised in the light of the new method of recording. Figures for reports after 1882 are for offences reported to the Police Magistrate; this figure is higher than for reports to the police alone, and seems to include them. Reports to the Police alone can be found elsewhere in these reports.

[2] Excludes cases before the Marine Magistrate.

[3] Data missing from Blue Book for 1899.

[4] Data missing from record for 1900.

between all men' instead of encouraging particular interests . . . The most blatant inequities occurred in the sphere of criminal justice policies. He believed that it was of vital importance that all sections of the community have faith in the fairness of the criminal justice system and that governance was premised on the rule of law rather than the parochial interests of British colonists. He also believed that there was a direct connection between securing the legitimacy of governance and the regulation of crime (Lowe and McLaughlin 1993).[102]

1880s–1920s: retrenchment and repression

With Hennessy's departure, retrenchment quickly set in. Various forms of governance were used to 'keep the Chinese in their place', including forced residential segregation and the full weight of colonial penality. A survey of penal matters in the 1880s and 1890s revealed, for example, that within a few years of Hennessy's departure, there were 'reports of overcrowding, increased punishments, flagrant abuse of power, prisoner revolts, escape attempts, deaths from floggings, and prisoner suicides'.[103] In 1882, the practice of arming Chinese police was abandoned. In the late 1890s, with the annexation of the New Territories (NT), repression also became the order of the day in response to strong native resistance. According to Welsh, on the night the British took over the NT in 1898, three Chinese villagers were murdered. Lockhart dealt with the crime by burning the suspects' houses and fining the village, actions which Blake (the Governor) criticised: ' "We have come to introduce British jurisprudence, not to adopt Chinese ways" ' (Welsh 1993: 331).

Lockhart apparently thought British jurisprudence fine in theory but not in practice (ibid). More qualified than Caine to understand Chinese culture, he nevertheless shared Caine's opinion that the local population was distinctly different from the British, rendering British punishments less effective than harsher Chinese penal forms. In this he was at odds with the Governor, Blake who, in line with Colonial Office thinking at the time, preferred to win over the native population of the NT 'by encouragement and fair measures [rather] than by bullying' (Welsh 1993: 332). But holding the belief that the people of the NT were 'different' was to persuade the authorities to delay any attempt to impose British law and standards on the NT (ibid). Local customs were allowed to continue (with a proviso of a prohibition on torture) but, in line with 'Indirect Rule', village customs, village leaders and village institutions were co-opted as an aid to governance.

This abiding belief in the 'difference' of the Chinese underpinned a longstanding desire of the Europeans for some sort of spatial separation between themselves and the Chinese population. With the encroachment of the Chinese elite upon the colony's decision-making institutions at the end of the nineteenth century, the social distance between the communities was reduced, but this seems to have strengthened calls for more physical distance. This was finally realised by a 1903 Ordinance setting aside 20,000 acres in Kowloon for European occupation only; the Peak Reservation Ordinance also excluded all non-Europeans from living on the Peak.[104] The Peak became a 'home from home' for the English, like 'Surbiton or Wimbledon', a place of tea dances, bridge parties and dinner (Welsh 1993: 42). This residential segregation of the races, which hardened between the 1880s and 1910, was not abolished until 1946.[105] Meanwhile, the leading European clubs (the Cricket Club, the Hong Kong Club, the Jockey Club and the Freemasons Lodges) all barred Chinese membership. According to Welsh, in 1908 there were even some proposals to reserve some areas of parks and public transport for foreigners, whilst within the colonial bureaucracy, higher office was still restricted to 'whites' and inter-racial marriages were looked on with disapproval (Welsh 1993: 381).

Faced with numerous protests, boycotts and demonstrations between the 1880s and 1930s (see below), the European elite retrenched further, their insecurities deepening as they faced mass opposition from the Chinese 'coolie' class. They responded with repression, using the full force of the criminal justice system as well as administrative and political means to suppress destabilising forces. Deportation, for example, was widely employed before and after the 1911 revolution to rid the colony of subversives, but also other 'undesirables' such as vagrants and criminals. Though as Governor, Lugard was willing to allow diverse political groups to stay in the colony (provided they abided by certain rules of conduct) he nevertheless opted to send army patrols into areas hit by 'bandits' (those who came to Hong Kong at the height of the celebrations of Sun Yat-sen's victory) whom the authorities accused of looting, obstructing the police and engaging in anti-foreign behaviour (Welsh 1993: 354). Simultaneously, he proclaimed the Peace Preservation Ordinance, enabling magistrates to impose summary flogging in public (ibid).[106] In 1912, this punitive approach continued. A Boycott Prevention Ordinance was introduced allowing the authorities to penalise areas submitting to the tramways boycott (ibid). During the 1922 Seamen's' Strike, Emergency Regulations were also passed, giving the government extraordinary coercive powers (see below).

Crime

The mood of repression that began in the 1880s was reflected in criminal justice. It had a great deal to do with politics and little to do with recorded crime, though of course repressive measures themselves operated to swell the crime figures.

The 1880s, years of internal unrest had seen peaks of crime and disorder; this continued into the 1890s, as the colonial state faced increasing challenges from organised labour and nationalist movements. Recorded

Table 5.5 Reports of crime to police 1890–1900

Serious crime	*1890*	*1891*	*1892*	*1893*	*1894*	*1895*	*1896*	*1897*	*1898*	*1899*	*1900*
Murder	11	9	3	3	6	3	8	8	1	6	4
Robbery with violence	248	202	49	19	29	11	8	22	15	85	59
Burglary/Larceny in dwelling	382	366	83	66	41	81	120	159	170	247	316
Assault with intent to rob	16	12	3	4	3	–	–	1	2	3	7
Kidnapping	377	370	86	72	320	43	62	59	40	35	37
Piracy	36	30	–	–	–	–	–	–	–	1	5
Unlawful possession	1,529	1,738	411	327	278	428	273	398	436	389	434
Larcenies	10,534	10,936	2,304	2,156	2,163	2,126	1,770	2,079	2,124	2,432	2,477
Other felonies	374	338	44	78	67	75	73	170	147	194	193
Total serious crime	3,100	2,994	2,983	2,725	2,578	2,767	2,314	2,896	2,935	3,392	3,532
Minor crime	*1890*	*1891*	*1892*	*1893*	*1894*	*1895*	*1896*	*1897*	*1898*	*1899*	*1900*
Assault	1,032	1,335	1,111	1,057	1,007	1,240	1,135	1,404	1,765	1,414	1,531
Gambling	29	523	595	319	218	171	126	145	265	199	324
Miscellaneous	3,952	5,656	4,341	4,328	3,806	5,400	4,342	4,122	4,531	3,170	3,265
Drunkenness	150	133	221	192	302	378	336	132	161	133	182
Nuisance	111	140	399	510	538	1,223	1,245	780	939	715	1,039
No pass or light	50	88	80	57	191	2,196	3,477	150	–	–	–
Total minor crime	5,324	7,875	6,747	6,463	6,059	10,608	10,661	6,733	7,661	5,631	6,341
Total crime	**8,424**	**10,869**	**9,730**	**9,188**	**8,637**	**13,375**	**12,975**	**9,629**	**10,596**	**9,023**	**9,873**

Source: Blue Books 1890–1900.

Table 5.6 Trials for serious crime (on indictment) 1901–1913

	1901	*1902*	*1903*	*1904*	*1905*	*1906*	*1907*	*1908*	*1909*	*1910*	*1911*	*1912*	*1913* [1]
Total	98	98	178	97	76	67	70	59	120	122	139	104	50
Murder	6	3	28	6	5	11	9	6	22	3	4	6	3
Manslaughter	5	13	13	6	12	10	16	5	3	9	5	2	3
Attempted murder	1	–	–	3	1	–	–	–	–	–	–	–	–
Concealment of birth	–	–	–	–	–	–	–	–	–	–	–	–	–
Abortion	–	–	–	–	–	–	–	–	–	–	–	–	–
Rape	–	1	–	–	–	–	–	–	–	1	–	–	–
Unnatural crimes	–	4	2	2	–	–	2	–	2	–	1	1	–
Other offences against the person	29	13	25	19	38	21	27	16	18	53	84	19	11
Robbery with violence	22	39	45	27	6	1	–	4	27	8	10	40	–
Other offences against property	10	11	44	12	5	11	2	3	33	24	24	32	21
Miscellaneous offences	25	14	21	22	9	13	14	25	15	24	11	4	12

Source: Hong Kong Government Annual Reports 1901–1913.

[1] Data for 1913 missing from Annual Report.

crime rose also steadily in the early years of the new century, and for similar reasons. The colonists' obsession with imposing order and attaining a morally hygienic environment pushed up the absolute numbers for recorded minor crime from 5,768 in 1901 to 37,951 in 1940. Recorded serious crime also rose from 3,404 in 1901 to 15,476 in 1940; reports for miscellaneous offences almost tripled in the 1920s, and doubled again in the 1930s.

If the use of public forms of punishment is related to insecurities within the state, it comes as no surprise to see that, in the years up to the First World War, the numbers convicted and punished for serious crime grew, as did the numbers sentenced to physical punishments such as flogging, thrashing, and exposure in the stocks. In 1900, for example, only one person had been sentenced by the magistrates to exposure in the stocks. By 1904 this had risen to over 1,000, and remained at around 500 until 1915; whippings rose from 84 in 1900 to 178 in 1912.[107]

The use of banishment and deportation by the courts increased, joined in the late 1920s by the sentence of expelling defendants from the colony. The early 1920s also experienced the rise of administrative deportation, enabling the government to by-pass the courts especially where it wished to expel political subversives, such as those it detained during its crackdowns on Communist and Nationalist agitators in the territory.

Marked rises in recorded crime occurred from the mid-1930s onwards. In 1930, the total numbers of serious crimes recorded stood at 6,036. By 1940 this had more than doubled to 15,476. In the same period, minor recorded crime also doubled in absolute terms from 18,895 to 37,951. Overall, total recorded crime increased from 24,931 to 53,427 in 1940, having peaked at 60,943 in 1938. This shift is marked in both the police records and the records of magistracy cases. The biggest rise in reports was for offences classed as 'other'. The increase in offences under this classification is especially marked for the mid-1920s, a period of tremendous industrial strife in the colony. Magistracy records for the 1930s indicate a rise in cases 'against public justice', which included breach of banishment orders. The sheer number of people brought before the magistrates also increased exponentially – from 18,401 in 1910 to 42,325 by 1930. The burden of criminal cases became so heavy that, by the end of the 1930s, a second magistracy was established in Kowloon and two more in the NT.

Despite the general trend in repression, some new penal practices were adopted in this period. Records suggest a brief experiment with juvenile prison in the 1920s, followed in the early 1930s by new sanctions such as industrial schools, reformatories, binding over, as well as cautioning for juvenile offenders (also short-lived). In the late 1930s, the trial and sentencing of juveniles began to be recorded separately, as (reflecting British practice) specific attention was paid to this group of offenders. But alongside these more reformist practices other new, physical punishments appeared, such as caning in court (for boys only) as well as imprisonment with birching (for

Table 5.7 Reports of crime to police 1901–1910

Serious crime	*1901*	*1902*	*1903*	*1904*	*1905*	*1906*	*1907*	*1908*	*1909*	*1910*
Murder	4	5	7	5	6	8	14	15	9	19
Robbery	82	66	99	54	48	45	32	51	62	100
Burglary/Larceny in dwelling	301	401	481	374	330	299	357	400	374	486
Assault with intent to rob	2	5	5	5	7	5	5	5	6	12
Kidnapping	22	33	49	90	90	99	109	114	81	109
Piracy	2	–	1	1	–	–	–	–	–	–
Unlawful possession	388	491	526	427	284	550	321	297	209	248
Larcenies	2,421	2,742	3,281	2,338	2,036	2,126	2,235	2,134	2,407	2,420
Other felonies	182	255	412	239	183	201	233	217	197	214
Total serious crime	3,404	3,998	4,861	3,533	2,984	3,333	3,306	3,242	3,345	3,608
Minor crime	*1901*	*1902*	*1903*	*1904*	*1905*	*1906*	*1907*	*1908*	*1909*	*1910*
Assault	1,620	1,287	1,169	1,160	1,239	1,136	1,119	932	946	643
Gambling	265	259	204	166	178	299	315	302	314	423
Miscellaneous	3,267	3,653	4,134	5,466	5,842	5,085	5,177	4,265	4,288	3,917
Drunkenness	150	167	160	191	161	112	118	69	48	45
Nuisance	466	1,057	723	1,297	1,113	1,179	1,505	752	878	1,513
No pass or light	–	–	–	–	–	–	–	–	–	–
Total minor crime	5,768	6,423	6,390	8,280	8,533	7,811	8,234	6,320	6,474	6,181
Total crime	**9,172**	**10,421**	**11,251**	**11,813**	**11,517**	**11,144**	**11,540**	**9,562**	**9,819**	**9,789**

Source: Blue Books and Hong Kong Government Annual Reports 1901–1910.

Table 5.8 Reports of crime to police 1910–1920

Serious crime	*1911*	*1912*	*1913*	*1914*	*1915*	*1916*	*1917*	*1918*	*1919*	*1920*
Murder	11	16	14	14	13	12	11	24	31	23
Robbery	101	129	92	40	70	65	70	89	115	101
Burglary/Larceny in dwelling	450	481	472	455	401	422	443	347	375	519
Assault with intent to rob	19	16	12	9	5	–	6	5	7	7
Kidnapping	97	113	146	69	57	58	54	95	126	113
Piracy	–	4	2	1	–	–	–	–	–	–
Unlawful possession	278	540	388	312	281	337	322	288	472	440
Larcenies	2,369	2,769	2,095	1,891	2,059	2,400	2,309	2,526	3,132	5,303
Other felonies	258	207	229	192	237	225	214	205	279	280
Total serious crime	3,583	4,275	3,450	2,983	3,123	3,519	3,426	3,579	4,537	4,986
Minor crime	*1911*	*1912*	*1913*	*1914*	*1915*	*1916*	*1917*	*1918*	*1919*	*1920*
Assault	603	752	615	479	474	472	412	312	365	455
Gambling	355	538	766	521	370	375	315	238	380	437
Miscellaneous	3,736	5,440	5,635	3,622	4,365	5,668	4,207	3,749	4,561	4,689
Drunkenness	36	55	56	55	60	35	22	19	35	79
Nuisance	976	1,600	1,489	1,157	1,068	1,250	1,126	552	664	1,266
Total minor crime	5,706	8,385	8,561	5,834	6,337	7,800	6,082	4,870	6,005	6,926
Total crime	**9,289**	**12,660**	**11,981**	**8,817**	**9,460**	**11,319**	**9,508**	**8,449**	**10,542**	**11,912**

Source: Hong Kong Government Annual Reports 1911–1920.

Table 5.9 Trials on indictment 1915–1930

	1915	*1917*	*1918*	*1919*	*1920*	*1921*	*1922*	*1923*	*1924*	*1925*	*1926*	*1927*	*1928*	*1929*	*1930*
Total	104	106	102	96	102	77	129	209	164	190	118	199	118	140	78
Murder	6	2	11	13	11	9	11	9	6	6	12	8	5	11	11
Conspiracy															7
Wounding															13
Forgery															2
Arson															3
Criminal intimidation															1
Manslaughter	9	7	1	2	8	1	4	7	4	4	8	5	4	1	–
Piracy												26	5	–	–
Attempted murder	–	–	–	–	–	–	–	–	1	–	4	–	–	–	–
Rape	–	1	–	1	–	–	–	1	–	1	–	–	1	2	–
Unnatural crimes	–	–	–	–	–	–	–	1	–	–	–	–	–	–	–
Other offences against the person	13	16	16	10	24	9	14	29	15	10	11	18	23	14	7
Robbery	–	–	3	1	–	1	–	1	–	52	36	52	40	47	10
Other offences against property	58	50	52	48	38	36	58	61	60	27	13	15	5	–	–
Miscellaneous offences	18	30	19	21	21	20	42	100	78	90	34	75	35	64	24

Source: Hong Kong Government Annual Reports 1915–30.

Table 5.10 Offences reported to police [1] or magistrates [2] 1898–1930

REPORTS		*CONVICTIONS*							
	Total cases	*Against the person*	*Gambling*	*Offences against property*	*Other*	*Convictions*	*Acquittals*	*Total persons*
1898	13,341	1,181	369	1,844	9,947	13,530	1,289	15289
1899	11,446	–	–	–	–	–	1,641	– [3]
1900	14,041	1,169	392	6,210	6,306	10,054	2,651	– [4]
1901	14,531	1,232	401	6,123	6,775	10,221	2,276	– [5]
1902	16,070	1,462	387	2,199	12,022	11,829	2,236	18,087
1903	14,268	1,108	285	6,079	6,796	12,864	2,271	16,442
1904	14,505	984	183	4,815	8,523	11,050	2,176	16,459
1905	13,450	934	205	1,886	10,445	12,561	2,323	18,475
1906	13,871	905	301	1,751	10,914	14,576	2,400	20,128
1907	13,414	998	317	1,531	10,568	12,875	2,723	19,716
1908	10,555	788	315	1,375	5,591	10,020	3,028	15,966
1909	10,771	1,020	320	1,431	5,663	12,664	2,973	16,660
1910	11,688	853	421	1,320	4,293	13,628	3,933	18,401
1911	10,471	716	346	1,317	4,280	11,484	3,049	15,269
1912	13,450	775	561	1,729	5,681	16,829	3,356	20,944
1913	14,218	665	705	1,221	6,581	16,458	2,739	23,998
1914	11,192	463	492	1,204	6,108	10,575	2,516	16,190
1915	12,263	436	342	1,336	7,389	13,049	2,163	15,766
1916	15,057 [6]							
1917	11,992	482	288	1,396	7,603	12,168	2,260	14,881
1918	9,805	344	239	1,462	6,035	8,296	2,140	12,535
1919	12,961	358	360	2,134	8,006	11,588	1,933	16,680
1920	15,267	463	393	1,956	9,891	13,466	1,740	18,525
1921	17,374	515	589	1,491	5,283	9,497	2,539	22,693
1922	18,221 [7]	444	425	1,640	9,450	14,524	2,094	21,557
1923	21,720	536	723	1,817	9,302	18,422	3,262	27,123
1924	27,724	676	672	2,394	16,566	29,567	5,326	35,484
1925	25,790	500	777	1,848	16,439	27,493	4,339	32,358
1926	30,516	576	607	1,828	20,681	32,739	3,689	36,978
1927	32,122	629	758	2,066	21,578	34,420	3,661	38,746
1928	28,468	489	580	2,459	21,829	27,196	3,379	31,276
1929	31,558	501	541	2,654	24,428	28,631	5,075	34,368
1930	38,646	646	531	2,948	30,548	35,411	6,395	42,325
1931 [8]								

Source: Hong Kong Government Annual Reports 1898–1931. The crime figures provided by the Police Magistrate differed from those provided by the police, mainly due to different methods of recording. Uniformity was pursued in the 1930s.

[1] From 1881, the compilation of the crime figures changes. The Blue Book Annual Report for 1881 contains tables summarising the crime figures for the years from 1872, revised in the light of the new method of recording. Figures for reports after 1882 are for offences reported to the Police Magistrate; this figure is higher than for reports to the police alone, and seems to include them. Reports to the police alone can be found elsewhere in these reports. [2] Excludes cases before the Marine Magistrate. [3] Data missing from Blue Book for 1899. [4] Data missing from record for 1900. [5] Data missing for 1901. [6] Data missing for 1916. [7] The prohibition of opium after Ordinances in 1914 and 1922 produced a subsequent rise in the number of persons arrested

(continued overleaf)

Table 5.11 Conviction and punishment in the Supreme Court 1912–1940

	Convicted	*Acquitted*	*Death Penal servitude*	*Hard labour over 1 year*	*Hard labour 1 year and under*	*Publicly flogged Privately flogged*	*Solitary confinement*
1912	76	27					
1913	66	28	1	60	5	27	
1914	35	14	–	25	10	6	
1915	70	30	2	59	9	24	
1916	65	22 [1]					
1917	85	20	1	77	6	36	
Fined							
1918	79	22	8	60	8	30	2
1919	78	16	6	66	6	41	
1920	81	19	8	63	10	27	
1921	54	19	3	48	3	17	
1922	101	22	7	84	9	19	
1923	167	36	4	137	26	30	
1924	137	20	5	124	8	34	
1925	141	32	3	125	12	1	[2]
1926	74	18	11	61	2	9	
1927	112	47	17	87	8	12	
1928	73	41	3	60	10	14	
1929	82	39	3	74	3	19	1
1930	35	32	2	25	6	9	
1931	49	31	–	40	9		
1932	83	15	4	60	18	6	
1934	97	26	2	72	22	–	2
1935	122	18	2	111	7	–	–
1936	196	40	4	154	35	1 birched + imprisoned	1
1937	229	41	6	181	41	1 caned + imprisoned	–
1938	347	40	5	292	47	3 caned + imprisoned	2
1939	381	34	18	319	43	51 thrashed + imprisoned	2
1940	403	70	8	280	113	42 thrashed + imprisoned	5

Source: Blue Books and Hong Kong Government Annual Reports 1868–1940.
[1] Data for 1916 missing from Annual Reports.
[2] In 1925, 'Imprisonment with Hard Labour' was altered to 'Imprisonment'.

and convicted. Increases in the mid-1920s are mainly for 'other offences', probably arising from the strikes and demonstrations of the period. [8] Records change in 1931, introducing seven categories of crime: Against Property; Against the Person; Offences of a Public Nature; Against Public Justice; Against the Public Peace; Against Trade; and Against Public Morals and Police. Offences Against Public Justice included returning from banishment; Against Public Morals included gambling, hawking, vagrancy, drunkenness – the vast majority of recorded offences were for hawking. This is also the first year separate returns are provided for Hong Kong and Kowloon Magistracies.

Table 5.12 Reports of crime to police 1921–1930

Serious crime	*1921*	*1922*	*1923*	*1924*	*1925*	*1926*	*1927*	*1928*	*1929*	*1930*
Murder	25	35	28	19	30	27	17	19	22	23
Robbery	115	242	151	109	173	119	100	99	113	56
Burglary/Larceny in dwelling	479	631	599	587	467	557	675	726	695	715
Assault with intent to rob	2	2	4	3	1	2	5	4	4	3
Kidnapping	96	63	68	65	10	23	23	49	44	70
Piracy	–	5	4	3	–	3	7	6	2	–
Unlawful possession	294	336	331	365	336	258	326	332	322	355
Larcenies	2,861	2,671	1,949	2,142	1,787	2,155	2,615	1,652	3,386	3,727
Other felonies	258	275	225	639	841	827	1,111	2,644	1,082	1,087
Total serious crime	4,130	4,260	2,457	3,932	3,645	3,971	4,879	5,531	5,770	6,036
Minor crime	*1921*	*1922*	*1923*	*1924*	*1925*	*1926*	*1927*	*1928*	*1929*	*1930*
Assault	528	542	279	304	217	310	332	291	299	257
Gambling	460	471	412	393	445	335	791	612	532	591
Miscellaneous	6,073	7,221	563	9,577	9,157	14,881	18,170	12,915	14,296	17,275
Drunkenness	114	57	65	36	55	38	24	20	22	25
Nuisance	937	1,388	220	273	326	513	248	239	321	647
Total minor crime	8,112	9,679	5,452	10,583	10,200	16,077	19,565	14,077	15,470	18,895
Total crime	**12,242**	**13,939**	**7,909**	**14,515**	**13,845**	**20,048**	**24,444**	**19,608**	**21,240**	**24,931**

Source: Hong Kong Government Annual Reports 1921–1930.

Table 5.13 Reports of crime to police 1931–1940

Serious crime	*1931*	*1932*	*1933*	*1934*	*1935*	*1936*	*1937*	*1938*	*1939*	*1940*
Murder	18	30	14	22	14	16	16	19	43	42
Robbery	79	66	63	57	83	56	97	109	215	186
Burglary/Larceny in dwelling	715	804	615	534	398	377	675	802	610	805
Assault with intent to rob	6	5	3	2	–	9	5	7	5	10
Kidnapping	33	22	22	14	25	12	14	9	4	11
Piracy	–	–	–	–	–	–	–	–	–	–
Unlawful possession	270	294	321	309	238	344	504	300	242	260
Larcenies	3,499	3,685	3,657	3,591	4,247	6,602	9,527	8,697	8,883	10,947
Other felonies	934	1,096	1,246	1,329	1,606	1,966	2,100	1,745	2,044	3,215
Total serious crime	5,554	6,002	5,951	5,858	6,611	9,382	12,938	11,688	12,016	15,476
Minor crime	*1931*	*1932*	*1933*	*1934*	*1935*	*1936*	*1937*	*1938*	*1939*	*1940*
Assault	311	341	402	487	738	668	563	674	683	468
Gambling	824	609	859	772	424	285	363	489	722	1,233
Miscellaneous	14,878	13,707	23,015	25,209	30,859	35,636	42,603	47,604	33,875	35,939
Drunkenness	22	19	16	14	8	11	26	14	13	14
Nuisance	1,139	394	1,046	942	733	605	626	474	505	297
Total minor crime	17,174	17,988	25,338	27,424	32,762	37,205	42,784	49,255	35,798	37,951
Total crime	**22,728**	**23,990**	**31,340**	**33,282**	**39,373**	**46,587**	**55,722**	**60,943**	**47,814**	**53,427**

Source: Hong Kong Government Annual Reports 1931–1940.

Table 5.14 Magistracy cases [1] 1931–1940

	1931	*1932*	*1933*	*1934*	*1935*	*1936*	*1937*	*1938*	*1939*	*1940*
Total	38,573	33,573	46,087	53,817	56,727	62,293	68,311	72,793	57,445	61,982
Against property	3,350	no data		3,884	3,813	7,131	9,056	9,541	10,210	13,760
Against person	444	no data		504	518	534	454	570	774	326
Offences of a public nature	1,599	no data		4,079	3,705	3,474	3,180	5,486	7,153	6,614
Against public justice	232	281		553	905	927	969	890	966	2,086
Against public peace	436	372		485	460	405	360	326	516	401
Against trade	57	124		67	218	265	282	275	304	32
Against public morals and peace	19,233	26,563		44,153	46,819	49,528	47,469	52,895	38,432	39,199
Convicted	37,164	31,588	44,727	45,436	47,841	53,163	63,315	67,601	56,835	61,094
Acquitted	4,478	4,647	3,851	5,146	8,174	8,128	8,044	8,396	5,391	7,469
Total persons	42,466	36,333	48,618	56,370	58,472	62,965	71,554	76,257	62,395	68,898

Source: Blue Books and Hong Kong Government Annual Reports.

[1] Includes cases at Hong Kong and Kowloon Magistracies and, from 1939 for the first time, cases tried at Tai Po and Ping Shan Police Magistrates Courts, NT, and the Police Magistrate's Court at District Office South, NT are included in the official returns.

Table 5.15 Punishment for summary offences 1900–1940

	Fine	*Imprisonment in lieu of fine*	*Peremptory imprisonment*	*Whipping*	*Bound over*	*Reformatory*	*House of detention*	*Exposed in stocks*	*Total*
1900	10,366	1,500	1,604	84	213	–	54	1	13,824
1901	11,119	1,421	1,586	56	312	–	36	1	14,531
1902	11,819	2,024	1,708	62	290	–	81	10	16,002
1903	8,809	2,219	2,008	88	232	–	42	314	13,747
1904	9,236	2,757	732	72	247	–	104	1,040	14,188
1905	10,972	2,800	891	45	380	–	53	673	15,814
1906	12,516	3,249	620	56	341	–	32	736	17,550
1907	11,710	2,900	834	29	480	–	40	757	16,750
1908	8,750	2,209	1,114	31	405	–	54	226	12,789
1909	8,857	2,396	850	35	791	–	42	482	13,455
1910	10,098	2,260	689	14	463	–	64	493	14,088
1911	8,083	2,118	539	21	450	–	92	631	11,934
1912	12,051	2,938	964	178	553	–	147	551	17,382
1913	14,945	4,013	434	90	512	–	175	669	20,838
1914	10,731	1,268	466	105	318	–	7	555	13,450
1915	7,359	1,390	659	87	570	–	24	570	10,381
1916 [1]									
1917	9,839	1,071	854	83	282	–	10	317	12,456
1918	7,606	1,044	1,012	87	264	–	13	264	10,290
1919	10,074	1,742	1,882	276	273	juvenile prison	56	118	14,421
1920	13,335	879	1,920	147	85	27	23	42	16,458
1921	16,972	1,041	1,515	124	194	22	30	41	19,939
1922	15,781	1,186	1,785	167	141	2	32	–	19,094
1923	18,404	3,706	1,432	216	324	–	32	–	24,114
1924	22,259	1,740	5,386	317	441	–	32	–	30,175
1925	21,329	1,938	3,798	379	324	–	23	–	27,791
1926	27,618	618	4,136	343	440	–	24	–	33,179

1927	26,815	2,547	4,585	426	570	expelled from colony		46	–	34,989
1928	22,067	64	4,598	420	610	1		48	–	27,808
1929	23,364	88	4,700	449	515	4		26	–	29,146
1930	29,250	132	5,470	462	462	4		41	–	35,873
				Imprisoned and birched	*Caned in court*	*Expelled from colony*	*House of detention*	*Convicted and cautioned*	*Bound over*	*Total persons*
1931	29,069	3,420	2,193	43	415	7	29	3,066	796	39,183
1932	22,121	3,627	1,553	35	10	10	29	3,374	1,052	32,812
1933	no data									
1934	32,378	8,842	2,726	36	–	37	25	4,399	555	49,240
								Industrial school		
1935	32,477	11,389	3,162	48	–	75	25	12	2,380	51,200
1936	43,303	10,291	3,683	65	–	57	24	13	3,621	47,167
1937	40,623	9,908	5,327	176	–	164 [2]	41	–	3,293	54,387
1938	47,182	8,616	5,657	229	–	78	34	–	2,606	65,222
1939	38,182	9,891	6,078	291	–	160 [3]	25	69 [4]	3,239	50,919
1940	39,780	8,513	10,040	241	–	640	8	92 [4]	2,633	56,908

Source: Blue Books and Hong Kong Government Annual Reports.

[1] Data missing for 1916.

[2] In 1937, this includes 117 persons 'sent back to country'. Figures for 1936 include 167 juveniles sent to remand home; figures from 1937 exclude juveniles but see separate table for details of disposals.

[3] Figure for 1939 includes 126 'sent back to country'; figure for 1940 includes 82.

[4] Cautioned.

Table 5.16 Male and female juveniles: punishment at Magistrates Court 1937–1940

	Total persons	*Caned in court*		*Fined*		*Remand home*		*School or orphanage*		*Bound over*	
		M	*F*	*M*	*F*	*M*	*F*	*M*	*F*	*M*	*F*
1937	1,610	49	–	611	254	90	14	13	–	199	39
1938	1,338	132	–	491	121	99	26	8	1	73	8
1939	1,609	147	–	397	111	232	36	31	–	231	24
1940	1,902	326	–	341	97	203	32	23	–	48	5[1]

Source: Blue Books and Hong Kong Government Annual Reports.
[1] Figures for 1940 show another 45 girls imprisoned.

male prisoners). At the same time, the number of offenders fined tripled between 1900 and 1930, and almost quadrupled by 1940. The number of offenders sentenced to imprisonment also grew almost fivefold: in 1930, for example, those sentenced to imprisonment by the magistrates reached a high of 5,470, compared with just over 1,600 in 1900. This reflected an immense increase in the number of people being drawn into the criminal justice system itself. For summary offences alone, this rose from 13,824 in 1900 to 56,908 in 1940.

The insecurities felt by the colonial regime and its European elite in the 1880s continued throughout the troubled years of the 1920s and 1930s. At the same time, however, sections of the elite itself, as well as the colonial authorities in London, favoured more liberal, humane and scientific penal practices that mixed welfare with punishment. Hong Kong was seen in these quarters as outdated. It had to be dragged into the twentieth century by London, which insisted on the end of the legalised use of opium, *mui tsai*, and licensed prostitution. Exposure in the stocks and flogging were similarly out of kilter with liberal thinking at home. On the ground, however, Governors resisted such pressures, arguing that instabilities within the colony (as well as turmoil in China) made Britain's grip on Hong Kong highly tenuous. In this climate of general anxiety, reformist penal measures made little impact on colonial criminal justice. It was not until after the Second World War that they proved more successful, driven by UK experts with a different vision of colonialism and a regime altered by the War and Mao's victory in China.

Notes

1 It was only the Chinese who were presented 'matter of factly' as desperate pirates, disreputable adventurers and seasoned criminals (Chan, W.K. 1991: 2). By contrast, European fortune-seekers were described as entrepreneurial merchants, even though 'they were as much opportunistic fortune-seekers as the Chinese' (Chan, W.K. 1991: 72) whilst at least some were also criminals and outcasts. The

absence from Europeans from this story of crime contributes to what has become an over-integrated image of the European community and an under-integrated view of the Chinese (ibid).
2 Munn 1995: 232.
3 Later, the British similarly incorporated the office bearers of other Chinese organizations, such as the Man Mo Temple, the Nam Pak Hong, the Tung Wah Hospital, the Po Leung Kuk and the District Watch.
4 Lockhart, J.H.S. 'Report on the New Territory', 7 February 1900, HK Sessional Papers 1900: 252 cited in Endacott 1964: 131.
5 The North–South division lasted until after the Second World War, as did the principle of administering the NT separately from Hong Kong. See Endacott 1964: 133.
6 The lack of suitably qualified lawyers and commercial courts meant that traders used a system of arbitration to resolve their disputes.
7 Norton Kyshe 1971: 37, 39.
8 Ibid.
9 Norton Kyshe 1971: 59.
10 Norton Kyshe 1971: 65.
11 Munn 1995: 233.
12 See Sirr 1849: 26–7.
13 The allegations formed part of a feud with the Governor, Davis. *The China Mail* argued that Hulme was, in fact, held in high esteem by the public. He was reinstated when Davis left. See Bard (ed) 2002: 23.
14 Munn 1995: 234.
15 Munn 1995: 236.
16 This could be extended to number nine members but the jury was never to number 12 'good men and true' as in England.
17 Juries Ordinance No 6 of 1887. See Endacott 1964: 153.
18 The Magistracy, Police Station and Victoria Gaol formed a complex between Old Bailey Street and Wyndham Street, Central. The site was relinquished in 2005.
19 Munn 1995: 238.
20 By 1842, the rest of the judicial establishment consisted of Samuel Fearon in the Registrar's General's Office, C.G. Holdforth, the Coroner, Notary Public and Deputy Sheriff; and Lieutenant Pedder, RN as Marine Magistrate and Harbour Master. See Norton Kyshe 1971: 14. The six Justices of the Peace included representatives of the large trading houses, such as D Matheson, along with F.W. Bruce, A.E. Shelley, J.T. Edgar, A. Fletcher and G. Smith – members of the Chinese community were appointed much later, with the emergence of a Chinese merchant elite; although Indian merchants were already well-established in China, they too had to wait until much later for inclusion into the legal and political establishment.
21 For example, a man might act as Chief Justice at one point and as Acting Governor at another – in the early 1900s, for example, the former head of the Police Force (May) became Colonial Secretary and then Governor.
22 Ibid.
23 Norton Kyshe 1971: 39.
24 Norton Kyshe 1971: 58.
25 William Tarrant, cited in Munn 1995: 216.
26 Norton Kyshe 1971: 80.
27 Norton Kyshe 1971: 103.
28 See Munn 2001 for further development of this argument.
29 Remnants of this differential treatment persisted well into the late twentieth century. In the 1990s, for example, Europeans held in police cells and prison were

offered a mattress to sleep on, whilst Chinese detainees were provided with bare boards on the basis that this was the cultural practice they were used to.

30 Official concerns with safety and sanitation, for example, brought local festivals and lion dances within the remit of colonial regulation.

31 This Ordinance was adapted from the provisions of the Metropolitan Police acts in England, where the government had embarked on a similar mission to control and civilise the labouring classes.

32 See Munn 2001 for a detailed analysis of cases.

33 Munn 1995: 238.

34 Norton Kyshe 1971: 82.

35 Magistrates have tended to be drawn from Commonwealth countries such as Australia and Fiji, as well as from England. As with the rest of the judiciary and other posts deemed important, the Colonial Office thought it desirable that office-holders in the colony should be drawn from a distance, 'unconnected with any of the parties and cliques into which such societies usually become divided' (Governor Bowen to Secretary Earl Derby dispatch 84, 23 May 1883, CO129/209 cited in Miners (1995): 151. Cadets, a body of men drawn principally from the English public schools and Oxbridge and specially groomed for service in the Empire, were eligible for the post of Police Magistrate (see Miners 1995). As with other public servants, however, this 'distance' between those who administered justice and those who received it was to become a liability. As Lau has pointed out, by the 1960s the Hong Kong government was seen by local people as remote and distant, unfamiliar and unconcerned with the affairs of the ordinary Hong Kong Chinese. See Lau (1982).

36 See, for example, Coates 1968.

37 See Miners 1987: 40.

38 Hillier's lack of proper legal qualifications was the main stumbling block to his promotion, in the 1850s, to Chief Magistrate over and above the rival candidate, a lawyer favoured by the Chief Justice, John Hulme.

39 For further details of Bowring's character see Welsh 1993: 192ff.

40 See the chapter on early policing for more details of the Caldwell inquiry. See also Welsh 1993: 212–3 and Munn 2000.

41 *Mui tsai* were 'little daughters in law', usually sold by poor mainland families to wealthy members of the Chinese elite in Hong Kong for the purposes of domestic labour. See Miners 1987; Smith 1995.

42 Ho Ch'i (later Sir Chi Ho Chi (Kai Ho Kai), member of LEGCO and mentor of Sun Yat Sen. He and Ng Choy undertook their legal studies in England (Welsh 1993: 246). They were sons of the elite who generally represented elite values, though Ho Ch'i proved much less amenable to 'Anglicisation'.

43 This prompted the emergence of a small clique of Chinese 'leftist' lawyers – trained in the UK – who provided a weak but significant corrective to the exercise of power. The core of the legal profession remained solidly conservative, pro-government, and pro-capital. By the late 1940s, Brook Bernacchi, a barrister, had become associated with constitutional change but, for the most part, the use of repressive measures by the government met little opposition from the legal profession.

44 Vagg, J in Gaylord and Traver (eds) 1994: 145.

45 Crisswell and Watson, 1982: 32.

46 Chan, M.K. 1994: 33.

47 Ibid.

48 Munn 1995: 213.

49 Norton Kyshe 1971: 6.

50 Ibid.
51 Norton Kyshe 1971: 20.
52 Crisswell and Watson 1982: 15.
53 Ibid.
54 Ibid.
55 Norton Kyshe 1971: 92.
56 Davis to Grey No. 98 Legislature, 11 September 1847: 24–5.
57 Norton Kyshe 1971: 110–11.
58 Ward 1991: 21; Sinclair 1983: 23–4; Chan 1994: 23.
59 Chan 1994: 11.
60 Crisswell and Watson 1982: 27.
61 Chan, S. 1994: 16.
62 For details, see Chan, S. 1994: 17.
63 See Foucault 1979; Spierenburg 1984.
64 Regulations for the Government of the Gaol at Hong Kong, 1853.
65 Ibid.
66 Chan 1994: 24; Radzinowicz and Hood 1990: 570.
67 Garland 1985.
68 Despatch 28 June 1845 by Lord Stanley on an Ordinance for the Suppression of Triad Society, No 1 of 1845.
69 CO129: 213.
70 Chan 1994: 35; Sinclair 1983: 28, 33.
71 CO129: 213.
72 CO129: 214.
73 The 1872 Police Commission is discussed more fully in the chapter on policing. See also Kerrigan 2001.
74 Report of Police Commission 1872 para 78; see also Kerrigan 2001.
75 CO129.
76 CO129: 209.
77 In addition, a number of offenders were sentenced to solitary confinement – 1899: 13; 1900: 1; 1901: 1; 1902: 8; 1903: 35; 1909: 2; 1910: 7.
78 Ibid.
79 Ibid.
80 MacDonnell to Kimberley April 1872, CO129.
81 Extract from statement made in LEGCO 17 September 1877, CO129.
82 Hennessy to Hicks-Beech No 10 16 October 1878; Kerrigan 2001.
83 May to Colonial Secretary No 31 11 July 1878; Kerrigan 2001.
84 *China Mail* 8 October 1878.
85 Lowe and McLaughlin 1993, 57–89; see also Lowe and McLaughlin 1992: 239–40.
86 *China Mail* 22 August, 1877 cited in Lowe and McLaughlin 1993: 72.
87 Supplement to *Hong Kong Daily Press* 10 October 1878; CO129/182: 210; Kerrigan 2001.
88 When the Chinese asked permission to hold their own meeting, Hennessy discouraged the idea that a public meeting could be used to bring matters to government attention.
89 Hennessy's statement to Legislative Council 6 November 1879, CO129/188: 90.
90 As Howell and Lambert say, Hennessy was well known at the Colonial Office for 'stirring up trouble' wherever he was appointed. His antipathy to slavery had already made him enemies amongst the planter elite of Barbados; he was 'disdainful of the white settlers' claims to racial superiority' and came with a reputation for 'a pronounced sympathy for the subordinate races'. It was thus

'entirely foreseeable' that he would provoke apprehension amongst the British merchant community. See Howell and Lambert 2006: 228–56.

91 Lowe and McLaughlin 1993: 70–71.

92 Lowe and McLaughlin 1993: 68–9.

93 Tallack to Bulkeley Johnson, 10 January 1882, CO129/197, 440 cited in Lowe and McLaughlin 1993: 83.

94 Lowe and McLaughlin 1993: 74.

95 Ibid.

96 Ibid. Hennessy had also provoked elite resentment for his attack on the practice of *mui tsai* and the system of licensed prostitution in the colony, likening both to slavery. Under the system, brothels for European men were sited in the Central district; those for Chinese clients were located in the Western. Unlicensed or 'sly' brothels were suppressed, though police corruption allowed them to continue in business. Women in licensed brothels for Europeans had to undergo a monthly medical check for venereal disease and, if found to be infected, subjected to forced hospitalisation in the Lock Hospital; women in Chinese-only brothels were exempt. See Howell and Lambert 2006: 245; Howell 2004: 229–48; Report of the Commissioners Appointed to Inquire into the Workings of the Contagious Diseases Ordinance 1867 in Hong Kong (C.3039).

97 Creagh attributed the increase in crime to famine and floods on the Mainland, factors which pushed up the numbers of refugees into the colony throughout the 1870s.

98 Lowe and McLaughlin 1993: 80.

99 Ordinance 8 of 1882.

100 Lowe and McLaughlin 1993 argue that Hennessy's sympathy for the Chinese had its roots in his Irish background, and that England's oppression of Ireland had made him sympathetic to the underdog. Howell and Lambert, however, regard this analysis as too simplistic. They argue instead that Hennessy was not simply 'an apostle of enlightened imperialism' or a 'deluded idealists and ideologue' but that his ideas and practices altered and evolved as he moved from colony to colony across the Empire, each forcing him to deal with numerous conflicts between principle and pragmatism. See Howell and Lambert 2006: 237.

101 The Po Leung Kuk, created to protect women and children against being kidnapped and sold, had its own army of detectives who would, for example, search houses and boats for stolen girls. This detective force operated independently of the police. In addition, those it caught trafficking in women and children were brought before a tribunal presided over by Directors of the Kuk.

102 Lowe and McLaughlin, 1993: 83–4.

103 Ibid.

104 The Ordinance allowed the Governor in Council to permit exceptions to this rule. In practice, the only one made was in favour of Sir Robert Ho-Tung.

105 Welsh 1993: 379–80.

106 Lugard also supported the founding of a local university (the University of Hong Kong) with a view to preventing students becoming indoctrinated with revolutionary ideas abroad by providing them with a tamer education at home. See Welsh 1993: 357.

107 Blue Books and Hong Kong Government Annual Reports 1900–15. The records for 1914 write of floggings in private, indicating that public flogging had come to an end, probably after Hennessy's reforms of the 1880s.

Part 2

Colonial Rule, Second World War to 1997

Chapter 6

The Second World War, the Japanese occupation and the '1946 outlook'

On 8 December 1941, only hours after the raid on Pearl Harbour, Japanese forces landed in Hong Kong. There was resistance by combined British, Canadian and Indian forces, and the Hong Kong Volunteer Defence Forces, but by 18 December the Japanese had fought their way from the NT to Hong Kong Island and on Christmas Day, 25 December 1941, the Governor, Sir Mark Young, formally surrendered at the newly-established Japanese headquarters at the Peninsula Hotel.

General Rensuke Isogai was appointed Japanese Governor of Hong Kong on 20 February, and the territory was ruled under Japanese martial law, with Sir Mark Young himself and some 7,000 British soldiers and civilians kept in prisoner of war camps. Under Japanese administration, the police force was reorganised, and a wide range of new controls – including over banks, factories, trading and currency – imposed. As the Second World War progressed in the Pacific, further controls were imposed including the rationing of essential foodstuffs such as rice, flour and cooking oil. Meanwhile, many people were forcibly repatriated to the Mainland, so that the population declined from approximately two million in 1941 to 700,000 by 1945.

The occupation was not without resistance. There were strikes and boycotts of Japanese goods. Chinese communist guerrilla forces were active in a range of ways, including killing Japanese collaborators, mounting attacks on police stations and other targets, rescuing some prisoners of war and rescuing American pilots whose planes had been shot down. There was also a 'British Army Aid Group', formed in 1942 and based on the Mainland, which carried out intelligence operations, smuggled supplies into prisoner of war camps and rescued prisoners of war. Meanwhile, various far-sighted individuals in the camps were already planning for the resumption of British rule over Hong Kong.

In August 1945 the US dropped atomic bombs on Hiroshima and Nagasaki, and Japan surrendered on 15 August. The effect on Hong Kong was not immediate, however; the formal surrender of the territory to British forces did not take place for another month, until 15 September.

The Second World War and the Japanese invasion

The Japanese invasion of 1941 was only one part of a much larger pattern of Japanese aggression and occupation. Ten years previously, in 1931, the Japanese had occupied Manchuria and in the following year set up their puppet state of Manchukuo. They had moved to occupy Shanghai, Nanjing and surrounding areas in 1937 and by 1940 were fighting on a broad front across northern and central China and the coastal regions. Japanese attacks on Shanghai and Canton caused many refugees to leave for Hong Kong, and as Hayes points out, by 1941, almost half the colony's population had entered since 1931 (Hayes 1993: 34).

The Sino–Japanese war had already led to a State of Emergency being declared in Hong Kong, the government deploying its powers under both the 1886 Peace Preservation Ordinance and the 1922 Emergency Powers Ordinance to place all life in the colony under state control. Identity cards were issued and a food control office set up. In 1940, the prospect of invasion caused the government to embark on the compulsory evacuation of British-national women and children. The process aroused controversy, for 'those with white skins' were sent to Australia, whilst those with 'brown or yellow complexions were dropped off in Manila' (Welsh 1993: 418).[1] Such discriminatory practices were taken for granted in the pre-war Hong Kong world. Though the war itself – and the decolonisation process which followed – put an end to such notions elsewhere, in Hong Kong they were to remain embedded in the social, political and legal institutions despite the efforts of some leading reformers to effect change.

The war had, however, forced the Hong Kong authorities to face the fact that some old colonial certainties were dissolving. The movement for independence in India spread ripples throughout the British Empire, for Indian troops and police were integral to British colonial forces around the globe. A number of minor incidents signalled that the Indian contingent of the Hong Kong disciplined services was rapidly becoming politicised, anti-British sentiment making some of its members 'politically unreliable'. According to a Hong Kong Police Force War Diary for December 1941, the loyalty of the 'Asiatic' contingents was being undermined by subversive activity within the Indian section of the police before the war.[2] When war was declared in 1939, an order was issued to the Indian Army to wear steel helmets. To do this, Sikhs would have to cut their hair, 'thus violating their religious vows as baptized members of the Khalsa' (Sundaram 2006: 9). The reluctance of Sikh troops to even carry the helmet prompted the general officer commanding Hong Kong to order that steel helmets be carried by all ranks to whom they were issued, be they British, Indian or Chinese (ibid).

When the order was read out, assembled troops were required to sign a register to say that they had heard it. One Indian officer refused to sign. In subsequent days, others followed his example; some went on hunger strike. Other incidents escalated this collective subordination so that, by 28 December, the commanding officer observed that as many as 800 Sikhs might mutiny (ibid). Those who did disaffect were court martialled. Subsequent investigation, Sundaram notes, blamed the incident not on the insensitivity of the British army towards Indian sensibilities but on the 'cloak and dagger' activities of spies and Sikh priests, who had been 'filling the heads of Sikh soldiery with seditious propaganda . . . which played on the themes of Indian nationalism and Sikh identity' (Sundaram 2006: 10). This was found to be more widespread than first thought:

> The inquiry found that seeds of discontent were present in the Hong Kong police force, in which served a number of Sikh constables, and among the colony's Indian expatriate community. Moreover, it was maintained that known Indian extremists were actively disseminating anti-British propaganda among Indian troops, and that they were aided and abetted in their activities by German and Japanese spies who were known to be operating in the area (Sundaram 2006: 11).

As the steel helmet affair was gaining momentum in Hong Kong, Sundaram notes, three Sikh civilians, charged with disseminating seditious propaganda amongst the troops, escaped and made their way to Japanese-occupied Canton, where they gained Japanese co-operation to travel to Bangkok to establish links with a Sikh revolutionary cell devoted to the overthrow of the Raj. Establishing contact with dissident anti-colonial groups was deemed by the Japanese to be advantageous to their goal of incorporating all of Southeast Asia into the Japanese empire (Sundaram 2006: 11).

Like so much else about Hong Kong's development, therefore, even an issue so apparently 'domestic' as the composition of the police force was tied to wider geo-political currents. An internal memo from 1940 recounts a number of desertions to Canton amongst the Sikh police, and raised the spectre that 'some unidentified source' was subverting the Indian police in Hong Kong.[3] The authorities in Hong Kong informed MI5 of their concerns about the number of Indian desertions, some of which were followed by the loss of secret papers; one deserter, traced to Canton, was found to be in possession of anti-British literature 'apparently emanating from Shanghai'.[4]

Since the early 1900s, the British had worried that Sikh members of its armed forces might, on their departure, fall into the hands of 'foreign powers'. It was now suspected that 'some unidentified organisation' was subverting the police in Hong Kong, and a request was made to India to send Sikh interrogators to Hong Kong to investigate this possibility and protect the Indian troops from subversive influences. Seditious pamphlets were found in Hong Kong aimed at encouraging the Indian police to desert the British in their fight against the Japanese. The Sikh element of the police force was described as 'mutinous . . . but by careful handling . . . remained sullen and non-co-operative' (ibid). The Chinese detective force was also described as 'definitely hostile', though many detectives did remain loyal, as did the rest of the Chinese contingent. Policing of the civilian population thus fell chiefly to the European contingent, though British military intelligence was supplemented by representatives from the Chinese secret service sent to support the authorities by Chiang Kai-shek.

As Japanese forces moved into the NT, many villagers fled to the hills and outlying islands, whilst others returned to China (Hayes 1993: 35). Those who remained were said to have accepted Japanese domination, the general feeling being 'one of dazed surprise at the debacle and a sad disillusionment with the British' (Endacott and Birch 1978: 114). The civilian police were withdrawn to Hong Kong Island, leaving behind a few Chinese police and their families. This withdrawal of the police allowed the spread of triad activity, with triad extortion, looting by 'abandoned boys' and looting of food by the 'poorer classes' described by the authorities as a 'serious menace'.[5]

According to Hayes, in the lull between British withdrawal and the imposition of authority by the Japanese, the NT villages around Tsuen Wan were beset by bands of lawless robbers and petty bandits, some of whom even attacked those walking back to China in an attempt to escape Japanese forces. These bandits, Hayes says, were:

> . . . seeking to take advantage of the confusion and uncertainty of the time . . . A gang of robbers attacked shops in the old market town of Tsuen Wan, and upon meeting armed resistance from one of the larger premises, set fire to the whole street. Such attacks were apparently a common experience in the period of transition, and the bandits seem mostly to have been outsiders from the districts adjoining Hong Kong (Hayes 1993: 35).

In the urban area of Hong Kong the police were sent to control crowds at rice shops to prevent rice riots, set up road blocks, guard vital posts, help with the evacuation of the European population, maintain blackout regulations, put out fires, assist with bomb explosions in the streets, help with food control, and generally assist in the maintenance of public order. The political police (Special Branch) rounded up Japanese males in the colony, sealed the Japanese consulate, and attempted to detect and prevent 'fifth column' activities. Some triad leaders were 'bought over' and assisted the police[6] but during the period of Japanese occupation, triad leaders appear to have co-operated with the Japanese forces in return for which, it is generally believed, all existing criminal records of triad activity were destroyed.

The Japanese administration

When Hong Kong fell to the Japanese on 25 December 1941, the European police were disarmed and interned along with other members of the British administration, in camps at Stanley and in Kowloon. As in other areas, the Japanese co-opted criminals – such as triads – into the police, along with the remaining Indian and Chinese police.

The Japanese police were modelled on the police forces of nineteenth century France and Prussia, the basic Kempeitai unit consisting of 40 men (Lamont-Brown 1998: 13; 35). Militaristic in character, they assumed a wide range of duties beyond crime prevention, protection of life and property, the apprehension of criminals and maintenance of public order (Lamont-Brown 1998: 14). Along with the Japanese army, they assumed responsibility for law and order but also kept prisoners of war under surveillance, controlled business, issued permits, regulated public health, screened and controlled those transported to camps in Japan, organised the movement of labour, monitored political activities and censored the press (ibid).

The system of administration adopted was one of decentralisation under three main bureaux in Hong Kong, Kowloon and the NT, each controlled by the Japanese with a Chinese staff (Hayes 1993: 36). In Tsuen Wan, police headquarters and the centre of authority was established at a large private house on Castle Peak Road (ibid). Sentries were posted outside it and, since it was a symbol of Japanese imperial authority, all passers-by were expected to bow before it (ibid). Failure to bow, Hayes says, brought 'cuffs and slaps':

> . . . a Hakka man from Wai Yeung . . . who worked in Hong Kong [said] 'I was passing the checkpoint at TsuenWan carrying vegetables and wearing a big straw hat. And I forgot to touch the brim of my hat and bow. So as I passed they bashed me across the back with a club . . .' (Hayes 1993: 36).

The Kempeitai were also key administrators of the organisation of 'comfort women', forced into prostitution in brothels serving the Japanese forces (Lamont-Brown 1998: 44). Relatively little is known about this practice in Hong Kong, though elsewhere enslaved women who survived the War have since brought actions for compensation against the Japanese government for the suffering they endured. As elsewhere, the Kempeitai also permitted gambling and promoted cheap drug dens 'to undermine native resistance' (Lamont-Brown 1998: 72). Another means of establishing Japanese power involved the public torture, punishment and execution of suspects, such public spectacles being intended to 'humiliate the enemy' and strike fear into the hearts of the public (Lamont-Brown 1998: 85).

Despite all this, the Japanese were said to have 'an arbitrary and ineffective control over the Chinese population', some of whom courted danger by helping the British resistance (organised from Guangdong by Leslie Ride), gathering intelligence and helping with escapes.[7]

When in 1932 the Japanese assumed power in Manchukuo, they had appointed a 'consortium of local civilian officials, businessmen, Kempeitai officers . . . army officers' to act as a 'puppet' government (Lamont-Brown 1998: 65). Similarly, in Hong Kong they appointed leading members of the Chinese community (such as Sir Robert Kotewall, Sir Shouson Chou, and Sir Man Kam-Lo) to assist with government, these three having apparently been asked by former members of the British administration to collaborate with the new regime in order to preserve peace internal security, protect life and property and restore order (Welsh 1993: 422). The Indian section of the police was likewise asked to assist with policing the colony. Most of the Europeans were interned but certain leading Government officials were commandeered to ensure that the administration of Hong Kong did not collapse (Woodcock 1969: 227). The Governor, Sir Mark Young, was kept at the Peninsula Hotel, which served as the Japanese headquarters throughout the war (ibid).

In Tsuen Wan, a District Bureau was established consisting of elders and local village leaders (Hayes 1993: 36). This was charged with applying 'the doctrine of "mutual responsibility" within the area' (ibid). Those in charge of households, groups of households and villages were, in this way, made responsible for the good behaviour of those residents under their charge (ibid). As Hayes notes, this represented a return to traditional Chinese methods of policing (the *pao chia*) also used in Japan and in Japanese colonies such as Taiwan (Hayes 1993: 37). In Hong Kong, however, people had become used to the British system, which emphasised an individual's responsibility under the law (ibid). The *pao chia* system altered this. It provided the police with a great deal of information about individuals, but it brought:

> . . . great pressure to bear throughout the community. [It] bore most heavily on the village elders who served as unit heads . . . The reimposition of mutual responsibility in Occupied Hong Kong under severe and much more stringent police controls was assuredly one of the most feared and detested aspects of Japanese rule . . . Some of the Tsuen Wan village leaders found themselves gravely pondering their position under the new arrangements. They knew full well that the newly imposed requirement of 'mutual responsibility' and membership of the 'self governing office' could spell danger for themselves should they fail to control crime or prevent 'subversive' (that is, anti-Japanese) activities (Hayes 1993: 37).

The civilian population of Hong Kong was subject to an intensity of surveillance unknown before the occupation. The gendarmerie and the Kempeitai amassed information on individuals and enforced 'mutual responsibility' through its extensive bureaucracy, the heads of households, village elders and local leaders:

> Aided by their own network of informers, their strict oversight of the population could quickly degenerate into a reign of terror if anything went wrong . . . the [Kempeitai] . . . was greatly feared for its arbitrary and brutal methods for it functioned more like the Nazi Gestapo . . . Its infamous behaviour in Hong Kong was on a par with that it exhibited in Singapore (Hayes 1993: 40).

Citing the recollections of older Tsuen Wan residents, Hayes records that the Japanese also forbade people from gathering fuel on the hillsides or moving amongst the hills, in order to prevent collusion with the resistance. Where men and women from one village defied this ban, they were said to have been caught by the Japanese and shot (ibid). In one incident reported by Hayes a villager recalls a 'great inspection' by Japanese troops in Tsing Yi:

> Somebody played a trick on Tsing Yi and said there were guerrillas here. A thousand Japanese came, and they searched from 8.00 in the morning to 6.00 or 7.00 in the evening, and arrested over ten people. I was one of them. I was tortured (Hayes 1993: 42).

Other extreme sanctions were also taken against those who offended against public order. Hayes cites the case of a villager from Shing Mun who was caught and executed for having bought a fish that turned out to be stolen property (Hayes 1993: 41). Raids and searches in villages resulted in houses being burnt and pigs and chickens killed; some villages were deserted as their inhabitants fled to avoid persecution and hunger (ibid).

Elsewhere, however, Hayes notes that villagers led peaceful and untroubled lives, and avoided doing anything that brought them trouble. Welsh also notes that the Japanese went 'further than the British ever had in extending Chinese participation in the decision-making process. District and area bureaux and central councils were established which exposed a much larger number to some nominal share in government' (Hayes 1993: 49). The duties of the 'self-governing' Tsuen Wan Bureau, for example, included issuing ration tickets, birth, death and marriage certificates, census-taking and, along with the street guards, the supervision of people in the district (Hayes 1993: 37). In Tsuen Wan another local body (which Hayes says may be equated with the street guards) was recruited from locals as well to assist the Japanese military police; others, including Chinese and Indians directly recruited by the Japanese, were recruited into a gendarmerie to assist with general police duties (ibid). Hayes reports that none of these men were well-regarded but were viewed as collaborators; those in the 'self-governing' office were viewed differently, being obliged to carry out their duties 'by virtue of their position in and responsibilities for their own communities' (Hayes 1993: 38).

A Hong Kong-wide police committee was set up (under the chairmanship of Chou Shou-son) to ensure Chinese co-operation. New residency permits were issued in an effort to combat crime, and passes were required to move around the colony. Each household was required to post a list of its occupants on its door, listing the names, age, sex and occupation of all inmates (Hayes 1993: 38). Local bureaux everywhere were charged with issuing the permits and licences that were required for many aspects of daily life. Some gambling house owners were given 'police powers' to help the Japanese control the colony, in return for receiving their gambling licences. This 'intensely bureaucratic' nature of life under the Japanese encouraged officials and citizens to resort to bribery and corruption, for eventually 'they could not get very far without it'.[8]

In early January 1942, some former members of the police force were recruited into a new Japanese gendarmerie, with new uniforms. Numbering between 1,500 and 3,000, they were supported by 150 Japanese secret military police as well as 200 auxiliaries.[9] The Japanese regime also experimented by recruiting women police officers, trained by Chinese members of the new police force at the old police headquarters at Boundary Street (ibid). Though Chinese members of the former police force participated in the interrogation of suspects, they were apparently not involved in their torture.

The gendarmerie itself lost control of policing when Lieutenant General Tanaka assumed authority over the police and set up a police bureau in the Governor's Office; thereafter, the police operated independently.[10] In April 1942, street guards and private protection guards (installed by the Japanese in the first months of the regime) were disbanded and replaced by this newly-formed police force which, by May, included an Emergency Police, which merged the 'protective guards' with a new corps of special police. These were scathing described by the local population as a lot of brothel keepers and their runners' who were 'sullenly accepted' by the Chinese (ibid).

New Regulations for Police Punishments were issued by the Japanese regime in May 1942. These listed 74 offences punishable with a three-month jail sentence or a 50 yen fine. They applied to everyone living in Hong Kong and included getting drunk in the roadway, dancing, singing or making other noise at night, failing to chain up a fierce dog, spitting in a public place, and urinating in a public place. Crimes such as burglary, robbery and murder 'were not regarded as seriously as political offences such as working against the Japanese, impeding the Japanese war effort, espionage, communications with the enemy' (ibid). Post-war, it became clear that the occupation had also been a time of widespread rape and plunder – according to Welsh, tens of thousands of Hong Kong civilians were executed between 1941 and 1945.

Meanwhile, in the internment camp at Stanley, the defunct Hong Kong administration was reformed as Camp Committee under the former Colonial

Secretary, Gimson (Welsh 1993: 419). As noted above, there was some clandestine resistance to the Japanese, and as discussed below, some far-sighted individuals laid plans for the resumption of British control of the territory. That said, the racism that characterised pre-war life is said to have resurfaced within the camp itself (ibid), whilst outside, it provided the conquering Japanese regime with legitimacy, for it was able to present itself as liberating the Chinese of Hong Kong from the discriminatory British (ibid). The local population was said to be disillusioned with the British.[11] A *Hong Kong News* editorial described them as 'vaunted supermen of the white race' who had 'melted like butter' (ibid). The fall of the British had shown the 'unconquerable British' to be 'men like others' (Woodcock 1969: 226).

The '1946 outlook'

With the end of the war in 1945, the question arose of whether Hong Kong should be returned to British rule or allowed to revert to Chinese sovereignty. The USA in particular favoured the assumption of sovereignty by the Nationalist government in China, but it was an interim British administration, under Gimson, and others interned in Stanley, which assumed control until British forces arrived to accept the surrender of the Japanese. Between August 1945 and May 1946, Hong Kong was administered both by the military and colonial civil servants under the direction of Brigadier David McDougall.

Initially, law and order was maintained by the Japanese, released internees and prisoners of war.[12] The only persons available to act as police in the colony were 'some seven hundred Chinese gangsters who had been allowed by the Japanese to run gambling dens in return for maintaining law and order . . . [they] were used as police in the hope that they would keep themselves out of mischief and the rest of the Chinese underworld under control' (Welsh 1993: 432). The Navy was ordered to take over the job of policing under the command of Colonel C.H. Samson.

The period of military administration was characterised as one of 'hasty improvisation, desperate overwork, a sense of close community of interest between the people, the civil officials and the fighting services', a period of short-term crisis management without any long term policy.[13] The economic life of the colony was dead, with no shipping, no industry, no commerce, and the utilities were 'barely functioning' (ibid). When the civil administration of Hong Kong was finally restored in May 1946 (under the governor, Sir Mark Young), the re-establishment of law and order was regarded as essential to the revival of trade and commerce; law and order were needed to assure the physical security of merchants, goods and money.[14] The speed with which the economy, law and order were re-established restored Chinese trust in the British. It was an administration that 'put business first' (Welsh 1993: 433).

Many Chinese began to arrive in Hong Kong, some returning after the occupation, others some fleeing the Civil War between Nationalists and

Communists which was still ongoing in China. This influx of refugees from China was not a new phenomenon, since the Sino–Japanese conflict in the 1930s, as well as ongoing skirmishes between Communists and Nationalists, had previously caused many inhabitants of China to seek safety in Hong Kong. The 'problem of people' – often depicted in the Hong Kong story as entirely post-war issue in Hong Kong – had only diminished during the war itself because many people had escaped to China during the Japanese occupation, or been compulsorily deported by Japanese measures to bring the population down to a size it could feed. In 1946, the population stood at about 1,600,000. About 150,000 were thought to be living on junks, whilst refugees from China squatted in huts on the hillsides or in makeshift rooftop dwellings. These lacked sanitation and fresh water, and were vastly overcrowded.

The influx of refugees and returnees forced the Government to provide free food for the destitute, labour to clear and clean the streets, and other relief work such as the distribution of rice through local area kitchens. According to the Government's own figures, it fed about 25,000 people per day through this means, as well as supplying food rations to orphanages; it also opened centres for the destitute to provide accommodation, food and clothing, as well as shelters for street sleepers. A system of repatriation and free transportation was also set up for those wishing to return to China.

The late 1940s and 1950s became what Jones (1990) has called the 'Golden Age of Aid', during which the Government relied heavily on the help of local charities and international aid agencies such as the Red Cross, the Salvation Army, the Society for the Protection of Children, the Hong Kong Social Welfare Council, the Boys and Girls Clubs association and various other local, non-governmental organisations. By the end of 1946, a Social Welfare Department had been established, but only as a sub-department within the Secretariat for Chinese Affairs; an administrative officer was also sent to the UK for social work training.[15] The establishment of a Colonial Development and Welfare Fund in the UK in 1945 also offered the possibility of more extensive welfare provision in British colonies, and a committee was established in Hong Kong to look at plans for the future. The government used it to invite Sir Patrick Abercrombie to the colony to survey the town planning needs of Hong Kong and prepare a report on development of the urban area. Other reforms included proposals for road building in the NT, public health improvement (including anti-epidemic measures and a crackdown on scavenging) and the development of Kam Tin.

The population continued to increase rapidly – figures for 1948 put it at 1.8 million, with just under two million entering, and two million leaving by air, sea or rail. By 1950, refugees were said to be pouring in at an alarming rate; the population had risen to about 2,360,000, the highest in the colony's history. Official estimates were that about 30,000 people were living in hillside squatter villages. On the government's own admission, however, these figures were estimates – the true number of those living in overcrowded accommodation on sea or land was probably far higher. The post-war administration of Hong Kong, as in many colonies, simply lacked accurate statistics on a number of social and economic issues, and collected data only when forced to by the Colonial Office in London. In Hong Kong, it was clearly evident however that thousands of people who 'in more settled times would have a house, flat or cubicle' were living in 'small overcrowded spaces or even in the crude squatters huts and shacks without water or sanitation . . . Squatter colonies . . . have arisen on the more accessible and conveniently situated open spaces, even in the heart of the city itself'.[16] Declaring these a threat to public health, the government wished to see such 'colonies' eliminated, but did little apart from permitting displaced squatters to build a hut of standard design, at low cost, on other, prepared sites.[17]

This *laissez-faire* approach to social welfare reflected the fact that, despite the war, older divisions and habits of mind remained intact. The year 1946 saw the repeal of the Peak District (Residences) and the Cheung Chau (Residence) Ordinances (which had stipulated that no Chinese person could reside on the Peak or Cheung Chau without the governor's permission) but stark inequalities and segregation remained. Whilst the mass of local Chinese lived in overcrowded conditions, the European elite favoured 'suburban-type villas, flats or small houses not unlike those of the UK'; a number of such suburbs had developed between 1930 and 1940, 'the houses being not unlike those in an average London suburb with the addition of servants' quarters and, in most cases, of verandahs which the semi-tropical climate requires'.[18] It was admitted that local government servants were amongst those living in the squatter villages, although there were plans to ensure that the local police did not live in too close proximity to slum areas. A similar discrimination existed concerning the supposedly different accommodation needs of European officers and the local rank and file.

As government reports of the time make clear, the dominant view of Hong Kong's post-war population was that the majority did not regard Hong Kong as their home:

> Most of them come here solely to seek a living, more money, recreation or political asylum, and strike no roots. Hence the colony's interest in social welfare had tended to be focussed more on short-term and sometimes unproductive relief work, than the goal of enabling every resident to become a reliable neighbour and useful and informed fellow citizen.[19]

The question of whether Hong Kong people were to be encouraged to become such 'useful and informed citizens' now became an issue both in London and in Hong Kong. The governor (Sir Mark Young), in keeping with the widespread sentiment of post-war decolonisation, favoured the development of a more democratic form of self-government and more equitable treatment of the local population (see Tsang 1988). This '1946 outlook' included plans to recruit more local officials, the Chinese and Portuguese officials having 'established their credentials' by helping out in the immediate post-war period.[20] Young himself proposed plans for representative government (the 'Young Plan') and it was these proposals that formed the core of the debate about the future government of Hong Kong up until 1952, when a combination of British indifference and the opposition of the Hong Kong elite and a new governor, Alexander Grantham, effectively put an end to the idea.

Post-War Hong Kong: social, political and economic issues

Hayes notes that people of the NT saw the occupation as a time of great tribulation, signifying a 'major divide' or marker between life before and after the War (Hayes 1993: 44). He also notes a recognition 'in high places' that everyone, regardless of race, had shared great suffering in their endurance of the Japanese regime. In some respects, then, the occupation served as unifying factor that should have brought rulers and ruled closer together in the post-war reconstruction of Hong Kong society. However, Woodcock likens the resumption of civil administration in May 1946 to a 'Bourbon Restoration', which seemed to 'forget nothing of the past and learn little from it' (Woodcock 1969: 237). As in pre-war Hong Kong, the system of government consisted of an EXCO and LEGCO; all members of the LEGCO were nominated by the governor, except two who were nominated by the Justices of the Peace and the Chamber of Commerce (ibid). In many respects the pre-war situation was restored:

> The head of Jardine Matheson was a member of both executive and legislative councils. The three Chinese representatives [who sat on both councils] were men who had become absorbed into the British trading community. It was estimated in the 1950s that a solid group of twenty men controlled government, public utilities and foreign trade in Hong Kong. The masses of the colony's vast Chinese population which reached 1,600,000 in 1945 . . . had no representation at all . . . Not only was the old system re-established, the old people came back to operate it . . . the officials who emerged from Stanley formed a tight clique [and] for a long time formed the most powerful group in the administration . . . The returning officials and businessmen . . . attempted to recreate not only the political structure of old Hong Kong but also its characteristic social life . . . The Cricket Club kept its greens free from the taint of Asian participation . . . [but] efforts to maintain segregated bathing places were unsuccessful and the Jockey Club, which had been opened to carefully selected Chinese in the late 1920s, was now thoroughly infiltrated by

> native merchants and industrialists . . . The districts which had formerly contained only British houses were now occupied largely by Chinese millionaires and it was only in the blocks of apartments specially built for government officials and in the military cantonments that the Europeans still lived apart among their own kind (Woodcock 1969: 238).

Old racial barriers, Woodcock argues, thus changed slowly rather than radically. Life for the British became gradually 'less ample' and less exclusive than before but old attitudes persisted until the 'old guard', which had returned from Stanley, was eventually replaced by Cadets joining the colonial service after the War, bringing with them new ideas about colonial governance (ibid).

The '1946 outlook' was thus short-lived, partly because in 1949 the Communist Party under the leadership of Mao Tse-tung emerged as the victors in China's civil war. This event, and the retreat of the Nationalists to Taiwan, had a profound effect on Hong Kong, shaping its character for the next 50 years. In the 1950s, the colony became caught up in the Cold War. It became a conduit for troops passing through on their way to the war in Korea and a listening post for those who wished to eavesdrop on the closed world of the People's Republic of China (PRC). The impact of the Korean war on Hong Kong's economy made 1951 a year of depression, poverty and unemployment. China's intervention in Korea caused the USA to impose an embargo on all shipments to China, effectively throwing a trade barrier around Hong Kong and Macao. This made development over the next decade all the more remarkable; by the 1960s, Hong Kong had recovered from this situation to become a leading centre for trade.

The following chapters take up this story of social change, population increase, economic development, reformist plans and social welfare provision, as well as the administrative and political caution that informed the re-establishment of the police, the courts and prisons in the immediate post-war period.

Notes

1 The Philippines, being as much a target of Japanese attacks and air raids as Hong Kong, was a far less safe place for 'non-white' evacuees than Australia was for the 'whites'.

2 Hong Kong Police War Diary 1941: 1, internal unpublished document, Hong Kong Police.

3 18 July 1940 Government House to the Colonial Secretary.

4 Secretary of State to Government of India 4 November 1940. CO 129/587. The authorities' interpretation of the 'Steel Helmet Affair' seems to have arisen out of, and also reinforced, such concerns. In April 1940, a seditious letter from an Indian Commissioned Officer to an English woman living in Patna, Northern India was intercepted by military censors in Singapore. As Sundaram (2006) explains, the

letter occurred in the context of resistance to the elevation of Indian 'native officers' amongst some English officers. In Hong Kong, however, disaffection amongst the Indian troops concerned 'other ranks'.

5 HKP War Diary: 1.
6 HKP War Diary.
7 HKP War Diary: 348.
8 HKP War Diary: 347.
9 HKP War Diary: 135.
10 HKP War Diary: 136.
11 HKP War Diary: 136.
12 HK Yearbook 1946.
13 HK Yearbook 1946: 2.
14 HK Yearbook 1946: 26.
15 HK Yearbook 1946: 59.
16 HK Yearbook 1948: 85.
17 HK Yearbook 1948: 85
18 HK Yearbook 1946: 55.
19 HK Yearbook 1948: 88.
20 HK Yearbook 1946: 6.

Chapter 7

Re-establishing the police, 1945–1950

The Japanese occupation saw several developments that, while understandable as strategies for an occupying power, proved to be problematic for the re-establishment of British rule over Hong Kong. Some Chinese police officers had, for example, been co-opted into the Japanese 'Emergency Police', which included known brothel keepers and triad members. Secondly, the complex structure of the administration, along with its perceived arbitrary and illegitimate character, had also spawned widespread corruption and 'black market' activities. A third problem was that many of those who were to figure in the post-war criminal justice system had spent lengthy periods in internment, from which they emerged physically weakened. Finally, as the occupation ended, thousands of people returned from the Mainland, creating acute problems of housing, food shortages, sanitation problems, and a demand for welfare that was met, as far as possible, by charitable agencies. More fled to the colony in 1949, following the end of the civil war in China and the Communist victory. Despite London's commitment to the 'post–1946 outlook', on the ground this 'problem of people' made post-war reconstruction a difficult undertaking. For most of the period, no one in the bureaucracy had any idea of the number of people in the colony – registration of the population had begun again in 1949 and by 1951 there were 1,627,608 persons on the register, but it was thought that thousands, including children, remained unregistered.[1] The official estimate in 1951 reckoned that the population had risen to 2,000,000. More were to arrive, posing an immense challenge to Hong Kong's resources.

Yet despite these challenges, a profound transformation was wrought over the ensuing decade. This chapter concentrates on how, in the midst of these modernising changes, the civilian criminal justice system was re-established in the post-war period.

Post-war, Hong Kong quickly established itself as an economic power, facing a range of taxing social problems along the way. The physical and social landscapes of Hong Kong were altered dramatically. The year 1951 alone saw a swathe of new public buildings, including new Government Offices, the Tai Lam reservoir, urban reclamations in Central and Causeway

Bay, the upgrading of Kai Tak to give Hong Kong an international airport, plans for a sports stadium for thirty to sixty-five thousand people, and the start of the City Hall project, designed to give Hong Kong a cultural centre consisting of a library, banqueting hall, museum and theatre.[2]

Though resources were said to be scarce, as the table below indicates, annual spending between 1953/4 and 1956/7 on law and order rose by roughly 20 per cent, education by 63 per cent, the labour department 68 per cent, subventions by 54 per cent, and capital building (non-recurrent public works) by 365 per cent. Clearly, a programme of intensive modernisation of social institutions and infrastructure was commenced in a very short period of time, despite post-war shortages. Intensive redevelopment and the construction of large blocks of flats was also under way on both sides of the harbour; several office blocks were torn down to make way for new buildings of a 'more

Table 7.1 Spending on law and order and other major departments

	1953/4	*1954/5*	*1955/6*	*1956/7*
Police	31,802,576	34,622,221	35,024,254	38,255,664
Auxiliary police	–	1,802,378	1,222,473	1,211,591
District watch	258,556	271,947	306,452	302,429
Prisons	5,693,933	5,107,071	5,266,299	6,193,447
Legal department	669,641	684,294	784,207	850,304
Judiciary	1,938,811	2,063,912	2,232,407	2,538,937
Total	40,363,517	44,551,823	44,836,092	49,352,372
Defence	31,641,832	30,267,284	23,825,554	24,065,150
Education	11,336,113	12,955,710	15,668,807	18,281,409
Medical department	23,704,484	25,105,401	27,002,383	30,048,868
Social Welfare	2,529,908	2,077,036	2,444,241	2,435,091
Secretariat for Chinese Affairs	384,144	395,620	447,274	439,029
Labour department	688,641	748,429	775,088	1,156,050
Subventions	27,639,261	34,645,531	34,727,237	42,772,652
Public works department	17,480,063	17,876,137	19,909,432	22,032,712
Public works (recurrent)	19,628,634	17,479,925	18,628,799	21,112,864
Public works (non-recurrent)	30,607,359	45,099,178	81,433,819	112,836,529
Resettlement department	–	3,574,550	5,499,235	5,408,936

Source: HK Government Yearbooks 1953/4–1956/7.

modern, functional design' with low ceilings and air conditioning.[3] Hong Kong had more cars, more roads, a new City Hall and piers, and new spaces for recreation, such as a park at Causeway Bay (ibid). The Tai Lam reservoir, 'more than any other material project', was said by the government to 'symbolize the confidence in Hong Kong's future of the Government and the people' (ibid). A UK Advisor[4] on education advised Hong Kong to do more by way of expanding primary education, higher education, and teacher training, and UK social work approaches were gradually assuming greater influence in Hong Kong penal practice.

The police

This modernising drive affected criminal justice institutions. New District Courts came into operation in 1953; a new Police Headquarters was built on the waterfront, along with two new police stations, eleven schools, new government offices, and new quarters for government staff. Immediately post-war, the so-called '1946 outlook' permeated plans for police reform (though, with hindsight, change had started pre-war, with plans which were never fully developed prior to the Japanese occupation).

The Commissioner of Police, John Pennefather-Evans, arrived in Hong Kong from his previous post in Malaya in September 1941 and quickly compiled a brief Preliminary Report to London on the state of the police force.[5] Some six weeks later, and about three months after his arrival in Hong Kong, he found himself interned in Stanley Prisoner of War Concentration Camp. In common with other senior civil servants, he spent his internment writing a plan (his 'Interim Report') for the post-war administration of the territory.

Pennefather-Evans's 'Interim Report' on the Hong Kong Police built on the recommendations of his Preliminary Report. It is worth particular scrutiny. A far-ranging and even visionary statement, it stated the principle that 'every opportunity shall be given to locally recruited persons not only to enter but to rise in the service of the public up to the highest points and to fulfil the highest responsibilities of which they are capable or can be assisted to become capable'.[6]

However, it did not fall to Pennefather-Evans to implement his plans. When British control was re-established in 1945, policing was briefly taken over in an interim military administration by Colonel C.H. Sansom. While Pennefather-Evans clearly had some role in this administration (he was given the duty of vetting European police officers for their prior involvement in corruption and determining which should remain in the force), by December 1945 Sansom was making it known to London that he did not think Pennefather-Evans should be allowed to resume his post as commissioner.[7] The job went instead to Duncan MacIntosh, a policeman since the age of 16 whose previous experience included the Irish Constabulary, the Straits

Settlements (he himself was interned by the Japanese in Malaya) and, briefly, Singapore (where he was Acting Commissioner). The Pennefather-Evans 'vision' was, though, largely (if slowly) implemented by MacIntosh and his successors over a period of several decades, shaping much of the architecture of the modern police force.

Pennefather-Evans and police reform

Pennefather-Evans's preliminary report, completed in November 1941 for the Colonial Office in London, was both a stock-taking of the situation and an agenda for action.[8] It pulled no punches. He acknowledged the fact that he had been unwilling to accept the posting, and the 'tremendous resentment' that the appointment of an 'outsider' to the post had created locally, although six months after his arrival he took the view that the force now accepted him and co-operated with him 'one hundred per cent' (ibid). He commented that he found his predecessor to be 'very unpopular' and that most of the officers were 'relieved when he went' because it brought to an end the 'over-centralisation' and excessive bureaucracy that had, under his direction, come to characterise the police force and that had relegated 'thief-taking' to second place:

> We had a pretty rotten state of things in Hong Kong normally. Narcotics, gambling, corruption and prostitution were all right out of hand. [The European police were] held in low repute by the non-Government members of the British community, who liked them individually but, with few exceptions, [saw] them as incompetent, lazy or corrupt (ibid).

Outlining what he saw as the main structural problems of the force, Pennefather-Evans described the Indian contingent as 'lackadaisical', having been 'allowed to deteriorate . . . The Senior NCO is useless and the NCOs appear to have no grip' (ibid). The force is described as generally 'inert', suffering from corruption, especially in the water police and detective branches, and lacking in pride.[9] He was also keen to remedy what he saw as the 'individualistic' character of the police force and the absence of a corporate identity. This he hoped to address by establishing an officers' mess, police colours and other 'symbols of the soul':

> It is most important that, in addition to training in police duties, an officer should be instructed in his obligations as an officer and in the traditions, history and customs of the Force to which he belongs; and that he should learn to cherish, enhance and transmit a feeling of special pride in that Force. This can best be inculcated in an Officers' Mess . . . The Mess would provide: (1) a meeting place at mess functions for Police officers and leading official and unofficial members of the British and

> other communities in Hong Kong in an atmosphere of informal hospitality; (2) a depository for the emblems and traditions of the Force; (3) quarters for junior bachelor members of the gazetted rank; (4) accommodation for junior gazetted officers of other police forces visiting Hong Kong; . . . The Mess should be situated in a suitable locality in a European residential area on Hong Kong Island (ibid).

At the same time, he lamented the bad effects the pre-war evacuation of women and children was having upon the marriages of the European contingent, and the departure of a senior European officer, occasioned by his marriage to a woman of Australian–Chinese extraction. Permission was still required for inter-racial marriages, which were generally discouraged; Pennefather-Evans indicates that he himself had attempted to persuade the officer in question to 'see sense' but to no avail (ibid).

Prefiguring his discussion of the ethnic composition of the police in his 1943 interim report, Pennefather-Evans set about delegating more responsibility for the policing of areas to European officers and their Chinese – and White Russian – subordinates. There was a special and intense campaign against gaming syndicates, and another against corruption – an anti-corruption sub-branch of the Detective Branch was established (ibid).

In terms of crime control, opium and heroin divans were brought under control and 'cleaned up' – in fact the report speaks of a 'general desire' amongst all Hong Kong people to get the place 'cleaned up'. On prostitution, Pennefather-Evans argued that this was 'chiefly economic' but sought to put measures in place to end soliciting, 'which is the objectionable part of prostitution to the man in the street' (ibid).

Pennefather-Evans had, however, a much wider perspective on the social and economic conditions that caused crime, and on the importance of good government. Without social improvements in education, medical care, housing and labour conditions, he argued, Hong Kong stood to lose her pre-eminence in comparison to post-war China:

> It is essential that Hong Kong should lead, not follow, China in these matters. It would appear that Hong Kong must turn her attention as a first consideration to the art of good government, to be an example to a modern and progressive New China, if she is not to lose in the eyes of the Orient of today the justification for her existence as a British outpost in a new Far Eastern Asiatic world.[10]

Somewhat unusually, therefore, Pennefather-Evans saw the policing of Hong Kong not simply in terms of fighting crime but in terms of a wider narrative of British colonialism in the Far East. This had long depicted the British as bringing civilisation, order and modernity to the region, and still justified British rule in Hong Kong in the post-war world. His report is also remarkable for the weight it places upon the wider social, political and economic conditions of crime – it was, he argued, overcrowding and lack of legal employment opportunities that drove people to hawking, crime and illegality.

In his later, interim report, he observed that the influx of refugees from the Sino–Japanese conflict had meant that in pre-war Hong Kong the streets were 'crowded with the homeless', tenements 'were packed', and narcotics, gambling and prostitution rife, making the enforcement of law and order difficult. Post-war, he anticipated, many of these problems would remain and, if restrictions on immigration were not feasible, some other means would have to be found of dealing with the situation. In place of immigration controls he preferred a more enlightened solution to the 'problem of people' – and of crime. Though it would continue to be necessary to monitor the post-war population figures, the government should carry out social improvements, and encourage the extension of living accommodation and the provision of employment. Only if the population 'shows signs of increasing to an extent which will choke social progress we shall have to consider ways of restricting immigration'.[11] Meanwhile the 'complete break with old Hong Kong' brought about by the War provided a 'unique opportunity to start afresh' and build up an improved police force.

The interim report, produced over 1941–3 while Pennefather-Evans was in internment, re-stated many of his earlier concerns but was much more wide-ranging. The pre-war police had, he argued, been handicapped by unsuitable promotions, 'resulting in the weakening of authority and lack of respect on the part of the juniors to the seniors'; by lack of support by senior officers for the rank and file when carrying out their duties 'with certain members of the public who considered themselves privileged and not amenable to rules and regulations governing the general public';[12] the recruitment of 'unsuitable men' for the police; the lack of 'any sense of tradition or esprit de corps'; a feeling that the European police were looked down on by the rest of the European community and the lack of a sense of pride in belonging to the force; the lack of any attempt to 'improve the quality and usefulness of the rank and file' of the Asiatic contingent, resulted in little incentive to work effectively or to obtain promotion. It seems to have been assumed that the Asiatic rank and file could not be trusted with any responsibility (ibid).

In order to address these problems, Pennfather-Evans made a series of proposals of which the most detailed were in relation to the ethnic composition of the police (and the allocation of particular tasks to different ethnic groups), a reduction in the number of Europeans in the force and improved career structures and opportunities for Chinese officers.

In place of a large contingent of 'lower standard of intelligence' Europeans, Pennefather-Evans wished to see a 'small body of high quality' European officers in charge of training up a better-educated Asiatic force which would then be in a position to take over the posts presently occupied by 'Europeans of moderate quality'.[13] Cadet officers from the UK should be trained in police duties by the Metropolitan Police in London, then sent for one year's education in colloquial Chinese in Canton. Better training for local recruits would be provided by a 'proper Police Training School outside the town area', equipped with new buildings and sports facilities, a modern revolver range, and a model courtroom; Europeans would be instructed in Cantonese by a specialist Chinese teacher, whilst all recruits would be exposed to an extended curriculum, including riot drill and simulation of actual policing situations.[14] Those on leave in the UK were also able to attend courses at Bramshill and other police training centres. This opportunity was closed to locals until, after the 1957 riots, five local inspectors were sent to the UK. Cadet courses were designed to give selected members of the rank and file an opportunity for promotion to inspector, to 'broaden the mind' and improve their professional ability.[15]

To prevent senior positions being filled by unsuitable candidates, Pennefather-Evans also suggested a system of examinations and promotions boards that would consider a candidate's conduct as well as his 'temperament, capacity for leadership, and power to maintain discipline'.[16] Selected candidates would also be given the opportunity for accelerated promotion and exchange with other colonial police forces to broaden their outlook. To foster wider contacts and understanding, Europeans should be encouraged to travel to neighbouring countries in their holidays, and 'every effort should be made to enlarge the outlook and contacts of the European members of the force'.[17]

Ethnic divisions occupied a hierarchy in Pennefather-Evans's plans, which placed the White Russian contingent almost on the same footing as European inspectors, with the Northern Chinese and Portuguese slightly above the local Cantonese; post-war, the Indian contingent was to be given the same rate of pay as local Cantonese officers, with additional benefits to induce them to join a police force so far from home. However, mixing of the races was not encouraged. Pennefather-Evans was clear that the Indian and Wei Hai Wei contingents ought not to be accommodated or trained with the local and European members of the force at the new Police Training School. Those European officers in charge who were stationed in the NT were to be provided with separate bungalows for their families, for it 'is not at all pleasant for their families to live in such close proximity to the Asiatic police'.[18] These pleasant, spacious bungalows were described as compensation for the lack of social activities for Europeans, who would be forced to spend much of their time in the NT at home.

Married European officers in the urban areas were also to have their own apartments, outside the police station, in blocks provided by the government. To attract the kind of 'better educated' Europeans, Pennefather-Evans also proposed that they be given an allowance to send their children to school in Britain, an incentive which, he suggested, might be extended to all European government officers in Hong Kong.[19] What Pennefather-Evans refers to as 'Asiatic single men' were to be housed in barrack-style quarters inside the police station since 'Asiatics do not mind communal living'; Asiatic married quarters were to be provided since

> . . . 90% of the Asiatic force is married [and] it does no good to the police to have police sergeants living in slum conditions in the town. These quarters can best be provided in the form of blocks of flats. Sites for these will not be so difficult as for European quarters.[20]

Moreover, a handwritten note on the Interim Report points out, increasing the pay to the Chinese contingent was 'likely to result in more relatives living on them. The remedy is to provide married quarters and limit the residents to a man, his wife and children'.[21]

The idea that there should be paternalistic controls of the social lives of police officers remained strong in Pennefather-Evans's vision. European single policemen throughout the Colony were to be accommodated in their own quarters outside the police station to prevent the 'mixed marriages', which communal, barrack-room living was thought to have encouraged. He took the view that Europeans marriages should still require the written approval of the Commissioner of Police:

> The disadvantages to the Police service of marriage with undesirable Europeans are obvious. Not so obvious are the disadvantages of marriage with Orientals and Eurasians. They are:
>
> (1) That such officers do not usually avail themselves of long leave, which is necessary for their health and morale;
> (2) That Asiatic women of the class who usually contract such marriages have low standards of morality. If such a marriage is not contracted for the opportunity it affords to obtain graft, the opportunity is there and is often taken, pressure being brought to bear on the woman by interested relatives and friends;
> (3) The difficulty of housing mixed partners in European quarters without causing dissatisfaction;
> (4) That leakages of information to interested parties take place via the Asiatic wives of police;
> (5) That the type of Asiatic wife usually taken tends to lower the social status of the Police as a whole . . .
>
> Should a police officer marry without official approval he should be required to leave the Police service within six months.[22]

While it was Pennefather-Evans's view that the European inspectorate should be reduced, leaving more openings for 'Asiatics' in more responsible posts, this was not based on a completely uncritical assessment of their past performance. In a handwritten note appended to his report he stated:

> I have not lost sight of the fact that there have been occasions from time to time when the Asiatic police have not proved entirely reliable, particularly so in the recent hostilities in Hong Kong. On the other hand, during the 1925 general strike organised from Canton, which was a great test of their fidelity, only a handful failed to perform duty. With better recruitment, training and living conditions, I believe that the Asiatic rank and file would remain on duty and even if they did not do so, I believe that the Special Entry [recruited directly as sub-inspectors] . . . would, if properly trained, adequately fill the place of a proportion of the Europeans.[23]

Pennefather-Evans planned to recruit Northern Chinese from Wei Hai Wei for use in the Hong Kong Police Emergency riot unit for, whilst language problems made it difficult to use them for ordinary policing, 'They are more amenable to discipline than are Cantonese and it is desirable to have other than Cantonese to deal with Cantonese crowds'.[24] The strategy of 'policing by strangers' was well practised in the British Empire. Since it was suspected that recruits from the same ethnic group or area might side with their compatriots in a situation of conflict, recruits from another area or ethnic group were frequently deployed to police the population.

The Indian contingent in the Hong Kong police were, however, Pennefather-Evans argued, 'becoming increasingly politically minded and unreliable':

> Before the outbreak of hostilities in Hong Kong, the 'Tin Hat' trouble among the Indian troops occurred and during the hostilities the Sikhs in the police were quite useless. After the capture of Hong Kong they became definitely hostile. The Punjabi Mohammedans were, for the most part, loyal. Both inside and outside the police there has been a revulsion of feeling against the further employment of Sikhs in the Police Force. The Sikhs formerly employed were not of a good type; they were usually corrupt, clumsy in dealing with the public, and were inferior to the usual standard of Sikh soldier or policeman.[25]

Pennefather-Evans recommended that Sikhs no longer be recruited into the Hong Kong Police; if the Indian government pressured Hong Kong to take them he recommended their restricted use in the 'Frontier Constabulary'. He did, however, recommend the continued recruitment of 'Punjabi Mohammedans', though again he saw them as playing a restricted role as part of the 'semi-military Frontier Constabulary'. This would combine with the recruits from Wei Hai Wei to form the Emergency Riot Unit, and the unit was to be trained separately from the rest of the police force in its own base in the NT. Indians were to be recruited where possible but were to be more carefully selected than before, and whilst stationed in the frontier Constabulary and training school, every effort was to be made

> . . . to keep them from the town; this can only be achieved by providing all facilities for their training, service and recreation on the spot in the NT, so that both service and requirements and their own desires to go into town can be cut down to the barest minimum. The depot will require a senior European as Officer in Charge, assisted by the Officer in Charge, Emergency Unit NT and a staff of Indian instructor under the direct supervision of the Assistant Superintendent of Police, NT.[26]

A large block of quarters for Indian men and their families was proposed near the Depot at Fanling, along with a mosque, school, clinic and shops 'so that a complete Indian community will be formed' (ibid).

The Russian contingent of 31 men was to remain, but be given different tasks and more responsibility. Formed in 1930, it was charged chiefly with anti-piracy duties, though 11 Russians had been seconded to Special Branch, were also engaged on passport duties and, during the war, had been put in charge of supervising the Indian armed patrols.[27] Those interned alongside the British in Stanley had proved 'reliable'. Pennefather-Evans now proposed to use them on 'special shore jobs such as Special Branch enquiries, passport enquiries, passport examination, waterfront searches, ship searches, this relieving the European police for ordinary police duties'.[28] They were also to receive a level of remuneration 'to enable them to enjoy a standard of living more commensurate with other white employees of government than is the case at present'.[29]

Special Branch, incidentally, whose functions Pennefather-Evans described as chiefly 'political' and 'security', was seen as defective in two main ways. Firstly, it lacked an 'underground' system of informers in potentially subversive organisations to provide intelligence about their activities 'before anything serious could come to the surface'.[30] It thus relied on information gained from raids, arrests and questioning, methods which were seen by the political police in other countries as 'clumsy'. Secondly, there was a lack of personal contact between members of the Hong Kong Special Branch and the political police of other countries, where methods were 'more delicate' (ibid).

To remedy this, Pennefather-Evans recommended that Special Branch be placed, for a time, under the control of an officer seconded from Malaya 'who has been trained in security work', and that an officer from Hong Kong also be sent to Malaya for training. This arrangement had, in fact, been agreed before the war but had been interrupted by the Japanese occupation. In addition to more funds for Special Branch work, Pennefather-Evans also suggested that those selected need not necessarily be police officers; men should be selected for their 'aptitude' for this type of work; whilst the head of each section should be European, the number of Europeans involved should be kept as small as possible: 'We had too many Europeans in Special Branch before the War' (ibid).

In pursuing his earlier comments on the need to improve morale, Pennefather-Evans expanded on the plan for an officers' mess that he had first mooted in the preliminary report. There should also be a police band and a police magazine, while:

> The establishment of a Police Officers' Mess should play a great part in preserving the traditions of the Force. Aids to the preservation of an esprit de corps such as police colours, police Christmas cards, the adoption of a universal police badge and motto to be worn by all ranks, police sports, police dances and entertainments, etc. should all be encouraged . . . In short, the tone of the Force should be regarded as of equal importance to its efficiency. A tradition of impartial public service needs to be established.[31]

Police restaurants were also to be established in Hong Kong and in Kowloon to provide good meals, in pleasant surroundings: 'where hospitality can be returned at low cost. Ladies would be admitted. Both alcoholic and non-alcoholic refreshments would be available. Dances and dinners could be held here'.[32]

Beyond these 'symbols of the soul' he also planned for a comprehensive updating of the police infrastructure. He recommended that the force update its photographic and fingerprinting branches, introduce women officers as 'searchers' and wardresses (women police constables were recruited from 1950 onwards), improve its communications system by introducing a teleprinter (as in Shanghai) and police telephone boxes, circulate monthly reports and routine orders via a police printing office (as in Singapore and Kuala Lumpur), replace motorcycles with high speed cars and buy more flexible and faster launches so that the water police were better able to pursue pirates ('still the chief danger to the Colony'). The lack of a commercial crime sub-branch 'in a commercial city like Hong Kong' was remarked upon, as was the need for specialist police squads to deal with commercial crime, immigration, gaming and brothels. What Pennefather-Evans calls a 'Preventative Branch' was needed – either as a branch of the police or separate from the police – to intercept the manufacture, trafficking, sale and use of narcotics. This, he says, was originally suggested by Sir Geoffrey Northcote and, in the absence of such a branch, LEGCO had authorised the police to raid opium and heroin divans and seize drugs and equipment. The increase in heroin divans, he argued, necessitated a specialist branch that should be modelled along the lines of the Malayan Customs Service. It would require secret service funds, which the head of the service would be able to disburse with complete discretion, mainly to informers who gave information in secret about shipments of drugs and so on. In terms of private security, he wished to retain the Private Watchmen, though recommended that Indians be appointed only after approval from the Commissioner of Police.

There was a great deal of discussion in the interim report of policing structures for the NT. In an addendum to the report, G.S. Wilson noted that the existing NT police stations were too small, too far apart, too distant from centres of population, and badly placed to catch criminals coming in by water or cutting across the mountains.[33] Policing still fell primarily to Village Penetration Patrols consisting of three or four men. These visited each village for four days at a time, eating and sleeping amongst the villagers to gain their confidence and goodwill, liaising with the Village Guards, and gathering intelligence about criminal and subversive activities; the bill for their stay was presented by each village headman to the local police station. The Village Guards were based on what the British saw as an 'ancient system' of self-help, using men originally elected from within the villages to protect crops. In the decade after the War, their numbers varied between 300 and 600 each year.[34]

Though this 'self-help' system was, from time to time, supported by the Emergency Unit in 'fire brigade policing' in the Frontier area, Pennefather-Evans and Wilson clearly saw it as inadequate as a means of detecting and apprehending the criminals operating in and around the NT. Their report describes Yuen Long as 'a big receiving centre for food and goods from Chinese territory', and the areas around Deep Bay as 'wild and rough and teeming with robbers'.[35] As Pennefather-Evans noted, chief amongst the most regular crimes affecting Hong Kong was piracy, closely followed by smuggling, which had occupied the customs authorities on both sides of the border throughout the nineteenth and early twentieth centuries. The high customs duties imposed by China in the 1940s was thought to have acted as an incentive for smugglers taking a wide variety of goods from abroad into China via Hong Kong, whilst the Hong Kong authorities remained concerned about the level of narcotics flowing from China into the colony. The virtually roadless and rugged landscape of the NT, combined with its numerous fishing villages and isolated coves, made it a centre for smuggling of goods and people to and from China, a reputation it was to maintain throughout the decades. The NT was said to have 'special and peculiar problems' which required 'the utmost tact and resourcefulness'.[36]

Pennefather-Evans wished, however, to see the abolition of the Street Guards and Special Constables (employed during the war), Village Scouts, and the Village Guards in the NT. The district watch, formerly maintained by private subscription, was still under the authority of the Secretariat for Chinese Affairs[37] (SCA). It now came under government control, paid for out of public funds, and was required to engage in normal police duties.[38] In May 1946, 103 men had reported back for duty, falling to 99 in 1947 (Hayes 1996: 103). Their duties were 'patrolling the streets, conducting enquiries in connection with boarding houses, guilds and the protection of women and girls, and in making general investigations on behalf of the Secretariat' (ibid).[39]

Certain issues, though, Pennefather-Evans regarded as intractable – he took the view that it was, for example, impossible to place effective controls on immigration to Hong Kong from China. Immigration controls had in fact begun in 1923, with the enactment of a Passport Ordinance. In 1934, this had been replaced with an Immigration and Passport Ordinance, which introduced the need for travel documents and established a prohibition on the entry of 'undesirables'; it authorised the police to examine the passengers, crew and documents of all vessels entering Hong Kong.[40] Previous registration ordinances had, of course, long attempted to keep some record of persons residing in Hong Kong. The 1916 Registration of Persons Ordinance had required all aliens to register with the police, though by 1934 only non-Chinese aliens were required to so register. A record of Chinese residents had been kept by the Secretary for Chinese Affairs office, but the issuance of passports and visas remained in the hands of the police, specifically the Special Branch. A brief experiment with an Immigration Department was attempted in 1940, but its failure led to the resumption of passport controls by Special Branch after the War.

Control of immigration from the Mainland was made difficult by Hong Kong's long land border with China, as well as the ready access by sea at numerous coves and fishing villages. In the view of Pennefather-Evans, Hong, Kong provided a safe, stable and orderly environment for those fleeing upheavals and poverty in China.

> . . . the better Hong Kong is governed, the more is it likely to attract the masses of China who thus, by the pressure of their numbers, introduce social problems of an acute kind, for there is only a limited amount of employment and accommodation available in the Colony. Overcrowding, hawkers, beggars, prostitutes, opium divans, gambling as well as ordinary crime, increase with the excess of population until the police are taxed to the uttermost to cope with these social evils.[41]

In contrast to later policies, which sought to deter migrants from bringing their families, Pennefather-Evans took the view that 'united families were to be preferred to separated families'.[42] Instead of seeing indigent workers as cheap labour, Hong Kong should aim at a:

> . . . higher ideal in keeping with the progress of the times. Cut throat commercial competition is steadily giving way to the practice of ensuring good pay, healthy working conditions and security of employment. Hong Kong cannot afford to lag behind in this respect without risking loss of her reputation as a city of good government. If the social conditions of Hong Kong are to be an improvement on those of China, the standard of living of the Chinese workers in Hong Kong must be higher than that of his compatriot in China.[43]

Pennefather-Evans's programme for change was not taken up immediately.

For one thing, in the immediate post-war period there were pressing practical problems such as rebuilding police stations, re-equipping the force, establishing whether those who had worked under the Japanese were still trustworthy and considering how many of the pre-war officers should be taken back onto the force strength. For another, Colonel Sansom, the commissioner of police under the interim administration, appears not to have considered Pennefather-Evans suitable for reinstatement to his previous position. He assigned to Pennefather-Evans the task of drawing up the list of European officers whose conduct was free from question, and who were thus allowed to return. In a memo of December 1945, he expressed the view that:

> . . . Pennefather-Evans will be 52 years of age on 4.1.46, it is very clear that he did not have the confidence of the officers under him and that he should not resume duty in Hong Kong. He probably will not wish to return . . . If Mr Pennefather-Evans is not to return to Hong Kong where is his replacement to be found? His importation from Malaya had a bad effect on the morale of the Force with a competent officer like Mr Perdue available locally . . . There seem to be two things to guard against in the future in the Hong Kong Police: (a) permitting gazetted officers to serve their careers in Hong Kong without having experience of police work elsewhere; (b) the appointment as Commissioner any officer who is likely to hold the post for longer than seven years.[44]

Pennefather-Evans's ideas[45] were highly influential in the reorganisation of the police that followed, shaping much of architecture and ethos of the police for the next fifty years. But in 1947, when the military administration handed over to a civilian one, the new commissioner was Duncan MacIntosh[46] and the credit for the reorganisation of the force was his.

Rebuilding the police

It was acknowledged in London and in Hong Kong that the post-war police force had to be 'shaped along different lines' from pre-war patterns.[47] They broadly accepted Pennefather-Evans's view that the police needed to recruit a better-educated 'superior type of Chinese' who, with training, could 'produce first class police material'.[48] An extempore Police Training School, set up in 1945 along the lines he suggested, set about the recruitment and training of local Chinese, with a view to increasing the responsibilities of the local Chinese inspectorate, reducing the total non-gazetted European ranks, and abolishing the rank of European sergeant. The School had a record of poor facilities – in 1949, it had been re-located from the Chinese YMCA to what were pre-war food storage godowns, and later to a small refugee camp at Brickhill. The accommodation was described as 'extremely austere with a poor water supply and . . . no amenities in the way of playing fields or covered

Drill Shed'.[49] A more 'magnificently appointed' school was scheduled for construction in 1949/50 (ibid).

Corruption amongst European officers pre-war made the authorities determined not to waste money that could be used to rebuild a better police force on the return of 'undesirable' European officers. Only certain Europeans were to be allowed to return to the force, with the remainder – the 'inefficient' and 'corrupt' 'men of the old type' – being eliminated by transfer to other dependencies 'where the temptations which have been their undoing in Hong Kong do not exist'.[50] If this were to prove impossible, or if it were thought unfair to 'saddle other dependencies with corrupt men', they were to be offered the chance to retire on full pension; those who did not accept but chose to return would have to be kept under close observation (ibid).

New laws on corruption were introduced in 1948, broadly based on existing UK laws designed to make proving the offence easier. These allowed the suspect's bank account to be investigated by the authorities, and the court to receive evidence of the suspect suddenly becoming richer than he should be, or spending unusually large amounts of money.[51] The judge was also relieved of the obligation to warn the jury of the dangers of convicting on the evidence of an accomplice without corroborating material implicating the accused (ibid). Pennefather-Evans had recommended the formation of a special anti-corruption branch, along the lines of Federal Agents in the USA, to ensure the prevention and detection of corruption inside the police. Since 'the corruption of detectives', he says, was 'notorious', to make this body effective against graft within CID or the uniformed police, the new branch would 'not be connected with the Criminal Investigation Department but would work directly under the Commissioner'.[52]

Immediately post-war, however, there were more pressing operational problems. The police force was well below strength with about 321 men, of whom 98 officers were of the rank of inspector and above.[53] For a period of time, before the civilian administration was re-established, policing fell to members of the armed forces. Some British officers had been left medically unfit for duty by their internment, many pre-war police stations had been damaged and, of 38 such stations, only 14 were in sufficient repair to be occupied; 13 temporary stations were established, but policing in the NT remained sparse. Only two out of six of the launches used by the water police were in working order.

Sansom drew up his own plans for the police in the immediate post-war circumstances of 1945.[54] He proposed to create four divisions of the police on Hong Kong island, and four in Kowloon. On the Island, Central Division would encompass Central, Gough Hill and Wanchai; Western Division was to cover West Point, the Upper Levels, Pokfulam and Aberdeen; Eastern Division included Wanchai, Happy Valley, Bay View and Wongneichong; Shaukiwan Division covered Shaukiwan, Quarry Bay, Shek O, Stanley, and Tai Tam Gap. In Kowloon, Yaumatei Division would encompass Yaumatei and Tsim Tsa Tsui; Shamshuipo covered Shamshuipo, Mongkok, Tsuen Wan and Sai Kung; Kowloon Tong included Kowloon Tong and Hung Hom; and the NT Division would cover the area around Tai Po.[55]

Sansom's immediate task, however, as the man responsible for policing under the interim administration, was to train sufficient numbers of local Chinese to take over from the European inspectorate when the civil administration was restored, whilst ensuring that the force contained sufficient numbers of trained officers to supervise the rank and file.[56] However, by the end of 1946, the force still stood at 600 below its authorised strength, the army had to be used to police the border and the outlying islands, and 'the strength, discipline and training of the Force left much to be desired'.[57]

Some of the former Chinese members of the force gradually 'drifted back', as did a few members of the Indian contingent. There was, however, now a question as to whether the British administration would accept all Indians back into the police, the loyalty of some having been brought into question by their support for Indian independence, whilst the collaboration of others with their Japanese occupiers was also thought to have gone above and beyond what might be expected to preserve law and order.

How to handle this issue occupied the minds of civil servants in London and Hong Kong, where the absence of the Indian police contingent had left the force seriously under-strength. They were anxious, on the other hand, to avoid making any commitments to the Indian police officers until Britain's attitude towards them was clarified. The Indian contingent had thus been sent away temporarily on 'recuperative leave' after the War. Internal UK government memos indicate that the authorities were willing to extend this leave until they were convinced that there was no further cause to doubt the loyalty of the Indian recruits.

It was also becoming clear that the question was not merely a local one. During the late 1940s, after partition, both the Indian and Pakistan governments began to discourage their nationals from joining the colonial police or prison services. In 1948, the Hong Kong government had asked the British High Commission in Pakistan to pursue the recruitment of 150 persons for the Hong Kong police force and another 100 for the prison service. Permission from the Pakistan government to recruit had been 'turned down flatly . . . no reasons being given'.[58] As a similar request had been made to recruit Pakistanis for the Aden Air Force, the British wished to discover the reasons behind this refusal and the chances of its being revisited. An internal memo from 1949 addresses the reasons underlying the decision of the Pakistan government to ban further recruitment of Pakistanis into the Hong Kong Police:[59]

> We now learn from a reliable source in the Pakistan Government that the Cabinet's decision was due to their feeling that, in view of the disturbed conditions generally prevalent in Asia, the police in places like Hong Kong

> and Singapore are bound, sooner or later, to come into conflict with the local population. They consider, therefore, that it would not only cause embarrassment but also reflect discredit on the name of Pakistan, if they permitted their nationals to serve in police forces in other Asiatic territories, where they might perhaps be compelled, should commotions arise, to open fire on the local inhabitants. We understand that there is virtually no prospect of the Cabinet's decision being reconsidered in the foreseeable future. Copies of this letter are being sent to Hong Kong and Aden as well as New Delhi (17 February 1949).

Despite similar anti-colonial sentiments being expressed by the Indian government, there were, nevertheless, a considerable number of former Indian police who wished to take up their duties in Hong Kong. Their status as Indian nationals now made this problematic, since police and military posts in the British Empire required post-holders to be British nationals or subjects. Indian independence had altered the status of former Indian recruits to the Hong Kong police, and there was in addition the lingering doubt that Indian recruits might prove disloyal or, worse still, subversive.

Plans to reorganise the Hong Kong Police post-war were delayed by the fact that, by 1945, it had also become 'politically difficult' to recruit men from Northern China and Wei Hai Wei.[60] Migrants from Northern China who 'drifted down to Hong Kong' were thought, in any event, to prefer a career as house servants to joining the police.[61]

Progress in re-establishing law and order was, Young admitted, 'very much slower than had been hoped, especially in Kowloon'.[62] Without the Indian contingent (which, pre-war, had numbered 779, mainly from the Punjab) members of the armed forces were having to undertake police duties. The governor took the view that it was, therefore, important to retain the remaining 300-strong Indian contingent but restrict their role to a 'striking force' consisting of 'riot squads, fixed guards and frontier posts. The intention is to keep Indians from direct contact with the Chinese in policing Hong Kong' (ibid). He also recommended that, whilst 'all former Mohammedans, if fit, should be taken back into the Police Force . . . [the] balance of Indian policemen should be discharged.' A Punjabi-speaking officer was to be sent to India to supervise recruitment and to 'discharge those policemen who are not (repeat not) wanted' (ibid). Internal correspondence makes plain Young's view that 'it is essential that a number should not return, even if fit and willing, in view of their activities during the Japanese war and occupation'.[63] He wished to 'dispense with all Sikhs, except two or three, and only employ Muslims' (ibid). This proposal was welcomed in London, where it was said that 'The India Office and the Indian government would, in fact, welcome an opportunity of preventing Sikhs from 'straying up and down the China coast . . . [since] before the war they had been anxious to control the chain of Indian political agents which linked up with America'.[64]

Sir Mark Young was aware that if the Sikh contingent alone was abolished 'we shall be open to a charge of discrimination' (ibid). To circumvent this issue, he proposed that the entire Indian contingent be abolished and a new, Indian Special Force, established:

> My proposal to abolish the whole contingent will avoid a considerable amount of administrative difficulty involved and invidious distinction between different sects. It will make it possible to select on more satisfactory basis those who are to return to Hong Kong and to avoid retaining undesirable persons . . . (ibid).

Young also proposed to pay both the Indian and Chinese contingents the same rate, as well as provide additional incentives to entice suitable Indian recruits back to Hong Kong.[65] His vision of the role to be played by Indian contingent clearly confined them to three small, semi-military units for use in emergency situations on Hong Kong Island, Kowloon and at the Frontier.

In the interim, some men were recruited from the London Metropolitan Police and other British police forces. Early in 1946, European inspectors who had previously worked in the Shanghai Municipal Police were also recruited on short-term contracts.[66] Questions arose as to whether these men were to be retained, and as to whether other Europeans who had formerly been members of the police force were to be allowed to return.

In 1946, the number of police rose to about 2,401, the majority of whom were rank and file Cantonese officers from Hong Kong or Guangdong, some of whom were former police officers returned from China. A Shantung contingent had also been formed consisting of men from Wei Hai Wei, prized for their supposedly 'superior physique'.[67] The Indian contingent, drawn mainly from the Punjab, which had numbered almost 800 before the war, now stood at only three; just over 200 Europeans held positions as inspectors. By

Table 7.2 Hong Kong Police 1946–47: strength and distribution

	Approved	*Actual number*
Gazetted officers	27	25
European inspectors	277	228
Local inspectors	89	88
Russian inspectors	23	16
Cantonese contingent	1,298	1,507
Northern Chinese contingent	305	193
Indian contingent	325	3
Portuguese (emergency unit)	50	99
Asiatic detectives	243	242
Total	**2,637**	**2,401**

Source: HKPARs 1946–7. See CO129/611.

November 1948, the entire force was headed by three British superintendents, 18 assistant superintendents under a British Commissioner and two Deputy Commissioners.[68] The police force remained under strength at 2,957 officers, of whom 222 were European, 400 from Shantung, 180 from India, and the remainder (2,140) local Cantonese.

Plans to supplement the shortfall in strength with men from the Indian contingent came to a sudden halt when the Indian government placed a ban on recruitment and on the proposed visit to India of a Punjabi-speaking Superintendent of Police. An internal Whitehall memo labelled the ban 'part of Nehru's general nationalist drive' and went on:

> But if (as seems probable) India goes out of the Commonwealth on or before 20th June 1948, it surely fits in very well with out own interests. It seems to me that it would be most embarrassing to Colonial Governments to have a police force which, one fine day, would turn out to be composed of foreign nationals owing allegiance to another, and not necessarily friendly, state . . . I see that . . . the existing Indian Contingent of the HK Police Force is to be discharged, so that – assuming the project of recruiting a new force in India is dropped in the face of the Govt. of India's ban – there will be no problem there. I would suggest that . . . we should consider very seriously before attempting to overcome the Indian ban. It seems much better to leave things as they are . . .[69]

London informed Hong Kong that its proposals to retain an Indian contingent would have to be abandoned.[70] The possibility that other colonial police would also be banned from seeking recruits in India led to the circulation of similar memos to Ceylon, Sarawak, North Borneo, Aden, Gibraltar, Trinidad, Jamaica, Nyasaland, Malaya, and Singapore, where the government requested permission to replace the Sikh members of the police force with Gurkhas, since Gurkhas were 'not be subject to Nehru's ban'.[71] The matter did not stop there, however, for it was quickly realised in Whitehall that Indian nationalism posed problems in relation to all Indian employees in government service throughout the Empire, although the police were in a special position because of their concern with security. In Hong Kong, Sir Mark Young sought clarification as to whether the ban only affected new recruits or extended also to those who had formerly been members of the Hong Kong Police.[72] He continued to seek the return to Hong Kong of former members who were medically fit, not known to be of bad character, or due to retire, and willing to return. The reply from the government of India was that it did not:

> . . . wish to associate themselves in any way with the encouragement of employment of Indians as policemen in countries outside India. They regret, therefore, that they must refuse to be party to any arrangements

> for early return to Hong Kong of former members of Hong Kong Police and cannot in any case agree to sending of officers to India for organising their return.[73]

London hoped that the government of Pakistan might 'adopt a different policy to India' but this was not to prove the case. Though the Hong Kong government had, in June 1947, issued letters to all former police in India asking whether they wished to return to Hong Kong, in January 1948, they were served with notices of retirement on the grounds that the Indian contingent had been abolished.

The political difficulties hindering recruitment of Indian police led Sir Mark Young to advise that 180 local Cantonese and 21 Portuguese police be recruited instead.[74] An increase in police strength had been made more urgent by the fact that the police were due to take over the policing of the border area from the military in April 1947.

The immediate post-war need for police with prior experience and training led the Governor to ask London for the transfer of police from Palestine and other Colonial Police Forces.[75] The contracts of the 28 men secured from the Shanghai police were due to expire, and the issue of whether the Indian police were to be allowed to return had not yet been resolved, leaving a shortfall in force strength (ibid). By 1948, the Governor was arguing for further senior appointments to the police since

> . . . the size of the population, the political situation and the aftermath of war have created problems of a complexity and delicacy unknown before the war, and there appears to be little prospect of any advantageous change in this situation. Hong Kong now bears the burden of all the former Treaty Ports and its importance has increased in the political field. The foundation of the prosperity of the colony is the law and order which it provides, and the maintenance of law and order depends in very large measure upon an efficient Police Force over which gazetted officers exercise a degree of supervision far beyond the superficial control considered adequate before the war. Moreover, if the European Inspectorate is to be replaced by local officers in conformity with general Colonial Policy, it is essential that the ultimate supervision and training of the new local inspectorate should be in the hands of trained and intelligent gazetted officers rather than of European inspectors.[76]

Twenty-eight men were meanwhile sent from Palestine to strengthen the garrison and London promised further assistance in the event of an emergency.[77]

By 1950, the size of the force had risen to 3,899 but remained below strength, despite the recruitment of women police officers. Between 1945 and

Table 7.3 Hong Kong Police: strength and composition 1947–60

	1947	*1949*	*1950*	*1951*	*1952*	*1953*	*1954*	*1955*	*1956*	*1958*	*1959*	*1960*
Gazetted officers	22	29	138	39	38	42	49	57	57	72	79	84
Inspectorate		**357**	**386**	**375**	**436**	**432**	**444**	**478**	**515**	**562**	**599**	**639**
European	191	229	(238)	(226)	(286)	(280)	(282)	(294)				358
Women					1	2	2	1		4	4	
Local	84											281
		128										
Russian	18											
Rank and file			**3,228**	**3,489**		**4,106**		**4,152**	**4,214**	**5,586**	**6,022**	**6,416**
Cantonese	1,557	2,205			450	(3,922)	(3,974)	(4,046)			5,986	
Northern Chinese/ Shantung	289	446	510	552	675	581	565					516
Indians	64	127										
Portuguese	80	57										16
Asiatic detectives	290											
Pakistani					212	(184)	(178)	(168)				139
Women					30	31	69	66		118	174	182
Total	**2,595**	**3,326**	**4,164**	**4,455**	**5,022**	**5,194**	**5,281**	**4,749**	**6,169**	**6,778**	**7,272**	

Source: HKPARs 1947–60.

Gaps in available data produce approximate totals for each year.
(Figure in brackets represents sub-totals of figure in bold type)

1955 the force also lost a number of officers to sickness (such as tuberculosis) and death – 51 officers were killed on duty in these ten years.

By the end of the 1950s, the majority of the police (4,795 out of a total of 7,562) had less than ten years experience in post; 364 out of 7,562 had served 20 years or more, indicating that they had joined the police before the war. Revised terms of service, a new ranking and in-service training scheme were introduced at the start of the 1960s to encourage more junior officers to apply for promotion. Although more locals and more women were being recruited, Pennefather-Evans's vision of a force that incorporated Chinese at the senior levels remained unrealised. By the end of the decade, most locals remained in rank and file positions. Equal opportunities for the locals to rise in the force did not exist, and the number of Europeans increased, consolidating their monopoly on the higher ranks.

However, other aspects of police organisation were improved, largely in line with Pennefather-Evans's proposals. The first part of the 1950s were clearly regarded as an exceptionally pressing time for all the law enforcement agencies struggling, as many still were, with poor resources following the war but under pressure, too, to 'modernise' their services in keeping with the spirit of the times. This modernising push included changing the way in which crime was recorded. In December 1946, the Governor consulted the Chief Justice on the question of crime statistics, following a memorandum written by a Mr A Lonsdale, Crown Counsel.[78] This had pointed out that before the war, statistics were kept both by the police and by the magistrates in Kowloon and Hong Kong Island. The magistrates' returns were compiled annually. They were divided under two main headings: offences against individuals (e.g. against property, against the person) and offences of public nature (against public peace, against Crown and government, trade, public morals, and against the police). The total number of charges and defendants was shown, as was the number of convictions against male and female offenders and number of previous convictions. Separate returns were made for juvenile delinquents. The police returns separated minor and serious offences, dividing each category into 20 specified offences, with a 'residue' of unspecified offences. Their returns, compiled monthly, showed cases charged, persons convicted or discharged, and the value of any stolen property.

These two systems of data collection remained in use after the war. Lonsdale's argument was that, 'in view of the abnormal conditions in the Colony', more frequent recordings of crime were needed. He suggested quarterly returns from both police and magistrates using the same categories of offences but a much more specific breakdown of offences, including detailed figures for armed robbery, possession of arms, break-ins to houses and godowns, and opium cases. He also wished to see the type and extent of punishment imposed recorded, something that, he argued, had not hitherto received attention. Both the police and the magistrates were to be encouraged to draw attention to offences they thought were becoming more prevalent, more difficult to detect or more difficult to convict, and to report on any difficulties encountered in detecting or convicting certain types of crime 'so that any steps necessary to reduce the crime incidence in the Colony can be taken at an early date'.[79] Two offences drew their attention: possession of firearms and armed robbery.

In 1954, a new crime recording form, circulated by the Secretary of State for the Colonies to all British colonies, provided a uniform standard of data collection.[80] This was needed, it was said, in view of the 'importance of statistical records in appraising the efficiency and achievements of the authorities responsible for law and order in Colonial Territories' (ibid). Though some variations between colonies were expected, specimen tables were supplied to provide some sort of uniformity of classification. This classification 'accords with the standard form issued by the United Nations . . . under article 73e of the Charter' (ibid). Two tables were proposed – one for cases reported to and dealt with by the police during the year, the other referring to persons dealt with by the courts. The tables listed six main headings for offences. Colonies were instructed that whilst they need not strictly follow these headings, they should show all 'the more serious offences whose character or frequency make them important' (ibid).

The police saw little point in using the new form and objected that, since no extra staff were to be appointed to collect the data, it imposed an additional administrative burden. Reluctantly, they eventually agreed to use it from 1955 onwards. Crime figures were recorded by three areas: Hong Kong island (Central, Bay View, Eastern, Western); Kowloon (Yaumatei, Sham Shui Po, Kowloon City, and Hung Hom); and the New Territories (Frontier, Tsuen Wan, and Marine). The form (based on a standard UK form) did not require the police to collect the details of the age and sex of those apprehended but it did divide crimes and offences into different categories:

- Class 1 crimes included offences against lawful authority (such as public order, perjury, unlawful society);
- Class 2 crimes were those against public morality (such as rape, indecent assault, other sexual and 'unnatural' offences);
- Class 3 crimes were those against the person (such as murder, manslaughter, attempted murder, sexual assault, abortion, kidnapping, and criminal intimidation);
- Class 4 included offences against property;
- Class 5 included offences against the penal code; and
- Class 6 referred to offences against local laws.

The category 'miscellaneous offences' was extremely wide-ranging, and included common assault, drugs, dangerous goods, drunk and disorderly behaviour, firecrackers, gambling, hawking, obstruction, vagrancy, spitting, night noises, prostitution, suicide, keeping an opium divan, and smoking opium or heroin.

The Criminal Records Bureau was reorganised in 1956, and a new 'modus operandi' was also introduced to improve detection.[81] In 1959, the system of recording crime was altered yet again, and a new distinction made between 'serious crime' and 'true crime'. Serious crime was recorded separately whilst 'true crime' applied to cases where the facts showed conclusively that an offence had been committed. This category did not include reports of crimes deemed too trivial, false, or where no case in law was disclosed.[82]

Several specialist branches had been developed, including a Commercial Crime Unit, and Anti-Corruption Unit, an Emergency Unit and a Special Branch. The first female police inspector was appointed in 1949, a police laboratory with forensic expertise was opened and a police surgeon appointed; CID, Traffic and Statistical Branches were all mechanised; a single fingerprint index was established, and a better system of communications was to follow, accompanied by the design and procurement of four armoured cars.[83]

In a foretaste of things to come, the assistance of the press was also harnessed by the police. In 1955/6, meetings were held between the police and the editors of the colony's newspapers to discuss 'problems of mutual interest' designed to 'foster a closer understanding between the Police and the press'.[84] In 1956, the police observed that 'The satisfactory and tranquil state of law and order which has prevailed throughout the Colony for some time past . . . has been the subject of favourable comment in the World Press' (ibid).

To keep track of 'undesirable persons' and maintain this level of orderliness, more police – especially more beat officers – and improved police records were thought to be required. The Modus Operandi section set up in October 1955 collated information about crime and criminals. Another new system of recording crime was also introduced, excluding many items included in previous years, thus reducing the level of recorded crime.

The police also began to compose 'crime maps' of the territory, showing the location of particular types of crime by area; these highlighted Kowloon as a major area of criminal activity. These maps noted premises of particular interest to the police on a street index; a newspaper cuttings index and triad index were also established.[85] What the police referred to as the 'weight and complexity' of policing Kowloon meant that by the end of 1956 a plan was devised whereby Kowloon would become a separate new district in April 1957; the NT and Marine were to form another new district.[86]

Other 'modernising' changes were introduced. The professionalisation of the force was evident in the 'keen appreciation' within the inspectorate of 'the status conferred by professional qualifications', leading to support for a proposed staff college for higher training. The year 1951 also saw the introduction, for example, of the 999 system for emergency calls, as well as the recruitment of the first ten female constables. By the mid-1950s, the government was proudly advertising the success of the 999 system and the work of the police forensic science laboratory. The detection rate (54.7 per cent) was the highest since 1945 and in many respects the force began to feel that it had re-established itself after the war.

This view was strengthened when, during his visit in 1951, the Secretary of State for the Colonies praised the police force for its handling of a difficult situation, whilst the government complimented the police for the role they played in 'restoring harmony'. Official reports speak of a 'high degree of public confidence in the police' and paint a picture of a community-friendly force organising cinema shows in outlying schools and villages' (ibid), conveying urgent cases of illness to hospitals, delivering and collecting mail, and putting on performances by the Police Band.[87] Pictures chosen for the Hong Kong Yearbook 1952 contrast the 'smartness and efficiency' of the police with the old-style policeman of 1910, and show a smiling policeman holding hands with small children as he helps them cross the road.[88] Under the caption 'the raised hand of welcome' the 1955 Yearbook depicts a penetration patrol being greeted by waving villagers as they arrive at a New Territories village.[89] This was said to show how much the public appreciated the police, how willing members of the public were to seek help and advice from the police on a variety of problems, and how active they were in the fight against crime – members of the public arrested over 1,000 offenders in 1952.

There was also said to be no shortage of locals lining up to join the police. By 1952, 500 more police had been recruited, and courses were available for members of the rank and file 'who have displayed potential fitness for promotion to inspector'.[90] However, the recruitment of women remained low and none occupied high ranks (the number of inspectors stayed in single figures until the 1960s, the majority remaining at constable level, though some did rise to station sergeant). Mostly, they were intended to deal with prostitution and 'social hygiene', and were lauded as 'patient, efficient and courageous'.[91] They were provided with a two-month long training regime, compared to the 14 weeks provided for their male counterparts. (Following the 1956 riots, these periods of training were extended to four months for women and six months for men). For another decade or so, women were generally confined to traffic duties (they were trained to ride scooters), school crossing patrols, crowd control and anything to do with women and children. For male officers, training included unarmed combat and weapons training, as well as team sports to build 'the team spirit so essential in police work' (ibid).

Most policing was still carried out on foot, though some radio-equipped patrol cars were used on patrol 24 hours a day to deal, among other things, with 999 calls. A radio network linked the Border and NT to Headquarters and two main command operations rooms used in times of emergency. This radio-telephony link was supposed to enable sub-stations to keep in touch with each other and with Headquarters. A new, six-storey Headquarters building in Wanchai housed the main administration, Special Branch, CID, Immigration, Accounts, armoury and Central Radio Control Room.

By the mid-1950s, the police force in Hong Kong was already double the strength it had been ten years earlier, and had more experienced officers among its ranks (in 1947, almost half the force had less than two years' experience).

Policing, politics, social and public order

In numerous ways, therefore, the recommendations of the Pennefather-Evans report shaped the nature of policing in 'modern' Hong Kong. But many policing issues, while appearing relatively trivial and straightforward, were made more complex by virtue of wider social and geopolitical concerns. For example, unlicensed hawkers were viewed as a perennial problem. In the Hong Kong Report of the Committee on Hawking, 1947, Megarry (Acting Secretary of Chinese Affairs) lamented the problem they caused in terms of obstructing traffic and pedestrians, endangering public health, competing with shopkeepers and market stall holders, attracting criminal activity in the form of criminal gangs extracting 'protection money', and attracting large numbers of destitute people to Hong Kong 'who might be the receivers of stolen goods'.[92] As Lock points out, almost all unlicensed hawkers were blackmailed by triad members for protection money (Lock 1993: 31), while they also found themselves the subject of routine raids by the police Hawker Squad and Urban Services. Lock cites one incident from 1946 in which an unlicensed hawker (Huang Yongxiang) died during a police raid on unlicensed hawkers in Mong Kok, provoking a riot in which crowds gathered to throw stones and bricks at he police; though the riot was suppressed, it erupted once more at Huang's funeral (ibid).[93]

As Lock argues, many local people regarded the problem of unlicensed hawkers as a social welfare, rather than a criminal or public order, issue (ibid). He cites arguments in the local press that the Hong Kong government should follow the 'world trend' and be 'responsive to public opinion', which in this case sympathised with the hawkers as being amongst the poorest section of Hong Kong society (ibid). The spirit of these discussions was that of a population which wished to see the government become more concerned with its livelihood and grievances, something which – given the '1946 outlook' – London was also thought to favour:

> [I]n all Colonial territories, the first aims of the administration must be the well-being and education of the native inhabitants; their standards of life and health; and their preparation for self-government without delay.[94]

However, in the case of Hong Kong, such issues became complicated by both the influx of refugees from the Mainland and the rise of a communist government there. On the one hand, democracy, decolonisation and self-determination were seen, Lock says, as the best way of preventing the spread of communism. However, as the refugees began to arrive in large numbers towards the end of the 1940s, the Hong Kong government began to adopt a more cautious policy of retrenchment.

Between them, Grantham (Governor from 1947 to 1957) and business interests effectively stymied Young's plan for self-government. Suspicions about the political loyalty of the local police resurfaced in the wake of the communist victory in China; the government, enforcing the Immigration Control Ordinance 1949, imposed immigration controls. This department, headed by R.A.D. Forrest (senior police magistrate) also handled the issuance of identity cards to all persons entering Hong Kong.

By 1950, it was said that immigrants from China were crossing the border at a rate of 500 per day, resulting in the need for further reorganisation of immigration controls. Some years later, in 1958, the Immigration (Control and Offences) Ordinance started the process of establishing a separate Immigration Department and service, placing immigration under the control of a deputy immigration officer; the police were, however, still to control border crossings. At the same time, it was suggested that one way of deterring migrants from bringing their families with them to Hong Kong would be to raise the price of rice, making it impossible for a family to survive on the low wages paid to migrant labour (Pennefather-Evans had, by contrast, wished to encourage the migration of family units rather than individuals, on the grounds that it would be less socially disruptive).

The '1946 outlook' thus gave way to a 'Cold War outlook'. Hong Kong became part of the 'Bamboo Curtain', a significant geopolitical point in the West's fight against Communism in the region and, most immediately, in Korea. The Police Force Ordinance, introduced in 1948, put in place many of Pennefather-Evans's proposals but here, too, the '1946 outlook' was reined in by Cold War *realpolitik*. As a result, although the Cantonese contingent of the force did enjoy more opportunities for promotion than in the pre-war police force, senior posts and major decision-making remained in the hands of a European officer elite whose political loyalty the authorities did not doubt.

Notes

1 HK Yearbook 1951: 1.
2 HK Yearbook 1951: 1.
3 HK Yearbook 1953: 9.
4 N.G. Fisher, Chief Education Officer for Manchester.
5 Pennefather-Evans Preliminary Report on the Hong Kong Police 11 November 1941, CO129/588.
6 Pennefather-Evans 1943, Interim Report.
7 Sansom to Civil Affairs Headquarters 27 December 1945, CO129/611.
8 Pennefather-Evans Preliminary Report on the Hong Kong Police 11 November 1941, CO 129/588.

9 Colonial Correspondence, Preliminary Report, CO129/588: 16.
10 Pennefather-Evans Preliminary Report: No 220 of 1946.
11 Pennefather-Evans Interim Report: 3.
12 Rank and file members of the police were said to be especially aggrieved for being 'rapped over the knuckles' by European officers for carrying out their duty towards influential members of the public who then complained to those in high authority. Pennefather-Evans saw this as undermining relations between the ranks and insisted the superior officers must support the actions of their subordinates 'whoever is affected by them' (Interim Report: 32).
13 Interim Report: 28.
14 Interim Report: 12.
15 HK Yearbook 1957: 232.
16 Interim Report: 14.
17 Interim Report: 15.
18 Interim Report: Appendix A: 5.
19 Interim Report: 25.
20 Interim Report: 16, 17.
21 Interim Report: 23.
22 Interim Report: 36.
23 Interim Report: 2.
24 Interim Report: 5.
25 Interim Report: 5.
26 Interim Report: Appendix A: 7.
27 Interim Report: 6.
28 Interim Report: 9.
29 Interim Report: 10.
30 Interim Report: 30.
31 Interim Report: 39.
32 Interim Report: 18.
33 Interim Report: Appendix A.
34 Although they lacked any official connection with the police, were not paid by the government and had no police powers, the Guards were referred to in police reports, which describe them as 'highly reliable people', 'an important factor in the maintenance of law and order . . . especially along the frontier with China' (where they helped detect and arrest illegal immigrants) and commended them for doing 'specially good work' (HKPAR 1946/7: 8, 17). In the aftermath of the war, in the late 1940s, they were the only form of day-to-day policing in many parts of the NT, and were permitted by the administration to carry firearms; these the villagers either bought themselves or had supplied on free loan by the police – the 1946/7 Police Annual Report refers to 300 rifles having been loaned in this way to villagers, along with ammunition and obsolete battle dress (HKPAR 1946/7: 8).
35 Cited in HKPAR 1946/7.
36 HKPAR 1946/7: 3. Partly, this sensitivity was due to long experience of villagers resisting the imposition of foreign laws and regulations, something that was to characterise the entire history of policing in the NT. Later police reports speak of the strength of NT customs and carry anecdotes of village elders investigating matters such as the pregnancy of a Hakka widow, of a serious clash caused by a boy caught stealing fish from a pond in a neighbouring village, and so on (HKPAR 1956: 17, 86). Partly, however, policing the NT needed greater tact because of the political volatility of the border region, an area penetrated by Communist supporters and, between 1946 and 1949, the site of serious armed engagements with Communist troops. After the erection of a border between Hong Kong and China

in 1950, the NT were also the corridor by which millions of refugees made their way into Hong Kong. As in the urban areas, policing these refugees involved a good deal of 'peacekeeping' and service activities, providing assistance in the aftermath of the fires, floods and landslides that devastated squatter areas such as Shek Kip Mei in 1953.

37 The SCA was the department formerly known as the Registrar Generals' Department, with the Registrar as Protector of the Chinese.
38 1946/7 HKPAR: 7.
39 Hayes 1996. Hayes notes that the District Watch gradually dwindled in size and was disbanded in 1969, though its members continued to do some work within the reorganised SCA – by then the Home Affairs Department.
40 See previous chapters on pre-war Hong Kong. See also colonial memoranda CO1030/1446.
41 Interim Report: 40.
42 Interim Report: 40.
43 Interim Report: 41.
44 Sansom to Civil Affairs Headquarters 27 December 1945, CO129/611.
45 Ie those contained both in his Preliminary Report of 1941 and his Interim Report on the Hong Kong Police, 1 October 1943.
46 MacIntosh is remembered in Hong Kong for, among other things, giving his name to the string of lookout towers strung along the border with China.
47 HK Yearbook 1946: 75.
48 Interim Report: 4.
49 HKPAR 1948/9: 13.
50 Civil Affairs Hong Kong to Colonial Office, London January 1946, CO129/607.
51 HK Yearbook 1948: 94.
52 Interim Report: 28.
53 See HK Police War Diary: 265.
54 Sansom to Civil Affairs Headquarters, 24 December 1945, CO129/611.
55 Sansom to Headquarters, Civil Affairs Secretariat, 24 December 1945; Hong Kong Annual Review 1949: K22.
56 Cf Pennefather-Evans Interim Report: 4.
57 HK Yearbook 1946: 74.
58 Heppel, British High Commission, Karachi to Rumboldt, Political Department, London CO129/607.
59 Heppel, Office of the High Commission, Karachi to Gibson, Political Department, London CO129/607.
60 Sir Mark Young to Secretary of State for the Colonies 7 June 1945, CO129/607.
61 HKPAR 1946/7: 19.
62 Young to Secretary of State for the Colonies 19 June 1946, CO129/607.
63 Young to Secretary of State for the Colonies 19 September 1945, CO129/607.
64 Internal memo 29 November 1946, CO129/607.
65 Young to George Hall, 10 September 1946, CO129/607.
66 Memo from HM Treasury to Mr Bayle 26 November 1946.
67 HK Yearbook 1946: 73.
68 HKPAR 1946–7 CO129/611.
69 Internal Memo 14 March 1947, CO 129/607.
70 Secretary of State for the Colonies to Hong Kong 9 March 1947, CO129/607.
71 Internal memo 15 March 1947.
72 Young to Secretary of State for the Colonies 11 March 1947.
73 India Office to Governor of Hong Kong 10 May 1947, CO129/607.
74 Young to Secretary of State for the Colonies 27 January 1947, CO129/607.

75 Governor of HK to Secretary of State for the Colonies 27 November 1947, CO 129/608.
76 Young to Creech-Jones, Secretary of State for the Colonies 15 October 1948, CO129/611.
77 Secretary of the State for the Colonies to Hong Kong 3 November 1948.
78 HKRS 41–1–1315 17 December 1946.
79 Lonsdale memorandum 8 October 1946, HKRS 41–1–1315.
80 Savingram Hong Kong to Secretary of State for the Colonies 30 June 1956, in response to communication of 14 October 1954, HKRS 41–1–8200.
81 HK Yearbook 1956: 189.
82 HKPAR 1960/1: 18.
83 For further details see HK Yearbook 1950.
84 HKPAR 1955/6: 68.
85 Ibid.
86 HKPAR 1956: 2.
87 HK Yearbook 1954: 162.
88 HK Yearbook 1952: 34.
89 HK Yearbook 1952: 133.
90 HK Yearbook 1956: 188.
91 HKPAR 1956: 22.
92 Megarry cited in Lock 1993: 29.
93 See also *South China Morning Post* 29 October 1946.
94 Frost 1945: 320 cited in Lock 1993: 32.

Chapter 8

Crime and courts 1945–1960

In the immediate aftermath of the Japanese Occupation, looting of properties left empty or abandoned during the war was common. In November 1946 EXCO was complaining that 'crime in Hong Kong is getting too serious'.[1] In a replay of nineteenth-century discourses, it was held that 'desperate characters' were coming to Hong Kong from China because:

> (1) in Hong Kong the punishment is far too lenient; (2) imprisonment for a certain period is nothing to this class of people, they are being fed and housed comfortably. This is only a holiday or rest time to them; (3) carrying fire-arms or dangerous weapons without licence is very common amongst this class of people. If they are found they can well afford to pay a fine and get off. To minimise the present crime the following suggestion is worthy of consideration:
>
> (1) To take more drastic action by amending the present law with more severe punishment;
> (2) Unless corporal punishment in introduced mere confinement in a prison house or heavy fine will bring no good result;
> (3) Possession of fire-arms or dangerous weapons be subject to death penalty. Every one who commits crime with such weapons has good intention to kill against any resistance.
>
> Dealing with Chinese criminals should be entirely different from dealing with foreigners. Experience in the past history of China has proved that the old ways of dealing with criminals had very good result; but the present civilisation in prohibiting such actions has brought more sufferings and difficulties to the villagers. Punishment with bodily pain to this class of people for return of their actions is the only way to bring them to their senses. Corporal punishment as a minimum penalty and death sentence as a maximum will surely reduce the existing crimes in the Colony.[2]

One memorandum from EXCO, containing the following handwritten note, also indicates that the government still looked to the Chinese elite for hints about how to deal with the 'coolie class':

> The returns indicate, to my mind, a need to increase the penalties against persons possessing arms and convicted of armed robbery. I attach notes left with me recently by an elderly Chinese minister who argued the necessity for the Government to take sterner measures. It is indicative, I submit, of the attitude of the educated Chinese.[3]

A second handwritten note simply stated:

> What about reviving the 'stocks' for this type of case? They used to have a serviceable set at or near No. 7 Police Station. An armed guard would be necessary as otherwise someone would steal the stocks for firewood (ibid).

Such unreconstructed attitudes had no justification in the official crime reports. Indeed, the police report for 1946 described the increase in crime that year as 'less than might have been expected'.[4] Between May and December 1946, serious recorded crime stood at 25 per cent above the pre-war 'norm', at a total of 9,908 cases, mainly of robbery, burglary and store breaking (ibid). There were a few cases of assault with intent to rob (20), an increase in piracy, and the appearance of a 'new type of crime' as proprietors of hotels, restaurants and theatres received demands for money accompanied by threats of bombing. Twelve explosions actually took place, and one gangster blew himself up with his bomb. According to official reports, the gang responsible operated on both sides of the border, which made detection difficult (ibid). The increased use of firearms in the course of crime left two police officers dead and eight wounded.

The 'crime problem' was seen locally as having much to do with Hong Kong's 'peculiar geographical position and its land and sea frontier with turbulent and unsettled China'.[5] Chinese criminals as well as subversives could freely pass over the border between Hong Kong and China, posing what were termed 'political and other problems' for the police (ibid). There were a number of border incidents after 1950 (when the British recognised the Central People's Government) and Hong Kong shipping found itself fired on from time to time by Chinese patrols. Firearms, said to have already been widespread before the war, were now increasingly used in domestic crime. In January 1947, a 'railbus' from Fanling to Kowloon was held up at gunpoint. One passenger, a Mr Collins, who was on the bus with his wife and children, was shot and killed when he went to the driver's assistance. The incident provoked comment not only because Collins (whose father was Deputy China Secretary in Ceylon) had been killed, but because none of the Chinese passengers on the bus had supported Collins when he tackled the robbers:

had they supported him, 'the robbers would not have succeeded in their object and he would not have died'.[6] It was estimated that 5 to 10 per cent of those admitted to the casualty wards of government hospitals had been wounded by armed robbers, leading to demands that the bill for those wounded be waived. The government was, however, divided on the issue.

The official figures for serious crime showed a slight fall between 1947 and 1948 (13,704 and 11,008 respectively) with falls in robbery (375 to 227), burglary and larceny (1,651 to 1,198), and an overall fall in prosecutions for serious crime (5,233 compared to 6,303 in 1947). However, some concern was expressed in EXCO about the penalty for armed robbery with violence during which the accuracy of the figures for armed robbery was questioned, there having been some change in the manner in which these statistics were maintained. Miscellaneous offences rose from 34,783 in 1947 to 84,377, forming the vast majority of total crimes recorded (98,032).[7] By 1949, total reported crime stood at 197,443, of which 9,331 constituted serious crime; miscellaneous offences numbered 110,159.

By 1950, these figures had risen. Total reported crime reached 264,204 but of these, 102,245 disclosed no offence after investigation; recorded crime reached 161,959 of which 12,462 (7.7 per cent) consisted of serious crime.

Offences against public morality continued to be a target of policing. Police reports described the Hong Kong population as a 'moral community' made immoral only by overcrowding and the disproportionate number of males to females in the colony.[8] The war, having broken up families and led to the rise in refugees, had 'lowered moral standards' and produced a 'crime wave'. In these changed times, 'notwithstanding the wishful thinking of those whose standards go back to the days of normal serenity, the abnormal is now the normal'.[9]

Crime in the early 1950s was interpreted by officials as a side-effect of the chaotic circumstances of Hong Kong's overcrowding and economic distress, brought about by the 'problem of people'.[10] Large numbers of petty crimes were committed by poor people scraping a living by whatever means they could find. Officials clearly understood that the refugees' usual source of livelihood – working the land – was closed to them, Hong Kong's rural areas already being home to more farmers than they could support.[11] The refugees thus looked to the city – to Kowloon and Hong Kong – to make a living. The dominant impression given by the crime figures is of Hong Kong streets crowded with poor people whose everyday activities gave rise to litter, nuisance, disorder, and a myriad petty offences. Many of these were petty thefts of food and clothing, of 'bits and pieces of no great value to their owners but of considerable value to the thief who sees in them the price of his next bowl of rice'.[12] Pickpocketing and snatching were, for example, twice as common on the streets of Kowloon, where most of the squatters were located, than in Hong Kong.

According to Strickland, Acting Attorney General, 'these immigrants commit crimes very shortly after they have entered the colony'.[13] The police also believed that many of the refugees were criminals, gangsters, and 'potential criminals of all kinds'. They were 'difficult to absorb'.[14] Official reports for the early years of the decade paint a picture of police resources being taxed:

> . . . for only one week in 1950 were the police free from a state of extraordinary precautions or operations. The upheavals caused by the civil war and change of government in China brought to Hong Kong as a place of refuge a large number of unscrupulous men supplied with arms and well-versed in their use. The change of government also created frontier problems amongst which was the gradual disintegration of co-operation between the Chinese and British police on duty at the frontier. This in its turn made the apprehension of criminals more difficult.[15]

In the midst of all this, however, serious crime fell in 1950 and the police clear-up rate (44.7 per cent) was 'the highest in the last five years'.[16] Official figures for 1951 show that the magistrates' courts dealt with 20 per cent more cases than in 1950 (201,377 and 167,976 respectively). The police, echoing Strickland, held that many of those convicted had arrived from China only days or weeks before they committed an offence.[17]

The crowded urban areas experienced the major problems of housing, unemployment, poverty and crime. For the authorities, both the squatter villages and the resettlement estates posed problems of impenetrability. Their inhabitants were able to organise themselves 'for protection against the various authorities'[18] including the forces of law and order; 'sympathy and co-operation with Government were withdrawn' and 'the whole situation was opened up for the insidious political influences that were never far from the squatter settlements'.[19] The resettlement programme, when it came in 1954, offered at least some prospect of penetration for by assuming direct responsibility, the government itself entered the field of resettlement and the lives of the resettled.

The sense that many of the less serious crimes of the era were committed out of economic necessity is evident in official reports of the time. The Hong Kong Yearbook for 1955 stated quite plainly that the government saw over-population and economic distress as the main causes of what it saw as the high crime figures for the year.[20] In 1955, the population was said to be rising at a rate of 1,360 people per week, and by 1956 it was estimated to stand at 2,535,000, and increase of 135,000 on 1955. Most of this increase was due to the large number of births registered in Hong Kong and to a brief relaxation in immigration controls which had allowed 56,000 more persons into the colony from China. The majority were still living in squatter huts, on roof-tops and in poverty. It was this hardship that the criminal justice institutions saw as the main cause of crime amongst juveniles. A Social Welfare Office, instigated by the government in 1947, concentrated on youth work, though this was outside the prison and aimed mainly at non-delinquent children. Its duties included visiting adopted and trafficked children (*mui tsai*) and the provision of leisure activities and youth clubs for 'street arabs'.[21] The opening of a Girls' Approved School, run by the Salvation Army and financed by the government, was lauded as a 'great advance', as was the appointment of a psychiatrist in the Medical Department to whom child and juvenile welfare workers 'could turn for advice'.[22] But as the Chief Justice was to state in his speech at the opening of the legal year in 1950, juvenile delinquency was not seen as a serious problem. This was despite the fact that the official crime figures showed that roughly 29 per cent (45,208 of 154,503) of convictions for that year were of juveniles.[23]

By March 1951, Hong Kong was estimated to have 300,000 squatters living in approximately 47,000 huts on the hillsides or in makeshift rooftop dwellings; by 1953, almost one-eighth of the population lived in such flimsy housing. Most were very poor, some were completely destitute, others thought to be quite well-to-do; not all were refugees, some being from old established Hong Kong families forced into squatter areas by the severe shortage of housing. According to the official statistics, in the midst of this poverty, overcrowding and dislocation – and the influx of a disproportionately high number of young people into the colony – serious crime briefly fell. In 1950, there were 402 convictions for serious crime compared to just 219 in 1951 and 108 in 1952. A fall in armed robberies was explained locally as due to the introduction of the death penalty for that offence.[24] In the mid-1950s, it began to rise again, with the increase in serious crime in 1954 being blamed on the increasing number of persons who had unlawfully returned to Hong Kong after deportation.

Table 8.1 Overall reported crime 1950–60

	Total reported	*Serious crime*	*Miscellaneous offences*	*No offence disclosed*	*Total recorded crime*
1950	264,204				
1951	289,377	13,903	197,705	77,763	211,614
1952	314,438	18,306	169,777		126,355
1953	416,024	19,053	174,956	173,837	242,187
1954	468,426	27,876	248,561	191,989	276,437
1955	422,811	23,265	241,453	158,093	264,718
1956	428,948	23,427	203,605	184,235	
1957	396,414	18,992	225,045	152,377	
1958	372,381	15,662	179,207	173,831	
1959	406,795	14,970	177,910	211,222	
1960	353,672	13,599	99,778	239,277	

Source: Hong Kong Yearbooks 1950–60. Excludes deportation offences and membership of triads.

Table 8.2 Crime in pre-war and post-war Hong Kong 1938–60, absolute numbers

	Reported crime	*Murder*	*Serious assault*	*Rape*	*Robbery*	*Burglary*	*Theft*
1938	60,943			data missing			
1939	47,844	37				220	11,915
1946/7	48,537	26				682	11,602
1947/8	98,032	17	21		318	1,432	12,272
1948/9	141,745	23			226	658	7,817
1950	153,608	19			236	251	6,634
1950/1	279,576	30	3		262	634	6,403
1951/2	329,980	3		data missing			
1952/3	436,549	31	134	7	149	915	10,651
1953/4	463,855	29	212	3	105	919	11,962
1954/5	487,019	34	340	2	109	951	12,825
1955/6	428,948	28	315	4	154	850	13,597
1956/7	369,191	36	410	1	128	618	14,516
1957/8	403,427	19	364	5	126	349	11,190
1958/9	407,395	28	436	2	95	429	9,848
1959/60	406,795	25	447	3	72	463	9,987

Source: HKPARs: 1946–1959/60; format reflects style of Hong Kong Police Reports in 1950s.

As these figures indicate, the vast majority of reported offences were against property, rather than the person. In most years, offences against the person numbered less than 600, compared with fifteen to twenty thousand for all offences against property, the highest number being for larcenies of various types (e.g. larceny from the person – such as pickpocketing and snatching – and from ships and wharves, of bicycles, from dwellings, and from vehicles). The number of serious assaults rose slightly over the decade, but numbers remained low (rising from 192 in 1953 to just over 400 in 1956), as did the number of reported murders (under 40 cases in most years). Each year saw a small number of assaults by throwing corrosive liquids (acid) at the victim, and a small number of rapes and indecent assault were reported to the police, their numbers kept artificially low by a reluctance to report such offences. (Though the new resettlement blocks were depicted as happy and safe communities, the communal bathing blocks were often perilous places for women and girls.)

Despite the government's talk of high crime levels, the figures for 1955 showed a slight fall in overall crime – the 422,811 reported crimes were down by 45,615 on 1954. Of these, 158,093 disclosed no criminal offence; there was also a fall in serious recorded crimes such as murder, burglary, housebreaking, serious assault and larceny from the person. Armed robbery had, however, increased.[25]

In 1956, the total number of reports made to the police again dropped (from 422,811 to 410,427) and of these reports, 184,235 were recorded as disclosing no crime, 22,587 were recorded as serious crimes, compared to 23,265 in 1955.[26] The most common type of recorded crime was common assault, the vast majority of which the police regarded as trivial domestic disputes not requiring prosecution (for example, the police prosecuted only 736 out of 13,782 such cases in 1956, 562 out of 12,266 in 197 and 555 out of 12,896 in 1958). But serious crime was thought to have reached record levels following the prohibitions on deporting known criminals to China or Taiwan. Deportation has become increasingly difficult by the mid-1950s resulting, the police argued, in a large number of serious crimes being committed by triad members left stranded in Hong Kong.[27]

Nevertheless, 1957 saw another fall in recorded serious crime (from 22,587 in 1956 to 18,992 in 1957). The total number of reports made to the police showed a similar reduction: 396,414 reports were received, 14,013 fewer than in the previous year; of these, 152,377 disclosed no criminal offence.[28] The police now claimed that the fall in serious crime was due to the success of their preventative measures against 'criminal secret societies' (triads) coupled with the effectiveness of the more comprehensive 1956 Police Supervision Ordinance. This enabled them to keep under surveillance triad members and others whom the authorities were unable to deport from the colony; in the first year of its use, 2,384 persons were placed under police supervision and by 1957, a total of 5,280 people had been placed under such supervision by the courts. Some of these were political agitators; others were persistent offenders (77 per cent of those convicted in the colony had a prior record), and drug traffickers linked to international drug syndicates. In short, the police supervision orders and the Emergency (Detention Orders) Regulations enabled the police to detain, deport or control anyone whose release into the community was deemed 'contrary to the public interest'.[29] Despite a rise in the number of persons arrested for breach of deportation orders, the fall in serious crime recorded in 1957 was said to be due to the detention and deportation of major triad figures and police disruption of triad activities following the 1956 riots.

Their new powers were said by the police to be of 'great value' against triads – they had earlier argued that their inability to deport or detain 'the worst of the Colony's alien criminals' had led to the upward trend in serious crime in the first half of the decade. According to the police, many of the crimes committed in the colony were committed by triad members: 'Such persons are usually to be found amongst the baser criminal elements engaged in gambling, prostitution activities, dealings in narcotic drugs, extortion and other forms of vice.[30] It was their alleged involvement in the 1956 riots, however, which caused the police to intensify operations against triad societies in September and October 1957, during which time 'positive action was taken against 1,040 known members of these societies' (ibid). The crackdown, it was claimed, created confusion within the societies, causing many active members to leave the colony to avoid arrest; a total of 1,887 people were arrested for membership of unlawful societies (ibid).

Though serious recorded crime was pushed upward by the riots of 1956, it now began a decline that continued until the end of the decade. Reports for 1960 note four cases of manslaughter, 26 murders (mostly the result of quarrels or disputes, though one had a political background) and five attempted murders. Serious assaults (551) included four cases of throwing corrosive fluid at the victim. Offences against public morality rose slightly – from 172 in 1958 to 180 in 1960, and there were 148 recorded cases of indecent assault on a female, one recorded case of rape, 19 cases of under-age sex (four with girls under 13) and four cases of trafficking in women and girls.[31]

Typically, throughout the decade the vast majority of serious recorded crime comprised offences against property rather than the person – these too dropped towards the end of the decade, from 13,999 cases in 1958, to 12,697 cases in 1959 and 12,418 in 1960. Many of robberies and house breakings occurred in the new multi-storey housing blocks. These were high-density residential developments on land previously occupied by farmers and squatters, for which the police had adopted methods of semi-rural policing.[32] The density and complexity of the new estates made it easier, the police argued, for criminals and drug addicts to elude detection; a spate of breakings at office blocks in the Central district in the mid-1960s also defeated the normal beat police. Though older methods now gave way to 'concentrated urban police coverage' (ibid), beat policing remained at the core of what the Hong Kong Police did.

Minor crime and nuisances

As before the war, the vast number of offences reported in the official statistics represented miscellaneous and minor crimes. Social hygiene and concern with 'insanitary conditions' provided justification for new laws against spitting, the control of vagrancy and prostitution, and the clearance of thousands of squatters. The squatter control operations, directed by Health Department officials and Urban Services, required the police to maintain law and order in the face of the anger of those forcibly removed. One of worst incidents of the post-war period occurred in Wanchai, where squatters were cleared from shacks and rooftops. This was described as 'perhaps the first time that such a measure had been either necessary or executed'.[33] An earlier clearance operation in 1947/8 at Kowloon City resulted in an attack upon the police by a hostile mob. Warning shots were fired, six squatters and eight police officers were injured and tear gas used to disperse the crowd.[34]

The post-war years established the use of police to assist in such clearances. The police became, in effect, an adjunct of development, ensuring that squatters, rooftop dwellers and those whose homes stood in the path of new developments were cleared. No one was allowed to stand in the way of Hong Kong's modernising new order.

Mendicants and vagrants were another group regarded by the police as 'undiscovered or potential lawbreakers'. Many of the destitute, beggars and streetsleepers who were arrested were sent to the Social Welfare Department or, where possible, voluntarily repatriated. Adults were taken to court and referred to the probation service.[35] Dealing with 'legal vagrants of the Chinese race' proved especially problematic for the police, however, due to 'an ancient anomaly' in law, which the police sought to have revised.[36] In 1960, a Vagrancy (Amendment) Ordinance accordingly gave the courts new powers to increase the prison sentence passed on vagrants and mendicants convicted of a third offence.

As before the war, hawkers were a constant source of irritation to the police. In 1948/49 hawking constituted half of all recorded non-serious offences (51,628). In 1955, unable to stop hawking altogether, the police adopted a policy of containment and control, setting aside certain areas where hawkers could trade; this resulted in less unlicensed hawking, but offences by hawkers creating an obstruction increased markedly.[37] The figures for the years between 1950 and 1960 show a rise in arrests for hawking, peaking in 1953/4 (though given the extent of police corruption, it is likely that much illegal hawking was unofficially 'tolerated'). However, hawker cases saw a dramatic decline at the end of the decade – from 59,589 in 1958 to 42,528 in 1959 and 9,064 in 1960. This stemmed from a new method of controlling hawkers, begun in 1960, which removed the need for large-scale arrests for minor infringements of the law.[38] This said, by the mid-1960s, the number of hawker arrests was once again rising – statistics for 1963 show, for example, that 23,162 reported hawking offences and over 57,000 cases

Table 8.3 Principal miscellaneous (non-serious) offences 1946–60

Year	*Total*	*Common assault*	*Hawking*	*Nuisance*	*Drugs*	*Prostitution*
1946/7	34,783					
1947/8	84,377					
1948/9	103,596	3,208	51,628	3,898	2,890	277
1949/50	104,044	5,310	47,689	7,914	2,270	482
1950/1	178,320	7,314	83,132	20,507	3,342	1,560
1951/2		8,081	87,232	15,287	1,707	
1952/3	181,077	10,307	98,536	12,240	1,553	
1953/4	266,082	13,425	147,165	24,076	6,235	1,302
1954/5	269,779	13,648	135,116	37,761	10,010	1,593
1955/6	234,838	13,782	93,377	34,668	17,910	2,950
1956/7	191,756	12,266	56,201	33,039	18,334	2,523
1957/8	231,696	12,868	60,604	7,060	17,264	1,820
1958/9	214,229	12,896	59,620	6,261	14,238	1,805
1959/60	206,514	12,707	46,781	7,006	10,771	1,582

Source: HKPARs: 1946–60.

of obstruction by peddlers and holders of licensed and unlicensed food stalls.

Other 'street nuisances' included touts, shoeshine boys, beggars, street-sleepers, and drug peddlers. The police described the majority of the boys engaged as 'shoeblacks' as 'decent youngsters in hard circumstances concerned only with earning a daily living', though they seem to have annoyed tourists who declined their services, and thus become a target for police activity.[39] As in the UK during the same period, prostitution also became a target for police action aimed at clearing the streets of women whose activities might offend the 'respectable' citizens of the city. In the mid-1950s, arrests for soliciting or loitering for the purposes of prostitution far outnumbered arrests for keeping a brothel, dance hall, unlicensed massage parlour or other vice establishment. In 1958, for example 2,099 persons were arrested for loitering or soliciting, compared with 94 arrested for keeping a brothel, unlicensed massage house or lodging house for prostitutes.[40] The police were regarded as the bulwark against the descent into immorality, crime and lawlessness. Though the colony might be 'minute' its population meant that it ranked 'with many of the world's principal cities'.[41] The density of the population was seen as one of the 'conducive elements that usually result in the corruption of morals and conduct' (ibid). This said, arrest for prostitution also declined towards the end of the 1950s, from 1,792 recorded cases in 1958 to 690 in 1960/1.[42]

The vast majority of offences reported were minor in nature, and the increase in overall crime was due mainly to a rise in petty larcenies, often of articles that were of little or no value, officially blamed on the 'economic conditions and unemployment'.[43] In 1954, for example, of the 248,561 miscellaneous offences reported, most (221,995) resulted in a prosecution, including a number of people arrested for obtaining free meals under false pretences following the squatter fires. Overall, almost 60 per cent of the offences recorded in 1954 resulted in an arrest and prosecution. Of the 15,441 persons arrested, 358 (just over 2 per cent) were juveniles.[44] Though 1951 figures show juveniles alone accounting for 54,372 offences – mainly minor larceny – by 1952 this had fallen to 34,920 and 29,068 in 1953.[45] Given that it is unlikely, in the conditions of the time, that fewer juveniles were committing the offence, the explanation for this drop seems to lie with a shift in policing policy – it is clear, for example, that the police increasingly came to regard such minor offences as a product of poverty and hardship rather than 'real' criminality.

However, by the mid-1950s policing priorities were shifting. The police had identified Kowloon as the place where 75 per cent of the colony's major crime was committed, and home to an even higher proportion of its persistent offenders, racketeers, and gangsters.[46] By 1958, it was observed that 71.5 per cent of all juvenile crime in Hong Kong was also committed in Kowloon, compared with 23.5 per cent in Hong Kong and 5 per cent in the

NT.[47] These observations produced a shift in the deployment of police and, by 1964, Kowloon would be sub-divided in two police districts.

In 1956, the ratio of police to population on Hong Kong Island stood at 1 to every 678 persons; in Kowloon, it was one per 721; and in the NT it was one per every 416 persons. (Hong Kong's population was estimated at 1,000,000, Kowloon's at 1,040,000 and the NT at 500,000.) In Hong Kong there were 46 police per square mile, 3.5 per square mile in the NT and 85 per square mile in Kowloon. But by 1957, Kowloon already had more inspectors and chief inspectors than the other districts, as well as the highest concentration of women police (30 in all, out of a total of 62 force-wide, rising to about 350 by 1964). By 1965, Kowloon would have 2,301 officers, more than any other police district (Hong Kong had 1,755, the NT 1,439, and Marine 1,071). And by 1969, the number of police deployed in Kowloon would double its 1956 level, whereas in Hong Kong and the NT, the numbers increased less than one and half times over the same period. By the mid-1960s most reported cases of serious crime were said to originate in Mongkok and Wong Tai Sin.[48]

The identification of Kowloon as a 'criminal area' led not only to increased policing, but also to intensified policing. More officers were drafted into the area and more experienced officers were charged with specialised policing tasks. The building of resettlement estates to re-house squatters presented police with new challenges, as they sought to adapt their methods to the policing of multi-storey, densely populated high rise blocks. In the 1961 census, the population of the area between Lo Fu Ngam and Lei Yue Mun in the Northeast area of Kowloon was estimated at 332,000, but by the end of the year it stood at 622,000. Beat constables on normal duties were thought to

Table 8.4 Shift in the distribution of force establishment 1956–66

Year	*Police strength (excluding civilian staff)*		
	Hong Kong Island	*Kowloon*	*NT*
1956/7	1,489	1,455	1,222
1957/8	1,516	1,569	1,483
1958/9	1,566	1,626	1,573
1959/60	1,632	1,744	1,711
1960/1	1,670	1,894	1,866
1961/2	1,730	2,074	1,867
1962/3	1,748	2,150	1,978
1963/4	1,762	2,154	1,303
1964/5	1,775	2,301	1,439
1965/6	1,859	2,522	1,751 [1]

Source: HKPARs 1956/7–1965/6.

[1] In 1965 the NT and Marine were divided into two districts. The figure given from 1965 is for the NT alone.

be unable to cover these densely populated areas and special squads were deployed instead.[49]

Despite these concerns about crime and the immense increase in population, between 1956 and 1960, serious recorded crime in Hong Kong actually fell and overall crime decreased. However, much crime went unreported simply because police officers were 'on the take' from criminal enterprises. They were, in any event, themselves committing criminal offences.

The courts

In the immediate post-war period, the only courts that operated in Hong Kong were the military courts, presided over by a barrister or solicitor attached to the Legal Branch of the administration.[50]

As elsewhere, the end of the war saw a number of measures taken in Hong Kong to deal with war crimes committed by members of the Japanese forces, as well as locals who had collaborated with them. Ordinance No. 7 of 1946 dealt with Chinese collaborators and set up a procedure for the surrender to the Chinese authorities of persons sheltering in Hong Kong who had collaborated with the Japanese.[51] Special Courts were set up in March 1946 in Hong Kong, under the presidency of a Scottish lawyer (later succeeded by a British barrister from India) to try Japanese personnel accused of war crimes in any part of what was known as the South East Asia Command Theatre. The men charged with handling these prosecutions were Canadian, Australian and Indian lawyers, whilst the officer in charge of the investigations was a Chinese man qualified in English law.

Out of the 10,000 Japanese who surrendered to the British, 239 remained in detention as war crime suspects. Others were brought to Hong Kong for trial from elsewhere in the region. The accused were defended by Japanese lawyers assisted in procedural matters by British advisors. At a trial in Mui Wo in 1946, 12 Japanese soldiers were convicted of atrocities against villagers on Lantau; three were sentenced to hang. According to a newspaper report of the time, they had beaten, tortured and killed a number of villagers, tying them to the verandah at the Japanese headquarters on the island, inflicting torture, burning houses, and beheading some by sword; one woman was said to have been beaten with a wooden rod for about 20 minutes, until she vomited blood.[52]

By the end of 1946, a total of 50 Japanese had been tried in Hong Kong, nine of whom were sentenced to death, nine to ten years or more in prison and 26 to shorter terms of imprisonment. Six were acquitted; some remained in detention awaiting trial.[53] However, a number of Kempeitai in the region were said to have escaped trial due to the sudden death of a Colonel Cyril Dalrymple Wild, a Japanese speaker and investigator of war crimes in South East Asia. His flight from Kai Tak mysteriously crashed in September 1946, destroying key prosecution documents (Lamont-Brown 1998: 148).

According to official reports, ordinary crime increased after the war, and for a time in 1945 and 1946, it was dealt with by summary courts presided over by a barrister or solicitor sitting alone. Review of all convictions fell to the chief Civil Affairs officer, who was also required to confirm all sentences of death, as well as those amounting to more than two years' imprisonment or a fine exceeding HK $2,000. With the return of the civil government, the sentences passed by the summary courts were validated by ordinance and their powers of review and confirmation were vested in the Chief Justice.

Almost all records of the proceedings of these summary courts have been lost. Records for the Supreme Court in 1946 show that 315 persons were tried on indictment, compared to 426 in 1938; 255 were convicted, compared to 347 in 1938.[54] Records for the re-established Magistrates Courts in Kowloon and Hong Kong Island also indicate a reduction in the overall number of criminal cases compared with 1938, though these figures are difficult to interpret since there are only rough estimates of the population level in Hong Kong in the immediate post-war period and, as we noted above, there was a continuing influx of people into the territory.

By 1948, the mainstream courts were said to be back in full swing, though there was no ceremony to mark the opening of the legal year.[55] Something of

Table 8.5 Criminal cases, Hong Kong and Kowloon Magistrates Courts, 1938 and 1946

	HK	*Kowloon*	*Total May–Dec 1946*	*Total 1938*
Prosecutions against adults and juveniles	25,518	10,730	36,248	72,752
Convictions, adults and juveniles	N/A	N/A	29,284	67,600
Adults				
Fined	9,394	5,755	15,149	47,182
Imprisoned for fine default	721	346	1,067	9,317
Imprisoned without option	1,766	2,023	3,789	5,886
Bound over	1,319	105	1,424	2,606
Cautioned or discharged	5,632	1,805	7,437	7,888
Fined and allowed time to pay	15	10	25	967
Juveniles				
Fined	589	30	619	1,544
Sent to reformatory	99	66	165	292
Committed to approved institution	15	70	85	16
Bound over	45	45	90	313
Placed on probation	45	33	78	23
Cautioned or discharged	2,579	101	2,680	508
Whipped	55	63	118	190

Source: HK Yearbook 1946: 72. Figures for the NT show that 749 prosecutions were brought by the District Officer but no details are given.

the '1946 outlook' was reflected in the appointment of women jurors, first used in 1947, but women remained excluded from the ranks of the judiciary and magistracy. Another new idea designed to relieve the workload of the magistrates was the deployment of a Justices Court consisting of two unofficial Justices of the Peace (one of whom was to be a solicitor) sitting jointly. In addition to the three Magistrates' Courts on Hong Kong Island and two in Kowloon, District Officers in the NT exercised the powers of a magistrate at Yuen Long and Tai Po. By the early 1950s, there were four magistrates' courts in operation on Hong Kong Island, three in Kowloon and a Justices of the Peace court in the NT, presided over by the District Commissioner and District Officer. By 1954, both Kowloon and Hong Kong had four magistracies each; the magisterial duties hitherto carried out by District Officers in the NT were also handed over to the lower judiciary, a magistracy being established at Tai Po and Pingshan; in 1955, a fifth court was added to the Hong Kong magistracy to deal with what was seen as an increased workload. In addition, a juvenile court also operated in the mornings and a JP court in the afternoons in both the Hong Kong and Kowloon Magistracies. The number of cases heard before the magistrates subsequently showed a brief increase – in 1953, just over 266,800 cases were prosecuted in the magistrates' courts and in 1954 this rose to 276,577. However, in 1955, the number fell again to about 200,600. A new District Court came into being in February 1953, with one branch in the existing Supreme Court Building in Central and another in the Kowloon Magistracy. This took some of the work out of the Supreme Court and created a new tier of judiciary in the colony. The new District Court in Kowloon dealt with more cases than its Hong Kong counterpart.

As in the nineteenth century, most of Hong Kong people gained their experience of the criminal justice system at the lower level, i.e. in the magistrates' courts. The small numbers of persons processed by the courts immediately after the war had, by 1948, given way to substantial increases for both adult and juvenile accused (see Table 8.2).

As these figures indicate, the fine was the favoured penalty handed down by the lower courts, followed by imprisonment for adult offenders; a substantial number of juvenile offenders were subjected to corporal punishment.

Prosecutions and convictions for serious crime also fell in the Supreme Court, with only 68 convictions in 1954 compared to 89 in 1953, mostly for crimes of violence such as murder, robbery wounding, and manslaughter.

The majority of offences coming into the criminal justice system were heard by the magistrates. They were overwhelmingly minor in nature (hawking without a licence, obstruction breaches of traffic regulations etc). Many involved juveniles (29,068 in 1953; 39,700 in 1954; 34,584 in 1955) and though juveniles committed few serious crimes, their minor offending was regarded by the Chief Justice as one of the colony's major problems.[56] However, as the decade progressed, magistrates courts saw a falling off in respect of juvenile

Table 8.6 Cases heard in the lower courts 1947 and 1948

	Hong Kong	*Kowloon*	*Total 1948*	*Total 1947*
Prosecutions: adults and juveniles	77,889	55,112	133,001	103,847
Convictions: adults and juveniles	73,174	47,719	120,893	82,221
Adults				
Fined	37,425	26,173	63,598	46,808
Imprisoned/Fine default	9,980	9,791	19,771	9,266
Imprisoned without option	2,688	2,665	5,353	5,765
Bound over	587	536	1,123	1,114
Cautioned/Discharged	3,175	5,466	8,641	6,998
Fined and allowed time to pay	–	425	425	304
Expelled from colony	934	846	1,780	1,755
Juveniles				
Fined	19,914	2,591	22,505	7,317
Sent to reformatory	24	33	57	131
Committed to approved institution	57	13	70	106
Bound over	229	179	408	571
Placed on probation	–	21	21	70
Cautioned/Discharged	564	1,708	2,272	18,514
Whipped	234	4,297	4,531	1,307
Imprisoned	424	53	477	94

Source: HK Yearbook 1948 (magistrates at Tai Po and Yuen Long decided another 2,634 criminal cases).

Table 8.7 Prosecutions and convictions before the Magistrates' Courts 1954

	Hong Kong	*Kowloon*	*Total*
Total no of charges	69,026	55,607	124,633
Prosecutions against adults and juveniles	106,044	170,533	276,577
Convictions against adults and juveniles	84,017	93,095	177,112
Prosecutions against juveniles only	17,368	38,258	55,626
Convictions against juveniles only	16,614	23,086	39,700
Summonses issued	17,895	23,279	41,174

Source: HK Yearbook 1954: 158.

Table 8.8 Prosecutions and convictions before the Magistrates' Courts 1955

	Hong Kong	*Kowloon*	*NT*	*Total*
Total no of charges	79,006	60,800	2,300	142,106
Prosecutions against adults and juveniles	96,689	118,342	5,237	220,268
Convictions against adults and juveniles	93,379	117,110	4,721	215,210
Prosecutions against juveniles only	9,403	25,393	16	34,812
Convictions against juveniles only	9,193	25,383	8	34,584
Summonses issued	28,696	27,518	2,283	58,497

Source: HK Yearbook 1955: 138.

Table 8.9 Prosecutions and convictions before the Magistrates' Courts 1956

	Hong Kong	*Kowloon*	*NT*	*Total*
Total no of charges	72,627	67,531	3,911	134,069
Total defendants: adults and juveniles	84,044	99,794	8,063	191,902
Convictions: adults and juveniles	78,618	96,986	7,192	182,706
Total adult defendants	78,050	86,739	8,030	172,819
Total adults convicted	72,670	83,853	7,189	163,712
Total juvenile defendants	5,994	13,055	33	19,082
Total juveniles convicted	5,948	13,043	30	19,021
Summonses issued	37,295	29,359	3,770	70,424

Source: HK Yearbook 1956: 181

Table 8.10 Prosecutions and convictions before the Magistrates' Courts 1957

	Hong Kong	*Kowloon*	*NT*	*Total*
Total no of charges	56,051	62,341	7,285	125,677
Total defendants: adults and juveniles	61,753	115,802	8,748	186,303
Total convicted: adults and juveniles	57,702	111,422	7,987	177,111
Total adult defendants	58,617	102,546	8,713	169,876
Total adults convicted	54,633	98,218	7,956	160,807
Total juvenile defendants	3,136	13,256	35	16,427
Total juveniles convicted	3,069	13,204	31	16,304
Summonses issued	28,634	47,007	43,94	80,035

Source: HK Yearbook 1957: 227.

trials and convictions – in 1951, for example, 54,372 juveniles were convicted by these courts, compared to 34,920 in 1952 and 29,068 in 1953.[57] Figures for 1956 also showed a sudden and dramatic fall in the number of juveniles brought before the magistrates' courts from 34,812 in 1955 to 19,082 in 1956, possibly due to the introduction of alternative methods of dealing with youth crime.[58] There seems, however, to have also been a more general change in policing as regards other minor offences. For example, hawking without a licence and obstruction also fell from 71,985 in 1955 to 44,038 in 1956.

It was the magistrates on Hong Kong Island who experienced an increase in their workload – their counterparts in Kowloon actually saw their workload fall. By the late 1950s, however, this situation had reversed: Kowloon Magistracy became the busier of the two main magistrates' courts. Chances of acquittal had not improved: in 1952, for example, the Hong Kong magistrates tried 140 offenders of whom 100 were convicted; the Kowloon Branch tried 83, of whom 78 were convicted.[59] This picture remained similar at District Court level – in 1955, for example, of the 157 tried before the District Court in Kowloon, 110 were convicted; in Hong Kong, 104 of the 135 persons tried were convicted.[60]

Deportation and detention without trial

In addition to the normal operation of the criminal justice system, since the 1920s the Hong Kong government had developed an administrative system for dealing with 'undesirables' within the colony. This ran in tandem with the judicial sentencing of convicts to banishment and deportation. The late 1940s saw increased use of the government's power under the Deportation of Aliens Ordinance 1935 and its amendment in 1948, to banish and deport undesirable aliens from the colony. Banishment or deportation could be recommended by a magistrate for a person who had not been resident in the colony for a year preceding the committal of an offence. The order could be made in addition to, or in lieu of, sentence. If the defendant claimed to be a British subject, or disputed the time s/he had been resident in the colony, the claim was to be investigated by the Secretary for Chinese Affairs. Deported prisoners were held at Victoria Jail immediately prior to their departure, which was overseen by a Police Deportation Officer in the Deportation Office at Central Police Station. British subjects could also be deported under the Deportation (British Subjects) Ordinance. A series of emergency regulations and shifts in policy in 1949, 1950 and 1956 were also designed to increase the government's powers of deportation.

Deportation took two main forms ('political cases' appear to have been dealt with by a third procedure). Summary deportation, first used in the 1914–18 war as an emergency measure, was seen as an exceptional procedure in which the decision to deport was made by the Governor in Council on the advice of the Attorney General after an application had been made by the police; there was no judicial or independent oversight of the process. The 'normal' procedure was known as 'long procedure deportation' in which the evidence for deportation was considered by Administrative Officers in the Secretariat for Chinese Affairs.[61] However, official figures showed that, since the end of the Second World War, summary deportations had outstripped 'long procedure' deportations by three to one in most years.

The exile to China of political prisoners and criminals had, as we have seen, been part of Hong Kong's criminal justice practice since the early days of the colony. From the 1930s onwards, there were several examples of co-operation on such matters between the Hong Kong and Chinese authorities. The Sino–Japanese conflict had, in effect, put an end to this, especially when Japanese forces took control of Canton. Immediately after the war, co-operation with the Nationalist regime resumed and it remained possible to deport Hong Kong's 'undesirables' to China. With the victory of the communists in 1949, the situation altered. Between 1949 and the mid-1950s, foreign powers (including Britain) were working out their relationship with the new regime in China. During this period, it was also still possible – though perhaps more difficult – to return detainees to China, despite the erection of a physical barrier at the frontier. From the mid-1950s onwards,

Table 8.11 Total of deportation orders made 1946–60

Year	*Number of deportations*
1946	153
1947	1,072
1948	3,210
1949	3,532
1950	3,562
1951	2,946
1952	2,682
1953	2,262
1954	1,743
1955	1,090
1956	141
1957	302
1958	330
1959	278
1960	159
Total	**23,462**

Source: Internal Memo 24 January 1961, J.R. Oliver, Chairman, Committee of Review of Deportation Process to Colonial Secretary.

Table 8.12 Persons held in detention 1953–60

Year	*Number of persons detained in Chatham Road Centre [1]*				*Number of persons put up for confidential banishment [2]*	*Number of orders rescinded*
	Male	*Female [3]*	*Juvenile [3]*	*Riots [4]*		
1953	6,116	151	81	–	364	–
1954	11,843	151	17	–	128	–
1955	5,975	196	9	–	457	2,565
1956	1,404	63	16	1,234	250	1,643
1957	2,945	86	39	–	453	725
1958	1,034	–	–	–	313	566
1959	594	–	–	–	190	516
1960	304	–	–	–	149	321
Total	**30,215**	**647**	**162**	**1,234**	**2,304**	**6,336**

Source: Internal Memo 24 January 1961, J.R. Oliver, Chairman, Committee of Review of Deportation Process to Colonial Secretary.

[1] Chatham Road Centre was the centre at which those awaiting a deportation order were detained while their case was investigated. It also held those under deportation orders whose deportation to China or Taiwan was impossible.

[2] 'Confidential banishment' appears to refer to 'political' deportees whose deportation was subject to a separate, confidential procedure.

[3] The juveniles and females shown in the figures were said to be nearly all illegal immigrants.

[4] Figures for 1956 refer to those detained in lieu of deportation as a result of the 1956 riots.

however, relations between Britain and China meant that deportation ceased to be an option – those detained for criminal and political activities in Hong Kong had thus to remain in detention in the colony unless and until China – or Taiwan – signalled a willingness to allow them to return. The effective cessation of deportation was to come at a time when Hong Kong was faced with new problems of political subversion and agitation by both Nationalist and Communist sympathisers who fled to the colony following Mao's victory in 1949. For the next two decades, Hong Kong criminal justice was to be inextricably linked to the colony's geopolitical position and the 'realpolitik' of the Cold War era. As we shall see, the practice of deporting and detaining people without trial was to remain part of the government's repertoire until the 1970s.

Notes

1 EXCO Secretariat File 1/2/2406/46 1 November 1946.
2 Notes in EXCO Secretariat file 1/2/2406/46 1 November 1946.
3 EXCO Secretariat File 1/2/2406/46 1 November 1946.
4 HK Yearbook 1946: 75.
5 HK Yearbook 1948: 105.
6 HKRS 41–1–2869 Crime 1947.
7 HKPAR 1947/8: 10.
8 HKPAR 1946/7: 1.
9 Ibid; see also HKPAR 1956/7: 29.
10 HK Yearbook 1956: 1.
11 HK Yearbook 1956: 8.
12 HKPAR 1955/6: 51.
13 Hong Kong Hansard 20 October 1948: 286 cited in Lock 1993: 66.
14 Police Report 1956/7: 2 cited in Lock 1993: 114.
15 HK Yearbook 1950: 73.
16 HK Yearbook 1950: 74.
17 HK Yearbook 1951: 88.
18 HK Yearbook 1956: 14.
19 HK Yearbook 1956: 20.
20 HK Yearbook 1955: 141.
21 HK Report 1948: 89.
22 HK Yearbook 1948: 90.
23 HK Yearbook 1950: 71.
24 HK Yearbook 1951: 88.
25 HK Yearbook 1955: 141.
26 HKPAR 1955/56: 82; 1956/7: 41.
27 HKPAR 1955/56: 44.
28 HK Yearbook 1957: 233.
29 HKPAR 1956/7: 5.
30 HK Yearbook 1957: 233.
31 HKPAR 1960/1.
32 HKPAR 1963/4: 1.
33 HKPAR 1948/9: 29.
34 HKPAR 1947/8: 16.

35 HKPAR 1960/1: 26.
36 HKPAR 1948/9: 29. The 'anomaly' effectively allowed Chinese persons to claim a kind of 'sanctuary' in the Walled City on the basis that this remained under Mainland jurisdiction.
37 HKPAR 1955/56: 41.
38 HKPAR 1960/1: 26.
39 HKPAR 1956/7: 15.
40 HKPAR 1958/9: 27. Accounting for a similar crackdown on prostitution in the UK at this time, Smart argues that prostitutes presented a challenge to the government's attempts to re-establish a moral order in the aftermath of the upheavals of war, which had disrupted the dominant norms of wedlock and childbearing in British society. See Smart 1995.
41 HKPAR 1955/6: 1.
42 HKPAR 1960/1: 27.
43 HK Yearbook 1953: 127.
44 HK Yearbook 1954: 161.
45 HK Yearbook 1953: 123.
46 HKPAR 1956: 29.
47 HKPAR 1958/9: 25.
48 Maurice Heenan, Attorney General, quoted in *South China Morning Post* 14 January 1966.
49 HKPAR 1963/4: 2.
50 HK Yearbook 1946: 67.
51 HK Yearbook 1946: 67.
52 *South China Morning Post* 26. April, 1946; HKRS 256-4-1.
53 HK Yearbook 1946: 73.
54 HK Yearbook 1946: 67.
55 HK Yearbook 1948: 96.
56 HK Yearbook 1955: 136.
57 HK Yearbook 1952: 120; HK Yearbook 1953: 129.
58 HK Yearbook 1956: 181.
59 HK Yearbook 1952: 123.
60 HK Yearbook 1955: 136.
61 Internal Memo 24 January 1961, J.R. Oliver, Chairman, Committee of Review of Deportation Process to Colonial Secretary.

Chapter 9

The 'red menace': post-war instabilities

As before the war, labour issues remained a trigger for disputes in the colony. The police were called upon to control disturbances wherever these escalated into public order incidents. In 1948 the Hong Kong government introduced a new Trade Unions and Trades Disputes Ordinance, designed to take the heat out of labour disputes; one of the first arbitrations under the Ordinance took place between Dairy Farm Ice and Cold Storage Company and its employees in 1948. The Labour Affairs office established before the war, in 1938, also resumed responsibility for settling disputes, but the politicisation of the labour unions had, by the 1950s, become an obstacle to this kind of negotiated settlement. The left-wing unions in particular were thought by government to be under orders from the Central People's Government (CPG) to turn labour disputes into anti-colonial as well as anti-capitalist issues.

The Hong Kong government countered their influence by arguing that their activities had more to do with the CPG than with the welfare of the worker. According to the government, the workers had begun to realise this and turn away from the 'unsuccessful violence' and 'ideological campaigning' of the right-wing and left-wing unions towards 'honest unionism'.[1]

Throughout the decade, however, the Federation of Trade Unions (FTU) continued to provide welfare facilities for large numbers of non-affiliated workers. Hong Kong continued to suffer from a series of labour disputes and stoppages throughout the 1950s, some of which saw the police deployed against pickets.[2] In 1952, the police were also kept busy by various labour disputes that required their 'constant surveillance', including a sit-in at a factory which lasted 42 weeks.[3]

By the mid-1950s, the trade union movement had become highly politicised, hijacked by the two principal political groupings in Hong Kong, the Federation of Trade Unions (FTU) affiliated to the Communist cause and the Trade Union Council (TUC) affiliated to the Nationalists. As industrialisation took off, especially in new towns such as Tsuen Wan, labour disputes reflected this political factionalism as much as grassroots grievances. According to the government's own analysis, infighting between these groups was the biggest obstacle to the development of effective trade unionism in the colony.[4]

While the number of disputes remained relatively stable, the potential for a strike to develop into a major political conflict increased with this politicisation, especially since the left-wing unions were thought to have the better resources, organisation and backing. The government accused these unions of using intimidation and threats to gain the support of workers whose relatives still lived in China, though support was also fostered by the provision of welfare, food and facilities to workers, even if they were not union members (ibid).

The Labour Affairs office thus had limited success. Instigated by London, where the Colonial Office was increasingly anxious about its ability to stave off pressure from the International Labour Organisation in Geneva, it provided information about labour in the colony, often as part of a wider strategy to forestall the application of ILO conventions to Hong Kong. Many Chinese workers worked seven days a week for nine hours a day; in the textile industry, a 10 to 12-hour day was the norm. These hours and conditions prompted concern amongst liberal Europeans, who raised the issue in Hong Kong and, *via* their friends, in London.

In addition to the potential for labour disputes to spark conflict, a new flashpoint emerged in the early 1950s. The post-war period witnessed numerous disasters in squatter areas occupied mainly by refugees. These did not, however, initially give rise to any official co-ordinated attempt to house or otherwise integrate the refugees into Hong Kong society more generally. Government was far removed from the people. It was also late to follow post-war UK thinking on the responsibilities of the state towards the people in its colonial possessions. As Hayes notes, Hong Kong in the 1950s still resembled its pre-war days, with its 'racial divisions and social cliques' which made life 'seem friendly and sociable but resulted in making it narrow and restricted' (Hayes 1996: 11).

Like the vibrations on a spider's web, however, a number of incidents in the early post-war era should have alerted the government to the potential for relatively small domestic incidents to spark off wider disorder. One of the first post-war incidents to ruffle political sensibilities was a 1947 order, by the Hong Kong government, to squatters in the Kowloon Walled City to quit the area in which they had taken up residence within two weeks. The government announced that it wished to clear the area (described as a 'cesspool of iniquity, with heroin divans, brothels and everything unsavoury')[5] to make way for a park. But the integration of the Kowloon Walled City into urban Hong Kong had long been a thorny issue, fraught with political sensitivities. Approximately 25,000 squatters 'resisted their dispossession', arguing that the British had no rights over the area (Smart 2006: 60). A Chinese magistrate declared the eviction orders invalid because, under the Treaty of Peking, the Kowloon Walled City was Chinese territory. Organised resistance came from the Kowloon Walled City Residents Association. This petitioned the Nationalist government in China for help and, when the evictions were announced in November 1947, diplomatic protests quickly followed from China. When the evictions started in January 1948, what was described as the 'Battle of the Kowloon Walled City' commenced. The residents clashed violently with the 150 police and Public Works officials sent to clear the area (Lock 1993: 54). The police met 'an enraged mob and a shower of bricks and stones and had to use tear gas bombs and open fire' (Smart 2006: 61). One squatter was killed, dozens injured and 14 police officers were hurt (ibid).

In China, the incident was interpreted as yet another example of the unfair treatment of the Hong Kong Chinese by the British colonial administration. As Lock points out, the eviction orders to the squatters came at a time when Hong Kong faced a severe housing shortage as well as a huge influx of destitute people. Many in Hong Kong were thus critical of the government's push to evict the squatters, seeing it as a sign of a government that cared little for people's livelihoods. In the post-war world, there was also a sense that the rights accorded to Britain over the Walled City under the 'unequal treaties' were illegitimate (Lock 1993: 52, 56).

The evictions sparked off anti-British demonstrations in Beijing, Shanghai, and Canton, where a crowd attacked targets in the foreign concession of Shamian, such as on the British Consulate, the Dutch Consulate and the headquarters of Butterfield-Swire and Jardine Matheson (Lock 1993: 56). Diplomatic manoeuvres apparently prevented the matter from escalating any further, and in Hong Kong the government decided to 'leave the area to its own devices' (Smart 2006: 61). China sent a comfort mission to tend to the needs of the Kowloon Walled City residents,[6] whilst British policy was to 'soft-pedal' the issue 'in the interests of good neighbourly relations'; the plan to convert the Kowloon Walled City into an open space was forgotten (Endacott 1978: 315). The police maintained their patrols of the Walled City but 'did not care to prosecute malefactors in the courts, lest the controversial issue of jurisdiction be raised by the defence. We preferred to deport – an executive and not a judicial act – those who committed offences in the City'.[7] What was not forgotten, however, were the activities of the Kowloon Walled City Association. These remained a focus of Special Branch into the 1960s, when a government survey of the Walled City sparked a hostile response from residents.[8] The resistance put by the Kowloon Walled City residents was also not forgotten. In the discussions about cutting fire lanes through Shek Kip Mei, for example, caution was urged because its residents were seen as 'well-organised and capable of putting up very vigorous resistance', not only having their own fire brigade but also their own police force and legal advisers (Smart 2006: 68).

The next major confrontation occurred on 1 March 1952, in the wake of a fire in the squatter area of Tung Tau. The Tung Tau fire, in November 1951, came at a time when diplomatic relations between Britain and Communist China had yet to be established. After the fire, the government refused to allow its displaced victims to rebuild on the site, insisting that they be relocated to other, approved sites. The victims refused this offer, as the cost of rebuilding to plan on the approved sites was too high for them (Lock 1993: 168). According to the government, an already difficult situation was made worse when the Canton press misrepresented its actions, prompting some organisations in Canton to call for a 'comfort mission' to travel to Hong Kong to aid the victims and urge the government to accede to their demands. The 'comfort mission' would carry out its own investigations as to what was required, and interview those affected.

The authorities in Hong Kong made it clear that they were 'not prepared in the circumstances to admit such a mission in the colony, although all facilities would continue to be given for distributing any frontier relief funds which might be sent from Canton'.[9] Despite this, the Canton mission went ahead, though the organisers undertook not to make any political speeches (Lock 1993: 169). On this basis, the Hong Kong authorities agreed to allow its delegates into the colony.

In the colony itself, left-wing organisations made preparations to greet the mission when it arrived on 1 March. On the day itself, a reception party was sent to Lo Wu. It was, however, stopped by the police and persuaded to return to Fanling (Lock 1993: 169). Later, its members were informed that the arrival of the Canton mission was postponed. According to the government's version of what happened next:

> . . . considerable crowds which had assembled at the Kowloon Railway Station were not given this information until the afternoon, when a welcoming party which had earlier left to meet the mission at the border returned to Hong Kong. The crowds at first began to disperse peaceably but a series of incidents subsequently occurred and developed into large-scale rioting, possibly owing to the false rumours being spread that the mission had in fact arrived but was being held up in the border area . . . Order was restored after about 2 hours and casualties amounted to no more than 30, mostly with minor injuries. One Chinese demonstrator, however, died some weeks later.[10]

Police initially reported the crowd of twenty to thirty thousand at Tsimshatsui as 'gay, cheerful and good-tempered' (Lock 1993: 169). Even when, at 3 pm, it was informed that the mission had been postponed, the crowd dispersed peacefully.

According to the local Chinese press, however, this mood changed when, at Jordan Road, a police vehicle ran into the crowd, injuring a young girl. Shouting started and the conflict soon spread 'like wildfire along the route of Jordan and Nathan Road'.[11] Armed police later used tear gas against the crowd and, when a lone police officer was surrounded by the crowd, he opened fire and riot broke out (ibid). The rioters then attacked Europeans, burned police cars and army trucks, and stoned Mongkok police station; the rioting lasted for about two hours, during which time around 30 people were injured (12 civilians and two police officers) (ibid).

The *South China Sunday Post Herald* of Sunday 2 March 1952 carried the following report of the disturbances:

> Serious rioting occurred in Kowloon yesterday when a disorderly mob clashed with Police forces in Nathan Road shortly after 4 pm. A Police squad car was overturned and burnt at the corner of Austin Road, where a Police motorcycle was also thrown down and set afire. A big Army lorry was stoned and partly damaged also by fire. Twelve civilians, including three Europeans, were treated for injuries and three were detained in hospital. Two European Police inspectors were also injured, one still being in hospital. The extent of the injuries suffered by military personnel is unknown. Mongkok Police station was stoned by an attacking crowd about an hour later and a defending Police officer opened fire with a riot gun peppering three Chinese . . . The disturbance arose first at the rear of a ragged procession of some twenty to thirty thousand Communist sympathisers who were returning up Nathan Road from Kowloon Station and Salisbury Road where they had waited without avail for some two hours to greet an expected 'comfort mission' from canton which failed to materialise. It spread up the long column of hitherto happy, singing demonstrators, turning them into a raging uncontrollable mob which the Police only dispersed with great difficulty in the direction of Mongkok, where they finally broke up under tear gas shelling by riot squads at about 5.45 pm. Under a hundred arrests were made in the course of the cleaning up operations' (*Post Herald* 2 March 1952).

The *Hong Kong Standard* reported that 'thousands of Communist-led workers and students' had marched along Nathan Road, attacking policemen, smashing property, and engaging in a 'roaring riot'.[12]

The incident that sparked off the riot occurred by the Alhambra Theatre. There was no damage to shops but a police car, driven by an Inspector Cowie, was attacked at Jordan Road, overturned and set on fire, as was a police motor cycle. Other police cars and army trucks also came under fire from a shower of missiles thrown by the crowd, including chunks of cement. According to the *Post Herald*, both the attacks and the 'ammunition' had been pre-prepared. A European taking pictures was jeered by the crowd and had his camera taken from him:

> . . . he sought shelter in a staircase but was dragged out and beaten up savagely. Jumping on a bus, he was again dragged out and maltreated. When an ambulance arrived, the crowd dragged the driver out of the ambulance and thrust two Communist flags into his hands, telling him to wave them. Police intervention drove them off (ibid).

A crowd who had been watching an afternoon show at the Liberty Theatre, Nathan Road, emerged to tear gas shells; hundreds of others found their way home barred by road-blocks at Argyle Street. Police and army reinforcements drove the crowd towards the Broadway Theatre, where the 'rioters stopped to tear down all the posters, wider elements avoiding the hail of tear gas shells by ducking away from the mainstream down side streets, and their numbers had dwindled considerably by the time Prince Edward Road was reached:

> Military jeeps full of grim-looking MPs [military police] in their red caps circulated with loud speakers and posters calling on all troops to return to units immediately ready to stand by in case the Police needed assistance. Flashes were put on at various cinemas also telling them to get back to barracks . . . two Americans . . . were attacked while riding in a taxi from which they jumped and fled . . . An injured Police inspector, during the rioting, tried to borrow the use of a telephone to summon aid but was refused admission into barricaded shops by the frightened owner . . . Out in the NT, the Police took precautions all day, checking traffic at road blocks and searching vehicles . . . Last night . . . the US Navy was given the order to return to its ships . . . to avoid any possible incidents in the city. The Hong Kong special Constabulary was called upon to reinforce members of the regular force (ibid).

According to the police, only 200 police officers had faced the 20,000 or so rioters until reinforcements arrived. Then, the armed Chinese constables were said to have been 'wonderful in the way they showed forbearance under great provocation, maintaining their discipline throughout . . . The constable who opened up on his attackers at Mongkok did exactly as he should have done . . . it was his duty to defend the station' (ibid). At the trials of those arrested, special precautions were taken at the magistracies, with 'steel helmeted' police on guard inside and outside the courts. Those arrested were mainly males in their early twenties (including students, waiters, hawkers, and weavers) as well as three juveniles.

In Hong Kong, the Chinese and English language press generally praised the government for its handling of the 'March First Incident' and its determination to maintain law and order, seen as necessary for the residents 'to live and work in peace and contentment' (Lock 1993: 175). In China, however, the *People's Daily* attacked the Hong Kong government for suppressing the people. This article, reprinted in a local Chinese newspaper (*Tai Kung Po*) on 5 March, accused the government of being imperialist (Lock 1993: 170). The proprietor, publisher and editor were accused by the government of publishing a seditious article, fined and ordered to cease publication for six months; the *Wen Wei Po* and *New Evening Post* were also charged (ibid). Later, the courts reduced the period of suspension to 12 days; charges against the other two newspapers were dropped. The Hong Kong government accused the press in Canton of exaggerating the trouble. It praised the 'firmness displayed by the Government', the 'restrained but efficient handling of the situation by the police', the restraint shown 'in difficult circumstances', and the swift restoration of 'law and order'.[13] The Commissioner of Police, reflecting the widely held belief of the authorities, described the clash as a trial of strength between left-wing political agitators and the government, together with opportunists out to loot whatever they could.[14]

The belief that the incident was a 'Red Riot' appears to have been shared by the general public – local newspapers reported that the riot was a pre-arranged attack on the British authorities, aimed at promoting political propaganda (Lock 1993: 172). Local and Mainland Communists, it was argued, wished to make political capital out of the Tung Tau fire. However, in 1952 local Communists had adopted a more co-operative stance towards the authorities, and during the 1 October anniversary of the founding of the People's Republic, only about 100 red flags flew in Hong Kong (Lock 1993: 190). It thus seems unlikely that the 1 March riot was a deliberate, pre-arranged attack on the government.

The incident was understood by the government to demonstrate the readiness with which dormant political sensitivities could be inflamed by communist agitators stirring up trouble around relatively trivial incidents. This, more than an armed attack on its borders, was seen as the most likely line of attack by Communist China. A confidential memo written by Grantham later in March that year identified the ability to foment internal disturbances such as strikes, riots and sabotage as the 'most potent weapon' that the Communist government in China could use against the British:

> An examination of the position on March 1st when the disturbances occurred in Kowloon leaves no room for doubt on this point . . . By withdrawal of labour, and the internal disturbances that would certainly ensue, Hong Kong . . . could be made untenable quickly and without much effort on the part of the enemy . . . [can] the internal security position be held'.[15]

What these and other incidents taught the police was the need for intelligence about subversive activities and triad organisation on the ground, in the squatter villages and resettlement estates. Smart notes, for example, that Special Branch actively monitored the situation in the squatter areas, and observes that one of the leaders of the Chinese Chamber of Commerce which set out to greet the comfort mission was deported for life for his 'extreme left-wing activities' (Smart 2006: 77). The Chinese Chamber of Commerce was itself described in confidential reports as an 'indirect agent' for the CPG, which used it to carry out its United Front campaign in the colony (ibid). The likelihood of direct military attack was, thus, regarded as a less serious threat than 'internal unrest used by China as an excuse for intervention' in

Hong Kong, the authorities being 'extremely concerned by the colony's vulnerability to communist insurrection'.[16]

In the years after these disturbances, policing strategy emphasised the presence of the beat police officer and his contacts with local people. In this way the authorities hoped to prevent seemingly trivial and unimportant incidents from developing into a major disorder. At the same time, however, echoing a recurrent theme, Grantham regarded the Chinese members of the police force as 'wholly unreliable', and set about introducing a set of initiatives to deal with their suspect loyalties.[17] One of these was ensuring that the Chinese did not dominate the Hong Kong Regiment and Reserves, deployed in times of internal unrest. Smart cites a defence Review in which it was decided:

> That the racial proportions between Europeans (including Portuguese) and Asians (including Indians) be confirmed at a 50:50 ratio until the Hong Kong Defence Force reaches its approved establishment . . . [and] . . . Asians should in future be directed to the Royal Hong Kong Defence Force only as required by the Commandant . . . [and] . . . that a review of European manpower at present enrolled in the Essential Services Corps should be undertaken with the aim of ensuring that the strictest economy in holdings of European manpower is observed by that Corps, and of making available to the Special Constabulary and the Royal Hong Kong defence Force any European manpower that can be released by the Essential Services Corps without endangering services.[18]

The Essential Services Corps maintained services such as electricity and consisted of Europeans and 'reliable non-Chinese'. They were issued with pistols to defend their plants in case of civil disturbances (Smart 2006: 79, 80). A second initiative was to establish a secret Chinese (Emergency) Advisory Committee to 'keep the Government in the closest possible touch with current Chinese opinion before and during an emergency', and assist with censorship and propaganda (ibid). Other policies which, Smart says, reflected the 'widespread distrust of the loyalties of the Hong Kong Chinese' included shutting down communist-infiltrated schools, the promulgation of the 1949 Societies Ordinance 'to prevent subversion', and the deportation by executive fiat of 'undesirables' (ibid). Though the squatter villages were not the same as 'the scattered and inaccessible hotbeds of Malaysia', they did potentially harbour large numbers of people who, in an emergency, could 'constitute a very real potential threat'.[19] As far as the police were concerned:

> No single factor in the Colony has so much bearing on the crime situation as the squatter problem. Because of the geographical nature of squatter settlements, the complete lack of planning and the absence of lighting of any kind, no proper police supervision can be exercised and patrol work is almost impossible at night in these areas . . . these areas

> [also] . . . provide shelter and meeting places for political agents of all kinds.'[20]

As we shall see, however, when rioting did break out in the resettlement estates in 1956, the authorities were keen to play down the degree to which 'political agents' of any kind were involved. Criminals – specifically triads – were blamed instead. Though government continued to employ deportation and detention to rid the territory of political activists, putting the blame on criminals helped it to maintain the myth that Hong Kong was a stable, apolitical society.

Notes

1 HK Yearbook 1952: 38.
2 HK Yearbook 1950: 25.
3 HK Yearbook 1952: 125.
4 HK Yearbook 1954: 29.
5 Grantham 1965: 132 cited in Lock 1993: 53.
6 Some English-language accounts of this can be found in Lock 1993: 55; Endacott 1978: 315; Welsh 1993: 444.
7 Grantham 1965, cited in Smart 2006: 61.
8 See Smart 2006: 62.
9 HK Yearbook 1952: 6.
10 HK Yearbook 1952: 6.
11 *South China Morning Post* 2 March 1952, cited in Lock 1993: 170.
12 *Hong Kong Standard* 2 March 1952 cited in Smart 2006: 76.
13 HK Yearbook 1952: 6.
14 Police Report 1952: 47 cited in Lock 1993: 171.
15 Inward Telegram to Secretary of State for the Colonies, 22 March 1952, COS37-17669 cited in Smart 2006: 76.
16 Mark 2000: 837–71 cited in Smart 2006: 78.
17 Grantham 1965 cited in Smart 2006: 78. Goodstadt (2005) also notes a confidential memorandum from 1959, which complained that, since the Hong Kong Chinese were only interested in economics (money and a living) they had little loyalty to the administration and their 'secret loyalties' might lie with China. See Goodstadt 2005: 40.
18 HKRS 369–1–15 'Defence force review' cited in Smart 2006: 79.
19 McDouall report, cited by Smart 2006: 81.
20 DCI Johnston's appendix to the McDouall report, cited in Smart 2006: 81.

Chapter 10

Corrections, juveniles and 'disciplinary welfare'

The 1950s saw some very significant shifts in the way offenders, and in particular young offenders, were dealt with in Hong Kong. The Prison Department, as it was then called, was able to build new establishments and develop prison regimes that, if still strict in many respects, were nonetheless oriented to concerns such as the United Nations Standard Minimum Rules for the Treatment of Prisoners (1955). The probation service, having existed for some time as a rather minor appendage to the criminal justice system, became a part of the Social Welfare Office and was able to expand; and provisions made for discharged prisoners.

The Social Welfare Office, by the mid-1950s, had become the key agency dealing with juvenile offenders; juvenile offending was not in fact considered a major problem at that time, but this development meant that the precepts of social work were applied to these young people, who were often regarded as having committed their offences because of the circumstances of the time (with the rapid influx from China and creation of squatter areas, etc). That said, the type of interventions made with these offenders tended to be rather more authoritarian and disciplinarian than in, for example, the UK.

In addition, extensive efforts were made by the Social Welfare Office and voluntary agencies to engage young people generally in positive activities that would encourage them to grow into good citizens.

Post-war prisons

Pre-war, Hong Kong had three prisons but by 1946 only Stanley prison (opened in 1938) was in use. A former prison for females in Kowloon (Lai Chi Kok) had been severely damaged, necessitating the temporary removal of female inmates to Stanley, where they were housed in the old printing shop and segregated as far as possible from the male inmates of the prison. The Victoria prison, closed and abandoned when Stanley opened in 1937, was reopened in 1939 when it was realised that herding all convicted and unconvicted prisoners into Stanley was a mistake.[1] It had since come to function principally as a remand prison. It had suffered some damage during the war but its proximity to the central courts meant that it was quickly brought back into use in 1946, though the building was described as far from satisfactory 'being the remains of an old Victorian gaol, the colony's first prison and a dungeon-like relic of Victorian prison design'.[2]

These three makeshift penal institutions housed 8,963 inmates (compared to 16,146 in 1938), with a daily average of 1,214. By 1947, this figure had risen to 14,743 and by 1948 to 24,941. The majority were Chinese, though figures reveal a small number of European inmates (23), Indians (four) and Japanese prisoners. The figures also included 3,596 females and 64 boys sent to the reformatory in 1947, rising to 75 in 1948; as the Prisons Department itself pointed out, the statistics on children and young people were contained in the annual reports of the magistrates rather than the Prison Department. By 1948, Victoria was said to have been refurbished to a 'fairly satisfactory' standard. Able to accommodate up to 416 inmates it actually housed 437 prisoners, most serving one month or less, as well as prisoners awaiting deportation, inmates on remand, vagrants and debtors. By the end of 1949, accommodation for another 200 convicted prisoners was planned.[3]

On average, in 1946 only 35 female inmates were in custody on any day, though by 1948, this had risen to 224. By 1948 too, Lai Chi Kok had been repaired. It now housed 287 females in two large dormitories of 80 beds each, 24 cells for convicted prisoners, and a separate facility for holding the 22 inmates waiting deportation. Young offenders and female offenders were held in dormitory-type accommodation; adult males were held in single cells, though overcrowding had on occasion led to three prisoners (never two) sharing a cell. Stanley, which had been overcrowded since the day it opened in 1938, by the end of 1947 held 2,672 inmates in accommodation for 1,578. Some 104 prisoners with tuberculosis were housed in a separate cell block with double windows for the supply of fresh air.[4] Showers were permitted once per week, and an in-cell bucket system provided sanitation. Exercise was provided for all inmates. In Lai Chi Kok, the discipline was said to be strict 'as is proper' but not severe.[5] The women performed mainly domestic chores such as laundry, sewing and gardening. They were described as 'quiet, industrious and well behaved . . . There is instruction in domestic science and suitable minor trades' (ibid). From 1954 onwards, nursing infants were allowed to stay with their mothers inside the prison, though internal Prisons Department memoranda indicate that it was Chinese custom to separate them soon after birth.[6]

Internal documents indicate that it was common practice in the late 1940s and 1950s to separate triad prisoners according to their common territorial origin and dialect (e.g. Cantonese, Chiu Chau, Hakka). Struggles for power between these triad societies resulted in fights and assaults. In 1948, Stanley Prison saw 22 gang fights, mainly between local Cantonese and Hakka triad society members. In the early 1950s, with the influx of prisoners from amongst the refugee population, these ethnic divisions gave way to division along 'more orthodox' triad lines. There were four main triad societies in Stanley:

(i) 'Sze Tai Juk': composed of four 'big families' (Dan Yee, Macau, Luen Kwan Ying, and Tung Sun Wo societies);
(ii) 'Tai Huen': formerly a Cantonese triad society composed of splinter groups from the 'Wo' group;
(iii) 'Chiu Chau': originally limited to native Chiu Chau and Hoklo but later affiliated with several other societies of Chiu Chau origin (e.g. Sun Yee On, King Yee, Yee Hing);
(iv) 'Sap Sei': (14K), originally a pro-Nationalist society from Canton; once affiliated with the Chiu Chua but grown independent and divided into many sub-divisions.

Material about the origins, structure and organisation of triad societies was distributed to prison staff as part of their training. According to these internal documents, new inmates were particularly vulnerable to recruitment – fearing for their personal safety, they would join a society believing it could guarantee them safety.[7] The various triad leaders tried to agree amongst themselves what they would control in each prison (e.g. cigarettes, sweets, food, toothpaste, soap; drugs were apparently traded by other, independent, ventures). To thwart their authority, the Prisons Department emphasised staff control, careful work, cell and dormitory allocations, categorisation and control of movement within the prison so as to constantly change the pattern of engagement and prevent any particular group from organising. Later, the regime of young offender institutions, with its frequent changes in working parties and constant evaluations of inmates, was thought to deter the recruitment of young offenders, seen by the authorities as 'quasi-triads with a scanty knowledge of triad procedures'.[8]

In addition to prisoners on remand, in the late 1940s Victoria also housed convicted juveniles. A temporary reformatory was also set up in some concrete storage huts in Stanley for boys under 16. This 'large, airy, somewhat bare and Spartan' facility was described as Hong Kong's first 'open institution for delinquents'.[9] It was 'admirably suited' for its purpose, the boys being situated:

> . . . in one of the healthier spots in Hong Kong on the slopes of Maryknoll overlooking Tai Tam Bay on one side and Stanley Bay on the other. A maximum of 100 boys can be accommodated, but the average population is 70. There is a competent staff of schoolmasters and trade instructors. The boys are divided into progressive grades, but the community is treated as a whole and no attempt is made to impose the barriers of the 'hate' system. The happy and creative atmosphere of this camp has been

the subject of favourable comment by visiting justices and other members of the public among whom the Reformatory has many friends.[10]

Like the adult inmates of Stanley, the boys were put to work on clearance and reclamation, clearing Stanley of the 'rubbish and filth left behind by the Japanese', and transforming a level piece of ground, which had deteriorated into 'a wilderness', into a market garden with a piggery and poultry farm (ibid). The Maryknoll Boys' Reformatory in the old concrete storage huts housed up to 72 boys. The boys' regime was supplemented by technical education in rattan work, carpentry, cookery and photography. Adult males received training in shoemaking, tinsmith work, tailoring, carpentry, gardening, laundry, and domestic work.[11]

As Law Yick Man has pointed out, the British Criminal Justice Act 1948 provided for the establishment of detention centres for young offenders aged between 14 and 21 years of age.[12] It would be another 20 years before Hong Kong followed suit. In the meantime, however, Hong Kong did choose to adopt another UK practice. A Borstal institution was felt to be necessary for boys of Borstal age kept in Stanley. Subsequently, an Industrial and Reform School Ordinance was mooted to set up a training centre of this sort at Stanley. Unlike the Borstal system in the UK, however, it would not cater for boys aged 16 to 21 but rather for boys aged between 14 and 18.

The regime of existing reform schools was modified in 1953, under the Training Centre Ordinance.[13] The Training Centre regime was to be based on the ideal 'of membership of and service to the community'. This theme was carried through to associations for 'street children' outside the prison, with organisations such as the British Council encouraging the formation of boys' and girls' clubs. Two training courses were established in 1948 to train leaders for this movement, some of whom were sent to the UK for experience in social work. One such leader took over the running of the clubs on his return to the colony; from 1949 onwards, other courses on child psychology were organised locally. By the end of 1949, 1,500 children were involved in such clubs, rising to 2,380 by the end of 1950. By the mid-1950s, these clubs were to be found on rooftop dwelling areas and in all the resettlement blocks.[14] Though leisure pursuits and physical exercises such as swimming and outward bound were provided, there was also an educational side to the movement, boys being taught handicrafts such as how to make brooms and rattan baskets, whilst girls were taught sewing, weaving and knitting, with articles made by the children sold to support the family budget. Teaching them some form of trade was seen as giving them the assistance they needed to take a 'proper place in the life of the community as independent members of society' (ibid). Though the 'experiment' was attempted with older boys and girls, it met with less success amongst boys over 16 whose 'characters are already formed' and could not settle down into 'club life' (ibid).

Within Stanley, boys were segregated as far as possible from adult inmates, though there were no fences or walls around the centre. The daily regime consisted of rising at 6 am, when the boys were to make their beds before proceeding to physical exercise from 6.30 to 7.00 am. From 7.00 to 7.30 they breakfasted, and from 8.00 until 11.00 am, participated in vocational training. A break between 11 am and 12 noon was followed by classes between 12 noon and 3.00 pm. Between 3.00 and 3.45, games were organised, followed by dinner at 5.00 pm. Between 5.30 and 8.00 pm the boys enjoyed free time for hobbies and games; at 8.00 pm they went to bed, and at 9.00 pm the lights were out. This curriculum, it was explained, was based 'on a full, active and useful life in the community'.[15]

Echoing nineteenth-century clashes between costs and regime reform, the post-war prison authorities wished to put the prison population to industrial and unskilled labour so that they might 'contribute to the cost of their maintenance'.[16] Plans were made to construct what was described as a 'penal labour camp' in 1949 to provide accommodation for another 700 inmates.[17]

Discipline within the prisons also retained some pre-war features. It included the use of corporal punishment, which, it was said, had a 'markedly deterrent effect'.[18] However, an internal memo for 1946 shows that the Secretary of State for the Colonies had written to the Hong Kong government requesting it to reduce its use of corporal punishment.[19] Officially the Prisons Department was to aim at individualisation of punishment, though internal memoranda indicate that in practice overcrowding was thought to make this difficult.[20]

Prison staff remained mostly local, under European supervision. Post-war, they were divided into two grades. Grade 1 consisted of officers from the UK or other colonies, such as Sarawak and Brunei (whose officers were trained in the UK) and those promoted from Grade 2. Grade 2 staff were generally local officers, though it also included three Pakistani officers who had returned after the war. Most of the former Indian and European staff had been mobilised to fight against the Japanese; some were killed or interned; others returned to duty but were found medically unfit as a result of their internment and given recuperative leave. A nucleus of three British officers remained in charge until the colonial administration was in a position to resume control, and some staff were recruited from Shanghai. As with the police, the absence of the Indian contingent led to a shortage of trained staff.[21] The Indian contingent were said to have been 'outstandingly loyal and courageous during the occupation' and were recommended for honours for their conduct during the war. Of the staff at Stanley in 1947, 19 were either Indian or Pakistani; others were expected to return 'shortly' – a British officer was to be sent to India to assist with their return.

By 1948, things were said to have improved as rates of pay for prison staff rose, attracting a different 'type of man' as well as a 'higher standard of efficiency in the locally recruited staff'.[22] All staff were now required to undertake a period of training, emphasising reform and rehabilitation, before they commenced work, and salaries were placed on a par with those in the police force. The result, it was said, was an influx of better candidates and 'signs that it will be possible in due course to create an efficient and reliable local staff' (ibid). The focus on local staff reflected the general prohibition on the recruitment of Indians to the colonial service in the wake of Indian independence. Localisation thus began to take root rather by default than by design.

The 1950s: prisons and probation

In keeping with the '1946 outlook' and the then-current UK penal thinking, post-war prison staff training in Hong Kong emphasised the reformative aspects of prison life and work, and the need to train inmates to become 'useful citizens'. The administration of probation for juveniles, and plans to extend it to adult offenders, was however delayed by the fact that Hong Kong needed to import a qualified probation officer from the UK. Probation and probation homes were not introduced until 1956.[23] In this, Hong Kong lagged slightly behind other colonies – a probation service had already begun in Sarawak in 1949, for example, to deal mainly with juvenile delinquents; Brunei had considered introducing probation but felt that, still being a largely agricultural, Islamic and family-based society, a formal agency was not required.

Until the mid-1950s, Hong Kong had a very small probation service. Before the war it had only two probation officers. By 1956 it employed a staff of ten officers whose job it was to provide courts with background reports on 'mendicants', supervise juveniles, oversee camps, welfare centres and hostels, and investigate cases. It was not until 1957 that a Discharged Prisoners' Aid Society was registered to assist adult ex-offenders.[24]

There was, in any event, some dissent within government as to the desirability of such innovations as probation, open institutions and reformatories. One internal report claimed that they were 'looked on with favour' in Hong Kong, but the line was crossed out and a handwritten note appended explaining that the government had not yet made up its mind on the issue.[25] Another internal memo of February 1955, from the Commissioner of Prisons, emphatically denied that it was the Prisons Department that had thought of setting up open institutions like Castle Peak Boys Home. Indeed, it argued, 'the exact opposite is the truth'.[26] C.J. Norman, who had become Superintendent of Prisons in 1947, was himself the former headmaster of a Borstal institution and had previously worked in Chelmsford, Wormwood Scrubs, and Pentonville prisons in the UK before joining the Hong Kong Prison Service as Assistant Supervisor in 1940 and being promoted to Commissioner in 1953.[27]

Norman was one of the few Commissioners to speak Cantonese. In the early 1950s he faced the task of responding to calls to modernise the prison system both from within the department and from outside. In 1954, he applied a new Prison Ordinance enforcing what were then still-new UN minimum standards regarding the treatment of adult prisoners to Hong Kong. Under these rules, there was to be no discrimination on the basis of race, colour, religion, or political affiliation; no arrows were to be marked on prisoners' uniforms; there were to be no 'dark cells' or instruments of restraint used for discipline, though corporal punishment was to continue; special diets were to be introduced so as not to offend any ethnic groups; and all prisoners were to be granted equal privileges and required to perform an equal amount of work. New legislation was required, it was argued, because 'new conceptions as to the treatment of prisoners rendered previous legislation obsolete'.[28] The set of Prison Rules established in 1925 were now 'inadequate' and would be replaced by the new Prisons Ordinance.

However, unlike the police – where Pennefather-Evans had encouraged links with professionals in other countries – the Prisons Department did not favour broadening the horizons of its staff by sending them to overseas conferences. It remained unconvinced that it could learn much from other jurisdictions. Hong Kong prisons staff knew nothing of the penal systems of neighbouring countries, nor was it thought that they had anything to gain from by acquiring such knowledge. Hong Kong, it was argued, was 'almost unique'.[29] Thus, when a principal officer sought permission from the Commissioner of Prisons to attend the first UN Seminar of Crime Prevention and the Treatment of Offenders in Rangoon, in 1954, support was less than enthusiastic. Instead of sending anyone to the conference, the Commissioner reluctantly allowed staff to submit four written papers, all of which were subject to internal censorship before they could be sent to the conference organisers.

In keeping with the modernisation of the criminal justice system and the regime in Hong Kong more generally, the early 1950s did however see the increased classification and segregation of prisoners according to whether they were long-term, short-term, first offenders, juveniles, male, female, long term 'habitual' offenders, and young recidivists. At Lai Chi Kok (then used for women prisoners) long-term first offenders were housed separately in unlocked 'rooms' (former cells) whilst other inmates were housed in communal dormitories.[30] Of the six cell-blocks in use at Stanley, one contained long-term prisoners, three contained long-term first offenders, and two housed short-term prisoners. There were separate wards for European prisoners, for prisoners under punishment and for previous offenders serving five years and over.[31] 'Stars' were first offenders or those treated as such; 'ordinaries' were older offenders, divided into short-term and long-term groups. There were also young prisoner 'stars' who were allowed to work outside the prison walls and young prisoner 'ordinaries'. There was provision of cells for separate confinement, for those awaiting the death penalty (at Stanley, and some at Lai Chi Kok) but these were said to be seldom used.

Along with this more detailed system of classification came more individuated penal programmes. It was hoped, for example, that young offenders could eventually be removed from the prison and placed in a new camp where they would work outside in the fresh air.

The general pursuit of rehabilitation as a goal of the penal system was also extended to a group hitherto detained completely separately from the general Hong Kong community. A leper colony had been established much earlier on Hei Ling Chau, four miles from Hong Kong. In 1954, the government decided that its isolation perpetuated social prejudice and made the rehabilitation of lepers into the community impossible. It therefore adopted a new policy: treatment would be given to lepers in outpatient clinics 'unless they are badly disfigured'.[32] Another leper colony, at Sandy Bay in Pokfulam, was cleared in 1956 to make way for a hospital for crippled children. At the same time, however, the relative isolation of Hei Ling Chau recommended it to the government for use as a drug addiction treatment centre, whilst Stonecutters Island became the principal penal establishment for British forces stationed in the Far East. The ability to throw a *cordon sanitaire* around certain types of troublesome populations made islands like these popular locations for penal establishments and detention centres in the decades to come.

By 1954, Hong Kong had five main penal establishments operating under the Prisons Department (Stanley, Victoria, and Lai Chi Kok prisons, as well as the Stanley and Tung Tau Wan Training Centres for 14- to 18-year-old boys). A sixth prison, at Chi Ma Wan, was established in 1956 on the site of a former Social Welfare centre for the disabled on Lantau.

Established under the Training Centre Ordinance 1953, training centres were an experiment for Hong Kong. They were to provide both punishment and vocational education to young offenders. They received some unwelcome publicity, however, when in 1959 one of the warders at Cape Collinson Training Centre was murdered. A Commission of Inquiry, held in camera, fuelled public speculation. It examined the incident itself and the general administration of such centres. Only one 'bad beating' and 'certain administrative defects' were brought to light, leading some to wonder why the government had gone to such lengths to investigate the matter:

> The chief merits of the report seem to be implied rather than stated. The experiment of the training centres as an alternative to prison for juvenile delinquents has revealed no serious or insuperable difficulties. The general lines of the camp's administration appear, with some small exceptions, to be endorsed. Slackness of discipline is not a fundamental weakness while the lack of suitable staff is a common complaint today. The hope is that the eight recommendations made by the Commission set matters aright and that this institution is able to play its part usefully in the rehabilitation of wayward youngsters . . .[33]

The composition of prison staff was almost entirely local, though Europeans still dominated the higher offices of the Prisons Department. All the Pakistani and Sikh male staff who had left before the war were replaced by locals, though some of the Europeans, Pakistanis, Sikhs and Portuguese who had stayed through the war remained on staff. At the female prisons, the female staff were all either local Chinese or Portuguese. Despite its poor condition, Victoria remained in use principally because its proximity to the Central Magistracy made it convenient as a remand centre. Throughout the 1950s, it was used to house prisoners awaiting deportation, vagrants, convicted prisoners awaiting sentence and those serving a sentence of under one month, as well as remand prisoners (it was not until 1954 that the government opened a separate remand centre for juveniles). According to the official reports, these groups were 'strictly segregated', whilst newly-sentenced prisoners were held for two weeks at the start of their sentence for medical examination and classification.[34] Plans to open a camp for short-term offenders in the New Territories were laid but set aside on cost grounds.

Hard work was a key component of the Hong Kong government's approach to social welfare. In its penal establishments it combined with welfarism to produce a distinct brand of 'disciplinary welfare'.[35] Whilst young offenders were to be 'treated', those inside Hong Kong's adult institutions were still made to work: 'Every prisoner physically able to work now has a job to do.'[36] Adult offenders in Stanley received training in industry and crafts; young offenders were generally put to work on reclamation projects, whilst the female inmates of Lai Chi Kok worked on the local forestry plantation. When Chi Ma Wan prison opened on Lantau in 1956, its short-term inmates were required to do work on the island, also in conjunction with the forestry officer.[37] The Prisons Department was anxious to avoid the notion that life on the 'inside' was more comfortable than outside: 'the knowledge that a hard daily task awaits him is the best deterrent for the idler and loafer on the streets who might otherwise regard prison as a refuge'.[38] Many of those received into prison were described as being in 'pitiable physical condition'; some had tuberculosis, some were drug addicts, and some had venereal diseases; others simply showed the effects of poor diet and housing. For all these prisoners, an earnings scheme was introduced in 1953. This allowed inmates to earn a small amount of money, which could then be spent in the prison canteen or remitted to their families. Prisoners sentenced to one month or more also became entitled to a maximum of one-third remission. The women detained in the maximum-security prison at Lai Chi Kok were said to 'work willingly at simple tasks' in a 'bright and cheerful' atmosphere.[39] Those on short sentences only had time to learn 'the usual domestic duties' (ibid).

Of those sent to prison in 1950, 8,750 received sentences of less than one month; much the same number (8,529) were imprisoned for a month or less in 1951 and 1952 (9,564). The same pattern occurred throughout the decade.

Table 10.1 Population by institution

	Stanley		*Victoria*		*Lai Chi Kok*		*Stanley & Tung Tau Wan Training Centres*		*Chi Ma Wan*	
	Rec.	*D/A*	*Rec.*	*D/A*	*Rec.*	*D/A*	*Rec.*	*D/A*	*Rec.*	*D/A*
1950										
1951										
1952						109	41	41		
1953	7,396	2,692			1,539	120				
1954	5,174	2,099	14,839	695	1,418	102	58	58		
1955	6,160	1,665	11,636	880	1,559	98	39	111+55 [1]		
1956	13,434	2,461	8,248	530	1,247	92	121	184	139 [2]	
1957	10,473	2,420	8,207	479	1,470	119	175	126+86	4,134	501

D/A = daily average population.
[1] Tung Tau opened in February 1955; figures thereafter are for both centres.
[2] Chi Ma Wan opened December 1956 for short-term first offenders.

Juvenile delinquency

In the 1950s, everyone in authority agreed that the 'problem' of juvenile delinquency was nonexistent. Throughout the decade, the number of juveniles involved in crime and coming before the courts remained low. Even so, there was a good deal of enthusiasm for developing the 'Stanley Reformatory School for the training of young delinquents',[40] and for the idea of developing a programme of after-care in conjunction with voluntary societies. The two juvenile courts, established under a Juvenile Offenders Ordinance of 1933, had been explicitly modelled on the UK system. Until this point, juveniles had been treated as adults in the criminal justice system, though there do appear to have been some experiments with different penal regimes for young offenders in the 1930s. The new courts were said to be 'sympathetic and understanding' and seldom meted out a sentence without first making background inquiries about the offender. The Ordinance had forbidden the imprisonment of juveniles aged under 14. The juvenile courts also rarely sent juveniles aged between 14 and 16 to prison, placing most of them on probation for between one and three years, though some it sent to orphanages, children's homes and approved schools.[41] Industrial Schools and reformatories for the detention and correction of juveniles had also been introduced by the 1933 Ordinance but, as we have already seen, relatively little use was made of these before the war.

After the war, the Prisons Department entered what Chan has described as a more 'humanitarian period', adopting a social work model especially in relation to young offenders.[42] It was felt that the Social Welfare Office, rather than the Prisons Department, was the more appropriate location for the care of juveniles, reflecting contemporary UK approaches to juvenile delinquency.

Indeed, the remand home opened at Mau Tau Wei Road was run by a superintendent who had trained in the UK in the administration of remand homes.[43] Senior staff within the Prisons Department seem to have been reluctant to embrace these new ideas and approaches. It was the relocation of probation to Social Welfare that allowed it to thrive and that provided the impetus for the growth of 'disciplinary welfare' throughout the decade. In 1950, a principal probation officer was appointed and the supervision of young probationers was finally transferred from the Prisons Department to Social Welfare. The lack of trained youth workers also led to the establishment of a course provided by the Social Welfare Office in 1951. By 1952, it was reported that the courts were showing a greater willingness to place young offenders on probation. Juveniles on probation were supervised either by government probation officers or by private agencies; only about 30 per cent of the workload of the Probation Section comprised adult offenders. However, the 1956 Probation and Offenders Ordinance also extended probation to adults who were 'not yet hardened criminals', and who were thus thought to be still open to reform.

Some influential voices in the criminal justice system clearly regarded juvenile crime as the consequence of the deleterious effects on family life of economic hardship and dislocation. They blamed it on the breakdown of the environment, which had severed or weakened traditional social ties, and on economic necessity. In July 1954, for example, a paper on juvenile delinquency written by a Mr Poon Cheok, acting principal probation officer, was sent to the United Nations conference on offending in Rangoon (mentioned above) outlining what it claimed to be the 'Hong Kong approach' to the prevention of crime and treatment of offenders. This placed juvenile delinquency firmly in the context of dislocation, poverty and family breakdown, blaming extraneous circumstances such as a 'defective environment', a 'breakdown in home discipline', lack of employment opportunities and a lack of schooling facilities. In only one respect – 'lack of self-discipline' – did it imply that the 'defect' might lie with the offender's individual 'pathology'.[44]

This paper was influenced by the views of others in government and advisers from overseas. In a letter sent to the author of the Rangoon paper, one adviser argued that:

> . . . the under 16s are not a great problem in HK. They are not numerous, nor are their crimes of a serious nature. The institutions for their care are – or will be when the Remand Home is opened next year – quite adequate to cope. There seems to be a downward trend in the incidence of reported juvenile crime. We are worried, however, by the number of vagrant and mendicant youngsters who, when they reach adolescence or young manhood, may resort to crime, or live on the margins of it because they have no work or belong to any stable unit of society. There seem to be enough orphanages to cope with the absolutely derelict and the Shanghai Street

> Children's Centre and the Juvenile Care Centre are an attempt at helping without absolutely taking over the care of the juvenile. About one probationer in ten so far has defected, but four years is too short a period to be significant.[45]

Another internal memo of the time linked juvenile delinquency to 'abject poverty, poor housing and housing shortage leading to over-crowding [giving] rise to easy irritations, anxieties, broken and apparently affectionless homes which in turn affect the children'.[46] By the mid-1950s, the population had increased by at least two-and-a-half times its pre-war level:

> Discipline at home breaks down as anxiety is focussed on the 'bowl of rice' and children are sent out to the streets to beg, to hawk or to shoe-shine without some basic training in self-discipline. This state of affairs is most congenial to the growth of delinquency among the children as they come into contact with, and are undoubtedly influenced by, the local 'bad hats' for whom they work, to whom they pay protection money and by whom they in turn are protected . . . Another group is the destitutes and their children. These, too, can fall easy prey to gang activities.[47]

The Chief Justice echoed this view, arguing that most crimes, especially juvenile crimes, were petty in nature and a reflection of economic hardship: 'no less than 30,000 of the juveniles' convictions were in connexion with offences which may be described as being of a quasi-criminal nature, such as hawking without a licence, and obstruction' (ibid). This remained the case throughout the 1950s – a 1955 report stated clearly that juvenile delinquency in Hong Kong was:

> not a serious problem . . . the majority of offences are committed by boys and girls who were brought before the two Juvenile Courts . . . [they] arose more from poverty (illegal hawking to supplement family income etc) rather than from any intrinsically anti-social motive.[48]

Other internal documents are equally clear on the matter:

> Statistics show that in the two years of 1953 and 1954, the total number of juveniles (aged 8–16) charged in court with offences is 33,768. Of this 26,034 are boys and 7,734 are girls. This appears alarming but should not be so in view of the fact that 97% of the juveniles commit only the technical offence of hawking or shoe-shining without a licence. Of the remaining 3%, again, allowances must be made for some mendicants and others who commit minor offences like riding a bicycle at night without lights. Even assuming 3% of the total of 33,768 for two years, the incidence of juvenile delinquency in Hong Kong is comparatively low.[49]

> Delinquency amongst juveniles and young persons in Hong Kong does not on the surface constitute a problem which can compare to that of large towns and seaports in the UK. Most juveniles appear before the courts of Hong Kong and Kowloon on charges of illegal hawking [and larceny].[50]

The thrust of youth policy throughout the decade was to establish youth clubs that would remove young people from the 'harmful influences of undesirable homes and malignant secret societies' so that their lives 'might be shaped within an atmosphere of spirit, example and constructive training calculated to fit them for a responsible place in society'.[51] Rescuing children – and especially young women – from moral danger and reforming them into responsible citizens were the twin aims of penal and welfare youth policy.

It was only with the reorganisation of probation in 1952 that the collection of statistics on juvenile delinquency became possible. The reorganisation, led by an adviser from England in 1951 and 1952, prompted the government to bring work with young offenders more 'up to date'. It abolished the reformatory and set up a remand home and detention centre for juveniles, as well as an approved school for boys and another for girls. These institutions were to be run not by the Prison Department but by Social Welfare, though the approved schools were still to be run by the Salvation Army using locally recruited and trained staff.[52] A few social welfare staff were sent to the UK to train and learn from UK voluntary institutions, the absence of locally-qualified social workers to handle such issues eventually prompting the government to consider a scheme for training social workers locally, including the establishment of a social science diploma and degree at the University of Hong Kong.

By 1952, the Stanley Reformatory School, under the charge of Social Welfare, had become an institution for Borstal-age boys (up to 25); its numbers were to be reduced once a New Training Ordinance came into effect providing for the 'indeterminate' Borstal sentence, as introduced in the UK by the 1948 Criminal Justice Act. Sentences ranged from nine months to three years, plus supervision on discharge, an approach that was to shape the approach to young offenders in Hong Kong for many years to come. Young recidivists were also to be segregated in a separate, 72-cell hall where they would receive education and training under prison discipline. As an experiment, their education was to be provided not by Prison Department or Social Welfare staff but by two Chinese schoolmasters, the senior of whom had recently returned from a Colonial Development and Welfare Fund course in the UK.[53] An approved school for boys serving terms periods up to three years was also opened at Castle Peak. The approved school originally run by the Salvation Army on behalf of the Prisons Department was handed over, 'in line with modern practice', to Social Welfare in 1953, and extended in 1955. Its mission was to provide 'education in good citizenship and vocational training in shoe-making, carpentry, rattan-work and agriculture'.[54] In 1953, the Boys' Reformatory School at Stanley was also transferred to Social Welfare; in 1956, the Shanghai Street Children's Centre was also placed under the supervision of the probation office. Two other centres, operated by philanthropic organisations, were opened for delinquent boys whose offences were not serious and seen as resulting from some sort of 'social deficiency'.[55] Each centre consisted of a hostel and a club where children were taught tailoring, rattan weaving, and broom-making. Government youth centres and privately run youth clubs like these were to try to prevent the growth of juvenile delinquency by providing a 'healthy recreational life to poor boys and girls'.[56]

The experimental all-day club and probation hostel opened in 1952 provided the model for further developments. Most of the boys sent there were sent by the Juvenile Courts, police or welfare agencies who had 'uncontrollable boys in their hands'.[57] The club was established to 'fill in the gaps in the social life of a child which have started him on the road to a criminal life'.[58] In 1953, a special children's centre was opened for young offenders, aimed at cutting recidivism. The first of many such centres, it provided clubs in handicrafts and games, training in a trade, as well as elementary schooling; child vagrants and street sleepers also slept on the premises.[59] Attendance was said to be 'enthusiastic' and recidivism dropping.[60] By 1954, Hong Kong had 87 youth 'clubs' or hostels, many of them rooftop clubs, run by the Boys and Girls Association, and another 13 under the supervision of the Principal Welfare Officer. Official estimates put the number of non-school children at 60,000, 'constituting a considerable challenge to youth welfare organisations'.[61] In 1956/57 a club leaders' training centre was established on land granted by the government between Jaffe Road and Lockhart Road, Wanchai; funds to cover the cost of the building were provided by the Rotary Club. The four-storey building housed the headquarters of the Association, a training centre for youth workers, and club facilities for activities such as the Scouts and Girl Guides.

There was, however, no special centre for juveniles held on arrest or remand until 1956, when a remand home was opened in Kowloon for juveniles on arrest and those serving periods of detention of not more than six months. In 1956 alone, it was estimated that about 300 children passed through the home each month. The Hong Kong yearbook for 1956 speaks of fifty to sixty thousand children living on the streets 'without any form of family discipline and without any education, formal or otherwise', their families' preoccupation with finding food, shelter and making a living leaving little time for family life.[62] The government expressed concern that these 'street children' were growing up 'without any ethical standards, in fact without standards of any kind, except the will to survive'.[63] It thus welcomed the setting up of clubs, hostels and orphanages to remedy this problem, as well as nurseries for the children of working mothers and low-cost hostels for working girls. By 1952, some 300 to 350 orphan children and homeless juveniles were being housed in 21 orphanages run by non-governmental organisations (NGOs). By 1954, this had risen to 29 homes for abandoned children and orphans, together with numerous 'relief camps', day nurseries and other centres run by NGOs and Social Welfare. These catered for children and babies from poor, squatter families, and aimed to provide basic education in infant hygiene for their mothers. Only one centre – the Juvenile Care Centre – provided entirely voluntary institutional care. Run by 'a Committee of public-spirited individuals', it took children with 'behavioural difficulties' referred to it by the courts.

The problem of homeless and parentless youth, as well as the trafficking in children, eventually persuaded the government to appoint a Children's Officer to investigate cases of suspected child trafficking and the welfare of children separated from their parents who were thought to be in 'moral danger'. These included young girls 'who have gone astray', unmarried mothers and juvenile prostitutes, some of whom resided in a home (Pelletier Hall) run by the Sisters of the Good Shepherd. In 1954, a sub-committee of the Social Welfare Advisory Committee set out to conduct a study of these 'wayward girls', focussing in particular on juvenile prostitutes. Most were thought to have been forced into prostitution by economic pressures, some having been 'sold' to brothels by their destitute parents.

According to official reports, crime amongst women and girls was 'very low'.[64] There were, nevertheless, a number of penal and welfare establishments for young women, some a legacy of the anti-*mui tsai* movement. In 1948, an approved school for girls had been set up by the Salvation Army on behalf of the Social Welfare Office. The Kwai Chung Girls Home, like all the institutions for females, provided vocational training in domestic work. Although committed to the school by the courts, its 'youthful girl offenders' were not kept under lock and key, the atmosphere was to be that of a school and, if their behaviour was good, girls were allowed home visits at the weekends.[65] The Salvation Army and Young Women's Christian Association (YWCA) also ran special hostels for young factory girls, such as the YWCA hostel at Shamshuipo. In 1955, the Moral Welfare section of the Social Welfare Office became the Women and Girls Welfare section, increasing its remit. The Social Welfare Office, the Secretary for Chinese Affairs, and the police enforced a ban on the keeping of *mui tsai*, now expanded to apply to both boys and girls and the illegal trafficking of women.[66] By 1953, 4,000 were being supervised by the Secretariat for Chinese Affairs.[67] As in UK and US cities of the late nineteenth century, the task of Social Welfare was to 'reclaim and rehabilitate them', that of the Sisters of the Good Shepherd was to train them.[68]

Plans were made to extend youth clubs into rural areas, and to link up with other youth movements such as the Boy Scouts and Girl Guides. Like the Stanley Sea School, a juvenile care centre on Hong Kong Island, the emphasis was on healthy, outdoor pursuits, good citizenship and – in the case of the

Stanley Centre – training young boys to supply the demand of the big shipping companies.

To coordinate all these welfare activities for all the young people of Hong Kong, a new body was established – the Standing Conference of Youth Organisations. This ran holiday camps and outward-bound camps (such as the one at Mui Wo) and assisted voluntary associations in their running of 75 clubs catering for about 3,000 children from poor homes. Recreational facilities, such as playing fields and sports grounds, were provided for urban youth, along with twelve Children's Libraries provided by the Hong Kong Chamber of Commerce to keep 'boys and girls away from street libraries where the reading matter provided is not always suitable'.[69] In 1955, an aftercare officer was appointed to the Prison Department staff to be responsible for all boys after their release (the Salvation Army and the Family Welfare Society provided aftercare for adults). In the mid-1950s, probation received firm backing in the form of a new Probation and Offenders Ordinance. This enabled the courts to place on probation persons of either sex, juvenile or adults, first offenders or recidivists. It also established Probation Homes and Hostels and a Probation Committee to oversee the operation of probation in the colony. A Police Supervision Ordinance also extended 'the class of persons over whom a close eye may be kept'.[70] The system of supervision was made more stringent and, in theory, more difficult to evade.

By the mid-1950s the government was claiming that 'marked progress' had been made in the treatment of young delinquents', and that juvenile vagrants were now subject to supervision and placement.[71] Though the government lacked any general employment statistics even by the mid-1950s, it acknowledged that Hong Kong's rapidly growing industrialisation had solved some of the 'youth problem' by absorbing large numbers of young men and women into work.[72] Internal documents indicate, however, that the government still saw the 16 to 20-year-old age group as problematic. Some argued that the scope of the Juvenile Offenders Ordinance should be enlarged so that offenders up to 18 could be 'treated by the more sensitive machinery of the Juvenile Court'.[73] It was also argued that the real solution to offending in this age group was jobs, but 'There just aren't any and this frustrates our attempts at probation and aftercare. I marvel that so many of this older group do stay on the rails when every meal represents a problem to them – much less clothing, pleasure and the press of adolescence' (ibid). According to this Social Welfare Officer writer, what was needed was:

> . . . a sociological survey of the families which are producing our criminal population – something like attempted by the Gluecks in America or by Stott in England (*Human Nature and Delinquency*) or Cyril Burt (*Fifty Juvenile Delinquents* – I think it's in the SWO library . . . [It is] . . . impossible to be more specific . . . because we haven't the material. I have broken down about two hundred cases we've had so far looking for such

> things as the incidence of foster parents, or the effects of concubinage or some other factor which may be unique in H.K. but I have not found it. Maybe in another five years there will be enough material to work on. Certainly in the greater proportion of those children referred to SWO or WCA as 'uncontrollable' we find a broken family, divided loyalty and parental rejection of the child. That is true of everywhere else it seems and there is nothing new to say about it. Our problem seems to be less baffling than that of other communities probably because we have a law-abiding community (of juveniles anyhow). We want schools and jobs. The other refinements – child guidance clinics, elaborate recreational and social activities for youth, special schools and classification centres can wait until the social fabric has been changed and the more stable family life gives way to the blessings which accompany the products of western science (ibid).

For this observer, the nature of probation in the Far East would probably prove to be quite different to that done in western countries:

> The concept of the 'permissive' relationship which is the essence of case-work in the West has to develop in the minds of social workers here and we may not be able to skip the period in which social work is more directive, assumes authority and gives advice and lays down rules. Social workers . . . cannot be expected to develop faster than their times. Consequently, I think the pace should be set by private agencies rather than by government, at least for after-care or where assistance in the form of money or institutional care is concerned. I think the present set up in Hong Kong is healthy; with technical assistance and financial help from government available on the one hand, and the advice of the Council of Social Services and its sub-committees available to government for the shaping of policy on the other (ibid).

The influence of UK social workers and advisers was clear. In 1949, for example, the Secretary of State for the Colonies (Creech-Jones) forwarded a critical report from his Social Welfare Adviser (W.W. Chinn) to Grantham, which stressed the need for a separate Social Welfare Department and for the preparation of an official plan for the treatment of juvenile delinquency.[74] It was Chinn who pressed for something to be done in order to prevent delinquency degenerating into crime and imprisonment, something he saw as a distinct possibility given the unsettled circumstances of 1950s Hong Kong (ibid). As Smart observes, one result of this was that, when the Hong Kong government did get around to spending on social welfare, 'the main points highlighted concerned an initiative to create a reform school' (ibid).

Throughout the late 1950s and early 1960s, trainee social workers in Hong Kong would read UK social work texts, digest their ideas, and attempt to put them into practice in the very different environment of colonial Hong Kong. In relation to juveniles and young people, in particular, this influence was to be very evident in the report compiled in the aftermath of the 1966 riots (see below). Within the prisons, however, the shift towards welfare was slower. Though rehabilitation was the official goal of the system, staff remained poorly trained in this regard, whilst the presence of rival triads within the prisons meant that containment and control was, in effect, the primary objective. With the increase of young – primarily male – offenders in the 1960s, this tension between discipline and welfare was resolved in favour of the former. It was not until the 1970s, in the context of wider social reforms, that this was to alter.

Notes

1 HK Yearbook 1950: 75.
2 HK Yearbook 1946: 77.
3 HK Yearbook 1948: 195.
4 HK Yearbook 1948: 105.
5 HK Yearbook 1950: 76.
6 23 February 1955, HKRS 41–11315.
7 Correctional Services Restricted File.
8 Correctional Services Restricted File.
9 HK Yearbook 1950: 76.
10 HK Yearbook 1950: 76.
11 HK Yearbook 1946: 77.
12 Law, Yick-man 1996.
13 Ibid.
14 HK Police Magazine 1956/7: 20–21.
15 HKRIS 41–1–1315.
16 HK Yearbook 1948: 105.
17 HK Yearbook 1948: 105.
18 HK Yearbook 1948: 106.
19 Memo 11 November 1946, HKRS 41–1–1315.
20 HKRS 41–1–1315.
21 HK Yearbook 1946: 76.
22 HK Yearbook 1948: 106.
23 See Law, Yick-man 1996: 33.
24 HK Yearbook 1957: 239.
25 HKRS 41–1–1315.
26 23 February 1955 HKRS 41–1–1315.
27 Borstals were penal institutions for young offenders, and were intended to offer a significant level of regime activity including vocational training and education for inmates. The name arose from the original model institution at the village of Borstal in Kent, UK, which was founded in 1902. They ceased to exist in 1982, being replaced by Youth Custody Centres.
28 HK Yearbook 1954: 150.
29 Internal memo 5 May 1954, HKRS 41–1–1315.
30 Later, the main female prison became Tai Lam, though a female prison was established next to the reception centre at Lai Chi Kok in 2006.
31 HK Yearbook 1956: 193.

32 HK Yearbook 1954: 7.
33 CO1030/1386257, *South China Morning Post* 9 February 1960.
34 HK Yearbook 1954: 163.
35 See Garland 1985.
36 HK Yearbook 1951: 94.
37 HK Yearbook 1956: 194.
38 HK Yearbook 1950: 75.
39 HK Yearbook 1954: 138.
40 HK Yearbook 1951: 95.
41 HKRS 125–3–636: 2.
42 Chan, S. 1994.
43 HK Yearbook 1955: 126.
44 HK Statement to UN Seminar on Prevention of Crime and Treatment of Offenders in the Far East 25 October 1954, Rangoon, HKRS 41–1–1315.
45 Letter dated 14 June 1954 HKRS 125–3–636: appendix.
46 HKRS 125–3–836.
47 HKRS 125–3–636: 1.
48 HK Yearbook 1955: 126.
49 HKRS 125–3–636: 2.
50 HK Yearbook 1956: 166.
51 HK Yearbook 1956: 167.
52 HK Yearbook 1952: 112.
53 HK Yearbook 1952: 130.
54 HK Yearbook 1954: 141.
55 HK Yearbook 1954: 141.
56 See HKRS 125–3–636: 1.
57 HK Yearbook 1952: 111.
58 HK Yearbook 1952: 112.
59 HK Yearbook 1953: 114.
60 HK Yearbook 1953: 116.
61 HK Yearbook 1955: 123.
62 HK Yearbook 1956: 168.
63 HK Yearbook 1956: 171.
64 HK Yearbook 1956: 168.
65 HKRS 125–3–636: 2.
66 HK Yearbook 1952: 110.
67 HK Yearbook 1953: 110.
68 HK Yearbook 1956: 166.
69 HK Yearbook 1954: 143.
70 HK Yearbook 1956: 174.
71 HK Yearbook 1953: 114.
72 HK Yearbook 1956: 38.
73 HKRS 125–3–626: letter to author of Rangoon paper.
74 Secretary of State for the Colonies to Grantham 4 March 1949, HKRS 41–1–5404 cited in Smart 2006: 107.

Chapter 11

Building order and stability in the 1950s

The fact that Hong Kong maintained domestic stability and a low crime rate despite the tumultuous circumstances of the 1950s intrigues those for whom periods of modernisation are usually associated with rising crime, internal turmoil and social instabilities. There were, as we shall see, a number of integrating forces which government deployed to help build and maintain the colony's post-war social fabric.

Politically, not much changed. Local elections for the Urban Council were planned for 1952, a wider franchise recommending itself to the then governor, Sir Alexander Grantham, as a substitute for the higher-level constitutional reform demanded by significant numbers of the population. The question of whether Hong Kong people would be granted democracy was still very much a live issue. By October, however, it had become clear that there would be no further constitutional development. The colony's powerful business elite had informed the Secretary of State for the Colonies that there was no majority demand for democracy, despite popular support – including religious groups, the Reform Club and labour unions – or for constitutional change.

Elsewhere in the 'Western' World, 1950s Hong Kong was seen as the place from which to eavesdrop on Communist China, a place where academics and spies could interview refugees about life inside China's closed world. It also became a transit route for various commanders of the armed forces in the Far East, and a base for 'rest and recreation' for the thousands of US service personnel stationed in Korea. The boom in triad-run prostitution triggered by this was famously represented by Hollywood in *The World of Suzie Wong*.[1] For the next few decades, this mixture of exotic women, fishing junks, vice, underworld crime, gambling, and triads, remained the abiding image of Hong Kong in the West.

The Communist victory in China in 1949, and the erection of a border between Hong Kong and the Mainland in 1950, had a major impact on the 'post-1946' outlook. Plans to localise Hong Kong's government services, including its criminal justice agencies, were placed on hold. Suspicions that the Indian police would prove subversive had already led to their reduced role in the Hong Kong Police force, but this did not lead to an automatic increase in local recruitment, as envisaged by Pennefather-Evans. The existence of Communist and Nationalist sympathisers amongst the Hong Kong population, coupled with the infiltration of triads into all walks of life, now gave rise to suspicions in some quarters about the 'reliability' of locals. Though the 'post-1946 outlook' had initially favoured localisation, the Hong Kong Police now continued to recruit, and promote, expatriates.

Even before the Communist victory in 1949, sympathisers of both the Communist and Nationalist causes had been active in Hong Kong. In 1947, for example, some students and teachers had mobilised to support a Mainland students' movement to stop the civil war and put an end to the hardship it was causing (Lock 1993: 45). Public outrage concerning the rape of a female Beijing university student by a US marine in 1946 was also said to have been orchestrated by left-wing elements in Hong Kong (ibid). This increased the sensitivity of the authorities to incidents likely to provoke hostility amongst the local population. A case in which an unlicensed peanut hawker was killed by a policeman led to a trial for manslaughter at which the officer was acquitted. The verdict provoked a boycott and was seen by the government as one of many incidents contributing to 'ill-feeling' feelings amongst the Chinese, said to be 'always susceptible to the treatment of Chinese in Hong Kong'.[2]

After Mao's victory in 1949, concerns about restoring the colony after the occupation were joined by anxieties about the threat of Communism and the 'problem of people' generated by the millions fleeing China. These twin concerns underpinned much of 1950s social and political policy, as well as law and order. A Public Order Ordinance of 1948 provided the authorities with 'the means to deal rapidly and effectively with serious threats to law and order', and to forestall the development of such threats.[3] The Ordinance gave the government the power to impose a curfew within a specific area, close an area to all except certain permitted persons, order the evacuation of an area, and prohibit the movement of craft in waters around the colony. Such measures were justified to the public as necessary to 'curb the activities of political organisations which seek to advance their views by force' and to preserve 'the right of public meetings of ordinary peaceful citizens' (ibid). The 1948 Hong Kong Yearbook refers to a 'number of dissident Chinese political groups out of sympathy with the Chinese government' taking asylum in Hong Kong:

> There was a tendency for a certain number of them to abuse the hospitality granted to them by using the principles of freedom of the press and freedom of speech enjoyed in the colony to attack in immoderate terms the established Government of China. It was therefore necessary for warnings to be given to them that they should not abuse the privilege of asylum they enjoyed.[4]

The presence of rival political groups within the territory lent a political dimension to local issues throughout the 1950s, as a series of small skirmishes punctuated Hong Kong's fragile post-war internal stability and security. Instability in China, which had such an impact on social, political and economic life in Hong Kong in the late 1940s, now propelled increasing numbers of refugees to the colony in the early 1950s. Although the economy recovered remarkably quickly, by 1951 unemployment and poverty rose: these were side effects of the US embargo on all shipments to China imposed during the Korean War. There were also continuous sporadic incidents along the border with China, as well as numerous occasions on which naval craft and merchant shipping bound for Taiwan were fired on at sea by Chinese launches. Attacks by the Communist and Taiwanese governments on shipping and air traffic occurred every year, and the armed forces were repeatedly faced with sporadic incidents along the border. Domestically, there was also always a possibility that the simmering conflict between Nationalists and Communists would trigger disorder within the colony. This air of anxiety was said to reflect 'the troubled situation in the Far East generally'.[5] That the Hong Kong government saw itself standing on the frontline of the 'Bamboo Curtain' was reflected in its donation, in 1952, of HK$8 million to the UK to 'help relieve the expenditure incurred on the defence of the free world and on the reinforcement of the garrison of the Colony'.[6] This came in addition to the HK$16 million spent annually on reinforcing the garrison.

In the early 1950s, Hong Kong's future was still unsettled and its population far from stable. According to the government, the business of eking out a living worried Hong Kong's poverty-stricken people far more than 'the delicacy of [Hong Kong's] position in the Far East'.[7] In London, the Colonial Office spoke of the Hong Kong Chinese as 'resilient' and 'ingenious', 'hard-working' and 'industrious'. Shanghai entrepreneurs, who had fled China, were beginning to transform Hong Kong from an entrepot to a centre of manufacturing requiring industrious, hard-working, cheap and plentiful labour. The fact that Hong Kong struck London as financially self-sufficient justified its reduced spending from the Colonial Welfare and Development Fund on Hong Kong – it was better spent in other colonies, such as Malaysia, where the battle against Communism needed more resources to win the 'hearts and minds' of the people. Indeed, it has been argued that because Britain was at war with communists in Malaya and Singapore, it was important for Hong Kong to be seen as a stable and successful commercial colony, the symbol of British power and status in the Far East (Tang 1993, cited in Lock 1993: 63). So important was this role that the British government went so far as to seek American approval for a nuclear strike at China should the Communist government attack the colony.

Official reports for the 1950s convey something of a 'siege mentality'. The social as well as material infrastructure of Hong Kong had hardly recovered from the depredations of war before they were hit by a massive influx of refugees. The 'problem of people' was singled out as the single most pressing issue of the decade, affecting everything from finance, social welfare, education and labour to policing, prisons and political relations.[8] By the mid-1950s, the government estimated that for every pre-war resident of the colony, there were now four residents (ibid). Of the 2.5 million living in Hong Kong, a UN survey estimated that about 700,000 were refugees (ibid). As in the nineteenth century, the attraction of Hong Kong was seen as lying in its role as a 'safe and ordered sanctuary' to those who sought to escape from the political instabilities of Mainland China, welcomed 'as long as they did not continue whatever struggles they were engaged in from within [Hong Kong's] borders'.[9]

In the first part of the decade the government had assumed that many of these asylum-seekers would return to China once things settled down. It even relaxed its immigration controls for a time in order to facilitate this return. It found, to its dismay, that immigration increased. By the end of 1956, quotas had been restored in an attempt to control the influx. According to the government, these immigrants were predominantly farmers. Their usual source of livelihood (working the land) was closed to them. Hong Kong's rural areas were already home to more farmers than they could support.[10] Officials feared that, without land, they would become discontented:

> If they were to remain and become good citizens they had to be weaned away from their discontent and transformed by some social alchemy from the mentality of the farmer to that of the industrial worker. Until that transformation was achieved, the seeds of discontent would remain.[11]

This discontent, the government surmised, made such people susceptible to Communist and Nationalist propaganda, as both sides sought to win the hearts and minds of the Hong Kong Chinese. To 'prevent China's battles being fought on the streets of Hong Kong', the government held itself 'aloof from the internal politics of China', a policy that required 'considerable dexterity . . . a subtle combination of firmness, perspicacity, patience and understanding'.[12]

In addition to these 'asylum-seekers' and recent immigrants from China, the government identified another group which it said were neither refugees nor immigrants. Both groups settled in squatter villages:

> Virtually every sizeable vacant site which was not under some form of physical or continuing protection was occupied, and when there was no flat land remaining they moved up to the hillsides and colonised the ravines and slopes which were too steep for normal development. The huts were constructed of such material as they could lay their hands on at little or no cost – flattened sheets of tin, wooden boarding, cardboard, sacking slung on frames . . . Land was scarce even for the squatters and

> the huts were packed like dense honeycombs or irregular warrens at different levels, with little ventilation or light and no regular access. The shacks themselves were crowded beyond endurance. In some cases five or six human beings existed in a cubicle measuring 40 square feet. Density was at a rate of 2,000 persons to an acre in single storey huts. There was, of course, no sanitation and there was seldom any organised system of refuse disposal . . . Chickens, ducks and pigs shared the huts or the narrow congested areas around them . . . Some of the squatters had work in the towns; others started cottage industries, which were sometimes more akin to small primitive factories, in the settlements . . . In such conditions every kind of vice flourished. Drugs were manufactured, sold and stored; there were divans, brothels and gambling houses; every form of crime was sheltered by the anonymity of these dark places . . .[13]

In the absence of any co-ordinated state response, the task of helping and organising the refugees fell mainly to some 60 voluntary organisations, churches and charities, such as the Tung Wah. Government yearbooks for the 1950s speak of generous gifts of aid and substantial shipments of clothing pouring in from voluntary organisations in the UK, Australia and America. The UK government provided some assistance via the newly established Colonial Welfare and Development Fund, but it used this sparingly to support Hong Kong's welfare and social services. Some help was provided by way of an exchange of expertise. Staff from the various services (including the police, housing, and social welfare) were sent to Britain and Europe to gain knowledge and experience, while foreign advisers were sent to Hong Kong from Britain and from other colonies.

Communicating with the massive influx of very diverse groups of people arriving or returning to Hong Kong after the war was a problem for the government. Few possessed proper housing or electricity, television or radio sets; many did not speak Cantonese. Though a government Public Relations Office and Information service was established in 1955 to disseminate news of government activities and explanations of government policies, there was no reliable means of conveying this information and propaganda to the public. To overcome this problem, the government installed prominent broadcasting points in playgrounds and football fields, broadcasting via Radio Television Hong Kong (RTHK) to the entire population. Until 1953, RTHK remained part of the government Public Relations Department. Part of its job was to publicise the affairs of the Hong Kong, UK and Commonwealth Governments.[14] Officially, RTHK's mission was to broadcast programmes that reflected all sections of the community (it broadcast in English, Cantonese, Swatowese and Mandarin). In practice, it was the mouthpiece of government, its plays and dramas sending out messages on issues relevant to current drives by the police and medical authorities. In 1953, it played its part in disseminating the notion that Hong Kong belonged to the larger, 'Family of Commonwealth nations' by joining Hong Kong to the UK and the Commonwealth with an all-day, territory-wide, coverage of Queen Elizabeth II's coronation. A 'loyal address' was read to leading citizens in the council chamber and 'broadcast to the whole colony'; an enormous dragon dance processed through the streets,

> . . . a popular and friendly beast which Hong Kong seems slowly but firmly to be adopting as its heraldic emblem . . . Its scales were of gold and its large head was decorated and painted with all the emblems of ritual ferocity. It was 180 feet long and was borne by 90 energetic men. Before it and around it danced its tormentors, twisting and turning their high sticks on which were impaled fanciful and highly coloured baits . . . perhaps a million people rejoiced in its serpentine progress through the wide streets and to all there it was a recognised and welcome symbol of a great occasion.[15]

RTHK provided a direct relay of events in London for seven hours. Grand illuminations along the waterfront, fireworks in the harbour and numerous other events also commemorated Coronation Day. RTHK programmes emphasised Hong Kong's relationship to the British 'Motherland'. Throughout the 1950s and 1960s it also delivered all sorts of public service announcements, conveying the message that, although the government might not be a very visible part of people's lives, it maintained a 'night watchman role'. This role was to expand dramatically, however, during the 1970s when RTHK became integral to government propaganda about, and its mass campaigns against, crime, corruption, and the need to keep Hong Kong clean.

In the mid-1950s, it was decided to send the Chinese section of RTHK out and about to visit Hong Kong's disparate communities, as well as the more remote villages on the islands. The recordings it made during these visits were compiled into a programme entitled *We Are Living Below Victoria Peak*, a forerunner of the later *Below the Lion Rock* programme.

The media were thus an important aspect of the colonial government's efforts to mould some sense of identity in the 1950s, melding Hong Kong's diverse groups into a more homogenous population with shared experiences. The efforts were, however, rather poor and their effects were consequently weak. For most of the 1950s, Hong Kong people remained highly disparate. Though the common language of Hong Kong was Cantonese, a number of different dialects were spoken. A quarter of all films made in the colony were in Mandarin; about 400 American and 50 British films – rather than Cantonese – were shown every year. Local theatrical performances celebrated traditional Chinese culture; some troupes were sent by the Mainland to perform plays extolling Communist values while others came from Taiwan to promote more traditional culture. The government, eager to appear even-handed and anxious to avoid conflict with either side, allowed both to perform before Hong Kong audiences. Its new-found desire to promote tourism also led it to welcome American film makers and luxury liners to Hong Kong, contributing not only to the colony's reputation as a consumer's paradise but also to the dissemination of 'Western' culture. By the end of the 1950s, the youth of Hong Kong had begun to listen to British and American pop music, wear 'teddy boy' fashions, whilst their elders still listened to Chinese opera, sang traditional Mandarin songs and watched Mandarin films. The constant bickering about the building of City Hall – between those who thought Hong Kong should become a centre for high culture and those who thought it never would be – reflected a long-standing ambivalence about Hong Kong's role in the Far East as a means of transmitting 'Western' values.[16]

Kaifongs

Possibly the most influential integrating and stabilising force of the 1950s were the *kaifongs*. The Hong Kong government harnessed these quasi-traditional groups to assist with its organisation of the refugees, promoting the *kaifong* movement as a means of ordering the population.

Based on traditional Chinese 'self-help' organisations, the Kaifong Welfare Associations aimed to promote welfare amongst their communities through self-help, good neighbourliness and assistance for those in dire need.[17] This chimed well with the government's espousal of the *laissez-faire* approach to social welfare. But, as Hayes observes, unlike the original *kaifongs*, the post-war *kaifongs* were not spontaneously produced within the local Chinese population but 'owed a great deal to government prompting and support' (Hayes 1996: 90). In 1947 it set up a special office within the Secretariat for Chinese Affairs to stimulate the *kaifong* movement, and liaise with *kaifong*, clan and district leaders, especially in the Resettlement Areas. In 1957, this office became part of the Social Welfare Department. Its officers liaised with the *kaifongs* to promote community development, care for the disabled, and engage in measures to address child welfare, moral welfare, juvenile delinquency, youth organisations and emergencies (Lock 1993: 148). In 1956, these officers intensified their *kaifong* connection by visiting clansmen and district associations.

In the true colonial tradition of 'indirect rule', in order to organise and govern the people through the *kaifongs*, government needed to know about them. By helping *kaifongs* to improve their districts, the government hoped to encourage people to 'take a pride in belonging to it' as well as 'a personal interest in developing the physical, mental and moral well-being of their own community'.[18] They were to help establish a sense of belonging amongst the 50 per cent of the population who, in 1954, still did not regard Hong Kong as their home; otherwise, they 'might threaten local stability and prosperity'.[19] For the Social Welfare Office, the *kaifongs* would:

> . . . enable every member of the community to develop a reliable neighbour and a useful and informed fellow-citizen . . . [these] citizens [should have] a much more highly developed social consciousness and sense of social responsibility than had existed previously (ibid).

Despite this official sponsorship, the government presented the *kaifong* movement as a 'spontaneous expression' of service to the community. As Lock notes, the *kaifong* organisations were a traditional form of community organisation but they had never been recognised by the government before the late 1940s, when it needed help to deal with the wave of Chinese immigrants. Under its encouragement, the movement grew rapidly from four associations in 1949 (the Shamshuipo Kaifong Welfare Advancement Association being the first) to 14 associations in 1950, 18 in 1951 and 20 in 1952. By 1951, it was estimated that one adult in 15 belonged to a *kaifong*. By 1952, the movement had a total membership of 209,400, rising to 222,771 in 1953.[20] Between 1949 and 1957, the number of associations increased six-fold, from four to 26; in 1957, their membership stood at 370,000 (Lock 1993: 148). Their mission was to 'give mutual help and protection', 'be bound by a common cause', 'go through thick and thin together' and 'transform social traditions' (ibid). Thus, although to outsiders the scattered population of Hong Kong might look rootless, disorganised and ramshackle, in practice it organised around *kaifongs* and other quasi-traditional groupings based on native place, linguistic group, craft or industry.

In addition to their welfare role, the *kaifongs* were co-opted by government to assist with its various aims (such as the registration of persons), campaigns (such as fire prevention), and the spreading of propaganda (about such matters as free clinics, hygiene, and water-saving). The *kaifongs* were said to be 'always ready and eager to co-operate with the government in any emergency relief measures'.[21] This co-operation extended to providing relief in the wake of the 1956 riots. Theatrical shows with didactic themes were organised to 'improve the moral tone of the community and restore traditional values'.[22] They also shouldered a wide range of responsibilities, which in the UK, with its commitment to the welfare state, were provided by government. They organised free schools and dinners, provided new recreational facilities, and ran domestic science classes. During 1952, a women's section was begun which organised free maternity services, sewing classes and 'Little Mothers' for the education of young mothers. They also lobbied government on local matters such as water supply, street lighting, markets, hawkers, and squatters,[23] conducted one of the first ever surveys of youth in Hong Kong, and even sent representatives overseas to Singapore and Malaysia to study welfare work in these territories.[24] Along with the government, they encouraged women to become more involved in local welfare and civic work, as well as providing them with the basic skills to make a living and improve their own health.

Such voluntary associations, by the government's own admission, carried out most of the welfare work for adult destitutes, providing free meals, shelter, loans, and a free repatriation scheme for those wishing to return to China. They also assisted the government in relief work following serious fires in several squatter areas. Although the Shek Kip Mei and the Tung Tau fires are the most well known, hundreds of smaller fires regularly threatened squatter villages throughout the 1950s. In 1954, for example, there were ten separate fires in squatter areas, leaving over 40,000 people homeless.[25] In November 1951, a fire at Tung Tau Village left two dead and over 10,000 people homeless in a matter of hours.[26] The fire at Tai Hang Tung in 1954 left 24,000 homeless, the third worst squatter fire in the colony's history.[27] In the same year, fires at Li Cheng Uk and Tai Po Road left 7,000 and 6,000 people homeless respectively; another 11 smaller fires affected some 5,000 more.[28]

These disasters were followed by the collapse of squatter huts in Ngau Tau Kok, caused by a typhoon, which struck in August. In 1955, further hardships followed when the colony was struck by frost in January followed by a severe drought in the summer, resulting in water restrictions and crop failure. At the start of the 1960s, the police were called upon to assist when typhoon Mary caused havoc in the colony, close on the heels of torrential rainfall, which had caused severe flooding in the NT.

A UN survey estimated that, by the mid-1950s, there were at least 667,000 refugees living in Hong Kong, 'probably the biggest displaced person problem on earth, given its size'.[29] Poverty and susceptibility to flooding, landslides, and fires was the experience of the majority. Relief was provided by a variety of religious and charitable organisations (such as the Lutheran Church and the Hong Kong Family Welfare Society). Because most people had no ready access to sanitation, night soil collections were necessary, especially in the densely populated urban areas, and bath houses were opened by the Urban Council to provide free baths in Kowloon and Hong Kong. For several years, these old methods of handling the 'problem of people' persisted, without any organised response from government. Though the squatter villages presented a fire and public health risk, clearing them entailed demolishing thousands of huts, leaving their occupiers homeless and aggrieved – providing them with public housing was not something the government yet envisaged.

Squatter fires, floods and landslides are routinely presented in Hong Kong yearbooks of the period as adversities over which government and people triumphed. But as Smart points out, these incidents and the government's response to them were also permeated by political, geopolitical and internal security dimensions. As the Commissioner of Police observed at the time, unless displaced squatters were compensated or given new housing, removing them could cause 'bitterness' and create an 'explosive' situation; he thus urged caution (Smart 2006: 70). Smart also notes that the civil unrest which was sparked by inadequate provision for fire victims (particularly at Tung Tau) was 'significant enough that Governor Grantham pointed to them as evidence for the precariousness of Hong Kong's internal security position', whilst his 'discourses about his concerns reveal how the Chinese of Hong Kong were seen as a profoundly unreliable population whose fundamental loyalty was to China' (Smart 2006: 73). For Smart, the government's decision to embark on its massive Resettlement Programme in 1954 was, in part, regarded as a means of containing this threat to internal insecurity.

Resettlement and reorganisation

Whilst the lack of proper housing for squatters clearly created dissatisfaction, which could provoke civil unrest and invite communist agitation in the colony, attempts to clear squatter areas were equally fraught with similar problems.[30] In these early years of the Cold War, the British were anxious to do nothing that would provoke intervention by China into Hong Kong affairs. It was this, Smart argues, that drove the Hong Kong government's decision to embark on large-scale resettlement after the Shek Kip Mei fire (Smart 2006: 84). The Tung Tau fire demonstrated how easily small, localised issues could trigger far more serious public order problems. This realisation contributed to the more 'caring' response adopted by the government when further fires occurred in squatter areas.[31] Previous fires (for example at Kowloon City in 1950, which left 20,000 people homeless) had met with a less compassionate response than the fire Shek Kip Mei in 1953. In 1952 alone, there were seven serious fires in areas mainly inhabited by people who had been 'driven out of China' by the Communists or who had simply moved back to Hong Kong after the war, when accommodation was in short supply:

> . . . these displaced persons in hundreds of thousands settled on the hillsides and in the valleys, building for themselves wooden shacks literally touching each other for hundreds of yards and separated by lanes which are often no more than a yard wide. Fire and health risks are consequently serious, and the difficulties of re-settlement are enhanced by the fact that there is no other suitable land and that some congestion is in consequence inevitable.[32]

The government's initial response was to construct fire breaks to limit the effects of the fires and set aside 'approved resettlement' and 'tolerated squatter' areas for re-settlement, but fire breaks still displaced those living in huts demolished to make way for the lanes, whilst 'approved areas' were mainly intended for families with the longest residence in the colony who could afford to build a house, rather than the new impoverished immigrants.[33] Smart observes that the Commissioner of Police also stressed the importance to internal security of keeping a record of every single family that moved into 'approved' areas (Smart 2006: 81). Those seeking permission to move would have to establish that they had the necessary financial resources and were 'law abiding and useful citizens' (ibid). Initially, a new sub-department of the Urban Council was established to re-settle the squatters 'by degrees' into 16 'bungalow towns' and three semi-permanent hut areas,[34] which the government described as 'cottage-areas' and 'miniature villages' with schools and essential services, essentially echoing quaint images of English village life. The government was still not prepared to consider wholesale resettlement of the squatter population into decent housing (even though it had been criticised by London in the 1930s for its poor housing provision and the state of its housing stock, particularly its urban tenements. The war and the influx of refugees had worsened the situation). The population in 1952 was estimated at 2.25 million; in 1954, the government estimated a rise to 3.5 million over the next ten years, ringing alarm bells amongst those departments faced with providing services for this increased population. The prospect of such a commitment appears to have caused the government to hesitate before accepting responsibility for squatter re-housing. Over 80 per cent of the population lived in the 36 square miles of the urban areas.[35]

As the somewhat limited resettlement plans got under way, the government applied its own notions of 'deserving' and 'undeserving' cases. It was keen to 'weed out' from those applying for resettlement 'imposters whose only aim is to obtain cheap accommodation for which they were ineligible under the resettlement scheme'.[36] Only 'genuine' applicants were to benefit. A 1952 survey conducted as part of this screening process estimated that of the 70,000 in the survey, about one quarter were aged under ten, and a large number were aged between 25 and 40; it also reported 'an exceptionally low proportion of youths and old people'.[37] About half had no regular employment and earned a living by doing casual work; over 90 per cent were said to originate from Guangdong 'though a substantial number are old Hong Kong residents'

Table 11.1 Population immediately pre- and post-War

Year	*Population*
1931 census	948,751
1941 estimate	1,600,000
1945 estimate	500,000
1946 estimate	1,600.000
1947 estimate	1,800,000
1950 estimate	2,360,000
1952 estimate	2,250,000
1953 estimate	2,500,000
1954 estimate	2,500,000
1955 estimate	2,500,000
1956 estimate	2,535,000
1957 estimate	2,677,000

Source: Hong Kong Yearbooks.

(ibid). By 1953, the Social Welfare Department was reporting growing destitution amongst the elderly, physically weak and unskilled who could not return to China:

> Some of these people are juvenile vagrants, the subject of expulsion or banishment orders, while others are physically or mentally handicapped from competing in the Colony's limited employment market . . .[38]

By the early 1950s, the government realised that the refugees were not going return to the Mainland. The 'problem of people' that now arose related not only to the sheer number of persons entering Hong Kong but also to their poverty, age and health. Even Hong Kong's commitment to the free market could not deny welfare facilities to the aged, the orphans, the sick and the mentally and physically infirm who were unable to earn a living in the market place.[39] It became necessary for the Social Welfare Office to take care of 'blind boys, and crippled and mentally defective persons' but this was done under makeshift conditions whilst long term plans were made' (ibid). Many of the institutions catering for these groups were built in this period, though most were run not by government but by charitable, religious and other voluntary organisations.

As part of its obligations under the 1951 Protection of Women and Juveniles Ordinance (amended from 1938), the government embarked on measures to improve the 'moral welfare' of young women, especially juvenile prostitutes and children 'in moral danger.[40] Forty juvenile prostitutes were placed by the Moral Welfare Officer in a home for up to 100 girls established by the Catholic Sisters of the Good Shepherd in 1954. 'Qualified social workers experienced in moral education' came from Shanghai, some probably drawn from amongst the missionaries fleeing the city in the aftermath of the Communist victory. Nationalist and self-help groups provided 'welfare camps' in places such as Rennie's Mill for the old, blind, crippled amongst those refugees whose plans to travel to Taiwan were scuppered by Taiwan's refusal to admit them.[41]

The need for large-scale reform in the colony's housing supply had been highlighted by the D'Almada Committee in 1946, and by Sir Patrick Abercrombie in his 1948 report on town planning in Hong Kong. The 'post-war mood of Europe . . . favoured the planned re-building of blitzed cities', and Abercrombie had been commissioned to draw up plans for the re-building of London. Visiting Hong Kong, he had noted its shortage of land for urban expansion and its 'unlimited reservoir of possible immigration', and recommended the building of new towns on the outskirts of Kowloon and in the NT; the zoning of the colony into industrial and residential areas; the removal of military bases from urban centres; and the construction of a cross-harbour tunnel linking Victoria and Kowloon.[42]

Anxious to stave off criticism about its slow progress on the housing front, the government pointed out that Hong Kong's planners had had to deal with the more pressing problem of housing large numbers of refugees. It was already 'packed to the limits of its tattered fabric' and had one of the highest urban densities in the world at over 50,000 people per square mile.[43] That a number of people were still left in the squatter areas did not, thus, reflect any 'callousness or indifference' on its part to the welfare of the people.[44] Rather, it was said to reflect Hong Kong's humanity, its 'long and proud tradition as a free port . . . and a place of refuge for anyone in China who cared to step across the border' (ibid). The influx of refugees since 1949 presented the government with:

> . . . the complicated moral predicament of a squatter population which includes, perhaps to an increasing extent, Chinese British subjects, people who have lived in Hong Kong for generations and whose only home it is, people for whom the Hong Kong government has a very special responsibility.[45]

Despite this rhetoric of moral duty, the government relied heavily on voluntary agencies to distribute free meals and other relief and looked to the refugees themselves to re-build their huts in designated areas. In keeping with its free-trade and self-help principles, neither the provision of government housing nor relief was, it argued, the answer:

> It is a question of rehabilitation in such a way that the people concerned can be absorbed into the economic life of the basic community. It is not therefore a simply matter of building cheap, manageable fireproof houses. It is a matter of building these houses in areas where industry can absorb the occupants and of stimulating and assisting industry so that it is in a position to increase employment.[46]

Turning the refugees into productive citizens, it was hoped, would enable them to lift themselves out of poverty. Employers in industrial undertakings were encouraged to provide basic dormitory accommodation for their workers on land provided by the government at a special low price; some of the expense of site formation on the difficult hilly slopes, and of the provision of water, electricity and sewerage, would also be met by the government. The construction of the tramline to East Point and Shau Kei Wan in 1904 had led to the growth of 'working class suburbs' but industrial areas remained scarce.[47] With the growth of manufacturing in the 1950s, land was needed for new industrial developments and for low-cost housing for factory workers. Since Hong Kong's hills meant a shortage of suitable land for industrial development, squatter villages on the flatter land became highly desirable. Plans were developed to clear the squatter areas using squatter patrols and, since the government owned the freehold of almost all the colony's land, it was in a position to force through its plans without too much public consultation.

By 1953, areas in Kowloon Bay and Tsuen Wan were designated as new towns for this kind of industrial development. In Tsuen Wan, surveyors investigated the possibility of building a road link to Tai Po, another possible new town site. Negotiations also began with villagers to relocate their homes and ancestral halls to make way for the construction of new factories, roads, dormitories, gardens, playing fields, swimming pools and sports grounds. The possibility of building 'in the beautiful and fertile valley of Shatin' was mooted[48] but the government was keen to avoid taking land from agriculture, preferring instead to reclaim land or reuse what was already under-utilised.[49]

Meanwhile, the government cut fire lanes through existing squatter areas. It also announced plans to eventually 'clear the various squatter areas and rebuild them', but the possibility of speedy resettlement was seen as an 'impossible task'. It experimented instead with two new subsidised housing schemes at Sheung Lu Uk and Sham Shui Po 'for the poorer sections' of the population. These were regarded as pilot schemes for more ambitious plans 'to reduce the deplorable congestion which now exists in the tenements of the city'.[50] Five million dollars was made available to make housing loans available at low rates of interest to junior civil servants provided that 'they organise themselves into housing societies'.[51] Grants were made available from the Colonial Development and Welfare Fund to assist the newly established Hong Kong Housing Society build low-cost, new model housing and to assist with the costs of site formation.[52]

By the end of 1952, however, it was clear that these schemes would not reduce the squatter population fast enough. By 1953, 32 per cent of the government's budget was being spent on social services, at a time when government revenue was dropping. The 'problem of people' clearly required more radical thinking.

At the end of 1952 the government finally announced its resettlement policy for the 'gradual elimination of the unhealthy squatter colonies in the urban areas of Hong Kong'.[53] 'Healthy Villages' – such as the ones constructed at North Point, So Uk, and Kennedy Town – were one model.[54] They provided relatively low-density homes for white collar workers, incorporating separate living room and bedrooms, a kitchen, toilet, shower, lifts and refuse chutes; the complex included a post office, schools, clinics and a bus terminus. Another model existed in the form of the 'garden city' of Kowloon Tong, an area of low-density housing developed in the 1920s and 1930s and occupied almost exclusively by Europeans. As a large-scale remedy for the poorer sections of the population, however, these models were deemed far too costly. Something else had to be designed.

Shek Kip Mei and the Shek Kip Mei 'myth'

The fire at the largest squatter settlement, Shek Kip Mei, on Christmas Day 1953, left over 50,000 people homeless overnight. Though, as Smart argues, it alone did not finally propel the government to launch an ongoing multi-storey resettlement programme, the decision to re-settle these fire victims in government-financed housing blocks 'as a single emergency response . . . was indeed momentous' (Smart 2006: 103). The government's own account of how it reached this point talks of humanitarian impulses, the immediate provision of free food for the homeless, mobile relief teams sent out to help the aged, collect stray children and the sick, the distribution of warm clothing and the provision of emergency sanitary and washing facilities.[55] Public baths and latrines were provided in the urban areas for those living in makeshift dwellings that lacked such facilities. A special 'night-scavenging' service was introduced to clear the streets of rubbish and cleanse the latrines.

More recent histories of the event have, however, revealed less altruistic motives behind the massive resettlement programme that followed Shek Kip Mei. Principal amongst these was the need for land upon which to develop the industrial undertaking essential to Hong Kong's 'miraculous' economic growth of the 1950s and 1960s.[56] Smart also notes the considerable world media attention to the plight of those left homeless meant that the prestige of the colonial government was at stake, and that earlier incidents had already demonstrated the problems which disaffected squatters could cause for internal security (Smart 2006: 104).

According to the 1953 government yearbook, following the Shek Kip Mei fire, 'A vast scheme for re-housing of the homeless in the devastated area was immediately launched with government funds and government backing'.[57] Though there were, as Jones (1990) says, clearly some in government who did manifest a humanitarian concern with the plight of the fire victims, by 1954, it was also becoming clear that the costs of continuing the vast relief programme were roughly the same as constructing new homes for the victims. The first Commissioner of Resettlement's report in 1955 also stated that:

> Squatters are not resettled simply because they need . . . or deserve hygienic and fireproof homes; they are resettled because the community can no longer afford to carry the fire risk, health risk and threat to public order and prestige which the squatter areas represent and because the community needs the land of which they are in illegal occupation. And the land is needed quickly (cited in Jones 1990: 184).

Some individuals in the government did see the plight of the squatters in more compassionate terms. The introduction to the 1954 government report speaks of how fires, landslides and flooding:

> . . . [H]ave made many tens of thousands of desperately poor people completely and finally destitute . . . Shelter for tonight and tomorrow is of little consequence when one is faced with a problem of these

> dimensions. It would be tolerable to be homeless for weeks ahead if there was some reasonable hope of finding security in the future.[58]

Many fire victims were still living in 'pathetic cabins built against walls of side streets and cul-de-sacs', and in 'deplorable squalor between the fire breaks in the old settlements'.[59] But, more pressingly for the colony's commercial interests, the squatter settlements were hindering Hong Kong's industrial and economic modernisation by occupying valuable land which could be used for building by business and industry, making a powerful economic case for squatter clearance (Jones 1990: 184). Clearance had been done before without re-homing the squatters. Now, however, 'there were just too many people involved for simply removal. En masse, they were capable of stirring up trouble' (ibid). Another influential argument was that, unless they were re-housed, the squatters would remain a threat to the territory's law and order. Internal stability was paramount.

Economic and political factors thus finally prompted the government to 'set itself firmly upon the new course of merging the newcomers and their children into the fabric of Hong Kong society'.[60] The fire site was bulldozed and plans approved for over 10,000 domestic 'units' to be built, at government expense, to be rented to the homeless at a minimal rent. According to the government, this building programme would effectively re-house about a quarter of the squatter population (between 40,000 and 60,000 people) in 'sanitary, fire-proof quarters adjacent to their place of work' (ibid). The new blocks were also to follow the trend of modern, functional design:

> Soon the old porticoed, heavily-pillared building with its high ceilings, fans and broad verandahs would be as out of date as the pith helmet. The new trend, in both commercial and domestic architecture, was for functional blocks, many air-conditioned'.[61]

The relocation of cheap labour to areas where it was required also made resettlement potentially advantageous economically. By the end of 1954, one year after the Shek Kip Mei fire, thousands had been re-housed in fireproof, sanitary dwellings 'far beyond what they could have envisaged when, a year ago, they racked through the rubbish heaps for sheets of cardboard and tin with which to shape walls and a roof' (ibid).

The idea that this massive resettlement programme came as a humanitarian response to the Shek Kip Mei fire has become part of Hong Kong folklore, earning a government short on political legitimacy plaudits locally and worldwide. From 1954 onwards, it embarked on a massive public housing construction programme (the Mark 1 Resettlement Blocks). The first blocks, built at the Tai Hang Tau fire site north of Boundary Street, provided the model for the rest. It consisted of H-shaped blocks in which the crossbar provided communal toilets, washing spaces and bathing cubicles. Two wings contained anything from 80 to 128 rooms on each floor, each room measuring 12 feet 6 inches by 9 feet 6 inches; the total number of rooms in an average block was between 500 and 600, and the rent per room was fixed in 1954 at HK$10. Squatters who had previously operated shops in the squatter villages were given the chance to rent a ground floor room for domestic and business use.[62]

Officially, the rationale for resettlement seems to have had little 'had little need for mere humanitarianism' (Jones 1990: 184). The question was raised as to whether the land needed for re-settlement could be justified for a single section of the community, most of whom were recent immigrants with no legal rights to land.[63] Other citizens had a better claim to these resources (ibid). In keeping with its tradition of prioritising economic matters, the government's approach to the 'problem of people' was rather 'hard headed' (Jones 1990: 184). The solution hit upon was 'intensive vertical development' rather than intensive horizontal development, which would use up too much valuable land.[64] In the years to follow, the abundance of cheap labour, the 'know-how' of refugees from Shanghai, and the existence of cheap, nearby housing allowed employers to keep wages low, all of which contributed to Hong Kong's economic take-off.

By 1957, 120,000 people lived in the basic Mark I Blocks:

> Basic they were indeed: 24 sq.ft. of usable floor area per adult, arranged in back-to-back, tenement-like 'family' units of 120 sq.ft. each, with communal sanitary facilities and with access only via communal balconies which were also . . . to be used for cooking; the whole being organised in 'H blocks' consisting of six or seven lift-free, electricity-free floors (Jones 1990: 185).

'Modernisation', the watchword of the 1950s, was reflected in the design of public buildings throughout the colony, including these new resettlement estates. Old Victorian and Edwardian colonial-style buildings, such as the Hong Kong Shanghai Bank, were demolished to make way for 'loftier buildings' such as the Bank of China (1951) and the Chartered Bank building (1957); 'slim towers of concrete' were built to accommodate more people on the same ground area; lawns and gardens were turned into sites for garages and car parks (ibid). A building boom was under way in both the public and private sector; projects were to 'offer the quickest and most profitable return'.[65] Government architects broke away from traditional designs: 'the bold design of buildings erected by the government from 1948 onwards put the official seal on the architectural "New Look" . . . these buildings, repeated in later constructions, followed the same basic pattern, thus achieving the economy of series-production. Quarters built for the Police Force showed that official architecture was now as elegant and clean-edged as the most advanced private buildings anywhere' (ibid).

In respect of poor people's housing, the government likewise built less elegant, but equally 'modern', six- or seven-storey, reinforced concrete H-shaped resettlement blocks to accommodate large numbers of squatters and refugees. These were built on the same pattern and thus also achieved 'economy of series production' and maximum use of land. The flat rooftops were fenced to be used for recreation and welfare facilities such as roof-top schools and clinics. Each block could house over 2,000 people. The government estimated that the cost of building such a block was more or less the same as it was already spending every fortnight on the victims of the Shek Kip Mei fire.[66]

By 1956, 40 separate blocks had been built in four estates, housing some 103,000 persons (ibid). By 1957, the northern perimeter of Kowloon was described as 'an almost solid phalanx of H-block resettlement estates'.[67] The estate at So Uk was the largest domestic housing development carried out as an integrated scheme in the Far East,[68] accommodating up to 30,000 people in 12- to 16-storey blocks. Tenants were, however, subject to selection and had to meet certain criteria. They had to be over 21, to have lived in Hong Kong since at least mid-1948 (by 1956, less than 50 per cent of the population had lived in Hong Kong for more than 10 years), to have an income of HK$300–900 per month, and to have a recognised housing need. All were now direct tenants of the government.[69]

As their landlord, however, government was reluctant to evict troublesome tenants, for 'these people cannot be evicted without recreating those very dangers the establishment of these tenancies was designed to remove' (ibid). Evicted tenants with nowhere to go could, in other words, easily return to being disaffected squatters, tinder for communist agitators in the colony.

Large numbers of squatters did remain reluctant to relinquish the relative independence of their villages. A housing survey of 1957 found that 56.3 per cent of the population was unwilling to live in resettlement estates; 53.5 per cent refused to move to Housing Authority estates.[70] Thus, towards the end of the 1950s, substantial sections of the population still lived in squatter villages, cubicles and 'bed spaces' (ibid) beyond the main reach of government. Though there were said to be some 'undesirable elements' amongst those who did accept the new housing, most were said to 'appreciate what is being done for them by the Government' and respond well 'to the efforts of staff to train them to be decent, law-abiding citizens of Hong Kong'.[71]

Housing and social order

The government's presence in the new resettlement estates came in the form of the Resettlement Department, described as being run along military lines and comprising many ex-soldiers as resettlement officers.[72] This presence was crucial because, as it finally appreciated after the 1956 riots,

> . . . possible threats to public order . . . may be sparked off and spread

> like a forest fire in such conditions. And it would be criminally foolish to overlook the opportunities which these estates offer to political or even subversive agitators . . . On the other hand, such compact and uniform communities probably present a unique field for experimental education in the social and civic spheres . . . (ibid).

The Resettlement Department was separate from the Housing Authority, established in 1954 to oversee non-resettlement, low-cost housing (Smart 2006: 114). The Housing Authority comprised members of the Urban Council and three members nominated by the Governor. It supervised estates at North Point, Cadogan Street and So Uk, low-costs housing estates 'of a scale never before attempted in Hong Kong'.[73] North Point was built to accommodate about 12,000 people and So Uk, about 31,000, each estate matching the size of a small town in England. But, echoing orthodox accounts of crime and the rise of the police in the industrialising Britain of the nineteenth century, the government saw the high density of the population in these urban areas as 'carrying with it all the elements conducive to the corruption of morals and conduct . . . demanding from the Police Force continuous vigilance and a frequent reassessment of ideas and methods'.[74] The flow of migrants to the urban areas was, thus, thought to necessitate more police and different kinds of policing. The Housing Authority and Resettlement Department would each have their own officials responsible for the day to day running and management of the estates, for the monitoring of standards and the enforcement of policy.

The new multi-storey estates thus had a place in the ordering and disciplining of this potentially unruly society. They were administered by area officers in the Resettlement Department whose main task was:

> . . . one of educating the inhabitants to observe ordinary rules of hygiene, pay their rents, and in general become good citizens. When it is considered that these persons have formerly been living in insanitary squatter areas where almost all activities were illegal, it can be appreciated that the work of administering these estates requires constant vigilance, coupled with a high degree of tact and understanding.[75]

As with the housing provided by large charitable foundations in nineteenth-century British cities, ideas of discipline and good citizenship were to be conveyed through the rules regulating the renting and occupation of such housing. By ordering the lives of those living in the housing, the government might produce good, law-abiding citizens. By becoming the largest public housing landlord in the world, the Hong Kong government thus provided itself with a major means of discipline and regulation. The fact that it used voluntary organisations to deliver many of the services in the estates did not detract from its ability to influence the lives of their inhabitants, since the voluntary associations worked in close association with the Social Welfare Office and Secretary for Chinese Affairs. Voluntary effort was thus co-opted to government purpose.

This was the case even outside the housing estates, in those congested urban areas where hundreds still squatted in rooftop dwellings. By 1956, the government had organised squatter prevention units to patrol these rooftop areas on a regular basis, and to demolish any illegal huts or structures. Smart also observes that, following a fire at Tseun Wan, the government introduced a programme of 'regulated street sleeping', overseen by special police patrols to control those permitted to sleep in the streets, on recreation grounds, and in other public places.[76]

Supervision of the anti-squatter patrols was taken over by 'a young and active officer whose training thoroughly fitted him for planning and carrying out this type of [zero tolerance] . . . operation' (Smart 2006: 165). Squatter patrols consisted of an Area Officer from the Resettlement Department, accompanied by six labourers and a Demolition Squad (Smart 2006: 168). Area Officers were recruited from former Army Sergeants Major, Senior Customs Officers, ex-Police Magistrates, ex-Naval Commanders, and ex-Commissioners of Police (ibid). Squatter Control squads were also said to suffer from low morale, their work making them unpopular with the public and placing them in physical danger (ibid). The clearance of squatters and creation of the new resettlement estates was, after all, fraught with confrontation.[77] For example, when land was cleared for the building of the So Uk estate, an angry clash ensued between those already cultivating the land and police and Resettlement officers; the clearance of new Kowloon Villagers for the building of Wong Tai Sin in 1957 also provoked controversy (Smart 2006: 147). In his account of his role as District Officer in post-war Tseun Wan, Hayes also catalogues the numerous confrontations that occurred between residents and police during the course of clearance operations, both for industrial development and for the construction of large infrastructure projects such as the Mass Transit Railway (Hayes 1993; 1996).

By the mid-1950s, the government was reporting a 'growth in civic-mindedness . . . throughout the community'.[78] By the late 1950s, it was calling the years between 1947 and 1957 the 'decade of development'. At the ceremony to mark Grantham's departure as Governor in 1957, it was said that he had presided over a decade of material progress and the development of community spirit 'unprecedented in the annals of the Colony [and] . . . perhaps unique in any land'.[79]

By 1959, the new Resettlement estates housed a population of 215,405; by 1963 this rose again to 462,582 (Smart 2006: 149). The government acknowledged that the density, ventilation and amenities for the Resettlement blocks were less than satisfactory, but argued that they were designed to allow alterations to be made later, and that 'it was thought better to provide all with minimum standards of hygiene, safety and security before thinking in terms of the optimum for everyone'.[80]

By the end of the 1950s, these densely populated 'vertical housing estates' were, however, proving a challenge to traditional policing tactics. Government publications spoke of the resettlement blocks in glowing terms – they became part of the 'Hong Kong story', places which – although crammed with thousands of people earning very little money – were safe, crime-free, graffiti-free, and orderly. There is some truth in this, partly because the Housing Authority and Resettlement Office employed their own guards to monitor the estates. However, the experiences of those who lived in them suggest a different picture. Anecdotal stories abound of women being harassed in the communal bathing and toilet facilities. Families too few in number to fill a flat were forced to share their living quarters with complete strangers. As the government was later to realise, the estates also provided new opportunities for those engaged in political subversion as well as criminal activity. The 14K, in particular, proved a different kind of triad society from pre-war triads both in its organisation and activities. It recruited widely amongst the rootless young men living on the new housing blocks.

The potential for aggrieved squatters to generate internal security problems clearly occupied the minds of the government in the 1950s. As Smart says, 'if squatters believed that the colonial government was acting unjustly and illegitimately depriving them of the only homes that they could find, organised protest and violence became more likely . . . routine injustices were accepted. It was when government actions went beyond certain expectations, or when groups were left with no alternatives, that grievances could spark social unrest' (Smart 2006: 188). In 1956, however, it was the more ready mobilisation[81] of aggrieved residents within the resettlement estates themselves that played the major part in the structure of the 1956 riots (considered in the next chapter) and which intensified what Hayes has called the 'tin hat under the bed' mentality of foreigners – 'the view that one should always be ready for trouble'.[82]

Notes

1 Released 1960, directed by Richard Quine. Based on a 1957 novel of the same name by Richard Mason. There is also a stage play based on the novel, while in 2005 the Hong Kong Ballet staged a dance version.
2 Endacott and Birch 1978: 314.
3 HK Annual Report 1948: 96.
4 HK Yearbook 1948: 2.
5 HK Yearbook 1952: 4.
6 HK Yearbook 1952: 21.
7 HK Yearbook 1954: 12.
8 HK Yearbook 1956: 2.
9 HK Yearbook 1956: 4.
10 HK Yearbook 1956: 8.

11 HK Yearbook 1956: 9.
12 HK Yearbook 1956: 10.
13 HK Yearbook 1956: 13.
14 HK Yearbook 1953: 82.
15 HK Yearbook 1953: 3.
16 HK Yearbook 1955: 1.
17 HK Yearbook 1950: 11.
18 HK Yearbook 1956: 174.
19 *Hong Kong Telegraph* 2 September 1950; Social Welfare Office 1954: 33, 39 cited in Lock 1993: 146.
20 HK Yearbook 1952: 107–8; 1953.
21 HK Yearbook 1956: 173.
22 HK Yearbook 1954: 147.
23 HK Yearbook 1952: 108.
24 HK Yearbook 1954: 147.
25 HK Yearbook 1954: 2.
26 HK Yearbook 1951: 85.
27 HK Yearbook 1956: 24.
28 HK Yearbook 1954: 147. For more detail about these incidents see Smart 2006.
29 HK Yearbook 1954: 138.
30 See Smart 2006: 82.
31 What Smart calls the 'Shek Kip Mei' myth masks, he says, the real story of the gradual emergence of public housing in Hong Kong, which was 'a much more complicated and multi-stranded affair'. He also argues that it seems probable, even if there had been no fire at Shek Kip Mei, that something like the Mark 1 Resettlement Blocks would have been built sometime around 1954. See Smart 2006: 96.
32 HK Yearbook 1952: 7.
33 HK Yearbook 1956: 18.
34 HK Yearbook 1951: 84.
35 HK Yearbook 1957: 35.
36 HK Yearbook 1953: 116.
37 HK Yearbook 1952: 114.
38 HK Yearbook 1953: 110.
39 HK Yearbook 1952: 107.
40 HK Yearbook 1953: 113.
41 HK Yearbook 1952: 110.
42 HK Yearbook 1957: 13.
43 HK Yearbook 1957: 13.
44 HK Yearbook 1953: 12.
45 HK Yearbook 1953: 12.
46 HK Yearbook 1953: 12.
47 HK Yearbook 1957: 5.
48 HK Yearbook 1953: 105.
49 HK Yearbook 1957: 33.
50 HK Yearbook 1952: 110.
51 HK Yearbook 1952: 19.
52 HK Yearbook 1957: 21.
53 HK Yearbook 1952: 94.
54 See Smart (2006) for a more detailed discussion of this strategy.
55 HK Yearbook 1953: 13.
56 See, for example, Smart 2006 and Hayes 1996. In his earlier book on Tsuen Wan,

Hayes quite explicitly describes the squatter clearance and public housing programmes as less a decision to build public housing than to ensure that land could be cleared for development. Land was scarce and squatters had to be cleared to make way for new industrial towns like Tsuen Wan. See Hayes 1993.

57 HK Yearbook 1953: 13.
58 HK Yearbook 1954: 2.
59 HK Yearbook 1954: 4.
60 Hong Kong Annual Report 1956: 21; Hong Kong Annual Report 1959: 3, cited in Lock 1993: 132.
61 HK Yearbook 1957: 17.
62 HK Yearbook 1955: 117.
63 HK Yearbook 1954: 2.
64 HK Yearbook 1954: 4.
65 HK Yearbook 1957: 30.
66 HK Yearbook 1956: 26.
67 HK Yearbook 1957: 31.
68 HK Yearbook 1956: 151.
69 HK Yearbook 1956: 28.
70 Maunder and Szczepanik 1957 cited in Lock 1993: 135.
71 HK Yearbook 1956: 154.
72 See MacKay 2000: 466 cited in Smart 2006: 114.
73 HK Yearbook 1957: 24.
74 HK Yearbook 1856: 184.
75 HK Yearbook 1955: 119.
76 See Smart 2006: 123.
77 Smart also documents the confrontation that ensued during the clearance at Diamond Hill in 1963, when a 'near riot' occurred. See Smart 2006: 178. Many of the clashes surrounding the building of Hong Kong's massive infrastructure projects remain undocumented, creating the misleading impression of an apathetic, inactive public and a peaceful colonial past.
78 HK Yearbook 1956: 184.
79 HK Yearbook 1957.
80 HK Yearbook 1954: 5.
81 See Lam 2004, cited in Smart 2006: 186.
82 Hayes, quoted in Goodstadt 2005.

Chapter 12

The 1956 riots

The potential for civil unrest, which had so occupied the minds of the Governor and top officials through the early 1950s, was translated into reality in 1956, when riots exploded in Kowloon and Tsuen Wan. The rioting began on 10 October, the Nationalist anniversary of the founding of the Republic of China by Sun Yat-sen in 1911, sparked off by the removal of Nationalist flags in the Li Cheng Uk housing estate by a minor Resettlement Department official.

Aware since the late 1940s of the possibility of disaffection turning to unrest in the squatter areas, the government had become increasingly sensitive to politically significant occasions, such as 1 October (anniversary of the founding of the People's Republic of China) and the Nationalist celebration on 10 October. Just after the war, in 1947, it prohibited any public celebrations of the Double Tenth unless they were approved by the Commissioner of Police or the Secretary for Chinese Affairs.[1] However, both anniversaries were routinely marked by rival groups in the colony with the discharge of firecrackers, the decoration of buildings with flags, and the holding of indoor political meetings.[2]

Passions arose on these key days and conflicts had already occurred on previous occasions – riots broke out on the 10 October anniversary in 1952, for example, when 'unruly groups' of Nationalist sympathisers 'attacked and stoned leftist union premises' and pulled down the five-star flags that had been hoisted by the Communists on 1 October. Thousands of people attended various rallies throughout the colony; Nationalist flags flew on buildings, cars and bicycles. The large crowd gathered on vacant land near Bute Street had proceeded to throw stones at nearby buildings and march down the street towards a left-wing factory. A number of incidents occurred when leftist and rightist workers clashed. Nationalist workers had stoned Communist workers' clubs and torn down the PRC flag from buildings in and around Sung Wong Toi Road and Kowloon City Road. On that occasion, the police used tear gas bombs to disperse the crowds.[3] Over 20 people were arrested, including a 15-year old boy who was sentenced to two strokes of the cane. Nineteen people were convicted of various offences:[4]

> Charges ranged from disorderly conduct – stone throwing and inciting crowds to throw stones; illegal posting of anti-Communist handbills – these abused Mao Tse-tung as a devil, wife-stealer and slave-driver; and participating in an unauthorised procession – the Police claimed the procession was heading for a left-wing factory.[5]

By the mid-1950s, police precautions were, in short, the order of the day whenever these political anniversaries approached. In 1956, prior to the Double Tenth, police patrols were increased in Shamshuipo and Yaumatei (where many labour unions were located) and all police leave was cancelled (Lock 1993: 191). Officials in the Resettlement Department, Housing Department and Urban Services Department were under instructions to remove political symbols such as flags when they appeared on buildings, road bridges and street signs. In Li Cheng Uk, resettlement staff were instructed that residents were not to stick Nationalist flags on the buildings.

At about 9am on 10 October, a junior member of the Resettlement Department removed some flags stuck to the walls of Block G. By 11am a small crowd had gathered outside the resettlement estate office, demanding money back for the flags and an apology; firecrackers were discharged. By the afternoon, the mood of the crowd had grown angrier and one member of the resettlement office staff was assaulted. The police put an end to the disturbance by discharging tear gas into the crowd.

That night, however, rioting broke out again in Li Cheng Uk, Shamshuipo, Mongkok and Tai Hang Tung. According to the police, at about 8.30 pm a crowd of about 5,000, 'probably including hooligans from other parts of Kowloon', gathered at Li Cheng Uk. A private pro-communist school (Heung To School) was fired on and looted; shops were set on fire and looted, and vehicles stoned and set on fire. The Garden Bakery was set on fire, a car carrying two Europeans was attacked, police and fire brigade vehicles were damaged, and 'the police were attacked with bottles and stones throughout this period . . . reinforcements were called in and a broadcast announcement was made advising people to keep away from the areas affected.[6] A roadblock was erected on Castle Peak Road; baton charges and tear gas were deployed. The police sought to confine the rioting using minimum force and the situation was said to have been brought under control during the early hours of 11 October.

However, more serious rioting broke out again on the morning of 11 October. In one incident police were stoned by 'a large and disorderly crowd'.[7] A 'Grave Warning by the Government' was issued:

> No further assembles in the affected areas will be tolerated, and severe action will be taken against further outbreaks of lawlessness. Residents of the Shamshuipo and Li Cheng Uk areas are strongly advised to stay indoors for the remainder of today both for their own protection and in

> order to assist the authorities in maintaining law and order. Troops are being moved into the Kowloon area (ibid).

By noon on 11 October it had been decided to call in the army to cordon off affected areas.[8] Despite this, rioters continued to attack buildings and vehicles, stopping motorists as they passed through Kowloon and forcing them to buy and display the Nationalist flag before they could pass. During the afternoon of 11 October, the Swiss vice consul and his wife were attacked as his car drove through the area; the wife later died of her injuries. The offices of left-wing organisations were targeted and ransacked. Overall, the police recorded 25 incidents extending from Kwai Chung village on the eastern limits of Tsuen Wan to Shum Cheng village on the western side.[9] A curfew was imposed in Kowloon from 7.30 pm until 10.00 am the following morning; all ferries were stopped at 7.15 pm and all other public transport at 7.30 pm. The public were advised to listen to the radio for further information; the Governor was to make a broadcast about the disturbances (translated into Chinese) after the 8.00 pm news.[10] By 6.25 on the evening of 11 October, troops had been mobilised to cordon off the affected area. Sporadic rioting occurred along Nathan Road and in one incident the police opened fire on a crowd attempting to set fire to the Canton Provincial Bank, near the Alhambra Theatre. Another crowd erected a road-block on Clearwater Bay Road, near Kai Tak, and police used Greener gun fire to disperse the crowd; official reports indicate that two persons were killed in this incident.

The first major incident of 11 October had taken place at the Pao Hsing Cotton Mill on Castle Peak Road. A PRC flag, hoisted in the dormitory on 1 October, was removed by a non-communist worker. Pro-communist workers complained to the management, the flag was replaced and the worker apologised (see Lock 1993: 193). On 9 October, Nationalist workers had attempted to erect Nationalist flags, decorations and slogans in the same mill but, because they were too big, the workers were persuaded not to put them up. A rumour then began to circulate that the mill had refused to allow workers to celebrate the Double Tenth (see Lock 1993: 194). On 10 October:

> . . . a group of Chinese girls who were from the South Sea Textile . . . assembled in the Castle Peak Road near the bridge slightly to the west of the Pao Hsing Factory. They commenced to sing songs and called on the factory management to replace the Nationalist Flags. On being approached by the Police, the girls stated they were present in support on the Pao Hsing workers, in their efforts to obtain agreement from the factory management for Nationalist flags to be flown. Many other persons collected near where the girls were standing, some of whom were carrying Nationalist flags. The crowd gradually increased in size and many commenced to shout abuse at the factory management. A party of

> police had arrived at the scene and they warned the crowd to keep the peace. This temporarily quietened the crowd, although the group of girls continued singing. Persons in the crowd were seen to be inciting others, whose numbers were increasing. The temper of the crowd was beginning to become ugly and Police attempts to reason with them were ignored. More people joined the mob and more Nationalist flags appeared and by this time the crowd had become entirely out of hand and demanded the immediate hoisting of the Nationalist flag, otherwise they threatened to burn down the factory. (Persons were seen in the crowd carrying tins of what appeared to be kerosene). As the mob gathered outside the factory one of the watchmen . . . informed one of the senior staff . . . of this . . . however . . . [they] did not feel it was important and . . . nothing was done. At 17.00 hours a motor van . . . was overturned by the crowd and set on fire. This incident was also reported by the watchman but no instructions were given by the persons in charge of the factory. The crowd continued to be hostile and to threaten the factory and Det/Sgt Chung Hon entered the premises and informed the Works Manager . . . of the danger and of the hostility of the crowd and suggested that it would be advisable to fly the Nationalist flag. [He] . . . refused to do this and pointed out that the flags had been removed by the workers themselves and not by the management' (ibid).

The police tried to disperse the crowd. Management issued a notice asking for patience and for proper negotiations. Five right-wing workers then entered the factory to talk to the works manager. They demanded that all left-wing workers be dismissed, that Nationalist flags should be flown, and that the man in charge of the general office be dismissed. During the negotiations, a group of rioters gained access to the factory and set fire to the cotton and machinery:

> The crowd, following the fire and apparently feeling that there was unlikely to be any satisfactory co-operation from the factory management, became completely out of hand. They blocked Castle Peak Road with boulders and held up vehicular traffic. A motor cycle on which there were two Chinese males was stopped and, even though there was a Nationalist flag displayed on the cycle the crowd compelled the two persons on the motorcycle to dismount. The passenger . . . managed to escape . . . and ran away but the driver . . . was seriously assaulted. He was eventually rescued by Police and taken to Tsuen Wan Police station . . . the motorcycle was then set on fire by the crowd (ibid).

The factory management again refused to hoist the flags but agreed that the workers could do so if they wished. According to the police, the crowd had by this time become quite antagonistic, 'completely out of control and worked up into a frenzy'. The police were:

. . . completely unable to cope with the situation which had developed into a riot involving in the region of 500–600 people. A number of them climbed the factory gates and opened them, allowing the crowd to rush inside and pushing the Police back into the factory compound. Cotton was dragged out and set alight, as was another motor van, a sports car, and two more motor cycles. The crowd also attacked workers' dormitories on the first floor of the complex, and set these on fire; the factory's clinic had its windows broken; ten left-wing workers were assaulted. The Police were said to be helpless to stop the crowd rampaging through the factory. They were . . . eventually able to escape, whereupon they had to reinforce the 16 officers at the Police Station, where the crowd had begin to move. Inside the factory, negotiations continued after the fires – a Mr Wong, described as being from Rennie's Mill (a Nationalist stronghold) and 'the overall commander of the area', demanded that the Works Manager himself hoist the Nationalist flag, that 'the largest firecrackers in the Colony' be set off to accompany the act, and that HK$1,000,000 'tea money' be handed over. The sum was handed over by the factory's cashier. The fires were extinguished by 23.30.

Whilst the management was considering these demands, part of the Mill was set alight and left-wing workers were assaulted. Attacks followed on other left-wing premises in the Tsuen Wan area. The police and army called up reinforcements, opened fire, and later imposed a curfew to bring the situation under control. About 1,100 police were in action throughout the 10th and into the early hours of the 11th. These were later supplemented with 200 Auxiliary Police and joint police/military operations rooms were set up in Kowloon and Hong Kong. According to official reports, the police deployed baton charges, tear gas and 'sickening gas' to disperse the rioters, and only a 'few, isolated revolver shots' were fired by individual police officers in self protection, none causing any casualties (London Press Service, August 1957). On more than one occasion on the 11th, the police found themselves surrounded and stoned by the crowds of rioters and had to fight their way out or await reinforcements. Shamshuipo police station was, for example, attacked and the police opened fire with Greener guns to defend it. Anecdotal reports from officers involved in the riots indicate that some police officers fired indiscriminately into the crowds without shouting any warning. When it became clear that the incidents on the 11th were no longer 'attributable primarily to the crowd excitement which might have been engendered by the Double Tenth celebrations' but were 'clearly being fomented by hooligans and criminals', the Commissioner of police decided that the situation required 'firm handling' to bring it under control. He thus issued 'emphatic instructions that all necessary force must be used to disperse the mobs, including, if necessary, the use of Greener gun fire. This appreciation was reinforced by the arrest during the morning of two

> confessed Triad society members who admitted that Triad societies were among those directing the mob attacks (ibid).

Other incidents on the 11th followed a similar path – crowds demanded that the management of factories hoist the Nationalist flag and dismiss left-wing workers; they entered factory premises, broke windows, damaged vehicles and set them on fire. In the Kowloon Textile Factory, some men from the crowd forced open the guard room and took away three shotguns and a quantity of ammunition. At the Textile Corporation, left-wing workers were assaulted by the rioters outside the factory. Later the same day, a crowd outside the factory dormitories shouted 'Burn down the mill'; the police described the situation as 'extremely ugly' (ibid). Thirty left-wing workers who agreed to resign tried to leave the factory by a side entrance but were caught by the crowd, beaten and forced to '*kau tau*' on the roadway and shout anti-communist slogans (ibid). Other left-wing workers inside the factory were forced to march, two by two (with a female worker forced to carry the Nationalist flag) to and from the Pao Hsing Mill. Other targets included the South Sea Textile factory and South Textiles Limited (ibid). Elsewhere, rioters lit fires in the street to attract fire appliances, which they then stoned, immobilised and used to block streets; eventually, the fire service was instructed not to answer fire calls without a police escort.

The situation was brought under control temporarily by the British army and a curfew order imposed to clear the streets. A broadcast by the Governor on the evening of 11 October announced that order had initially been restored at 5.30 am but that at 9.00 am the disturbances had resumed. In his broadcast, the Governor portrayed the rioters as an atypical, 'lawless minority' whose activities were wrecking the daily lives of 'ordinary law-abiding citizens':

> Now I know that these disorders are the work of a group of lawless elements – of gangsters and hooligans – who are trying to turn the situation to their advantage. I know that their actions will be roundly condemned by the natural law-abiding people of Hong Kong . . . Now I want to say a word to . . . those who are instigating and perpetrating these riots. Last night the Police exercised great care and restraint in their natural desire to avoid inflicting fatal casualties. As you heard at mid-day, Military Forces have now been moved into the area in support of the Police. I give you fair warning now that if you continue this lawless behaviour you will run the risk of being shot. Although the Security Forces will only use the minimum of force required to maintain order they will not hesitate to use that force and to use it quickly. The government is determined to put down these disorders without delay and will take whatever means are necessary to ensure that this is done . . . Tomorrow is the Cheung Yeung Festival. The government has no desire

to interfere with the observance of the religious rites associated with this festival but in the present situation it cannot allow any large gatherings of people. I therefore appeal to all of you to make the task of the government easier by cancelling any plans you might have to go out tomorrow . . . I very much regret the inconvenience which is being caused to the law-abiding citizens of Hong Kong through the misguided actions of a small number of lawless elements, but the government is determined to restore law and order in the shortest possible time and you can best help to make that time short by doing what you are asked to do. I very much hope the situation will be brighter tomorrow morning. Goodnight.[11]

On 12 October, however, the rioting continued in parts of Tsuen Wan where Nationalist and Communist workers were employed. The premises of some left-wing unions were damaged and several of their members were killed or injured.[12] The driver of a burnt out car was killed and its European passengers were seriously injured.[13] Military detachments were sent into Tsuen Wan town, where inter-factional fighting was reported to have resulted in 30 deaths; by the early hours the town was reported to be quiet, as were the rest of NT and Kowloon (ibid). A government bulletin, broadcast on the radio after the BBC News at 8.15 pm on the 12th, reported that, since the riots began, 26 people had been killed, 176 injured, and 179 charged, with other arrests pending. To reassure the public, it was added that the border at Lowu was open and vegetable markets were operating normally.

Another bulletin the following day (13 October) indicated that there was no evidence of prior planning but that 'from the very early stages of the disorders following the original incident . . . the violence has been planned and directed by Triad Societies and similar criminal organisations which have taken advantage of the emotions peculiar to a national celebration to stimulate rioting under cover of the symbol of their celebrations'.[14] On the evening of the 13th, the Colonial Secretary broadcast to the colony reassuring everyone that things were back to normal. This was followed by yet another broadcast by the Governor on the Sunday night (14th) in which he expressed his sympathy with those who had been injured or suffered losses in the riots, and insisted that the government would 'deal with the evil ones' according to their deserts and to prevent them from committing further misdeeds. The government and the majority of the people were, he argued, on the same side, fighting a 'common enemy':

It is one of the primary duties of governments to ensure the maintenance of law and order, so that decent self respecting citizens can go about their normal avocations in peace and without fear. That duty is fully recognised by this government and thanks to the prompt firmness of the authorities the situation is now under control . . . As you know, the curfew orders have already been substantially modified. But I cannot, and

> do not, promise you the removal of all restrictions until law and order has been completely re-established. In this, you yourself can help . . . I now ask you, nay, I demand of you, that you throw your weight whole-heartedly behind the forces of law and order, who are fighting your battle and who are immeasurably stronger than the common enemy . . . It is also your duty to assist the Government . . . Don't allow yourselves to be bullied by gangsters. The majority of them have already been rounded up. Together we'll deal with the remainder.[15]

By 26 October, the casualty figures had been revised: at least 60 people were known to have died, 43 of them males killed by gunshot wounds; two women were also killed by a fire engine which had run off the road after being stoned. A total of 232 people were known to have been admitted to hospital.[16] The total costs of the damage caused stood at HK$4.77 million; over 1,000 factories had also been forced to cease production in Kowloon.[17] Over 6,000 'criminals, hooligans and Triad societies gangs' were arrested on charges connected to the riots, including five persons who were charged with murder, convicted and sentenced to death.[18] However, nearly 2,500 of these were released after evidence against them was not forthcoming; a further 1,455 were detained for breach of curfew orders – 1,241 were sentenced to periods of imprisonment ranging from seven days to two months; another 214 were bound over, fined or discharged. Between 13 and 16 October the police conducted further raids on premises to obtain evidence against them. Of those arrested, 591 were charged with more serious offences such as murder, riot, possession of arms, triad membership, looting, and breach of deportation order. Others (about 1,400) remained under investigation and another 400 were awaiting trial.[19]

Despite the fact that no 'emergency' was ever declared, the Emergency (Detention) Regulations were brought into force, allowing the Governor to extend the period of detention for suspects.[20] The trials were moved from Kowloon Magistracy to Hong Kong, and were surrounded by considerable security.

The official report on the riots, compiled by a board appointed by the Governor, was published on 2 January 1957. Figures for the casualties were updated in February 1957 and again in August 1957, as prosecutions progressed. These showed that at least 60 people were known to have died as a result of the riots, one in January 1957 of Greener gunshot wounds.[21] However, it is clear from both the report itself and from subsequent research that no systematic record of the dead and injured was compiled at the time, and the actual number of casualties was never fully established.[22] As Lee says, rumours circulated that the white truck containers at Hunghom were used to store piles of corpses, which were then transported to Sha Ling (a remote Closed Area near the border) for cremation and burial (Lee 1995: 32).

Some 3,700 persons (out of over 6,000 arrested) were released after questioning; 1,455 cases of breach of curfew orders were disposed of; 26 people remained in custody awaiting further investigation; and 967 others were charged with more serious crimes. Many of those arrested had to be released due to insufficient evidence; others were held in a 'temporary' holding area at Chatham Road, an old Gurkha barracks in Tsimshatsui (Lee 1995: 30). Of the 6,200 arrested, most received minor convictions for breach of curfew orders – many were workers making their way to work in the early hours of the morning, unaware that they were breaking a curfew. Far fewer were convicted of the serious offences (Table 12.1).

Sentences of imprisonment ranged from six months to six years for riot and looting, one to three years for riot with membership of a triad society, and six months to two years for membership of a triad society (ibid). A further report issued in August 1957 decided levels of compensation to be paid to riot victims and provided the official account of what had happened.

At the official inquiry, the Governor stated that all the indications were that the riots had started spontaneously, but were subsequently exploited by:

> . . . gangs of criminals, hooligans, and Triad societies . . . it is significant that nearly half the reported crime in the Colony occurs in the northern part of Kowloon, which was the main centre of the rioting. As a result of the intensive police action taken during the disturbances, many members of these gangs are now in custody.[23]

In the government's view, the original incident at Li Cheng Uk had been hijacked by Nationalist agitators, aided and abetted by triad gangs (known to be of a pro-Nationalist persuasion) for the purpose of redressing old scores and attempting 'to win a dominant position in the labour world'.[24] The

Table 12.1 Charges and convictions from 1956 riots

Offence	*Convicted*	*Awaiting trial*	*Acquitted/ Discharged*	*Total*
Murder	5	–	4	9
Arson	1	1	–	2
Riot and unlawful assembly	232	–	299	531
Looting	145	–	27	172
Wounding	2	–	1	3
Malicious damage	2	–	7	9
Triad membership	154	–	42	196
Possession of arms	5	–	6	11
Breach of deportation order	31	–	–	31
Criminal intimidation	–	15	–	16
Total	**577**	**16**	**403**	**980**

Source: Government Daily Information Bulletins: 1 January 1957; 5 February 1957; 24 August 1957.

labour movement was, by the mid-1950s, dominated by pro-Nationalist and pro-Communist unions.[25] As far as the government was concerned, Communist influence had been evident in almost every labour dispute of the decade.[26] Industrial strikes in the economically unstable years of 1951, 1953, 1956 and 1959 were serious (Lock 1993: 101). By October 1956, there had already been ten strikes and three lockouts, some of them lasting longer than any other strike in the 1950s.

In Taiwan, the riots were seen as a 'Communist show', there being no good reason why, seven years after the establishment of the PRC, the Nationalist sympathisers in the colony should suddenly start attacking communist organisations (Lock 1993: 198). Grantham dismissed this theory, arguing there was no evidence to indicate that the communists had provoked any disorder during the civil disturbance.[27] At least some of the local press similarly acquitted the communists of any blame, noting instead the involvement of Nationalist groups in past incidents of public disorder and the fact that the main target of attack had been communist organisations and premises (ibid). There was, indeed, no evidence that the Communists were behind this incident.[28]

Locally, the *South China Morning Post* described the initial removal of flags by a Resettlement Department official as 'tactless in the extreme in view of the tensions between Communists and Nationalists in Hong Kong', but went on to praise the firmness with which the riots had been suppressed, complaining only that the Army had not been called in earlier.[29] Lock also concludes that the public, though critical of certain aspects of the police response (particularly the mistreatment of suspects and the arrest of persons who had unintentionally broken the curfew order), remained broadly supportive of the way in which order had been restored. He cites reports from numerous Chinese language newspapers as an indication of this quest for 'Peace and Stability'. Many encouraged those involved in the rioting to return home, observe the curfew orders, assist the government to restore order and 'observe a citizen's duty' (Lock 1993: 209). Some, however, also reminded the government of the need for restraint so as not to provoke further unease, and urged it to compensate riot victims for their losses (Lock 1993: 207). In startlingly prescient editorials, the *Hong Kong Times* argued that part of the problem lay in the absence of a good channels of communication between the government and the people, whilst the *Sing Tao Jih Pao* recommended the appointment of 'more approachable officials [who would] . . . be careful to deal with public affairs such as customs, religious affairs, or any sensitive issues that might provoke negative public sentiment in the future'.[30] This was a message that, as Lock points out, was not heeded until the1970s, by which time Hong Kong had experienced successive years of serious rioting in 1966 and 1967.

The riots received considerable coverage in both the English language and Chinese press. In the UK, however, they received little attention. Welsh notes that a short (half-hour) adjournment debate was held on 8 November in the House of Commons[31] in which, he says, the MP John Rankin, gave a 'reasonably accurate account of the riots'. The *Manchester Guardian* and the London *Times* argued that the riots were 'in no way an expression of hostility to British rule' but must be 'firmly quelled [as] they are like primers for atomic bombs'.[32] The *Times* tried to explain the disturbances in terms of Hong Kong's high population density, its overcrowding, high rate of unemployment, huge flow of refugees, and its severe water shortages.[33] The *Far Eastern Economic Review* also argued that 'the best way to prevent the poor from being provoked by political elements was to enhance the living standards of the poor'.[34]

Certainly, there was some truth in these explanations. Worker support for the strikes of the 1950s had derived, for example, as much from poor working conditions as political rivalry – most worked a nine to ten-hour day, seven days a week, with Chinese factories offering no holidays to workers for occasions such as Chinese New Year (Lock 1993: 25). There was also a highly unequal distribution of wealth in the colony – over 95 per cent of the population earned around HK $300 per month, and accounted for 60 per cent of the national income: 'simply put, the remaining 5 per cent of people shared 40 per cent of Hong Kong's national income' (ibid). In 1957, the top 10 per cent of the richest earned 42 per cent of Hong Kong's total national income, while the rest, 90 per cent of people, only obtained 58 per cent.[35] At the same time, unemployment was made worse by the number of migrants desperate for work and, despite the resettlement programme, many of the poorest people still lived in overcrowded and insanitary conditions as bad as anything they had left behind in China. It is likely that, for at least some of those engaged in fighting in Tsuen Wan, their own grievances formed part of the mix that led them to support riots triggered off by a dispute about political symbols.

However, by the time the riots erupted in 1956, life for many in the colony had actually improved in terms of health, living conditions, and law and order. Reported crime had fallen, and people living in resettlement estates such as Li Cheng Uk were much better off than those left behind in the squatter areas (Lock 1993: 197). Grievances rooted in material inequality could not, therefore, account for the degree of activism and disaffection indicated by the riots.

The police and government blamed the triads. Many, they argued, had entered Hong Kong as refugees. Being known supporters of the Nationalist government in Taiwan (which itself contained triad members) they had proceeded to stir up trouble in the colony whenever they could.[36] During the civil war in China, the Nationalists had recruited thousands of troops from the 14K to 'bolster public opinion behind the Nationalist cause and to prevent or reduce communist infiltration into the Armed Forces and civil administration' (ibid).

Writing in 1969, Fletcher[37] repeated the claim that the main 'trouble-makers' behind the 1956 riots had been criminals (triads) rather than political agitators. Over the years – and in the absence of any countervailing theory – this has become accepted as the official view of the matter.

However, it is clear that the government was by 1956 already aware of the potential for civil unrest amongst the refugee communities, and of the salience of political anniversaries as rallying points for trouble. The Far East was a key battleground in the post-war battle against Communism. In another year, the Emergency in Malaysia would end with independence but the spectre of communist-influenced insurgencies remained in other parts of the region. Moreover, involvement in the riots for opportunistic reasons does not exclude the possibility that triads also saw the riots as a political cause. Crimes committed during the riots – such as looting, assault, and protection rackets – were indeed committed by criminals and gangsters, but only 25 per cent of those convicted following the riots were convicted of belonging to a triad society (Lock 1993: 210) mainly the 14K. This percentage is not in itself surprising, given that in 1940, about 8 to 9 per cent of the Hong Kong population belonged to a triad society,[38] a number that had risen with the influx of refugees from the Mainland. According to the main published authority on the subject, post-war triads controlled public markets, transportation coolies, construction workers, and even into the labour sections of government departments.[39] By the 1956 riots, the 14K alone was said to number 50,000 members, giving them numerical supremacy over more established triad societies in the new resettlement estates. Described as more ruthless than the more established triads within which older members exercised their authority over disputes,[40] the 14K was particularly active in the Shamshuipo, Kowloon City and Tsuen Wan areas, and was also pushing for a dominant position in north-west Kowloon.[41]

It thus seems likely that a number of the men involved in the riots belonged to a triad society of some sort, perhaps especially the young male factory workers of the Tsuen Wan industrial area. But as Hayes says, this was also a heavily unionised workforce, and highly partisan. With their large numbers of non-Cantonese workers, 'Tsuen Wan's factories were among the problem areas of the Colony' (Hayes 1993: 62). When, in the early 1960s, the government began to clear the villages of Tsuen Wan to make way for the 'New Town' housing and industrial development, further confrontations were to occur here.[42]

The fact that, after 1956, Tsuen Wan was 'carefully monitored by the civil and police authorities' to prevent any recurrence of the riots indicates that the authorities recognised that something more than 'criminal' influences were at work. In the early 1950s triad societies were far less well organised than they were later to become, and posed no real challenge to authority. An attempt in 1946 to unite the different societies by Lieutenant General Kot Sin-wong had failed and, when he died in 1953, the 14K split.[43] Sub-branches of the 14K then 'abandoned all pretence at patriotic motivation and developed into wholly criminal associations to exploit the refugee areas of the Colony', and a power-struggle began as their leaders jockeyed for position (ibid). In 1955, the year before the riots, 148 of the 'most troublesome' officials and members of the 14K were arrested and deported, further weakening triad influence in the territory (ibid).

Whilst the triad presence was widespread, it is therefore doubtful whether triads possessed sufficient strength and unity to plan and organise the riots, though they were clearly involved in many of the criminal activities that took place during the disturbances. Placing the blame on criminal rather than political elements did, however, allow the government to depoliticise the affair and avoid antagonising the political sensibilities of Taiwan and Communist China, something it remained anxious to do throughout the Cold War era.

Its efforts in this regard have proved highly successful. Modern Hong Kong knows little or nothing of the 1956 riots, and few academics have paid them any attention.[44] The official view that they were triad-inspired remains largely unchallenged, perpetuating the myth that the post-war population was essentially politically apathetic. However, the reorganisation of the police in the aftermath of the riots, along with the activities of Special Branch, suggest that inside government itself, the internal stability and security of Hong Kong was never taken for granted.

Notes

1 Hong Kong Executive Council Minutes, cited in Lock 1993: 190.
2 *Report on the Riots in Kowloon and Tsuen Wan, October 10th to 12th, 1956* (hereinafter the 'Riot Report') and covering despatch from Grantham to Secretary of State for the Colonies, 23 December, 1956, Hong Kong, Hong Kong Government Printer.
3 *South China Morning Post* 11 October 1952.
4 HKPAR 1952–3: 44; Tsang 1988: 180–81, cited in Lock 1993: 191.
5 *South China Morning Post* 12 November 1952.
6 Police press release 11 October 1956.
7 Special Government Press Release, 1.15 pm 11 October 1956.
8 HK Yearbook 1956: 191.
9 Internal DCI report 'Recommendations – Tsuen Wan Riot prosecutions', 1956.
10 Special Government Press Release 6.45 pm 11 October 1956.
11 Daily Information Bulletin, Hong Kong Government 8.35 pm 11 October 1956.
12 HK Yearbook 1956: 45.
13 Special Release 2.00 am 12 October 1956.
14 1.00 am bulletin 13 October 1956.
15 Government Daily Information Bulletin 8.15 pm Sunday 14 October 1956.
16 Special Government Press Release 26 October 1956.
17 Riot Report 1956: 44–6. See also Lock 1993: 194.
18 HK Yearbook 1956: 191.
19 Special Government Press Release 2 November 1956.
20 Hong Kong Government Gazette 1956: 485–6 cited in Lock 1993: 193.
21 'Greener guns' were shotguns made by W.W. Greener of Birmingham, England, and designed initially for use by the Egyptian police. They were also called 'Tiger

guns' because they were used in Africa to shoot tigers. They used unusual calibre shells and were useless if stolen because standard ammunition would not fit them. The company is now based in Chippenham, England.

22 See, for example, Lee, Hong-nee 1995. Lee interviewed several police officers from the period. One respondent recounted seeing a person shot dead by a Greener gun at close range. The body 'had a nasty big hole at the front' (Lee 1995: 29). The respondent also claimed that the police lacked organisation on the ground, were left to make decisions for themselves, including when and where to fire; they were, he said, 'trigger happy'. Dead bodies were brought to police stations where staff, overwhelmed by the numbers of persons arrested, often made no attempt to trace relatives.

23 HK Government Compensation for Riot Damage and Injury August 1957.

24 HK Yearbook 1956: 45.

25 The Trade Union Council (TUC) and the Federation of Trade Unions (FTU) being the largest groupings. The FTU had approximately twice as many members as the TUC.

26 The Tramwaymen's Strike of 1949/50 had developed into a riot when police had attempted to suppress a meeting of the FTU in Russell Street (Lock 1993: 24). The government saw this and other strikes of the 1950s (such as the Hong Kong Tramways strike and Hong Kong China Gas Company strike of 1957) as politically motivated, waged by the Communists in support of the Beijing government, intended to disrupt the economy (ibid).

27 *South China Morning Post* 13 October 1956 cited in Lock 1993: 200.

28 Lock 1993: 27; Tsang 1988: 129–30.

29 *South China Morning Post* cited in Lee 1995: 75.

30 *Hong Kong Times* 13 October 1956; *Sing Tao Jih Pao* 14 October 1956, cited in Lock 1993: 208.

31 Welsh 1993: 456.

32 Ibid.

33 *The Times* 12 October 1956, cited in Lock 1993: 196.

34 *Far Eastern Economic Review*, cited in Lock 1993: 196.

35 Chow 1977: 166, 227, cited in Lock 1993: 100.

36 Morgan 1960: 71–2, cited in Lock 1993: 202.

37 Fletcher 1969, cited in Lee 1995: note 54.

38 Wong 1972: 108, cited in Lock 1993: 202.

39 Morgan 1960: 75, cited in Lock 1993: 202.

40 HKPAR 1956: 59.

41 Riots Report 1956: 4; *Eastern World* 11 November 1956; Qun-zhong Publication Society 1957: 79–80 cited in Lock 1993: 202. Some of these sources put 14K numbers as high as 80,000 by 1956.

42 See Hayes 1993: 64–89.

43 Lock 1993: 203; Morgan 1960: 84ff.

44 The most recent notable exception is the work of Lam Wai-man, who revisits the 1950s political landscape. Her work underscores the degree to which a certain hegemony has prevailed in the social science literature, perpetuating an elite version of history, which depicts the Hong Kong Chinese as politically apathetic and immature. See Lam 2004.

Chapter 13

Post-1956: paramilitarism, hearts and minds and political policing

The 1956 riots confirmed what the police force leadership of the 1950s already knew, i.e. that a 'police force on the British model cannot be organised on the lines of a military establishment and in consequence is not adapted for internal security duties in strength'.[1] The question thus arose as to whether the kind of 'military' and counter-insurgency policing used in Malaya during the 'Emergency' should become a template for the organisation, training and equipping of the Hong Kong Police. This had already been raised by a police advisor, seconded from the Home Office in 1948 to review 43 colonial police forces in the Colonial Police Service.[2] When, in 1949, he visited 11 colonial forces, he noted that in many colonies, policing was confined to the European quarters, with 'native administration' holding jurisdiction beyond. The growth of political consciousness meant that these 'native administrations' needed to be watched. The police needed be trained and encouraged to 'provide an impartial and efficient service for the preservation of law and order, independent of tribal, political or other influences, and imbued with the desire to give service justly as between all peoples' (ibid). He also emphasised the need to introduce such reform as would secure the loyalty and support of native police forces:

> Taking a broad view of the present social and political conditions in the Colonies and having regard to the possibilities of unrest and disturbances inspired by subversive influences, I cannot over-emphasise the importance which must be attached to the role of the Police not only within the system of Civil Administration but also in the much wider implications of internal security generally (ibid).

Native peoples must be made to feel that their police force had not been 'imposed upon them'; closer relations must be developed between the police and local populations. Sooner or later, he advised, the authorities would be forced to accept some form of representation from the rank and file. There must be 'an absolute prohibition upon membership of any trade union' but, in line with Pennefather-Evans, he argued that the rank and file might be permitted to form organisations to enhance the welfare of members: 'Happy home life, with a family housed under proper conditions, will do more to inspire and maintain an efficient and loyal service than any other aspect of the policeman's daily life' (ibid).

Post-war, internal security required consolidation in a number of Britain's colonial possessions. Hong Kong, on the frontline of the 'Bamboo Curtain', was no exception. Following a notice to all colonial governments in 1948, by 1949 most forces had introduced a Special Branch, though these were still inexperienced and could not yet be regarded as satisfactory; policing organisation, training, communications and equipment were also 'completely out of date' (ibid). Building on the idea of a Colonial Police Force (established in 1936), it was suggested that the commissioners of all major colonial forces hold a conference in London in 1951 to exchange ideas and experience.[3] It was at this point in the early 1950s that academics began, for the first time, to talk of an identifiable form of 'colonial policing', and to draw up a list of its supposed characteristics.[4] Within the colonial forces themselves, ideas and personnel were exchanged – some officers, with experience of insurgencies elsewhere were, for example, transferred to Hong Kong.

Unlike other colonies, however, a specialised 'paramilitary' gendarmerie was thought inappropriate for Hong Kong. In the heightened atmosphere of the times, all arms of the colonial government had to appear impartial and politically neutral to avoid providing China or Taiwan with any excuse for intervention. It was thus decided that the entire force (i.e. all male officers) would be trained in two distinct structures – as a civil force for normal policing duties, and as a paramilitary body for use when the occasion arose,[5] but it was not until after the 1956 riots that the force actually established the Police Contingency Unit as a specialised 'paramilitary' capability. On a day-to-day basis, the felt need was for a police force seen as more representative of, and responsive to, the local community. However, the presence of both Nationalist and Communist sympathisers in the colony made the authorities wary of employing locals, since their entry into the police opened up the possibility of subversion. Since the Nationalist cause was also associated with triad societies, there was the additional possibility that locally recruited police might have criminal, as well as political, ties. The need to carry on recruiting and retaining European officers was thus regarded as a necessity (even though they cost more to employ) and the control of the force remained firmly in the hands of this European elite. Grantham's distrust of the Chinese contingent, coupled with internal security concerns, meant that localisation was placed firmly on the back burner. Command and control was to remain in British hands, with Chinese officers in a subsidiary position.

The riots revealed a number of other weaknesses in police force capacity that the authorities now sought to remedy. One step was to improve the technology of repression, by implementing changes to systems of command and control, purchasing new communications equipment, re-styling police riot control uniforms, producing a force Riot Manual, and buying more modern types of armoured vehicles road-tested in other colonial insurgencies. The more visible side of maintaining internal security came in the form of the Police Contingency Unit (later re-named the Police Tactical Unit) formed at Fanling in 1958 to provide a trained internal security reserve. It introduced a fundamental change in the way the police approached internal security. Training involved weekly riot drill and the development of a paramilitary capability. This replaced the Emergency Unit, composed of Indians and Portuguese, established shortly after the war. (Even in the late 1940s, the Hong Kong police had been recruiting police capable of tackling internal security problems – it had, for example, recruited 30 expatriate sub-inspectors, transferred from Palestine, in 1948.)

The standard weapon carried by all police was the .380 Webley revolver, though gazetted officers could be issued with a .450 Colt automatic if they preferred; the same weapons were issued to inspectors at stations along the frontier. The Emergency Unit, the Northern Chinese, the Marine Police and rank and file employed in the NT were issued with a .303 rifle, although certain NCOs and the inspectors were also taught to use Bren guns, hand grenades; the 2" mortar guns were normally carried by inspectors and NCOs on patrol.[6]

All police divisions were supplied with Greener riot guns and '92' smoke grenades for emergency purposes, as well as tear gas and other special smoke; the 'entire force is taught how to throw grenades. Each man has his individual gas mask and riot stick as part of his kit for immediate use and wicker shields are used for anti-missile protection . . . Courses are given in revolver and automatic weapons twice a year and in the rifle once a year' (ibid). Between 1945 and 1962, the police also acquired locally designed and constructed armoured personnel carriers. These were thought to provide all-round protection to the police taking action against armed men, against bomb blasts, splinters, and mines, to provide a means of escorting bomb disposal teams, to be useful in patrolling the border area and for escorting VIPs, and for providing quick and easy entry and exit for its occupants (an officer and section, plus ammunition). As a last resort, small arms could be fired from their turrets. As it turned out, they were completely unsuitable for internal security duties. Their tyres proved vulnerable to attack, they provided poor visibility from the driver's position, were difficult to manoeuvre, became extremely hot inside, and were under-powered. Some of the defects were to be reduced after their use in the 1966 and 1967 riots, but the consensus was that they had to be phased-out or replaced with another type of armoured vehicle (the US Avenger, the Shoreland Armoured Patrol Car, the FV432 Armoured Personnel Carrier or the Saracen – the latter was the preferred option but without its Browning machine gun). Though the water tanker was used for riot suppression in the 1950s, by the time of 1966 its usefulness in congested urban areas was being questioned, the deployment of tear gas being seen as a more effective means of dispersing crowds away from the rioting and clearing Hong Kong's busy streets.

Some other force reorganisation also took place. Throughout the 1950s, the police had been aided by two auxiliary forces: the Police Reserve and the Special Constabulary. The Reserve was founded before the war and consisted entirely of Chinese volunteers; it assisted the police in times of emergency and with crowd control on special occasions. The Special Constables were a volunteer and conscript force of various nationalities who occasionally performed the same 'watch and ward' duties as the regular police. Neither branch received much in the way of training as most of their members were employed in the existing supply of essential services such as water, electricity, and communications.[7] As we have seen, however, internal security fears in the early 1950s had already resulted in their being equipped with firearms to defend their sub-stations in the event of civil unrest in the colony. Following what were identified as problems in mobilising two separate forces during the 1956 riots, in 1957 basic training was provided and the two were merged to form the Auxiliary Police in 1959.[8] Their amalgamation placed them under a single chain of command, making the force more administratively convenient and easier to operate for emergency duties.[9]

Winning hearts and minds

The rapid expansion of the police force between 1957 and 1961 prompted anxieties about reducing costs by reducing the army's presence in Hong Kong and the authorities' ability to maintain internal security:

> Neither increases in police strength nor any other measures that may be taken to improve the capacity of the force to deal with riots could (because particularly of Hong Kong's geographical position and the racial composition of its people) provide a substitute for military aid in conditions of widespread internal disorder. While such increases should improve the ability of the Hong Kong government to deal quickly with spontaneous riots before they develop, it will be necessary to be able to continue to call on strong military aid immediately there is any sign that rioting may spread; and disorders of any real size would in any case be quite outside the competence of the police to suppress unaided. If, therefore, Hong Kong is faced with a grave threat to law and order, military aid will almost certainly be required just as soon, and in just as great strength, whether the increased forces planned are in the field or not . . . The Police force is over 90% Chinese, a proportion which cannot be reduced. The deputy Inspector-General finds it is a good police force. But Chinese police can be expected to stand firm on the orders of a British government against Chinese rioters in Hong Kong just so long as they believe in the British government's will and ability to back them. The

> garrison provides evidence of both. Any reduction in it is therefore not simply a reduction in the armed strength available but also lowers the confidence of the Police – and the public ... Because of the special position of Hong Kong, where the problem of 'internal security' cannot be divorced from the external threat across the border, there is no possibility that the proposed further increase in the strength of the police can justify a reduction in the strength of the British garrison. If, however, the Governor found it possible to recruit a Gurkha striking force, it might then be feasible to effect a small reduction in the garrison equivalent to the strength of the Gurkha force.[10]

An earlier memo from the Governor, Robert Black, to the Colonial Office also mentioned the potential for conflict with local people if the police were used to suppress internal disorder. Black suggested that a programme of community service by the forces might go some way towards convincing local people that the police and army 'were not the stuff of which oppressors are made'; it might also counter propaganda that tried to paint them as oppressors and reduce the likelihood of disturbances arising in the first place.[11] Although, in his view, the forces were generally seen in a benevolent light by local people, propaganda might depict them as:

> ... something alien to Hong Kong, and with alien interests, rather than as an integrated part of the community ... it is much better that the Services should be seen at all times on friendly terms with the local people, identifying themselves with them as far as possible, helping them and generally being their good neighbour, so that, when seeming conflicts do occur, these may be already largely discounted in advance in the minds of people of goodwill ... It is for these reasons among others that the Services put so much effort into their relations with the civilian population. All ranks and units of the services, and service wives, devote much individual time, trouble and money to foster good relations, and they are generally responsible for much genuine welfare work ... (ibid).

Black's strategy was to embed the disciplined services in the community. This kept the police committed to what was seen in some quarters as 'non-police' work, such as providing help and relief to the population during fires, floods and landslides, but such measures were designed to win the 'hearts and minds' of the native population. Such measures had, by 1956 already been developed in Hong Kong's near neighbour, Malaysia. The Hong Kong Police already had a track-record of assisting with such 'civil defence' tasks as helping those made homeless by squatter fires, supervising feeding queues, keeping fire-sites clear, and assisting with what the government euphemistically called resettlement scheme 'problems' when those reluctant to be resettled resisted removal from their homes.[12] By the mid-1950s, such duties were said to have won the force the support and co-operation of the public.

Before 1956, the authorities were already talking of the 'proper and sufficient' deployment of the beat police officer as especially important', but the events of 1956 meant that the emphasis now firmly shifted to making him 'part of the familiar scene, readily available and constantly in touch with the public's needs ... a steadily growing number of Hong Kong's citizens are coming to regard the policeman as their friend and the guardian of the peace'.[13] Other methods of policing, such as the use of patrol cars, were disparaged for whilst they were 'more economical' they were 'too impersonal to meet basic requirements and to fulfil the public need'; they were to remain ancillary to the man on the beat (ibid). The beat officer, officially depicted as helpful, friendly, and community-oriented was, however, clearly never going to be entirely a servant of the people.

This emphasis on the beat officer stemmed from the need that was felt after the 1956 riots to maintain a presence in the housing estates, the beat officer being more likely than a patrol car to pick up intelligence from people on the streets about crime and/or subversive activities. This was crucial given the ever-present possibility of internal clashes between rival political groups and Hong Kong's sensitive geopolitical position adjacent to Communist China. Along the frontier, where immigration and smuggling were seen as the main problems, the potential for clashes with the Chinese frontier guards was at its highest, calling for 'the utmost tact and resourcefulness in police work'.[14]

In the NT, the force still relied on the village penetration patrols, two or three constables and a non-commissioned officer visiting villages for three or four days at a time at regular intervals, assisted by village guards, elected by the villagers to serve as a link between villagers and the police. The guards were issued with ammunition and weapons but received no money from the government except for 'specially good work'.[15] The village penetration patrols were said to have had 'remarkable results which have contributed in no small measure to the maintenance of law and order in extremely difficult country during this troubled period' (ibid).

Echoing what was known as 'Operation Concord' in Malaya, after 1956 the police and army were thus encouraged by the government to foster better relations with, and win the 'hearts and minds' of, these borderland villagers by providing cinema shows and putting on performances by the Police Band; the Army undertook a whole range of community services, including laying electricity power lines to outlying island villages and running sports events and open days.

Early in 1960, the government specifically requested money from London to fund this 'Concord-type' operation more widely in the colony, on the basis that it would be useful to help it prop up the public's flagging faith in the government.[16] London took the view, however, that such an operation was a 'luxury' and offered limited help. The Hong Kong government was free to spend money on such matters, and the armed services were free to help the community when requested to do so. They should be presented as an integral part of the community, and any servicemen involved in drunkenness or assaults should be dealt with firmly, as this generated bad feeling locally. However, in London's view, the main role of the military was to prevent widespread disorder and preserve internal security. It had no evidence that Hong Kong people had reacted badly to the sight of troops on the streets during the 1956 riots; the same was said to be true of Singapore: 'Perhaps the truth of the matter is . . . that if it comes to a choice, even our bitterest enemies much prefer to be occupied by British troops' (ibid).

In Singapore, 'Concord' had been developed to foster goodwill at a time when political changes (in Malaya) were due to take place that could cause relations to deteriorate. The maintenance of a British base in Singapore had to be made 'as palatable as possible' to Malaya because it formed part of the Far East military defence strategy. One essential feature of a 'Concord' scheme was 'to put across the idea of the British serviceman as a friendly helpful member of the community, by a variety of welfare and public relations activities . . . the second feature – and this is the reason for our refusal to underwrite such a scheme in Hong Kong – is that "Concord" operations are launched to improve the British political position in an overseas territory in the context of "cold war" activity' (ibid). Such operations involved holding Christmas parties for local children, sports days, the adoption of local schools, and the teaching of English, all done on a voluntary basis by servicemen.

In Hong Kong, British troops already carried out this type of voluntary welfare-type activity, which 'no doubt helped to present the British servicemen as friendly and helpful members of the community' (ibid). As far as London was concerned, therefore, there was no 'overriding political necessity' for the Colonial Office to provide any further funds for an 'Operation Concord' in Hong Kong, though it was quite happy to allow the local administration to foot the bill for any such operation. This it did, since this 'public interest' role of the police and army served the wider political purpose of countering Communist and Nationalist representations of their work as serving factional or imperialist interests.

Political policing

Apart from putting in place a striking force capable of dealing with internal disorder and developing 'hearts and minds' strategies, after the riots the Hong Kong government was equally keen to obtain intelligence about those it suspected of fermenting discontent. Whatever was said in public about 'criminal' as opposed to 'political' agitators, Grantham regarded the dangers presented by persons sympathetic to the Nationalist and Communist causes as sufficiently serious to warrant exempting Hong Kong from international conventions on human rights:

> Broadly speaking, I should wish this Convention to apply eventually in Hong Kong [but] . . . I consider that the Colony is, in fact, faced with such a public emergency threatening the life of the nation as is contemplated in Article 15 of the Convention. The Colony is severely overcrowded, with a floating population, much of which comes in from Communist areas where violence and the complete negation of human rights are the order of the day; and to deal with the day to day administration of such people calls for rapid and sometimes arbitrary action such as could not, rightly, be tolerated in normal conditions.[17]

Similar derogations were being made by a number of colonies at this time, particularly in Africa and Malaya, where 'a favourite technique' of governments faced with insurgency 'was vigorous repression action against "ringleaders", "troublemakers", "agitators", "subversives" and the like who occupied a special place in the demonology of colonialism as corrupters of the basic loyalty of colonial subjects . . .' (Simpson 2004: 837). Thus, though Hong Kong's 'emergency' was never officially declared, the Governor clearly deemed it sufficient to derogate from European human rights standards.

The task of monitoring suspected subversives within the colony fell to Special Branch intelligence. In the late 1950s it turned its attention, for example, to the political affiliations of competing factions of the Heung Yee Kuk. Special Branch was not only tracking the activities of the Heung Yee Kuk factions in Hong Kong but also in London, where dissident factions involved in the 1959 struggle for leadership of the Kuk had been 'indoctrinating' young men from the NT now working in the UK. Such men were reported to be returning to Hong Kong with 'positive left-wing inclinations'; pro-Communist elements in Hong Kong itself had not, apparently, shown much interest in the Kuk's dispute.[18] Special Branch memoranda from the early 1960s noted a number of 'friendly' visits by left-wing associations to the Kuk, and donations given to the Kuk by such associations for the relief of villagers affected by Typhoon Wanda in 1962:

> Also, it is noteworthy that for the first time the local office of the New China News Agency invited representatives from the Kuk and its 27 affiliated rural committees to attend a function in celebration of the CPG National Day on 1st October . . . It is believed that one of the leading pro-communist elements in the Heung Yee Kuk is Kan Chung Hing (4675/2646/5281) an ex-member of the communist dominated Society of Plantations which was dissolved in May 1959 because of its subversive activities in the New Territories.[19]

The NT was always a recalcitrant part of the colony. Bordering the Mainland, its villages and coves provided hidden pockets of smuggling, illegal gambling, arms stashes, general resistance to the colonial bureaucracy, and suspect political allegiances. Until 1957, the government had managed to govern the NT through its District Officers and the Heung Yee Kuk, which it recognised as the official voice of rural society. In 1957, however, the government withdrew its recognition during a contest about the operations of village elections.[20] Two factions emerged from this struggle, both of which drew Special Branch attention. A Bill was also introduced to recognise the Kuk (under new leadership) as a statutory body and regularise village elections.

The government needed the Kuk to help it negotiate with villagers whose land and homes had to be cleared for urban development. However, some members of the Heung Yee Kuk were opposed to this clearance programme and were observed by Special Branch to have visited villages to 'conduct a propaganda campaign' against the government's policy of converting agricultural land for development.[21]

As with most forced relocations, the police were required to maintain order when clashes did ensue. This was to remain a force role throughout the 1950s, 1960s and into the 1990s, as older places of habitation were bulldozed for roads, pubic housing, and private property development. Some, like the Rennie's Mill settlement established by Nationalist refugees in the 1950s and the Kowloon Walled City, would ultimately be erased in the run-up to the 1997 handover.[22] Efforts to assert British jurisdiction in the Walled City had already proved a flashpoint for Sino–British conflict. The 1948 attempt to assert British jurisdiction had resulted in the destruction of the British Consulate in Canton. Subsequently, the government tried to avoid clashes with the Walled City Residents' Association, lest they invite intervention by Beijing in the colony's affairs and/or provoke further agitation. It was also concerned not to antagonise the Nationalist government in Taiwan, since Nationalists could also lay claim to ownership of the Walled City. The possible international repercussions of clearance meant that correspondence about the area was copied to both Washington and the UK. The place represented a claim to Chinese jurisdiction inside the colony and, as such, was viewed by many as being outwith the control of the Hong Kong police, as well as sanitation and fire regulations. Nevertheless, Special Branch kept a watchful eye on the Kowloon Walled City anti-clearance organisation.

With the establishment of a communist government in the PRC, control over the Walled City assumed greater urgency. Seen as a place of refuge and a rallying point for political activists, as well as a den of crime, attempts to clear it were opposed by the Committee, described in intelligence reports as a 'left-wing unregistered committee', which intended to disguise itself as a *kaifong* association 'no doubt with the object of using a more respectable front to induce the undecided to support its cause'.[23] Leftist leaders were observed by Special Branch visiting Guangdong to gauge PRC government thinking on the issue. A fire that destroyed some buildings provided an opportunity for clearance but this was vetoed by London.

The Hong Kong authorities declined to make any public statement about its intentions towards the Walled City. However, secret internal papers reveal that in 1959 the government had been advised that Beijing was unlikely to object to the police arresting drug dealers and other criminals inside the area. Heartened by this, the Hong Kong government hoped to clear within it in two years. It had 'cautiously penetrated' the Walled City by initiating 'normal' prosecutions in a few cases of murder and wounding, and initiating an anti-narcotics drive in the Walled City which had led to over 1,000 arrests for gambling, drugs, prostitution and the selling of dog meat; only 5 per cent of opium divans, along with about 40 per cent of heroin pill divans and 20 per cent of tinfoil divans, were said to have maintained their 'precarious and fugitive existence'.[24]

A 1960 court case – seen as 'the long-expected challenge to British jurisdiction in Kowloon Walled City' – raised the whole question of British jurisdiction.[25] Wong Hon was accused of murder inside the Walled City but his lawyers claimed that the crime occurred outside Hong Kong jurisdiction and applied for a writ of habeas corpus. The court ruled in the government's favour. The fact that this provoked no reaction from the Mainland was seen to indicate that the PRC government was not, at that time, eager to use the occasion to embarrass the British in Hong Kong. The activity or inactivity of local leftist groups on issues such as this and the use of deportation orders was also used as a barometer of the PRC's attitude towards Hong Kong.

Throughout all this, Special Branch monitoring was strengthened and control was further supplemented by revised ordinances governing immigration control, the deportation of aliens, the Emergency (Detention Orders) Regulations 1956, and the Emergency (Review of Detention Order) Rules 1956. These new ordinances sat alongside prior legislation, some of which continued to be used.

The Emergency Regulations were particularly repressive. They allowed the government to detain and deport 'undesirable elements' without trial. Those affected included anyone who, under the Societies Registration Ordinance (1949), could be expelled for having political affiliations with political parties (Lock 1993: 71). Following the 1 March riots in 1952, for example, the government deported a number of 'undesirables' such as left-wing cultural workers and labour union leaders who 'threatened public security and disturbed the peace'.[26] According to Lock, although some FTU members objected to the provisions of the ordinance, the public generally regarded it as necessary to secure law and order in the colony.

On the same basis, the government had introduced a Citizens' Registration Ordinance in 1949, which saw residents over the age of 12 issued with an identity card (ibid). This was intended to aid the maintenance of law and order and assist with the distribution of food.[27] Again, despite some objections (mainly to the inclusion of fingerprints on the cards) the measure was accepted largely because, Lock argues, most people were willing to support anything that kept the colony free from the kind of political instabilities they had experienced in China, and which threatened to undermine their livelihoods in Hong Kong.[28]

The Emergency Regulations were described as the colony's main defence against triad societies, narcotics traffickers, and Nationalist and Communist agitators. The Emergency (Principal) Regulations 1949, made under the Emergency Regulations Ordinance 1922, were brought into force in 1951.[29] The Emergency (Detention Orders) Regulations extended deportation to those involved in the 1956 riots, be they political activists or triad members. Some 298 were scheduled for deportation immediately after the riots. Whilst both Taiwan and China accepted political deportees, neither was keen to accept known criminals.

Up to 1955, the Deportations of Aliens Ordinance had 'served fairly well as a means of ridding the colony of undesirable alien elements'.[30] In 1955 and 1956, however, the Central People's Government (CPG) refused to accept any more deportees. The Hong Kong government responded with the Emergency (Detention Orders) Regulations 1956, allowing deportees who could not in fact be deported to be detained without trial in Hong Kong. Thousands of people were detained following the riots; the government wished to deport as many as it could. Though it was now impracticable to do so, deportation orders continued to be made and deportees were simply kept in detention in Hong Kong, unless they opted for voluntary repatriation. Even then, there was no guarantee that either China or Taiwan would accept them back.

Deportation orders had earlier been used by the Hong Kong government in 1912 to deal with agitators involved with Republican Revolution in China; scattered records exist in Hong Kong of persons banished or deported at this time for political activities, as well as for vagrancy. During the First World War, 'summary deportation' was used as an emergency measure though it could only be imposed as an adjunct to a deportation order.[31] Before that, 'in ALL cases some constitutional safeguard existed by way of an enquiry being available to the potential deportees'.[32]

'Summary deportation' was initially looked upon as 'exceptional' step. What was known as the 'long procedure' form of deportation was more usual. In summary deportations, the decision was made by the Governor in Council, with advice from the Attorney General following evidence presented by the police at a consultation in his chambers.[33] In long procedure cases, evidence was collected by the Secretary of Chinese Affairs (SCA) both as to whether a person was an 'alien' and whether he was 'undesirable'; advice from the SCA was then considered by the Governor in Council. The final decision lay with the Governor.

After 1945, however, summary deportations exceeded long procedure deportations in most years by a ratio of about three to one.[34] Accurate figures are hard to discover but records do show that 153 deportation orders of both types were issued; between 1946 and 1960, 23,462 orders had been issued, the vast majority for summary deportation.[35]

Table 13.1 Number of persons held under Deportation of Aliens Ordinance

Year	*Number*
1947	2,627
1948/9	7,107
1950	6,800
1951	8,986
1952/3	6,581
1953/4	6,211
1954/5	10,338
1955/6	4,000
1956/7	1,356 [1]
1957/8	1,155 [2]
1958/9	795
1959/60	543

Source: HK Police Annual Reports 1946–59/60.

[1] Another 2,603 were placed under Police Supervision and 14 deported under Emergency Regulations.

[2] Another 3,064 were placed under Police Supervision and 232 deported under Emergency Regulations.

The official rationale for the Regulations was that triad elements had played a major role in the 1956 riots. This rationale continued to provide the official underpinning for Hong Kong's deportation and detention policy well into the mid-1960s. A brief for the Secretary of State's visit to Hong Kong in 1966, for example, still cited the triad problem as a major rationale for the system. The fact that the number of triad members arrested had markedly declined since the late 1950s was also claimed by the police as evidence of the system's success, though it seems likely that the fall in the number processed by the criminal justice system was accompanied by a rise in those processed without trial via this administrative regime.

Though it in practice used the Emergency Regulations to rid the colony of 'subversives', the government publicly endorsed the argument that they were principally a means of crime control. In 1960, for example, it argued that it was 'most unlikely that it is pure coincidence that there were some 4,500 less cases of serious crime committed in 1959 than there were in 1956' when deportation and detention had been used against triads detained during the riots (125 were still in detention in 1959). The relaxed procedures associated with detention, the lack of legal representation, the lack of charges – whilst all these could be said to infringe the principle of not convicting a man without proof, this principle was 'never intended to frustrate the enforcement of the criminal law'.[36] A review of the system in 1962 reiterated the belief that triads still constituted 'an occasion of public danger', justifying its retention.[37]

Certainly, criminals and triad members fell within the net of this method of control. By the end of the decade, the police were talking of 'a sustained drive against secret societies, the detention of undesirable aliens under the Emergency (Detention Orders) Regulations and the selective application of police supervision to habitual criminals'.[38] Between 1956 and 1962, a total of 9,120 police supervision orders were made. Between 1956 and 1960, most of those detained in Chatham Road Detention Centre (under police control) were males (30,215) though a few were women (647) and juveniles (162); a further 1,234 were held after the 1956 riots, making a grand total of 32,258. But a further 2,304 were put up for 'confidential banishment' under a separate procedure, and most if not all of these were political suspects.[39] Between 1956 and 1960, a small number objected to their detention and were recommended for release.[40] Records show that the approximate number of persons arrested under the Deportation of Aliens Ordinance in 1957 was 455 (365 under summary procedure and 88 long procedure); in 1958 these numbers were 313 (205 and 108 respectively); and in 1959 they were 190 (52 and 158 respectively). The highest number detained in the 'House of Detention' was 125 in 1959, but secrecy still surrounds this centre and it remains unclear as to how many 'political prisoners' were detained in Kennedy Town.

By the late 1950s, however, the Regulations were attracting criticism and seen as problematic on a number of grounds. They did not, for example, provide for the deportation of what officials saw as the increasingly large number of locally born 'undesirables', whether or not these were involved in criminal or political activities. (The authorities wished to employ the regulations against locally born triads, since they saw this as a way of effectively dealing with the 'triad problem'). The government tried to devise a scheme whereby detainees born outside Hong Kong could be 'voluntarily repatriated' (i.e. assisted to leave the colony on the understanding that they would be re-detained if they returned) but the non-co-operation of the PRC made this difficult. The existing system was also proving time-consuming, and deemed likely to attract international criticism because, as the Attorney General's office realised, the impossibility of sending deportees back to China meant, in effect, that they were being held in indefinite, preventative, detention without trial. This was deemed 'unreasonable'; at minimum, it was felt, there ought to be some judicial oversight of what was an administrative system in which the detention of individuals was decided in secret.[41] In the 1960s, a new system was to be devised, with rather more judicial involvement but equally controversial and secretive.

Cumulatively, then, Hong Kong ended the 1950s with a series of highly repressive laws and processes – some of them criminal justice measures, others administrative. This picture of the colony jars with the received wisdom, which presents the 1950s as a time of development and growth, when an industrious but politically apathetic people triumphed over adversity to build a 'miracle economy'. There is clearly some truth in the latter – the 1950s was a decade of 'modernisation' and remarkable achievement, but it was also fraught with conflict and contestation. The measures adopted by government in these years – criminal and administrative sanctions, its resettlement programme, its paramilitary and public order capability, its political policing and its 'hearts and minds' policy – all indicate a nervousness about civil unrest. Policing and criminal justice in this context were inevitably tools of government, and to some extent tools for social engineering, a means of maintaining social order in the face of a range of threats, and of repressing political dissent and protest. Fortunately for the British, in the 1950s, the most obvious threat came not in the form of explicitly anti-colonial protests but of Nationalist versus Communist tensions. This would change in the 1960s.

Notes

1 HKPAR 1957/8: 2.
2 W.C. Johnson, Police Advisor to the Secretary of State for the Colonies 28 December 1949, CP3/214/50.
3 Memo Colonial Police Forces 28 April 1950. CP3/214/50.
4 See, for example, Jeffries 1952.
5 HKPAR 1957/8: 2.
6 HKPAR 1949/50: 18.
7 HK Yearbook 1956: 243.
8 Lee (1995) says that rivalry existed between the two reserve forces, those in the Police Reserve being seen as richer expatriates, compared to the Chinese and Pakistani members of the Special Constabulary. See Lee 1995: 98. Legally, they were part of what was known as the Essential Services Corps, called upon to assist the Defence Force in times of emergency.
9 HK Yearbook 1957: 231.
10 Note by the Colonial Office to Cabinet Committee on Future Developments in South East Asia 4 August 1960, CO1030/1352.
11 Black to Wallace 19 July 1960.
12 HK Yearbook 1954: 158.
13 HK Yearbook 1956: 184.
14 HK Yearbook 1956: 185. By 1960, it had been decided that police responsibility for overseeing migration across the border should be transferred to the newly created Immigration Department, independent of the police.
15 HKPAR 1948/9: 8.
16 5. May 1960, CO1030/1346/74.
17 Telegram 16 July 1952, CO936/156 cited in Simpson 2004: 837.
18 Colonial Secretariat Hong Kong to Colonial Office, London 1 March 1960, CO1030/1278/37.
19 Special Branch Report September 1962.
20 A little later, in 1961, elections to the Shap Pat Heung Rural Committee resulted in clashes between rival factions. When trouble erupted, the police had to intervene to prevent more injuries and impose order.
21 Special Branch report September 1960, CO158–1 222–34.
22 Rennie's Mill (so called after the Canadian businessman who established a mill there) was later called Tiu Ken Leng ('Hanging Ridge') following the business's failure and Rennie's suicide and subsequently changed to Tiu King Leng. In 1950 the government settled a considerable number of Nationalist/Kuomintang

refugees there. Intended as a temporary measure, it became a Nationalist enclave. Though plans were drawn up in 1962 to redevelop the area the last of its residents was only finally evicted in 1996, making way for the expansion of Tseung Kwan O new town. The timing of this led to the widespread belief that it was a move to please the PRC government prior to its resumption of control over Hong Kong in 1997. The Walled City was originally a Chinese magistracy or *yamen*, comprising a small walled estate. Though abandoned by China in the late 1800s, since it was technically Chinese territory it remained unpoliced and thus something of a haven for criminals, drug dealers and triads. After several unsuccessful or partly successful attempts, residents were evicted and it was demolished in 1991/2 to make way for a park.

23 Monthly Intelligence Reports September 1962, C01030/ 1338 LIC.
24 LIC Monthly Intelligence Report December 1959, CO1030/1338.
25 Governor of Hong Kong to Secretary of State for the Colonies 1 February 1960, CO 1030/1338.
26 *China Mail* 1952, cited in Lock 1993: 182.
27 This was revised in June 1960 by new legislation that required all persons in the colony to register and everyone over six years of age to have an ID card. In the 1967 riots, mobile ID card units would be used to round up everyone who could not produce their ID card on the spot. In 1969, more legislation was introduced giving the government the power to demand that people carried their ID cards at all times.
28 The one measure that, Lock says, was widely regarded as the best safeguard against Communism – a democratic government – had already been rejected by the Governor and by the business elite in Hong Kong. They had persuaded the government in London that there was no popular support for the idea.
29 The 1922 Emergency Regulations Ordinance had been passed to deal with the seamen's strike of that year.
30 Detention and Deportation Preliminary Note for Consideration by the Working Party, 1962.
31 J.R. Oliver, Chairman, Review Committee to Colonial Secretary 24 January 1961; HKRS 179/1/5.
32 Chair of the Committee of Review to Colonial Secretary 24 January 1961.
33 Ibid.
34 Ibid.
35 Ibid.
36 CO1030/1386-295.
37 CO1030/1538/19.
38 HKPAR 1959/60: 18.
39 Ibid.
40 21 per cent in 1957, 33 per cent in 1958, 16.9 per cent in 1959.
41 Report of the Working Party, 16 February 1961.

Chapter 14

The China factor: the early 1960s

In the 1960s, Hong Kong was in the midst of rapid economic restructuring. It was gaining a world-wide reputation as a manufacturing economy – plastic flowers and ornaments with 'made in Hong Kong' stamped on them became synonymous with the era of cheap, mass-produced goods. It was, however, also synonymous with cheap labour, overcrowding, and Dickensian working conditions. At the same time, the children of the 1950s refugees had grown into teenagers. Fifty per cent of the entire population was under 21; 40 per cent was under 16. The social and demographic landscape of Hong Kong had thus altered quite dramatically.

The political landscape, however, remained doggedly unaltered. EXCO and LEGCO were still dominated by (principally European) business interests – so much so that the government was nicknamed 'Hong Kong Inc.' in popular parlance. The administration was still colonial, with little localisation at the higher levels. Society remained marked by social, economic and political exclusion, run by an oligarchy for business, with no popular representation except at the Urban Council level. The gap between rich and poor was as wide as ever, and there were long-running allegations that the police force was deeply corrupt. As Jarvie, writing in 1969, argued, the situation was riot-prone (Jarvie 1969). All it needed was the trigger, which was to come in 1966.

In addition, there were concerns about drug-smuggling and triad activity that ran alongside and were intertwined with the growing concerns about police corruption. Meanwhile a series of political issues and developments on the Mainland put the Hong Kong government in a difficult position. Some of these revolved around the problem of Hong Kong becoming a place in which Mainland Communists and Taiwanese Nationalists both sought to extend their influence, while there were also periodic influxes of migrants and refugees from China following the turmoil of the 'Great Leap Forward' in 1957 and the beginning of the Cultural Revolution in 1966.

In terms of 'everyday' crime and justice issues, it is worth noting that the rates of serious crime actually fell in the early part of the 1960s (see Table 14.1) and ended the decade, in real terms rather than absolute numbers, only about 10 per cent higher than at the beginning. There was also some concern

Table 14.1 Crime Hong Kong 1959/60–1969/70: absolute numbers and crime rate

Year	*Total no. of reported offences*	*Recorded as serious crime/key crime*	*Crime rate*
1959/60	406,795	17,433	597.23
1960/1	353,672	14,465	485.24
1961/2	350,905	14,852	460.38
1962/3	419,334	14,660	415.65
1963/4	453,759	14,245	391.02
1964/5	557,638	17,076	465.59
1965/6	580,840	20,022	523.70
1966/7	635,051	21,516	580.07
1967/8	489,009	24,047	620.14
1968/9	665,119	22,380	563.52
1969/70	833,669	26,979	668.67

Source: RHKPARs and HKPARs 1959/60–1969/70.

about what a police report of 1963 flagged up as 'the growing numbers of juvenile offenders'.[1] According to the police, small gangs of youths, the *ah fei* or 'teddy boys', were the main cause of the 'youth' crime problem, especially on the new resettlement estates (see below). By the end of the decade these would become the 'crime problem' of the period. In the meantime, the police expended time and resources tracking the 'enemy within' and maintaining the integrity of the border with Communist China.

Communism, education and culture

The riots of 1956, coupled with growing concern throughout the 1950s about triad activities and political subversion, led the government to increase the resources of the political police (Special Branch). Throughout the 1950s, it drew on the experience of police and military personnel familiar with counter-insurgency work in other parts of South East Asia (in particular from Malaya) and in the African colonies. Special Branch – with its immigration responsibilities – monitored the movements and activities of 'undesirable aliens' in the colony, as well as those of 'home grown' subversives. These included members of the left-wing FTU union and communist controlled organisations.

The remit of Special Branch also included advising (along with specialists in London) on ways to combat communist influence in everyday life. This included the surveillance and questioning of suspected subversives, as well as the routine monitoring of schools in which Communist or Nationalists were thought to be active. As Lock points out, some private schools were funded by Beijing and Taiwan to indoctrinate students, something which the Governor, Grantham, acknowledged when he described leftist schools as 'the focus for communist penetration, some being completely communist dominated and centres of communist and anti-British indoctrination'.[2] Special Branch reported on 'patriotic' activities within communist schools – one memo noted that the students and teachers of the Pui Kiu Middle School had been told by their headmaster at an end of term assembly that 'a good education alone was not sufficient, since being one hundred per cent pro-communist was a pre-requisite to achieving success in life'.[3] The Education Ordinance had already been amended in 1948 to empower the Director of Education to withdraw his approval of any registered teacher or registered school whose conduct was considered 'to be prejudicial to the interests of the pupils of the Colony'.[4] A few teachers had already been charged with being unsuitable to teach in the colony because of their political activities and, in 1949, one school (Tat Tak School) was forced to close for being prejudicial to the interests of the colony, being a centre for communist activities and teaching (ibid). Other schools suspected of teaching communist thinking were also reformed or replaced (ibid).

However, in the absence of comprehensive subsidised state education, many poor parents continued to send their children to whatever schools set up in their districts, including those funded by the trade unions. As Lock notes, some 105,000 school-age children did not receive any formal education in the late 1940s; over 60 per cent of these studied in private schools. These numbers grew as the birth rate of the post-war population rose (Lock 1993: 69).

In the late 1950s, concerned about the growth of Communist schools and the rise in the number of Communist teachers the government sought to limit their expansion. However, the schools utilised the appeals system within the Education Department to review adverse decisions. An internal government memorandum of the time wearily noted that, 'where the Communists are making a determined effort to expand in new or existing schools, they would take advantage of the right of appeal'.[5]

Legal contests were, however, preferable to the closing or banning of schools. Such 'heavy-handed tactics' had, officials noted, already allowed left-wing organisations to make political capital out of accusing the government of 'driving the workers' children out of schools.' Repression was not, London felt, 'justified by the present threat'.[6] Instead of confrontational politics, the government should take a sideways approach to the issue: school places were in short supply; parents were sending their children to Communist schools simply because they lacked an alternative. A better way to counter Communist influence, therefore, was to promote more government-funded and subvented schools. The expansion of existing Communist schools should be contained not by a legal crackdown but by administrative refusal of their requests for expansion. The registration of Communist schools could, it was noted, also be revoked on the grounds of the personal political affiliation of principals and teachers.[7]

Special Branch reports from the mid-1960s indicate, however, that the authorities continued to keep a close eye on Communist schools. There were reports of increased political indoctrination in the schools. In October 1963, Han Wa Middle School and Ching Wa Middle School were said to have undergone a 'general revival of political training', including a 'Study from comrade Lei Fung' campaign.[8] When faced with what it saw as a Communist 'cultural offensive' on Hong Kong during the early 1960s, the government responded with a crackdown on social events organised by cultural troupes (such as the Red Women's Detachment and the Central Union of Chinese Students) and propaganda film shows. Alarmed at press criticism of what was seen as censorship, London queried whether the threat of a 'Communist monopoly of popular culture' was really so great as to merit this outright repression. Officials in the Colonial Office and Foreign office counselled that:

> The need to limit and control presentations which have an obvious political content and a direct political impact (e.g. modern Chinese drama) is of course acknowledged, and we fully support your policy of laying down conditions regarding the approval of scripts, avoidance of propaganda, etc. But within these limitations, we would be inclined not to take too rigid a position, reminiscent of the most severe 'cold war' measures, and to maintain a certain flexibility with regard to the presentations of traditional cultural activities for which there must be in Hong Kong a considerable nostalgic demand of a genuine non-political nature. We agree that such presentations should not be too regular a feature in Hong Kong in case they become (as you say) a target for right-wing demonstrations; nevertheless, we feel that a fixed annual limit (and to such a low number) strikes precisely the same uncompromising attitude as we object to in the CPG's (Central People's Government) handling of cultural relations with the West . . . we would like you consider whether the somewhat wider considerations to which we have drawn your attention might not justify some softening of your policy in regard to those cultural activities that have no obvious political significance.[9]

In Hong Kong, however, it was felt that whilst a 'balance has to be struck,' the government needed to avoid accusations from Nationalists that it was favouring visiting Communist cultural groups by allowing them to stage propaganda performances:

> Whether or not it proves possible to hold these visits to their present level, however, we here are in no doubt that it is most important to try to keep the situation under control and not allow them to get out of hand. While there is no doubt a certain amount of genuine non-political nostalgic demand for these shows, they are not the only manifestations of Chinese culture available here. At the same time, the CPG's aim is certainly not just to satisfy this demand. What they are after is the

> propaganda and prestige dividend. It is not in our interests that the CPG should have things all their own way in this field, nor do we wish to see rivalry between Peking and Taipei intensified. If an unlimited number of troupes from China were allowed to enter and perform in the Colony, we should undoubtedly be faced with embarrassing demands along the same lines from Taiwan. As you know, it a major object of our policy to try to prevent the Colony from becoming the cockpit of Communist/KMT political conflicts: rivalry in cultural matters may be on the face of it a good deal less objectionable, but one thing is apt to lead to another. In the circumstances, and since we are not under any serious pressure to relax our controls, we do not think it would be to our advantage to take any initiative to do so. This does not, however, imply rigidity: clearly such application has to be examined and treated on its merits in the light of conditions at the time. All this may, as you suggest, be somewhat reminiscent of cold war measures, but Hong Kong is in some ways in a permanent cold war situation and cannot always apply the same standards as is possible in countries less delicately situated.[10]

A handwritten note in the margins of one document argued 'it might be worth linking up with the censorship legislation' locally to deal with the troublesome material. Essentially political decisions could thus be made to appear as the moderate and 'even-handed' application of the law, allowing the government to escape accusations by China or Taiwan of treating their sympathisers unfairly.

Throughout the 1960s, Special Branch informants kept the government informed as to the attitude of the Chinese leadership towards Hong Kong, monitoring meetings and speeches by key leftist figures. In August 1965, for example, Special Branch noted that at a meeting in Canton, a Chinese leader stated that Hong Kong's status would not be affected if the Vietnamese war expanded because Britain had not engaged in any hostility towards China, had not permitted Hong Kong to be used as a base for 'US aggression,' and because 'the Hong Kong Government did not persecute patriotic workers and organisations in Hong Kong'.[11] The same dispatch reported that Chinese leaders had let it be known to a Special Branch inspector that if, in the event of China/US hostilities, the Hong Kong government 'continued to maintain strict neutrality and refrained from any action which would antagonise the CPG' the latter 'would not attempt to disrupt the economy of the colony'; it was also reported that the CPG 'appreciated' the Hong Kong government's return of illegal immigrants and its refusal to recognise them as refugees.

Deportation and detention

In 1959, the entire procedure of detention in lieu of deportation was reviewed by a Working Party. The police lobbied for a system that would make it easier for them to deport and/or detain the 'menace of locally born triad members'. Their argument was put in full to the Working Party:

> The problem facing us is that in respect of persons against whom the allegations of triad or narcotics activity have been made. The triad setup especially, if it is to be combated effectively, requires that persons involved be completely removed from within the community. Their presence alone, if tolerated, and even if they themselves do not engage in unlawful activities, acts as a powerful morale boost to other members of the societies . . . The difficulties of bringing active important triad and narcotics personalities before the Courts I am sure are well appreciated . . . Considering our ever increasing alien population and the hard core alien criminal element now with us because of our present difficulties in removing it entirely from the community, I feel that the principle of the Deportation of Aliens Ordinance is realistic and necessary . . . It is not my contention that all criminals should be deported but I do maintain that the weapon of deportation . . . is our most effective measure and the best deterrent as far as triad members are concerned. Without this we would not have been in the position we are today nor would we have accumulated the wealth of information that we now possess about these societies and personalities. It is also a necessary factor if, as our law now stands, we are to get at the major narcotics personalities who seldom if ever themselves handle consignments . . . Deportation has for many years been a major weapon against the criminals within this Colony and it is so considered by the criminals themselves . . . the position at present is that deportation . . . to [China] is not possible. When deportation virtually ceased in 1955, a decision was made to rescind numerous [almost 6,000] deportation orders. A new Police Supervision Ordinance was brought into force and it was hoped that this . . . would be a satisfactory substitute for deportation. Unfortunately such was not the case. The breakdown of deportation and the wholesale recission [sic] of orders had an adverse effect. The criminal element . . . decided that the police were powerless to deal with them by deportation and in the case of triad members they felt reasonably safe from being proceeded against in the Courts owing to the fear in which they were held by those they persecuted. Consequently, they have lost their fear or respect for the forces of order. I am convinced that this feeling of security on their part was one of the major factors which aggravated the 1956 riots. The riots brought into operation the Emergency (Detention Orders) Regulations. A section was formed at CID headquarters to take action against the triads, making use of these Regulations. For a period from about mid-1957 to mid-1958 deportation to China was resumed on a limited scale . . . However since 1958 deportation to the Mainland has become increasingly difficult and is now virtually impossible. In the three years during which use has been made of the

> Emergency (Detention Orders) regulations, a marked improvement has been made in the triad situation in this Colony. Overt violent triad activities have markedly decreased and the triads to some extent are being contained. This has not been accomplished easily. Action has been taken in the Courts against thousands of triad members but as a whole this action, although spectacular, apart from placing on record known targets, has been of little real worth. In the majority of such cases sentences have had little deterrent value either to the member charged or to the potential member. What the triads fear is deportation or detention if they cannot be deported . . . though it is conservatively estimated that there are 10–20,000 active triad criminals in the Colony only 455 persons have been placed in emergency detention and today [1960] there are only 188 detained. The relatively satisfactory state of affairs today must not give us a false sense of security. The triad problem has been with us for over a hundred years and during that time the triads have never lost an opportunity to exploit any breakdown in authority which has been caused by riots or war. Their use by the Japanese in the last war is well known and their continued existence provides a tool for any party intent upon embarrassing this Government. Any upsurge of triad activity has usually brought counter action from Government but when the triads have become acquiescent action has diminished. I am satisfied that the foundations of the triad societies are intact and any signs of faltering by Government will result in renewed and increased triad activity. In short, in my opinion, the Emergency is still with us. The object is to destroy these societies. Time is against us and unless vigorous and, what may appear at times, harsh action is not sustained we will in the future be faced with masses of locally born members and in their respect our hands will be even more tied. I should add that given the power and continued support, I believe triads in this Colony can be destroyed . . . In due course it will probably be necessary to have special provisions in law to deal with the non-aliens who are members of these societies. At present however our campaign is primarily against aliens and it is hoped that if this can be sustained and effective it will act as a deterrent against locally born persons joining the triads.[12]

In 1960, an internal memo from the Chairman of the Working Party acknowledged that emergency detention was, however, 'open to the most searching criticism'. Minutes from the Secretariat, the police, and the SCA had, he said, opened his eyes to its 'worst features'.[13] Moreover, those scheduled for deportation were mostly stateless persons who could not return to their countries of origin. For them, deportation represented 'a very severe punishment indeed'. In addition, although deportation and detention was an administrative measure it was, in effect, being used as a form of punishment, imposed in secret without trial. This was seen by the police as especially useful for dealing with triad members whom, they surmised, would be hard to convict in a court of law, as witnesses would be too frightened to testify.

The authorities were also open to criticism for failing to take into account the period of an alien's residence in the country, the fact that deportation would separate a married woman from her husband, that an alien might have a family domiciled in Hong Kong, whether an alien was likely to be put to death on his return to his own country,[14] and how long a person should or could be detained. Under the existing system, this was determined by referring to the weight of evidence against him, but according to the legal advisors this was simply wrong – a person was detained not because he had committed a crime but because he could not be deported. The Attorney General's memo to the Chair of the Working Party notes:

> On reflection, I am not happy at this method of dealing with the problem. I think it might well be open to the objection that it provided for the imprisonment of British subjects and aliens for offences we could not prove in the courts . . . What I feel may well be the short term solution of the problem with which we are faced is to modify the Deportation of Aliens Ordinance by providing for a hearing into the allegations upon which the deportation is sought by a tribunal consisting of a Judge or Magistrate in lieu of the present statutory interview by the SCA representative and to empower that tribunal to recommend that, if deportation proves to be impracticable, the subject of the deportation order to be detained in custody for a specified period. Detention under a deportation order over and above a short period of say three months would then be permissible only in accordance with the recommendations made by the tribunal . . . The advantages of this proposal (which I have mentioned to the Chief Justice) would be . . . that we would get rid of the Emergency Regulations, limitless detention, and combine in one tribunal the functions of the Committee of Review and the statutory interview.[15]

The suggestion that the judiciary replace the SCA did not find favour with the Colonial Secretary. He argued that, since the SCA tended to treat aliens more sympathetically than the courts, it was in the best interests of the alien to be dealt with by the SCA where:

> There is no formality and no atmosphere of a tribunal or judicial hearing . . . [SCA officers] are very patient with the simple folk with whom they have to deal. They put up with a mass or irrelevancy and apply, much of the time, trouble and understanding in the attempt to reach the basic facts of the case . . . A tribunal on the other hand has none of the appearance of a personal interview. It is bound to be somewhat awesome to a simple person. It is likely to pay more attention to the strict rules of evidence and to conduct its proceedings in a language and form which

> are more difficult for a simple person to understand than proceedings before the Assistant SCA and his interpreter . . . These proposals will involve legislation, and it (is) almost inevitable that they will also involve very considerable publicity for our deportation and detention arrangements. Any subject on which there are strong local feelings seems nowadays to reach the House of Commons very easily. If facts and figures in respect of the years since the Kowloon riots were asked for in the House, I have little doubt that we should come in for some pretty severe criticism. I suppose we shall just have to face this possibility. Before we face it, however, I think we should be absolutely sure that the police have tried every possible means of getting rid of those deportees who are still on our hands. What I have in mind is that if some scheme could be devised which would rid us of the main bulk of the backlog in say 6 or 9 months.[16]

The Attorney General, on the other hand, thought SCA officials inexperienced and easily bamboozled.[17] Nevertheless, he held that, 'whether they were good, bad or indifferent there is no real continuity in the place, which counts most, at least from the defendant's point of view, in the interviewing room.'[18] He was, however, unhappy about the SCA being both the adviser to the Governor in Council and 'one of the judges of his own advice':

> I have found no difficulty in this dual role myself but it would give at least a greater appearance of impartiality (e.g. in the event of some Parliamentary Question) if as a member of EXCO the SCA has had no previous direct part in the preliminary investigation into a defendant's character and way of life.[19]

The Attorney General, himself a law officer and member of the government, used his speech at the opening of the legal year in 1960 to defend the idea that a person ought not to be convicted without proof. It was, he argued, the basis 'of our administration of the criminal law and its principal safeguard against wrongful conviction'.[20] However, he added, this was 'never intended to frustrate the enforcement of the criminal law'. There were circumstances in which the rules of evidence and procedure might justifiably be modified. What was proposed was a new tribunal, employing relaxed rules of evidence and procedure. However, this was criticised as an 'extra-judicial' system trying certain offenders by different standards to the ordinary criminal law. A proposal to send all deportation cases to a tribunal presided over by a judicial officer was also objected to, since deportation was an Executive – not a judicial – matter:

> The expulsion of aliens is a matter, at an international level, in which the government of sending country is liable to be involved in dispute with the country to which a person is deported and it is therefore with the

> government and not with any domestic tribunal that the decision to deport an alien must lie. This is not to say that the courts of law . . . may not have a part to play; indeed it would seem desirable that the facts upon which the Executive comes to its decision should be found by a tribunal separate and distinct from that which makes the administrative decision.[21]

Internal documents indicate that the Working Party was concerned that no pressure be brought 'upon any person to return to a country where he would be liable to be punished for his political opinions'.[22] In this regard, Hong Kong needed to abide by international conventions on human rights established post-war. Involving the judiciary in the decision to detain, and giving the detainee the choice to return to his own country voluntarily, would also hopefully offset international criticism.[23] It was also felt imperative that the detainee be informed of the tribunal's recommendation:

> . . . as not to do so would be contrary to all concepts of natural justice . . . the Deportation Committee will be a quasi-judicial body answerable for its decisions by way of the normal prerogative writs . . . The Deportation of Aliens Ordinance, which largely came into operation in 1912, is out of touch with the realities of the situation which exists in the world today, and Hong Kong in particular . . . The most important points for consideration by the Committee will be:
>
> (i) whether the procedure of summary deportation is to be allowed to continue in its present form. There is little point in creating an efficient tribunal headed by a member of the judiciary if that tribunal can at any time be by-passed at the will of the Executive – that is to say by making use of the summary form of deportation. As the colony has the largest per capita 'alien' population in the world, to keep the summary form of deportation in existence would make a mockery of the whole rule of law;
> (ii) whether deportation is to be an executive or a Judicial act; and
> (iii) the detailed procedural changes which will have to be made . . .
>
> If a good inquisitorial system could then be devised . . . which proves workable and efficacious, one could look ahead to the possible extension of that form of 'hearing' to other cases – I have in mind particularly allegations of Triad activities – dealing with Narcotics – and Corruption. Criticism that these cases would be taken away from the normal courts would only be true in the narrowest sense; what would be of more importance is that all cases would be heard and decided by the Judiciary . . . This 'ready made' alternative procedure would be of vital importance if an Emergency had to be imposed at a moment's notice, as happened in 1956.[24]

The Commissioner of Police, however, argued that Hong Kong was already in an 'emergency' situation. It was imperative to remove offenders from the community altogether as quickly as possible. Even so, he did not favour summary deportation – it was still preferable for a detainee 'to have some form of hearing and an opportunity to rebut the allegations made against him'.[25] He also supported certain due process aspects of the revised system such as having a judge or magistrate oversee the revised tribunal process; the granting of bail; and the right of the detainee to appeal the tribunal's decision.

The Working Party held that indefinite detention was undesirable. The existing system had 'few constructive features and with no more than a formal review, by the Governor in Council, at certain prescribed intervals'.[26] The six-monthly reviews by the Governor in Council were inadequate 'to ensure a through review of the detainee's case'.[27] The taking of pleas to deportation charges also made 'it appear that one is treating deportation as a punishment for quasi-criminal charges which are based on inadmissible evidence'.[28] A new format for a tribunal system was eventually agreed upon. The police would be present alongside a member of the judiciary and a legal representative for the alien.[29] A single magistrate would preside who would have the power to detain for a maximum of five years; detainees could however, be released (subject to good behaviour) and allowed to leave the colony; locally born detainees could be released under police supervision. This 'more fluid' type of tribunal would:

> . . . give rise to far less ill informed criticism, which any kind of legislation involving the liberty of the person always brings to the surface. 'Five years detention' is the kind of 'catch phrase' which, taken out of its context, might cause a great deal of harm; especially as its consequences could be made to apply to such a large segment of the population . . . if the more fluid system is adopted (the average period of review) should be three years . . . I think the 'more fluid' type of recommendation gives the New Tribunal far greater scope for acting in a manner so that justice is done to the individual whose case is being considered. All cases of deportation must differ enormously one from the other, and . . . it will be very difficult to give advice which will result in justice being done which will in any way differentiate one case from the next . . . difficulty . . . will arise if too rigid a system is adopted.[30]

The tribunal would, however, still hold its sessions in camera. Some modifications of the existing law of evidence and standards of proof would also be permitted, but it would be possible to appeal against the tribunal's decisions (though whether such appeals should go to a second tribunal or review by a District Judge was not clear).[31] A new and separate detention camp would also need to be established under the Prisons Department; special emphasis would be placed upon rehabilitation. Political prisoners could, it was suggested, be dealt with in a different way and be held at a separate camp. International conventions would apply to the conditions of these detention camps.[32]

The Working Party's Report was considered by EXCO in 1961 and a new draft of the Emergency (Deportation and Detention) Regulations was prepared. Although the usefulness of the existing system in the war against triads ('undesirable aliens of an evil character') was acknowledged, the Working Party felt that, in view of the increasing importance of triad affairs, consideration should be given to setting up another process, separate from deportation, for dealing with the 'triad menace to peace and good government'. In the short term, however, it was agreed that the threat posed to Hong Kong by triads constituted an 'occasion of public danger' under the Emergency Regulations Ordinance. They would, therefore, still be dealt with by deportation and detention, which served at least to keep them out of circulation without having to go through the normal process of law. A person held in such detention might also be 'brought to the point where he is willing to leave Hong Kong of his own volition'.[33]

EXCO agreed that all proposals for deportation were to be referred to the new tribunal, except such 'political' cases 'as were certified by the Governor to be unsuitable for such procedure'.[34] Its proceedings would be presided over by a qualified lawyer appointed by the Chief Justice (Sir Michael Hogan) with members drawn from a lay panel. The power to issue further warrants for detention was to be transferred from the Governor to the President of the tribunal: 'It is thought that the exercise of this power by a quasi-judicial tribunal might go a long way toward meeting the criticism of the present practice whereby the executive may continue week by week to hold in custody persons whose enquiry proceedings may drag on indefinitely'.[35] The new process would achieve 'the maximum degree of just dealing consonant with the need to preserve peace and good order in the Colony coupled with the maximum attainable administrative simplicity'.[36]

By now, the British section of the International Commission of Jurists (*Justice*) was monitoring these developments. It argued that there was a distinct lack of judicial review of existing deportation and detention orders, and that 'whatever the circumstances in which such orders are made, there should always to be safeguards'.[37] *Justice* also insisted that a detainee should be brought before a magistrate within 48 hours of being detained, have the right to representation by Crown counsel, to cross-examine witnesses and to have their case aired in public. Thus, though initially welcomed by many as an improvement on past practice, from the outset the new system had its critics.

Throughout the early 1960s, both the press and a small section of the bar kept a watchful eye on the new system. A fall in the numbers detained for criminal activities (from 125 in 1959 to 67 in 1963) suggested that there had been some change in the process. The *China Mail* described the new tribunal system as a 'step in the right direction' since 'Our procedure for deporting undesirable aliens, essential though it may be for defending the well-being and security of our city, had long been subject to severe criticism because these summary actions could often lead to injustices and the misuse of discretionary powers'.[38] Though not 'strictly a judiciary organ', the tribunal would at least provide some quasi-judicial protection and provide detainees with legal representation at a hearing of their peers:

> Such a hearing and a thorough review of the evidence would serve as a useful and effective check against any possible abuse of the discretionary administrative powers – real or imagined . . . The protection which our law courts give to our people is, without a doubt, the best available in South-east Asia. Our judiciary system is in fact one basic and important reason why people and capital from nearby regions have migrated to our city . . . But our legal structure, admirable though it is, has several inevitable loopholes. These come mainly as a result of discretionary powers enjoyed by the administrative personnel of our Government. More and more, if justice, harmony and administrative efficiency are to prevail here, we have to subject these discretionary powers of our public servants to the proper checks. The Deportation and Detention Advisory Tribunal was therefore an historic step: it gave testimony to a significant change in the thinking and policy of Government on the matter of minimizing the possible tyranny of discretionary powers exercised by its employees.[39]

Whilst acknowledging that the new system did not live up to the ideals of the 'Anglo-Saxon system of jury trials and open hearings', it took the view that it at least provided some quasi-judicial oversight of the discretionary powers of those in charge of what was essentially an administrative system. In the circumstances, it was the best that could be hoped for.

However, the experience of the tribunal's first president, Mr Justice Briggs, raised questions about this quasi-judicial oversight. Shortly after his appointment in 1965, Briggs resigned. He expressly disapproved of the way the tribunal operated, in particular that its recommendations were ignored by EXCO and the Governor in Council. In August 1965, he had presided over a review of the detention of Yu Kit and others, in which the tribunal had recommended the release of six detainees, all alleged to be members of triad syndicates who had collected protection money from operators of vice dens. The original tribunal, held in 1964, had found all allegations against them proved 'to the hilt' and ordered their detention. Briggs, as chair of the reviewing tribunal, advised that they be released since, had they been convicted at trial, their period of detention would have already expired. The Governor in Council rejected this advice. The detainees were returned to custody.

At the end of the tribunal, Briggs had informed the detainees of its recommendation for their release. They were, therefore, aggrieved when they were returned to detention.[40] The government tried to minimise the publicity surrounding Briggs's departure, but the detainees went on hunger strike and their plight soon reached the local newspapers. It was subsequently reported in the *Glasgow Herald* in November 1965, provoking an urgent demand from the Secretary of State for information on detention without trial in Hong Kong. He first sought the advice of the legal advisers[41] but they had difficulty finding any information about how long a person might be kept in detention in Hong Kong. A scribbled note in the margin of one internal document suggested that they could be detained: 'until deportation can be carried out or his release in the colony can be tolerated.' This could be indefinitely:

> On the face of it, the procedure whereby an enquiry by the Deportation and Detention Advisory Tribunal is necessary before a deportation order may be issued, seems liberal and in advance of the normal detention provisions in most colonies, particularly as the person concerned is entitled to be represented by counsel. What I am not clear about, however, is whether a detention order can only be made in cases where the Tribunal advises in favour of such a course, or whether the Governor in his Council has complete discretion to order detention even though the Tribunal advises that there are insufficient grounds to justify it. If the former is the correct interpretation I think we are on unassailable grounds . . . It looks to me, however . . . as if the Governor in Council has an absolute discretion to order a detention whatever the tribunal might recommend. If so, the procedure is much less liberal and defensible than it looks on the surface . . . a power whereby the Government can apparently keep a man indefinitely in detention notwithstanding a recommendation by the tribunal in favour of release seems to me very difficult to justify. If the reason for keeping him in detention is that his deportation is impracticable, one must face the position that owing to the attitude of the Communist Chinese Government, the man's deportation may never be practicable. Is he to be kept in prison for life? On this point I am bound to say that I am impressed by the argument of the Tribunal which . . . expressed the . . . view that 'If they had been charged and convicted of some offence covering these activities . . . an appropriate sentence would have been eighteen months which . . . would have expired by now.' Ought not detainees in such circumstances be given another opportunity of making good and if they then fail to do so they could be legitimately detained again, not for the original offence but for a repetition of it or some different offence?[42]

However, another internal memo noted that ridding society of triads had proved one of the Communist Government's most difficult tasks in the Shanghai of the 1950s, and that it had been achieved principally by executing them:

> . . . these men are not political prisoners nor indeed are they ordinary criminals. They are members of secret societies whose hold on the Chinese is very great indeed . . . Whilst I accept that we cannot use Communist methods or even use them to justify our own, it does suggest that some special powers are necessary . . . they are unfortunately going to remain in detention for a very long time indeed.[43]

In a speech made to LEGCO in December 1965, however, Mr Cheong-Leen pointed out that it was not the triads so much as the police power to detain that now scared people in Hong Kong. This discouraged them from criticising the government even on minor matters for fear that they would be arrested by mistake and detained in Stanley '. . . the Chinese community, especially local intellectuals, have an intense dislike of the Emergency (Deportation & Detention) Regulations . . . There are very grave misapprehensions in the minds of the local community as to the efficacy and fundamental justice of the . . . Regulations . . . No one can deny that Government has a serious obligation to provide order and security . . . [but] the Government should seek the active cooperation of local residents by creating a local citizenship, and give people a sense of belonging, of civic pride and of local loyalty'.[44]

The Hong Kong government insisted that the detainees were a menace to society and were being treated fairly: they had been brought before a tribunal presided over by a judge, represented by a barrister and a solicitor, and the tribunal's decision had been reviewed by a judicial officer. Detentions were not legally problematic – the government had absolute discretion to deport an alien from its territory. This was a normal and internationally accepted power.[45] The system was open and transparent – the numbers detained were reported every year to the House of Commons library (in 1965, 17 were awaiting deportation under normal procedure, and 28 under the Emergency Regulations, a fall from 67 in 1962). However, London noted that, whilst the number of detainees had indeed fallen from 67 in December 1962 to 28 in December 1965, '[t]his substantial fall has not been due to deportation . . . (and) can therefore only be accounted for either by release or death in prison'.[46] This raised the alarming possibility that some detainees had died whilst being held without trial. Moreover, even where a person had been convicted, sent to prison, and released, he might still receive another deportation order and end up in further, unlimited, detention. In one such case, an accused acquitted at trial in the Supreme Court was re-arrested on the steps of the court and returned to detention. This, it was felt, almost amounted to contempt of court.

London took the view that the majority of detainees were, indeed, not political but 'criminals of an anti-social type', drug and vice racketeers who were all triad members'.[47] As of October 1965, 17 people were in detention pending deportation, and another 28 were being held under the Emergency Regulations, down from the 67 held in 1962 (ibid). At the tribunal hearing of the six aggrieved detainees in 1964, 80 people had given evidence in camera which they would not have given in open court, for fear of retribution from triad members. The Emergency (Deportation and Detention) Regulations of 1962 allowed the government of Hong Kong to detain them since neither China nor Taiwan would accept those deported for criminal activities. Nevertheless, the scope of the administrative discretion involved in the system was felt to be 'extremely wide' and information about its application was 'defective.' A colonial official was thus sent to Hong Kong to discover what happened in practice. Meanwhile, as the memo cited earlier had observed, the six aggrieved detainees would have to remain in detention 'for a very long time'.[48]

The government kept a close eye on a number of political activists. Special Branch were monitoring the activities of left-wing groups in the colony, including their cultural activities and their contacts with China. It noted, for example, that 'friendly relations' were being developed between the Heung Yee Kuk's left-wing faction and local left-wing organisations. It also uncovered a group of Taiwanese guerillas working under Taiwanese Military Intelligence in Hong Kong, whose task its was to infiltrate the Mainland, subvert the local population, and proposition them to join forces with groups invading from Taiwan. Their presence was linked to an incident in Shenzhen in August 1962, when an explosion took place. The 1956 Emergency (Deportation and Detention) Regulations were amended to empower the police to detain such persons, against whom a deportation order had been made after consideration by the Governor in Council, acting upon the advice of the Advisory Tribunal.[49]

Ascertaining the numbers of 'political or 'triad' detainees after 1962 is problematic. Internal documents show that 42 'political' detainees were held in custody in 1962 of whom 38 were detained for triad activities. In 1963, 67 persons were detained. The secrecy surrounding the process meant that no information was publicly available concerning who was detained or why. It fell to journalists to press the Government Information Office for details, but their requests usually met with stony responses, 'We have no information to give on the subject,' and 'we are sorry that details of the action taken under this ordinance are not available'. According to one newspaper report from 1962, the first anyone knew of 'guests' in the Victoria Road detention camp in Kennedy Town were when the 'lights burned late'.[50] The report noted that more than 20 people had been arrested under the Emergency Regulations and detained at the new Detention Camp, 'set up a few weeks ago to replace the Chatham Road Camp' (ibid). Queried by the reporter, an official spokesman said, 'There has been no unusual activity whatever at the centre' (ibid). According to the press, however, most of the 20 inmates were political detainees under deportation orders.[51] A similar report of June 1962 referred to the fact that 20 people were being detained for political reasons.[52] The existence of Taiwanese detainees in the detention camp also only became known when they were released in 1964. They complained of ill treatment in the centre at the Victoria Road camp and revealed that another seven Chinese newspapermen remained in detention.[53] Questioned by a Reuters correspondent, the Government Information Service disclosed that 30 people had been detained on espionage charges by Special Branch. In 1965, the press also reported that Special Branch (acting on information given by the Chinese government) had detained 15 people under the Deportation of Aliens Ordinance for subversive activities.[54] Earlier the same year, nine people (including a former Special Branch member) were deported to Taiwan after engaging in political activities in Hong Kong.[55] A *Hong Kong Standard* article in October 1970s referred to the detention of two KMT spies in Victoria Detention centre, and the deportation by Special Branch of ten others. The Regulations were also used to deport youths engaged in anti-Japanese and anti-Vietnam War protests in the late 1960s and early 1970s.

In the mid-1960s an Urban Councillor, Elsie Elliott, informed officials in London that the police were using the threat of deportation and detention to silence those trying to expose police corruption. This, she argued, had a chilling effect on everyone campaigning for social reform. There were, she felt, many members of the police who were 'tired of corruption and who would welcome the chance of trying to clean it up'; about 12 people, 'many of whom are in the Police Force' were said be in contact with her reporting various corruption cases: 'She said they were afraid to reveal their identities before the Hong Kong authorities because they felt they would be "framed" . . . I believe common people are very decent . . . and it is because of this the Colony is able to manage without being completely rotten'.[56] Unless something were done, Hong Kong would soon 'be ruled by crime and become just like Chicago was with a capital "C" – meaning crime' (ibid).

Two MPs were sent to Hong Kong in 1966 to investigate these allegations and examine the workings of the Deportation and Detention of Aliens Ordinance.[57] On their departure from the colony they stated that they would call for its review. The English language press, whilst acknowledging that the system had its defects, opposed its modification on crime control grounds:

> Where criminal elements such as drug-peddlers and members of Triad organisations are concerned the comparatively simple process of deportation is generally ruled out. Resort is therefore necessary in a few cases, for the protection of the public, to the unpopular procedure of detention and the tribunal; the reason that there is no open trial being that witnesses are usually impossible to obtain where drug trafficking and secret societies are involved. The hope is that during the period of detention the rings organised by detainees will have broken up. This is admittedly a far from ideal situation; but Hong Kong's geopolitical situation is also far from ideal in several respects.[58]

Because so many of the internal documents regarding emergency deportation and detention are classified, the practice remains shrouded in mystery, speculation and rumour. Used extensively from the 1950s onwards, and again to great effect during the 1967 riots, questions remain about the legality of the Emergency Regulations, the system of deportation and detention, the methods used to interrogate detainees (particularly those suspected of political activities who were detained at the Victoria Road Centre) and the numbers subjected to deportation and 'Confidential Banishment' on the basis of their political activities.

For the police, the Regulations were seen as a major weapon in their armoury against triads, whose activities they regarded as 'real and continuing'. But it is clear that they were also used by the Special Branch to detain without trial political activists regarded as 'undesirable aliens', and to keep under surveillance and/or detention the local Hong Kong activists whom they were unable to deport to another country. The practice drew increasing international criticism especially when, in 1969, the Hong Kong authorities colluded with the Macau police to return a political activist, Joao Teixeira, to Portugal, where he was sentenced to a penal colony for political prisoners (his offence was to write critical letters to the Macau newspapers).

Illegal immigration

At one level, many of the crimes that plagued Hong Kong in the 1960s were similar to those of the nineteenth century. Smuggling, narcotics, and the movement of criminals in and out of the territory still occupied the police, as did more local crimes such as vice, triad activity and gambling. Keeping track of the population (though somewhat eased by the fact that there was now a physical barrier with Mainland China) still remained a priority, especially for the marine police whose task it was to police Hong Kong waters for illegal immigrants. About 1,500 illegal immigrants from the Mainland were detected in a 'normal' year in the 1960s. Many crossed the bay or entered by boat across the sea, but some attempted to cross illegally at land borders such as Lo Wu, control of which was handed over by the police to the Immigration Department in 1965.

From time to time, there was also some two-way traffic across the border with China by Hong Kong residents and their families in China. Special Branch files also note the movement of a number of political subversives into Hong Kong both from Mainland China and from Taiwan. It was, however, illegal immigration from China that was to become the policing problem of 1962, prompting the establishment of the Anti-Illegal Immigration Branch.

The responsibility for immigration control at this time still lay with the police force. Immigration controls had first begun in 1923, when the Passport Ordinance was enacted. This was replaced in 1934 by an Immigration and Passport Ordinance that retained the need for travel documents but prohibited entry to 'undesirables' and permitted the police to board craft, examine passengers, its crew and their documents. The 1916 Registration of Persons Ordinance was one of a long line of laws that also allowed the police to keep track of aliens entering the colony. This was repealed in 1934. All aliens except those coming from China had been required to register with the police; the Chinese were required to register with the Secretary for Chinese Affairs. In 1938, Special Branch had taken over the issuing of all passports and visas, and in 1940 an Immigration Department had been set up but its failure led to these responsibilities being handed back to the police after the War. In 1949 an Immigration Control Ordinance placed the registration of aliens within the scope of immigration (i.e. in the hands of the police, typically Special Branch).

Immigration from China in this post-war period had led, in the early 1950s, to the reorganisation of this police department, an increase in staff, and the establishment of a quota of 50 persons a day being allowed to cross the border into Hong Kong. Enforcement of the quota proved highly problematic; it was relaxed and re-established several times during the 1950s. A certain number of school-age children and certain others were, for example, allowed to cross into Hong Kong during the school holidays and festivals to visit relatives living there. Over the years, fewer and fewer returned to China after these breaks – in 1962, 3,500 children aged 11 to 21 entered Hong Kong and 3,000 failed to return. Interviews with these migrants provided the authorities (and academics) with some insight into conditions on the mainland.

In 1958 the Immigration (Control and Offences) Ordinance placed immigration under the control of a deputy immigration officer operating under the Commissioner of Police. The police remained responsible for border controls but this was, in effect, the start of a separate Immigration Service. It was this service which, in 1962, was reorganised to deal with the massive influx of immigrants from China.

The spring of 1962 saw a marked increase in the number of illegal immigrants – up to 6.000 daily – crossing the frontier from China. Initially rounded up by the police and returned across the border, as their numbers grew, reinforcements had to be called in to assist. A Special Branch internal document for May 1962 reported:

> . . . an extraordinary mass influx of Chinese across the land frontier which created a serious emergency and necessitated the extensive reinforcement of the police division covering the frontier, not only with the police from the urban areas but by British and Gurkha military personnel.[59]

Special Branch estimated that about 60,000 illegal immigrants from Mainland China had been arrested in the border area in that month alone, compared to the usual number of about 150 per month (the police put the figure at 62,000). During the six weeks up to 26 May 1962 over 62,000 persons were arrested and returned.[60] The influx of more students and illegal immigrants was reported throughout July and August, alerting the government to the possibility that new and further restrictions on immigration might be needed to combat the flow.[61] The Hong Kong police were hampered in their attempts to intercept the arrivals by the fact that many locals along the border area sympathised with the illegal immigrants and helped them to evade arrest. Those caught were detained at the PTC Unit in Fanling; female police officers were transferred to the Frontier to deal with women and children in transit. In June, the numbers intercepted were down but still higher than normal – 879 illegal immigrants were arrested trying to cross the land border and 1,009 by water. The military, observing activities across the border, 'have daily reported large numbers of Chinese peasants to be held in a compound in Shum Chun' (ibid). Increased security in Guangdong and a curfew appeared to have reduced the numbers leaving.

The explanation for the huge increase in migrants lay in the relaxation of controls by frontier guards on the Chinese side, and their encouragement or ignoring of the illegal immigrants. The Special Branch view was that the guards' attitude had produced unintended consequences – they had:

> . . . merely decided, in response to numerous complaints, to issue exit permits somewhat more freely. But distorted rumours of this decision, which came at a time of acute food shortage and widespread apprehension of a further deterioration as a result of the movement of the population from the towns to the countryside, touched off a mass exodus (ibid).

At this point, the government in London decided not to approach Beijing about the problem. Instead, the Anti-Illegal Immigration Branch was reinforced by the police, navy and the army and, in August, in an operation that was to continue all year, the Anti-Illegal Immigration Branch was detailed to deal with illegal immigrants entering the colony by sea. In September, an 'all-out' operation to stop illegal immigration was begun involving a fleet of marine police launches, a Royal Navy ship and reserves, the RAF, marine auxiliary police, and police stationed at a new division in Yuen Long. By the end of the year, over 13,529 craft had been searched, and 2,841 illegal immigrants arrested.[62] In November, however, secret internal documents acknowledged that many illegal migrants were evading the patrols, still entering the colony at a rate of 10,000 per month. This made illegal immigration 'the most pressing and serious problem at this present time'.[63] The special measures taken since September were said to have resulted in relatively few interceptions, prompting the suggestion that an approach might be made to the PRC government itself to stop the flow of migrants across the border by restricting exit visas.

For Special Branch, the incident shed light on the conditions of widespread dissatisfaction in South Guangdong, as well as the 'extraordinary capacity' of the Communist government for 'misappreciation of the effect of their decisions' and its problems of exercising administrative control (ibid). Most of the immigrants had valid Chinese exit visas. An internal police memo noted that, whilst the PRC's motives for issuing these was unclear, it did not suggest that the PRC regime was on the verge of collapse, as some had speculated.[64] When the implications for internal discipline and external publicity did dawn on the Chinese leadership, the barriers to leaving were re-established. At its height, however, over 6,000 people were rounded up on a daily basis at the frontier for deportation back to China.

The 'immigration crisis' of the early 1960s prompted changes in operational policing but also brought home to all involved how easily one small change in PRC policy could stretch Hong Kong's resources and threaten the colony's 'peace and stability'. It also highlighted the fact that certain areas of Hong Kong's internal security required highly sensitive handling. The police handling the mass migration of the early 1960s operated with one eye on international relations. Hong Kong's geopolitical position in the Cold War era thus added an extra dimension to policing in these years, and was to provide the context for other events as they unfolded in the late 1960s.

Notes

1 HKPAR 1963/4: 2.
2 Grantham, cited in Lock 1993: 67.
3 CO1030/1541/8.
4 Education Department 1948: 30–31; cited in Lock 1993: 68.
5 Quoted from memoranda contained in the file CO1030/1541: 30.
6 Ibid.
7 Colonial Secretariat Memo, 'The Chinese Communist Threat in Schools' 17 April 1963, CO 1030/1541: 19.
8 Special Branch Intelligence Reports, 1963, CO1030/1541–3–10.
9 Higham, Colonial Office to Willan, Colonial Secretariat Hong Kong 18 January 1963, CO 1030/1542: 5.
10 Colonial Secretariat to Higham, Colonial Office London 19 February 1963, CO1030/1542: 4.
11 Cipher from Trench to Secretary of State for the Colonies, and to Peking and Washington 11 August 1965, CO 1030/1556: 63.
12 Heath, Commissioner of Police to members of the Working Party 18 January 1960.
13 Memo 26(1) HKRS 179 1/5.
14 Ibid.
15 Hooton, Attorney General to Chairman, Committee of Review 18 January 1960; CO/1/425/59.
16 Burgess, Colonial Secretary to Committee Chairman.
17 McDouall, Secretary of Chinese Affairs to AG memo 84 9 January 1961.
18 Ibid.
19 Ibid.
20 CO1030/1386/295.

21 Ibid.
22 Draft Report of the Working Party 16 February 1961.
23 Oliver to Hooton 9 February 1960.
24 Ibid.
25 Heath, Commissioner of Police to Attorney General 11 April 1960.
26 Colonial Secretariat to Chairman of the Committee 8 July 1960; CR1/2706/58.
27 Ibid.
28 Ibid.
29 Ibid.
30 Committee Chairman to Colonial Secretariat 14 October 1960.
31 Ibid. at Preliminary Note 5.
32 Final Report of the Working Party 16 February 1961.
33 EXCO Memorandum HKRS 179/1/5 1961.
34 Memo 30/1 HKRS 179/1/5 Executive Council.
35 Ibid.
36 Ibid.
37 Memo 5 April 1963 from the President, the Deportation and Detention Advisory Tribunal to Commissioner of Prisons.
38 *China Mail* 31 July 1962.
39 Ibid.
40 *South China Morning Post* 20 November 1965.
41 CO 1030/1538: 7.
42 Mr Wallace 3 December 1965 CO 1030/1538: 8.
43 8 December 1965, CO 1030/1538.
44 Mr Cheong-Leen's speech to LEGCO, HKRS 70–3–66.
45 Read, Internal Memorandum December 1965. CO 1030/1538: 9.
46 Wallace, Internal Memorandum 8 December 1965, CO 1030/1538: 10.
47 CO 1030/1538.
48 Ibid.
49 HKPAR 1962/3: 7.
50 *South China Sunday Post Herald* 17 June.1962. This is the same centre previously used in the 1950s for detention of 'political prisoners'.
51 Ibid.
52 *Sunday Post Herald* 17 June 1962.
53 Government Press Office, press cuttings 8/10/64 HKRS 70–3–66.
54 *Hong Kong Standard* 21 April 1965.
55 *South China Morning Post* 3 March 1965.
56 *China Mail* 25 March 1966.
57 *South China Morning Post* 27 September 1966.
58 Ibid.
59 LIC Monthly Intelligence Reports 1962, CO 1030/1436.
60 HKPAR 1962/3: 3.
61 CO 1030/1436–10.
62 HKPAR 1962/3: 33.
63 Internal intelligence memos dated 18 October 1962 and 8 December 1962, CO 1030/1436.
64 Confidential memo Governor of Hong Kong to Secretary of State for the Colonies 5 October 1962, CO 1030/1254.

Chapter 15

Policing and crime in the mid-1960s

The 1960s continued some of the 'modernising' tendencies of the 1950s, set out in Pennefather-Evans's original blueprint for a post-war force. The 1966 and 1967 riots were to reinforce the view that Hong Kong needed a strong, well-resourced force. They also emphasised the need for officers to be loyal to the government. Reform, however, came slowly, and it was not until junior officers took action in the mid-1970s that terms of service for local recruits improved. Thereafter, the provision of housing, welfare, and of leisure facilities made membership of the police an attractive proposition. After 1974, when the government acquired powers of summary dismissal, dissidence within the force carried a high personal cost.

The 1960s saw the recruitment of more officers, the construction of a new twenty-storey Police Headquarters at Arsenal Street, a new depot for the PTU, another nine police stations (including Lamma, Pok Fu Lam, Ping Chau and Aberdeen) as well as various marine operational bases and more police accommodation. The old Police Training School at Aberdeen was rebuilt; more quarters were provided for the rank and file, and air-conditioning was introduced into some police report rooms. In January 1964, a new station opened at Wong Tai Sin to house 400 officers. There were other new police posts in Nam Sang Wai, Deep Water Bay and Lau Fau Shan, mainly to cope with illegal immigration in remoter parts of the colony. In 1965/6, several more stations were opened at Kwun Tong, Mongkok and Yuen Long, the Divisional station at Mongkok housing 800 officers. The new stations built in Kowloon lacked the traditional gun turrets around the perimeter, since these became obsolete once stations were located in areas where missiles and gunfire could be discharged from nearby high-rise buildings. Annual reports show a continuing rise in the cost of maintaining the force throughout the decade (from HK$61,091,016 in 1960 to HK$143,344,734 by 1969). In the earlier half of the decade the police had been divided into three territorial districts (Hong Kong Island; Kowloon; the NT and Marine). However, population growth and urban density had persuaded the government to divide Kowloon into two sub-districts by the mid-1960s.

As Tables 15.1 and 15.2 show, the 1960s saw the police establishment

Table 15.1 Police force establishment 1960/61–1969/70[1]

	1960/1	*1961/2*	*1962/3*	*1963/4*	*1964/5*	*1965/6*	*1966/7*	*1967/8*	*1968/9*	*1969/70*
Men										
Gazetted officer	89	91	98	105	105	119	131	148	153	148
Inspectorate	685	668	721	742	789	863	905	955	962	989
Rank and file	7,147	7,351	7,435	7,513	8,225	9,786	9,530	9,830	10,665	10,825
Total	7,921	8,110	8,254	8,360	9,119	9,858	10,566	10,933	11,780	11,962
Women										
Gazetted officers	1	1	1	1	1	1	1	1	2	2
Inspectorate	8	8	12	14	16	18	21	21	23	25
Rank and file	205	233	330	378	393	469	408	428	448	550
Grand Total	**8,135**	**8,352**	**8,597**	**8,753**	**9,529**	**10,346**	**10,996**	**11,383**	**12,253**	**12,512**

Source: HK Police Annual Reports 1960–70.

Table 15.2 Racial composition of Hong Kong police 1960–70

	1960/1	*1961/2*	*1962/3*	*1963/4*	*1964/5*	*1965/6*	*1966/7*	*1968/9*	*1969/70*
Senior officers (Overseas)	84 [1]	88	98	91	93	104	114	123	127
Senior officers (Local)	–	–	–	7	8	16	16	18	19
Junior officers (Overseas)	358	353	359	374	376	394	409	413	443
Junior officers (Local)	281	307	346	367	411	422	499	537	554
Rank and file									
Cantonese	5,986	5,839	6,167	6,615	7,297	8,169	8,759	9,330	9,904
Northern Chinese	516	494	477	469	460	458	438	389	379
Pakistani	139	182	175	166	163	155	151	132	129
Portuguese	16	16	17	16	15	15	15	12	10
Women police	182	198	261	346	364	454	408	517	515

Source: HKPARs 1960–70.

[1] Figure for 1960–63 is for all gazetted officers.

increase by a little over 50 per cent. Groups such as northern Chinese and Pakistanis, who had constituted a significant proportion of police strength in times past, were now small minorities, with almost all the rank and file being recruited locally. The number of women police officers grew even more rapidly, though the actual figures were tiny – they constituted about 2.5 per cent of the force in 1960 and 3.3 per cent in 1970.

By the late 1960s, the number of women police in the force had risen from about 350 in the early part of the decade to just over 400. Hardly any occupied higher ranks; in 1965, a woman officer (Miss A.H. Calderwood) was seconded from Glasgow City Police and appointed as a senior inspector and, in 1966/7, women were admitted for the first time into the Auxiliary Police, mainly to perform communication duties.[2] Police women were paid less than their male counterparts – in the mid-1960s, for example, a male inspector was paid a minimum of HK$1,030 and a female HK$770; a male constable's basic monthly pay was HK$240 and a female HK$180.[3] Moreover, enlistment standards for local officers specified that, whilst a male applicant for the position of constable could be either single or married, women had to be single. As with all government service, marriage between ranks was not permitted and inter-racial relationships were strongly discouraged.

Though officially used in all police duties without concessions to their gender, women police were seen in very traditional terms, suitable for dealing with missing persons enquiries, juvenile casework, liaison with Social Welfare, and traffic enforcement duties that required 'friendly contact with the public'. The public, apparently, appreciated the sight of 'cheerful' women policing pedestrian crossings, busy thoroughfares and on point duty. The force regarded them as particularly successful in crowd control at festivals and parades (they were responsible for maintaining order outside the hotel and theatre when the Beatles came to Hong Kong). They also accompanied medical and dental teams visiting remote island villages. One of the principal benefits of employing women seemed, however, to be to relieve male officers of court and station duties, enabling them to pursue 'outdoor crime prevention duties', probably regarded as more like 'real' police work. Women officers were also detailed to handle all juvenile court proceedings ('a particularly appropriate duty for women and one which they enjoy') and provide escorts for female juveniles from the Girls' Remand Home to Court 'ensuring that these young girls do not mix with women and male juvenile prisoners'.[4] They were assigned to the arrest of prostitutes and mendicants, as well as school crossing duties. Some change seemed to be afoot in 1969, however. For the third time, a female inspector was sent to the UK to study how the British utilised women in the police force; one was sent to Australia, and another to Japan, as part of promotional visits.

These somewhat complacent attitudes were shaken by events in 1966 and 1967. These marked a watershed not only for policing but also for government more generally. These events are dealt with in a later chapter. We now turn to the development of the police in terms of specialist aspects of law enforcement.

Specialist policing

The organisation of the force indicated its priorities at the end of the 1950s. Its three main investigative branches were the CID, Special Branch and the Anti-Corruption and Narcotics branch, reflecting what were felt to be the major criminal activities of the colony. A major police campaign against narcotics had begun in 1958. A force Narcotics Committee was established in 1960 to co-ordinate all police action in the field, and a force-wide anti-narcotics drive was credited with the successful suppression of local heroin factories and opium use. Triads were also seen as a 'constant threat to law and order', resulting in an ongoing drive against the larger societies.[5]

In 1956, another specialist branch, the Anti-Triad Bureau, was set up at police headquarters to investigate triad-related activities in the world of gambling, prostitution, narcotics and extortion. The interests of these branches overlapped, triads being implicated in 'ordinary' crimes such as protection rackets, political crime in support of the Nationalist cause, drug offences, as well as corruption (including corruption in the police). By the 1960s, the use of deportation orders and detention without trial had, it was argued, fragmented the traditional triads, many of whom were now left without 'natural' leaders. In 1963, the police began 'plotting and indexing' the operational areas of triad activity and their membership:

> This survey has now enabled street gang leaders to be graded as targets for prosecution before the Courts of the Colony or, in the case of vicious thugs against whom there is insufficient admissible evidence to support a criminal charge, before the Emergency (Deportation and Detention) Advisory Tribunal.[6]

In 1963, the 'King of Narcotics', a known triad leader, was arrested and deported under the Deportation of Aliens Ordinance. In September 1964, a Reuters correspondent sought confirmation of a *Sing Tao Jih Pao* report that some 30 people had been detained on espionage charges, and was told by Special Branch that a number of people had been detained under the deportation of Aliens Ordinance. A 1964 breakdown by Reuters of all aliens deported that year found that 29 had been deported, 15 for triad activities, 11 for narcotics offences, one as an illegal immigrant and two for commercial crime.

By the end of the 1950s, as Hong Kong's economy began to grow, the police identified the growth of financial and commercial crime, often involving foreign criminals; this required more specialist expertise. In a Hong Kong which was becoming part of the international commercial world, government was keen to deter crimes that had a detrimental impact on the colony's reputation as an 'economic city' – business needed to be certain of a secure and orderly environment in which to conduct its affairs. In the 1940s, Pennefather-Evans had already highlighted the need for a Commercial Crime Unit but his recommendations produced meagre results. Nevertheless, if it was to combat 'commercial swindlers' for whom the colony was a 'convenient hideout'[7] the police needed to be outward-looking, and to liase with other police forces around the world.

Throughout the 1950s, a small branch had tracked crimes such as counterfeiting, forgery and fraud, mostly involving false driving licences and foreign currency. Many of the smaller, less complex cases had then been handled by non-specialist CID officers. By the 1960s, this unit (the Commercial Crime Office) had been relocated to the central business district (in the Li Po Chun Chambers) where it continued to investigate complex frauds, conspiracy offences, bankruptcy offences, and forgeries relating to currency, identity cards, passports and other travel documents. In 1967, it had to deal with what, in the distant future, would become a much more common type of crime – the manufacture and possession of gramophone records that infringed copyright.[8]

As with the Narcotics Bureau, the work of the Commercial Crime Unit often necessitated liaison with overseas forces to break up international syndicates of forgers and smugglers of currency, gold or goods between Europe and the Far East. Though Hong Kong was a small spot on a map of the world, the international nature of some its crime problems thus necessitated increasing specialisation and co-operation with overseas forces and other law enforcement agencies.

In part, this specialisation and professionalisation reflected the police force's wish to move away from dealing with minor infringements of the law (such as hawking) because these often engendered a great deal of public dissatisfaction. Police action in returning the thousands of Chinese who had crossed the border in 1962 had also provoked fierce criticism in some quarters. The police blamed this on a 'vociferous minority'. To counter it, the force sought to portray itself instead as a 'servant and guardian' of the people to whom members of the public could 'readily turn for help in times of personal need or worry'; 'even the fishermen and farmers' of the NT were said to turn to the police for help.[9]

But a remarkable preamble to the 1965/66 Police Annual Report hinted that public attitudes towards the police needed to be understood in the context of public apathy and resistance towards the government more generally. Hong Kong people, it argued, were competitive seekers after their own interests, with little time for anyone else. They had no sense of civil spirit and no sense of belonging to Hong Kong. This made them apathetic or resistant to government measures:

> The Police Force is the most visible arm of Government and it must of

> necessity become associated with measures which, although designed for the common good, may from time to time run contrary to individual and sectarian interests. The clearance of squatters, the restrictions within proper bounds of the hawker population, and the strict enforcement of parking regulations, these and other activities are not calculated to increase the popularity of the Police Force with the public . . . We have made increased efforts to present Police activities to the public in a frank way that can be easily understood by any intelligent person . . . We do not expect to create interest and sympathy in place of apathy and mistrust overnight, but we are confident that, by advising the great majority of decent law-abiding people in advance of Police policy and intentions, we shall create an increasing reservoir of goodwill and understanding . . .[10]

Throughout the 1960s, the police continued their 'servant of the people' role, mobilising to provide assistance, for example, during water shortages, typhoons and fires (such as the Sham Shui Po and the Chung Kiu Chinese Products Emporium fires in 1966). Such activities remained within their 'civil defence' ambit. Their role in enforcing unpopular government policies, such as the forcible eviction of squatters, was more problematic. These often took place in densely populated urban areas (such as Wanchai), were highly visible, provoked much hostility and generated highly problematic public order problems. 'Real' police work was, however, increasingly seen as crime fighting, the suppression of subversion and serious crime, especially after the 1966 and 1967 riots.

Throughout the decade, therefore, there was a sense that the force should cease to be quite so generalist, but should acquire a more professional and specialised role. Certainly this view was shared by some senior officers. Some specialist units were developed. There were, however, those who resisted greater 'modernisation', whilst some opposed any change that threatened the existence of their corrupt syndicates.

In regard to international linkages, too, the police were clearly ahead of the other disciplined services, especially the Prison Service, which had resisted overseas engagement on the basis that it had nothing to learn from foreign places. By the mid-1960s, the police were representing themselves as playing a major role in maintaining the colony's security and its prosperity, providing the law and order people needed to get on with their daily lives and their commercial activities. Ironically, though, many of those providing these conditions of law and order were, at the same time, themselves prospering from police corruption.

Overall crime and juvenile delinquency

At the start of the 1960s, virtually everyone in authority agreed that Hong Kong did not have a juvenile delinquency problem. By the end of the decade, however, they had identified a new problem with *ah feis* ('teddy boys' and youth gangs).

Serious crime actually fell in the first years of the new decade (Table 15.3). The figures for miscellaneous offences also fell in absolute terms between 1958 and 1962, and the vast majority of crime in Hong Kong in the 1960s still comprised such offences – they routinely accounted for over 200,000 prosecutions each year. The largest categories, as in the 1950s, were gambling, hawking, obstruction and larceny from the person or vehicles. The number of offences committed by juveniles declined as well, though they had begun to account for a larger proportion of those arrested – almost 17 per cent of those arrested in 1960/61 were aged under 17, up from 10 per cent in 1959; 9 per cent were aged 17 to 20, up from 7.7 per cent in 1959.[11] There was, however, little change in the extent or type of crime for which juvenile arrests were made. The vast majority of recorded crime was against property rather than persons, and the offence for which juveniles and young persons were mostly arrested was miscellaneous larceny.

Almost 95 per cent of the juveniles were arrested for offences against property, mainly of a minor kind, such as snatching and pick pocketing. Juveniles aged under 17, for example, accounted for 28 per cent of all arrests for larceny against the person, and 28 per cent of those arrested for miscellaneous simple larceny. Those aged 17–21 accounted for 31 per cent of all arrests for larceny from the person and 37 per cent of all miscellaneous larcenies. According to the police, the majority of juveniles they came across were:

> . . . of the street urchin class who congregate in the vicinity of theatres, hotels, restaurants and areas frequented by tourists. Juvenile offenders generally come from poor homes. Parental control over them is practically non-existent. Indeed, in some instances, they are encouraged by their parents to beg and steal. Triad society influence is also evident in the areas where juveniles engage in their illegal activities.[12]

The police allowed that, given the increase in Hong Kong's population overall, the numbers of young people arrested did not actually represent a notable increase in juvenile crime, nor was there 'any evidence of any abnormal tendency to crime amongst the youth of Hong Kong'.[13] Indeed,

Table 15.3 Reported serious crime 1960–65 (absolute numbers)

	1960/1	*1961/2*	*1962/3*	*1963/4*	*1964/5*
Crime against the person	697	818	849	836	1,129
Crime against property	15,113	12,748	12,517	11,964	14,064
All reports	17,426	14,852	14,660	14,245	17,076

Source: HK Police Annual Reports 1960/1–1964/5.

police Annual Reports consistently remarked on the absence of a juvenile delinquency problem. The official figures showed juveniles to be one of the lowest offending groups in the population.

In the late 1950s, the police had, however, begun to more closely monitor juvenile involvement in crime and from 1957 onwards, the official statistics specifically included a breakdown of juvenile crime (see Table 15.4).

The Annual Report for 1963/4 appears to have adopted a different system of counting. In its appendix it cites slightly different figures for the fiscal years 1959–1964 (Table 15.5).

Thus, although at the end of the 1950s and start of the 1960s, the official figures had charted a rise in juvenile crime, their rate of arrest was still far below that of adult males. The substantial increases in arrests of young

Table 15.4 Juvenile crime Hong Kong over 20-year period 1947–67 (fiscal years) [1]

	No of Juveniles (Under 16 [2]) and Young Persons (16–20)						
Year	*Age group*					*Sex (age under 16)*	
	14–16		*16–20*		*21–30*	*M*	*F*
	No	*%*	*No*	*%*	*No*	*No*	*No*
1947/8	856					819	37
1948/9	625					573	52
1950	507					483	24
1951/2	387					368	19
1952/3							
1953/4							
1954/5	333		1,450		6,663		
1955/6	445		1,105		5,241		
1956/7	838		1,225		4,312		
1957/9	601	(9.5)	1,069	(88)	3,826	94%	6%
1958/9	879	(6.6)	1,099	(8.3)	4,593		
1959/60	1,259	(10)	973	(7.7)	3,692		
1960/1	1,226	(17)	676	(9)	2,124		
1961/2	1,609	(21.6)	798	(9.5)	1,500		
1962/3 [3]	1,219	(16.3)	1,594	(14.1)	1,156		
1963/4	979	(14)	971	(14)	1,877	939	40
1964/5	1,612	(18.6)	1,399	(16.1)			
1965/6	1,490	(15.4)	1,533	(15.9)			
1966/7	1,558	(15.3)	1,822	(17.9)	–		

Source: HKPARs 1946–67.

[1] Based on police figures for persons prosecuted during the fiscal year, not calendar year.
[2] In 1959 this changed to under 17; by 1963 it appears to have reverted to under 16 again.
per cent = percentage of prosecutions for all reported crime that year.
[3] Beginning of Superintendent's Discretion Scheme (known as the 'Liverpool system' copied from an experiment in Liverpool, UK) whereby juvenile first offenders were diverted from prosecution and courts into the Juvenile Liaison Scheme.

Table 15.5 Juvenile and youth offending 1959–64

	Under 16	*16–20*	*20–30*
1959/60	1,151	1,081	3,692
1960/1	1,123	779	2,174
1961/2	1,495	822	2,122
1962/3	1,219	1,054	2,190
1963/4	979	971	1,877

Source: HKPARs 1959–64.

persons came, not amongst juveniles, but the 16 to 20 age group, principally for robbery (up 154 per cent on the previous year), theft from a vehicle (up 125 per cent), burglary and break-ins (up 71 per cent) and serious assaults (up 36 per cent). The police noted the increase in offending by this age group but, also, the decline in the number of serious offences committed by children under 14. Where juveniles did engage in crime their involvement was in property offences. About 95 per cent of all juveniles arrested between 1960 and 1962 were arrested for offences against property.[14] Although they were arrested for larceny, however, this was not predominantly a juvenile crime. The vast majority of those arrested were adult males.

By the mid-1960s, Hong Kong's population had risen to over 3.5 million, half of whom were under 21 and many of whom were single males, a section of the population which, research suggests, are more disposed to crime. The statistics for the period indicated a marked increase in the number of young males (16–20) arrested by the police. Some were, by this time, being diverted from the legal system by the Police Superintendent's Discretion Scheme. The Juvenile Liaison Office, established in 1963, dealt with first time offenders under 16 (in 1965, it became part of the new Prevention of Crime Office). Based on a scheme started in Liverpool, England, in 1950, the new unit was 'to collect useful information on all criminal offenders under 21 arrested in Kowloon and to obtain information on juvenile gangs and undertake prosecutions where necessary'.[15] In terms of dealing with young offenders, under this system (called the 'Liverpool system' after its city of origin) a young first offender was not sent to court but, after a personal interview, was given a warning by a Superintendent of Police.[16] Supervised by the Juvenile Liaison Office, s/he was then helped to obtain a job, join a 'reputable youth group', and generally encouraged not to get re-involved with crime. Aimed at crime prevention, work in this section also involved frequenting areas of Hong Kong where youth congregated for entertainment or other activities. It also involved close liaison with the social welfare department and voluntary agencies. According to police figures, by the end of the decade, over 2,693 juveniles had gone through the scheme, with only 5 per cent committing a second offence.[17]

Table 15.6 Serious crime (excluding minor narcotics offences) 1961–5: juveniles, adults and young offenders

	Adults and young offenders					*Juveniles*				
	1961/2	*1962/3*	*1963/4*	*1964/5*	*1965/6*	*1961/2*	*1962/3*	*1963/4*	*1964/5*	*1965/6*
Against lawful authority	387	356	392	580	597	7	16	10	26	23
Against public morality	152	135	107	107	148	27	14	19	21	17
Against the person	638	581	584	862	838	56	62	65	103	69
Against property	4,363	4,794	4,305	4,639	6,020	1,517	1,123	876	1,454	1,371
Other serious crime	313	389	313	374	294	2	4	2	5	6
Narcotics	[1]	[1]	245	498	269	[1]	[1]	7	3	4
Total	**5,865**	**6,255**	**5,946**	**7,060**	**8,166**	**1,069**	**1,219**	**979**	**1,612**	**1,490**

Source: HK Police Annual Reports 1961–6.

[1] Excludes narcotics.

Table 15.7 Persons prosecuted for serious crime 1959–65

	Juveniles	*Young offenders (16–20)*	*Adults*
1959/60	1,151	1,081	11,634
1960/1	1,123	779	6,314
1961/2	1,495	822	5,967
1962/3	1,219	1,054	6,255
1963/4	979	971	5,946
1964/5	1,082		7,060

Source: HK Police Annual Reports 1962–4

Tables 15.6 and 15.7 provide a further view of juvenile and youth offending, this time for serious offences. The number of juveniles involved in such offences remained consistently low in the early years of the decade, whilst the number of young offenders steadily rose. The vast majority of offences remained offences against property.

The police force itself held that there was no notable increase in juvenile crime and the number of juveniles prosecuted remained relatively low: out of a total of 918,000 persons aged 7 to 16 in the colony in 1969, only 1,535 appeared before the courts. Out of a total of 11,261 prosecuted in 1968/9, only 2,095 were aged between 16 and 20; another 630 were aged 14 to 15 years. For 1969/70 these figures were 2,914 for the 16 to 20 age group, 547 for those aged 7 to 13, and 988 for those aged 14 to 15, out of a grand total of 13,802.[18] Adult offenders aged over 26 remained by far the largest group represented in the crime statistics.

The mid-1960s showed a general fall in recorded crime, including crime by young offenders. Triad offences decreased and the only notable increase came in recorded narcotics crime, an ongoing feature of Hong Kong life.

There was a rise in overall crime in 1962 but youth involvement in crime had increased only slightly, from 17 per cent of all arrests in 1960 to 26 per cent in 1962. However, the involvement of juveniles in these kinds of offences now more visible as the police had started to compile special tables and graphs depicting the trend in juvenile crime – all crime figures now began to differentiate between adults and juveniles, as well as between male and female juvenile offenders.

The official figures for the first four years of the decade had actually showed some remarkable falls for offences such as larceny from the person, hawking, demanding money with menaces and criminal intimidation.[19] Miscellaneous offences fell overall – in fact almost halved – from 179,207 in 1958/9 to 99,778 in 1960/61.[20] Figures for hawking offences showed an even larger fall from 59,598 in 1958/9 to 9,064 in 1960/61.[21] This was put to down to new methods for controlling hawkers introduced in 1959. These obviated the need for mass arrests though, as already indicated, by the mid-1960s large numbers of hawkers (over 23,000 by 1964) were once against being prosecuted for illegal hawking and obstruction offences. Mendicancy also showed a sharp fall, from 3,954 in 1958/9 to just 492 in 1960/61; by the mid-1960s it had disappeared from the statistics as a specific category, and whilst vagrancy remained an offence, the numbers arrested were negligible.

Moreover, of the 246,531 reports of miscellaneous offences made, few were found to have sufficient merit to warrant further police action. About 58 per cent of all reported crimes for that year were eventually classified as 'reports disclosing no offence'.[22] The pattern of the 1950s thus continued throughout the early 1960s; changes in overall crime were often due to miscellaneous offences, not serious crime. Indeed, according to the official figures, serious crime continued to fall – by 1964, it had reached the lowest level for ten years.[23] This was despite the fact that increased police activity in regard to narcotics, triads, and young offenders meant that, by 1962, the downward trend in serious recorded crime (which had lasted since 1956) looked set to be reversed. However, levels of serious crime in 1962 were still below those of the 1950s.

Table 15.8 Reports to the police

	Total number	*Disclosing offence*	*Disclosing no offence*	*Miscellaneous offences*	*Crime*
1959/60	406,795	195,573	211,222	177,910	13,599
1960/1	353,672	114,395	353,672	99,778	13,530
1961/2	350,905	112,726	238,179	81,757	14,468
1962/3	419,334	174,435	244,899	143,596	14,660
1963/4	453,759	236,736	217,023	202,481	14,245
1964/5	557,638	295,843	261,795	259,492	17,076
1965/6	580,840	363,378	217,462	325,357	20,022
1966/7	635,051	422,737	212,314	382,890	21,516
1967/8	489,009	320,516	168,493	284,270	24,047
1968/9	665,119	440,517	224,602	401,246	22,380
1969/70	833,669	495,565	338,104	453,421	26,979

Source: HKPARs 1960–70.

Table 15.9 Crime reports per 100,000 population

	Serious crime	*All reports*
1962/3	415.65	11,889.26
1963/4	391.02	12,455.64
1964/5	456.59	14,910.51
1965/6	523.70	15,192.59
1966/7	580.07	17,120.97
1967/8	620.14	12,610.80
1968/9	563.52	16,747.30
1969/70	668.67	20,216.34

Source: HK Police Annual Reports 1960–69

Arrests continued for relatively minor offences such as loitering for the purposes of prostitution or keeping a brothel, but these too fell in the early 1960s. It is difficult to tell whether this was because the actual level of offending had decreased or because they were 'protected' by corrupt police. The police were responsible for issuing licences to, amongst others, massage parlours, dancing schools, public dance halls, billiard rooms and money changers. All offered ready opportunities for police corruption. Lethbridge has documented the close association between triad-run illegal activities and police corruption since the nineteenth century in Hong Kong, as well as the most notorious public sector corruption cases of the decade (see Lethbridge 1985: 159ff). The triad association with 'dance halls', illegal massage parlours and obscene film shows meant that such activities were keenly monitored by the Anti-Triad Bureau. Triads were thought to recruit among hawkers and prostitutes in particular. Crackdowns on these two groups had forced them to look for new members amongst factory workers. This tendency was being 'closely watched', given the association triad members had with pro-Nationalist forces and the 1956 riots.[24]

Despite the fall in crime through to about 1963/64, the following year (i.e. police figures for 1964/65) showed the highest level of recorded serious crime since the late 1950s. The figures for 1965 sounded an alarm bell – not only was serious crime at high levels but the number of crimes committed by youth also appeared to have increased to the highest level post-war.[25] However, most of the rise in overall reported crime was still due to arrests for loitering and other miscellaneous offences. Some of the apparent sudden rise in crime in 1965 may also have been due to the opening of new police stations in densely populated urban area such as Wong Tai Sin. The colony was booming economically and undergoing massive urbanisation. With more new towns being built in the NT, police presence in the urban areas and the NT also rose.

The increase in the size of the police force and building of such new police stations had a marked impact on reporting rates. For example, with the opening of the Wong Tai Sin Police Station in 1964, the number of reported serious crimes in that area to rose from 1,692 in 1963 to 3,005 in 1964; reported crimes of violence rose from 231 to 473. As Lethbridge has argued, 'The suggestion of a sudden crime wave in Wong Tai Sin in 1964 is not a sufficient explanation of the reported increase' (Lethbridge 1972). Another contributory factor was the installation of a new 'PO Box 999' service, aimed

Table 15.10 Reported serious crime 1961–70

1961/2	*1962/3*	*1963/4*	*1964/5*	*1965/6*	*1966/7*	*1967/8*	*1968/9*	*1969/70*
17,417	16,292	14,245	17,076	14,245	21,516	24,047	22,380	26,979

Source: HKPARs 1961–70.

at providing people with an anonymous means of reporting crimes such as drug dealing and gambling.

The police themselves did not see this rise in crime as evidence of a 'crime wave'. The Attorney General also argued that it 'was not one which justified really serious alarm'.[26] This did not, however, dissuade a number of legislators at the time from claiming there was indeed a 'crime wave' and that, moreover, juveniles were to blame.

The crime figures were, in any event, open to a number of interpretations – changes had, for example, made in the way the statistics were compiled and crimes were classified. In the late 1950s, police began to employ the term 'true crime' or 'true cases', by which they meant cases where 'all the facts showed conclusively that an offence had been committed'.[27] They also omitted from the official figures cases which they deemed trivial, false or where no 'case in law' could be established. The fall in the overall crime figures for the first two years of the 1960s may have been partly due to this policy. In addition, in 1964/65, though the number of reports of crime (as opposed to recorded crime) was 14,910 per 100,000, most of these were later re-classified as miscellaneous offences requiring no further action. Thereafter, miscellaneous offences were simply omitted from the crime figures. The term 'crime' now applied to 'serious crime' only – in reports for 1965/66, for example, the term 'recorded crime' refers to recorded *serious* crime only.[28] In addition, in 1962, the term 'juvenile' was changed to cover persons aged below 16 years of age, rather than 17 as in previous years.

Such changes indicate shifts in policy, practice and approach – the 1960s was a period in which 'modernisation' of the force continued but, increasingly, it did so with an eye towards UK policing and social work practice. How Hong Kong's criminal justice agencies responded to crime and other issues (such as illegal immigration) was thus never purely a matter of changes and developments in domestic penality. International practices were accorded great attention, regardless of whether these suited the situation of the colony at the time. At the same time, Hong Kong's criminal justice policy could never be divorced from the threat of internal unrest, always a highly sensitive matter in the political climate of the decade, when China, its next-door neighbour, was about to embark on the Cultural Revolution.

This confluence of British penal thinking and the 'China factor' meant that, whilst the presence of young offenders in the recorded crime statistics had been noticed at the start of the decade, by the end of the 1960s youth would become firmly established in official discourse as a 'problem' category for the agencies of criminal justice and government alike.

Notes

1 Establishment, not actual strength.
2 HKPAR 1966/7: 37.

3 HKPAR 1964/5: 46.
4 HKPAR 1968/9: 38.
5 HKPAR 1960.
6 HKPAR 1964/5: 23.
7 HK Yearbook 1956: 185.
8 HKPAR 1966/7: 25.
9 HKPAR 1962/3: 2.
10 HKPAR 1965/6: 2–3.
11 HKPAR 1960/61: 24.
12 HKPAR 1960/61: 24.
13 HKPAR 1966: 2.
14 HKPAR 1960/61: 24.
15 HKPAR 1962/3: 21.
16 The fact that a scheme hatched for dealing with young offenders in Liverpool, an industrial and port city in the UK, was seen as suitable for the colonies says much about (1) the influence of UK social work models at this time; (2) the propensity of the Hong Kong Police to look overseas for such models. 'Development' and 'modernisation' paradigms of the 1960s neglected the possible ill consequences of such transplantation.
17 HKPAR 1969/70: 23.
18 HKPAR 1969/70: 58–61.
19 HKPAR 1960/61: 18.
20 HKPAR 1960/61: 25.
21 HKPAR 1960/61: 26.
22 HKPAR 1962/3: 21.
23 HKPAR 1963/4: 21.
24 HKPAR 1960/61: 32.
25 HKPAR 1964/5: 5.
26 *South China Morning Post* 9 November 1970 cited in Lethbridge 1972.
27 HKPAR 1960: 18.
28 In 1969, the term 'recorded crime' was abbreviated to 'crime'. In 1977, police reports would refer not to crime at all but to 'cases', suggesting that they only counted reports of crime that resulted in a prosecution. In 1979, another new term, 'key crime', was to be introduced to encompass all recorded reports of serious crime.

Chapter 16

The usual suspects: triads, drugs, gambling and corruption

This chapter surveys developments in the 1960s in a series of interlinked issues, some of which had already begun to rear their heads in the late 1950s. The decade of the 1960s might be characterised as one in which these issues became matters of public and governmental concern, and a slowly growing willingness to address them – a slow growth that was given a major push following the riots of the late 1960s, with some of the 'fallout' from this extending well into the following decade. The riots themselves are discussed in more detail in the following chapter, and the comments below are largely confined to the matter of how and why some of these issues became matters of significant concern.

Triads

Triads were seen from the very beginning of Hong Kong's colonial administration as a threat to social order, as much because of their links with political struggles on the Mainland as because of their criminal activities within the colony. Membership of a triad became an offence as early as 1845, though triads continued to thrive and were a significant, if 'underground', part of the social structure of the territory. At various times in the 1960s, they were involved in the management of youth and martial arts clubs, protection rackets and opium dens; they had a hand in industrial disputes; some had been Japanese collaborators during the Second World War. They were multi-faceted organisations with a complicated history. Although it is unlikely such a history will ever be written, and while in some respects they were predatory criminals, for many men at the lower end of the socio-economic spectrum they were also a source of social solidarity and social welfare.[1]

During the 1960s the 'underworld' of triads assumed pubic and political significance because of perceptions that they had become powerful, hydra-like organisations with interests in a wide range of legal and illegal enterprises. They took protection money from shops in some parts of the territory; 'organised' and generated income from areas such as wet markets and minibuses, and engaged in or profited from clandestine trades such as prostitution, gambling, loan-sharking, smuggling, illegal immigration and narcotics. Beyond all this and even more importantly, there was an increasing understanding through the 1960s that they were heavily involved in corruption, and in particular the corruption of the police.

Official 1960s views of triads

For the police, the fact that many of the young male offenders arrested in the 1960s were charged with offences contrary to the Societies Ordinance indicated the growing presence of triads. These younger triads had replaced what the police saw as traditional, organised triads, some of which had been damaged by arrests and deportations following the 1956 riots. As the police saw it, these younger men formed less organised triad-style gangs: 'The present day triad organisation in Hong Kong exists only as individual splinter groups and gangs'.[2] The gangs were said to run various vice, gambling and drug rackets. No genuine triad ritual was required for membership, though leaders were thought to engage in some sort of quasi-triad ritual which mimicked the traditional form: 'It has become apparent that the old traditional initiation ceremony of joining a triad society has to a great extent been abandoned and instead a much more simplified system of verbal recognition has been introduced' (ibid). The political affiliation of triads to the Nationalist cause had, by the 1960s, also disappeared from official discourse. Since 1956, triads had instead been represented as self-seeking criminals though, as Lam says, this did not exclude their retaining some political intention (Lam 2004: 91). In an era of heightened political sensitivities, however, any identification of triads with politics was to be played down.

The decline in the 'traditional' triads was, the police argued, due to their intensive anti-triad actions since the late 1950s, since when the major triad factions had disintegrated. By the early 1960s, the number of persons arrested for membership of unlawful societies had dropped from over 3,500 in the late 1950s to 301 in 1962; some triads, detained pending deportation in the late 1950s, remained under police supervision orders. Certainly, some of those deported or detained in the late 1950s were major triad figures. However, the 'very fact of disintegration has led to a proliferation of loosely-led splinter groups' of young men running various vice and protection rackets.[3] They had 'stepped into the vacuum' left by the demise of traditional triads. They 'falsely claimed Triad identity in order to intimidate victims' (ibid). To stop this, an amendment to the Societies Ordinance was introduced in 1965 to make claiming to be a triad member or office-bearer an offence. Not only was membership of a secret society an offence, so too was possession of any documents or insignia relating to a triad society, both subject to a punishment of up to five years' imprisonment.

By the mid-1960s the police were claiming success in eliminating triads – the year-on-year decline in convictions encouraged them to talk of the 'ever-diminishing influence' of the triads (ibid). At the same time, they warned of the possible resurgence of triad activity, as new leaders emerged with the ability to control the splinter groups and turn them once more 'into a menacing whole' (ibid). However, a side effect of their success against the traditional triad leadership seemed to have been an increase in leaderless gangs of youths still involved in traditional triad activities. This may help account for the increased attention the police paid to young male offenders, and their heightened profile in the official crime figures at the end of the decade.

Narcotics

In 1958/9 the government had launched a campaign against narcotics. Heroin trafficking and its triad associations was seen as a major problem. The campaign to 'suppress the narcotics menace' [4] resulted in increases in recorded drug offences in the early 1960s. Figures for narcotics offences almost doubled from 9,041 to 17,885 between 1959 and 1961. Despite efforts to reduce drug offending, figures showed that 50 per cent of those placed under police supervision committed further offences associated with narcotics.[5]

Hong Kong had developed a specialised anti-narcotics policy, with police resources divided between detection, seizure and suppression of drug shipments (the Narcotics Bureau) with divisional vice squads policing day-to-day street distribution and use. A special committee was appointed in 1963 to examine enforcement issues, leading to an increase in resources for the Narcotics Bureau. Government statistics for the year indicated that about 70 per cent of all convicted prisoners were known to be drug addicts.[6]

The interception of drugs entering the colony fell to what was called the Preventative Service of the Commerce and Industry Department. The police were responsible for action against the movement, manufacture, distribution and consumption of drugs within the colony itself.[7] In 1960, a Dangerous Drugs Ordinance was enacted, which increased the penalties for the manufacture of drugs (ibid); the police also sought greater co-operation with Interpol to address the international dimensions of the drug trade. In 1962, a new Narcotics Squad was established (part of the Narcotics Bureau) to concentrate police efforts against organised heroin distribution syndicates. In 1963, the Narcotics Bureau began to liase with the vice squad, and in 1965 it made the largest single seizure of drugs (over two tons of opium and morphine) in the colony's history and, at the time, one of the largest ever made in the world.[8] Hong Kong's 'drug problem' had more to do with the manufacture and trafficking or drugs through the port than with their consumption – older members of the population still frequented opium dens and the practice was tolerated, as it had been for so much of Hong Kong's history. Increasingly, however, the police now found themselves concerned with syndicates responsible for the manufacture and trafficking of morphine and heroin in the Asia Pacific region. This was to necessitate a more international outlook and co-operation with overseas forces.

In October 1963, the government pursued an evaluation of its anti-narcotics policy and the effectiveness of its anti-drugs war.[9] A 'White Paper' of November 1959 (*The Problem of Narcotic Drugs in Hong Kong*) had set out some measures but these were felt to require revision in view of what was seen as a worsening situation. A Working Party on Narcotics was set up under the Narcotics Advisory Committee to conduct a wide review of the present position, the desirability of intensifying the measures being taken, and to examine how best to enforce the government's anti-narcotics campaign. This Committee produced a survey showing that, from data recorded between 1959 and 1963, most drug addicts were in the 30 to 50 age group; their supplies came partly from outside Hong Kong but also partly from illegal laboratories within the colony. Between January and June 1959, there were 5,143 'self-confessed' addicts in Hong Kong's prisons of whom only four were under 19. Most were coolies or hawkers.[10] Between January and June 1960, Stanley Prison had admitted 2,946 'self-confessed' addicts, Victoria

Table 16.1 Reported narcotics offences 1960/61–1969/70

1960/1	17,887
1961/2	16,042
1962/3	16,081
1963/4	19,914
1964/5	19,187
1965/6	17,913
1966/7	18,310
1967/8	12,364 [1]
1968/9	16,872
1969/70	15,154

Source: HK Police Annual Reports 1960–70.

[1] Figure for 1967 is for recorded rather than reported offences.

Table 16.2 Seizures of narcotics 1963/64–1964/65 (kilos)

	1963/4	*1964/5*
Raw opium	1,472.251	2,645.409
Prepared opium	61.385	47.962
Morphine and morphine hydrochloride	91.994	285.462
Heroin	109.750	75.157
Heroin pills	8.873	8.796
Barbitone	8.673	8.796

Source: HKPARs 1960–65.

602, Chi Ma Wan 905, Tai Lam 1,033, Li Chi Kok 211, and Stanley Training Centre four.[11] The Commissioner of Police acknowledged that hardly any were under 20 and that most were addicted to heroin. A 1960 Drug Addiction Treatment Centre Ordinance provided for centres at which addicts were to receive compulsory treatment. Those held at the Tai Lam Centre received medical treatment during drug withdrawal, as well as help with their physical and mental recovery and aftercare. New Life House, a voluntary treatment centre opened by Caritas in 1968, provided for the rehabilitation of former prisoners.

One report from the Deputy Commissioner of Prisons to the Commissioner of Police for 1966 showed that in 1964, 2,655 offenders were 'self-confessed' addicts, whilst in 1965 the figure dropped slightly to 2,624. In its 1968 annual report to the United Nations on Narcotic Drugs, the Deputy Commissioner for Prisons, T.G. Gartner, showed that the total number of persons imprisoned for dangerous drug offences stood at 8,075 males and 199 females out of a total prison population of 14,893 and 376 respectively; another 455 males and 6 females were held in Training Centres. In sum, drug offenders numbered 8,280 out of a total prison population of 15,724 – some 53 per cent of the prison population. The figures for 'self-confessed' addicts were higher – of 12,614 'self-confessed' addicts, 11,502 were addicted to heroin. Only 9 of these addicts were under 15, the vast majority falling into the 40 to 49 age group.

Convicted drug addict statistics for the early 1960s indicated that most of convicted, 'self-confessed' addicts were addicted to opium and heroin.[12] Figures for Stanley Training Centre in 1968 showed that out of 61 offenders admitted, only one had been convicted of a dangerous drugs offence, though another 34 confessed to taking heroin. Most were males (5,183 out of 5,353 in 1963; 2,580 out of 2,648 in 1964) aged between 20 and 25, mainly unskilled labourers, skilled workers or those engaged in street occupations. Most were males employed as waiters, coolies, delivery boys, factory workers or unemployed, though statistics for the entire 'self-confessed' addict population covered a wide spectrum of mostly low-paid jobs, including typing, hairdressing, spinning, shop work, laundry work, tram driving and so on. The biggest group, however, both in the prison population as a whole and amongst 'self-confessed' addicts, were the unemployed and unskilled.

Figures for drug addiction indicate that, by the late 1960s, the numbers of self-confessed addicts being convicted remained more or less the same as the early 1960s (3,245 in 1969/70, of whom 3,216 were males aged 20 to 25). The Drug Training Centre at Stanley held 15 to 19 year olds convicted of dangerous drugs offences – in 1969, this admitted 35 addicts. The Tai Lam Addiction Treatment Centre admitted 26 heroin addicts in 1969, mostly aged between 40 and 49 whose occupations included maid (3), housewife (5), prostitute (4), hawker (2), factory worker (3) and unemployed (9). In the same year, Victoria Prison admitted 3,216 'self-confessed' addicts of whom 2,968

Table 16.3 Seizures of drugs

	1959/60 (kg)	*1960/1 (kg)*	*1961/2 (kg)*	*1962/3 (kg)*	*1963/4 (lb)*	*1964/5 (lb)*	*1965/6 (lb)*	*1966/7 (lb)*	*1967/8 (lb)*	*1968/9 (lb)*
Raw opium	582.76	966.27	223.53	748.123	1,874	5,820	4,576	11,178	2,454	8,811
Prepared opium	–	–	29.198	44.751	98	106	59	70	42	265
Morphine and morphine hydrochloride	64.932	202.782	104.867	157.060	172	599	189	1,007	25	439
Heroin	54.078	63.907	32.042	83.370	193	136	24	68	45	114
Barbitone	–	–	35.532	90.037	43	161	121	151	953	829

Source: HKPAR 1959/60–1968/9.

Figures before 1963/4 are in kilos.

were addicted to heroin and only 248 to opium; most of these were unskilled (1,302), unemployed (444) or rickshaw pullers and hawkers (338). Li Chi Kok Prison admitted 46 'self-confessed' heroin addicts, two opium addicts and two persons addicted to hash; these were mostly aged between 33 and 79, only one person being under 19; most were unemployed (16), prostitutes (11) or housewives (7). When, in 1967, the Research Sub-Committee of the Action Committee Against Narcotics published a report on the number of narcotics addicts in Hong Kong, it estimated a figure of male addicts between thirty and sixty-five thousand; the figure for female addicts was about 3 per cent of that number.[13]

Drug use was, thus, mostly confined to adult males. However, the Acting Commissioner for Prisons argued that there had, in recent years, been an increase in the number of young persons under 21 taking drugs, as well as those admitted to prison for drug offences who were found, on admission, to have a drug addiction. A report in June 1969 showed that, out of 3,075 persons admitted with a heroin addiction, 369 were under 21; for those addicted to opium, the number was 20 out of 287. He forcefully argued that more should be done by way of prevention and drug education amongst the younger generation.[14]

The international nature of the drugs trade had propelled the police force into co-operation with overseas police forces quite early on. In the late 1960s, officers from the Narcotics Bureau were in touch with representatives from Australia, the Philippines, Japan, Afghanistan, South Korea and Thailand. Because the suppression of narcotics involved the detection and seizure of drugs smuggled into Hong Kong, usually by ship, close liaison was kept with the marine police. The principal drug seized (and used) in Hong Kong was heroin, little demand being said to exist for LSD. Opium continued to be used by elderly members of the population in small and ever-dwindling numbers, whilst cannabis was seen as a drug favoured mainly by a small minority of the expatriate community.

Gambling

The drive to clean up Hong Kong in the late 1950s, and bring triad activities under control, resulted in the introduction of several new ordinances regulating gambling, vagrancy, supervision of offenders and hawking. A Gambling (Amendments) Ordinance in 1956 enabled the police to supervise mahjong establishments and other games in places where a fee was charged. All such places were required to be licensed and police were given powers of entry which, they argued, would be of great value 'as mahjong establishments are known to be places of resort for bad characters'.[15] Street gambling, gaming house and lottery cases also rose.[16]

By the mid-1960s, however, these cases seemed to have mushroomed: there were over 17,000 reported cases in 1963/4.[17] Part of the explanation may lie in the fact that, in 1960, the Police Commissioner was suddenly alerted to the fact that large-scale gambling schools were operating in Hong Kong apparently undetected by the police. A police raid on a gambling school at the waterfront in Kennedy Town resulted in the arrest of five triad members and uncovered gambling on a large scale.[18] The Commissioner established an inquiry to discover how this had gone undetected for so long. It concluded that large-scale gambling was run by the triads and that there was no question of corrupt police having turned a blind eye to its existence. However, the Commissioner concluded that officers in Western District had clearly failed to perform their duty, and requested the retirement of one senior CID officer, an NCO, and a constable, whilst another twelve officers were demoted.

Figures for gambling offences in 1964 were three times higher than in 1962 (32,334). Gambling itself was said not to be the problem so much as the vice, crime, corruption and triad protection rackets associated with it. To control gambling, in 1965 the Advisory Committee on Gambling Policy recommended elimination of all mahjong schools, the legalisation of off-course betting on horse racing, and that all press reports of horse racing and greyhound racing be banned. This prompted criticisms that such a move encroached upon press freedom. Hong Kong would, it was argued,

> . . . lose its reputation it has been enjoying for some years for the freedom and democracy accorded to the populace, if news censorship, which has been dispensed with since the end of the last war, is reintroduced in a disguised form. Hong Kong will have no way to defend itself against allegations which have been prevailing at the moment that Hong Kong is a 'police state'.[19]

There was sufficient concern about the problem that the Government eventually agreed to hold a 'Hyde Park Forum' at City Hall to air the issues. In the Chinese press, tougher penalties and more severe legislation to suppress gambling were endorsed: 'The sooner the enforcement of an anti-gambling policy, the less damage to the community would be done. Government should not hesitate in dealing with this issue' (ibid). *Kaifongs*, the Heung Yee Kuk, rural communities and other community organisations were enlisted to help the police suppress gambling. Local leaders appeared, however, to be split on the issue of legalised gambling. One of Hong Kong's most respected community leaders, Sir Cho Yiu Kwan, remained staunchly opposed to its introduction, on the grounds that it would lead to moral and economic decline.[20] These 'anti-legalisers' were dubbed 'pseudo-puritans' by the press, which was otherwise supportive of stronger measures against illegal gambling. Some newspapers called for more lotteries, built on the existing 'Tse Fa' model but removed from triad control.

Corruption

The extent of syndicated police corruption continued to provoke questions both in Hong Kong and in London, and calls for a Committee of Inquiry. London was not, however, convinced that this was the way to proceed. It knew there was corruption but not the extent of it.[21] LEGCO's attention was drawn to the Singapore Commission Against Corruption.[22] The press called for an independent Commissioner from the UK. The Hong Kong government suggested a Standing Committee, chaired by someone (such as the Chief Justice) not associated in the public mind with the executive. This suggestion was, however, vetoed on the basis that it would not be appropriate for a person of such high status to chair such a committee. A proposal to appoint an expert to review the Anti-Corruption Branch of the police was also dropped. But, London argued, the Hong Kong government was tackling the issue 'energetically'.[23] The Attorney General was, trying to 'bust the rackets' by getting the public to report corruption to the police. The problem with this was that the police themselves were corrupt. During the raids on illegal gambling schools, for example, pieces of paper with the numbers of individual police constables were discovered.

MPs continued to demand that strong measures be taken against any police found to be discredited. Police in certain divisions (such as those in Kowloon and Wanchai, where most of the vice establishments were located) were notorious for 'squeezing' money – and receiving 'kickbacks' – from these enterprises in return for turning a blind eye to their operation. Chinese constables were said to be taking 'hush money' from unlicensed hawkers, and prostitutes were paying 'protection money' to the police. During a Commons debate in April 1960, Earnest Thornton, MP commented that:

> Bribery and Corruption in Hong Kong are very bad – indeed it is worse than before. In my judgment it has reached a critical stage and threatens the very stability of the Colony . . . it is evident that something is drastically wrong . . . I know that bribery and 'squeeze' have long been associated with the Eastern way of life, but things have got to a desperate pass and the situation has reached a dangerous stage. To a large extent, this arises out of the mad scramble for wealth which there has been in Hong Kong in recent years.[24]

The Anti-Corruption Committee, Thornton argued, did not inspire public confidence when it contained well-known local businessmen who were known to put private before public interest when these had clashed in the past. He went on to quote an editorial from the *China Mail* in February 1960:

> For all that is admirable in this Colony, for all our dazzling prosperity, the great achievements by Government and the genuine hard work that

> has gone into making the place what it is today, corruption is the millstone around our necks, dragging us down. It is impossible to exaggerate its incidence and perhaps the only reason that the Government could offer for not holding a public enquiry is that the resultant scandal and shock would rock Hong Kong to its foundations . . . the Government could never succeed in carrying out such an investigation for there are few who would dare to probe it to its depths. At its highest level, fortunes are passed over for favours, at its lowest the odd dollar or . . . 'tea money' . . . But perhaps Hong Kong needs the shock that a truly impartial investigation could give. Perhaps we have been telling ourselves how good we are for too long. And it would be a change for us as well as others to know how really rotten we are . . . (ibid).

Thornton's critique was, however, dismissed by the Secretary of State for the Colonies. Thornton was a well-known critic of British policy on Hong Kong. As far as London was concerned, he had 'nothing good to say about Hong Kong' (ibid). The Secretary of State for the Colonies refused to establish an inquiry on the basis that he had received no evidence of flagrant cases of corruption, nor any statistics that demonstrated an increase in corrupt activities. As the Hong Kong government itself was not pressing for an inquiry, neither was he (ibid).

The Governor, meantime, proposed to summon to the editors of the three British-owned newspapers for an 'off the record' discussion about corruption. It might be useful, he argued,

> . . . if I were to try to get as much information as I could from these gentlemen in the course of one of these off the record talks. I arranged therefore, on some pretext, to see them on the afternoon of the 13th. The discussion started on general topics but I managed to get them round fairly quickly to the subject of corruption . . . I asked them bluntly if they had any evidence at all that corruption in the public service was worse than it had been a year ago. They were all emphatic that they had no such evidence. . . I asked them whether there were really strong feelings in the town about corruption and their answer was no.[25]

In internal memos, the Governor blamed the public disquiet about corruption on the 'machinations of two men, Burns and Edwards' (aggrieved victims of corruption). After consulting London, he sought the news editors' advice about how the press might 'help the Government over corruption', since it was mainly the English press that had raised the issue – the Chinese press had simply followed its lead (ibid). He confessed to being 'worried by the whole business' but was frustrated because he could not find any evidence about corruption and could not see what else the government could do. He was, finally, worried that Thornton would use the issue to discredit Hong

Kong, whose products were seen as a threat to jobs in the cotton mills of his constituency. Countering Thornton would require a 'robust and positive stance . . . which would leave Thornton with the alternative of either producing the evidence on which his allegations are based or withdrawing them' (ibid).

The Governor's refusal to appoint a Commission of Inquiry should not be taken, London argued, to indicate complacency. What was lacking was:

> . . . not the will to act against corruption but a judgment on the best methods which can best achieve success as be can be reasonably looked for in the circumstances of Hong Kong. For the present, the Governor sees no reason to depart from the less spectacular but nevertheless constant war which he and his administration have been conducting against corruption. This has resulted in the 4 years 1956–59 in 92 prosecutions against public servants and private individuals of which 56 were convicted . . . [internal disciplinary action found that] charges were proved against another 204 others, including 116 police (ibid).

Tightening the law was not, London argued, the answer, for it was 'better that nine guilty men go free that one innocent man be convicted' – relaxing the standards of proof in corruption cases would jeopardise this principle:

> It is the need to balance conflicting considerations, the desire not to convict or dismiss innocent government servants on the one hand, and the necessity for swift action against corruption on the other, which makes it so difficult to proceed speedily and effectively against corruption and bribery.[26]

This failure to tackle corruption, especially in the police, meant that much triad activity – such as the running of illegal gambling dens, extortion, showing of obscene films, and protection rackets – went unrecorded. There was a widespread view that bribery and corruption were Chinese customs. Corruption was common throughout the public and private sectors; ordinary people dealing with officials and business people routinely expected to be faced with corrupt dealings. A letter to an MP from a Hong Kong expatriate asserted that local residents regarded corruption as rife in the colony, and that:

> . . . it is the common talk of the town that an indictment naming several senior government officials was filed with the recently appointed anti-corruption committee and included the name of one member of that committee . . . the committee was only a sop to the House of Commons and no-one here seriously believes that it will ever take any positive action.[27]

The familiar 'orientalist' view that corruption was an exclusively Chinese malady was challenged by one correspondent to the *South China Morning Post*:

> We often hear the weak excuse, 'It is a Chinese custom. They are offended when their gifts are refused. They lose face.' I must say the expatriate who is almost invariably the receiving principal is awful quick in catching on. . . . There is also a school of thought which contends that corruption is very difficult to detect and it is better to let it go on than to introduce drastic legislation. That is the line of least resistance used by people who 'never had it better', and sounds ridiculous when we already have many harsh laws, e.g. several forms of arrest without a warrant.[28]

As in earlier days, therefore, sections of the colonial elite itself questioned the complacency and discriminatory views of fellow expatriates, though to little effect.

An editorial on the subject in the *Hong Kong Tiger Standard* in the same year criticised the Colonial Secretary's proposal to set up special Advisory Committee to examine corruption. He had, it said, blamed rampant corruption on the public and the low moral standard of Hong Kong people:

> These are familiar alibis used by all governments which failed to act in a determined manner against corruption . . . They blame the public, they put the responsibility on the bribe-offerers, they lament the loopholes in the law, but seldom are they willing to blame themselves . . . Such alibis . . . produce one unfortunate impression: that the government, in its eagerness to whitewash itself, is perhaps unconsciously condoning corruption . . . It is the established procedure of all public administrations to appoint a committee and promulgate a law whenever they are criticized for their shortcomings. Our government is especially prone to follow the committee or commission procedure . . . What we need in fighting corruption is fewer paper tigers and more determination; fewer alibis and more action; better – and more visible – results instead of committees.[29]

The Anti-Corruption Branch (ACB) of the police, founded in 1950, had proved wholly ineffective, mainly because it recruited from amongst CID. The 1948 Prevention of Corruption Ordinance was, thus, equally useless as a tool for tackling corrupt behaviour since its enforcement lay in the hands of many who were themselves corrupt. A review of the Branch's organisation in the early 1960s had 'reluctantly' concluded that anti-corruption work 'must remain in the hands of the police' despite strong arguments that a separate body be established under a Director appointed by the Governor.[30]

Though a number of official bodies were appointed to examine the issue of corruption, the Government seemed disinclined to do anything about it. Its primary concern at the time was to maintain social stability: 'the economy was taken as the key to achieving that end . . . To launch an anti-corruption crusade on a large scale might, then, have perilous consequences and lead to a flight of entrepreneurs and capital to Taiwan, Singapore, or other places' (Lethbridge 1985: 197).

However, 1960 had seen the introduction of a Police Force (Amendment) Ordinance providing for the dismissal of any police officer unable to explain how they maintained a standard of living greater than that commensurate with their salary.[31] The Advisory Committee on Corruption had also recommended legislation to make it an offence for any public servant to be in possession of property acquired from corrupt transactions, with the onus being on the accused to establish that any property not commensurate with his income was not derived from corrupt activities. Such property could be confiscated. A Target Committee was also established within the Anti-Corruption Bureau to decide upon which allegations to investigate, which to pass on to other departments, and what information was currently available about corruption.[32] Twelve police officers were tried on corruption charges but only five convicted, though some 14 others were dismissed from the police following disciplinary proceedings. An anti-corruption drive and police raids in 1961 led to 85 arrests and the conviction of 75 people, but only three government servants were convicted of corruption (the rest were mostly convicted of drug or gambling offences).

Press releases by the Government Information Service sought to publicise the vigorous action taken against government servants suspected of corruption, but figures for the year after the Target Committee began work suggest that it made little difference: only seven officers (out of 138 reported) were charged and only four were convicted (two absconded and one was acquitted at trial). The Advisory Committee recommended a mass publicity campaign 'based on an appeal to the community spirit of the public on the moral issue of corruption' and also that the subject be introduced into the civics syllabus of secondary schools, something the ICAC was to do in the 1970s.[33]

Meanwhile, syndicated police corruption remained entrenched even though the otherwise uncritical 1966 Inquiry into the Star Ferry Riots observed that police corruption was a major source of public dissatisfaction with the police.[34] The government's failure to tackle it was one of a series of failures to deal with social problems of the time. Individually insignificant matters grew in an incremental fashion to produce a widespread sense of distrust in the government generally, and the police in particular. These grievances simmered away throughout the early 1960s but eventually found expression in the 1966 riots. These were, as Lam says, 'truly impressive in their scale, attracting . . . participants from nearly all walks of life' (Lam 2004: 122). Though often overshadowed by the 1967 riots, the 1996 riots had a vastly more profound effect on Hong Kong society and its governance. Much of what followed in the 1970s, both in terms of youth policy and policing practice, stemmed from these events and the challenge they posed to the legitimacy of the colonial regime.

Notes

1 For further reading see, for example, Chu 2000; Booth 1991.
2 HKPAR 1968/9: 26.
3 HKPAR 1966/7: 24.
4 HKPAR 1960/61: 34.
5 HKPAR 1962/3: 6, 7.
6 HKPAR 1963/4: 24.
7 HKPAR 1963–4: 21.
8 HKPAR 1964/5: 22.
9 Memo, the Secretary for Chinese Affairs to the Commissioner of Police 30 October 1963.
10 Memo from Commissioner of Prisons to Commissioner of Police 12 August 1960.
11 Memo, Colonial Secretariat to Secretary of Chinese Affairs 16.October 1963.
12 Memo Prison Department, PD1/179/57 II.
13 HKPAR 1966/7: 23.
14 PD1/179/57 II 1969.
15 HKPAR 1955/56: 64.
16 See HKPAR 1960/61: 26.
17 HKPAR 1963/4: Appendix 17.
18 Gambling in Western District 22 August 1960, CO1030/1386.
19 *Sing Tao Jih Pao* 31 July 1965, HKRS 70–3–94.
20 *China Mail* 14 October 1971.
21 2 January 1960, CO1030/1386.
22 This was appointed by Sir William Goode, Acting Governor in the absence of Singapore's then Governor, Robert Black.
23 10 January 1961, CO1030/1386–22
24 28 April 1960, CO1030/1386–149.
25 CO1030/1336–154.
26 CO1030/1386–196.
27 S.B. Mitford to Otho Prior Palmer MP 23 June 1960, CO1030/ 1386/106.
28 W.S. Edwards, *South China Morning Post* 2 April 1960.
29 *Hong Kong Tiger Standard* 24 March 1960.
30 Memo dated 19 February 1962, CO1030/1387.
31 HKPAR 1960/61: 4.
32 HKPAR 1960/61: 33.
33 Information Services Hong Kong to Secretary of State for Colonies 17 January 1962, CO 1030/1386/26.
34 *Report into the Kowloon Disturbances* 1966, Hong Kong, Hong Kong Government Printer.

Chapter 17

The 1966 Star Ferry and 1967 riots

In 1966 and 1967, Hong Kong experienced two sets of riots: the Star Ferry Riots of 1966 and the 1967 riots, often described as a 'spill-over' of the Cultural Revolution in China, which had begun in 1966. Of the two, the latter was the more prolonged and violent but both came as a shock to the British administration, and both were indicative of wider – if disparate – discontent. In terms of the political landcape of Hong Kong, both riots presented an immense challenge to the legitimacy of the colonial administration. In terms of law and order, both consolidated the image of the Hong Kong Police in the eyes of the world as yet another repressive colonial force, and in terms of criminal justice policy, both had a far-reaching impact on the organisation and character of policing and punishment for the next four decades. Two groups – youth and suspected 'subversives' – became particular objects of governmental attention.

As Lam says, the government continued its policy of depoliticising such incidents by blaming unrest on a few cranks and troublemakers, thereby implying that 'the meaning of the issues involved was insignificant because they were not related to the fundamental political or structural problems of the society' (Lam 2004: 139). But the 1966 and 1967 riots did fundamentally challenge Hong Kong's colonial polity and unrestrained capitalist economy. This challenge was so serious that the whole of Hong Kong society was, in the decade that followed, to be reshaped from the top down, with the aim of fashioning new citizens who identified with Hong Kong and were sufficiently invested in it to resist any future seductions by communism.

The 1966 Star Ferry Riots

In April 1966, the Star Ferry Riots (referred to in official reports as the 'Kowloon Disturbances') began with an incident at the Hong Kong Star Ferry terminal. They ran for two days from 6 to 8 April. During this time, a curfew was imposed on the streets of Hong Kong, and the police force was mobilised into emergency formation, along with the Auxiliary Police, the Hong Kong Regiment and other regular army units. Large crowds demonstrated, principally along streets in Kowloon, initially engaging in occasional stone-throwing at the police. The riots culminated in over 300 convictions and in damage of over HK$1 million to property; ten police officers and 16 civilians were injured and one civilian died of gunshot wounds. The subsequent Commission of Inquiry stated that most of the participants were young people.

The Commission's report is the main source of public information about the disturbances. Few members of the public participated in the inquiry, although statements were submitted by academics and social workers. The Commission placed the riots in the context of Hong Kong's rapid, economic restructuring and the economic slowdown, with a recession in real estate and a banking crisis, which had afflicted the colony in 1965; its housing shortage; its insecure international political situation; its dense urban population; rapid post-war increase in population (3.5 million by 1966); the fact that, according to the 1961 census, less than 40 per cent of the population had been born in Hong Kong and that about 40 per cent was also aged under 15 (ibid). By 1966, half the colony's population (around 2 million) was under 21.

The Commission's report argued that it was 'obvious' that overcrowding, the struggle to make a living, the underlying political insecurity of life in the colony, and economic conditions would be 'more than a sufficient cause for frequent disturbances' anywhere (Riot Report 1966: 6).[1] That Hong Kong had only experienced one riot in the previous ten years was, thus, seen as 'a tribute to the general patience and good sense of the population and the vigilance of the police force' (ibid). In an assertion unchallenged by most academics of the time (or since), the Commission declared that the significance of the riots was that they had to be seen in the context of the rarity of riots in Hong Kong (ibid). Such events were mere 'blips' on the otherwise tranquil history of a colonial power and its subjects. They had to be understood, however, because confidence in the Hong Kong economy depended on such disturbances being avoided in the future. As with most things, therefore, official concern with the economy drove the inquiry's concern to comprehend the causes of the riots.

This concern made the Commission of Inquiry open to what it thought of as a sociological analysis of the riots, though Jarvie castigated its report as singularly unsociological (Jarvie 1969: 364). Lam also argues that it played down the political activism of the participants by explaining the riots away as the work of 'misfits', 'cranks' and troublemakers, whilst attributing its causes to mere 'glitches in government management' (Lam 2004: 124). The Inquiry reflected Hong Kong's recent conversion to social work and the 'modern' belief that therapeutic knowledge could cure all social ills. It stopped short, as Jarvie and others have argued, of advocating a more sociological perspective, far-reaching structural reforms or a new political order, and offered instead structural changes that 'would both preserve the existing distribution of power . . . increase organisational links between government and people' and improve its image (Scott 1989: 105).

In a sense, what followed was an exercise in social engineering, the pacification of discontent by a level of 'welfare colonialism' hitherto unknown in Hong Kong, the creation of new channels of communication between government and grassroots, and the sponsorship of cultural changes designed to create a Hong Kong identity amongst the people. Generating this new order entailed, however, creating a new unity of purpose between rulers and ruled, a joint battle against certain common enemies: corruption, subversion and crime, especially juvenile crime.

The events of 1966

The trigger for the 1966 riots was a small increase (5 cents) in the first class fare for the Star Ferry cross-harbour ferry, proposed in October 1965. This occurred in the midst of public concern about other transport fare increases, as well as complaints about cost of living increases more generally – school fees and water charges had also been raised by the government. Newspapers of the time had been critical of these increases, of the service provided by the companies which had instigated them, and of their massive profits. There was, therefore, already opposition to such increases when the Star Ferry Company imposed its rise in fares. There was also pressure for the government not to permit any further rises. A mass meeting was scheduled for November to protest against the Star Ferry and other rises, and Elsie Elliott organised a signature campaign for a petition to the Governor; by the end of November, more than 23,000 had signed and a further 100,000 had promised to do so (Riot Report 1966: 12). A second petition was handed in on 12 January 1966 containing 155,000 signatures. Mrs Elliott argued that if the government agreed to the Star Ferry increases, this would give the go-ahead for other companies to follow suit, that this would lead to spiraling price increases, that the burden would fall on those least able to afford paying, that the company's past profits were excessive, and that the revenue from the proposed increase was more than that needed to improve services. It was, she stated, 'simply a case of the people's interest weighed against a few people who are by no means in need of the extra profit they wish to make out of the public' (Riot Report 1966: 13, 14). In her autobiography, she recounts that it had never been her intention to raise a riot over a small fare increase: 'I was simply appealing for an agreement to be observed, and for an additional hardship on the workers to be avoided' (Tu 2003: 105). The government nevertheless allowed the fare increase.

The announcement came at the same time as other proposed tax increases on petrol, tobacco, vehicle licensing, salaries and profits, as well as increased parking fees (Riot Report 1966: 16). The cumulative effect of what might, individually, be small rises, was widely criticised as dealing a serious blow to the poorer sections of the community (ibid).

On 4 April 1966, at the Star Ferry pier, Hong Kong side, a young man called So Sau Chung went on hunger strike. His jacket was emblasoned with various phrases such as 'Hail Elsie! Join hunger strike to block fare increase', 'Democratic' and 'Oppose gambling' (Riot Report 1966: 18). His presence attracted the attention of passers-by and the media; on the afternoon of 4 April he was joined by a youth called Brian Raggensack, and in the evening he was visited by Elsie Elliot. As she later wrote,

> I did not know him. However, when I found that a crowd was collecting around him, I went and spoke to him telling him that demonstrations in Hong Kong were not permitted, and that as a crowd was gathering around him he could be charged with obstruction, and I did not want his good intentions to destroy his career because, at that time, even the smallest offence earned a permanent police criminal record (Tu 2003: 105).

So's demonstration was widely reported in the press on 5 April, by which time he had been dubbed 'the man in black'. By 11 am on the 5th, he had resumed his position on the Star Ferry concourse, where he was later joined by some youths. So wrote placards for his supporters and eventually crossed the harbour with them to stage a demonstration on the Kowloon-side ferry concourse. At about 3.45 pm he was warned that he and his supporters were causing an obstruction, and that if he did not move he would be arrested (Riot Report 1966: 20). After ignoring this and a second warning, he was arrested, provoking some jeering and shouting from the crowd as the police led him away (ibid). A demonstration followed at Government House to petition the Governor to release So. This was dispersed by the police around 5 pm. The group then went to the Central Government Offices to see Mrs Elliott who was attending an Urban Council meeting. Mrs Elliott accompanied them to the Central Police Station to see if So was all right, to offer to stand bail, and to advise the young people that if they wished to demonstrate they needed to make a formal application to the police.

In the interim, one of So's supporters had informed the police station at Tsim Sha Tsui that they intended to hold a procession down Nathan Road that evening. The Police in Kowloon apparently took the view that the demonstration should be allowed to proceed so long as no obstruction was caused, but it was to be watched by uniformed and plain-clothes officers (Riot Report 1966: 22). At about 9.15 pm a group of about 20 people, carrying banners and placards, made their way from the Star Ferry down Salisbury Road, into Nathan Road as far as Bute Street, returning to the Star Ferry at about 1.20 pm. Along the way, more people joined the procession, now numbering about 150 people, mainly youths (ibid). At about 11.30 pm they were addressed by Raggensack and other supporters.

At this point the crowd was said to have grown rowdier and the speeches more inflammatory (ibid). The crowd then moved off along Nathan Road until it reached the Shek Kip Mei estate. It proceeded through the estate, on to Castle Peak Road and the Li Cheng Uk estate. The crowd of about 400 was described as 'boisterous', mostly youths and children shouting some slogans. At about 2.30 am, the police stopped the leaders of the demonstration near the junction of Prince Edward Road and Nathan Road and warned them to behave in an orderly way. The demonstrators returned to the Star Ferry where they were prevented from moving off again by a police cordon. Groups of five were allowed through the cordon on the basis that they were dispersing peacefully, but they linked up again and returned to the Star Ferry. The police officer in charge found himself surrounded by the crowd and cut off from other officers (Riot Report 1966: 23). He was struck in the back by a demonstrator, who was then arrested. A struggle ensued and three others were also arrested. The crowd dispersed, 'although it seems that these arrests caused a considerable measure of resentment' (Riot Report 1966: 24).

On 6 April, So was brought before Western Magistrates on charges of obstruction. The proceedings attracted public and press attention and the courtroom was packed. So pleaded not guilty and was granted bail. He was taken home by taxi, whereupon the crowd dispersed. Other leaders, including Lo Kei (described by the Inquiry as a leader of the riots and 'a witness . . . indifferent to the truth') went to the Reform Club to make statements and arrange a meeting with Brook Bernacchi, a barrister and Urban Council member who advised them that a demonstration required police permission. The demonstrators' statements alleged that there had been police violence at the previous night's demonstrations. Lo Kei also seems to have made a Commercial Radio broadcast calling for support for further demonstrations. According to the inquiry report, on another occasion he also questioned the continuation of the colony and of colonialism, stating that 'there was something abnormal in Hong Kong because, whilst America was sending rockets to the moon, an 18th century system prevailed here' (Riot Report 1966: 93). Lo Kei was eventually convicted of inciting a crowd to interfere with law and order; his evidence to the Riot Inquiry was dismissed as confused, chaotic, and 'studded with fantasy' (Riot Report 1966: 96).

The police, meanwhile, had been issued orders to form into their District Emergency Force Companies; five companies were placed on standby; the combined police and military operations room in Kowloon Police Headquarters was opened, as was the operations room at Police Headquarters on Hong Kong Island. The PTC was called in from the NT to stand by as reserve at Wong Tai Sin police station. The police had no evidence of triad involvement in the demonstrations but it was thought the situation was 'potentially dangerous' and 'could develop into disturbances and rioting if demonstrations by teenagers and youths continued' (Riot Report 1966: 25). The 'danger period' was identified as the evening of 6 April. The garrison was alerted, a company of soldiers brought in, and the police force was ready to be mobilised in emergency structure by 7 pm.

Full force mobilisation, including the Auxiliary Police, was ordered at 10.50 pm. This put 2,655 uniformed officers and 347 CID on the ground, including 947 in riot companies, 819 in stations, 127 on mobile patrols, 383 on foot patrols, 328 'special' and unallocated, and 51 at the police/military headquarters (Riot Report 1966: 25). In addition, the military provided armed support, as they were required to do in instances of a threat to internal security. A joint directive on the command of security forces and the internal Police Emergency Manual stipulated the arrangements for joint police and military actions (Riot Report 1966: 73). The inquiry report described what happened when the police swung into emergency mode:

> When the Police Force forms into emergency structure, each division mobilizes a para-military formation of company strength for riot suppression. Each riot suppression company consist of 128 all ranks, comprising a company headquarters of five and three platoons, each of 41 men. The company is commanded by a gazetted police officer and each platoon by an inspector. Each platoon, in turn, comprises four sections consisting of one NCO and seven men. These are variously armed to reflect the different situations which may be encountered by the company and the different degrees of force required to be used. One section is armed with riot batons and rattan shields; the second with CS tear smoke; the third with. 300 calibre carbines; the fourth section's task is to secure prisoners. In addition, a number of platoons engaged in riot suppression on this occasion carried the Federal Gas gun and used it to fire wooden projectiles only. The whole company is mobile and Company headquarters is equipped with a radio in a Land Rover for communications with each of its platoons and with District Headquarters. Each platoon is similarly self-contained with a wireless land rover for Headquarters and two large personnel carrying vehicles for the striking force . . . (Riot Report 1966: 25).

The police, as the civil authority, requested the Governor to authorise the deployment of the military; they retained their responsibility for law and order but liaised with the military through a joint command (although in certain circumstances, the military was permitted to exercise sole command). Police officers did not give commands to troops, nor army officers to the police (Riot Report 1966: 74). The Commission was at pains to point out that bringing in the army did not mean that the police had lost control of the situation (ibid).

At the protestors' meeting with Brook Bernacchi later in the evening, plans were made to seek police permission for a demonstration on 9 April.[2] Shortly after dark, scattered disturbances broke out in Kowloon, mainly along Nathan Road. One group of youths at the Jordan Road ferry was initially stopped from going further by the police but allowed to stand by the road provided they did not cause an obstruction. When the group swelled to about 500, the police informed them that the demonstration could no longer be allowed, and offered to take the four leaders back to the Star Ferry so they could return to Hong Kong. They accepted, but some in the crowd assumed they had been arrested and taken to Yau Ma Tei police station. Soon after, a crowd of about 300 people gathered in Public Square Street, moving towards Yau Ma Tei police station. Those involved, mainly young boys, were shouting: 'they had no banners but it was menacing, with an angry roar' (Riot Report 1966: 31).

The officer in charge, seeing this attack on the station, took his company outside and ordered a baton charge on the crowd, clearing the area and scattering its members into side streets. A little later the same officer took his company out on patrol down Nathan Road, where a crowd of about 500 people (led by youths) had gathered opposite the Princess Theatre, where cinema crowds were coming out. The police opted for restraint but when they later turned up Nathan Road, they confronted a crowd of about 1,000 people and were met by a hail of stones and bamboo poles; the crowd dispersed after a police baton charge. The crowd stoned the police, cars and buses. Flower pots were thrown from high buildings. Tear gas was fired, but blew back towards the police and towards bystanders. Small groups of youths repeatedly dispersed up side streets only to re-form on Nathan Road (Riot Report 1966: 36). One police officer stated that the rioters seemed to be enjoying themselves smashing things up for fun (Riot Report 1966: 44). A police mobile patrol car was attacked.

The Yau Ma Tei, Headquarters, Marine, and Kowloon City companies, as well as the PTC, were all ordered to Nathan Road. At different locations along Nathan Road and its side streets, they discharged tear gas and tried to disperse the crowd; police vehicles were attacked and one European officer was injured. By midnight, a great deal of damage had been inflicted on buildings and vehicles along Nathan Road; parking meters and traffic signs were smashed, fires were burning, and small crowds of youths continued to throw missiles at the police. Bottles and other missiles were also thrown at the police from higher buildings. The police opened fire at the rooftop rioters as well as at some youths who had surrounded and attacked a police patrol vehicle. About midnight, they were also instructed to use firearms to disperse another crowd, but no shots were fired as the crowd retreated when faced with police carbines. The police also fired at, or over the heads of, a crowd in Argyle Street and others in Portland Street and Soy Street (Riot Report 1966: 43). A curfew was imposed at 1.30 am. The police and army were then said to have the area under control; 427 people were arrested.

Rioting continued on 7 April despite appeals from the Governor and civic leaders. Police prepared to place 3,600 uniformed officers and 356 CID on the streets to deal with further disturbances. Military units were deployed to police stations. The streets were described as 'tense', with 'people waiting for something to happen'. Trouble broke out at 9.30 pm when a crowd of youths was dispersed by police at the junction of Argyle Street and Nathan Road; the crowds coming out of the cinemas again found their eyes stung by tear gas. As the evening wore on, large and hostile crowds of up to 1,000 people began to form in different locations on Nathan Road and its tributaries; curious bystanders were, apparently, prepared to join in by erecting a barricade against the police across Nathan Road (Riot Report 1966: 54). According to the Inquiry Report, the rioters' intention was to 'take' Nathan Road and the police objective was to prevent this from happening.

The rioters were mainly young people, hawkers, children from poor families, street boys and the unemployed (ibid). As on the previous night, the police were stoned and had a variety of missiles thrown at them, including a 'fuel bomb' (Molotov cocktail). In response, they used tear gas and opened fire on several occasions – on one occasion at an 'uncontrollable mob' around Mongkok, resulting in death and injury to some rioters (Riot Report 1966: 56). The Hong Kong Regiment, a volunteer force trained in internal security, was deployed, along with the rest of the military units. At 12.15 am a proclamation was made under the Peace Preservation Ordinance and a curfew was imposed at 12.30 am. The Ordinance gave increased powers of search and arrest to the police and the Justices of the Peace (ibid). Rioting continued for a time in various locations around Nathan Road. A large crowd eventually marched down Nathan Road in the early hours of the morning, but was dispersed by police and military. By 2.30 am the rioting had died down.

The Inquiry Report described the events of the night as more limited in area, the rioters smaller in number but more aggressive, more hostile and more determined than on the previous evening (Riot Report 1966: 58). It concluded that the presence of the military on the streets had 'a sobering effect on the crowds and contributed to the maintenance of public confidence in the Government's ability to restore order' (Riot Report 1966: 75).[3]

The following day, a 7 pm to 6 am curfew was announced. The police and army in Kowloon were ordered to cordon off the area of the previous night's disturbances, and eight companies were deployed inside the cordon to prevent crowds gathering. These measures seem to have proved 'almost entirely effective' at keeping the streets clear (Riot Report 1966: 59). Minor clashes between the authorities and small crowds of youths occurred throughout the evening, but no damage was reported and only a small amount of tear gas was used: 'The measures taken by the security authorities and the realisation amongst potential trouble-makers that firm measures would be taken to suppress any disturbances combined to ensure a complete cessation of the disturbances on this night' (Riot Report 1966: 60).

The use of the military seemed to the Commission of Inquiry to have hastened the end of the rioting. It was, thus, held to be 'fully justified'. Its only criticism was that the decisions to impose a curfew and to call in the military might have been made earlier (Riot Report 1966: 62). It dismissed charges of police brutality made by the protesters, arguing that rumours about such brutality were due to the unpopularity of the police amongst certain sections of the public because of their enforcement of anti-narcotic and anti-hawking laws (Riot Report 1966: 65). In the Commission's view, the police action 'was characterised by reason and restraint and fully consonant with the principle that no more force should be used than is necessary to attain the objective' (Riot Report 1966: 66). It also exonerated the police from any allegations that they had provoked the riots by their actions. They had, it argued, acted in a 'fair and reasonable manner'.

The rioters and their supporters were, by contrast, castigated by the Inquiry. In particular, it criticised one of the leaders, Lo Kei, as a pathological liar and cast suspicion on Elsie Elliot's actions during the riots and her evidence to the Inquiry. One of the allegations leveled against the police was that certain officers at Mongkok police station had set out to 'frame' Mrs Elliott as an *agent provocateur* of the riots – she was unpopular with the police because she had complained about police corruption to such high-profile bodies as the International Commission of Jurists (*Justice*). She had also complained to London that the police were using their deportation and detention powers to intimidate anyone thinking of reporting police corruption. In her evidence to the Inquiry, she recounted how she had been informed by 'a decent policeman' that, 'the ruffians who entered into the peaceful demonstrations and turned them into riots were *ah feis* from black societies, appointed by corrupt police, with the intention of forcing them afterwards to prove that (she) paid them to do it' (Riot Report 1966: 80).[4] In her autobiography, she recounts how a visitor came to her home:

> . . . she said she had two uncles working at Mongkok Police Station. They had discovered that some corrupt policemen at that station were beating boys and forcing them to sign statements that I had paid them to throw stones. They considered it unfair to me and she had come to warn me of the plot. I laughed this off, not believing for one moment that anyone would do that to me. However, the next day she came again and told me that it was quite a serious mater and I must believe it. She also gave me the names of her two uncles, which I noted own, promising that I would never betray their trust (Tu 2003: 107).

In the witness box at the Inquiry, the boys whose signatures were on these statements denied that they had been paid by Mrs Elliott to throw stones:

> The Chairman was taken aback because he seemed to believe that they had a clear case against me, so he asked they boys why they had signed statements if they were not true, to which each boy replied, 'The police

> beat us around the room to force us to sign'. Asked if I had in any way supported them in the demonstrations, they replied, 'No, we supported her but she did not support us' . . . When the boy witnesses exposed this treatment by the police, the government must have been in a quandary as to what to do next, but to admit to corruption in the police or in any of the civil service was not likely (Tu 2003: 108).

Instead of investigating these allegations thoroughly, the Inquiry instead lambasted Mrs Elliott for refusing to name her source within the police. It deemed her refusal an obstruction of justice: she 'not only defied the law of this territory and claimed to set herself above it but . . . also violated the oath she had taken on entering the witness box' (Riot Report 1966: 80). She was also blamed for having lent her support to the demonstrators' cause, for fostering 'an atmosphere of unrest', and for encouraging 'those feelings of insecurity and discontent which are bound to exist amongst the under-privileged in any big city' (Riot Report 1966: 111). The 'bar of public opinion', the Commission argued, would judge her.

This attack on Mrs Elliott turned the Inquiry, Lam says, into the trial of a political activist and 'astoundingly, this discourse was unashamedly transposed into a personal attack on Elliott in the Commission Report' (Lam 2004: 121). Elliott herself recounts that she was made to feel like a prisoner in the dock: 'they had no intention of letting me give my side of the story . . . They obviously wanted the blood of the policemen [who had warned me] . . . the Chairman warned me that if I did not answer the question I could be sent to prison or fined' (Tu 2003: 109).

However, the Inquiry's treatment of Mrs Elliott backfired. She later learned that 'some important person' had approached the Governor to warn him that 'the tempers of the people were rising over the case, and that if I was sent to prison there could be another riot' (ibid). The public's everyday experience of police corruption, the government's conspicuous failure to deal with it, and subsequent events were all to lend Mrs Elliott's claims credence. In the Urban Council elections in 1968, she received over 80 per cent of the votes (ibid). Her opposition to the ferry fare rise and her vilification by the Commission only served to increase her public standing, especially when investigations in the 1970s uncovered the true extent of syndicated corruption in the Hong Kong Police, and the depths to which they were prepared to go to cover it up.

The Commission's conclusions

Despite the fact that police corruption helped generate the discontent that fuelled the riots, the Commission of Inquiry completely exonerated the police and avoided explicitly tackling the problem of corruption. Other, rather vague and non-specific factors, were identified as its cause. In total, 905 people were arrested and charged; another 560 were arrested but released without charge. The typical age of those arrested was between 16 and 20. This was the age group identified by the Inquiry as the troublemakers (Riot Report 1966: 103).

In an attempt to understand their motives, the Inquiry studied the rioters rather as traditional anthropologists once studied exotic tribes. It gathered data on 313 prisoners held in Chi Ma Wan prison, whilst social workers obligingly provided other data on 24 young rioters held in the Begonia Boys Home. Scientific study, it was thought, would discover something in their social backgrounds, their attitude to government and public utilities, their reasons for participating in the riots. Over half those held in Chi Ma Wan had only received primary school education; 46.5 per cent had been in Hong Kong for less than ten years, and most said they had committed offences in the excitement of the moment (Riot Report 1966: 104). The 24 from the Begonia Boys Home (who represented only a fraction of the youths who had participated in the riots) were mainly aged between 13 and 17; most had been born in Hong Kong, had left school at the time of the riots, were mainly low-paid or unemployed, and half said they did not feel they had many prospects for the future. Apart from work, they spent their time going to the cinema, loafing in the streets, swimming, playing ball games and gambling (ibid). Most had no idea who owned the public utilities such as Star Ferry (this was taken by the Inquiry as evidence that the rioters lacked political consciousness); 16 felt the police force was bad; one said he and his friends had seen the riots as a good opportunity to take revenge on the police and let off steam (they had attacked a police van); 16 said they joined in out of curiosity or for fun; 17 said the main cause for the riots was the rise in ferry fares, one thought it was 'bad government', another that it was public hostility towards the police, and one that police brutality had provoked the rioters (Riot Report 1966: 106).

According to the social workers who conducted these surveys, the boys were not 'social misfits anxious for political or other reasons to cause unrest and trouble in Hong Kong', but came from ordinary, hard-working families, and themselves worked long hours in low-paid jobs that offered few future prospects. They felt aimless, bored and, because of their long hours, lacked opportunities for 'normal teenage fun'. They had used the riots as an 'outlet for this need' (Riot Report 1966: 108). This evidence proved very influential. The Inquiry concluded that the rioters consisted of these ordinary youngsters from the poorer section of society, led astray by leaders (such as Lo Kei) who were cranks or misfits (Riot Report 1966: 107).

On the question of how it was that such youngsters – poor but not destitute and not from the 'criminal classes' – came to be drawn into the riots, it concluded that the explanation lay in a mix of factors. The riots were not the result of any pre-planned organisation, neither were they the spontaneous explosion of general social unrest, though rather disingenuously the Inquiry accepted that they would have attracted less support if there had not been *some* 'underlying social and economic dissatisfaction in the community' (Riot Report 1966: 113, 114). It dismissed absolutely the idea that there had been any police plot to provoke the riot or discredit Mrs Elliott. The riots, it argued, were simply demonstrations that got out of hand, the 'youthful emulation of the precedents and pattern of demonstrations so familiar in other countries' (Riot Report 1966: 116). As to why they got out of hand, this too was down to pure coincidence – Tuesday 5 April was the Ching Ming festival. Many people were not at work but on the streets. The demonstrations had taken place in the busy area of Nathan Road, attracting the participation of those leaving its many cinemas and restaurants, all of whom were 'infected' by 'the contagion of mass action' (Riot Report 1066: 120). People living on the resettlement estates, the Inquiry concluded, were less likely to get involved because of their security of tenure, low rents and greater contacts with the authorities (ibid). This kind of explanation, which identified social ties with a propensity towards law-abiding behaviour, tallied with what was to become Hong Kong's favoured theory of social control in the 1970s.

In the official acount, the protest had turned into violence because 'normal youths' on the streets got carried away when caught up in a boisterous mob, started looting and throwing stones, 'getting drawn into actions which at first may seem rather fun', 'having a go' at 'the normal targets in teenage riots throughout the world' (Riot Report 1966: 121). In keeping with the tendency to depoliticise all civil action in this era, the Inquiry held that these youths had no overt political pro-Communist or pro-Nationalist agenda, and were 'less interested in the ideological struggles of which their parents had experience on the mainland' (Riot Report 1966: 125). Thus the riots were, in almost textbook terms, simply an example of the unconscious, mental unity of crowd psychology, the 'mass hysteria of the crowd' which, when the storm passes, resumes its normal character of quiet, law-abiding citizens.[5] Such an explanation located the 'cause' of the riots in individual psychology (albeit 'lost' in the crowd) rather than in sociological or socio-structural factors.

Nevertheless, the Inquiry did acknowledge *some* wider social and political causes of the riots. These were couched in terms of the dominant rhetoric of the day with its essentially economistic conception of Hong Kong people as apolitical, utilitarian, instrumental seekers after wealth. The job insecurity engendered by the economic downturn in 1965 had, it was held, caused the public to oppose anything that threatened general price inflation and their aspirations of a better economic situation. Some acknowledgement was made of the general feeling that big companies were making vast profits for the few at the expense of the many but this was couched in terms that suggested that the rioters' grievances were borne of frustration and jealousy at the gap between rich and poor, especially amongst those faced with limited life chances owing to inadequate opportunity, education or skills; and a widespread 'misunderstanding' of the reasons why the government had approved the Star Ferry fare increase.

The prevalence of 'uninformed opinion' amongst the general public about the 'reasoned conclusions' of the Transport Advisory Committee amounted, the Inquiry concluded, to a 'considerable and dangerous gap', which had led to the demonstrations (Riot Report 1966: 110). It was, then, simply a case of poor communication and, by implication, once the information gap was closed and the public properly understood the government's motives, its grievances would dissipate.

The Inquiry rejected the view that the government ought not to have sanctioned the fare increase simply because the majority of Hong Kong people opposed it. This it saw as an argument which went against the entire ethos of Hong Kong for it:

> . . . ignored the basic fact that the salvation and strength of Hong Kong in a hard and material world has lain in the stark realism of her economy . . . it has not had the resources to subsidize the unprofitable and the uneconomic. It must be efficient to live and, in a free economy, efficiency requires a fair return for labour, capital and management (Riot Report 1966: 110).

In the Inquiry's view, therefore, the fact that the government might flout the opinions of the majority was not an argument that carried any weight in Hong Kong. The fare increase simply represented a 'fair return' for the Star Ferry company. Whilst working conditions required improvement, the capital required to produce them would, it was argued, not be invested if anti-social behaviour threatened internal stability. If the 'man in the street' had understood these things, the riots would not have occurred. Consequently, it recommended that, in the future, the 'gap' between the man in the street and the government on issues of public interest should be bridged by giving people 'that measure of information and understanding, that capacity to form a sound judgment which will bring him closer to the council table' (Riot Report 1966: 122).

As Jarvie pointed out at the time, the Commission simply assumed that the rioters were misinformed – it never contemplated the idea that it might be the government that was misinformed (Jarvie 1969: 364). Instead, the Commission argued, the government could not leave the important task of proper communication to the free media, though it was 'highly desirable' that the media, as strong influencers of public opinion, should be 'encouraged' not to 'unduly prejudge or prejudice' government policy in its reporting. The government needed its own dedicated mechanism for pressing its case with the public. This was to become the Government Information Service (GIS) which, in 1971, first coined the term 'Hong Kong people' in its publications.

The Inquiry was inclined to agree with social workers' evidence that the riots revealed a feeling in Hong Kong of 'impermanence, of a lack of belonging, and of elements of misunderstanding between Government and people'

(Riot Report 1966: 125). These feelings, it was argued, arose from Hong Kong's status as a place where people were always on the move, where one worked for a time and then hoped to move on, enhanced by fears of deportation, producing a feeling of not having a real stake in the community:

> . . . but this feeling of not belonging applies not only to Hong Kong; it extends further than that; it is based on the realization by Hong Kong youth that their native home as their parents knew it no longer exists and the chance to recreate it either here or abroad is denied to them . . . To belong, our Chinese youth must be induced to accept Hong Kong . . . we endorse the view that there is a need to develop civic consciousness and a responsibility to Hong Kong . . . Lack of homogeneity in the population-tends to inhibit the development of a widespread and strong civic feeling as illustrated by the vigour of the clan and neighbourhood associations; we would, however, [warn] against weakening the support inspired by these ties before there is a broader but no less effective bond of cohesion to take their place. They could indeed provide the foundation for a wider loyalty . . . Nevertheless, with a new generation growing up who have never had experience outside Hong Kong it is important to develop avenues for participation in the life of the community and to give expression to young peoples' zeal for service . . . (Riot Report 1966: 126).

One means by which this new cohesion might be produced was civic education in schools. The inadequacies of the educational system were, in the Commission's view, a contributory factor in the riots, especially the lack of universal primary education, shortage of school places, and the lack of vocational and moral education. The emphasis on exams also produced a feeling of failure amongst the drop-outs, whilst those who completed their primary education at age 12 had to wait until they were 14 or 16 before they could be employed. Significantly, the Commission entitled one section of its report, 'The Special Problems of Youth'. This argued that youth was a category requiring specialised, social scientific understanding, an 'important and profitable field for further study (ibid). Youth needed a better social environment, more recreational outlets and 'healthier interests' so that 'surplus energy and emotion' could be diverted from 'deviant outlets' such as gambling, bars, dancehalls, brothels and 'undesirable films, books and magazines' (Riot Report 1966: 138). This echoed the 1965 Annual Report of the Hong Kong government and a UK government White Paper on Social Welfare in Hong Kong, which had highlighted the 'problem of youth', the need for 'assistance and guidance for youth', and the provision of 'healthy and character forming outlets' – including training them for industry (Riot Report 1966: 144).[6] Young people had less need of a 'cause' to induce them to riot, being attracted instead by any exhilarating, exciting or unusual way of spending their time; boys, more than girls, were held to be attracted to the 'spice of danger', the flouting of authority and to violence (Riot Report 1966: 142). Young people were felt to identify less closely with Hong Kong society, feeling neglected and misunderstood, uncared for by their parents, teachers, employers and the administration. They had a lower threshold of control over their dissatisfactions; they were affected to a greater degree than their parents by changing values, 'by the cross-currents set up by the contact of two cultures in Hong Kong', and by the exposure to Western values and Western modes of thought (ibid). They were more aware of social and economic conditions in the colony, felt a growing sense of frustration at their limited life chances and the gap between their aspirations and their achievements. They were, in sum, more vulnerable to any appeals from anyone showing an interest in their welfare. This, the Inquiry felt, explained their support for the demonstrations.

The kind of work done with youth by the Police Juvenile Liaison Office recommended itself to the Commission, since it sought to 'steer potential offenders away from trouble' (Riot Report 1966: 146). However, the Commission also highlighted a dual 'punishment and welfare' approach towards the 'youth problem' which was to characterise the government's approach to juveniles from this point onwards. The first indicated the need for more social work and welfare for youth if future problems were to be avoided. The second located the cause of the riots in individual pathology and its remedy in stricter discipline, moral training and the reinforcement of traditional moral values, character building, and the prevention of further weakening of family discipline (Riot Report 1966: 147). From the 1970s onwards, these ideas were to translate into a juvenile justice policy that mixed welfare and punishment, and the increased supervision of youth by welfare and criminal justice agencies, as well as their subjection to the harsh discipline of 'short, sharp, shock' centres.

To address the perceived lack of government responsiveness to the people at the grassroots, the Commission recommended the establishment of a body such as the Citizens' Advice Bureau, more personal contact between government servants and the public, the creation of improved channels of communication, readier access to government, and the use of community leaders to build bridges and stimulate 'a more informed and constructive approach to public issues' (Riot Report 1966: 127). The existence of a gap between government and people was 'a continual danger and anxiety for any form of administration', especially for a bureaucratic and colonial one, 'even though it may provide the most efficient administration and offer the best chances for . . . economic and social progress' (Riot Report 1966: 127). These ideas were, again, to be translated into a top-down re-engineering of state/society relations in the 1970s that avoided the need for more democratic representation.

The Commission acknowledged that the government had an image of 'detachment from the man in the street'; its laws and regulations were also written in a language not readily understood by most of the people. Despite the 'very high rate of crime detection achieved by the police in relation to ordinary crime', the police were seen as corrupt and inefficient, and there was a belief that their powers were used in an excessive and arbitrary fashion (Riot Report 1966: 130). This the Commission put down to a general world-wide tendency to criticise the police, declining respect for law and order everywhere, and the need to better educate the Hong Kong public about the 'real facts' regarding police powers and the enforcement of laws on deportation and detention (ibid). Another 'scientific survey' was needed of public attitudes towards the police to indicate what measures were required, but in the short term their public image could be improved by closer contact with the public, more press coverage of the measures taken by the police and the problems they faced in the fight against crime, more involvement with schools, and better public relations overall (Riot Report 1966: 131).

The issue of police corruption – a sore that had festered since the 1950s in the face of government inaction – thus remained completely unaddressed. In an extraordinary show of complacency, the Commission avoided discussing the institutional defects of the criminal justice system, the stunting effects of bribery and corruption on peoples' life chances, and the effects of police corruption upon the public's faith in justice and fairness. Only with the arrest of one of Hong Kong's most distinguished police officers (Peter Godber) in the 1970s was the government finally forced to act. In this sense, the riots themselves produced no salutary effect on corruption whatsoever.

The Commission also rejected the view that the government had deliberately ignored public opinion over the Star Ferry fare rise. There had, it held, been a 'degree of misunderstanding' of the government's aims and policies, and a failure to actively pursue the public's co-operation. Most people believed that 'administrative knots' could not be untied or legal rights obtained 'other than through influence or even bribery'; they were 'unaware of the Government's 'outstanding achievements' in many fields, resulting in a readiness to listen to those who claimed it was disinterested in their welfare, and to succumb to 'false rumours' that it did not care (Riot Report 1966: 128). There was, in addition, a general tendency everywhere to blame the government for all the failings of society and to demand more from it.

The answer was to decentralise some of the administration to facilitate better contact with the people, provide a better range of simple services, develop greater representation on local advisory and consultative bodies, help build a community spirit, and improve the public's access to government. These measures would avoid 'the weakening of confidence of the public in the administration', the 'slowing down of investment' and – foremost amongst the government's concerns – the 'flight of capital' (Riot Report 1966: 129).

In sum, the Commission concluded that political, economic and social frustrations were not the direct cause of the riots. Such factors had 'played a part', however, and needed to be watched 'lest they provide inflammable material which could erupt into disturbances should opportunity arise in the future' (Riot Report 1966: 148). It endorsed the conclusions of a 1965 report by the Director of Social Welfare that there was a need to 'take determined and unfaltering steps' to develop a sense of community and social responsibility in Hong Kong (Riot Report 1966: 141). This had argued that Hong Kong was 'an assemblage of people' with little feeling of neighbourliness and very little leisure in which to develop a sense of community: 'Such conditions present formidable difficulties in any attempt to encourage the new citizens to play a part themselves in the development of a coherent society' (ibid).

A rather different view is provided by Lam, who points out that the public's demands and criticisms of the government persisted even after the riots (Lam 2004: 123). The riots themselves signified the 'emergence of young people as political actors . . . [who] . . . had yet to be absorbed by established social organisations' (ibid). Their propensity to set up their own groups, Lam argues, reflected their 'diminishing confidence' in these established groups due partly to their failure to address 'the boiling social grievances of the times' (ibid). The Inquiry's very failure to address these deeper social, political and economic factors also contributed to the public's general disillusionment with the Hong Kong establishment.

The Inquiry's report exemplified the complacency of officialdom, and its failure to grasp opportunities to redress public grievances. At the same time, the scapegoating of 'cranks' and 'misfits' represented an attempt to persuade the public at large that these grievances were the idiosyncratic rantings of an irresponsible few rather than the reasoned demands of the many. The net effect of these tactics was to represent the riots as apolitical 'glitches' that did not require radical surgery. As a result, the 'simmering public rage' continued, erupting again in 1967 and, as we shall see, during the student movements of the 1970s (Lam 2004: 124).

Though the official line was the events of 1966 were 'apolitical' in nature, government's response in the 1970s indicates that, behind the scenes, officials understood them as a severe blow to regime legitimacy. The extraodinary depth and range of this response is discussed in later chapters.

The 1967 riots

In May 1967, Hong Kong experienced more serious and prolonged rioting. Because these riots developed into an overt challenge to the government by communists in the colony, they assumed a wider political significance and attracted the intervention of both the British and Mainland governments. Orthodox accounts represent them as a 'spill-over' of the Cultural Revolution, reinforcing the image that whenever unrest hit Hong Kong, it was fomented by 'outsiders', whilst 'ordinary people' were law-abiding, politically disinterested spectators.

Newsreel images of mass protests and riot police in Hong Kong made this a riot that attracted international attention. Although after the riots the

Hong Kong Police were awarded the accolade 'Royal' as a reward for their endeavours, they also acquired what was to prove a long-lived image overseas as a repressive colonial police force. Orthodox histories of Hong Kong, however, remain uniformly uncritical of the police handling of the riots. Tsang argues that the government benefited from reforms introduced after the 1956 riots, which included regular anti-riot training and the provision of a 'central mobile reserve' which could be deployed within minutes should the need arise. When the riots started, the government had in place:

> . . . an organised, equipped, well-trained and efficient anti-riot police . . . The capability of the police to restore order enabled the government to avoid calling for a large-scale deployment of British troops to aid civil power, a key factor that allowed it to make measured responses, maintain public confidence and keep a high degree of normality (Tsang 2004: 186).

The police 'riot manual' for 1967 had indeed been improved following operations in 1956 and 1966, as well as the numerous skirmishes with squatter clearances throughout the 1960s. By 1967, it contained instructions on how to disperse crowds, leaving open a route of dispersal and using tear-gas to move crowds down the preferred route; it also contained instructions on how to 'shoot to kill' in riot situations. Tsang acknowledges that the police did use tear gas, baton charges and live fire on occasion, but contrasts their 'policy of restraint' with the Maoists who 'resorted to violence like throwing stones, setting vehicles alight and storming police lines' (ibid). Their indiscriminate bombings antagonised the public, Tsang argues, and encouraged it to support the colonial government's efforts to restore law and order. But not everyone agrees with this view. As Tsang Yok sing puts it:

> The prevailing view now is that the police acted with a great deal of restraint at the time, and the people in the leftist camp were just a violent mob, throwing bombs and escalating the violence. This is not true, and the Government's firm action was neither necessary nor justified (Tsang Yok sing 1996: 96).

Since many of the documents relating to this period of law and order in Hong Kong remain classified, it is impossible to judge the accuracy of the comparison between the 'restraint' of the authorities and the 'indiscriminate violence' of the rioters. The push to depoliticise Hong Kong's history, and the fear of being labelled as a 'troublemaker', means that the riots have been rather neglected by academics. The main histories thus remain somewhat partisan. Alhough some of the less sensitive documents of the riots have been released in recent years, it will probably be more years yet before a fuller picture can be assembled (though in all probability some documents will have been completely destroyed by the 'sensitivity exercise' undertaken prior to Britain's departure from Hong Kong in 1997).

Accounts published at the time were highly polarised – the newspaper accounts, for example, were mainly divided between the pro-government English language press, the vehemently critical left-wing press, and the anti-communist right-wing press. Other accounts, published in the run-up to the 1997 handover, tended to adopt a strongly anti-British tone that depicted the entire period of colonial rule in a bad light; in the middle ground there are some whose descriptions of these riots (and the 1966 and 1956 riots) as 'blips' on an otherwise tranquil colonial past. These somewhat conservative accounts implied that the government in 1966 and 1967 enjoyed the support of the majority of Hong Kong people (who were, in any event, depicted as uninterested in politics). When rioting did occur, therefore, it was depicted as the work of an isolated minority, out to cause trouble for their own ends, inspired by forces outside Hong Kong.[7]

The events themselves, however, strain this theory. Thousands of people took the streets to protest, only one year after police and troops were mobilised to quell the rioters of 1966. The sheer size of this support is indicative of deeper, widespread grievances, and a more developed sense of politics amongst Hong Kong people than is usually allowed. Cumulatively, these riots were the most serious challenge to the legitimacy of the government in Hong Kong's history. They forced some serious re-thinking about the relationship between rulers and ruled and provided the impetus for wide-ranging changes (see Scott 1989).

The events of 1967

The Hong Kong police were always nervous about festivals, carnivals and parades, especially when they occurred on politically sensitive dates. The first of May was recognised internationally as 'Labour Day', and since Hong Kong contained a number of left-wing organisations and unions, the police, the Auxiliary Police and the Hong Kong Regiment were placed on standby at the end of April (Cooper 1970: 1). It was known that on 1 May, 153 unions representing hundreds of thousands of workers would be holding celebrations (ibid). As Cooper points out, elsewhere in East and South-East Asia, the authorities were also on standby – against anti-Vietnam War demonstrators in Tokyo, and to enforce a government ban on all demonstrations in Saigon. There was, as Cooper noted, a certain 'dormant restlessness' underlying workers' relations with management in Hong Kong, and had been for some time (Cooper 1970: 9). However, the day passed peacefully in Hong Kong, though workers were involved in minor disputes with management in several companies. These included the Hong Kong Artificial Flower Works at San Po Kong, where workers went on strike against the dismissal of several employees who had been made redundant (Cooper 1970: 2).

Scott (1989: 97–9) usefully divides the sequence of events which followed into three stages: (1) May–June: labour disputes and demonstrations supporting the strikers; (2) June–August: stoppages to disrupt the economy, some violent demonstrations that resulted in loss of life; and (3) August–December: bomb attacks and terrorism (though some bombs were still being set off into 1968).

Towards the end of the first week of May, a sit-down protest occurred at the Artificial Flower Works against the 'harsh working conditions which [management] had imposed since 13 April, including very long hours, a two-shift system, the requirement for a very high level of output, deduction of pay when the machines broke down, and no absence for any reason during working hours (Cooper 1970: 4). The management of the company had responded to the protest by dismissing 95 workers and, on 28 April, closed the plants without giving any reasons, arousing resentment. The sit-down protest ended without further disturbance but on the following day (a Saturday) the striking workers clashed with non-striking workers and a company foreman who were moving goods out of the factory onto a lorry. When the police arrived, the strikers demanded that they arrest the foreman for assault on a fellow worker; the worker, however, refused to accompany the police to hospital to check his claim (Cooper 1970: 6). The police now found themselves confronted by 'openly aggressive men' with whom they realised they could not reason and against whom they would soon have to take firmer action. They thus called in reinforcements from the PTU at Fanling and, when they arrived,

> . . . the police drew their batons, marched into the screaming mob and arrested twenty-one of them, who were later charged with unlawful assembly. As they were led away . . . the arrested men hurled abuse, shouted communist slogans, and a few . . . brandished aloft copies of Mao Tse-tung's quotations (ibid).

The police cordoned off the area and, amidst a large and hostile crowd, allowed cartons from the factory to be loaded onto the lorry. Twenty-one men from the works were arrested.

Another ongoing dispute at the Green Island Cement Company on the same day also resulted in a peaceful sit-down protest by about 200 workers until 5 pm, when they were joined by eight school children who brought them tea, carried Mao books, and sang communist songs (ibid). The following days (Sunday, Monday) were quiet but on Tuesday another demonstration took place at the Artificial Flower Works, when more than 70 workers put up 'big character' posters attacking the management, 'shouted slogans, sang songs, and recited Mao's thoughts for two hours' (Cooper 1970: 8). The sit-in also resumed outside the cement factory, where another left-wing 'comfort mission' arrived consisting of three local film stars (ibid). On Thursday 11 May, workers from other factories joined those outside the Artificial Flower Works at San Po Kong. They put up posters which, according to Cooper, had nothing to do with the factory workers' dispute but carried anti-British, anticolonial slogans; many also had copies of Mao's 'Little Red Book', recited it and sang revolutionary songs. By 3 pm they had started banging on the factory gates and the police were called and, although at 4.25 pm the strikers indicated to the police that they wished to break off, they were encouraged to continue by a number of youths who exhorted the crowd to resist the police (Cooper 1970: 11).

As Cooper says, the evening was then 'given over to violence' as the crowd, now guided by these youths, clashed with the police. As in 1966, this crowd was quickly joined by teenagers who threw stones at the police and jeered them, as well as by people throwing bottles from tall buildings in the surrounding streets. The police fired tear gas and wooden baton rounds, and the riot intensified and spread to the Tung Tau Resettlement Estate, at which point the area was placed under curfew (Cooper 1970: 12). However, in a replay of the tactics employed in 1966, youths on the estate continued to 'play cat and mouse with the police, disappearing as soon as they saw them coming and re-appearing as soon as they left' (ibid). Overnight, vehicles and property were set alight, and some arrests were made. Small demonstrations by other workers followed throughout Hong Kong on the following day (12 May); most apparently included youths brandishing the 'Little Red Book', wearing Red Guard uniforms, shouting communist slogans, and putting up anti-imperialist posters. Scott notes that the government contended that many of the rioters had been paid and that the violence was premeditated (Scott 1989: 100).

The authorities allowed these demonstrations to proceed; no violence was reported. On 13 May, crowds again arrived at the San Po Kong factory, put up posters denouncing the Governor, David Trench, ran off into side streets when the police arrived, throwing missiles at the police. Fires were lit and roads barricaded to prevent the fire service putting them out; other fires were reported in the Wong Tai Sin and Tung Tau Resettlement estates. The police fired tear gas and used baton charges to break up a crowd of about 500 in the Tung Tau estate, but extensive damage was caused to buildings before a curfew was imposed and the area was brought under control.

Protesters surrounded the court when those arrested were brought before the magistrates in South Kowloon. As Cooper points out, the Chinese language, left-wing, newspaper, *Wen Wei Po*, had interpreted the police action at San Po Kong as an intervention on behalf of management against the striking workers (Cooper 1970: 59). Whether this interpretation was correct or not, Hong Kong had by now a long tradition of this kind of state intervention on the side of the business elite. Moreover, the police themselves had previously been warned to avoid involvement in industrial disputes, where possible, for fear that their intervention would be construed as support for the management. Such perceptions and rumours were powerful drivers of the riots, as they had been in the past (see, for example, Cooper 1970: 61).

Demonstrations now also took place outside Government House, where protestors recited the thoughts of Mao and posted 'big character' posters at its entrance. Similar demonstrations followed the next day, when the crowd outside South Kowloon Magistracy in Gascoigne Road spilled into Nathan Road: 'The incessant shouting and chanting had given it a uniform voice and a uniform aim and it was obvious that anyone who sought to challenge them would be in for a rough handling' (Cooper 1970: 17). A journalist from the right-wing press was attacked and had to be rescued by police. When the police moved to disperse the crowd, road signs were smashed, stones were thrown and the crowd moved off into the side streets in Yaumatei. Elsewhere along Nathan Road another group appeared: 'From then on the game became serious. As far as the police were concerned, these mobs had to be pursued and dispersed; as far as the rioters were concerned authority had to be taunted and resisted . . . gas shells were used frequently' (Cooper 1970: 18). Other groups assembled at various points along Nathan Road and at one stage the crowd in the area of Public Square Street was estimated to number about 3,000 people. Fires were lit, stones were thrown, the police used tear gas and baton-shells, and one officer, who found himself isolated, drew his pistol to scare off the mob (ibid). A curfew was imposed at 7.30 pm but in the areas not under curfew, disturbances continued.

On 15 May, the FTU denounced the government's actions. The Ministry of Foreign Affairs in Beijing also released a statement demanding the release of all arrested persons, the acceptance by the government of all the rioters' demands, and the punishment of all those responsible for the 'sanguinary atrocities' committed by its fascist forces (see Scott 1989: 100). In the statement, China also accused the British of collaborating with the USA against China, and of providing a base in Hong Kong for US forces engaged in the war in Vietnam. It also apparently endorsed the 'anti-imperialist' struggle being conducted by local Hong Kong communists, eager to demonstrate their engagement with the Cultural Revolution. A year earlier, local communist cells had forced the Portuguese colonial government to agree to their demands; the fear in Hong Kong was that its communists wished to score the same kind of victory.

China's intervention, and anti-British demonstrations in China itself, confirmed the international dimension of the riots. A good deal of diplomacy followed. On 18 May, the government in London issued a reply to Beijing's statement. This argued that the disturbances arose from an industrial dispute, that the police had acted with restraint, that since the matter was one of industrial relations the Labour Department would advise on its resolution, and that the Hong Kong government had a duty to maintain law and order impartially for all in Hong Kong (cited in Cooper 1970: 71). In a speech by the Governor, reference was made to the need to 'hold the fabric of the community together', and to preserve the rule of law – 'the shield behind which all the community can live at peace free from arbitrary pressures or turbulent assaults' (ibid). As in the past, however, law and order in Hong Kong could not be separated from its geopolitical position, nor was the rule of law perceived by everyone in Hong Kong to be fair and impartial.

On 18 May, large numbers of demonstrators converged on Government House, the symbol of colonial power in Hong Kong. As Cooper notes, Hong Kong island contained most of the symbols of expatriate power and authority (including the Supreme Court and the Hilton Hotel), which made it a target for the leftist protesters:

> Accordingly, the following day, the left-wingers stepped up their campaign and the northern part of the Island became their battlefield. In mass marches through the Central District they held aloft their little red books and sang, shouted and chanted incessantly from the works of their hero . . . At Government House itself demonstrators were estimated at more than a thousand at one stage and were the noisiest and most violent to date . . . they kept up a day long stream of abuse . . . began to call out personal insults and to defame the character of the Governor himself. Whilst most shouted, others began to put up even more posters, using the trees as notice boards when all available wall space became occupied. (Cooper 1970: 21).

On Saturday 20 May, Government House was again a focus of protest which, in riot gear, police had difficulty controlling. In the afternoon, the crowd rampaged through Central District and marched between Garden Road and Upper Albert Road, home to the Central Government offices (ibid). According to Cooper, there were so many communist demonstrators that they were able to spread through the whole of Central in groups of about 100 each, chanting slogans, causing damage and showing great hostility towards Europeans; the crowd around the Bank of China shouted anti-British and anti-American slogans, and played communist songs from loudspeakers in the building. When more police were sent in to control the crowd, feelings intensified; some police vehicles were surrounded and forced to withdraw (Cooper 1970: 25). As events in Central died down, in Wanchai, buildings associated with the government were daubed in painted anti-British slogans.

At this stage the police seem to have adopted stronger measures; disorderly processions and unlawful gatherings were banned, but small groups presenting petitions would be allowed (Cooper 1970: 75). On Sunday 21 and Monday 22 May, however, the violence intensified. There was a major confrontation on 22 May when, as Scott recounts, crowds tried to reach Government House but were prevented from doing so by the police (Scott 1989: 101). The area around Garden Road, the Hilton Hotel, and Central Post Office was again the site of most of the incidents, the most violent of these occurring outside the Hilton Hotel. A curfew was ordered on Hong Kong island, the first since the Japanese occupation (Cooper 1970: 27). By Tuesday, the demonstrations had quietened down. However, legislation was introduced banning broadcasts by loudspeakers. This was aimed at the Bank of China which 'had constantly broadcast inflammatory speeches from its location in the very centre of Hong Kong' (Cooper 1970: 76).

Anti-British posters in Western District carried such messages as 'Who are the rioters? Hong Kong British are the rioters', 'Double our force to fight back', and 'The great sins of the HK British must be liquidated'. Police were detailed to remove them. An Emergency Regulation dating from 1949 was activated on 1 June 1967, banning the display of inflammatory posters inciting violence (ibid). The Emergency (Prevention of Inflammatory Posters) Regulations 1967 made anyone convicted of the preparation, distribution or display of inflammatory material liable to a HK$5,000 fine and two years' imprisonment (ibid). It gave the police special powers to seize, remove or obliterate the posters (ibid). Numerous police raids were conducted on premises where it was suspected that printing presses were being used to produce such posters (Cooper 1970: 82).

Scott notes that by this point, a number of civic and occupational groups had expressed publicly their support for the government. It is unclear, however, how many were spontaneous expressions of support, as the government was taking active steps behind the scenes to encourage local worthies and organisations to make such expressions of support, in the hope that public opinion would swing behind them.

The second stage of sporadic strikes and stoppages began when left-wing organisations attempted to damage the infrastructure of the colony (Cooper 1970: 33). These stoppages – including food stoppages – continued throughout May and June; several industries were badly affected; some came to a complete standstill for a time. Police were brought in to protect those who opted to work throughout these strikes and evict those dismissed. These actions resulted in some violent clashes and arrests, as at the Taikoo Dockyard and Dairy Farm company. The police kept meticulous records of labour disputes and of all property seized during raids. Officers were instructed to make it clear to all involved that their investigations were impartial, unbiased and according to law. Arrests for 'technical offences' were discouraged lest they alienate members of the public. Weekly intelligence reports recorded the names and addresses of the dismissed workers, listed all known leftist supporters in each district, and noted the premises where workers and activists were thought to meet.

Transport was badly hit as the Star Ferry Company, the Hong Kong & Yaumatei Ferry Company, and the two bus companies (China Motor Bus and Kowloon Motor Bus) were targeted by left-wing organisations for strike action, inconveniencing the mass of the population. This, Scott surmises, probably lost the communists a good deal of public sympathy. For a fee, lorries, informal 'mini-buses' and taxis filled the gap left by public transport (the forerunners of the green and red light buses, now part of Hong Kong's public transport system). The call for an all-out general strike on 24 June also met with a somewhat muted 50 per cent response (Scott 1989: 101). Throughout this period, the police acted both to protect non-striking workers and to conduct raids on union premises and other premises suspected of harbouring communist cells.

Towards the end of June, the situation in Hong Kong was debated in the House of Lords. This reaffirmed Britain's commitment to the colony and reiterated that there was no question of her withdrawing. By this point, however, a number of Europeans had already sold their properties and fled Hong Kong, fearing a Communist overthrow of the government. Property prices plummeted. In the last week of June, as the disturbances appeared to die down, the Governor (David Trench) left Hong Kong for a holiday in the UK. In a broadcast made before his departure, he too had reiterated the 'Government's determination to maintain law and order in spite of the communists. It was unthinkable, he said, that so few rioters could triumph over the great number of citizens of Hong Kong' (Cooper 1970: 85).

The most serious incidents came, however, on 24 June and 8 July. The police station at Sha Tau Kok was attacked, the second attack resulting in the deaths of five policemen and injuries to 11 others.[8] Sha Tau Kok village lies in what is known as the 'Restricted Area' along Hong Kong's border with Mainland China – the frontier runs down its high street (Chung Ying Street). In 1967, one side of the street was in communist China, the other in British Hong Kong (see Cooper 1970: 102). During May and June, it had been the scene of some violent demonstrations; on another occasion, when two car loads of police had arrived there to remove inflammatory posters from government offices, they had been attacked by villagers, and forced to retreat using tear gas (ibid). On 8 July, a crowd from the communist side marched to the police post waving flags and shouting slogans; they then pelted the police post with stones and other missiles. The police inside, taken by surprise, responded with tear gas and wooden baton rounds; the crowd moved back (Cooper 1970: 103). A company of police in riot formation outside the police post came under automatic fire; one officer died on the spot, another later. The company then made a dash for the rural committee building, where the entire contingent of police came under fire, pinning it down. The 68 men trapped inside the police post could do little as they were under orders not to fire across the border. Under siege, they called up military reinforcements, but this proved problematic as their deployment at the frontier could lead to a direct confrontation with an alien power and a major conflict between Britain and China (Cooper 1970: 105). The request for military assistance had, therefore, to be relayed to London, resulting in a delay before the decision was made to deploy troops to the village and rescue the police. Gurka soldiers were eventually sent to the village to end the confrontation, and thereafter the army remained on the border until the late 1990s.[9]

Tension and anxiety were by this time growing, with rumours of thousands of communists moving towards border crossing-points, leading to fears of a mass incursion into the colony (Cooper 1970: 106). By the end of the day, five police officers had been killed and 13 injured. Reports by the New China News Agency argued that the village demonstrators had, in fact, first been fired upon by British riot police when they returned from a demonstration on the Mainland side, that the police had ignored warning shots by Chinese border guards and had continued firing, killing one villager and injuring eight (cited in Cooper 1970: 108).

The incident sparked off more demonstrations in Kowloon and on Hong Kong Island and at this stage the government decided to take punitive action against the communists. The Colonial Secretary told the Legislative Council: 'We are convinced and determined now that the time has come to grasp and retain the initiative in this contest, we have no doubt in doing so we shall have the wholehearted support of the vast majority of the community and we have no doubt of the final outcome' (ibid).

The third stage of the disturbances lasted for several months and was characterised by sporadic bombings and killing. On Sunday 9 July there was a violent confrontation between crowds and police in Queen's Road West in which one police constable and one member of the crowd were killed (Cooper 1970: 112). Later the same day, riot police were called to deal with an attack by a crowd on a tram station in North Point. According to Cooper, police were hampered by hundreds of onlookers, who harassed them; the police dispersed them with tear gas (ibid).

Violence continued through the next two days – bottles of acid were thrown at the police from communist buildings, along with stones and firecrackers; fires were lit and property damaged; a man shouting anti-communist slogans was beaten up and stabbed in Johnston Road, Wanchai (ibid). According to Cooper, the violence in these urban areas was mainly directed at the police and public transport. A curfew was imposed on Hong Kong Island.

Numerous violent incidents followed on Hong Kong Island and, when violence erupted again in Kowloon on 12 July, a curfew was imposed both on Hong Kong Island and Kowloon. There were also further anti-British demonstrations in China. In Hong Kong, the Acting Colonial Secretary sanctioned a crack-down, including armed raids on known centres of communist activity with military support. According to Cooper, these uncovered numerous stores of explosives throughout the colony and resulted in the arrest of several leading left-wing supporters (Cooper 1970: 145–6). On 20 July, nine emergency regulations (on the books since 1949) were effected dealing with police seizure of weapons, the opening and closing of premises, the obligation to give one's name and address when asked by the police or a member of the armed forces, the power to disperse assemblies, the power to prohibit meetings held in private as well as in public, offences against police, army or emergency vehicles, obstruction, the power of the court to order that a trial might be held in a court from which the public had been excluded, and the offence of spreading reports or statements which might cause public alarm or despondency (see Cooper 1970: 157).

On 28 July another three emergency regulations were brought in to deal mainly with 'conspirators and instigators' who used others to do their work for them (ibid). Regulation 31 (i) allowed the Colonial Secretary to order detention, without trial and without reasons, for a year. On 2 August another Emergency Regulation (Principal Amendment No 2) extended the jurisdiction of the District Court to enable it to impose heavier sentences (up to 10 years) than normal (up to five years) for certain offences against the Emergency Regulations.[10] Amongst some members of the elite, disquiet was expressed about the repressive nature of these measures. Some who expressed this disquiet openly – such as Mrs Elliott – stood in danger of being labelled subversive themselves, public discourse allowing no other division than between 'them' and 'us'.

The indiscriminate bombing of trams and busy locations, which took place in the following months, provoked widespread outrage since those killed or injured (or likely to be) were innocent civilians, including children. Official targets, such as Wong Tai Sin Police Station, were bombed, as were the station at Yaumatei and the police married quarters at Western Police Station on Hong Kong Island. However, other bombs, such as the one at Whitty Street Tram Station, were in busy public thoroughfares (Cooper 1970: 150). Police and army bomb disposal units were heavily pressed to deal with numerous genuine and hoax bombs placed around Hong Kong.

According to Cooper, in the NT, the military adopted a tolerant approach towards demonstrations by villagers, anxious not to provoke any incident that might spark off confrontation with Chinese border guards or with Cultural Revolution activists in Guangdong. In August, the border was closed to all traffic except at Lo Wu, but between August and November, a number of people (including a police inspector, Mr Knight) continued to be abducted from the Hong Kong side and held in China (Cooper 1970: 196). The arrest of leading left-wing journalists in Hong Kong, and the ban on the publication of three left-wing papers, also provoked demonstrations in China, the sacking of the British Diplomatic Mission, and the house arrest in Beijing of the Reuters correspondent, Anthony Grey (not released until October 1969). In London, police clashed with Chinese protestors outside the Chinese Legation.

In the urban areas, police and military co-operation increased in the face of continued bombings and rioting throughout the August to December period. Raids uncovered explosive dumps and weapons, as well as acid stored as missiles to throw at the authorities. One raid at North Point in August, was 'big . . . [and] spectacular both in execution and in results':

> More than one thousand policemen and soldiers participated ... the security forces decided that a two-pronged attack, featuring both ground and air assault, was the only way of entering, searching and combing the premises within a reasonable time limit ... helicopters were to land soldiers and riot police on the roof at the same time as police attacked the building on the ground ... Three huge, low-flying Wessex helicopters took off from the aircraft carrier [HMS Hermes] at 6.30 am ... with their first load of riot police and soldiers, all of whom had received practical training in rope landing and commando assault tactics ... As the soldiers on the roof kept guard, their police friends began to descend ... they met no resistance but found plenty of equipment to absorb their attention ... Other police who had attacked the building from the ground began to move towards them (Cooper 1970: 162).

According to some commentators, this was a public housing block which had been extensively infiltrated by left-wing activists. They had knocked through internal walls between flats to create what was, in effect, a store, command centre and hospital. It was at this point that the elaborate command structure and resourcing for activists involved in the demonstrations became more visible to the public at large. In this sense, the 1967 riots were of a rather different order to anything Hong Kong had experienced since the war, showing an unprecedented degree of organisation and political commitment. Unlike previous periods of unrest, there was also no mistaking the fact that they were explicitly political, anti-capitalist and anti-colonial. In this respect, though government propaganda depicted the thousands of participants as an unrepresentative group of subversives and Hong Kong people as generally 'loyal', it was impossible to depoliticise the event in the same way as it had the 1956 and 1966 riots.

In August, an anti-communist radio broadcaster (Lam Bun) and his cousin (Lam Kwong-hoi) were burned to death when the Volkswagen car in which they were driving was hit by a petrol bomb thrown into the car by three men disguised as road workers; a list of others targeted for assassination was rumoured to exist (Cooper 1970: 183). A shopping centre, and police station, trams and tram stations were also bombed.

The government itself was anxious both about capital flight (luxury properties were quickly sold off as the elite left the colony) and about maintaining the confidence of its own staff. Confidential government memos were issued daily to staff to counter left-wing propaganda and sustain morale. The government's aim was 'to stand firm, win and keep the support of the bulk of the population; take limited counter-measures without provoking fierce response; anticipate predictable eventualities, and remain flexible enough to deal with them'.[11] Government employees had to be 'kept steady'. Left-wing organisations were said to be intimidating them and pressurising local organisations to support their cause, attempting to 'drive a wedge between

Government and people by making the Government appear stubborn and inflexible and unwilling to compromise in spite of the cost' (ibid). Government staff who had a relationship with semi-official groups were instructed to 'brief' them, taking care not to give away 'graded information':

> In order to induce non-Government people to show their support for government more actively i.e. appear on TV or be interviewed on the radio, it is hoped that senior officials . . . will be willing to be interviewed themselves when appropriate matters arise to which publicity can be given (Hayes 1996: 111).

Hayes also recalls that the government drove to establish more *kaifong* associations in the urban areas during the disturbances (Hayes 1996: 74). It felt, apparently, unable to rely upon the traditional *kaifongs* for support (Hayes 1996: 110). He recounts how a form of words was devised that allowed *kaifong* leaders to sign a statement calling on the authorities to maintain law and order, without being seen to oppose 'compatriots' by supporting a foreign, colonial regime. At the same time, staff of the Secretariat for Chinese Affairs were to encourage 'the steady build-up of public support among the leaders of local associations, though little urging was needed', even though there was 'a tacit recognition that it was no longer feasible – nor at such a critical juncture wise – to deal only with elites or associations' (Hayes 1996: 111). There was, he notes, a 'pressing need' for the government to establish a presence in the resettlement estates, and to gain more understanding and support in such places:

> I became a member of a public relations committee which coordinated and steered government efforts to combat the Communists' media campaign. A . . . group of government officers met almost daily in the earlier part of the emergency, and reported directly to the new second Deputy Colonial Secretary (Sir) Jack Cater. Our terms of reference were wide and gave us plenty of scope. Using information on public opinion gleaned by SCA staff and from other sources, we monitored the contents and direction of the Communist media in order to determine our line of action, paying particular attention to measures that would maintain and enhance public confidence and the general morale. A similar 'psych-ops' committee dealt with operational aspects of the emergency (Hayes 1996: 113).

The propaganda war continued in the press. Left-wing newspapers linked Hong Kong's fight to 'British military fascism and colonialism' in Aden and the Middle East and called upon people in Singapore to rise against 'the rulers of darkness'.[12] The British, meanwhile, monitored the Chinese press for comments from the PRC leaders condemning British action in Hong Kong;

when they found none, they interpreted this as a sign that the local communists lacked support from the Mainland.

The violence eventually tailed off by the end of December, partly, it has been suggested, because China's leaders intervened to prevent local cells causing further damage to the infrastructure of the colony, whose continued existence was of value to China economically. The official death toll at the end of the riots was 51 (including three children), 15 of whom were killed by bombs exploding (Scott 1989: 104). However, it seems likely that some of the pro-communist dead and injured were taken to unofficial medical facilities, leaving the true figures in doubt. The possibility that violence could re-erupt kept the authorities vigilant.

As Scott argues, faced with a choice between communism of this sort, and the colonial capitalist state 'most people chose to side with the devil they knew' (Scott 1989: 104). Some local people publicly stated their support for the government and the police, others demonstrated more tacit support by their silence and avoidance of trouble. Most commentators agree that the tactics adopted by local cells alienated support for the communists amongst the local population.[13] At the same time, however, the level of support for the riots had been a 'tremendous shock' to the authorities:

> The labour disputes, the strikes, the riots, and the bombs signified not only a threat to organized law, but also an open dissatisfaction with the present structure of the economy and with a Government which embodied for some the very worst and most repulsive elements of colonial rule. (Cooper 1970: 283).

For Cooper, part of the problem was that it was very hard for the residents of Hong Kong to regard themselves first and foremost as citizens of Hong Kong:

> The traders and businessmen live there principally to make money. The anticommunists generally look forward eagerly to a time when they can return to a free China. The administrators and government officials always identify with their country of origin. There are only a few who regard themselves as 'Hong Kongians' born and bred (ibid).

These comments echoed the conclusions of the 1966 Riot Report. Others also attacked the government for not giving the people a sense of belonging, for being outmoded, for not doing anything for ordinary Hong Kong people, for failing to ensure that everyone – and not just a few – shared in Hong Kong's rising prosperity, for substituting the extraordinary police powers of the emergency regulations for the rule of law, and for introducing a Pubic Order Ordinance which substituted the 'Law of the Ruler' for the rule of law (see Cooper 1970: 300). Labour laws were also heavily criticised and undertakings given that improvements would be made in working conditions. At the same time, however, there was a realisation that there were:

> . . . powerful interests in Hong Kong that have never been too reform-minded, for the obvious reason that reform costs money, and governments raise money from people and companies. These interests have always been able to bring enormous pressure on Governors in Hong Kong in the way that Big Business brings influence on government in most countries.[14]

As Tsang Yok-sing (1996) and Lam (2004) have both argued, one legacy of the 1967 riots was the leftist student activism of the 1970s, the start of life-long participation in the politics for others, and a deep scar on the memory of the colony. As Elsie Tu[15] says in her autobiography, for those who lived through the two summers of 1966 and 1967 'the memories will remain forever' (Tu 2003: 103). Tsang Yok sing recounts how, like thousands of others, his brother, aged 18, was arrested during the riots and imprisoned in Stanley for two years; his sister, aged 15, was imprisoned for a month:

> My brother was arrested for distributing anti-government leaflets. He was a Form 6 student at St Paul's and was a timid boy. Everyone linked his actions to me because I was obviously leftist by then and I didn't hide my political views. In fact I had no idea what my brother was doing. His actions surprised everyone. He printed some leaflets at home calling for the reform of the school curriculum, denouncing the British for the Opium War, and so on. He got a pile of those leaflets and handed them out during lunchtime at school. Of course, everyone saw him doing this, and when classes resumed, the riot police were there . . . My brother was arrested straight away, tried and sentenced to two years. He was sent to Stanley Prison . . . a couple of months later, my fifteen year old sister was also arrested. She was a Form 3 girl at Belilios Public School. She was in the playground with thirteen other girls and when the school bell rang they refused to go back into the classroom . . . the headmistress . . . called the police and all fourteen were tried, found guilty of breaching the emergency legislation in force during 1967, and sent to the women's prison in Lai Chi Kok for one month . . . My parents were very supportive . . . [however] after my sister, my mother began to break down (Tsang Yok-sing 1996: 97)

The experience made a deep and lasting impression on those detained as well as those who policed the riots. Remarkably, however, the events of 1967 attracted very little public or academic discussion until 1997, when Hong Kong's return to China stimulated a brief interest in colonial history. In a short story written at that time, Yu Feng reconstructed the memories of a young boy during the riots:

> . . . the air was filled with the hoots and shrills of police whistles. Helicopters threaded their way through the narrow gaps between the tall buildings . . . Military police paratroopers, each holding a rattan cane and wearing a gas mask, landed on the roof of the building opposite which housed the Chinese products department store, and took up positions among the huge slogan-bearing banners which had been hung there . . . In our room, we could hear the sounds of hurried, whispered arguments coming from the corridor outside. Sometimes there were rapid footsteps of pursuer and pursued. This ebb and flow of sound was punctured by the loud smash of something being struck to the floor, followed by the metallic crash of a steel security door being forced open then violently being pulled shut. I thought our door was gong to be the next to be smashed in, so I quickly dragged all the chairs over in front of it. My young brain stored these chaotic sounds and smells well, as all these years later I still clearly remember the atmosphere of terror which filled our home that day . . . The sporadic strikes, demonstrations and street bombings that took place . . . were just the tail end of a comet. Unfortunately . . . the tail of this comet killed my younger brother [killed] when one of those street bombs marked 'Fellow Chinese Keep Away' accidentally exploded (Yu Feng 1998: 18).

The riots clearly left a deep impression on whole generation, not least those serving inside government. Hayes recalled an incident when, on a JP visit to the Victoria Road Detention Centre during the disturbances, he had glimpsed 'a familiar figure' among the inmates, the headmaster of the Sai Kung Public School:

> I forget the contents of our usual report upon conclusion of the visit, but upon my return to the office I had felt sufficiently concerned to write to the Security Branch of the Colonial Secretariat, to voice my criticism of the overcrowded condition of the place, which had not been designed to be a prison or hold large numbers of people. I need hardly add that my letter was viewed unsympathetically. Those times were hardly propitious for showing undue concern for people who had been seeking to destabilise Hong Kong and overturn its government. Overcrowding in prisons and detention centres was inevitable in the circumstances and, on a visit to Stanley Prison – the colony's largest – not long after, I found that it, too, was grossly congested. Many years later, on another visit to the same institution, I was told by a senior officer who had served there in 1967 that the Prisons Department staff had been barely able to maintain control of the inmates at that time (Hayes 1996: 114).

Jack Cater[16] has also recalled the 1967 riots as a 'watershed . . . one of the 'most far-reaching occurrences to affect Hong Kong post war'. They raised the 'very real danger that Hong Kong could have been lost to the Chinese Communists in the Red Guard, just as Macau had been lost in 1966' (Cater 1996: 103).[17] In Cater's view, though the 1966 riots provided a 'first indication' of the pressures building up in Hong Kong society, the government 'may well have gone to sleep again thereafter had it not been for the events of the following year' (ibid). And whilst they are typically remembered as 'anti-colonial', and 'anti-imperialist', as Tsang Yok-sing implies, the rioters did not see their actions simply in anti-colonial terms but also as anti-capitalist. This was clearly understood by the elite of the day, who also saw the riots as a severe threat to the colony's economy. For Tsang Yok-sing, the government's handling of the riots was not only as 'very high-handed' and 'colonial' but also protected 'the interests of the capitalists and, in doing so, suppressed the workers' (ibid). The initial grievance at the plastic flowers factory may well have been exploited by local Maoist cells, but the strike itself arose out of worker discontent at a time when Hong Kong, known to the world for producing cheap plastic goods, was characterised by Dickensian working conditions:

> I personally knew many of the people, the workers and trade unionists, involved in the violence, and they were very good people. When we were together, none of those people was prone to violence. They were simple workers who had been exploited all their lives. Yes, they harboured a lot of resentment towards their employers and capitalists, but, no, they were not bandits; they were not taking to violence for violence's sake (Tsang Yok sing 1996: 96).

As Steve Tsang acknowledges, Hong Kong in the 1960s was facing serious social problems which were conducive to rioting and unrest (Tsang 2004: 188). Those who participated in the events of 1966 and 1967 were motivated by a mix of grievances against the 'arrogant, over-bearing and corrupt behaviour of the majority of government functionaries, who were normally the only officials the local Chinese residents dealt with on a daily basis', against the social injustice between rich and poor, expatriates and locals, and by dissatisfaction towards the gap between government and people (Tsang 2004: 189).

Although in 1967, the Maoists proved ultimately unable to harness these discontents, for Cater, the 1967 riots made possible reforms that would otherwise have taken 'light years' to push through (Cater 1996). From thereon, 'orderly progress' would require a more equal partnership between rich and poor, government and people.[18] After the 1960s, law and order came to be seen not purely as a matter of operational policing, but in terms of the wider social, economic and political context of governance and regime legitimacy.

Notes

1 *Report of the Commission of Inquiry into the Kowloon Disturbances 1966* (hereinafter, the 'Riot Report'), Hong Kong: Government Printer.
2 The Inquiry Report – almost in passing – noted that those present at the meeting were intent on discussing constitutional reform and Singapore's independence, politically charged issues of the kind in which the 'politically apathetic' Hong Kong Chinese supposedly had little interest.
3 Somewhat prophetically, in 1961 the police had noted that public confidence in the police force was more important than its reputation, 'for if the vast majority of people in Hong Kong were to lose confidence in the forces of law and order, the consequences would be appalling' (HKPAR 1961/2: 1).
4 'Black societies' were secret societies, triads and/or political subversives.
5 See Le Bon, Gustav 1885.
6 See also *Williams Report on the Feasibility of a Survey into Social Welfare Provision and Allied Topics in Hong Kong*, cited in Commission's Report: 144.
7 For a fuller discussion of studies of social conflict in this period see Leung (1996); Cheung Bing-leung and Louie Kin-sheun 1991.
8 Scott 1989: 102; Hong Kong Yearbook 1967: 310.
9 See Cater 1996: 110.
10 See Cooper 1970: 158; Jones 2007.
11 Internal Memo, Colonial Secretary to Heads of Department 25 May 1967.
12 *Wen Wei Po* 3 July 1967.
13 See, for example, Tsang 2004; Leung 1996.
14 *Hong Kong Standard*, cited in Cooper 1970: 308.
15 Formerly Elsie Elliott. A Wikipedia entry gives a short biography at http://en.wikipedia.org/wiki/Elsie_Tu.
16 Cater was at this time the Personal Assistant to the Governor 'with direct responsibility for the disturbances'. He had been in the colony since 1945, but in 1966 had attended the Imperial (now Royal) Defence College in London, returning in 1967 as Defence Secretary. His post was first re-titled Personal Assistant to the Governor, then Deputy Colonial Secretary, with direct responsibility for the 'confrontation'. See Blyth and Wotherspoon (eds) 1996: 103.
17 There had been 'Cultural Revolution' style riots in Macau in 1966, which had briefly ousted the Portuguese government.
18 This point was made by A. de O. Sales in a speech to the Urban Council, December 1967.

Chapter 18

The post-riot years

The 1970s was a pivotal decade both for the criminal justice system and for the governance of Hong Kong more generally. The changes wrought then radically reshaped the Hong Kong Police Force; their effects remain evident today. They also re-modelled Hong Kong society more widely, transforming the discontented 'non-belongers' of the 1960s into active citizens, albeit still without the right to elect their own leaders. This chapter gives an overview of these events, though some themes are dealt with in more detail over the next three chapters.

Though the government restored law and order in the aftermath of the riots, its legitimacy had been critically undermined. Its new 'right to rule' was to rest not on its success against the Communists nor on the delivery of prosperity, but 'on its claim that it consulted the public' and had the consent of the people to rule (Scott 1989: 105).

Scott argues that the 1966 Riot Report had identified a means of retaining the existing structure of colonial power whilst increasing organisational links between government and people (ibid). In addition, improvements had to be made in labour, social welfare, other public services, such as health and housing, and to relations between the police and the public. The beginning of the 1970s saw the arrival of a new Governor, Sir Murray MacLehose, whose personal drive and commitment associate him in the public's mind with these 'Golden Years'. His reforms included a ten-year public housing programme, subsidised secondary education for all, improved health care, community building, the reinvigoration of government at the grass-roots level and the establishment of new community groups with which the government could work to build a new kind of civil society. By 1978, 16 community relations officers had been appointed to establish and maintain close ties with such groups, and thousands of other people were involved with schools, *kaifongs*, Mutual Aid Committees, District Committees, youth clubs and the like.

But welfare policies alone could not answer the demands of the rioters. What the youth of 1966 had demanded was higher standards in public life, without which government could not claim to act as the 'moral umpire' within a metropolis given over to commerce and industry, trade and finance

(Lethbridge 1985: 81). What was required was clean, more responsive government. This entailed tackling corruption, opening up new channels of consultation and stimulating public participation in civil affairs. All were exemplified in the fight against crime and the remodelling of criminal justice.

After 1967, the challenge was also to create a Hong Kong which people felt proud of, a place they would defend. The government identified the enemies they had to fight to attain this goal: crime, criminals and corrupt officials who damaged Hong Kong's reputation, and critics like Mrs Elliott, regarded as disloyal if not dangerous political subversives, 'excoriated by highly conservative officials . . . for bringing the administration into disrepute, for making Hong Kong a more difficult place to govern' (Lethbridge 1985: 77). After 1967, both the government and the established elites remained nervous of politics. Very shortly into the 1970s, the government began a propaganda campaign to depoliticise the population. Its publications depicted Hong Kong as an economic city, and Hong Kong people as politically apathetic self-seekers after wealth. Both the academy and the polity talked of a 'refugee mentality', of a population willing to subsume individual rights and freedoms to the maintenance of social stability, of a Confucian culture that valorised harmony, stability, and of traditions of conflict avoidance and subservience to authority. Hong Kong people were represented to themselves in official reports as *homo economicus*, living in a depoliticised economic society benignly administered by a bureaucratic state. Academics talked of a 'remote bureaucracy', distant from the lives of the Chinese who, with their familial and particularistic ties, occupied a parallel universe.

Between 1970 and 1983, the MacLehose administration did what the report into the 1966 riots had counselled: closed the gap between the government and the people, and created a sense of belonging. Throughout the 1970s, new ways were developed to attach the local Chinese to colonial rule, and strengthen internal security. The fight against crime, which was so characteristic of the decade, formed part of an overall strategy to 'clean up' government, clean up the streets, and win the hearts and minds of the people. Whether intentional or not, by the end of the decade these measures had cumulatively transformed Hong Kong's reputation from one associated with crime, corruption, and sweated labour to one of clean streets, plate glass skyscrapers, an economic 'miracle', one of the most advanced cities in Asia. Government defined rising prosperity and public participation in civil society as the touchstone: as long as it delivered on the economy, and performed well as regards public consultation, democracy could wait.

Impressive new roads, new towns, hospitals, railways, an underground system and a cross-harbour tunnel were built. The country parks were created, along with an immense number of new recreational and leisure facilities. The building of City Hall was accompanied by the encouragement of new cultural forms – 'home-grown' Hong Kong styles such as canto-pop, local fashion, design, and art forms. Television started to produce locally produced shows featuring Hong Kong actors. Though the English language channel remained, more Chinese programmes were produced. Following a student-led campaign in the early 1970s, the government also finally made Chinese an official language of the colony. The Government Information Service (GIS) established in 1971 changed the word 'colony' to 'territory', re-titled the Secretariat of Chinese Affairs the Home Affairs Department, and coined the phrase 'Hong Kong people.'

The 'people' were mobilised on a staggering scale. A new civil society was, in effect, created from the top down, replacing the administration's reliance on old elites with the creation of new ones. In 1972, Hong Kong officials visited Singapore to observe first-hand Lee Kwan Yew's techniques of state building. On their return, they embarked on a series of almost Maoist-style campaigns, mobilising the community around the threats of crime and disease. The annual 'Fight Crime' and 'Keep Hong Kong Clean' campaigns were 'psych ops' mass events running alongside 'feel good' spectacles such as the Hong Kong Festival and the Miss Hong Kong beauty pageants.[1] The newly created City District Officers (CDOs) organised ceremonies to honour local dignitaries and hand out awards to what were now called 'civic-minded citizens'. Hidden subsidies supported the production of cheap rice, cheap transport and cheap car parking. The result was a real rise in living standards for the majority of the population. Many moved from rooftop dwellings and squatter huts into subsidised public housing. The worst excesses of the labour market were mitigated by legislation – wages were still subject to the market, but working hours, holidays and labour conditions all improved. Child labour was officially banned. Those who worked within the criminal justice saw a vast improvement in their terms of service, partly to keep them loyal and partly to obviate the need for corruption. 'Modernisation' of the criminal justice system involved embracing new technology and social scientific knowledge in the 'fight against crime'.

The MacLehose administration was also to be a government of laws. The ICAC, founded in 1974, sent a powerful message that no government official was above the law. Government was to become a neutral, impartial arbiter, even-handed and willing to listen to the people. The territory's first law school, opened in 1969, began to produce home grown lawyers and home grown legal critics.[2] Legal aid was increased – by the late 1970s, over 60 per cent of the population was eligible. The civil service, previously riddled by corruption and cronyism, was to acquire such a strong a reputation for integrity and professionalism that it came to be lauded as the 'bedrock' of Hong Kong's stability.

An unprecedented amount of legislation in the first years of the decade introduced new workers' rights, as well as accessible channels for bringing government officials to account. The 1970s also saw the development of numerous new bodies designed to air public grievances and transmit government policy down to the people. They included the Small Claims Court

(1973), the Land and Labour Tribunals (1973) the City District Officer Scheme (CDOs), a Complaints Against Police Office (1983), the Police Public Information Bureau (1968) the Police Community Relations Officers (1974), Neighbourhood Policing Units (1974), the Independent Commission Against Corruption (ICAC, 1974), and the Unofficial Members of Executive and Legislative Council Police Group (UMELCO). Mutual Aid Committees (MACs) were established in private housing blocks, ostensibly to provide a channel whereby residents could meet regularly with a government official to identify and remedy local problems but also, Walden tellingly observes, to 'stop grey blocks turning Red'.[3] When, in 1968, the government had placed CDOs in ten urban districts, it was adapting an old tactic of imperial rule to new circumstances. In rural areas of Africa and Asia, the District Officer had been the 'father and mother' of the people. When it extended this office to Hong Kong's urban centres, the government billed them as 'uncles' of the people, to whom anyone could take a complaint or grievance, and seek advice on anything from housing to finding a marriage partner. The intention was that they might develop into UK-style Citizens' Advice Bureaux, but this never came to pass. They operated from shop-front offices in busy thoroughfares, linked with Chinese community associations, initiated community projects and co-ordinated services in times of disaster. Since they were also JPs, they could provide simple legal services, such as the signing of sworn declarations. They conveyed public grievances up the political hierarchy, channelled government policy down to the grassroots, eased the acceptance of unpopular policies and acted as antennae picking up signs of unrest and political agitation. They were thus part of the political establishment. They needed the linguistic and personal skills to establish relationships of trust with local communities but, in case they were tempted to 'go native', only 'government men' were appointed.

The persistence of this style of governance owed much to the regime's continuing fear of the 'Red Menace'. CDOs, together with Hong Kong's new 'neighbourhood policing' units, were strategically placed to penetrate the nooks and crannies of Hong Kong's dense urban communities gathering intelligence. This all extended the reach of the colonial state. Government itself remained elitist and closed. Remarkably, however, by the end of the 1970s, no one seemed to mind. MacLehose's 'rose garden' strategy had worked. It had cultivated civic pride in the citizens. Extensive networks of consultation gave the appearance of a government that listened to the people (whilst also serving as 'listening posts'). Mass public participation in keeping the streets of Hong Kong safe from crime and clean of litter conveyed the idea that government worked in 'partnership' with the people. What happened to crime and criminal justice in this period was, then, inexorably tied to wider political goals.

After 1966 and 1967, the authorities became nervous about rising crime (seen as a possible plot to undermine stability) and about youth, the main perpetrators of the riots. Its response was five-fold: (1) the arrest, cautioning and locking up young offenders on an unprecedented scale; (2) the mass mobilisation of the population – but especially youth – in community action against crime; (3) the increased deployment of youth-oriented social work programmes; (4) a focus on a de-politicised pro-government education and the development of civic values in the school curriculum; and (5) the development of social science research into the 'youth problem'.

1967–70: the immediate post-riot period

Whilst policy post-1966–7 addressed some of the inequities of Hong Kong society, little was done immediately to address the issue of corruption. The 1966 Riot Commission had conspicuously failed to attend to this issue, preferring instead to vilify Mrs Elliott. In a speech to the Urban Council in 1966, Mrs Elliott had made a number of allegations against the police. According to Lethbridge, the Colonial Secretary was:

> . . . so enraged by her animadversions that he not only sent Mrs Elliott a letter disputing her facts but also sent a copy to the press. He asseverated, 'Such conduct on your part can only result in a loss of confidence by the public in the police force with a resulting reduction in the effectiveness of the efforts by that body to maintain law and order'. Ironically, Mrs Elliott's charges were often replied to by officers who were themselves corrupt (Lethbridge 1985: 76).

Lethbridge argues that the police hoped the Commission would hold prominent members of the Reform Club (Mrs Elliott and Brook Bernacchi) morally responsible for the riots. In his account, Lethbridge says that the attempt to 'frame' Mrs Elliott emanated:

> . . . from lower down the police hierarchy, among a number of grossly corrupt police officers, whose careers would later be investigated by the ICAC . . . [They were] . . . being made uneasy by Mrs Elliott and other reformers: what would happen if the Government started to take these claims seriously? Since 1945, the corrupt had not been seriously incommoded in their acquisition of illegal wealth (Lethbridge 1985: 59–63).

Ernest Hunt, one of the corrupt police officers later investigated by the ICAC, also engaged in clandestine investigations to gather sexually incriminating information on detractors of the police, to use as a bargaining chip should he himself ever be unmasked. Corrupt officers in Mongkok had a good deal to lose. This was a district:

> . . . well supplied with brothels, massage parlours, dance halls, opium

> divans, gambling stalls and other illegal enterprises. Over the years, Mrs Elliott had complained repeatedly of Triad activities and police corruption in the Mongkok division . . . the volume of [her] complaints, her constant references to corruption, must have made some guilty officers extremely uneasy. She was a woman who knew too much. In time, she might be listened to more sympathetically by those in authority. There might be a clean-up campaign . . . (Lethbridge 1985: 64).

The 1966 Riot Commission's final report blamed the riots on the 'problem of youth' but 'there was scant mention of corruption as a possible social irritant; no highlighting of the fact that that those who lived in the warrens of the poor, the tenement buildings, public housing estates and squatter camps, had little confidence in the integrity of the average constable or detective' (Lethbridge 1985: 65). No steps were taken to address corruption:

> Corrupt policemen, one imagines, breathed a sigh of relief at total exculpation. Some notorious police villains, and their partners in crime, remained in situ, apparently untarnished by the many revelations of dubious conduct uncovered by the Commission of Inquiry; but some of these activities had been registered by Mr Charles Sutcliffe, who became Commissioner of Police in 1969 . . . (Lethbridge 1985: 68).

For the time being, the police escaped censure. Instead, their performance during the 1967 riots meant they 'became heroes . . . They came into their own as a security force . . . the public reacted with enthusiasm and gratitude . . . In these circumstances, who could continue to make derisive remarks about "bent" policemen?' (ibid). Peter Godber, later unmasked as one of Hong Kong's most notoriously corrupt police officers, was described as a 'very good officer . . . a hero' in 1967 (Lethbridge 1985: 70).

The government itself failed to detect the degree to which corruption was undermining public confidence. In 1966, Lethbridge argues, the full extent of police syndicated corruption was not generally known. The poorer Chinese 'were well aware of what was going on' but the Secretary of Chinese Affairs 'only sampled the opinions of respected Chinese community leaders, of those not usually inclined to rock the boat or be too radical or critical of their views' (ibid). Government failure to act seemed to confirm grassroots beliefs that the regime itself, at the highest levels, condoned corruption. The community, Lethbridge argues, assumed that all government departments were corrupt, especially the police, immigration, transport, housing, public works, re-settlement and education. The European community saw allegations of corruption as undermining the moral justification for colonialism, that of bringing good government and a clean, efficient administration to native peoples (Lethbridge 1985: 78). They explained it away as an intrinsic part of 'Chinese culture', unamenable to change. Lam argues that corruption had led to a widespread loss of confidence amongst ordinary people in both the ability and impartiality of the police force, whilst police brutality in suppressing radical protest also generated an anti-law enforcement sentiment (Lam 2004: 157). It took a 1970 article in the *Far Eastern Economic Review* by Leo Goodstadt ('The Fixers') to alert the European community to the problem, but inaction, combined with fatalism on the part of ordinary Chinese, and complacency on the part of the government, allowed corruption to flourish. For several years after 1967, the police became, in effect, untouchable.

The Festival of Hong Kong

As part of the MacLehose administration's strategy, a series of measures were introduced to make people feel better about Hong Kong, and persuade them that life in the colony was better than in Communist China. Apart from the new infrastructure developments, the opening of the country parks, and massive upgrading of leisure facilities, in 1969, officials organised the first Hong Kong Festival (a 'Festival for the People, by the People'). The plan was to spend about HK$1,200,000 on a festival in December, (though some objected since Christmas was already a holiday, the government 'did not need to be Father Christmas in December but Santa Claus in July, if it knows about public relations').[4] The festival had to be seen, 'not as an end in itself' but as a 'mammoth community project, another means of bringing all citizens together in the common desire for a better Hong Kong'.[5] The government insisted that this was a festival for the people of Hong Kong, not for the tourists. It chose dates with the weather in mind so as to make it possible to make maximum use of outdoor venues and to secure the largest possible audiences. No one in the colony was to be left out of the entertainment: a fun fair was organised for factory workers in Tseun Wan; prisoners were put to work planting seedlings and making banners; visits were made to old people's homes; the Director of Education urged all schools to 'infuse the Festival of Hong Kong spirit' among their students. Competitions, walkathons, exhibitions, canoe races, and talent contests took place. Open-air 'Mod Pop-in dances' and 'marathon dances' were organised, with popular groups, such as 'D Top Notes', the 'Chopsticks', the 'Hong Kong Soul Agents', 'The Mystics', the 'Blackjacks', the 'Night Trippers', and the 'Menace'. Free appearances also were made by movies stars and celebrities, such as Lydia Sing, Peter Tao, Stella Chee and Linda Lee. The arts ranged from traditional Chinese calligraphy to martial arts, classical performances of Chinese ballet and music to Cantonese pop, Nepalese, Malayan and Polish dance. Hong Kong in 1969 was nothing if not inclusive and international. There was a particular emphasis on youth – a youth rally was held, there were lion dances, lantern processions, and the first of many Miss Hong Kong beauty pageants.

The final cost of the festival rose to HK$4 million, most of which was government money. An estimated three million people participated. The aim, it was said, was to bring 'some happiness and enjoyment to the hardworking man in the street'.[6] The festival motif was a bright yellow, bouncing ball incorporating the Hong Kong orchid, intended to represent 'the progressive and resilient spirit of the community'.[7] Government put out a press release claiming that it suspected that the colony's leftist activists had enjoyed it all 'as much as the rest of us' (ibid). The Chinese press called it 'a sort of social welfare for the people because it gives them an opportunity to have a joyous time'.[8] There was no festival in 1970 but by 1971 government carried out a survey to see whether it should hold another. This time, it would incorporate a procession both in Kowloon and on Hong Kong Island, and mass student rallies. Private firms were encouraged to give workers a holiday on the planned date,[9] the underground and railways were asked to provide late trains, a special stamp was issued to mark the occasion and *pai laus* were erected at various sites across Hong Kong.

Police and public

The 1970s was a time of unusually intense police activity. Concerned to repair its relationship with the people after the riots – and after the ICAC revealed the true extent of police corruption – the police force needed to assert its competence as a crime-fighting force. But it also needed to develop a more friendly and responsive face than the one that had faced the rioters in 1967.

Old familiar problems still made demands on police resources. Fires, landslides and water shortages required police assistance. A fire at the Tai Hang Tung Squatter Settlement, in December 1969, for example, had left some 5,300 people homeless; a football match at the Hong Kong stadium in 1969 (between an English side and a Hong Kong side) resulted in trouble amongst the crowd; several 'lightning strikes' by public light bus operators against police enforcement of a new law regulating their use led to public order problems. These, however, were well within the existing capability of the Hong Kong Police, and cannot explain why, in years after 1967, the force experienced rapid expansion and changes in the ways officers were deployed.

Table 18.1 Police force expenditure

Year	*HK$*
1971/2	200,038,734
1972/3	227,584,634
1973/4	286,534,738
1974/5	371,819,545
1975/6	Not known
1976/7	469,518,000

Source: HK Yearbooks 1971/2–1976/7.

The police force now developed in two directions: as an internal security force and as a beat police with its ear to the ground. It required its beat officers to develop closer and better relations with the general public, establishing better police/public relations but also improving the state's presence in – and closer surveillance of – housing estates and other areas of population. Basic training was amended to broaden officers' outlook and 'develop a sense of social responsibility'. Other mild reforms began to appear towards the end of the 1960s. The international nature of much Hong Kong policing increasingly brought the force into contact with overseas officers and practices. More police were encouraged to improve their educational qualifications, and more were sent on training courses with overseas forces than ever before, including work with the FBI.[10] The police started to become more open with – and responsive to – the public. Officers were provided with training in manners and courtesy, emphasising the need for politeness when dealing with members of the public.

Starting in the mid-1960s, the police had become sensitive to public criticism and the need for harmonious relations with the public, increasingly seen as essential to the force's ability to carry out its duties effectively. In 1966, the force even adopted the Riots Commission's terminology, speaking of Hong Kongers having 'no sense of belonging', lacking a sense of civic responsibility, and being apathetic or resistant to government policies.[11] In line with general government strategy, steps had to be taken to remedy this by establishing new 'channels of communication' with the people.

Immediately following the riots, the police established a Police Information Bureau, designed to keep the public better informed, and raise the profile of the police in the media. Those officers engaged in the Police Community Relations Bureau were to attend social functions, meet with people 'not as law enforcement officers . . . but as friends and confidants who offer advice and guidance to local residents and business people'.[12] The paramilitary image of the police, so evident in 1967, was to be replaced by a more community-friendly image. Closely linked to the Government Information Services department, this new bureau handled media enquiries and produced briefings and television programmes profiling the police force; exhibitions were organised creating 'a better understanding of the Force's organisation and role'.[13] The bureau organised a whole range of activities to stimulate better police/public relations, including open days, posters, leaflets, and television programmes. Camps were run for secondary school children; there were visits to police stations; the women officers of the Hong Kong Police Sports Association ran a scheme providing organised games sessions for 'needy children' every Saturday at a football ground in Boundary Street.[14] In 1969 the force felt able to report that the public was 'now better informed about the day-to-day activities of the Force'.[15] In the same year, the Queen accorded the accolade 'Royal' to the Hong Kong police force, in recognition of its role in suppressing the 1967 riots.

In 1969, the police embarked on a further, all-out public relations drive, opening up police stations to the public, liasing with *kaifongs* and factory management, watchmen and private guards, distributing leaflets to the public and working alongside the newly established District Fight Crime Committees. Competitions to design crime prevention posters amongst schoolchildren; appeals were made to the public to assist the police in the detection of crime. The 1969 Police Prevention of Crime exhibition at City Hall attracted over 200 visitors per hour. It aimed to 'show the public our problems with regard to crime prevention and solicit their support'.[16] At the start of 1967, it was decided to open a number of police stations up to the public, 'so that the man in the street may see for himself how a Police station functions and how the Police deal with their day-to-day work'.[17] An open day at Wanchai Police Station was thus intended:

> . . . To give the public a glimpse of the man behind the police uniform, and provide insight into the methods used by the police to render service to the community . . . we aim to impress you with our efficiency and ability to cope with every situation . . . We hope you will be impressed and in turn be our ambassadors of goodwill in your own sphere of activity, thereby strengthening the bond between the public and the police, which is so important to the well-being of the Colony.[18]

However, this drive to enlist the community's interest in crime prevention prompted an unanticipated rise in public interest not in the police so much as crime. The Chinese press, in particular, began to talk about the 'crime problem' – there were 25 editorials in one week on the subject in 1972.[19] One story, of two girls being raped in the Kwai Chung Resettlement Estate, prompted calls for heavier punishments and the greater use of caning (a report suggesting that caning failed as a deterrent had fuelled suspicions that it was to be abolished). Thousands of young girls, it was claimed, had to go to work in factories every day; the police should be protecting them. The police were exhorted to work harder to combat crime, put more police on the streets, and even to allow the residents of multi-storey blocks to form their own vigilante groups. A suggestion by the Inspector General of the Colonial Police, during his visit to Hong Kong, that the government should recruit some overseas experts to study the crime problem was met with derision in the Chinese press, who saw it as an insult to local Chinese in the police who knew the local situation and the 'mentality of the Chinese' better than any foreign expert.[20]

Faced with criticism about their failure to stem rising crime, police corruption, and their lack of responsiveness, the police looked to the 'fuller development of representative organisation at local level' to help interpret local opinion, guide and explain policies and laws guiding local affairs and 'remove any sense that the police enforce the law in an arbitrary way'. This would 'bring about a better understanding and acceptance of the need for action taken by the police'.[21] To this end, the police Press Office issued stories and information about the police and a new system – the 'PO Box 999' system – was established to enable members of the public to report illegal activities more easily.

But these changes in police image were not matched by changes in the composition of the force. Expatriates were still over-represented among the senior ranks; promotion of locals was difficult and slow. Women were still not regarded as equals: they were not, for example, eligible for the barrack-style accommodation provided in police stations to male married or single constables. Unlike their male counterparts, female constables and inspectors were also still required to be single. Operationally, they were confined to traditional roles, such as administration, liasing with social welfare as regards juvenile offenders. Few made it up the hierarchy into the senior ranks; a few expatriate women inspectors were recruited from Canada and the UK.

By the mid-1970s, women were being used more for operational roles in CID, the Public Relations Branch, and as plainclothes units patrolling Resettlement Estates and leisure areas, on the lookout for runaways and juvenile delinquents. The first few women Marine Police were also posted to

Table 18.2 Police establishment 1971–79

	1971/2	*1972/3*	*1973/4*	*1974*	*1975*	*1976*	*1977*	*1978*	*1979*
Gazetted officers	193	201	209	211	208	224	233	258	270
Inspectorate	1,201	1,235	1,356	1,291	1,286	1,419	1,567	1,720	1,731
Rank and file	12,379	13,527	14,497	14,713	13,708	15,481	16,770	17,086	18,893
Total	**13,773**	**14,963**	**16,062**	**16,215**	**16,177**	**17,124**	**18,579**	**19,064**	**19,507**

Source: RHKPARs 1971–8.

Table 18.3 Composition of police

	1973/4	*1974/5*
Officers		
Senior officers (Overseas)	311	298
Senior officers (Local)	123	133
Junior officers (Overseas)	321	303
Junior officers (Local)	529	625
Rank and File		
Cantonese	10,337	11,952
Northern Chinese	333	–
Pakistani	103	–
Portuguese	4	–
Women (Chinese)	719	1,214

Source: RHKPARs 1973–4. After the mid-1970s, police reports ceased to contain data on the ethnic composition of the force.

Islands Division on Lantau.[22] But it was not until 1974 that real reform began. That year was the twenty-fifth anniversary of the acceptance of women into the police. The occasion was marked by a ‘changing concept’ whereby women were to be more closely integrated into the force. Integration, it was said, ‘has now reached the stage where women officers are constantly required to exercise direct supervision over their male subordinates, a rare occurrence a few years ago’.[23] By 1976, women comprised 10 per cent of the force strength; they remained at this level for the rest of the decade. This made them ‘the largest female complement in the Commonwealth’ (ibid).

But understaffing and falling local recruitment in the mid-1970s led the force to look further afield, to Australia, New Zealand, Canada and London, for recruits. In 1974, for example, the recruitment of overseas inspectors was at its highest for many years.[24] In 1973, the Police Cadet School was established, providing education to young people with a view to their entering either the police force or one of the other disciplined services. A boarding school based in Fanling, it began life with 150 cadets and provided education in English, maths, Chinese and social studies, as well as Outward Bound and Character Training activities.[25] Larger premises (with space for up to 1,200 students) were planned for Shuen Wan, near Tai Po, and in 1977 another 600 students were admitted to larger premises at Dodwell’s Ridge. The erection of purpose-built accommodation at Plover Cove was put back to 1981.

The involvement of Police Cadets in community service work was meant to cultivate students’ sense of their ‘civic responsibilities’, but also to project ‘an impressive image to the public’, something the police force was anxious to promote.

Figures for the mid-1970s give us some idea of the priority attached to certain policing jobs at the time. Force strength in 1974 was, for example, 12,780 (out of an official establishment of 16,062). Although corruption was a major issue, the Anti-Corruption Office was staffed by only 84 of these officers. By contrast, the PTU numbered 1,081 and the Special Branch 638. The largest concentration of police was to be found in Kowloon (3,182), followed by the New Territories (2,039), Hong Kong (2,004) and CID (2,062).[26]

Internal security

Police force expansion had already begun before the riots, but the disturbances highlighted certain areas of need. Information about the resources committed to internal security and to Special Branch is not publicly available but the years after the 1967 riots saw increased police surveillance of potential subversives. In the rural areas, Village Penetration Patrols (*chuen shan kap*) were still used to maintain cordial relations with the rural population, and to maintain surveillance in parts of Hong Kong where supporters of Communism might be found. Otherwise, the police found the Frontier and

Table 18.4 Distribution of police establishment 1969

Police headquarters	166
Hong Kong Island district	1,977
Kowloon district	2,956
NT district	1,748
Marine district	1,114
CID	1,224
Anti-corruption branch	78
Narcotics bureau	93
Special branch	438
Police training school	182
Police tactical unit	1,070
Traffic branch	745
Communications and transport	60
Leave reserve, recruits under training	402
Total establishment	12,253
Total strength	11,471

Source: RHKPAR 1968/9.

the more remote reaches of the NT 'relaxed and tranquil'. They generally adopted the 'Concord' approach to policing the communities, becoming involved in the construction of bridges and footpaths, and generally undertaking community service-type tasks.[27] The Village Penetration Units (now re-titled the Village Patrol Units) consisted of locally born volunteers speaking Hakka. Movement in and out of the Frontier Closed Area was controlled by means of a special permit, though farmers were allowed to move within the border area to work their land. This style of policing was adapted in 1976 for the Rural Area Patrols in rural areas of Hong Kong Island, and in 1977, six more RAPs were established in the outlying islands during the clearance of land at Cheung Chau and Ping Chau for development, and when development began to take place on Lantau.[28] The job of the RAPs was, first of all, to provide a visible *government* presence in remote areas, secondly to maintain law and order, and thirdly to prevent and detect illegal immigrants.[29]

Vigilance along these areas bordering China was especially high during the Cultural Revolution, between 1966 and 1976. Following the 1967 riots, the Police Training Contingent at Fanling was disbanded and replaced by a new formation named the Police Tactical Unit (PTU). All (male) police officers now undertook training (or refresher training) in internal security duties, including drill, crowd control techniques, platoon and company exercises, map reading, first aid and special operations against vice, gambling and narcotics.[30] The new PTU was to provide an 'immediate reserve of manpower for use in any emergency'; an aid to large-scale crowd control duties (festivals, parades, football matches, natural disasters, etc); training in the use of modern weapons, armoured vehicles, and field craft; outward bound training; and advanced training in internal security duties.[31]

The police recognised that 'a large proportion of the force would have to be trained and then held for a time in Police Tactical Company formation, more or less divorced from ordinary police work', forming a reserve force for emergencies.[32] Ten 'riot suppression companies' received training in the first year; by 1972, it was anticipated, eight companies would be based at the PTU. After completing their 12-week course, each company of 'Blue Berets' was returned to the police district from which it was formed to undergo an 18-week operational attachment under the command of the police district commander.[33]

Hong Kong's approach to internal security attracted interest overseas. The PTU's training centre at Fanling began to receive visits from senior members of foreign police forces interested in Hong Kong's internal security drills and tactics. British police representatives were amongst these visitors. The Royal Hong Kong Police Riot Manual (revised in 1967 and issued to all officers at inspector level and above) later formed the basis of the manual employed by the London Metropolitan Police, and by the Royal Canadian Mounted Police. Colonial practices thus returned to the metropolis.

Political policing

In the Hong Kong of the 1970s, the government felt in need of resources like the PTU and Special Branch. The *New Life Evening Post* took the view that, after 1967, the police were very nervous about rising crime in case it was all part of a political plot to undermine peace and order in the colony.[34] The ongoing activities of various student groups also made government anxious. The student-led Chinese language campaign in the early 1970s reinforced the government's belief that Hong Kong's youth required special attention. After 1967, student unions were said to have 'veered to the Left'; there was 'an efflorescence of radical magazines and journals, mostly Chinese' (such as *70s Bi-Weekly*). Hong Kong had, it was said, become 'arguably a more difficult place to govern than at any time since 1945', and there had been 'an increase in overt criticism of the government, particularly from younger people' (Lethbridge 1985: 201). Throughout 1968, 1969 and 1970, left wing activists were still thought to be playing an active role in strikes; some newspapers reported that a 'Red terror' was intimidating workers. In May 1968, Hong Kong University students burned pictures of the leaders of the Soviet Union, in protest at the USSR's invasion of Czechoslovakia. This was 'not the first time that HKU student have protested against a regime which did not tolerate freedom of speech, freedom of information or independence of mind'; freedom, the *Hong Kong Standard* stated, had no frontiers.[35] So frequent had protests become that, in 1971, the Urban Council and Colonial Secretary had even agreed to establish a 'Hyde Park Corner' to provide an acceptable outlet for public opinion. However, groups wishing to use the area had to apply for permission to the Commissioner of Police seven days in advance, as stipulated by the new Public Order Ordinance. Police permission could be refused if it appeared to the Commissioner that a meeting might get out of hand or disrupt public order.

Such political activities confirmed the authorities suspicions about Hong Kong's 'dangerous youth'. Special Branch was tasked, for example, to discover whether those HKU students involved in the campaign to make Chinese an official language were Trotskyites. In January 1971, it was also reported that Special Branch had asked RTHK to pass on the names of everyone who participated in its phone-in programmes (its late-call programmes included the names and addresses of callers, given on the understanding that no use would be made of them). An article in the *Far Eastern Economic Review* stated that on two separate occasions, Special Branch had been given the full tapes and transcripts. The police argued that statements made on RTHK were public, and that they would continue to use them as a basis for probes. In April 1972, the *Hong Kong Standard* carried a report that nine radical students and two teachers had attempted to disrupt a garden party to be held on the Queen's Birthday at Government House by handing out anti-colonial leaflets and trying to storm the party.[36] April also saw a swoop by Special Branch on a flat in Hunghom and the arrest of 11 people, provoking subsequent protests by radical students. Anti-British posters mysteriously appeared in Tsim Sha Tsui, carrying slogans such as 'Down with Colonialism', 'British Get Out of Hong Kong', and 'Hong Kong belongs to China'. In May 1972, the *Hong Kong Star* noted the circulation of an anti-government bi-weekly edited by a student rebel (Mok chiu-yu). In July, anti-Vietnamese War protesters (some wearing Mao badges) had leafleted US servicemen at the Star Ferry and in Wanchai. A *Hong Kong Star* editorial observed that people were 'fed up with the regular demonstrations outside the US Consulate by anti-Vietnam War demonstrators', and by anti-Japanese protests; Hong Kong's 'delicate position' meant that it was inadvisable for people to have anything to do with international political disputes which had nothing to do with Hong Kong.[37] Several Chinese newspapers also stressed the need for stability and prosperity, and advised the government to 'kick out foreigners who threaten it'.[38]

Several protesters (mainly expatriates) were deported under the Emergency Regulations for participating in the demonstrations. One of these was a Christian social worker, another an academic. The *China Mail* claimed the government was expelling them because 'student power [was] something that causes government officials to wake up sweating at night'.[39] The government was afraid that Chinese students would be whipped up by radical overseas lecturers and students, as had happened in Europe in 1968 (Tariq Ali was, for example, refused permission to enter Hong Kong and put instead on a flight to Thailand). Others argued that the government was using its powers of deportation to quell the students into political silence. Letters to the press complained about the suppression of free speech and the chilling of anti-government criticism.

The demonstrations continued, however. In July 1972, 1,500 local teachers held a demonstration. In October 1971 (and again in 1972) there were student protests against Japan following the re-establishment of China's diplomatic relations with Japan despite the dispute over the Diaoyutai (Senkaku) islands. As Lam says, the episode demonstrated how nationalism and anti-colonialism came together to 'powerfully motivate local political activism and radicalism' (Lam 2004: 148). A protest at the Star Ferry was followed by a series of public demonstrations, a boycott of Japanese department stores in Monkok and a series of bomb hoaxes. One demonstration, organised by the 'Defend the Diaoyutai Islands Action Committee in Victoria Park in July 1971, led to 'some disorder' and the arrest of 22 people.[40] Lam argues that violent police tactics in suppressing the protestors generated wider support and consensus for their cause (Lam 2004: 151). The largest demonstration of 1972 combined groups from Victoria Park and Edinburgh Place in a march through Central. Scores of police kept watch on these protests, looking out for signs of trouble surrounding the 1 October National Day and the 'Double Ten' commemorations. Other student protests at the Star Ferry supported causes such as a united Pakistan, and called upon the English press to stop its 'anti-Pakistan' coverage. In 1974, students marched to Government House protesting about proposed increases in telephone charges; in August, about 5,000 government clerical staff marched from the Central Government Offices in connection with the terms of service.[41] In 1976, large numbers of local people held rallies against inflation. The furious debate about gambling that year also finally persuaded the government to set up the 'Hyde Park Corner' forum in Victoria Park to provide 'an outlet for the expression of public opinion' on this and any other issue.[42] In 1979, small-scale demonstrations took place around such issues as the re-housing of boat people from the Yaumatei typhoon shelter. Throughout the decade, the MacLehose administration had fostered community building. A number of social workers and housing workers had taken this injunction seriously. When, however, they helped the Yaumatei boat people and residents of poor housing organise themselves to march on government offices, they found themselves under arrest for unlawful assembly.

Clearly, this was not the kind of public participation the government had in mind. Another group of Revolutionary Marxists held a demonstration at Star Ferry to protest the police refusal to grant them a permit to hold a May Day rally in the park; arrests and convictions for unlawful assembly, disorderly conduct and loitering so as to cause a noisy assembly followed.[43] It was, however, to be the police themselves who mounted the biggest and noisiest demonstration of the year when they protested against the ICAC's targeting of police corruption – of which more later.

Notes

1 See Hayes 1996: 112–13 for an account of the political role of the District Officers during and after the 1967 riots.
2 John Rear and Henry Litton, for example, continued to campaign against Regulation 31, employed by the Colonial Secretary in the riots to detain anyone for a year without giving anyone any reason for his decision, including the detained person.
3 Walden, cited in Scott 1989: 145, note 45. See also Hayes 1996: 100.
4 Mr Rafeek, Urban Council Debate 27 November 1969.
5 Mr A de O Sales, ibid.
6 GIS Press Release 9 July 1969.
7 GIS Press Release 11 December 1969.
8 *Sing Tao Man Po* 26 December 1969.
9 More than 4,175 were contacted by the Labour Department and over 1,800 industrial undertakings agreed.
10 The first two women were sent in 1975.
11 HKPAR 1965/6: 2.
12 HKPAR 1978: 28.
13 HKPAR 1968/9: 5.
14 HKPAR 1968: 4.
15 HKPAR 1969/70: 6.
16 Press Release, Police Public Relations Bureau 3 April 1969.
17 HKPAR 1966/7: 5.
18 Police Public Relations Press Release 21 June 1969.
19 21 December 1972, HKRS70 DSNO 3–42–2.
20 *Sing Tao Jih Po* 22 December 1972.
21 HKPAR 1966/7: 2.
22 RHKPAR 1973/4: 32.
23 RHKPAR 1974/5: 28.
24 RHKPAR 1974/5: 12.
25 RHKPAR 1974/4: 17.
26 RHKPAR 1973/4: Appendix 3.
27 RHKPAR 1976: 35.
28 With the building of the ferry concourse, housing, and a bazaar at Mui Wo.
29 RHKPAR 1978: 49.
30 HKPAR 1968/9: 2.
31 HKPAR 1968/9: 17.
32 HKPAR 1968/9: 1.
33 RHKPAR 1976: 23.
34 *New Life Evening Post* 8 December 1969.
35 *HK Standard* 27 August 1968.
36 *HK Standard* 21 April 1972.
37 *HK Star* 8 May 1972.
38 *Tin Tin Yat Pao* 7 September 1970.
39 *China Mail* 25 September 1970.
40 HK Yearbook 1971: 136.
41 RHKPAR 1974/5: 8.
42 RHKPAR 1976: 23.
43 RHKPAR 1977: 34.

Chapter 19

The 1970s: re-forming the state and its citizens

During the 1970s, the strategy developed to secure popular support for the damaged regime combined a wide-range of social control measures, as well as measures to develop a new sense of civic responsibility. What followed was a massive exercise in social engineering, led by government and amounting to nothing less than the wholesale re-creation of a civil society with which it felt able to engage. Developments in crime and criminal justice in this period must be understood within this wider context. They formed one part of a much broader effort to re-make Hong Kong society, quell dissent and secure regime legitimacy.

Depoliticising education

Whether intentional or not, steps taken by the government in the early 1970s to reform education and provide more outlets for youth had the effect of creating a whole generation of exceptionally law-abiding and peaceable Hong Kong citizens. Nothing like the 1960s was to be seen again. When Hong Kongers took to the streets, as they did in 1989 following the Tiananmen Square massacre, they would do so in the kind of orderly fashion that was to become a characteristic of all street demonstrations in Hong Kong up to and beyond 1997.

As part of its wider package of 'welfare colonialism', the MacLehose administration introduced subsided secondary education for all. In 1972, it also established a Curriculum Development Committee to identify a 'common core curriculum at junior secondary level that would provide a 'well-balanced education . . . [including] the role of the citizen in the context of our own community'.[1] Civic education was to emphasise 'desirable qualities in people . . . to promote better and healthier relationships with the government and other members of society'.[2] These qualities included social awareness and civic responsibility; the role of government was presented in the curriculum in benign, paternalistic terms.[3] The criminal justice element of the curriculum dealt with government policies on juvenile delinquency, drug abuse, and punishment, and encouraging participation in crime prevention.

Responding to the message of the 1966 Riot Report and social science research on the 'problem' of adolescents in Hong Kong, social studies identified social control and deviancy, as well as 'adolescence' as specific topics for study (the 'characteristics of adolescent growth', the 'social environment of adolescents', the 'interaction between adolescents as their environment as a full members of the community', etc). The importance of law to society was stressed in the teaching of public affairs, where the government's role was also presented in positive terms as maintaining stability, encouraging economic growth and promoting equity in housing, education, social welfare and medicine. The syllabus for economic and public affairs stressed the classic *laissez-faire* notions of individuals as consumers and producers, although by the mid-1980s, it also addressed the idea of individuals as bearers of political and civic rights and obligations who could bring government to account through the various consultative and advisory bodies established in the 1970s.

Youth mobilisation

In accordance with MacLehose's policy of 'community building', much time and effort was expended on building bridges between the government and the people, as well as stimulating local organisations to become involved in social affairs. Critical to this programme were the City District Officers (CDOs), placed in the urban communities. They were able to liase with all local leaders and not simply the traditional *kaifongs*, which by the 1970s had begun to lose much of their traditional influence.

As part of this strategy, and to improve young people's perception of the police, great efforts were made by the police to liase with youth and the communities from which young people were drawn. Police open days – which focused especially on youth engagement – were instituted at the beginning of 1967. Police–public relations were also targeted for improvement, with special emphasis on the development of communications with youth and with local level organisations. Summer camps were organised, based on the principles of English 'Outward Bound' programmes, emphasising healthy living and outdoor pursuits. Youth activities of all kinds flourished, including the Boys and Girls Brigades, as well as Junior Police Call (JPC).

Junior Police Call, started by the police in 1975, was designed to enlist youth in positive community action. By the late 1970s, approximately 40 per cent of all Hong Kong youth were involved in the JPC – it became well known in the colony and quickly amassed a membership of over 200,000. By 1979, almost a quarter of a million young persons were involved, and by the 1980s, it had become the biggest youth organisation of its kind in the world.[4] Young people were encouraged to 'contribute unselfishly to society by cleaning beaches, raising funds for charitable organisations and needy institutions, visiting and tending the aged, the infirm, the retarded and the orphaned, and actively participate in road safety, crime prevention, fighting crime and Police recruiting'.[5] The JPC ran its own Chinese language television and radio programmes – the weekly 30-minute programme (*Voice of JPC*) broadcast by RTHK Channel 2 every Saturday night – covering such issues as fighting crime, civic education, culture, sports and entertainment. The JPC monthly newspaper (*JPC Monthly*) was sponsored by a local bank and, by 1996, had a circulation of 80,000. The JPC also ran its own 'JPC Award Scheme' – the Annual Young People's 'Help the Police' Competition – established in 1976 to promote awareness of police work amongst Hong Kong youth.

As the government rolled out annual campaigns in the 1970s, the JPC was mobilised to assist the police in a 'Help the Police Fight Youth Crime' competition sponsored by the Hang Seng Bank and Qantas Airways Ltd; another JPC summer camp was sponsored by the Royal Hong Kong Jockey Club and the Duty Free Shop. The police force itself argued that 'Harmonious relations with the public are essential if the Force is to carry out its duties in the community effectively and efficiently'.[6] A new Police Public Information Bureau had opened in 1968, and each year of the 1970s saw some 10,000 schoolchildren invited to visit police stations throughout the colony.

The Police Cadet School, established in 1973, also sought to improve recruitment among young people into the police. It emphasised improving a cadet's educational standards in the hope of recruiting better-educated constables. A Police Adventure Training Unit was set up in 1974, operating from this School; its courses stressed good character and leadership qualities, gained through physically challenging team activities such as canoeing, rock climbing, orienteering and survival exercises.

In terms of penality, however, a strong strand of punishment and discipline ran throughout youth custody at the start of the decade. Sha Tsui Detention Centre, opened in 1972, was to provide a 'short, sharp, shock' for young male offenders. Its regime was tough, silent and exacting. A short film (*To Make a Man*) was released as part of the 1973 anti-crime campaign. It opened with a shot of a young offender being shorn of his long hair; the regime shown included physical exercise at the crack of dawn, strict supervision and rules of politeness (total silence except at given times). The film ended with a close-up of an offender's blistered hands to demonstrate the regime's emphasis on hard labour.

At the same time, however, the government, whilst endorsing the 'swift and sharp' punishment of young offenders, also established a committee to study the social causes of crime. It was partly persuaded by the 'modernisation' view that, as Hong Kong had grown more materially prosperous, this was at the cost of traditional ties and family life. MacLehose's plans to build more and better public housing would go some way to alleviate the social conditions in which, it was thought, crime thrived.[7] The Social Welfare Department planned a 'comprehensive programme' of events for youth – such as rural work camps, donating blood, community service and social studies – aimed at mixing enjoyment with contributions to the community. The objective was 'to enable young people to understand the difficulties and needs of their own communities through systematic investigation so as to seek proper solutions'.[8]

The Fight Crime campaigns

One of the biggest changes in policing in the 1970s was the focus on involving the community in the fight against crime. The extent of this mobilisation against crime was quite staggering.

In a 1972 report, the *Hong Kong Standard* blamed public apathy for the failure to report crime. Whilst there were numerous social work theories about why people committed crime, juvenile protection and the rehabilitation of offenders, there was nothing, it observed, about this widespread apathy. Its own survey showed that one out of every seven residents of the Wong Tai Sin Resettlement Estate (population 80,000) had been a victim of crime, but that only 10 per cent had made a report to the police.[9] Only 20 per cent of the people interviewed said they would report a crime to the police, whilst only 12 per cent said they would render aid to a person being robbed (ibid). These were the very same people, the paper argued, 'who say they live in fear of being attacked and are afraid to leave their homes after dark' (ibid). Remarking on the success of seeing *Lap Sap Chung* being 'thrashed out of his hiding place' during the anti-litter campaigns, the newspaper concluded that what was needed was another massive public campaign to get people to report crime. This is exactly what the police did. Spurred on by the Governor's appointment of the Fight Crime Committee, district fight crime committees joined forces with the police in a series of mass 'fight crime' campaigns.

Most of this activity was organised through the Community Relations Bureau of the police. Its staff comprised a chief information officer, a police superintendent deputy, and 35 staff in the Bureau's headquarters, together with 16 divisional police community relations officers of chief inspector rank, with supporting staff in the field. A separate Information Bureau consisting of 25 police officers was responsible for keeping the public informed about police activities, producing the force's bilingual newspaper *Off Beat* (which started in 1973) analysing media reports, monitoring letters to the editor and editorials in 27 major Chinese newspapers, all Chinese TV channels and radio phone-in programmes, keeping the police force informed about public opinion and public discontent.

Each year of the 1970s was marked by a 'Fight Crime Campaign' organised by the Fight Crime Committee and targeting a specific type of crime. Most years, these campaigns focused on violent crime, with which both the police and public had become preoccupied. The 1978 'Beat Crime' campaign included, for the first time, the 'War Against Rape' focusing on sexual offences against women; the 1979 campaign mobilised mutual aid committees (MACs) and other local committees in a 'Community Against Crime' drive;

the 1980 'Stop Crime Now' campaign continued the campaigns into the new decade. Localised drives against crime in the various police divisions reflected local, as well as territory-wide, concerns.

The 1973 Fight Violent Crime campaign began in May, with posters showing a broken dagger, symbolising the breaking down of violence and the 'triumph of the community over violence'. The red and black colours of the design had been chosen 'because they are associated with terror and anarchy'.[10] The 6,000-strong auxiliary police were pressed into service, doubling the number of officers on the streets; by 1974, the number of auxiliary police was double that of 1971. The thousands of watchmen who 'policed' Hong Kong's multi-storey apartment blocks, as well as 'anti-litter wardens' from the Urban Services Department, were pressed into action to watch out for crime and keep the streets clean. Towards the middle of May, the police publicised the 'Dial 999 Immediately' system to make the public aware that they should dial this number when they saw a crime being committed and 'do your bit to rid Hong Kong of the menace of constantly rising crime'.

Having thus prepared the groundwork, the campaign began in earnest in early June. Every citizen was exhorted to participate, encouraged by the creation of a Good Citizen Award Scheme, which rewarded members of the public who helped the police. In 1973, the Chamber of Commerce provided cash awards to the 'Good Citizens Award Fund' for persons nominated for exemplary conduct in assisting the fight against crime.[11] In its first year, 3 per cent of all arrests in the colony were made by citizens. By 1980, this had risen to 11 per cent, 'one of the highest figures world wide'.[12]

Commercial firms also sponsored anti-crime football matches and stickers; CDOs gave talks and worked to mobilise the community; factories and schools joined in the campaign. The Department of Education asked head teachers to stress the campaign's importance to schoolchildren by bringing home its message in social studies, civics, economics and public affairs classes. Television films were and radio programmes reiterated the message of the campaign daily – Radio Television Hong Kong (RTHK) broadcasted the morning *Police Report* daily on the two Chinese channels, whilst the five-minute *Police Call* was broadcast on the English and Chinese channels. Schools were asked to make sure that they were watched and heard by all schoolchildren. The Shaw Brothers Film Company produced a film with an anti-crime message (*Police Force*) with police backing. Premiered at the Jade Theatre, it used local actors to tell the story of a young man who joined the police after a gang murdered his friend (he went on to become a leading detective). A short film by the police showing a bank robbery and the subsequent capture of the villains by members of the public was shown over 1,700 times in July. Kowloon Motor Bus (KMB) displayed the anti-crime symbol on all their vehicles.[13]

The issue for Hong Kong, according to one Urban Councillor, was that 'sometimes it is the honest man who feels afraid and the criminal who feels safe. Our task is to make the honest man feel safe again and the criminals isolated, afraid and marked'.[14] Joining the call for heavier penalties, he wondered whether the influence of the 'pity the poor socially deprived criminal' attitude was to blame for what, he stated, was a 140 per cent increase in violent crimes such as murder, manslaughter and serious assaults over the previous four years. The present 'epidemic of crime' had to be contained and 'these anti-social elements subjected to swift and . . . sharp punishment' (ibid). There was, he concluded, now a 'new mood' in Hong Kong and people were determined to 'reject, apprehend and punish the criminal in our midst' (ibid).

New slogans – such as 'You are helping a criminal unless you act to beat crime', 'Join the fight and beat crime', and 'bring the criminal to justice' – were broadcast daily. Weekly slogans were strategically organised to move the public on from simply listening to the anti-crime message to an 'action phase' when they would be asked to put into practice what had been said in previous weeks. Thus, week one of the campaign exhorted the public to 'Dial 999', week two to 'Report Crime', week three to 'Raise a Hue and Cry', week four to 'Protect Your Property and Yourself', and week five to 'Help the Police by Providing Information'. The daily slogans dovetailed with these – in week three, for example, one daily slogan encouraged the public not to walk away when they heard a hue and cry being raised, but to help the police, addressing the very issue identified by the *Herald*'s survey in Wong Tai Sin.

Within the police force itself, officers were instructed to get to know their beats more intimately, become involved with local residents and events affecting them, visit schools and civic organisations in their districts, go out and about with the City District Officers and liase with local *kaifong* leaders. In rural areas, a Civilian Information Team was dispatched by Land Rovers and marine launches to take films, slogans and leaflets to outlying villagers. Rural patrols were set up, based at Sai Kung. In the urban areas, the civil aid services were detailed to staff 14 'Fight Crime Kiosks', answering questions about crime and handing out information to members of the public. Stop and search operations at road blocks were stepped up, and officers were instructed to employ stop and search 'at all hours in many different places'. Mobile police patrols cruised the streets of high-density urban areas; new police posts were also set up in these areas to facilitate the public's reporting of crime.

In 1971, the first of these new police posts was established in the resettlement estates. During the 1973 campaign, they were rolled out to other areas, such as the Wah Fu and Lo Fu Resettlement Estates. Another 25 prefabricated Police Reporting Centres were also set up.[15] Teams of police were instructed to sweep known 'crime blackspots', moving off the streets to conduct 'vertical sweeps' of high rise buildings. More 'sweeps' were organised of drug peddlers and addicts, vice establishments, illegal gambling dens, and 'so-called music halls'. Watchmen in high-rise private apartments were trained and briefed by the police, whilst competitions were organised for residents in the same building to enable them to get to know and trust one another, and to ensure they were all aware of the need to combat crime.

New, specially adapted, Crime Complaint Books and Crime Report Sheets[16] were introduced as an experiment, first in Wong Tai Sin, but then into other Districts. These could be completed quickly, signed by the person making the complaint, and lodged by the beat officer as a crime report by telephoning a police station. Pressing home the message that all its resources were harnessed to the 'war on crime', the police force announced that even science was playing its part in the Fight Violent Crime campaign:

> One of the world's most sophisticated police forensic pathology departments is working relentlessly with powerful microscopes and expertise to help detectives track down criminals . . . The criminals become exposed under the magnifying glass of a microscope and justice is achieved rapidly on the strength of the pathologist's evidence in court . . .[17]

The 'Dial 999' system seemed to succeed – calls to the police on Hong Kong Island alone rose from 12,500 in 1969 to 19,300 by 1973; 999 calls in Kowloon rose from 19,500 to 32,900 in the same period. In 1977, police statistics showed that about 17 per cent of all calls to the police that year were connected with crime 'reflecting the improved reporting facilities and procedures'.[18] The problem with all this activity was, however, that it worked: the public did report more crime and, as a result recorded crime went sky-high.

Neighbourhood policing and Police Community Relations Officers

Neighbourhood policing, introduced in 1974, increased the visibility of the police on the ground, as well as opportunities for reporting and detection of crime:

> Through the medium of large scale publicity and the Government administrative machine the public was encouraged to form Mutual Aid Committees in multi-storey buildings. These bodies provided the basis for liaison with the Police and for seeking improved protective security of buildings and inhabitants. District and Area Committee, already in existence, had their roles extended to include a similar responsibility. Publicity and education emphasized the safe raising of a hue-and-cry and the emergency calling for Police assistance by members of the public affected by crime . . . It soon became evident that Police activity and exhortation of the public to co-operate should not be confined to a limited campaign period. Therefore, a number of the Fight Violent Crime Campaign policies and actions were adopted permanently and became a programme

> for regular review. As part of this programme it was decided that a greater stress and effort would be placed on improved Police community relations and to this end arrangements were put in place to create in all land Divisions posts of Police Community Relations Officers (PCROs).[19]

The success of the first Police Community Relations Officer (PCRO) in Wong Tai Sin persuaded the police to extend the idea to nine other places in Kowloon, Hong Kong Island and the NT in 1974, and to Yaumatei and Yuen Long in 1975. By 1977, there were 16 PCROs throughout the colony.[20] The scheme was heralded as having 'greatly contributed to the fostering of excellent relations between the Police and the public through contact with such organisations as the *kaifongs*, District Offices, Mutual Aid Committees, etc'.[21] Like the JPC and Police Cadet School, they 'projected a good police image', offering advice and guidance to the local residents and business people: '. . . [they] attend meetings, social functions, meet with people and are regarded as police friends rather than simply law enforcement officers'.[22]

To consolidate this united front against crime, it was also decided to establish Neighbourhood Policing Units, the first being established on the Un Chau and Mei Foo Sun Chun estates in May 1974. More were opened at Yau Tong, Choi Hung, Wah Fu, Ngau Tau Kok, Paterson Street Wanchai, and Queen's Road East Wanchai (the Tai Fat Hau Unit) later in 1974; another was planned for the Oi Man estate in 1975.[23] These small units of police were lauded for improving relations between the police and the public, particularly those in the densely populated housing estates.[24] The scheme involved setting up a unit of police officers to serve in an area for up to 12 months 'in order that they may gain better knowledge of the district and its residents' (ibid). Some of these residential areas were vast: Mongkok, for example, had a population density of 399,000 per square mile; Hong Kong as a whole comprised about 4.5 million people over some 30 square miles; some of the high rise complexes housed more people than an English town.[25]

By 1978, 106 Neighbourhood Policing Units and Reporting Centres were operating throughout Hong Kong.[26] In 1979, this had risen to 124. Twelve of these Neighbourhood Policing Units and 16 Reporting Centres were in Kowloon, where police attention continued to focus on vice establishments, hawkers, pickpockets, quasi-triad criminal activity, street gambling and drug trafficking. In 1979, Hong Kong Island had 15 Neighbourhood Policing Units and 17 Reporting Centres. In 1978, new police stations were also opened in the NT at Sha Tin and Sheung Shui; by 1979 there were 22 Neighbourhood Policing Units and 31 Reporting Centres in the NT. In total, by 1979 there were 124 Reporting Centres throughout Hong Kong, of which 53 acted as Neighbourhood Policing Units.[27] A report by the Working Party on Reporting Procedures and the Initial Investigation of Crime in 1978 concluded that the existing system of reporting was basically sound. By 1978, reporting facilities had in fact doubled since 1975.[28] Throughout the 1970s the police also adopted a policy of erecting small, temporary police reporting boxes in local communities, to facilitate the reporting of crime by the public.

The new weekly television programmes (such as *Police 15* in Chinese and *Police Report* in English) also appealed to the public to assist in solving outstanding crimes. Others, such as the popular weekly television soap opera, *On the Beat*, depicted the daily lives of fictional police officers (screened for the first time in 1979 with the co-operation of Radio Television Hong Kong). The police estimated that these programmes reached 98 per cent of the colony's population (between 1.7 and 2 million viewers) and that they were always amongst the 'top ten' television shows in the colony.[29] A police TV hotline was also set up to receive calls responding to the programmes.

In 1976, a number of other hotlines were established to make reporting crime easier. This resulted in more than 56,700 calls and 8,360 arrests. By 1980, a 24-hour police newsroom was issuing more than 250 press releases per month as well as organising press coverage of anti-crime campaigns, police parades, and major incidents. By 1980, television stations were required to show up to seven hours of government programmes per week, most of which consisted of injunctions to fight crime (ibid).

The Neighbourhood Policing Units ran in parallel with other methods of penetrating and governing such complex communities, such as the City District Officers and the Mutual Aid Committee. The job of these officers was to get to know their beat and become familiar with local residents, partly in order to act as a sounding board for residents' complaints, partly to transmit down to the grassroots official government policy, but more importantly to act as listening device, gathering intelligence on crime, discontent and subversion.

What is astonishing about the 1970s is the degree to which all this was achieved. Although the Neighbourhood Policing Units were said to be expensive and to draw police away from other kinds of policing, they were also deemed to be the most effective way of policing the densely populated high-rise blocks. Plans were therefore laid to adopt them territory-wide and build them into the new towns, currently under construction. This significantly increased police presence throughout Hong Kong. But as this presence became more extensive, so did reported crime. It thus became beholden on the police to deflect public criticism by pointing out that rising crime did not reflect poor policing but, rather, (1) improved facilities for crime reporting, (2) increased police activity, and (3) greater public awareness of crime. They also claimed that there had been 'a factual increase in crime'.[30]

Corruption

The emphasis on better police/public relations was one of two significant changes to Hong Kong policing during the 1970s. Of equal (if not more) importance was the government's decision, in 1973, to establish an Independent Commission Against Corruption (ICAC). Clearly, this represented a radical departure from the situation as it had prevailed throughout the 1960s and early 1970s.

According to some writers,[31] the police represented a force for the moralisation of the lower classes in society, 'the penetration and continual presence of central political authority throughout daily life'. But the sheer pervasiveness of corruption in the post-war suggests that the police operated more as a force for *demoralisation*, undermining the moral authority of the colonial regime. If anything, they symbolised a wholly impoverished set of 'aspirations and ideals' (Wilson 2005: 109).[32]

As Lethbridge points out, the establishment of an Anti-Corruption Squad had been suggested by Pennefather-Evans in the early 1940s (Lethbridge 1985: 84). He cites comments by Duncan MacIntosh, Commissioner of Police in the late 1940s and early 1950s, as evidence that senior police officers were well aware of the problem of corruption in post-war Hong Kong. At a meeting in 1946, MacIntosh is recorded as having stated that he had:

> . . . never seen such widespread corruption anywhere else before . . . he gave various instances of corruption which had been discovered in the Police Force . . . he considered that senior subordinates were retained too long in key positions and were thus enabled to create deep-rooted 'rackets' which were extremely hard to expose . . . (cited in Lethbridge 1985: 85).

Corruption post-war had flourished in conditions of scarcity, where there were strict controls over imports and exports, where smuggling was prevalent and where economic conditions encouraged black-marketeering (ibid). In 1948, the government introduced a Prevention of Corruption Ordinance to address this situation prompted in part, Lethbridge suggests, by an ideology amongst new recruits to the colonial service which favoured cleansing colonialism of old social evils. Moreover, the expansion of government provision in the field of public housing provided new opportunities for corruption in the construction industry, as did the private sector infrastructure projects that accompanied Hong Kong's economic take-off over the decade. More opportunities flowed from the embargo imposed during the Korean War and the erection of the border with China, both of which encouraged the smuggling of goods and opportunities for bribery and corruption amongst Customs officials (see Mannion 2004: 29). An anti-corruption branch was established within the CID department of the police to deal with these problems. In 1952, this branch separated from CID but its apparent autonomy was, Lethbridge argues, cosmetic as officers were seconded to the branch for a short time, with the result that no 'corps of anti-corruption specialists' was created (Lethbridge 1985: 87).

The police were thus responsible for investigating the police at a time when syndicated corruption existed throughout the force. Some police divisions were notoriously corrupt, the police extracting protection money from those engaged in illegal activities such as running a vice establishment or gambling house. According to Mannion, between 1952 and 1973, reports of police corruption exceeded reports of corruption in all other government departments combined (Mannion 2004: 30). For the public and the police alike, reporting corruption was deterred by the fear of reprisals. Even if a police officer wished to 'blow the whistle' on corrupt fellow officers, he had no guarantee that the officers within the anti-corruption branch itself were not involved in corruption. Though some of the triad leaders in league with corrupt officers were detained under the deportation and detention regulations, vice and the associated 'squeeze' exacted by corrupt police flourished. So thoroughly was the police force involved in protection rackets and 'squeeze' that recorded crime figures were inevitably distorted by the failure of corrupt officers to record criminal activities (such as the running of vice establishments and drug trafficking) from which they themselves directly benefited. The 'apparatus of control' was 'defective, out of date', with the result that, throughout the 1950s, 'the kingpins of corruption and the drug trade, as well as some senior police, were practically inviolate' (ibid).

The early 1960s saw some improvement on this situation when the Standing Committee on Corruption (established in 1956) finally began to take a serious interest in the problem. Re-named the Advisory Committee on Corruption, it produced six reports between August 1960 and December 1961 (Lethbridge 1985: 89). The last of these reports considered the possibility of transferring the functions of the anti-corruption branch to an independent body, as had happened in Singapore in 1952. This 'Singapore model' has been claimed by some (including a former Attorney General of Singapore) as the blueprint for the body that eventually emerged as Hong Kong's principal anti-corruption agency (the ICAC) in the 1970s. For reasons that are not entirely clear, the Advisory Committee decided against this separation, even though it acknowledged that the public were reluctant to complain to the police, of whom they were afraid; that nearly 50 per cent of all complaints of corruption were against the police, and that there was a strong feeling that that the anti-corruption body should not be part of the police (see Lethbridge 1985: 90). One of the arguments for keeping the investigation of corruption inside the police force made by the Commissioner of Police was that CID officers were already trained specialists who could, upon transfer to the anti-corruption branch, immediately investigate corruption without the need for further training.

However, during the 'show trials' of the 1970s, many of those unmasked as corrupt had previously served as CID officers (ibid). This much must have also been evident at the time, but nevertheless the committee supported the Commissioner's view and corruption investigations remained in the hands of the police. The Target Committee system, set up to select cases for investigation, was supposed to engender public confidence by making corruption a priority and bringing high-profile cases to court. However, as Lethbridge states, it was criticised for spending too much time on investigating the pattern of corrupt practices within certain departments of government. Moreover, if members of the anti-corruption branch were themselves corrupt, they were in a position to 'squeeze' fellow officers and the public and were, figuratively 'right at the centre of the spider's web' (Lethbridge 1985: 92).

When, in 1969, Charles Sutcliffe became Commissioner he initiated a number of innovations in the working of the Anti-Corruption Branch that quickly produced improved success in its investigations. In May 1970, the branch was reorganised so that it ceased to be part of CID and became directly responsible to Sutcliffe; in 1971, it was expanded and opened a new sub-office in Kowloon. The branch was re-named the Anti-Corruption Office in 1970. Its reorganisation under Sutcliffe and its improved campaign against corruption won it a reprieve, on the understanding that it would prove successful within the next four years. It employed more investigators; its Target Committee was reconstituted so as to consist, for the first time, mostly of non-police members (ibid). A new Prevention of Bribery Ordinance was also introduced in 1971 to combat corruption.

One of Sutcliffe's innovations (later to be adopted by the ICAC) was to investigate broader areas where opportunities for corruption existed, so as to prevent corrupt practices. The Target Committee also recommended to government Departments ways in which they could minimise opportunities for corrupt practices.[33] At the same time, the branch began to sift through complaints of individual corruption so as to separate out the most serious and most informative from those containing poor quality information, and thus less amenable to productive investigation.[34] Opening hours were extended to facilitate the public reporting of corruption, two investigative teams were placed on 24-hour call, and publicity about the branch was broadcast by television.[35]

One consequence of all this was a marked increase in reports towards the end of 1968. Most (85 per cent) were anonymous and most (between 45 and 50 per cent) were directed against the police. In seven cases, the allegations were substantiated by the Target Committee (resulting in one conviction) and proceedings instituted against the officers involved; some allegations were redirected to the relevant police department for further action; in others, the officer in question retired, resigned, or was transferred.[36]

Lethbridge attributes the improvements in anti-corruption work to the arrival of Charles Sutcliffe. His reign as Commissioner saw a marked upsurge in complaints of corruption. Sutcliffe was seen as a man of great integrity who 'took corruption very seriously indeed'; he, for one, *had* taken note of the deficiencies in the police revealed during the 1966 Commission of Inquiry (Lethbridge 1985: 93). In 1972 a senior Crown Counsel was permanently attached to the Anti Corruption Branch to improve the preparation of cases and seemed to bear immediate dividends: out of 50 persons brought to trial in 1973, 47 (94 per cent) were convicted. Despite this improvement, at the end of 1973 the creation of a new, Independent Commission Against Corruption (ICAC) was announced. It was Sutcliffe's targeting of police officers, such as Peter Godber, which set in train the series of events that eventually forced the government to divorce corruption investigations from the police and establish the ICAC. In February 1974, the branch was closed and the ICAC began.

As Lethbridge points out, Godber was one of a 'vintage year' for corrupt officers, having joined the force in 1952 along with Ernest Hunt, Walter Boxhall and Cecil Cunningham, all later imprisoned for corruption. For his services during the 1967 riots, he had been awarded the Colonial Police Medal for Meritorious Service, and in 1971 was posted as Deputy District Police Commissioner, Kowloon, where vice and triad activities were rife. Lethbridge recounts that, in 1973, Sutcliffe received information that Godber had been remitting large sums of money abroad. A file was opened on him by the Anti-Corruption Office. Investigators discovered that his fortune amounted to HK$4.6 million, almost six times his net salary from 1952 to 1973. When he requested permission to retire early, his request was refused and he was served with a notice under a 1971 Prevention of Bribery Ordinance, which required him to furnish a satisfactory explanation as to how he had come by his financial resources. He then fled Hong Kong for England, despite the fact that staff at the airport had been warned to look out for him.[37] His flight – and the fact that he had been able to evade security – both embarrassed the government and lent weight to rumours that Godber had been 'allowed' to escape by fellow corrupt officers, or by high-ranking officials who did not want him to stand trial for fear he might reveal 'too much' (Lethbridge 1985: 96).

Godber's flight from justice provoked a public outcry, demonstrations,[38] and calls for his extradition to stand trial. The trial itself provided, Mannion says, the catalyst that ultimately produced the ICAC: Godber became 'a symbol of police corruption and government impotence or, worse yet, government complacency' (Mannion 2004: 33). From 1967 to 1974, Lethbridge suggests, there had probably been an increase in corruption, as the riots had led to reduced policing of many areas, resulting in an explosion of vice establishments, drug trafficking and gambling (Lethbridge 1985: 203). There was, he argues, also likely to have been a concomitant rise in police corruption, some of which may have gone higher up the police hierarchy than Godber. Hong Kong was 'honeycombed with corruption'. The police – and Godber in particular – provided a 'fine focus for discontent' (ibid).

The government reacted to Godber's flight by appointing a Commission of Inquiry under Sir Alastair Blair-Kerr, a judge. Two reports followed but, whilst the possibility of creating an anti-corruption body independent of the police was aired, Blair-Kerr expressed no preference and made no recommendation. However, having admitted that he had failed to appreciate the extent of corruption hitherto, the Governor (MacLehose) now declared that he had resolved to create a new, independent, anti-corruption body:

> I believe that it is quite wrong, in the special circumstances of Hong Kong, that the police, as a force, should carry the whole responsibility for action in this difficult and elusive field. I think the situation calls for an organization, led by men of high rank and status, which can devote its whole time to the eradication of this evil . . . A further and conclusive argument is that public confidence is very much involved. Clearly, the public would have more confidence in a unit that was entirely independent, and separate from any department of the Government, including the police (cited in Lethbridge 1985: 101).

MacLehose's acknowledgment of the extent of corruption – and of its existence within the police – was noted by the media and described as 'the frankest commentary on this issue ever heard by the legislature from a Hong Kong Governor'.[39] MacLehose 'took the issue of public confidence seriously . . . accepted that an effective anti-corruption effort would require the cooperation of the community [and] . . . recognised that cooperation would not be forthcoming without a fundamental change in the arrangements governing anti-corruption work' (ibid). As Mannion says, he staked his reputation on reforming corruption. In announcing the creation of the ICAC, MacLehose had his eyes firmly 'fixed on the public, his constituents' (Lethbridge 1985: 102). Given that Hong Kong is not – and was not – a democracy and the Governor never answerable to the public, this was a somewhat strange argument – there were no citizen constituents in the Hong Kong of 1973. However, the riots of 1966 and 1967 had marked a watershed in the history of colonial governance, undermining the regime's legitimacy and highlighting its democratic deficit. For the government to retain its 'right to rule' it had to be seen to be governing in the public good – and in other respects the MacLehose administration had embarked on a programme of intense social engineering to re-create the administration as a caring, listening government rather than a remote colonial bureaucracy. The revelations about corruption that finally surfaced in 1973 further threatened to damage confidence in the administration just when it was seeking ways to regain public support.

As Mannion argues, when corruption becomes so widespread and expectations set in about how public officials normally transact business, the informal system subverts the formal one and 'in doing so, it subverts the role of government in supplying a social order roughly consistent with a publicly proclaimed theory of the state'.[40] Widespread corruption, she argues, breeds the suspicion that the government is conniving at and approves corruption, and it becomes obvious to all – including the corrupt – that 'the authorities are not reliable or impartial enforcers of prohibitions against official venality. Indeed, law enforcement is perhaps the most commonly exploited opportunity for official extortion' (Mannion 2004: 14).

Public knowledge of the extent of corruption thus subverted the colonial state's attempts to renew itself in the wake of the 1960s riots. The government had generated a raft of policies designed to convince the public that Hong Kong was a fair and open society, providing equality of opportunity for all on a level playing field. Driven by MacLehose, the administration increased spending on welfare and public services (welfare colonialism), embarked on an ambitious programme of public housing, created extensive country parks and local recreational facilities, subsidised health care and education for all, engaged in a frenzy of community building and mobilised the public to fight crime and disease. The Hong Kong of the 1970s was to be recreated as a city of clean streets, low crime, clean government and opportunities for social mobility unhampered by obstacles such as nepotism, bribery, and corruption. The creation of the ICAC fitted perfectly into this agenda. Its success was critical to the goal of re-building public confidence in the administration.

The ICAC was established in February 1974 under the Independent Commission Against Corruption Ordinance. From the beginning it was a relatively small body, with an initial strength of 369 officers, some recruited from the UK, some from the old Anti-Corruption Office. Though criticised for this reliance on former police officers, the ICAC was to prove its independence by instigating a thorough anti-corruption drive against the police force, so acquiring the reputation amongst the force as an anti-police body. Its structure, which remains largely unaltered, split the new body into Operations, Prevention and Community Relations branches. Its powers of arrest and investigation – often described as 'draconian' – enabled it to disrupt both syndicated police corruption and corruption in the private sector. The Commissioner himself was appointed by, and was made formally and directly responsible to, the Governor, though even at this early stage an Advisory Committee was set up to review the ICAC's work. Its remit was to receive and investigate corruption complaints, to investigate the conduct of any government servant conducive to corrupt practices, examine the practices and procedures of government departments and public bodies to discover corrupt practices, educate the public against the evils of corruption, and enlist and foster public support in combating corruption. To this end, the ICAC embarked on what Mannion describes as a 'massive public education effort' (Mannion 2004: 24).

The creation of the ICAC, the appointment of Jack Cater as its first Commissioner and John Prendergast as Deputy Commissioner, its independence from the police and extensive powers 'sent an unambiguous signal to ordinary citizens that "the authorities mean business"'.[41] The image that the ICAC quickly acquired of an elite, ruthless, efficient, crime-fighting machine 'was largely created by Prendergast and his colleagues' (Lethbridge 1985: 110). Mannion's analysis of the surveys measuring public beliefs about corruption conducted by the ICAC since 1977 also indicates that 'a sudden, large shift in mass public beliefs about anti-corruption enforcement' occurred. The figures on reported corruption suggest 'enormous public confidence in the ICAC . . . as an anti-corruption body' (ibid).

In 1974, the first year of its operation, the ICAC received more than double the number of reports (3,189) received by the former Anti-Corruption Office in 1973 (1,457); this level of reporting continued in 1975, suggesting that the figures for the first year were not a 'one off' reporting of past grievances (ibid). The arrest of Godber in 1974 and his trial in Hong Kong in 1975 were seen as ending the era of 'blatant, bare faced, institutionalised corruption' (Lethbridge 1985: 112). The trial also provided the ICAC with an early propaganda opportunity, conveying the message 'that no-one was above the law, that the government was prepared to act harshly to put down corruption' (Lethbridge 1985: 114).[42]

The public's support for the ICAC was enthusiastic, but that of the business community became less so when the ICAC began to investigate corruption in the private sector. Some lawyers, academics and journalists also questioned the methods it employed (such as the granting of immunity to witnesses in return for their testimony against Godber). But, Lethbridge argues, MacLehose believed that something needed to be done if the colony was not to slide into disorder, the crime statistics for the early 1970s having already indicated increases in commercial crime, juvenile delinquency, sexual offences and corruption. The fight against corruption thus coincided with his wider, mass mobilisation of the public in the 1973 'Fight Violent Crime Campaign' (Lethbridge 1985: 107).

Such mass campaigns, with their echoes of Maoist China, were common in Singapore. Hong Kong officials visited Singapore in the early 1970s and it seems likely that they copied the idea of mass campaigns. Henceforward, Hong Kong witnessed a continuous round of 'Keep Hong Kong Clean' anti-litter campaigns, as well as regular anti-crime campaigns. Mass mobilisation became a familiar feature of the landscape of criminal justice and was brilliantly adapted by the ICAC in its anti-corruption education campaigns. Quite apart from the distribution of leaflets and posters, the ICAC employed dramatic television commercials and hired one of Hong Kong's top film directors, Ann Hui, to direct a series of weekly television dramas. These dramas, broadcast from 1975 onwards, proved hugely popular. Such sophisticated use of media propaganda against crime was new to Hong Kong. The Community Relations Department of the ICAC 'placed ICAC success prominently in the public eye', providing press releases that the media used to build 'its dramatic stories of anti-corruption actions' (Mannion 2004: 44).

This intense early publicity helped to 'transform the beliefs of ordinary citizens in Hong Kong about what was possible' (ibid). Public education and community relations were part of what Mannion describes as the ICAC's three-pronged strategy to reduce corruption: (1) the enforcement to investigate corruption and prosecute the corrupt; (2) education to mobilise ordinary citizens to report corruption and increase the psychic costs of corrupt activities; and (3) institutional design to reduce opportunities for corruption in the organisation of work (Mannion 2004: 27).

The revolution in attitudes was more difficult to achieve within the police force itself. When, in 1976 and 1977, the ICAC focused its investigations on syndicated corruption, 'it became known that . . . every police division contained its own corruption syndicate' (Lethbridge 1985: 117). In one case, 15 policemen were brought to trial and convicted; other conspiracy trials involved police divisions in Wong Tai Sin, Mong Kok, Bay View, and Tsim Sha Tsui (ibid). Those who ran the syndicates were, Lethbridge says, station sergeants, many of whom fled to Taiwan and Canada once the ICAC began its crusade against police corruption:

> The ICAC's unmasking of so many bent sergeants helped in demolishing most of the long-standing and deeply rooted corruption syndicates . . . in doing that, the ICAC practically brought life in the Royal Hong Kong Police to a stop . . . The Government and the ICAC were to pay a heavy price for the suppression of so much traditional corruption (Lethbridge 1985: 125).

More resignations, of commissioned officers and rank and file police, followed in 1976 and, Lethbridge argues, the police began to feel increasingly beleaguered and boxed in by an organisation that enjoyed the backing of the government and the public. Between 1974 and 1977, the ICAC prosecuted 269 police officers for corruption, more than four times the number prosecuted in the four years before 1974 (Mannion 2004: 40). Morale declined but was also affected, Lethbridge suggests, by the reduced income corrupt police were receiving, especially after 1973, when the Fight Crime Campaign closed down numerous vice, gambling and triad-related enterprises. In October 1977, some 140 police officers were arrested by the ICAC on suspicion of involvement in syndicated corruption; later in the month another 34 were detained, including three British superintendents. Lethbridge describes what happened next:

> A number of policemen then met privately in Kowloon to examine ways of resisting the Commission. They decided to organize mass rallies so as to advertise claims of unfair treatment and harassment by the ICAC . . . the following morning the Kowloon police contingent was still simmering. About three hundred gathered in the Kowloon Police Headquarters canteen and drafted a nine-point letter [to] . . . the Commissioner . . . The nine points were published in Off Beat, the police newspaper, and in the English and Chinese press . . . When the petition reached the Commissioner, he at once appointed a senior officer to liaise with the

> delegates and to discuss with them the nine points. That same evening, about two hundred and fifty members of the rank and file held a meeting at Wong Tai Sin Police Married Quarters . . . On Thursday evening, several thousand police officers and their families gathered at the Police Sports Association premises in Boundary Street, Kowloon. Agreement was then reached that off-duty policemen should be urged to assemble the next day at the Colony Headquarters on Hong Kong Island. The following morning at around 9 a.m. about two thousand police congregated at Edinburgh Place, [in Central Hong Kong] . . . they moved off, shouting slogans, to Police Headquarters in Wan Chai. The scene was reminiscent of the Maoist street hubbubs of 1967 . . . (Lethbridge 1985: 138)

During the delegates' meeting with the Commissioner of Police, it was agreed that a rank-and-file association could be formed (the Junior Police Officers' Association). Most of the crowd dispersed on hearing this concession but a breakaway group marched to ICAC Headquarters:

> It was to be no lightening commando strike or SAS assault. An unruly, jostling, sweating mob of serving, retired, and dismissed police officers scrambled into lifts or up the stairs to debouch into the lobby that led to the Commission's offices. They found the doors closed; they broke a glass panel; the entrance doors were then unlocked; and the raiders swarmed into ICAC territory. A scuffle . . . then took place between police and ICAC teams. Five of the latter, outnumbered by their assailants, were injured . . . Differing accounts of the incident were given by the two law-enforcement agencies. The ICAC claimed one hundred intruders; the police put the figure at a modest forty and did not state that there had been cries outside Caine House for the Commissioner's resignation (Lethbridge 1985: 139).

Only one person was subsequently prosecuted for the raid on ICAC headquarters, a decision which, Lethbridge argues, was political: the government did not want a 'yet more fractious force' (Lethbridge 1985: 140). Further meetings took place amongst disgruntled police officers, however, and in early November over 1,000 of them met behind closed doors, some demanding a police strike; the junior and non-commissioned officers were, Lethbridge says, 'quite out of control' and there was much jeering and cheering as those present debated how to react to the Commissioner's response to the nine-point petition. In response to what Cater called these 'shameful and degrading events' (Mannion 2004: 40), the following day, the Governor announced a partial amnesty for corrupt police officers, news that 'stunned the public, for he had asserted on numerous occasions that the need for the ICAC was absolute' (ibid). The partial amnesty stated that the ICAC would in future not normally take action concerning complaints or evidence relating to offences committed before 1 January 1977. If there were to be any exceptions to this – for example, particularly heinous offences of corruption committed by fugitive policemen – the Governor would have to be consulted before action was taken. As Lethbridge notes, the legality of this directive was questioned at the time but was given belated legal effect by an amendment to the ICAC Ordinance in 1978.[43]

The granting of the partial amnesty did not, however, bring the disturbances to an end. Those officers excluded from the amnesty met and announced a march on Government House on 8 November to demand further concessions. According to Lethbridge, the Governor held a series of meetings with his aides, including the Acting Commander of British Forces, mobilised the support of over 100 community groups, brought together their leaders and other prominent persons at a press conference and arranged an emergency sitting of LEGCO at which the Police Force Ordinance was amended to grant summary powers of dismissal to the Commissioner (Lethbridge 1985: 144). This effectively put a check on what Lethbridge calls the 'recalcitrant portion' of the police, since further demonstrations on their part now entailed the possibility of dismissal.

The partial amnesty was seen by the police as a major victory but it was 'devastating to the prestige of the ICAC and to the morale of its officers . . . the amnesty [also] dampened public confidence' (Mannion 2004: 41). The 1978 ICAC report sought to alleviate public fears that the Commission was to be wound up, though it admitted that the events of 1977 had dented public confidence. It reiterated that the ICAC had no intention of reducing its anti-corruption efforts, and reassured the public of its determination to fight corruption. However, a drop in reports to the ICAC over the following year, and surveys of public beliefs, indicated that a good deal of damage had indeed been inflicted on the organisation's standing and credibility. The fall in the number of corruption reports – from 729 to 487 – indicated that complainants felt they could not trust the ICAC and did not see it as truly independent.

The ICAC managed to recover from this setback. By the 1990s it was widely regarded as one of the most important institutions in Hong Kong, its integrity crucial to the government's legitimacy and to the maintenance of business confidence in Hong Kong as an international financial centre. Reports of corruption within the police fell throughout the 1970s and 1980s and, probably for the first time in Hong Kong's entire colonial history, the public no longer automatically assumed that the police were corrupt.

For Lo, the 1977 partial amnesty was a resolution to the government's competing hegemonic goals. The riots had faced the colonial state with probably the most serious challenge in its history. It needed to regain the consent of the people by eradicating corruption and making Hong Kong a fairer society. But the riots, and ongoing internal dissent, also underscored the need to keep the police force loyal (Lo 1993). However, there has never been any satisfactory official explanation of MacLehose's decision to grant the amnesty, and official papers concerning the incident remain closed. One suspicion is that the government feared that, unless it appeased the police, revelations would appear about the sexual habits of prominent members of the community.[44] This allegation later resurfaced in the MacLennan Inquiry. Another plausible explanation is that the government was afraid that a police strike, and the sight of soldiers on the street yet again, would damage Hong Kong's economic image.

For Lethbridge, the standoff between the police and the Governor in 1977 had some positive effects. A three-man advisory team from the Home Office in the UK visited Hong Kong in 1978 to advise on the reorganisation and operation of the police force; a new channel of consultation between the rank and file and the police hierarchy was also established. The creation of a Junior Police Officers Association (JPOA) proved initially problematic, as for some months after the partial amnesty the JPOA continued to agitate for wildcat strikes, demonstrations and protests. However, after some officers were dismissed, this agitation subsided, and the JPOA became more involved in issues of pay, housing, promotion and welfare (Lethbridge 1985: 156). The JPOA model was later copied by other disciplined services, which, had hitherto also lacked a channel for junior ranks to air and settle grievances. A police Staff Relations Unit was also established as a vehicle for organising welfare services for force members and their families. The police force had long provided services such as a welfare fund for loans, distress funds, and pensions and education – a special school for the children of the Pakistani contingent was, for example, provided at Fanling, and another six primary schools were provided for the children of police officers in the main urban areas. These provisions continued but the JPOA now assumed many of the responsibilities of the force welfare officer, hitherto assigned to rank and file welfare. It was hoped that, in future, the use of official JPA channels would reduce discontent and defuse conflict before it had chance to escalate. In addition, reforms within the police followed partly because the ICAC developed a policy of providing advice and assistance to all government departments, on improving systems of work so as to eliminate conditions conducive to corruption (what Mannion calls 'institutional design').

Mannion also argues that the amnesty had positive benefit for the ICAC, allowing it to shift its focus from difficult and time-consuming investigations of past offences to the more efficient pursuit of recent offences (Mannion 2004: 41). She also argues that it produced more cooperation from those who, hitherto, had feared assisting the ICAC in case they themselves were prosecuted for past offences. The decline in reports of police corruption also enabled the ICAC to turn its attention towards private sector corruption, as well as corruption in other government departments.

As Scott argues, the ICAC was eventually able to convince the public that it could ensure that 'public office was honestly held'. Beyond straightforward crime prevention, it stood for 'certain moral standards in government' and helped enhance the government's legitimacy (Scott 1989: 152). It did this partly by promising that a level playing field obtained on which the individual's life chances would not be distorted by bribery, cronyism, or other corrupting forces. The Hong Kong of the MacLehose era was recreated as a fair society built on merit, a society open to talent. Government officials were more responsive to the public; public consultation documents legitimated government decisions: 'what constituted the consensus was what the government said constituted a consensus after the view of the public had been considered' (Scott 1989: 164). The city was a more pleasant environment in which to live; citizens enjoyed new legal rights and the ability to enforce them. Social and administrative reforms 'strengthened the state machinery at the centre and administrative penetration at the local level gave the state civil capabilities which it had never before possessed' (ibid).

The new institutions of the MacLehose era closed the communication gap between government and citizens by a means of 'manipulating local sentiment' (ibid). This was as true for crime and criminal justice as it was for other governmental issues in this period. The commitment to clean government, which Scott identifies as the hallmark of the MacLehose era, won the administration general support and consent for other measures of social control. Though ultimately able to fall back upon its paramilitary capability, the reforms of the 1970s made it less likely that the state would need to do so, whilst increased state capacity also enabled the bureaucracy to act against crime more quickly and more effectively than before.[45] Meanwhile, as 'domestic missionaries' on the streets, the police contributed to new conceptions of state, citizenship and decorum (see Storch 1976).

Notes

1 Curriculum Development Committee 1985: 3.
2 Curriculum Development Committee 1985: 7.
3 After the signing of the Joint Declaration returning Hong Kong to China in 1984, political education was to focus on 'education for democracy' (though with the proviso in undemocratic Hong Kong that 'democracy means different things to different people'. In this instance it meant 'civic education' promoting stability and responsibility).
4 The JPC's popularity fell off in the 1980s, but by 1996, there were still over 183,053 registered members of JPC, 14,418 JPC leaders, 322 JPC school clubs and 25 JPC clubhouses in 20 police districts. JPC members were participating in over 10,344 community activities.
5 HKPAR 1978: 28.
6 HKPAR 1968/9: 31.
7 This mix of 'discipline and 'welfare' is discussed by Gray – see later chapters.
8 Press Release 23 June 1973.
9 *HK Standard* 17 December 1972.
10 Government Information Services Press Release 11 May 1973.
11 HKPAR 1979: 21.

12 HKPAR 1980: 21.
13 Alongside this, and to provide more facilities for children and young people, land (probably the most precious commodity in the colony) was freed up by the government to make way for playgrounds.
14 Press Release of speech by John MacKenzie 12 June 1973.
15 RHKPAR 1973/4: 7.
16 These were based on ones used by the Hampshire Constabulary in the UK.
17 HK Police Press Release 18 June 1973.
18 HK Yearbook 1977: 119.
19 RHKPAR 1973/4: 1.
20 The effectiveness of the PCROS is discussed in Lo, Wing-hung, Carlos and Cheuk, Chun-yin, Albert. (2003) 'Police-Public Projects in Hong Kong: An Evaluation' *Asian Journal of Public Administration* Vol 25 No 2 pp 287–313.
21 RHKPAR 1974/5: 4.
22 RHKPAR 1976/7: 13.
23 RHKPAR 1974/5: 5.
24 RHKPAR 1974/5: 5.
25 RHKPAR 1975/6: 16.
26 HK Police 1978: 1
27 RHKPAR 1979: 7.
28 RHKPAR 1978: 1.
29 HKPAR 1980: 20.
30 RHKPAR 1973/4: 4.
31 Silver 1967 cited in Wilson 2005; Gatrell 1980.
32 Kerrigan (2001) and Petrow (2005) both employ the argument laid out by Storch (1976) in which he says the UK police were 'domestic missionaries bringing civilisation and decorum to working-class communities' – see Petrow 2005: 123, and Kerrigan 2001.
33 HKPAR 1968/9.
34 HKPAR 1968/9: 20.
35 HK Annual Yearbook 1970: 139.
36 HKPAR 1969/70: 50. The most common complaints recorded against the police in the 1960s concerned not corruption but assault, the unnecessary exercise of authority and overbearing conduct, but of the 332 recorded in 1969/70, for example, only four resulted in court action; another 20 resulted in internal disciplinary proceedings. In the same year, 108 allegations of corruption were leveled against the police, most of which were referred to the reinvigorated Target Committee for further investigation, and eight referred on to the Anti-Corruption Branch. Figures for the year showed, however, that only 11 officers were prosecuted, four having their convictions quashed on appeal. Of the 19 offences of which they were convicted, convictions on ten offences were quashed on appeal; another 100 had disciplinary proceedings taken against them and were either transferred, dismissed, retired, resigned, or faced other punishment.

As these figures indicate, obtaining a conviction against a police officer for corruption was extremely difficult partly because the investigation into police corruption was carried out by the police themselves, and partly because syndicated corruption was so extensive.
37 The logic of this was that the specific offences for which he was being investigated were not covered by the framing of UK legislation. Ironically, therefore, he could not be extradited to Hong Kong. Ultimately he was charged with accepting bribes and of conspiracy, both offences known to English law, and after some 18 months

(10 of them in custody fighting his extradition) he was returned to Hong Kong to stand trial.

38 Students spearheaded the street protests, campaigning for Godber's extradition under the slogan 'Fight Corruption, Arrest Godber'.

39 Goodstadt, cited in Mannion 2004: 34.

40 Mannion 2004: 24.

41 Davies (1973: 28) cited in Mannion 2004.

42 Godber's trial in fact owed much to the Anti-Corruption office under Charles Sutcliffe, but it was the ICAC that was able to benefit from his conviction and the attendant publicity.

43 See Lethbridge 1985: 143 for details.

44 Homosexuality was still a crime in Hong Kong and remained so until 1991.

45 See Scott 1989 for further development of this argument.

Chapter 20

Crime, policing and punishment in the 1970s

Though efforts had been made in the 1960s to reduce the vast number of hawking and other miscellaneous offences, courts in the 1970s were complaining that the biggest portion of their caseload, especially in the magistrates' court, was taken up with such matters. In his speech at the opening of the legal year, the Chief Justice, Sir Ivor Rigby, noted the 'tremendous expansion' of the judiciary since the mid-1950s. In 1955, he observed, all Hong Kong's courts had been accommodated in three buildings – the Hong Kong Magistracy, the Kowloon Magistracy, and the Supreme Court building, which also housed the Victoria District Court. In 1970, by contrast, Victoria District Court occupied its own building (in Battery Path), there were nine magistracies and plans for three more in the next three years, seven Supreme Court judges where there had been three, eight District Court judges and 36 magistrates where there had been 11. The non-legal staff of the courts had risen from 181 to 618 and all this expansion, he suggested, was due to the failure to tackle 'trivial' offences. He also expressed an interest in providing young offenders with community-based punishments as an alternative to imprisonment. The government should look to Singapore, the Chief Justice advised, to solve this 'great human problem', the 'great mass of mainly honest, decent people, pouring into the courts, swelling the lists'.[1] The government, it seemed, took his advice, for the anti-litter 'Keep Hong Kong Clean' (*Lap Sap Chung*) campaigns of the 1970s bore a remarkable resemblance to Singapore's.

The use of fixed penalties, begun in the late 1960s, greatly appealed to the Hong Kong judiciary as a means of taking 'trivial' cases out of court. There were concerns in some quarters, however, that police corruption would undermine such a system. Distrust of the police also prompted the recommendation that suspects be allowed to make their confessions before a magistrate instead of the police, due to allegations about the police's methods of interrogation. The *Hong Kong Star* criticised the police for attempting to combat Hong Kong's rising crime by forcing false confessions from suspects in order to make the statistics look good.[2]

Crime in the post-riot years actually showed a slight falling off. The official statistics show that many of the minor crimes were much as they had been previous decades – prostitution, gambling, obscene publications, and minor narcotics. As in previous decades, a large number of reports (around 40 per cent in each year) disclosed no offence (Table 20.1).

During and after the anti-crime campaign of 1973 and 1974, when the focus was on serious and violent crime, the prosecution of these miscellaneous offences dropped significantly. Nevertheless, in 1974/5 the police conducted 170 raids on gambling establishments connected with prostitution, another 176 raids on vice establishments and, in 1974, they arrested over 41,000 people for gambling and vice offences, and repatriated 26 of the 51 foreign prostitutes found working in the colony.[3] An Obscene Publications Ordinance, enacted in 1975, prompted another crackdown, on pornography and on 'Hong Kong's most notorious blue movie/live sex shows syndicate'.[4]

In 1971, the police noted a 'worrying concern' in the increasing numbers of juveniles and young people involved in crimes of violence.[5] However, the number of juveniles prosecuted at the turn of the decade had actually fallen slightly since the mid-1960s. In the early 1970s it rose briefly to about 10 per cent of total prosecutions, but by 1975 had dropped back below this level. It was the prosecutions for young offenders that showed the real increase.

In October 1971, the Governor, Sir David Trench, referred in LEGCO to the 'disturbing and continuously rising incidence of robberies and crimes committed against the person'.[6] The marked increase in recorded violent crime in 1969/70 alarmed the police and public alike.

A self-fulfilling spiral now began. The outcry over rising crime prompted more intensive policing and calls to the public to report crime. As noted previously, this produced ever-increasing crime figures. The figures for 1971 were greeted with calls for sterner measures, which were again answered by greater police activity. The police force increased its 'preventive crime controls', particularly stop-and-search operations; the auxiliary police was rapidly strengthened.[7] As a result, by 1972, the crime figures showed another rise. The press were critical; the public became 'vociferous in condemning the rising crime rate'.[8] The police further encouraged the public to 'play their

Table 20.1 Reports to the police, 1970–75

	1970/1	*1971/2*	*1973*	*1974*	*1975*
No offence disclosed	246,114	229,832	262,843	226,107	196,369
Offence disclosed	327,540	348,697	350,456	309,946	299,128
Recorded as crime	N/A	N/A	34,975	43,595	57,016
All reports	**573,654**	**578,529**	**613,299**	**536,053**	**495,497**

Source: RHKPAR 1973/4.

Table 20.2 Miscellaneous offences 1969–78

	1969/70	*1970/1*	*1971/2*	*1972/3*	*1973/4*	*1974/5*	*1975/6*	*1976*	*1977*	*1978*	*1979*
Gambling	44,498	49,770	55,231	60,712	48,228	41,889	44,590	42,593	13,689	14,766	13,104
Hawking	10,049	123,108	129,880	144,035	125,280	121,765	111,844	115,887	93,004	81,250	64,689
Obstruction	70,339	95,081	99,931	77,164	55,108	46,237	51,516	74,575	73,201	54,157	34,197
Prostitution	1,067	1,085	1,227	1,214	1,470	1,430	2,354	4,308	3,885	3,085	1,219
Other	17,294	14,242	14,158	13,945	16,666	14,799	14,109	20,641	21,936	18,387	17,167
Objectionable publication [1]										60	113
Money lending offences [1]										1	–
Minor narcotics [1]										1,528	5,558
Total	**243,247**	**283,286**	**300,427**	**297,070**	**246,752**	**226,120**	**224,413**	**258,004**	**213,687**	**180,071**	**138,232**

Source: RHKPARs 1969–76.
[1] Counted as miscellaneous offences since June 1978.

Table 20.3 Reported crime: actual numbers: immediate post-riot years 1966–70

Crime	*1966/7*	*1967/8*	*1968/9*	*1969/70*
Class I offences				
(Against public order, perjury, escape & rescue, unlawful society, other offences against lawful authority				
Total	1,270	1,902	625	976
Class II offences				
Rape	10	22	12	37
Indecent assault on a female	283	221	293	387
Other sexual offences	76	134	187	301
Unnatural offences	8	8	6	10
Other offences against public morality	31	29	23	41
Total	408	414	21	776
Class III offences				
Murder and manslaughter	43	80	44	55
Attempted murder	8	4	1	7
Serious assault	1,059	1,092	1,045	1,312
Abortion	3	4	5	–
Kidnapping	1	2	–	–
Criminal intimidation	17	49	32	38
Other offences against the person	71	150	135	143
Total	1,202	1,381	1,262	1,555
Class IV offences (Property crime)	17,740	19,592	18,864	22,073
Class V offences (Forgery, bribery and corruption, conspiracy, breach of deportation order, possession of arms and ammunition)				
Total	688	551	832	629
Class VI offences (Narcotics)	208	207	276	970
Grand total	21,516	24,047	22,380	26,979

Source: HKPAR 1966–70.

Table 20.4 Crime Hong Kong 1966–69: absolute numbers and crime rate post-riot years

Year	*Total no of reported offences*	*Key crime/serious crime*	*Crime rate per 100K population*
1966/7	635,051	21,516	580.07
1967/8	489,009	24,047	620.14
1968/9	665,119	22,380	563.52
1969/70	833,669	26,979	668.67

Source: HKPARs 1966–9.

part' by reporting 'all cases in which they were involved or which they had witnessed' (ibid).

After the brief downturn in crime following the riots, Hong Kong now experienced what was interpreted as an 'explosion of criminality'. Recorded crime rose from 29,979 in 1969 to 43,595 in 1974. Minor narcotics offences

Table 20.5 Crime rate 1969–74 (reports per 100,000 population)

	1969/70	*1970/1*	*1971/2*	*1972/3*	*1973/4*	*1974/5*
Total reports	15,453.31	13,897.33	14,301.26	15,041.43	12,886.20	11,662.32
Serious crime	668.67	716.97	808.66	857.78	1,047.98	1,341.96
Miscellaneous offences	6,028.88	6,862.88	7,426.57	7,285.77	5,931.68	5,322.10
Minor narcotics offences	375.59	354.38	383.43	450.39	470.92	376.40

Source: RHKPARs 1973–5: Appendix 10.

rose from 15,154 to 19,590. Miscellaneous offences shot up from 243,247 in 1969 to 300,427 in 1974.[9] The crime rate rose year on year (Table 20.5).

There had been a steady increase in recorded crime during the 1960s, and the riots themselves had produced a temporary rise in serious and violent crime – the police noted that in 1966, serious crime in the colony was at its highest since 1956/7. The official crime statistics for 1966/7 had recorded a 10-year high in serious crime (a total of 21,516). This was mainly due, it was argued, to public order offences, robberies and miscellaneous larcenies committed in the course of the riots. Then, in the later years of the decade, overall recorded crime and violent crime fell; in 1968 overall crime dropped by almost 7 per cent on the previous year (from 24,047 to 22,380). Prosecutions for crime also fell by almost 9 per cent.

In 1969, however, reported crime rose by 20.5 per cent over the previous year. Looked at overall, in the five years between 1965 and 1970, the total number of recorded crimes had risen from 19,790 to 26,979. In 1969/70, the statistics continued to show an overall rise in crime (29,052) and again in 1971, recorded crime grew still higher. These figures caused alarm – they were the highest annual figures recorded since 1954/5.[10] More was yet to come, however.

By 1974, recorded crime stood at just under 45,000; by 1975, it had risen again by 30 per cent to 57,016.[11] This represented over a three-fold increase in crime in the ten years since 1965. Between 1970 and 1975, overall crime had doubled from about 25,000 offences to over 50,000. Between 1972 and 1974 alone, it grew dramatically by 64 per cent.[12] The upward 'trend' in violent crime also continued. In 1973, serious assaults increased by almost 39 per cent, robberies by almost 19 per cent, rape by 36 per cent and criminal damage to property by 102 per cent.[13] Over 46 per cent of robberies involved the use of an offensive weapon, including firearms; 29 out the year's total of 103 homicides stemmed from robberies.

The following year (1974) reported crime was again up by over 40 per cent. The total number of arrests was also up by 42.1 per cent and, after a drop in 1973, prosecutions for adults and young offenders rose by over 45 per cent (to 18,827) and by over 14 per cent for juveniles.[14] One in nine young persons aged between 16 and 20 were said to have committed an offence; more than 40 per cent of these were involved in recorded crimes of violence.

Recorded violent crime had shot up sharply, from almost 4,500 offences in the middle of 1968 to over 20,000 by 1975. In the one year between 1973 and 1974 alone, the figure for serious assaults went up by 70 per cent (from 2,503 to 4,256); robberies went up by 30 per cent from 9,661 to 13,046) and there was no sign of things improving.[15] Public concern about violent crime prompted the police to specifically address this issue. Crime in Hong Kong was, the police argued, low by comparison with other major world cities. But public feeling was that the colony was sliding into moral decline; 'sterner measures' were demanded. The police acknowledged that it was 'cold comfort' for Hong Kong citizens to be told their city had a relatively low crime rate, or that it was following a 'worldwide trend in increasing crimes of violence'.[16] The force was under-staffed; crime had to be dealt with more effectively; 'more positive measures had to be adopted to counter the situation' (ibid).

Accordingly, the crime figures again rose, in 1973 by over 17 per cent to 33,778.[17] Again, the most noticeable rise was in serious crime (robberies, burglaries, serious assaults, and offences against public order); more minor offences (such as snatching) fell. When the Fight Crime campaign began in May 1973, more members of the public were encouraged to get involved in cracking down on crime.

Most of the serious crime was reported in Kowloon District – in 1973/4, for example, out of a total of 43,595 crimes, 26,143 were in Kowloon; the next highest was Hong Kong Island at 12,874. Breaking this down further, out of a total of 9,636 robberies in the colony as a whole, 7,172 were in Kowloon, and out of a total of 34,224 property offences, 21,219 were in Kowloon – the next highest was Hong Kong Island at 9,479.[18] Much of the rise was blamed on young offenders (aged 16 to 21).

In the late 1970s, the police altered the way in which the crime figures were presented. They were reorganised in terms of 'key crime', 'other crime' and 'preventive crime'. Within key crime, the figures first addressed violent crime,

Table 20.6 Crime 1970–76

	1970	*1971*	*1972*	*1973*	*1974*	*1975*	*1976*
Class I	1,276	1,386	1,424	2,445	4,647	5,971	6,205
Class II	775	841	1,118	1,329	1,639	1,589	1,695
Class III	1,617	1,982	2,108	2,533	4,275	5,485	5,628
Class IV	23,553	26,404	27,052	31,059	42,991	40,768	44,895
Class V	640	627	920	939	898	1,089	869
Class VI	1,191	1,221	1,377	1,473	1,461	1,621	2,717
Grand total	29,052	32,461	33,999	39,778	55,911	56,520	62,009

Sources: HK Yearbooks 1970–74; RHKPARs 1974–9. The RHKPAR give slightly different totals, i.e. 1974: 43,595; 1975: 57,016.

Table 20.7 Reported crime 1975–79

	1975	*1976*	*1977*	*1978*	*1979*
Violent crime	20,912	21,211	17,571	16,993	19,169
Other key crime	21,806	24,033	23,867	26,904	32,521
Total key crime	42,718	45,244	41,438	43,897	51,690
Other crime	6,261	8,286	7,190	6,636	7,004
Preventive crime	7,541	8,479	8,121	6,543	5,959
Total	**56,520**	**62,009**	**56,749**	**57,076**	**64,653**

Source: RHKPAR 1977:52.

then other key crimes such as theft, followed by offences against public order, financial crime, narcotics, and preventive crime, which included being a member of an unlawful society, going equipped for stealing, and so on.

By 1976, however, the police were claiming to have contained the crime problem – official figures began to chart a small decline overall in crimes such as murder, robbery and burglary. Serious assaults, however, remained unchanged. A sharp drop in violent crime was also noted by the police, but this began to rise again before the decade had closed.

Narcotics

All forms of recorded crime apparently increased in Hong Kong during the 1970s. The argument that the rise in crime in the late 1960s was simply a 'blip', and that crime would fall again to pre-disorder levels, initially seemed to be borne out. Figures for 1967/8 show that recorded crime fell by almost 7 per cent (from 24,047 in 1966/7 to 22,380). There were, however, increases in certain kinds of recorded crime, such as narcotics offences.[19] The police attributed this to the fact that the force had returned to its normal law enforcement duties, and resumed its war against drugs. Even so, reported narcotics offences were still below the figure for 1966/7 (18,518) and represented a steep drop from the early 1960s, when even minor narcotic offences stood at over 19,000. This was the high point of reported and recorded narcotics offences – though numbers rose immediately after the riots, they declined thereafter (Table 20.8).

The profile of the 'typical' Hong Kong drug addict in the 1970s was much as it had been in the 1960s: male, over 21, unskilled or semi-skilled, usually single, in a lower income group and generally with a low level of education.[20] In 1976, the police knew of some 60,000 addicts in the colony, almost all of whom (50,000) were addicted to heroin and the rest to opium. Cannabis and LSD were still reckoned to be the drugs of choice only within the expatriate community, and then only in small numbers. A reorganisation of the Central Registry of Drug Addicts in September 1976 provided more detailed information. By 1977, addicts were described as people who had (1) usually

Table 20.8 Narcotics offences 1959–77

1958/9	9,041
1959/60	12,615
1960/1	17,885
1961/2	16,038
1962/3	16,081
1963/4	19,914
1964/5	19,647
1965/6	18,159
1966/7	18,310
1967/8	12,157
1968/9	16,872
1969/70	15,154
1970	15,751
1971	16,674
1972	18,284
1973	20,886
1974	19,699
1975	14,629
1976	13,519
1977	9,940

Sources: HKPARs 1960–70 (for 1958/9 to 1969/70); RHKPARs 1970–76; HK Yearbooks 1970–76 (for 1970 to 1977)

become addicted before the age of 25; (2) became involved from curiosity and/or peer group influence; and (3) were usually separated from their families.

Police crackdowns on narcotics had, however, an unanticipated side effect: they pushed up the price of heroin and drove more addicts into methadone clinics. The crackdown on street sellers, local heroin refineries and the smuggling of drugs in 1976 doubled the price of heroin (see Table 20.9 for recorded seizures).

Table 20.9 Narcotics seizures 1970–76

	1970/1	*1971/2*	*1972/3 [1]*	*1973/4*	*1974/5*	*1975/6*	*1976/7*
Heroin	31	120	87	68.1	82.5	48.4	20
Morphine	170	659	528	317	238.2	67	137
Opium	–	12,291	3,802	2,164	4,789	–	–
Raw opium	877	9,104	–	–	309.2	–	3,186
Cannabis	–	113	8.5	17.5	27.3	1.2	–
Barbitone	72.8	17.5	26.7	3.9	3	–	

Source: RHKPARs 1970–76; HK Yearbooks 1970–76.
[1] Figures before 1972 are in lbs; after 1972, in kilos.

Triads

Since the major campaign against triads in the late 1950s, the police had spoken of conventional triads as a spent force, their remnants merely 'fragmented' gangs of young hooligans. Their offensive against triads continued into the 1970s, but it was not until the middle of the decade that this discourse altered. Then, triads were once more described as an 'organised menace' to society.

During 1968/9, 277 triad cases were detected, up 167 cases on 1967; in 1969/70, 43 gangs were said to have been broken up, 695 triad cases detected, 626 triad members convicted – both large increases on previous years.[21] This was still far below the level for the early 1960s – and in any case, any increase in triad activity was put down to triads having exploited the fact that the police were otherwise engaged during the riots to recruit more members and run more rackets. What the police referred to as the 'conventional triads' were said to be under control. It was the not so well organised, loosely-led gangs of violent youths – quasi-triads – which were problematic. To deal with these 'violent, quasi-triad youth gangs'[22] the Anti-Triad Bureau had been strengthened in the late 1960s. It paid special attention to young people associating in groups 'and conducting themselves in a manner which might lead to triad type behaviour'.[23]

This 'special attention' to 16–21-year-olds meant that the numbers arrested in this age group rose notably at the end of the 1960s. It was not until the mid-1970s, however, that the police explicitly related the number of fights taking place between gangs to triads attempting to expand their area of influence. The view that these 'quasi-triad' gangs were somehow less problematic than 'conventional' triads then altered. Organised police action was said to be necessary to smash triad syndicates and neutralise their influence.[24] In 1974, the force conducted an in-depth survey of triad activities as a precursor to mapping out what action to take against them. In July 1974, the police mounted an operation to 'strike at and disrupt' triads and gang activities, arresting 1,200 people in Kowloon alone;[25] by the middle of 1975, some 2,623 persons had been arrested, the highest figure for some time. Over 62 per cent of them were under 21.

The collection and dissemination of triad intelligence now became a prime objective of the Anti-Triad Bureau. Press reports on the activities of triads in other countries 'gave the impression that triad elements constitute a criminal syndicate of global proportion'. This view of triads as 'the Mafia of the Orient' was, the police argued, 'sensationalism . . . [it] is simply not true'.[26] Triads, they insisted, were simply gangs of thugs who usurped the name 'triad' and exploited the triad myth. Nevertheless, in 1976 the strength of the Anti-Triad Bureau was doubled, first from 87 to 189, then to 216. In January 1977, a new and streamlined system of processing triad intelligence was put into effect throughout the force and was 'proving invaluable as a basis for offensive action against criminal personalities and syndicates'; in March, a new offensive against triads was launched which continued into 1978 and 1979.[27]

The police now ceased to describe triads as 'disorganised, quasi-triad gangs of youths' and started to talk of them as 'organised criminal syndicates' and 'deep-seated criminal monopolies'.[28] The leaderless gangs of the early 1960s had, it seemed, transmuted into a serious (and often violent) crime problem. By 1974, there were said to be 38 separate triad societies active in the colony. Though no central triad body or executive existed, liaison between triad societies was said to occur through contacts between senior triad officials.[29] The 'fragmented gangs' of the 1960s now had 'a degree of organisation'.[30] In 1976, the Commissioner of Police described triads as the 'kernel' of the problem of organised crime:

> The gangs, mainly groupings of not more than 15 each, probably have a total of 8,000 active followers; in short, about 500 gangs. They are the leeches of our society and prey on those least able to protect and fend for themselves. Fear is their greatest weapon – fear created through the myth of a long-dead giant and fear generated through their operation in packs. Individually, they are insignificant and cowardly little men . . . We are aiming to hit the higher eschelons of criminal syndicates, be they involved in violent crime, drugs, gambling, prostitution or whatever . . .[31]

A crackdown on triads followed; some 4,700 extortion offences were discovered, almost double the previous year.[32] The first prosecution of a syndicate head for conspiracy to keep a common gambling house was held to have eliminated the largest illegal bookmaking syndicate in the colony; an amendment to the Gambling Bill led to the suspension of the triad-run 'Tze Fa' lottery; a telephone system relaying information on Macau dog races was put out of action (ibid). One consequence of these crackdowns was an increase in the turnover of lawful betting run by one of the 'pillars' of the Hong Kong establishment, the Royal Hong Kong Jockey Club (ibid). The police also cracked down on the organisation and protection of prostitution, hawkers, and 'significantly reduced the venues for organised criminal activities' (ibid).

The aim of the police force was no longer simply to contain triads, as it had been in the 1960s, but to eliminate 'these leeches and hooligans from society' (ibid). Irrespective of whether they were 'real or pseudo triads' or 'a group of thugs', they were described as:

> . . . a menace to society . . . Any distinguished background or patriotic aims have long disappeared, just as central control has been dissipated. The result has been a proliferation of interest-group disputes over

'territorial rights' or spheres of influence, thus increasing violence and danger to the community.[33]

Having persuaded the community to participate in the wider 'war on crime' the police now hoped to encourage it to 'unmask this major threat to the security of Hong Kong' (ibid). However, the triad renunciation scheme, introduced to enable young people to leave triads, was to prove rather unsuccessful. Throughout the last years of the 1970s, gang fights between triad members continued, at a rate of about 40 a month. By the end of the decade, there were an estimated 33 different triad societies active in Hong Kong, comprising some 80,000 members, all engaged in extortion and protection rackets around prostitution, gambling, bars and nightclubs, billiard rooms, bowling alleys, public light buses, and decoration companies.[34] The Anti-Triad Bureau now amalgamated with the Organised Crime office into the Organised Crime and Triad Bureau (OCTB) and a 'new initiative against triads' began.[35]

Violent crime and violent youth

The decline in arrests of what were termed 'conventional triads' towards the end of the 1960s was matched by an increase in the arrest of young men aged 16 to 21, the 'young thugs' identified by the police as 'quasi-triads'.

Since 1964, when they had made up about 16 per cent of all those prosecuted for serious crime, arrests for this age group had been in decline. The years 1966 and 1967 were, of course, unusual: many of those involved in the riots had been under 21. They had been arrested in large numbers, mainly for public order offences (up by 347 per cent in 1967 on the previous year) and membership of unlawful societies (up 94 per cent). Apart from the 1967 riots, however, throughout the 1960s their numbers had remained more or less below 2,000 prosecuted for any crime. In 1965, youths in this age group had represented almost 16 per cent of those prosecuted for serious crime, rising to about 17 per cent in 1966. By the end of 1967, their numbers were down again – their arrests for public order offences dropped by almost 90 per cent; for possession of unlawful instruments by 54 per cent; for larceny from the person by 62 per cent; for unlawful possession by 33 per cent; and for murder and manslaughter by almost 78 per cent.

But in 1969/70, this changed. The total numbers of young offenders prosecuted rose by 39 per cent over the previous year. In 1970/71, the number prosecuted for crimes of violence (such as robbery) rose by 59.8 per cent.[36] Figures for arrests for serious assault and robbery between 1967 and 1969 showed young offenders to be the largest single group prosecuted – the number arrested for serious assault alone went up by almost 50 per cent. Serious gang fights were said to have 'frequently resulted in serious injuries'.[37] Youth in this age group were characterised as 'quick to take offence' at a personal affront, inclined to 'form groups', engage in 'group anti-social behaviour', be 'indifferent to law', have a willingness to 'take a chance', and to start gang fights over trivial insults or girlfriends. Police activities were increased to cope with this trend. By 1972, the police recorded a 45 per cent rise in young offenders arrested for serious assaults. This came as something of a shock to the police and public alike. By 1973, young offenders represented almost 30 per cent of *all* prosecutions. In 1974, the police stated categorically that it was the 16 to 20 age group that caused the most concern: 'Based on 252,264 as the estimated male population of the age group, it is estimated that one in every 49 of such male persons was prosecuted for crime, and more than 35 per cent of them were involved in crime of violence' in 1974/5.[38]

This participation in violent crime was seen, not as a product of policing, but as a *real* change in youth behaviour. It did however reflect the heightened attention that the police were paying to this age group. Young offenders were the newly identified 'crime problem', gangs of youths 'given to violence'[39] (Table 20.10).

As in the 1950s and 1960s, however, the crimes for which *most* young offenders were being arrested were still miscellaneous larcenies (up by 155 per cent in 1968) such as snatching, loitering, trespass, and stealing a bicycle. In 1973, for example, 82 per cent of all offences committed by juveniles were against property. By the end of the 1970s, the police would note the deployment of juveniles as street couriers, but in any year, by far the highest percentage of offenders prosecuted for any type of crime was adults aged 21 and over. Moreover, whilst the number of young offenders and juveniles prosecuted rose in the early 1970s, the numbers *convicted* dropped between 1967 and 1969, as it had for juveniles aged under 16 and children aged 7 to 13 (Table 20.11).[40]

Juveniles were still not regarded as a 'crime problem'. The number of juveniles arrested and prosecuted had been more or less steady since the late 1950s. In 1957, for example, just less than 600 juveniles were prosecuted; by 1961 this had risen to just less than 1,600[41] and by the end of 1961, juveniles accounted for over 21 per cent of all arrests for serious crime. But

Table 20.10 Percentage of young offenders prosecuted for crime (percentage of all offenders)

	1973/4	*1974/5*
Crimes of violence	32	27
Robberies	39	34
Burglaries	21	18
Homicide	46	38
Sexual offences	33	26
Theft from person	19	10
Narcotic offences	2.4	2.9

Source: RHKPARs 1973–5: Appendix 16.

Table 20.11 Convictions in the magistrates' courts 1971–6

	1971	*1972*	*1973*	*1974*	*1975*	*1976*
Adult defendants	606,060	601,693	667,246	773,923	581,917	641,917
Adults convicted	537,487	539,066	608,482	508,826	536,310	604,982
Juvenile defendants	4,458	3,297	3,060	3,787	3,540	4,387
Juveniles convicted	4,240	3,137	2,900	3,615	3,252	4,074

Source: HK Yearbooks 1974–7.

this percentage had fallen steadily throughout the decade, to 15 per cent in 1965/6, to 11 per cent in 1968, and to 9 per cent in 1969. In 1970, it rose slightly to 10.5 per cent, where it more or less remained for the next three years. Numbers throughout the ten-year period from 1964 to 1974 never rose much above 1,500, and in 1976 the police noted a 17.6 per cent drop in prosecutions of juveniles.

In fact, police reports throughout the 1970s insisted that there was no 'Juvenile Delinquent problem' in Hong Kong; their involvement in crime had shown no 'dramatic change'.[42] They nevertheless remained 'alert to the potential' of juvenile delinquency, and were 'studying means and ways to ensure as far as possible that no such problem develops'.[43] A number of reports and studies were initiated. The Juvenile Liaison Office, set up in 1963, was said to be in 'close liaison' with statutory and voluntary bodies concerned with the welfare of juveniles 'with particular emphasis on the rehabilitation of young prostitutes' (ibid). As this activity indicates, all these agencies were watching for the first signs of the 'newer and more specific problem' of youth.[44]

Police specialisation and professionalisation

In the midst of its 1970s mobilisation against crime, and in line with its commitment to maintaining better police/public relations, the police force continued its traditional civil aid role. In 1973, for example, its assistance was required when Typhoon Dot hit the colony, and when fires occurred in the Chai Wan and Mau Heung squatter areas. They were also called upon when a hijacked aircraft landed at Kai Tak.

But the 'modernisation' and professionalisation of the police force, started by Pennefather-Evans, became a priority following the riots and corruption scandals of the era. Modernisation was visible both in the conduct of everyday policing (computerisation, increased use of forensic science and new technology, growing 'civilianisation' of the force), and in the adoption of more specialised units, such as the Criminal Intelligence Unit, formed in 1973 during the anti-crime campaign, and the Special Crimes Squad, formed in 1972 to tackle both one-off crimes (such as big robberies or particularly violent crimes) as well as ongoing organised crime syndicates, and crimes with particular political or social implications. The premise on which the squad was founded was that Hong Kong contained a number of highly sophisticated, organised criminal syndicates that demanded a sophisticated, specialist response. Police reports talked in terms of a small section, which used 'accurate tactical intelligence' and 'targeted investigations'. In 1973, for example, the Special Crimes squad mounted a series of dawn raids following the killing of a police officer who had raised the alarm during a bank robbery. This was one of a series of bank robberies that had taken place that year. In the years that followed, the squad continued to be involved in the investigation of some of Hong Kong's more spectacular robberies. In 1976, its strength was increased and its attention turned more fully to bank and goldsmith shop robberies, and robberies involving firearms.[45] Re-named the Special Crimes Bureau in 1977 (all the specialised units were thus renamed that year), the squad was expanded from 32 officers to 94. In line with the force-wide thirst for more information and detailed statistics, it began to compile 'a comprehensive index of information on crimes, personalities, modus operandi etc. in respect of certain groups'.[46]

Another specialised crime 'squad' – the Homicide Squad – was also formed in November 1972 to concentrate on protracted or complicated cases. The need for such a specialist squad was based on the belief that homicides (such as the still notorious 'Box Murder' case) attracted massive publicity and unsettled the public. Unsolved homicides unsettled it even more, left the people feeling insecure and weakened their confidence in the police.[47]

In 1974, in an example of the new 'joined up' policing, the Homicide Squad joined forces with the Narcotics Bureau to pursue two drugs syndicate 'barons' in what the police called 'probably the most significant break through the police have ever had in Hong Kong against top level syndicated crime'.[48] In 1974, the Organised Crime and Triad Bureau (OCTB) was established, reflecting the need for another specialised unit to combat what had once more come to be seen as the 'menace' of triad activities.

The OCTB led the way in police use of research to plan strategy. As the decade wore on, the force would become more interested in developing intelligence, seeing science and knowledge as keys to innovation and the making of 'a twentieth-century law enforcement agency'.[49] It was this quest for more knowledge about crime, its reporting, its characteristics, its trends and its incidence that eventually led, in 1976, to the Planning and Research Division of the police force taking an interest in US studies on crime victimisation. The plans for strengthening and centralising the statistics unit in 1977 now came together with the idea of conducting US-style crime surveys in Hong Kong. The first crime survey was eventually conducted by the Census and Statistics Department in 1979.

Illegal immigration was still the responsibility of the police, along with the Immigration Department. The marine police, in particular, patrolled the waters around Hong Kong. With the Cultural Revolution still ongoing from China, and the triumph of the Communists in Vietnam, a number of people tried to flee to Hong Kong. In 1973 a total of 6,472 illegal immigrants were arrested, rising to 6,610 in 1974. Most of these had attempted to swim across Mirs Bay or Deep Bay, though some came by boat, some by land, and some from Macau.[50] In 1974, a further 6,171 immigrants were arrested. At midnight on 29 November, a new policy came into effect whereby immigrants intercepted coming into Hong Kong were repatriated, mostly to China. Later in 1974, there was a demonstration by students and relatives of the deportees at Kai Tak Airport, as 118 illegal Vietnamese immigrants were returned to South Vietnam.[51] An inter-governmental agreement to allow Vietnamese illegal immigrants to land and be resettled by European countries meant that later arrivals were accepted rather than repatriated. The 'true' number of illegal immigrants was, as ever, unclear since there was no indication of how many entered Hong Kong undetected, helped, perhaps as in the early 1960s, by sympathetic NT villagers. As the decade wore on, however, Hong Kong was to see far greater numbers arriving from Vietnam.

In the NT, the old-style Village Penetration Patrols were still operational, maintaining a continuous police presence in such far-flung places as Ping Chau, Kat O, Yuen Long and Shatin. As the 1970s wore on, massive infrastucture development (roads, rail, the first cross harbour tunnel, new towns) would bring these places into greater proximity with the rest of Hong Kong, transform the rural landscape, and swell their populations.

Hong Kong was by now a thriving economic city. Its reputation as a financial and industrial centre made it a magnet for what the police described as 'unscrupulous criminal and business operators' from around the world.[52] Though the financial sector remained largely unregulated, the Commercial Crime Office was investigating increasingly complex cases, including long-term frauds, forgery (for example, of letters of credit, share certificates) and international currency counterfeiting cases. Increasingly, crimes committed by the powerful – company officers and directors – came to its attention but few were prosecuted. A stock market boom in 1972–3 threw up a series of company frauds, some of which required lengthy investigation. In 1974, for only the second time in Hong Kong's history, the Financial Secretary appointed inspectors to examine the affairs of three public companies under section 143 of the Companies Ordinance.[53]

The office reported a much-increased workload following the swathe of legislation relating to commodities, securities, chit fund businesses and stock exchange controls, as well as a 'discernible trend' in more sophisticated and international commercial frauds. Its officers became more closely involved with Interpol, as well as in investigations in Iran, Indonesia, South Korea, Singapore, the USA and the UK.[54] In December 1976, the government approved the appointment of 20 'high-grade' staff to investigate company fraud. Increasingly, the unit also attracted the interest of overseas forces such as the City of London Police.[55]

In the mid-1970s, the Commercial Crime Unit also became involved in the investigation of what was to become a long-standing feature of Hong Kong life, the sale of counterfeit watches, pirated books and fake music cassettes and records.[56] In 1974, the responsibility for policing fake watches was shifted to the trade investigation branch of the Commerce and Industry Department; its copyright unit also took over the policing of pirated records. That other feature of Hong Kong life – a crackdown on the display and sale of fake watches – remained the job of the police. (Said to be of benefit 'both to the local consumer and tourists', its continued prevalence suggests an active market amongst both). By the end of the 1970s, the Commercial Crime Office had become the Commercial Crime Group, reorganised into even more specialist units – the Company Fraud division, a General Fraud division and a Counterfeit division.

In September 1973, a new Complaints Against Police Office (CAPO) was established. This stemmed from the need for a separate Force Complaints Office to investigate all complaints against the police except those involving criminal or corrupt conduct.[57] Though not independent of the police, it did reflect a recognition that the force needed to at least be seen to be more accountable than hitherto. It also reinforced the message that it was now a right of the public to make complaints against public servants about the abuse of power. However, the fact was that CAPO was still the police investigating the police – not a recipe for public confidence given the force's track record on corruption. As in the 1960s, most of the complaints made against the police in the mid-1970s were of assault. Out of a total of 448 complaints in 1973/4, only 88 were found to be substantiated.

This move towards slightly greater public accountability was followed shortly afterwards by the establishment of the ICAC, which quickly demonstrated that it had the power to bring corrupt police officers to book. Such steps were part of a wider push to convince the public that the government was (1) clean; (2) more accountable; and (3) able to provide a level playing field on which any Hong Kong citizen could, by dint of hard work and merit alone, become more prosperous.

The late 1970s: a changing picture of crime

The first real drop in recorded crime during the decade was in 1976. The police explained this as the result of new and more effective police strategies and techniques, the improved economic climate, the increased educational and recreational facilities, as well as better housing, provided by MacLehose's 'welfare colonialism', and the public's participation in the anti-crime campaigns themselves. Violent crimes went down by about 10 per cent; robberies alone fell by 20 per cent. At the same time, however, more arrests were made

– 21,918 of the 23,485 persons arrested were classed as adults (up by 10.6 per cent on 1975) and 1,567 as juveniles (up by 9.4 per cent on 1975). Greater police action against narcotics, stealing, loitering, and extortion also produced rises in the figures for these types of crime, up by almost 10 per cent on 1975.[58]

By 1977, the police seemed to have finally brought the dramatic rise in crime under control – overall recorded crime declined from 52,812 reports in 1976 to 51,610 in 1977. Reports of violent crime fell from 21,211 in 1976 to 17,571 in 1977.[59] The crime rate was down to about 1,000 cases per 100,000 head of population. Robbery (including armed robbery), burglary, dangerous drugs, frauds, and blackmail all fell, robbery to its lowest level since 1971.[60] The new gambling laws had hit illegal gambling hard and police intensified their offensive against vice (ibid). The Narcotics Bureau was hailed as having eliminated several major drug trafficking syndicates; the street price of heroin doubled. Hong Kong was now recognised as 'no longer a major drug exporting centre' shipping drugs from the Golden Triangle.[61] People were said to be less apprehensive about crime than before, the police were convinced that the public had more confidence in the force and – even if there was no way of knowing how much crime there really was in Hong Kong – the public certainly seemed happier about reporting it.[62]

There was to be no let-up, however in the police presence on the streets. Crime, the police stated, was still a 'principal social problem in Hong Kong'.[63] A maximum presence on the ground, aided by the auxiliary police, was held to be necessary to nip crime in the bud and improve the police image 'to bring about greater public co-operation with, and confidence in, the Force' (ibid). Thousands of people were, the police claimed, now involved in the fight against crime; they served in a variety of capacities in widely different bodies but worked to a common aim, the prevention of crime (ibid). This 'cornerstone' of the fight against crime was the 'triple alliance' between the government, the public and the police (ibid). The Fight Crime Campaigns went on, with District Fight Crime Committees 'at the hub' of the campaign. In 1978, this took as its slogan 'Beat Crime' and included a 'War on Rape' campaign with its own co-ordinating committee (ibid). The Neighbourhood Policing Units continued to provide a 'full-time, visible police presence'; more were planned for the new towns. By the end of 1977, there were 87 police reporting centres and plans for another 50; by 1978 the number had grown to 106.[64]

The immediate legacy of the anti-crime campaigns was two-fold. They made law and order 'Hong Kong's No 1 internal problem', legitimising a massive increase in policing, and they co-opted the public in the fight against crime. The police–public partnership became the dominant motif of policing:

> While it is to members of the Force that the primary role of enforcing the law on behalf of the community falls, this does not obviate the

> responsibility of each citizen to play an active part. Indeed, the crime battle can be won only if it is fought on the broadest possible community front so that criminals have to fear not only 'the man in uniform' but the mass of our law-abiding citizens. This ground-swell of public response is something that is relatively new to Hong Kong. It began to gain momentum with the 1973 Fight Violent Crime Campaign and has been growing steadily ever since.[65]

By 1976, not only was the chair of the government's Fight Crime Committee the Secretary for Home Affairs, but another 17 District Fight Crime Committees had been formed, and there were more than 1,200 Mutual Aid Committees with responsibility for assisting the police.[66]

Like the Fight Crime campaigns themselves, community relations and the enlistment of the public were to remain part of Hong Kong policing into the next century. The JPC stayed active, and by 1979, its membership was almost a quarter of a million. This began to decline as the youth who had joined in the 1970s grew older and fewer young people joined, but nevertheless, it stayed part of the fabric of Hong Kong society. The Police Cadet School had its best ever recruitment in 1979. Other measures – such as the Police Call television programme, the Good Citizen Awards, the police hotlines and the 'Help the Police Competition' (begun in 1975 and said to have attracted over 600,000 young people by 1978) also remained an established part of Hong Kong life. A new docu-drama about the police, started in 1979, attracted more than two million viewers and maintained popular billing for the next two decades (see the discussion of these points in previous chapters). The police force now had at least 35 minutes' television and three hours' radio time per week, not counting the Public Service Announcement slots carrying paternalistic messages from government to the people, a routine feature of Hong Kong life.

By the end of the decade, the annual fight crime campaigns and public mobilisation in the 'war of crime' had become a familiar part of the criminal justice landscape. Equally familiar were the regular 'Keep Hong Kong Clean' campaigns, the Miss Hong Kong contests and all the other public spectacles generated by the MacLehose regime. In 1971, the GIS had coined the phrase 'Hong Kong people'; by 1979, it meant something. The economy was booming, there were more leisure facilities, more shopping malls, and a sense that Hong Kong was developing a distinctive identity through its music and culture. A revamped Police Public Relations Bureau was now expanded to become the Police Public Relations Wing, headed by a Chief Superintendent. Its staffing was increased from 36 to 71, two of whom were seconded from the Government Information Service (GIS). The Community Relations Bureau was tasked with consolidating the success of the decade by continuing to motivate the public to co-operate with the police. To this end, it produced a flurry of audio and visual aids, leaflets, television programmes, and exhibitions, organised the JPC, the Young Person's Help the Police Competition, the Neighbourhood Police scheme, the Good Citizen's Award Scheme, the *Police Report* television programme, the PCROs, and the anti-crime campaigns.[67] A public survey in 1977 had discovered that victims of crime were dissatisfied with the level of courtesy they received from police officers, and in 1978 the Force began seminars for all officers stressing courtesy in their dealings with the public. An annual award was created for courteous officers.

In the wake of the 1977 protests by police, the need to keep the police loyal also translated into better provision of police welfare and recreational services, and more consultation between the rank and file and the police hierarchy. However, a visit by Home Office Advisers in 1978 concluded that the force's preoccupation with the fight against crime, and its rapid expansion and redeployment to combat crime, had resulted in 'imbalances'. It produced some 'fresh ideas' for the further updating, reorganisation and consolidation of the police force, including a re-examination of Neighbourhood Policing. There was also felt to be a need for better intelligence about crime (particularly about triads). This drove future collection and collation of information by police and other disciplined services. More use was also to be made of science, technology and research. All the major CID squads had been revamped – in 1977 the Homicide Squad became the Homicide Bureau, headed by a Senior Superintendent and with 120 staff; in 1978, the Triad Society Bureau became the Triad Society Division of the Organised Crime Bureau; in 1977 an expanded Criminal Intelligence Bureau replaced the Criminal Intelligence Unit to provide information and intelligence to the rest of the force; in 1979/80 the Commercial Crime Bureau was also strengthened, growing to 124 officers.[68]

Immigration

With the end of 1979, the 'crime problem' seemed to be under control. However, new problems presented themselves. The situation in Vietnam drove large numbers of migrants to seek refuge elsewhere, including Hong Kong. With the opening of the door to the West in China in 1978/9, Hong Kong also saw the highest number of illegal immigrants from China since 1974.[69] A change in policy also saw the arrival of many more migrants who were allowed to stay. In 1978, over 6,600 Vietnamese arrived by small fishing craft, some of whom had to be rescued at sea before their boats sank; in 1979 the trickle turned into a flood (the police described it as 'an armada'). Over 5,000 Vietnamese a month were arriving, mainly by boat. In May, 18,688 arrived; in June, another 19,651; by the end of the year, over 73,000 had landed. Those who wished to stay in Hong Kong under the 'touch base' policy were housed in temporary accommodation ranging from factories to old military camps. Two refugee camps were established in Sham Shui Po, one housing 9,000 and the other 7,000 people; three more were set up at Argyle

Street – one, run by the Housing Department, housed 10,000 people, the other two (run by the Prisons Department) housed 1,000 and 400 people (ibid).

Chinese illegal immigrants were also entering the territory in large numbers – nearly 2,000 in January, over 14,000 in May, 11,000 in October, and over 15,000 in December. Over 36,000 were thought to have crossed over the land border into Hong Kong in search of what, in China, were rumoured to be streets of gold. China's opening up in 1978 raised awareness on both sides of the border of the degree of poverty in the Mainland. Many of those now living in Hong Kong still had relatives there, mostly in Guangdong. Many were thus willing to assist illegal immigrants to evade detection. The total number of Chinese illegal immigrants (dubbed by the police and press, in a somewhat de-humanising fashion, as 'IIs') arrested during the year was almost 90,000, with a further 100,000 estimated to have evaded the authorities.[70]

The Hong Kong authorities clearly felt under siege: the Anti-Immigration Department of the police was supported by the military – the Hong Kong regiment was deployed, along with the Auxiliary Police; the Hong Kong garrison was strengthened by a battalion from the UK, two companies of Gurkhas, two Royal navy hovercrafts, a fast patrol boat and helicopters[71]. A new law was also introduced making it an offence for anyone to aid or abet illegal immigrants, and the border fence was reinforced (ibid).

The deployment of almost 2,000 police to the border area meant reduced coverage elsewhere. The year 1979 saw an upsurge in crime, particularly in violent crime such as robberies and burglaries; overall, violent crime rose by over 16 per cent.[72] The racketeers smuggling Vietnamese and Chinese into Hong Kong by boats (such as the 'Skyluck' and 'Heuy Fong') also posed a new kind of crime problem. The arrival of so many people was said to have stretched police resources, leaving them unable to combat crime effectively. Minor domestic disputes and assaults amongst the Vietnamese were also said to explain the rise in recorded crimes against the person. Illegal immigrants from China were blamed for the rise in petty crimes, such as pick pocketing and petty larceny. By the end of the 1970s and early 1980s, female illegal immigrants were being trafficked into Hong Kong by 'snakeheads' for work in the vice industry. Chinese organised crime syndicates were identified as the main smugglers of contraband goods across the border. The extent of illegal immigration and its connection with crime were themes that were to recur throughout the remaining decades of the twentieth century.

Crime reporting and the topography of crime

In 1979, Hong Kong's first crime survey cast doubt for the first time on the effectiveness of the police's campaign to get the public to report more crime. It revealed that, despite the rising crime figures of the 1970s, only one in five crimes was reported to the police. The *less* serious crimes (such as pick pocketing and household theft) occurred *more* frequently but were *less* well reported; serious crime was 'over-reported' by comparison. The 'Fight Crime Campaigns' of the 1970s had also fuelled the impression that Hong Kong was becoming a more violent place, but the survey demonstrated that official statistics were an unreliable guide to the level of crime in society. Its findings challenged some popular myths about crime, especially the stereotype of young offenders. Throughout the decade, Hong Kong's young men had been typified as violent offenders or potential offenders. However, the crime survey showed them to be the people *most* likely to fall victim to crimes of personal violence, and the *least* likely to report their victimisation to the police. Another widely held view was that both crimes against the person and against property had increased in the 1970s but, as Traver has shown, violent crime only ever accounted for between 19 and 25 per cent of all crime in Hong Kong over the 30 years up to 1990.[73]

Instead of averaging out the territory's experience of crime, the survey also provided greater insight into the experience of crime in different parts of Hong Kong. Since 'crime mapping' began in the late 1950s, the official figures had revealed different levels of recorded crime for different areas. Until the influx of refugees and illegal immigrants after 1978, most police attention still focused on Kowloon and Hong Kong Island. The Central district of Hong Kong Island was the colony's political and financial centre – LEGCO, the Supreme Court, the Stock Exchange, Consular offices and Embassies, company headquarters, shops, offices and hotels – all were concentrated in Central, making it a hot-spot for protests as well as crime. Much of the police activity here consisted of crackdowns on triads, vice and commercial crime. Towards the end of the 1970s, recorded crime rose in the area. Drug trafficking was said to occur on a small scale, except in Western, Chai Wan and Shau Kei Wan: a small number of prostitutes operated from old boarding houses along the waterfront and in Wanchai. In 1977, about half the population of Wanchai was under 25, many of the older residents having been relocated due to clearances. In 1976, the police decided to 'clean up' the area, declaring war of triads and vice, music halls, call girl centres, unlicensed massage parlours and triads (ibid). The crackdown spilled over into Causeway Bay and North Point, where more sex and illegal gambling establishments were closed down. The action against triads also took in Mongkok, where a number of triad-run vice establishments were raided, and Kwun Tong, where a number of extortion rackets and blackmail syndicates were targeted partly, the police argued, as a result of closer local contact between the police and a public more willing to report crime.

The general push to 'clean up' Hong Kong drove the police to continue this offensive against vice establishments, pornography and sex shows on a territory-wide basis. As before, however, a police crackdown on narcotics in 1979, coupled with a shortage of heroin (due to a poor crop in the Golden Triangle) pushed the price of heroin up on the street, sparking a 35 per cent rise in robberies as addicts stole to get money to buy drugs. Robberies rose from an average of 16 a day in 1978 to an average of 30 a day in mid-1979.[74] Most were 'quick cash' crimes, taking place on the streets, in lifts, corridors and staircases but, as the police realised, what captured the public interest was the spate of spectacular one-man bank robberies, described as a 'new phenomenon' in 1979 (ibid).

In 1976, the police began to break their figures down district by district. These showed that Kowloon still had the highest rates of recorded crime. Since most policing resources were also deployed in that area, this is perhaps unsurprising. Almost three million people lived in Kowloon alone (half of Hong Kong's population), mainly in densely packed housing blocks. Of the half a million people who lived in Kowloon City, almost a third lived in eight public housing estates. Mongkok housed almost 400,000 people to the square mile in 1976. Kowloon was also one of the main shopping and entertainment areas of the territory, attracting large numbers of tourists and pickpockets. It also had a high concentration of heroin divans, brothels and illegal gambling clubs, frequented by locals and tourists alike.[75] Following the new laws against illegal gambling in the mid-1970s, the area around Mongkok became associated with a number of 'social gambling' establishments where VIP rooms of restaurants were used for gambling by a 'known and exclusive clientele' who ostensibly paid only for the food.[76] Drug dealers and the organisers of gambling and prostitution became more mobile and more elusive with the advent of the electronic pager, which they could use to summons and disperse 'punters'.

Police figures for the late 1970s showed that Kowloon accounted for 65 per cent of all the colony's crime. The Walled City, that thorn in the side of the police and government, remained a 'source of entrenched dangerous drugs activity'.[77] The first crime survey in 1979 generally confirmed the status of Kowloon as the territory's crime 'hot spot'. Two-thirds of all victimisations did indeed occur in Kowloon. One-fifth occurred on Hong Kong Island, and the remainder in the NT.

In the NT, rising crime levels were also recorded in the late 1970s, around the fast-growing areas of Yuen Long, Tseun Wan and Kwai Cheung. By 1976, what had been a rural part of Hong Kong had become intensely urbanised by the construction of large new towns. Police contact with the public in these areas was seen as presenting more complex issues, as they had to liase not only with the urban population but also with rural committees, some on the outlying islands of Lantau and Cheung Chau. Unsurprisingly, recorded crime grew as fast as new police stations sprang up to serve these communities. Shatin, still a rural division in 1976, had a neighbourhood policing unit in one of the newest housing estates (Lek Yuen); plans were laid to open more as the town grew. A second tunnel through the Lion Rock in 1978, major road building, new rail links, the construction of Shatin Race Course and the gazetting of the country parks were all expected to bring more people into the area. But, for the moment, crime was mainly confined to robberies and assaults against holiday-makers in picnic areas. Tseun Wan, the oldest and most industrialised of the 'new' towns, captured more serious police attention owing to the number of triad societies operating there.

Elsewhere, large-scale clearances of squatters in areas such as Yuen Long, Kowloon Bay Temporary Housing Area, the Yuen Chau Tsai floating squatter area near Taipo, and Tuen Mun, were required to make way for new factories, roads, railways and housing. These operations were still occasions of potential confrontation. Unfortunately, they remain little documented. As in the 1960s, they still demanded the presence of the police – in 1979, for example, an attempt to clear squatters at On Lok Tsuen, Fanling in 1979 led to violent clashes. Over 150 people armed with bottles, axes and choppers confronted the police, forcing them to retreat. Tear gas was then fired into the area, 24 people were arrested and charged with unlawful assembly, assault on the police, resisting arrest, and possession of offensive weapons.[78] Scenes like this occurred all over Hong Kong in the course of its development. Clearance of a site at Sai Lau Kok, in Tsuen Wan, was resumed, for example, to make way for the Mass Transit Railway (MTR). The residents resisted, even sending a delegation to the UK Parliament in 1979. At a meeting in Hong Kong to discuss the dispute, a scuffle broke out, a crowd gathered, three police officers were slightly injured and two people were arrested. Another three incidents arose out of the same development. Such small-scale but violent resistance was seldom reported in the press and went undocumented by academia, thus preserving the idea of Hong Kong as a crime-free, politics-free city. Where they were reported, the protesters were accused of greed, but their demands for higher compensation were one of the very few means available for resisting a government policy backed by armed police and property developers. In the 1980s, the private developers involved in these large-scale infrastructure projects began to engage their own 'experts' to diffuse disputes with the indigenous people and squatters. What was once an issue of public governance now became a matter of project development.

By the late 1970s, there were more police on the streets than ever before. The ratio of police to population was one officer per 240 people, better than Tokyo (1:287) and London (1:282).[79] The force had expanded rapidly in the decade, from 12,800 in 1969/70 to 17,597 in 1977. By 1979, the force establishment stood at 20,894, with an additional 3,879 civilian staff and an auxiliary force of 5,000, making a total 29,773, one of the largest per capita forces in the world. Moreover, MACs, the watchmen, the ICAC and Customs and Excise (formerly the Preventive Service) were all now performing some sort of policing function. In addition, Hong Kong's large shopping malls, home to many chain stores, began to instruct their own store security officers to pursue a policy of prosecution in relation to shoplifting. Juveniles who, since the 1950s, had been associated with petty theft, were now arrested in increasing numbers for shop theft, a new category in the crime statistics. In 1978, juvenile crime stood at 190.3 per 100,000. This rose to 315.8 per 100,000 in 1979, and 477.7 per 100,000 in 1980 – statistics for 1980 revealed an astonishing increase of 46 per cent for juvenile crime. The number of juveniles brought to trial also rose from 3,540 in 1975 to 5,110 in 1977, prompting the Governor to make juvenile crime an issue in his address to the Legislative Council in October 1980. It formed the object of a special study by the Fight Crime Committee. In the 1980s, it was juveniles who were to become Hong Kong's new 'folk devils'.

The wider legacy of the 1970s public mobilisation against crime was to turn the discontented people of 1966 and 1967 into active citizens. Within ten years, the wreckers had become society's protectors. Their status as citizens did not extend to electing their own rulers, but they could help defend their 'way of life' against crime.

The sheer reach of policing in all its forms makes it impossible to tell whether the recorded 'crime wave' of the 1970s represented a genuine rise in crime. It could all have been simply due to increased reporting and the expansion of new types of policing. Recorded crime is widely acknowledged to tell us more about police activity than the 'true' level of crime. Changes in police–public relations made it easier to report crime, there were more specialist detection agencies, and the annual large-scale, state-sponsored mobilisations of the community. Whether intended or not, the measures adopted by police and government in the 1970s wrought a tremendous transformation, turned disorder into order and, somehow, managed to persuade the public that they 'belonged' to Hong Kong.

Imprisonment

The 1970s also saw notable developments in the use of custody, some of which are discussed later. Immediately following the riots, large numbers of people were detained, mainly under the Emergency Regulations, which permitted detention for a year without trial and without reasons. Some had their periods in detention commuted by the Governor or by the Prisons Board of Review. Those processed by the criminal justice system were sentenced to much longer terms of imprisonment. A number were charged with serious offences, such as possession of offensive weapons, handling explosives, and conspiracy to cause an explosion; others were charged with relatively minor offences such as obstruction, various public order offences, or participating in an unlawful assembly. Many were in their mid-20s, but some were even younger – one group released from Chi Ma Wan in February 1971 included one inmate who had been 14 on admission and was now 17. Two others released in 1971 had been 15 on admission but were now 17.[80]

The Prisons Department had to draw up new guidelines for the processing of such large numbers of inmates. It meticulously weighed each person upon entry and exit so as to confound any allegations of mistreatment whilst in jail. On arrival at the Victoria Prison remand centre, each was medically examined for injuries and asked whether they had any complaints; any injuries were officially recorded and notified to senior officers. Referring to an inmate at Stanley, the prison doctor there noted, for example, that 'This young prisoner during his arrest in July 1967 was assaulted by the police and along with other injuries he sustained an injury to his right knee'.[81] Worsening pain made hospital treatment a necessity for this inmate, but the request was refused. The boy's father, who had written seeking permission to visit his son in the Queen Mary Hospital, was informed that the boy was not seriously ill and that there was no need for him to make a daily visit: 'Should you wish to pay him a visit, please apply to the Superintendent at Stanley in the normal way' (ibid). Numerous relatives did write to the Prisons Department requesting that their sons and daughters receive fair treatment; communist sympathisers also petitioned for the release of inmates.

Detailed returns were regularly compiled to keep check of the numbers of 'confrontation prisoners' still in detention, as well as those due to be released. 'Disturbance prisoners' were freed outside the Victoria Remand Centre in Old Bailey Street 'with a minimum of fuss and without prior notification to the prisoners' families'.[82] A number demanded the release of fellow 'disturbance prisoners' and announced they were to make a claim against the Hong Kong government for compensation for illegal detention.

Following the riots, the Red Cross representative in Hong Kong (Mr Hefti) was asked by Geneva to conduct more frequent visits to Hong Kong's prisons to monitor the detention of 'disturbance prisoners'. His reports provide some insight into the state of Hong Kong's prisons at the time. Tai Lam replaced Li Chi Kok as a women's prison in 1970. Built to accommodate 222 prisoners, its inmates in 1970 included five female 'disturbance prisoners' aged between 15 and 36 (one apparently complained that she could not obtain a copy of Mao's 'little red book' in jail). Different kinds of detainee wore different types of clothing, a practice that continues and that differentiates, for example, drug addicted inmates from 'ordinary' inmates. The prison was described as very up-to-date and modern. In common with other Hong Kong prisons, it provided dormitory-style accommodation rather than single cells; family visits were limited to a 30-minute visit once a month. Pregnant inmates or those with very young children were allowed to keep their children with them up to the age of three, accommodated in a 'well-run, well-equipped, and impressive nursery'.[83] Inmates who breached prison discipline could be held on a rice and water diet and placed in solitary confinement for up to 28 days. A Training Centre for younger prisoners occupied a separate block. Its regime provided half a day's schooling followed by half a day's vocational training in subjects such as hairdressing, day care and cookery.

As a maximum-security jail, Stanley prison had more than its fair share of 'disturbance prisoners', including longer-term inmates serving sentences up to 1977 and beyond. Visited by the Red Cross in 1970, it was found to be overcrowded, three inmates to a single cell, with no integral sanitation. Prisoners were generally locked up between 7 am and 7 pm though a period of exercise was allowed between 5 and 7 pm every day. Discipline was said to strict; those who offended against it could be placed on a rice and water diet for seven days and placed in solitary confinement[84] for up to 28 days. The close cropping of a prisoner's hair as a punishment was not permitted.

As in other prisons, defiant inmates at Stanley saw challenging prison discipline as a continuation of 'the struggle'. They chanted slogans and generally refused to abide by the rules. Crowds of communist sympathisers, gathered outside the prison, shouted to those inside not to co-operate inside the 'British black jail'. The result was a major fracas in November 1967, which led to questions being asked in the Houses of Parliament. There were also separate factions of 'leftist' prisoners in Stanley, said to be divided on ideology and prone to conduct periodic 'purges' and engage in inter-faction fights, as well as clashes with the prison staff. These continued to disrupt the regime for some time.

In response to a letter from Mrs Elsie Elliot in November 1972, the Prisons Department confirmed that there were only seven 'disturbance prisoners' left inside Stanley, the authorities in Britain having conceived the notion of granting remission to most of the 'disturbance prisoners' as a bargaining chip with which to persuade the Chinese government to release a British subject, Mr Johnston, from captivity in the PRC. But the government's retention of Regulation 31, which permitted detention without trial, provoked criticism from lawyers and academics alike. Regulation 31 was officially lifted in 1969, but it continued to be used into the early 1970s. It was eventually dropped, reportedly in return for China's release of a Reuters correspondent, Anthony Grey. Much damage had been done meantime, however, since the detention of people without trial, and the deportation of 'undesirables', were taken by the foreign media to confirm Hong Kong's post-1967 reputation as a repressive colonial state. Local critics also alleged that the police were abusing their powers of detention to stifle 'whisteblowers' who might lift the lid on police corruption.

A riot in Stanley prison in 1972 gave rise to an internal overhaul not only of training but also of the ways in which inmates were classified, and the way visits were organised. It is from this date that the 'modernisation' and professionalisation of the Prisons Department began. A shift in ethos was later signified by a change of name to the Correctional Services Department. As we shall see, this name-change signified a more profound shift in the processes by which the state sought to maintain social control in a period of wider hegemonic restructuring.

Notes

1 Chief Justice Speech, Opening of the Legal Year 1970.
2 *HK Star* 20 January 1973.
3 HK Yearbooks 1974 and 1975: 109; 110.
4 RHKPAR 1977: 24.
5 HK Yearbook 1971.
6 HK Yearbook 1971: 137.
7 RHKPAR 1973/4: 1.
8 HK Yearbook 1972: 110.
9 RHKPAR 1973/4: Appendix 10
10 HKPAR 1969/70: 19.
11 RHKPAR 1974/5: 1.
12 RHKPAR 1975/6: 16.
13 RHKPAR 1973/4: 4.
14 HK Yearbook 1975: 109.
15 RHKPAR 1973/4; 1974/5.
16 RHKPAR 1973/4: 1.
17 HK Yearbook 1974: 108.
18 RHKPAR 1973/4: Appendix 12.
19 HKPAR 1968/9: 6–7, 18.
20 RHKPAR 1976: 20.
21 HKPAR 1969/70.
22 HK Yearbook 1971: 138.
23 HKPAR 1968/9.
24 HK Yearbook 1974: 109.
25 RHKPAR 1975/5: 2.
26 RHKPAR 1977: 24.
27 RHKPAR 1977: 24.
28 HK Yearbook 1975: 109.
29 RHKPAR 1973/4: 26.
30 RHKPAR 1976.
31 RHKPAR 1976: 1.
32 RHKPAR 1976: 18.
33 RHKPAR 1976: 19.
34 RHKPAR 1979: 8.
35 RHKPAR 1979: 10.
36 HKPAR 1969/70: 1.
37 HK Yearbook 1974: 109.
38 RHKPAR 1974/5: 1.
39 HK Yearbook 1970: 138.
40 HKPAR 1968/9: 63.
41 HKPAR 1961/2: Table E.
42 HK Yearbook 1974: 109.
43 HKPAR 1968/9: 27.
44 HKPAR 1966/7: 2.
45 HK Yearbook 1977: 120.
46 RHKPAR 1977: 23.
47 RHKPAR 1977: 23.
48 RHKPAR 1974/5: 20.
49 RHKPAR 1976: 1.
50 RHKPAR 1973/4: 31.
51 RHKPAR 1974/5: 7.

52 RHKPAR 1976: 19.
53 RHKPAR 1974/5: 22.
54 HK Yearbook 1977: 121.
55 RHKPAR 1974/5: 22.
56 HK Yearbook 1974: 11.
57 RHKPAR 1973/4: 12.
58 HK Yearbook 1977: 119.
59 RHKPAR 1977: 20–21.
60 RHKPAR 1978.
61 HK Yearbook 1978: 119.
62 RHKPAR 1977: 5.
63 RHKPAR 1978: 1.
64 RHKPAR 1977: 18; 1978: 1.
65 RHKPAR 1976: 1.
66 RHKPAR 1976: 18.
67 RHKPAR 1978: 28.
68 RHKPAR 1980: 11.
69 RHKPAR 1978: 2.
70 RHKPAR 1979: 7.
71 RHKPAR 1979: 15.
72 RHKPAR 1979: 33.
73 See Traver 1991.
74 RHKPAR 1979: 8.
75 RHKPAR 1979: 33.
76 RHKPAR 1978: 39.
77 RHKPAR 1977: 39.
78 RHKPAR 1979: 14.
79 RHKPAR 1977: 7.
80 Chi Ma Wan was commended for its management and conditions of detention. It placed no restrictions on family visits, but its remote location made visiting problematic.
81 Memo Dr. Kit Thomas to Senior Superintendent, Stanley Prison 21 July 1969, PD59/401/71I.
82 Prisons Department memo 25 February 1971.
83 Hefti, Report of International Committee of the Red Cross, 21 October 1970.
84 The term 'separate confinement' is used in Hong Kong.

Chapter 21

The 1980s: crime, moral panics and 'ungovernability'

As Cohen writes, every now and then 'A condition, episode, person or group of persons emerges to become defined as a threat to societal values and interests; its nature is presented is a stylised and stereotypical fashion by the mass media' (Cohen 1972: 9). A number of studies relate the outbreak of such moral panics to the existence of widespread anxieties and people's 'experience of powerlessness, helplessness and social disintegration in the face of social change' (Hunt 1999: 510). Generalised anxiety becomes amplified so that it 'manifests itself in some sort of outburst or panic' (ibid) about the perceived turbulence of vagrants, the poor or the working class, youth, immigrants or other stigmatised groups (Hunt 1999: 511). Crime itself is talked of in terms of changing, disrupted or fragmented communities. A 'pre-existing golden age' or prior period of stability is often invoked as the backcloth to such anxieties.

All these features were readily present in the 1980s in Hong Kong. Coming on the heels of the MacLehose 'Golden Years', they provided the underpinnings for a moral panic about youth, about illegal immigration, about a territory that was becoming 'ungovernable' in the years between 1984 and 1997, when Hong Kong would be handed back to China. Between 1984 and 1997, the territory's criminal justice system operated under the influence of two major political forces, one encouraging the application of more liberal, democratic principles of justice, the other favouring a gradual but distinct drift in the direction of authoritarianism.

Reading the official accounts of Hong Kong in the 1980s, one could be forgiven for failing to realise that anything profound had occurred in that decade. The picture painted by reports of the various criminal justice agencies was, for example, one of ongoing stability, of a confident legal system handling familiar types of crime in its usual professional fashion. There was nothing here to provoke anxiety. It was all very soothing and reassuring.

This was as it was meant to be. A good deal of care went into constructing the official accounts. Behind the scenes, however, there was talk of Hong Kong becoming more politicised and, potentially, 'ungovernable'. This followed the announcement, in 1984, that China and Britain had signed the

Joint Declaration agreeing to hand Hong Kong back to the PRC in 1997. This was a momentous event. It triggered a new crisis of legitimacy for the colonial regime. In 1989 it was followed by another event of deep significance, the June 4th incident in Mainland cities, which saw the armed forces of the PRC mobilise against demonstrators all over China. Tiananmen brought together different strands of Hong Kong society into 'a relatively cohesive whole' (Thomas 1999: 205) reinforcing the sense of a common identity, 'linked by a common fate . . . [and] radically aided the formation of Hong Kong's political consciousness' (ibid). It also confirmed latent suspicions that the Beijing government could not be trusted to uphold Hong Kong's civil liberties after 1997, prompting demands for their deeper entrenchment before the handover.

The subject of Hong Kong's future was broached in 1979 by Sir Murray MacLehose on a visit to Beijing. Talks proper began in 1982 and the Joint Declaration was signed in September 1984. This announced that when the lease on the NT expired in 1997, Hong Kong would become a Special Administrative Region (SAR) of China 'enjoying a high degree of autonomy'. For 50 years, its present capitalist system would be preserved, along with its legal system.

As Scott notes, the negotiations had already triggered increased local political activity, 'a direct consequence of uncertainty about the future'; the publication of the agreement now 'accelerated the growth of political awareness' (Scott 1989: 9). Whilst both the British and Chinese sides assumed the decision to return Hong Kong to China would not meet with any local opposition, in fact it sparked a great deal of local disquiet as the negotiations 'brought home to Hong Kong people the fact their futures were being discussed by foreign governments who were reaching decisions on which the local population had very little say' (Scott 1989: 17).

The announcement of the decision and the arbitrary manner in which it was imposed added fuel to the fire. Many, having fled Communism in 1949, feared direct rule by Beijing; others worried that if civil liberties were not entrenched in the law before 1997, they would be lost. People were presented with no choice at all about whether to accept the agreement. The only choice they had was whether they would choose to live under the rule 'of a new suzerain power' (Scott 1989: 219). However, leaving was not an option for those who lacked the resources to relocate to another country.

The period after 1984 was thus beset by general anxieties and uncertainties about the end of Hong Kong's present 'life-style'.[1] Mrs Thatcher, as Britain's signatory to the Joint Declaration, was openly criticised for 'selling Hong Kong down the river', reflecting a deeper sense that Britain had reneged on its obligations towards Hong Kong and its people.

Following the Joint Declaration, in November 1984 the government produced a White Paper on the development of representative government in the territory.[2] This was welcomed by liberal groups as a step in the right direction, but opposed by China-aligned conservatives, who saw it as a plot to retain British influence in Hong Kong after 1997 (Thomas 1999: 160).

The ensuing debate highlighted the fact that a new element had come into play in Hong Kong politics and society. The year 1997 meant 'convergence' with China. It also meant the intervention of China in Hong Kong affairs during the transition years, undermining the authority of the colonial regime since, whatever steps it took, nothing could be done if China objected.

Paradoxically for a country wishing to contain political expression, China's openly negative response to proposals for more representative government immediately accelerated the politicisation of Hong Kong (Thomas 1999: 163). New political parties were founded and public issues were 'debated intensely', mostly outside LEGCO (Scott 1989: 29). Controversy was also aroused by the composition of the Basic Law Drafting Committee (BLDC), established to draft the law that would, in effect, become the territory's 'mini-constitution' after 1997. The committee was weighted in favour of Mainland participants (36) whilst its Hong Kong members (23) mainly represented the territory's business and commercial interests (a group which, in the nineteenth century, the Colonial Office had deemed unlikely to rule Hong Kong in the best interests of all its inhabitants). The majority of members on both sides opposed the introduction of democracy; none wished to 'risk disruption to the present quiescent consensus or administrative climate' (Thomas 1999: 185).

The law that the BLDC began to draft in 1985 promised to preserve Hong Kong's economy and 'lifestyle'. It construed this as consisting of predominantly of shopping, eating and gambling on the horses. There was no vision of Hong Kongers as a political people. The handover was to proceed in a smooth, gradual and prudent fashion and the BLDC, in keeping with the stability imperative, drafted a conservative blueprint for Hong Kong's future (Scott 1989: 205).

As King says, the process of drafting the Basic Law itself 'could hardly be said to have helped China win the hearts and minds of the majority of the Hong Kong people' (King 1995: 115). The support of Hong Kongers for the Tiananmen protestors in 1989 prompted the BLDC to rewrite the first draft of the Basic Law to include Article 23, requiring the post-1997 administration to implement anti-subversion laws prohibiting sedition, subversion or acts of treason against the PRC (Wu 1996: 206). This conservative backlash by the Chinese side prompted the resignation of one BLDC member and the expulsion of two other pro-democracy members. After 1989, pro-democracy politicians were blacklisted as criminals by the PRC and denied the right to cross into Mainland China.

Between 1984 and 1989, the debate about Hong Kong's future sustained the process of politicisation. In 1986, over a million people signed a petition and participated in mass rallies protesting against the building of the Daya Bay nuclear power station in China, close to Hong Kong (ibid). In 1987, controversy and demonstrations were triggered by a proposed amendment to the 1967 Public Order Ordinance. This would make it an offence to publish 'false news likely to cause public alarm or disturb public order', and was widely seen as a threat to the freedom of the press and an attempt to restrict the mass media (Thomas 1999: 172). Reversing the presumption of innocence, the amended ordinance placed the burden of proof on the publisher rather than the plaintiff (ibid). As Thomas argues:

> Despite the fact that this section was repealed a year later, not only did the ordinance still contain restrictions on civil liberties, but given the government's willingness to pass the legislation in the face of the large-scale public demonstrations that took place, it appeared that the pace of . . . liberalisation had slowed down and had been replaced by the Chinese policy of convergence (Thomas 1999: 172).

'Convergence' also implied a move towards a more authoritarian regime, rather than the preservation of a liberal way of life promised by Deng Xiaoping's 'one country, two systems' formula. Before 4 June 1989, polls in Hong Kong already indicated that 55 per cent of the population did not believe China would keep to the 'one country, two systems' model after 1997; this rose to over 70 per cent four months after Tiananmen and provoked a crisis of confidence in Hong Kong (ibid). Whilst some British officials favoured a faster rate of democratisation to offset growing fears about 1997, the Chinese leadership saw democratisation as detrimental to stability and prosperity (ibid). One pro-China member of the BLDC described the reaction of Hong Kong people as 'quite natural and admirable but [also] an emotive response which did not take account of the consequences . . . the masses are always naïve and often behave just like children; they do not think sensibly or rationally.'[3] But, King argued:

> Hong Kong is no longer a purely economic city. It has become a city baptized by ever-growing politicisation. The demand for democracy can no longer be easily confined, let alone ignored. Indeed, it can well be argued that, if Hong Kong is to enjoy its stability, democratisation of the system is no longer a luxury but is now a necessity. It is no exaggeration to say that the governability of the sunset colonial government may become questionable during its remaining years if the demand for direct elections for LEGCO is totally unaccommodated (King 1995: 117).

The prospect of Hong Kong becoming 'ungovernable' in the twilight years of colonial rule permeated official thinking in the 1980s. Officials were alert for any sign of 'ungovernability', including crime. In this climate it would have been remarkable if the authorities had not let it be known to the police force that it was expected to do its bit to keep Hong Kong stable. Both the

Chinese and British administrations wanted the period of transition to be marked by smoothness, prudence, caution, firmness and co-operation. The determinedly 'factual' official accounts of crime and criminal justice in these years contributed to this impression. Given their place in the machinery of government, it is understandable that the police saw it as no part of their remit to place the facts and figures of crime and criminal justice in a socio-political context. Like other state agencies, they framed their reports in terms of their own priorities. As a consequence, they gave an anodyne account of the era. Like the government's own annual reports, they carried on depicting Hong Kong as if nothing had happened, describing it as an economically vibrant and stable place, proceeding smoothly through the years. Maintaining public confidence required that there were to be no alarmist reports of rising crime – indeed, official records of crime would chart a remarkable fall in crime in the handover years.

Juvenile delinquency

Three main themes emerged in talk about crime in the 1980s. The first was that the impending handover would spark a rash of 'get rich quick' crimes as criminals sought to make money and flee before 1997. The second was that Hong Kong would be struck by a rash of crimes committed by illegal immigrants, flocking from Mainland China to Hong Kong's 'streets of gold'. The third (and the one that was to define criminology for years to come) was the problem of juvenile delinquency.

With the exception of Lethbridge's study of corruption in 1985, the key criminological writings of the era dwelt on the 'problem of youth'. Since the 1960s, of course, juveniles and young people had become associated with political activism, a worrying predisposition for a government concerned to play down controversy during the transition. Throughout the 1980s, youth participation in the various protests which marked the decade (culminating in their support for the Tiananmen protestors) underlined their potential as a destabilising force. As two students of the time observed:

> Politics was quite a taboo subject in schools, never really discussed by anyone. That all changed in 1989 . . . Tiananmen and the suppression of the student movement had an enormous impact on the whole school. None of my classmates nor I attended our lessons. We spent the whole day discussing democracy, what it was all about and what it meant. It was really the first time I had thought about it . . . At home too . . . the whole family was glued to the television to find out the latest news from Beijing.[4]
>
> I spent all of the evening of 3 June watching television with my family. We all saw the flares go out and all of Tiananmen Square was very dark with nobody making a noise. We were just lost for words and I think all

> of us were stunned. At the time my feeling was that we were doomed. Although I was only a secondary school student, I had an affinity with those university students in Beijing . . . I did not believe that the Chinese government would use the army or heavy weapons to attack them. I wondered what hope there was for us if Hong Kong was to be ruled by such people. Like many other Hong Kong people, I went with some friends to protest on the streets. It was very moving.[5]

After 1984 – and especially after 1989 – the incorporation of young people as citizens became a priority for government. Youth were to be persuaded to identify with China, with ideas of nationalism and concepts of the ideal citizen (Lam 2005). This was limited, Lam argues, to 'renationalisation' and the promotion of citizens' ethnic nationalism and a sense of belonging to China, rather than 'an all-round political consciousness and activism' (ibid). Civic education stressed the 'Asian values' of neo-Confucianism. This emphasised deference, harmony, avoidance of conflict, family, filial piety, patriotism, co-operation, collective responsibility and self-reliance (ibid). The unemployed and others living in the margins were 'losers' whose individual failings explained their failure and their delinquency (ibid).

Given youth's track record in political mobilisation, it is perhaps unsurprising that they should have become such a focus of official efforts at discipline. As Hong Kong's economic restructuring got underway in the 1980s, it was also becoming clear that youth unemployment was growing. Since China's opening up in 1978, Hong Kong firms had taken advantage of cheap labour on – and from – the Mainland. Many workers in Hong Kong manufacturing were made redundant. This especially hit young, unskilled workers whose lack of educational qualifications made it difficult for them to seek work in the restructured job market. Hong Kong was able to reinvent itself as an international financial centre, but the skills required to participate in this new economy left many on the margins. Criminology did not, however, discuss crime in socio-economic or political terms. Instead, it stuck to a decidedly administrative perspective on the crime issues of the decade.

Public order

For Lam, the anti-government sentiments that had bubbled beneath the surface during the 1970s lingered into the 1980s: 'flourishing citizens' movements involving students, professionals, workers and consumers engaged in a variety of formal and informal political activities' (Lam 2004: 233). From the start there were public order disturbances that officialdom (and academia) played down.[6] Early on Christmas Day, 1981, for example, trouble broke out in Central and Wanchai. A crowd of between nine and ten thousand had gathered to watch the Christmas lights. Public transport had not been extended to take them home. A minor road accident late on Christmas

Eve, in which a car driver accidentally hit a pedestrian, led to an argument and a scuffle. The driver was beaten up; others began a riot (Lam 2005). Eleven were injured, seven cars damaged and 18 people arrested, mostly young people. According to the police report, gangs of youths went on the rampage, vehicles, road signs and bollards were damaged, and rubbish bins upset – but 'order was quickly restored' and 'small groups of irresponsible young men' were blamed for behaving in a 'boisterous and lawless manner'.[7] The number of policemen patrolling major business areas was increased and cars kept away from the Central District.[8] Eye-witnesses reported a degree of anti-British feeling. The police were detailed to usher Europeans off the streets, into the Hilton Hotel or the bars of Wanchai, or back to their homes. Another disturbance briefly broke out a few days later on New Year's Eve when two expatriate youths upset passers-by by dancing in the street, 'provoking hostility from the crowds that were celebrating' (ibid). Neither incident received much attention but it seems clear that the authorities sensed that minor grievances could turn quickly into something far more serious.

Like the 1981 disturbances, the 'Taxi Riots' of January 1984 were dismissed as sociologically insignificant. As Lam says, the narrative of Hong Kong people as socially and politically apathetic self-seekers after wealth has become very pervasive, not only in official discourse but also in academia (Lam 2005). Like the riots of 1981, the Taxi Driver riots were thus confined to the waste bin of history, dismissed as insignificant blips of no political or sociological importance.

The riots comprised two days of demonstrations by the taxi drivers, culminating in rioting on 13 January, when a crowd (estimated at 5,000 by the police) marched along Nathan Road smashing, looting and damaging property. The PTU took four hours to restore order. Unlike the 1960s, local people could watch live broadcasts of the events on commercial television. Tear gas was used to disperse the rioters and 178 people were arrested.[9]

The 1980s also witnessed numerous small-scale clashes between police and public as more villages and squatters were cleared to make way for infrastructure developments, such as the Mass Transit Railway (MTR) and private property developments. Clearing Hong Kong's nuisance people (squatters and hawkers) had been a police role since the nineteenth century. In the 1980s, the police assisted with Housing Department clearances of squatters from land in Kwun Tong, and houses at Tseun Wan and Tai Wo Ping. Reports maintain official quiescence on the subject, saying simply that the police 'overcame resistance'.[10] In 1983, however, in an episode typical of these undocumented clashes, the PTU and construction workers came under attack by people resisting the clearance of illegal structures in Hang On Street, Ngau Tau Kok; 20 people were charged with rioting and unlawful assembly.[11] In 1984, occupants of Lung Kwong Road, Kowloon City, attacked police with steel rods, sticks and hot water when they tried to clear illegal structures in the area – the police responded using batons, rattan shields and chemical mace.[12] The police also met serious resistance when they tried to enforce other unpopular policies (such as crackdowns on hawkers) or make unpopular arrests. On several occasions in the early 1980s, they found themselves surrounded by hostile crowds (some up to 200-strong), throwing stones.

In keeping with the dominant discourse of economism, the official interpretation of the conflicts blamed greedy people for seeking higher levels of compensation for their land and homes than the authorities were willing to pay. Such interpretations decontextualised resistance, riots and disturbances, which, although brief and sporadic, reflected a wider sense of powerlessness. They marked the anxieties of a politically and economically fraught time. The 1984 riots broke out, for example, shortly after the breakdown of Sino–British talks, which had already sparked the panic buying of rice across the territory. A major public rally of 1983 had also previously protested against price rises. Crises of confidence in the territory's future produced repeated falls in the Hang Seng Index, regarded as the barometer of local feeling (Blyth and Wotherspoon 1996: 185). The 1984 riots came close on the heels of an economic slump that had bankrupted some institutions, produced a decline in that bellwether of Hong Kong society, the property market, and led to the spectacular fall of the Carrian Group.[13] Like the 1966 riots, which had ostensibly centred on a trivial 5-cent rise in the first-class ferry fare, the minor disturbances of the 1980s momentarily expressed the frustrations of a people powerless to affect government policy.

Political policing

Earlier government policy, formed in the Cold War, held that politically partisan groups were free to organise and protest so long as they did not break the law of Hong Kong. In the potentially controversial debates over the future of Hong Kong, this approach allowed the government itself to appear as a politically neutral arbiter applying the rule of law equally to all. But fears that Hong Kong might become 'ungovernable' meant the continued deployment of Special Branch in the background. One group to fall under its surveillance was a set of young well-educated, middle-class Chinese, the Hong Kong Observers.[14] Founded in 1975, the group published articles criticising the government and position papers on a number of social and political issues, such as the need for greater political accountability and the establishment of an Ombudsman system. In November 1983, they called for people to express their opinions on what they would like to see in the future constitution, and in December sent a delegation to Beijing (Scott 1989: 209). Scott lists a number of other pressure groups that were also active, including the group Meeting Point, concerned about the territory's lack of democracy (ibid). According to Walden, such pressure groups:

> . . . were carefully monitored by the Government and the Special Branch of the HK Police, and where possible their activities were discreetly obstructed or frustrated, sometimes by the use of highly questionable tactics. This deliberate and active discouragement of the growth of the democratic processes by the Government continued right up to 1980 to my certain knowledge.[15]

Purporting to welcome constructive criticism from pressure groups, the government quietly did 'everything it could behind the scenes to immobilise them [either by] fraternisation and reasoning to win them over to the official point of view'; or by absorption; or if that did not succeed, by 'damaging their credibility' (ibid).

Localisation?

The push to localise criminal justice agencies before 1997 was to prove another potentially destabilising force, especially given the colonial regime's traditional distrust of the local population. China's resumption of sovereignty in 1997 should have heralded a drive towards greater localisation. Officially, 1997 would see 'Hong Kong people running Hong Kong'. Ostensibly, the British had been pursuing such a policy since the war, but there were few signs of it amongst the police or judiciary, still largely expatriate, especially at the senior levels. The situation in the disciplined services was apparently at odds with that in the civil service generally – 98 per cent of Hong Kong's population was Chinese and by the mid-1980s, this was reflected in civil service appointments at all levels.

Following the Joint Declaration, the police announced plans to increase the localisation of the force. However, in keeping with the official preference for continuity and a 'smooth transition', at the same time they argued that it was important not to make any sudden changes to the command structure at a time when Hong Kong required stability.[16] Though some 'training for leadership' was introduced locally, in practice a considerable number of expatriates were still being recruited. The Home Office review of the police in 1979 had generated more emphasis on localisation, and management and leadership skills as part of inspectorate training. The first CID training course for uniform branch inspectors with CID potential began in June 1980. It was not, however, until 1989 that the police had their first local Commissioner (Li Kwan-ha) and it was not until the mid-1990s that any government department or criminal justice agency began to consider how the legal system of China differed from their own, or to encourage the learning of Putonghua.

This failure to speed up localisation after 1984 may be read as an attempt to maintain continuity and avoid radical changes, but it also indicated a remarkable degree of complacency. As 1997 grew closer, the police force reiterated the view that it 'is even more imperative than before that the Force helps maintain a stable, tranquil, and secure territory'.[17] Clearly, it saw itself as being in the vanguard of the transition, safeguarding stability as its priority. In the years up to 1989, it did little to embrace 'convergence' with China – its officers knew little of the PRC's criminal justice system and had few contacts with the Public Security Bureau. After 1989, when stability came to be seen more in terms of pacifying popular calls for democracy, the police were forced to embrace a Bill of Rights, which sat uneasily with their traditional crime-control view of policing.

The judiciary was equally slow to localise. Majorie Chui, the first Chinese female magistrate in Hong Kong,[18] notes that large numbers of senior judicial posts were still filled mainly by expatriates (Chui 1999). Instead of grooming locals in time for the return of Hong Kong to China, expatriates held over 90 per cent of the higher judicial postings. Many locals felt, she says, that expatriates were making the most of the colony before the hand-over to China (ibid). The extension of the Chief Justice's retirement age, as well as that of his High Court judges and Supreme Court registrars, also thwarted the rise of local candidates and perpetuated the careers of expatriate judges at the expense of locals (ibid). The Chief Justice stated publicly that maintaining a substantial expatriate element in the judiciary was essential to the preservation of confidence in Hong Kong's system but, Chui says, patronage of expatriates was pervasive and 'It was not difficult to see that those who had a particular connection with or friendship with important people rose quickly up the judicial ladder . . . connections mattered more than personal integrity'.[19] At one point, five expatriates were promoted to fill all five senior judicial vacancies (what Chui calls 'five devils knocking on the door'). Nine expatriates were promoted to fill another nine judicial vacancies ('nine big devils having a feast'). As Chui notes, 'the clearest indictment of the appointments in this period is the fact that at the handover 13 years after the signing of the Sino–British Joint Declaration, the Judiciary was still dominated by expatriates'.[20]

Chui also records her doubts about the independence of the magistracy during the transition years. On her appointment, she held the 'naïve belief that I would be expected to administer justice fairly and independently at all times, without fear or favour'. But magistrates were appointed on contract terms and, when several failed to be reappointed, rumours abounded that they had been penalised for delivering judgments unfavourable to the administration. She also criticises Sir Denys Roberts, appointed in 1979 as Chief Justice having just retired as Chief Secretary, the head of the colonial civil service. Second in command after the Governor, he had acted as Governor from time to time, and had served as Attorney General. He had, therefore:

> . . . been a key official behind many of the government's policies. For that reason, his move to the Judiciary aroused much controversy, as it was

> seen to blunt the separation of power between the Judiciary and the Executive branch of government. In particular, there was concern over Sir Denys' previous posting as AG, in effect the head of the Crown's prosecution service, and the effect that might have on his policies as head of the Judiciary. It was amidst these fears over the continued independence of the Judiciary that Sir Denys became Chief Justice.[21]

Part of the value of Chui's observations lies in their rarity as a counter to the official story of Hong Kong as a stable society of the rule of law, a meritocratic society of happy citizens content to be governed by a benign colonial administration. Clearly, discontents simmered beneath the surface, depressed by the official emphasis on stability that characterised the period. There were, however, a number of potentially destabilising factors at work, one of which was immigration.

Illegal immigration and the Vietnamese refugees

In the 1980s, the agents of law and order were to become preoccupied with a vast influx of Vietnamese refugees and Chinese illegal immigrants. It is ironic that, whilst Hong Kong people were themselves 'anxious to obtain some form of security should they become political refugees after 1997', in the late 1980s they campaigned to refuse asylum to Vietnamese boat people fleeing Communist Vietnam (Blyth and Wotherspoon 1996: 172). Large numbers arrived in Hong Kong in the 1980s, pushed by geopolitical forces in Vietnam and the prospect of a better life in Hong Kong. Though most were not criminals, the criminal justice agencies were charged with their detection and detention.

At the end of 1979, the 'touch base' policy that allowed many migrants to land in Hong Kong legally was cancelled in the hope that this would deter future arrivals. It had some effect on the Vietnamese, whose numbers dropped from over 70,000 arrivals in 1979 to 8,428 in 1980; another 37,468 left for overseas resettlement, leaving about 24,000 in detention camps.[22] In 1981, another 11,886 arrived, and 17,818 departed, reducing the numbers left in Hong Kong to about 16,000. Others, who had originally settled in China but had later fled to Hong Kong via Macau (Ex-China Vietnamese Illegal immigrants or ECVIIs), were repatriated.

Two different policies were applied to these groups. 'Genuine' refugees were defined under international law as those with a 'well-founded fear of persecution' in their home country. They were eligible to apply for refugee status and resettlement in a third country. The ECVIIs, on the other hand, were repatriated to China, a policy that was subject to legal challenge throughout the next two decades.

By 1983, Hong Kong had the highest population of Vietnamese 'boat people' in the region, accommodated in both open and 'closed' camps.[23]

Amenities in most of the camps were basic; the dormitory-style accommodation was overcrowded; women – especially single women – faced sexual harassment, and young men formed themselves into opposing gangs. A number of children (some 600 were born in the camps in 1988) were to spend their early lives locked inside compounds. As detainees were not criminals, it was unclear what kind of regime should apply to them, or who was to pay for it. As in the past, the government relied heavily on voluntary agencies for help, and much of the welfare, education and health care were provided by non-governmental agencies and the UNHCR.

By the mid-1980s, the government was justifiably arguing that its resources were being stretched – the failure of partner countries to live up to their promise to accept refugees, and contribute to the costs of supporting them, meant that the burden was falling on the Hong Kong administration. It, in turn, needed a 'solution to the influx'.[24] In 1988, a new distinction thus emerged that discriminated between genuine Vietnamese refugees and Vietnamese 'economic migrants'. A process of screening was established, and new arrivals were told that they could stay and be screened, or sail on to another destination. Applicants for refugee status were interrogated to establish whether they had a 'well founded fear' of persecution. Those who were 'screened in' were entitled to await resettlement in a third country; those who were 'screened out' (now defined as Vietnamese Illegal Immigrants or 'economic migrants') were held in detention camps pending repatriation.

By 1988, the drawbridge was being pulled up. Of the Vietnamese, only those who 'deserved' to stay were allowed to remain awaiting resettlement in another country; the 'undeserving' remainder were held in closed camps awaiting repatriation. Those granted refugee status were held under a more 'liberal' regime in open camps run by the UNHCR.[25] For the time being they were acknowledged as temporary 'citizens', free to find work outside the camps; their movement in and out of the colony (to visit nearby Macau for the day, for example) was, however, prohibited.

By the end of 1989, Hong Kong housed over 56,000 Vietnamese. Over 8,000 of these were held in open camps staffed by the UNHCR; the rest were held in closed camps run by the police, the CSD and the Housing Authority. Law, order and containment dominated the running of these camps. Rival factions of Vietnamese engaged in occasionally violent conflicts; guards were vigilant for 'home-made' weapons and alcohol, as well extortion rackets. As police reports of the time laconically commented, the 'problems' were expected to remain for some time to come.

At the frontier, police faced another group of illegal immigrants, this time from Mainland China. The PRC's own programme of economic modernisation had produced mass internal migration from poor rural areas into the cities, supplying the demand for cheap labour.[26] Individually or collectively, these migrants found ways of entering Hong Kong. If caught, they were criminalised, repatriated, or sent to prison.

The irony of Hong Kong's stern policy on this kind of illegal immigration was that the vast majority of its existing population had entered the colony as 'economic migrants' in the 1950s and 1960s, when they too had fled poverty and turmoil in China. Police decisions about such immigration matters were shaped by policy-making at a higher level.[27] Until the border was established in 1949, people had been travelling to and from mainland China for hundreds of years; throughout the Cold War, Mainland migrants (such as children visiting relatives in their school holidays) had been allowed to cross the border at regular intervals; many never returned to China. In the late 1970s, changes in economic circumstances, as well as domestic and foreign policy considerations, had altered criminal law and criminal justice policies. A new Hong Kong identity card was introduced, enabling the police to stop and identify illegal immigrants. The new policy, introduced in October 1980, made it mandatory for anyone over 15 to carry an ID card or other form of identification at all times.[28] In 1981, the numbers of illegal immigrants arrested subsequently fell to 7,531, but the ID law led to the emergence of new criminal syndicates, engaged in smuggling illegal immigrants into Hong Kong, selling forged ID cards, and 'ferrying young children from China to join relatives here'.[29]

In October 1980 alone, the police arrested over 70,000 Chinese illegal immigrants; another 67,000 were said to have evaded detection and settled in Hong Kong. Seven were found suffocated inside freight trucks; some died jumping off trains; others were arrested at Hung Hom, the terminus of the Kowloon-Canton Railway (KCRC). Those arrested at the frontier were held in the San Uk Ling detention centre, then repatriated to China over the bridge at Man Kam To.[30] Police and security forces were stretched, with over 1,000 land and marine police, and a similar number of military personnel, posted daily to anti-illegal immigrant duties along the frontier. Joint police/military operations were organised by regional centres (PolMils); joint police/navy operations were co-ordinated by a regional PolNav based at marine police regional headquarters; this was also linked with Immigration and Customs and Excise. These operations occupied police throughout the decade, as numbers attempting to enter Hong Kong illegally waxed and waned. Policing the landings of small craft under cover of darkness gave rise to what was to become a regular feature of the night sky – the spotlight of police helicopters slowly traversing the waters of Hong Kong's shorelines, looking for small boats discharging their cargo of illegal immigrants.

In the early 1980s, the border fence was reinforced and floodlit; 28 observation posts were built along its length, enabling the security forces to spot illegal immigrants trying to cross from China. Once the 'touch base' policy was cancelled, the police formed road-blocks and Action Squads 'to flush out' illegal immigrants who had evaded the border guards. The year 1984 saw a dramatic 107 per cent increase in numbers of Chinese illegal immigrants, the result of false rumours that the Sino–British Declaration was to usher in an amnesty for illegal immigrants already in Hong Kong. The highest ever number since the cancellation of the 'touch base' policy arrived in 1986, when over 16,000 Chinese illegal immigrants attempted to enter; the number of children smuggled into the territory to join relatives also increased, but the cancellation of the 'touch base' policy for minors drastically reduced their numbers the following year.[31] In 1987, the overall number rose again – 33 per cent more 'evaders' were arrested, making a total of 22,425 by the end of the year.

Those who escaped detection worked illegally in Hong Kong. Some were arrested when they became involved in crime (about 30.9 per cent in the 1980s). Others were picked up by routine police checks of ID cards, the possession of a fake or illegal ID card being an easy crime to prove and process.[32] The unemployed, illegal immigrants, and other marginal groups whose daily routine involved hanging around the streets were, as in the previous century, more susceptible to policing and criminalisation.

The presence of Chinese illegal immigrants in the crime figures was taken as proof that they were more 'criminogenic' than other sections of society. They became a group especially associated in the public mind with crime, particularly violent crime. By the end of the decade, Chinese illegal immigrants had joined juveniles as Hong Kong's new 'folk devils'. Popular stereotypes painted them as ill educated, backward, uncouth and badly dressed (a clear status marker in a Hong Kong obsessed with fashion and designer labels). They were violent, immoral, strangers who crept over the border at dead of night, raided people in their own homes, tied them up and robbed them, before disappearing into the crowds.

These stereotypes echoed others, formulated in an earlier period, when the British colonial elite was still uncertain of its authority in nineteenth-century Hong Kong. As studies of that period indicate, however, the stereotype had only a limited basis in reality. Those who arrived in Hong Kong with contacts (family or clan members, for example) could look to them for support during the first weeks or months. As in this past, this helped minimise the negative consequences of migration and assisted social stability.[33] Those who did become involved in crime were readily identified and quickly fell within the criminal justice net. In 1980s Hong Kong, as in the past, the dominant view was that illegal immigrants were disproportionately involved in crime.[34] As victims of crime,[35] however, their victimisation went unnoticed in the official crime statistics. Because of their illegal status, they were also less likely to report their situation to the authorities.[36]

Crime and its distribution

The first year of the 1980s saw a rise in overall recorded crime, but also a notable rise in recorded serious and violent crime, as well as the number of juveniles arrested. The problem of juvenile offenders had come to the

Governor's personal attention, and the Fight Crime Campaigns of both 1980 and 1981 made 'Fight Youth Crime' their theme. The alarm, briefly sounded, subsided again when figures for 1981 showed the number of juvenile offenders falling off but issues of juvenile and youth crime continued to occupy a central place in the 1980s debates on law and order.

According to the police, deploying so many officers at the frontier detracted from normal 'crime fighting' duties. This explained why, in the rest of Hong Kong in 1980, people experienced a 17 per cent increase in crime reports, a 21 per cent increase in 'key crime' and a 20 per cent increase in violent crime that year.[37] Illegal immigrants were also blamed for some crimes, such as serious and high-value robberies and using genuine or imitation firearms known to the police as 'pistol-like objects' or 'PLOs'.[38] There were successful calls for new laws to make the possession and criminal use of PLOs an offence.

Illegal immigrants were said to be involved in about 14 per cent of all robberies in 1981, but also in an even higher proportion of armed robberies.[39] Sixty illegal immigrants were rounded up by police in Kowloon alone, mainly for violent burglaries (which left the occupants bound hand and foot) but also for shoot-outs between police and bank robbers.[40] Security advice to banks and goldsmith shops by insurance companies was credited with producing a drop in robberies in 1981, when bank robberies fell to a five-year low.[41] According to the police, most of these violent crimes were committed by 'Big Circle' or other Mainland gangs, said to be 'violent, ruthless and well-organised'.[42]

As Tables 21.1 and 21.2 indicate, recorded crime was at its highest in the mid-1980s; between 1979 and 1983 recorded crime grew by almost 25,000. By the end of the decade, the police were claiming to have contained crime to an average of about 81,000 throughout the 1980s; recorded crime in 1989 had, they argued, fallen back to one of the lowest levels of the decade in 1988. But it still remained almost 20,000 higher than in 1979, despite changes in the classification of certain offences in 1987, 1988 and 1989. The fall in miscellaneous cases towards the end of the decade also appears to have been almost entirely due to a sudden change in policy that reduced hawking prosecutions after 1987.

For the third year running, the crime figures for 1983 showed an increase in overall crime, though robberies and burglaries recorded slight falls. Overall recorded crime – particularly burglaries, pick pocketing, miscellaneous thefts and robberies – rose continuously. The police blamed rises in 1980, 1981, 1982 and 1983 on drug addicts stealing to fund the rising cost of street drugs (for successive years, however, bumper crops of heroin in the Golden Triangle resulted in increased quantities of the drug being smuggled into Hong Kong. Police crackdowns pushed up street prices).

In common with other official bodies, the press and public opinion, the police claimed that Chinese illegal immigrants were disproportionately

Table 21.1 Reported crime 1979–89

	1979	*1980*	*1981*	*1982*	*1983*	*1984*	*1985*	*1986*	*1987*[1]	*1988*[2]	*1989*
Violent crime	19,169	22,524	21,656	23,506	24,520	23,984	23,214	21,215	15,469	15,724	17,721
Other key crime	3,252	38,294	42,674	46,899	44,637	42,827	46,200	43,358	–	–	–
Other crime	7,004	7,851	9,264	1,207	11,082	10,476	11,877	11,962	62,964	61,056	60,324
Preventive crime	5,959	6,383	6,023	6,615	5,761	6,245	5,653	4,876	4,481	3,079	3,763
Total	**64,653**	**75,754**	**79,613**	**87,227**	**86,000**	**83,532**	**86,418**	**81,411**	**82,914**	**79,859**	**81,808**

Source: RHKPARs 1979–89.

[1] In 1987 the police began to present the crime figures differently, altering the total of violent crime for 1986 to 14,303 but increasing 'other crime' to 62,544. The category 'Key Crime' disappeared from the tables

[2] In 1988, a new way of counting burglaries was introduced.

Table 21.2 Miscellaneous offences prosecuted 1979–89

	1979	*1980*	*1981*	*1982*	*1983*	*1984*	*1985*	*1986*	*1987*	*1988*	*1989*
Gambling	13,104	12,963	14,294	7,368	2,646	2,419	2,567	1,630	1,238	1,154	1,353
Hawking	64,689	64,847	65,134	48,507	42,058	29,381	18,523	19,706	15,777	8,251	5,294
Obstruction	4,197	38,888	52,408	47,919	44,535	50,839	47,983	42,240	39,528	33,857	26,040
Prostitution	1,219	974	1,146	1,561	973	1,154	1,091	1,297	800	214	233
Objectionable publication	113	196	184	259	241	101	171	437	186	196	253
Other misc.	9,352	31,759	37,827	27,887	29,954	3,218	34,825	35,691	24,219	21,832	18,498
Minor narcotics	5,558	4,712	6,751	8,242	9,562	10,321	10,643	9,797	8,126	6,673	4,538
Total	**180,071**	**154,339**	**177,744**	**141,743**	**130,059**	**126,396**	**115,803**	**110,798**	**89,874**	**72,177**	**56,209**

Source: RHKPARs 1979–89.

involved in recorded crime (especially violent gun crime) and that Vietnamese refugees had a high rate of interpersonal crime. Indeed, the rise in violent crime in the early 1980s was officially explained in terms of the armed robberies committed by illegal immigrants. The police estimated that, by 1982, illegal immigrants represented about 10 per cent of the population of Hong Kong but almost 14 per cent of those prosecuted for crime.[43] This official picture of crime underscored the notion that Hong Kong itself was a community built on a law-abiding consensus, disturbed only by strangers from 'without'.

Containment of crime had by the 1980s become fundamental to the legitimacy of both the police and the administration more generally. However, by the end of the decade, recorded violent crime – especially involving firearms – had risen and was still rising. The public found unusual homicides especially disturbing. The early 1980s had its fair share of these. In 1983, the 'Jars Murderer' was discovered to have dissected his victims and placed their body parts in jars (the subject of one of the many Hong Kong gruesome crime films). In 1982, a man with a knife had attacked 44 people (mostly children in a kindergarten) in the Un Chau Street Estate, Cheung Sha Wan, leaving six dead. In 1984, another murderer was discovered to have buried his victim in a concrete flower box on the verandah of a flat; another stored the body of his victim in a refrigerator.[44] In 1985, two teenagers were found murdered at Braemar Hill. The incidents are remembered as part of Hong Kong's 'folk memory', part of the crime stories people tell about the territory.

As in the 1970s, much of the increase in overall recorded crime was actually due to a rise in police numbers and their presence in previously unpoliced parts of Hong Kong. The development of the NT in the early 1980s meant major changes in its demographics. Its rural nature remained intact in parts, but urbanisation proceeded apace. In 1982, the police noted that in the new towns of Shatin and Tuen Mun, crime shot up by 43 per cent and 26 per cent respectively. As the NT developed and the police established a presence via more Neighbourhood Policing Units, reported crime here began to overtake Hong Kong Island. High-class housing, Spanish-style villas now also sprang up in rural villages, and goldsmiths' shops littered the new shopping malls, all regarded by the police as high-risk premises.[45] Although crime rose overall in 1980, in the NT it rose by over 50 per cent. Between 1979 and 1989, it more than doubled. In 1981 alone, crime in the NT rose by 4.5 per cent. Over 21 per cent of all crime in Hong Kong that year was recorded in the NT, just short of the 23 per cent recorded on Hong Kong Island. In 1982, the NT finally overtook Hong Kong Island in the crime stakes – almost 24 per cent of all crime was recorded there compared with Hong Kong Island's 20 per cent.[46]

The vast majority of crime was, as ever, recorded in Kowloon (55 per cent) where most of the 9 per cent rise in 1982 was put down to illegal immigrants squatting on the hillsides around Kwun Tong, and 'outside criminal elements' penetrating Yau Ma Tei via the newly-opened MTR link.[47] Train terminals such as Hung Hom and the ever-expanding MTR network were also portrayed as places which attracted illegal immigrants engaged in pick pocketing and snatchings.

Kowloon thus maintained its status as the 'hot spot' of crime. More police were deployed there than anywhere else (6,139 compared to 3,694 in Hong Kong and 3,473 in the NT). But whereas, in the late 1970s, almost 65 per cent of crime reports emanated from there, in 1980 this had fallen to about 55 per cent. Much of this remained as it had done for the previous decade – the resettlement estates and private developments experienced relatively high rates of burglary, the 'Golden Mile' of shops, restaurants and night clubs attracted tourists and hence pick pockets, fraudsters, and triad extortion rackets. The area around Mongkok was still identified as the 'vice capital' of Hong Kong, with well known districts (such as Shanghai Street, Portland Street, Tung Choi Street and Sai Yeung Choi Street) housing 'short-time hotels', organised vice establishments, one-woman brothels and a smattering of 'lower class' street walkers. By the end of the decade, more of the women working in the principal vice establishments were being trafficked into Hong Kong from China by organised crime.[48] Their families in the Mainland often paid the costs of the journey, believing their daughters would earn enough money in Hong Kong to lift them out of poverty.

Newly developed areas of Hong Kong attracted more vice-related activities – for example, the bars, restaurants and hotels of Tsim Sha Tsui East became infamous as haunts of high-class prostitutes and rich businessmen, as well as 'rent boys'. Some older clubs and bars in Tsim Tsa Tsui retained the reputation they had acquired during the use of Hong Kong as an American base for 'R&R' during the Vietnam War (older prostitutes could still recite the name of every state in the USA). Of vice-associated areas on Hong Kong Island, only Wanchai maintained its reputation for sex shows and hostess bars, the 'red light' district held up to tourists as the 'Suzie Wong' area. Areas associated with opium dens and prostitution since the nineteenth century (such as Lyndhurst Terrace and surrounding streets in Western) saw increasing gentrification, gradually becoming more famous for antique shops and the proliferation of trendy restaurants, bars and nightlife that collectively became known as Lan Kwai Fung.

Though Hong Kong Island had been demoted to third place in crime topography, it status as the centre of colonial administration and tourist hot spot made it a policing priority. Central district was home to LEGCO, Government Offices and Government House, and the Governor's residence. The increased political activity of the 1980s saw almost daily processions, petitions, and protests in this area.[49]

A slight fall in overall crime (including violent crime) in 1984 was welcomed by the police as the first fall since 1977 (though how much of this was due to 1983 changes in the method of counting crime is unclear). Recorded serious assaults rose slightly, as did burglaries of dwelling houses, but robberies

Table 21.3 Crime by district 1979–89

	1979	*1980*	*1981*	*1982*	*1983*	*1984*	*1985*	*1986*	*1987*	*1988*	*1989*
Kowloon	39,539	42,248	44,051	47,803	46,832	45,788	46,745	45,084	44,538	40,659	39,908
Hong Kong Island	14,600	17,525	18,030	18,046	16,894	15,741	16,331	15,653	15,705	14,803	15,599
NT	9,873	15,037	16,920	20,659	21,546	21,347	22,744	20,047	22,095	23,707	25,360
Marine	334	585	616	719	728	656	598	627	576	690	941
Total	**62,346**	**73,838**	**79,617**	**87,227**	**86,000**	**83,532**	**86,944**	**81,141**	**82,914**	**79,859**	**81,808**

Source: RHKPARs 1979–89. Figures for 1982 were later adjusted downwards following new counting rules introduced in 1983.

with firearms of goldsmith shops, banks, and cash-in-transit dropped, as two robbery syndicates were put out of action (ibid). Overall recorded crime kept rising through 1984 and 1985, though recorded violent crime fluctuated. The demand for narcotics remained high. The failure of financial institutions (such as Dominican Finance, the Overseas Trust Bank, and the Hong Kong Industrial and Commercial Bank) drew a series of frauds to the attention of an increasingly over-burdened Commercial Crime Unit.

Reports of burglary rose constantly, despite the 1985 Fight Crime 'Crime Prevention' campaign. Then, in 1986, the first signs that recorded crime was falling were detected. Overall recorded crime fell by 6.4 per cent. After four years of declining figures, robberies dropped to their lowest level for 15 years; violent crime dropped by over 8 per cent; burglary fell; the number of young offenders brought before the courts also fell, as did the number of juveniles arrested for drug offences (down 17 per cent) and violent crime (down 5.8 per cent).[50] Arrests for triad-related offences also fell from 2,218 in 1985 to 1,845 in 1986, but in 1987 a rise in violent crime was attributed to high levels of triad activity.[51]

The fall in recorded crime in 1986 was undone by the figures for 1987 showing an 8 per cent rise in violent crime and a slight increase in overall crime. The police argued that these figures were still well below those for the early 1980s. However, the classification for violent crime was modified in 1987, burglary in 1988, and theft from a vehicle in 1989. It is unclear what effect this had on the statistics – burglary showed a slight rise again in 1988, mostly for residential burglary.

Recorded violent crime also rose again in 1989 and homicide reached its highest level since 1981. Wounding and serious assault rose by over 11 per cent, rape increased, as did burglary and robbery with firearms. The firearms and grenades seized by police in 1989 included some manufactured in China, reinforcing the belief that many of the attacks on the territory's goldsmith shops and banks were carried out by criminals hired in from the Mainland.

Narcotics

As in previous decades, drug use – and drug-related – offences went up and down with the price on the street. This, in turn, depended on crop production in the Golden Triangle and the effectiveness of official crackdowns. Though the police noted the production of drugs in Afghanistan and a new route of entry via Thailand and China, Hong Kong's supplies and transhipments still mainly originated in the Golden Triangle. The rises in crime in 1981, 1982 and 1983 were partly fuelled by an escalation in the street price of drugs following record seizures by Customs and Excise.[52] As in the 1970s, law enforcement in one area of narcotics policing was observed to produce crime elsewhere. This was equally true of prosecution, since successful convictions of some suppliers left a gap that was inevitably filled by others.

Anti-drug measures became significantly more severe in the 1980s. An amendment to the Dangerous Drugs Ordinance made ship owners strictly liable if their vessels were found to contain drugs in Hong Kong waters on two or more occasions within 18 months (imports entering the colony through the main airport were said to remain 'small-scale').[53] Drug use remained mainly associated with the adult population – it was not an activity that seemed to attract the young. By the early 1980s, Hong Kong had about 45,000 known drug addicts. They shared the same characteristics as their 1970s counterparts and the drug of choice was still heroin, to which over 90 per cent were addicted. Only a small number (mainly elderly men) still used opium – the numbers arrested for opium offences had continued to drop since 1974 and, by 1987, only 0.5 per cent of the 56,733 registered drug addicts used opium.[54]

What had noticeably altered was the type of heroin coming into the territory – where once No 3 heroin had been the most common form, by the 1980s it had been replaced by No 4 heroin, said to be preferred by the international market.[55] The trend of importing heroin 'base', which could easily be cut with additives, was also said to reduce the chances of detection. The police noted that drug couriers were now more mobile, using electronic pagers to arrange the handing over of cash separately from the handing over of drugs, and thus also becoming more difficult to detect. A number of 'small time operatives' had moved into supply – in 1981, the numbers prosecuted for dangerous drug offences rose to 7,866 from 5,757 in 1980 (ibid).

Record seizures were noted in 1983 and 1984, years during which bumper heroin crops in the Golden Triangle increased quantities entering the territory. In 1984, the police recorded their biggest ever seizure of heroin base (298 kilos) in a fishing net near Ping Chau.[56] The cosmopolitan nature of Hong Kong, overseas travel, 'Western' influences, and the growth of 'trendy' Hong Kong nightlife were all said to be explain the growing use of cannabis, Mandrax and Seconal amongst the younger generation (ibid). A rise in the use of cannabis and LSD was attributed to their use by young, middle class Chinese. Though young people were a minority of known drug users, more were said to be involved as couriers, lookouts and runners. Police reports for 1980 drew attention to a 46 per cent increase in juvenile crime – in 1981, juveniles were said to be responsible for 16 per cent of all recorded crime, prompting the Governor to intervene personally to ask the Fight Crime Committee to examine the causes of 'this upsurge' (ibid). Juveniles were also said to be increasingly used as couriers by drug traffickers, underscoring the negative effective of triad organised crime on Hong Kong's youth.[57]

Triads

The continued existence of triads was another destabilising factor during the transition years. Public opinion was exercised trying to predict whether 1997 would mean an exodus of leading triads, their expansion into Mainland China, or – as the favourable comments from Beijing seemed to imply – their elevation to respectability and power. The police maintained that triads were a shadow of their former selves, that they 'really' represented no more than gangs of teenage thugs, and that Hong Kong and Western cinema kept alive the 'romance' of triads in films which glamorised the triad life-style. At the same time, however, they also claimed that the triads were now 'sophisticated', 'well-structured' and with 'strong committees' – a threat to law and order and the state's monopoly on coercion and popular loyalties.

Despite all the talk of crackdowns, offensives and better intelligence, everyone was aware that triads were a routine part of life in the territory. They controlled monopolies for decorating the Temporary Housing Areas, illegal bookmaking rackets, Public Light Bus routes, markets, vice and the provision of such things as water supplies to squatters.[58] Some 70 per cent of all inmates in Hong Kong's prisons were rumoured to have triad affiliations; they were even said to help control the prisons, and to contain crime by enforcing order among their members and ensuring that crime was kept low in tourist areas so that money continued to flow into triad-run businesses and protection rackets.

The police blamed the rise in juvenile crime on a mixture of triad influence, poor parental control, violent films, poor recreational facilities and the 'tempting displays of luxury goods in department stores'. Triads were said to hold 'a dangerous attraction' for juveniles in the densely populated housing areas.[59] A 1981 police drive against triad societies (such as the Wo Shing Wo, Luen Lok Tong, and Fuk Yee Hing) netted 2,324 persons of whom 309 were charged (ibid). About 8 per cent of all those arrested in 1981 had triad affiliations.[60] This prompted the Fight Crime Committee to form a Working Party on Gangs, and in 1986 the government produced a report.[61] The public's response to this was taken as support for firmer action against triads,[62] prompting the anti-triad theme of the 1987/8 Fight Crime Campaign, and, in 1988, the introduction of a Triad Renunciation Scheme under which non-active triad members could renounce their membership.[63] The Fight Crime Campaign 1988/9 targeted triad influences on youth, seeking to 'expose the sordid nature and modus operandi of triads so that members of the public, particularly young people, could be warned of the serious consequences of associating with triad elements'.[64] The Fight Crime campaign of 1989/90 continued this theme, along with exhortations aimed at juveniles against shop theft and hooliganism.

The police were said to be taking daily action against 'street thugs' and engaging in longer-term, intelligence-led operations against triads. An amendment to the Money Lenders Ordinance was also said to have 'disrupted' triad loan-sharking, whilst an amendment to the Societies Ordinance in 1982 gave police more powers to investigate societies, such as martial arts associations, suspected of triad affiliation.[65] In 1987, a major operation against the Sun Yee On resulted in the arrest and charging of its 'dragon head' and nine other senior office bearers, all of whom were convicted and received long sentences.[66] In 1988, another successful prosecution was mounted against other Sun Yee On members, as well as what was described as the largest loan-sharking syndicate in Hong Kong. A series of other arrests were made for possession of firearms and armed robberies.

Though successful legal challenges to these convictions were to follow, these arrests were taken as symbolically significant in the war against triads. At the same time, Beijing's description of triads as 'patriots' unnerved the authorities. At one level, the continued existence of triads reflected misgivings that Hong Kong people would be able – after 1997 – to rely on the government for their 'lifestyle' as much as they had since the 1970s. The whole question of government – of who would govern and how – of whether 'connections', power and corruption would once again become the key everyday life – encouraged people to retain their links to older, non-government networks and ties. In the atmosphere of uncertainty that surrounded the transition years, rumours abounded as to the degree to which triad influence was declining or expanding. The rumour that the PRC leaders had endorsed triads fuelled public fears that 1997 would mean a decline in law and order.

Policing

The uncertainties of the 1980s discouraged people from reporting the illegal activities of those (such as triads) who were currently defined as criminal but who, in the future, might assume power and position. This said, the second Crime Victimisation Survey in 1981 showed an 18 per cent rise in public reporting of crime to the police since 1978. This was partly due to the requirement to report the theft of an ID card, but the police were also victims of their own success. In 1981 they received over half a million requests for assistance, of which a daily average of 1,100, in round terms two in three requests, had nothing to do with crime. In 1982, this figure stood at about 74 per cent of the 621,865 requests received, and in 1983 at 75 per cent of 641,000 requests.[67]

The Commissioner interpreted this as demonstrating greater public confidence in the police, an increased willingness to turn to the police in times of difficulty (ibid) and the degree to which Hong Kong people were turning to the state for help. To some extent, the police were hoist by their own petard. The annual Fight Crime campaigns of the 1970s had promised that together, the police and the community could 'beat crime'. But, perversely, the crime figures never seemed to fall, only to get worse. The respect of the community, the Police Commissioner acknowledged, 'must be earned and can only be achieved if the Force measures up to the expectations of the community'.[68] The problem was that in the 1970s, the police had raised these expectations to an unrealistic pitch. The public was, understandably, critical.

The task of the Police Public Relations Wing now became the much more modest – but difficult one – of lowering these expectations by educating the public about the limitations of policing. It did so by highlighting the ways in which the 'legal checks and balances' of the criminal justice system allowed criminals to go free, reinforcing the prevailing view that due process imposed limitations on the police that prevented them from doing a better job of crime control.

The Crime Prevention Bureau, expanded in 1979, now concentrated on publicising ways of curbing crimes (such as burglary and shop theft) that could have been prevented by the victim. The Neighbourhood Watch Scheme, introduced as part of the 1985 Fight Crime Campaign, mobilised communities and neighbours to 'unite to guard against crimes' particularly residential burglaries and vehicle thefts. By early 1988, there were over 63,000 families participating in the 5,900 Neighbourhood Watch units in the territory. The popularity of the scheme was reckoned to have generated a high demand for more schemes.[69] A new television programme, *Crime Watch*, was introduced in tandem with the new scheme. Featuring unsolved crimes, it was screened once a month at prime times, on Chinese television, inviting the viewing public to call in with information. The theme of crime prevention formed the basis of the 1986/87 Fight Crime Campaign, which concentrated on home security and shop theft.[70] The shop theft arm of the campaign, in turn, focussed on juveniles, whose involvement in shoplifting was said to be causing 'alarm' in the community. Schoolchildren were to learn that shop theft was not a game 'but a serious crime which can bring equally serious consequences' (ibid). (This turned out to be true – teenagers in Hong Kong who stole very low-value items found themselves sent to jail, and subject to post-release supervision, much faster than in most parts of the world.)

The public relations exercises of the 1970s continued throughout the 1980s. Television stations were mandated, under the terms of their franchise, to transmit up to seven hours a week of government programmes.[71] The two stations had 98 per cent coverage of the population. Police programmes were estimated to reach between 1.7 and 2 million people, and were 'never out of the top ten most popular local Chinese programmes' (ibid). As in the previous decade, dramas such as *On the Beat* were used to 'further the community's understanding' of the police, whilst current affairs and documentaries featuring police officers helped 'cement good relations with the public' (ibid). The annual Fight Crime campaigns continued to mobilise the community against crime, emphasising what individuals – rather than the police – could do to prevent crime.

Modernisation, expansion and police–community relations

Following the advice of Home Office Advisers in 1979 that the force was suffering from certain 'imbalances', the 1980s was also a time of police reorganisation. The 1979 visit was followed by a report compiled by a former HM Chief Inspector of Constabulary, Sir James Crane, after a visit in 1983. Expansion continued, however – recruiting went on; more marine launches were planned; the traffic police were strengthened; new police stations were opened at Tsim Sha Tsui, Sau Mau Ping, Kai Tak, Waterfront, and the NT; 40 more new police buildings were in the pipeline. By 1982 there were also 164 Neighbourhood Police and Police Reporting Units established throughout the territory. In 1984, after a review of its operation, the police created 75 Neighbourhood Police Co-ordinators to 'improve community relations and enhance better and closer co-operation with the public'.[72] In 1985, a Neighbourhood Watch Scheme was introduced, following the UK model, and especially intended to cut the ever-rising number of burglaries in the territory. More post boxes were placed throughout Hong Kong – in banks, post offices, district offices and police stations – to ease public reporting of crime (ibid). By the mid-1980s, the police force was the largest government department, comprising over 35,700 regular and auxiliary police and civilian staff, housed in 255 buildings, and amounting to 16.8 per cent of total government staffing.[73]

The focus on police/community relations was matched by a new commitment to modernisation in all aspects of policing. Crime fighting became a matter of science and technology. There was to be greater use of computerisation, information technology and specialist policing, including counter-terrorist policing (now one of the tasks of the Special Duties Unit). In 1987, plans were made to improve Hong Kong's internal security capability by replacing the outdated Saracen armoured personnel carriers with more modern Saxon armoured personnel carriers.[74] In 1988, new 'mini-ranges' and simulators for firearms training were installed, reproducing real-life scenarios in training. In 1981, a new Computer Development Branch was founded to develop computer applications 'relevant to the efficient policing of a fast-paced and cosmopolitan urban environment' and plans were laid for a Computer Assisted Command and Control.[75] By the middle of 1983, a new Police Operational Nominal Index Computer System (PONICS) was in place, providing 'immediate case enquiry support to all operational officers on a 24-hour basis' (ibid). This system, enhanced in the 1990s (EPONICS) formed part of the Criminal Records Bureau which, in conjunction with the Identification Bureau, now held extensive fingerprint records (later also computerised) used both to identify offenders and for security vetting. The computerisation of ID card checks in 1983 also enabled the police to detect more illegal immigrants and holders of forged ID cards. By the late 1980s there was also in place an Integrated Law and Order Statistical System (ILOSS), which brought together Correctional Services, the Judiciary, the police, Social Welfare and Security Branch in a system designed to collect, compile and analyse crime statistics.[76] A new Criminal Intelligence Computer System was also in train by 1988, as was a new Computer-Assisted Fingerprint Identification system.

At the end of the decade, the police said they were seeking the 'very best computer hardware, software and communications equipment available worldwide', so as to become a 'world-beater'.[77] Basic qualifications for constables were also upgraded; by 1981, 90 per cent of those recruited had completed secondary education. More were asked for qualifications in computing and word processing (the force had 23 word processors in 1984 and more, Chinese language, processors were planned).

Traditional attitudes to women officers, however, remained as entrenched as ever. Hong Kong was a decidedly patriarchal society in which men were valued more than women. This was as true for the British as for the Chinese – on this aspect of culture, their interests coincided. In 1986, women were given more specialised training, but only in the area of policing women and juveniles. They were still not allowed to carry firearms or wear trousers. In 1988, when the first all-female company was formed for the visit of Philippine President, Corazón Aquino, female officers were briefly allowed to wear trousers, something normally only permitted the female marine police. It was not until the 1990s, when cutbacks forced the police force to rethink its inefficiencies, that some women officers were allowed to undertake public order training. The Women's Internal Security Company (Tango Company) completed its training at PTU in 1992. A later proposal that women officers should be allowed to carry firearms eventually brought to a head the forces of 'tradition' and 'modernity' – women were deemed too weak to carry firearms, and vulnerable to criminals wresting their weapons from them.[78]

Other areas proved even more resistant to change. Complaints against the police were still handled internally, giving rise to criticisms about independence and a low substantiation rate. The Commissioner argued that the system was sound but the criticisms never subsided. In 1986, a Police Complaints Committee took over the role of the UMELCO Police Group. The new committee consisted of three members of EXCO and LEGCO, the Attorney General and at least eight JPs nominated by the Governor. Its remit was to monitor all investigations into complaints against the police. The complaints themselves were investigated internally, by the Internal Investigations Office and/or CAPO. Complaints had been on the rise steadily between 1974 and 1984; they continued to fluctuate throughout the 1980s.[79] Though later changes did increase public oversight of police the complaints system, retaining supervision over the process was a battle that the force continued to fight (and win).

Further changes followed in force organisation, notably the introduction of a new structure of command consisting of Regions, Districts and Divisions. This reorganisation coincided with reference, in police reports, to a 'Security Wing', (though Special Branch was to remain an intrinsic part of the police force until the mid-1990s). The stated aims of the reorganisation were to devolve authority and responsibility 'to the lowest practical and acceptable command level' and strengthen links with local communities.[80] Subsequently,

Table 21.4 Hong Kong Police Establishment 1980–89

	1980	*1981*	*1982*	*1983*	*1984*	*1985*	*1986*	*1987*	*1988*	*1989*
Total	**21,981**	**22,473**	**23,476**	**24,211**	**24,834**	**25,397**	**25,957** [1]	**26,626**	**27,367**	**27450**
Gazetted officers	287	329	384	406	425	435	449	471	475	–
Inspectors	1,818	1,993	1,982	2,019	2,107	2,179	2,223	2,300	2,362	–
Rank and file	19,876	20,151	21,110	21,786	22,302	22,783	22,285	23,855	24,530	–

Source: RHKPARs 1980–89.
[1] The RHKPAR for 1985 put this figure at over 30,000 by the end of 1985.

Neighbourhood Policing and community liaison were to be both increased and fine-tuned, 'to provide a more even-handed and visible police presence in areas and at times when it is most needed'.[81] In 1987, Kowloon was split into two divisions, Kowloon West and Kowloon East. Kowloon West was regarded as the busiest police division in Hong Kong. Kowloon East included Hong Kong's international airport, and a number of major temples where large numbers of worshippers gather at certain times during the year. In the 1970s and 1980s it also housed three of the main detention centres for Vietnamese Boat People. Kowloon West, by contrast, remained the centre of the territory's vice industry and associated organised crime (triad) activities.

In 1983, the police force experienced its first cutback in expenditure, as the budget for recruitment was slashed.[82] In 1988, it was also decided to phase out the Police Cadet School, the government having announced in 1984 plans to provide a longer period of subsidised secondary education.

Despite these setbacks, by the end of 1985 the force had a total establishment of 30,977 officers and a civilian establishment of 5,580. By 1988, expenditure on the police force totalled HK$3,405 million, or 6.1 per cent of the government's total budget. By 1989, it had risen to HK$4,460 million or 5.7 per cent of the government's total budget.[83]

In addition to the Auxiliary Police, the ICAC, Immigration, and Customs and Excise, Hong Kong also by now had a formidable armoury of 'private' forms of policing, in the form of its 40,000 registered watchmen, its MACs, its private security guards at public and private buildings, and its private security firms providing advice and assistance to banks and credit card companies. One of the most familiar sights in the Hong Kong of the 1980s and 1990s was that of be-turbaned armed guards outside the premises of banks and goldsmith shops. Within the housing estates, Housing Department guards also kept a watchful eye on residents, and in the camps under Housing Department supervision, they guarded Vietnamese refugees. Refugees held in other detention camps were guarded by police, auxiliary police and prison guards.

The JPC, meanwhile, also encouraged children to keep an eye out for crime, whilst the Good Citizens' and other public-minded people of Hong Kong themselves accounted for about 11 per cent of all arrests in any given year. By the end of the 1980s, the territory probably had one of the most policed populations – and intensively supervised youth – in the world.

These were the official stories of crime throughout the 1980s, though the crime surveys revealed a different story. Whilst the official statistics for the 1980s showed, for example, an increase in overall crime, the 1989 crime survey revealed a *decrease* in the total number of victimisations between 1986 and 1989, particularly in relation to personal crimes.[84] It went on to say that 'there was no appreciable difference in the broad pattern of crime for both personal and household crimes between 1981 and 1986' (ibid). Victimisation rates for these crimes did, however, increase again between 1989 and 1994, though the official figures for the mid-1990s would record a 15-year low in all recorded crime.

The crime survey also charted the start of a shift in the willingness of people to report crime to the police. From the late 1970s onwards, there had been a steady, if moderate, increase in the overall level of reporting to the police. However, over the 1980s, this was to show a marked decline. The 1994 crime survey would note a distinct falling off in the willingness of the public to report crime, raising fears that the impending transfer of power was giving rise to a general loss of faith in official institutions.

Notes

1 RHKPAR 1983: 14.
2 *The Further Development of Representative Government in Hong Kong*, Hong Kong: Government Printer, November 1984.
3 Raymond Wu, member of the BLDC, Beijing adviser, writing in Blyth and Wotherspoon 1996: 205.
4 Rosa Mok, writing in Blyth and Wotherspoon 1996: 261.
5 Isak Lung, writing in Blyth and Wotherspoon 1996: 267.
6 Ng L.Y.Y. 1995; Wong, E.K.W. 1996; Lam, W.M. 2005: 309–22.
7 RHKPAR 1981: 11.
8 *http://www.answers.com/topic/hong-kong–1981-riots*.
9 RHKPAR 1984: 10.
10 RHKPAR 1980: 14.
11 RHKPAR 1983: 14.
12 RHKPAR 1984: 10.
13 See for example *http://en.wikipedia.org/wiki/Carrian_Group*; *http://www.icac.org.hk/text/eng/cases/carrian/index.html*.
14 See Scott 1989: 209.
15 Walden 1985.
16 RHKPAR 1986: 5.
17 RHKPAR 1989: 6.
18 Chui was appointed in 1976. See Chui 1999.
19 Ibid.
20 Ibid.
21 Ibid.
22 RHKPAR 1980: 13.
23 RHKPAR 1983: 14.
24 RHKPAR 1988: 10.
25 RHKPAR 1988: 11.
26 The symbiotic relationship between Hong Kong and China clearly had consequences for the definition of crime and law enforcement. Until 1980, for example, Hong Kong had repeated and serious problems with labour shortages. In effect, it managed its labour supply by *not* enforcing immigration ordinances, provided that (theoretically illegal) immigration did not result in oversupply and that the immigrants were in fact capable of absorption into the labour force. This was not a deliberate and long-term policy, but the result of a series of short-term 'fixit' policies. In periods when the numbers of immigrants increased sharply, the laws were enforced more rigorously and immigration ordinances were more

tightly enforced (although the ultimate sanction of imprisonment for immigration offences, which had been 'on the books' since the 1940s, was not in fact used until 1989). From the early 1980s, Hong Kong was thus in the almost unique position of benefiting from the global restructuring of capital while simultaneously keeping at arm's length many of the problems consequent upon fast growth. These problems were experienced more keenly in China. The national border enabled certain forms of essentially economic activity (principally migration) to be treated as criminal when it was useful to do so. These fluctuations in policy meant that attempts to demonise the 'IIs' were never entirely successful. At the same time, Hong Kong people sometimes put loyalty to kith and kin above obedience to the law, helping friends and relatives from the Mainland escape detection in Hong Kong.

27 Vagg 1991a.

28 RHKPAR 1980: 7.

29 RHKPAR 1980: 11.

30 RHKPAR 1980: 43.

31 RHKPAR 1986: 9.

32 Ashworth 1994: 126. Research generally shows that such offenders are more likely to be selected by the police to go forward in the criminal justice process because their crimes involve less police time and resources than other crimes. Cicourel's 1968 study of the juvenile justice system makes a similar point.

33 See, for example, Munn 2001; Chan, W.K. 1991; Sinn, E. 1990; Smith, C.T. 1985; Lethbridge 1978b.

34 Clinard and Abbott (1973) develop the idea of economic dualism – a migrant population coming from a peasant-based and unskilled social world into a more technically demanding one in which they experience high unemployment rates – coupled with social factors such as the breakdown through migration of family structures, and the absorption of achievement-oriented values. Shelley (1981) links some of these factors specifically to violent crime, which increases because the incoming migrants not only lack resources, but also the cultural background that would enable them to solve disputes non-violently in an urban setting.

35 See Munn 2001 for an account of how this situation obtained in 'criminal enclaves' in early colonial Hong Kong.

36 After 1978, Hong Kong may have 'exported' crime to Mainland China. When China 'opened up the door to the West in 1978, officials were alarmed at the rising rates of crime that occurred. For the Chinese leadership, crime, vice, and immorality were 'flies' that came in from the West, through the open door. The possibility of such a transfer is suggested by the radical view of crime and development put forward by Newman (1990). He suggests that developed countries export high crime levels to 'developing' ones, both as business relocates hazardous industrial processes to countries that cannot afford to refuse them, and through their selective demands on their own and 'developing' countries' labour pools, leading to the creation of an urban underclass that survives on occasional crime in both developed and 'developing' countries – though proportionately more so in the latter, where the lack of social welfare structures leads to higher crime.

37 RHKPAR 1980: 8.

38 RHKPAR 1980: 8.

39 RHKPAR 1980: 7.

40 RHKPAR 1981: 10.

41 RHKPAR 1981: 5.

42 RHKPAR 1981: 9. Shortly before 1997, closer liaison was devised between the Hong Kong Police and the Guangdong Public Security Bureau, with shared intelligence concerning such gangs. This close liaison did not, however, amount to a

formal joint rendition agreement, and was to prove highly controversial both in the run-up to, and after, 1997.

43 RHKPAR 1982: 7.

44 RHKPAR 1984: 8.

45 RHKPAR 1980: 43.

46 In 1981 the population of Hong Kong Island was roughly 1.18 million while that of the NT was 1.3 million, so the implication was still that crime rates were lower in the NT. By 1986, however, while the population of Hong Kong island remained at about the same figure, that of the NT had risen to 1.8 million, making it less than surprising that in terms of raw numbers and irrespective of specific populations of 'criminal elements', crime figures in the latter would rise. The population of Kowloon fell slightly from 799,000 to 774,000 over the same time period, most of these people moving to the NT (population figures from *http://www.demographia.com/db-hkhist.htm*).

47 RHKPAR 1982: 7.

48 In the bars and casinos of Macau, Russian girls were trafficked by Russian organised crime and Chinese gangs.

49 RHKPAR 1980: 40.

50 RHKPAR 1986: 5.

51 RHKPAR 1987: 5.

52 RHKPAR 1982: 5.

53 RHKPAR 1982: 8.

54 RHKPAR 1980: 8; 1987: 7.

55 Conventionally, heroin is described in four types: No 1 heroin is a processed morphine base (diacetyl morphine); No 2 is the crude heroin base precipitate from No 1; purification of No 2 results in No 3 (heroin hydrochrolide), a brown/white granular form about 25 per cent pure and often used for smoking; further processing results in No 4 heroin, a 90 per cent pure white powder used for injection. The figures for purity are of course approximate, depending on what manufacturers – and subsequently also dealers – 'cut' with the heroin to increase profits. Descriptions of this process can be found in many places, for example *http://hangoverguide.com/factbook/opi_burma.html.*

56 RHKPAR 1984: 7.

57 RHKPAR 1982: 5.

58 RHKPAR 1983: 11.

59 RHKPAR 1980: 1.

60 RHKPAR 1980: 7.

61 *Options for Changes in the Law and in the Administration of the Law to Counter the Triad Problem.*

62 RHKPAR 1986: 7.

63 RHKPAR 1988: 9.

64 RHKPAR 1987: 12.

65 RHKPAR 1982: 8.

66 RHKPAR 1987: 8.

67 RHKPAR 1981: 5; 1982: 7; 1983: 8.

68 RHKPAR 1980: 5.

69 RHKPAR 1986: 12; 1987: 12.

70 RHKPAR 1986: 12.

71 RHKPAR 1980: 20.

72 RHKPAR 1984: 12.

73 RHKPAR 1984: 25.

74 RHKPAR 1987: 22.

75 RHKPAR 1984: 21.
76 RHKPAR 1987: 6.
77 RHKPAR 1989: 6.
78 In 1995, the question was finally resolved in favour of providing women with firearms training.
79 RHKPAR 1985: 23; 1987: 23.
80 RHKPAR 1982: 5.
81 RHKPAR 1983: 7.
82 RHKPAR 1983.
83 RHKPAR 1988: 27; 1989: 35.
84 Department of Census and Statistics 1986.

Chapter 22

The 1980s: discovering juvenile delinquency

The idea that Hong Kong had a particular problem with juvenile and youth crime had been slowly developing since the 1960s, encompassing issues dealt with in previous chapters such as the *ah fei* gangs and the role of young people in the 1966 Star Ferry riot. In terms of international comparisons, however, youths in Hong Kong were orderly, conformist and law-abiding. Nevertheless, by the 1980s there was widespread concern about juvenile and youth crime, extending over a range of issues from petty theft to their recruitment into triads, their use as 'runners' by drugs dealers, and drug use. Whilst in the past these concerns had related principally to young male offenders, in the 1980s girls increasingly became the focus of criminal justice and social work agencies.

The numbers of juveniles prosecuted increased in the 1980s, despite (or perhaps because of) the constant 'Fight Youth Crime' campaigns. Most were arrested for petty theft such as pick pocketing, snatching and shoplifting. Overall, the numbers of juveniles prosecuted fell in 1984 but the percentage involved in violent crime rose by over 12 per cent, and their involvement in drug related offences rose by almost 40 per cent.[1] A 66 per cent rise in shop theft recorded in 1985 was mainly due to juveniles being prosecuted by the department stores, which had spread through the territory. The number of juveniles caught in 1985, for example, was 2,926, over double the number of 1,253 in 1984; this dropped slightly to 2,574 in 1986, following a major publicity campaign aimed at potential juvenile shop-lifters, but the fall was to prove short-lived.[2] Despite the fact that the Fight Crime Campaign had specifically targeted juvenile shop theft offenders, the number of juveniles arrested or cautioned under the Police Superintendent's Discretion Scheme stood at 7,698; in 1988, the number dropped slightly to 7,123.[3] As before, many were arrested for shop theft or miscellaneous thefts (2,574 in 1986, 3,318 in 1987, 2,274 in 1988, and 1,758 in 1989) – much the same sort of offences with which juveniles of the 1950s and 1960s had been associated.

The percentage of juveniles arrested for violent crime also kept rising (by over 7 per cent in 1985), as did their arrest for involvement with drug offences. Juvenile arrests for violent crime went up by 32 per cent in 1987; their involvement in overall crime was said to have risen by almost 26 per cent.[4] However, as a distinct group, 'young offenders' – who had attracted so much attention in the 1970s – now barely deserved a mention in police reports.

These figures were to underpin one of the abiding beliefs of the 1980s, which was that juveniles were becoming more delinquent. The origins of this discourse can be traced back to the 1965 *Report On Causes of Violence Committed by Young Persons*. This, Lethbridge says, 'discovered' juvenile delinquency as 'a modern disease, the herpes of crime' (Lethbridge 1985: 205). The second most significant official document was the 1966 Riot Report, which had identified the rioters as youngsters. In 1966, 50 per cent of Hong Kong's population was under 21 and 40 per cent under 16. This was the group said to be most lacking in any sense of belonging to Hong Kong, the group in most need of becoming 'attached' to the territory and its institutions.

This said, no one in the in the late 1960s and early 1970s discussed juveniles as a 'crime problem'. Only a small minority featured in the crime statistics, and they figured mostly for the same kinds of petty larceny as the previous generation. In 1970, of the estimated 918,000 persons under 16 living in Hong Kong, only 1,535 were arrested for any offence – arrests in the 16 to 20 age group were far higher. It was not until the 1979/80 crime figures that the authorities became alarmed at the apparent rise in juvenile crime and began to investigate it as a distinct phenomenon. The 1981 Fight Crime Committee heeded the Governor's injunction to discover the causes of juvenile offending, and instigated research. It argued that juveniles needed stronger parental control. Its 1981 'Fight Youth Crime' campaign therefore encouraged parents to 'to take a personal and healthy interest in the activities of their children'. It harnessed 51 stars from television, film, sport and entertainment to join its 'Stars Against Crime' committee to deter youth from crime.[5] In 1981, the Government also formally recognised the JPC movement, and allocated HK$8.5 million to it. The JPC membership was still growing – by 1981 it numbered some 287,000 young people, with another 6,624 leaders.[6] As part of the 'Fight Youth Crime' campaign, letters were sent to all secondary school principals inviting them to form JPC clubs in their school. Sponsorship for JPC activities came from the Hong Kong and Shanghai Bank, the Ka Wah Bank, as well as government. The 'Good Citizen Awards' (whose motto was 'not to let the thugs get away with it') led in 1981 to 1,120 persons receiving cash awards totalling HK$1,262,400 (ibid).

When, by the end of 1982, prosecutions of juveniles had declined again by over 20 per cent, this was interpreted as proof that these measures had worked. However, the discovery that more juveniles were showing up in the dangerous drug offences figures prompted the campaigners to continue. In 1983, a major government anti-narcotics campaign was launched aimed specifically at youth.[7] A 6 per cent fall in the numbers of young males arrested in 1983 was again interpreted as a sign of campaign success.[8] However, concern was expressed about the number of juveniles arrested for shoplifting (up by over 42 per cent on 1982) a 13 per cent rise in juvenile involvement in violent crime, and a 13.6 per cent rise in their involvement in dangerous drug offences. The 1983 Fight Crime Campaign – the 'Fight Youth Crime' Campaign – specifically targeted males aged between 14 and 20, described as a group with a relatively high record of crime, especially serious and violent crime. The fight against youth crime was a 'high priority' for the police force and the government, symbolised by launch of the 1983/84 campaign by the Chief Secretary, Sir Philip Haddon-Cave.

The JPC was mobilised to spearhead the campaign; there was a 'Fight Youth Crime Photo Competition', a 25-minute drama-documentary series (*There is no glamour in crime*) aimed at 14 to 20-year-old males, which was screened over eight episodes on both TVB Jade and ATV 1. There were fight youth crime promotions in all police districts, a series of TV commercials, posters, leaflets, bulletins and a mobile Fight Crime Exhibition Centre that toured housing estates and community centres, and was visited by over 43,000 pupils and over 9,500 others.[9] Another mobile police exhibition, staffed by young police officers, toured secondary schools, both as part of the anti-crime campaign and, on the basis that 'youth attracts youth', to encourage more young people to join the police. When Michael Jackson visited Hong Kong in 1987, the PTU exploited the occasion for public relations purposes by joining him for a jog through the park.

Looking to explain the causes of youth crime, the police noted that the population structure of Chinese illegal immigrants was biased towards young males, generally acknowledged to participate in crime more than other age groups.[10] The popular view that Chinese illegal immigrants were responsible for rises in crime was not, however, borne out – a comparison of local young males with newly-arrived young males found little difference in their propensity towards offending. In 1983, for example, the prosecution rate for male recent arrivals aged 16 to 20 was 21.80 per 100,000 compared to 21.85 per 100,000 for long term residents in the same age group.[11]

In 1984, yet another Fight Crime Campaign took youth as its focus. The police drama *On the Beat* carried messages in each programme cautioning young people against crime. The same year also marked the tenth anniversary of the JPC – it now had 384,400 members, 17,098 leaders, with over 3,000 new members and 250 new leaders joining each month.[12] In 1985, it signed up its 400,000th member. As part of International Youth Year, it organised functions around the themes of peace, participation and development, opened new clubhouses, ran discos and organised a total of 14,000 different activities.[13] Lauded for aligning itself with law and order, the organisation was also heralded as preparing young people for 'responsible citizenship' (this was featured more explicitly in their civic education curriculum after the signing of the Joint Declaration in 1984). In 1987, moreover, JPC activities were specifically organised around themes of civic education, filial piety, public service and respect for the elderly, themes that stressed the subordination of the individual to the collective and respect for authority, and themes that had already been harnessed to great effect in Singapore, where Confucian values were held to underpin social order.

The anti-triad, anti-shop theft themes of earlier Fight Crime campaigns continued in the 1988/9 campaign: young persons were encouraged to report inducements or threats from persons trying to recruit them into triad societies, and their parents and teachers were requested to inform the police of any triad activities they encountered'.[14] All the familiar channels of fight crime campaigns were brought to bear, including the JPC and television special TV episodes were dedicated to 'the triad menace', 'loan sharks' and 'shop theft' (ibid).

Throughout the period, the nature of juvenile offending echoed that of earlier decades. The crimes for which young males under 16 were arrested and prosecuted were predominantly property related crimes, such as theft, obtaining money by deception, and robbery, as well as unlawful society (i.e. triad membership). Violent crime was associated more with males in the 16 to 30 age group. Female juveniles were mainly arrested for shop theft. In the middle of the decade, shop theft appeared for the first time as a distinct category of offence in the crime figures (Table 22.3). This reflected the growth of chain stores across the territory, including the shopping malls of the new towns where many youngsters now lived. Formerly, individual shop owners had exercised some discretion as to whether to prosecute for such offences. The arrival of chain stores with a store-wide policy of prosecution

Table 22.1 Persons prosecuted by age group and gender 1980–90

Year	*Age group*									
	7–15		*16–20*		*21–30*		*30+*		*Total*	
	M	*F*	*M*	*F*	*M*	*F*	*M*	*F*	*M*	*F*
1980	3,420	433	5,704	484	9,475	817	6,305	914	24,904	2,648
1981	3,298	387	6,115	487	10,601	920	6,874	1,056	26,288	2,850
1982 [1]	2,502	260	6,640	529	11,320	1,129	7,754	1,178	28,216	3,096
1983	2,708	280	6,609	619	12,499	1,287	9,312	1,459	31,128	3,645
1984	2,623	286	6,743	597	12,412	1,280	10,112	1,485	31,890	3,648
1985	2,772	391	6,637	747	12,779	1,614	11,001	2,000	33,188	4,752
1986	2,364	234	5,736	715	12,462	1,662	12,426	2,264	32,988	4,875
1987	2,938	322	5,891	660	11,863	1,644	11,893	2,350	32,585	4,976
1988	3,380	354	6,132	651	11,517	1,501	12,371	2,009	33,400	4,515
1989 [2]	6,573	864	7,545	738	11,518	1,463	12,921	2,062	38,557	5,127
1990 [2]	5,764	819	7,541	765	12,590	1,416	12,791	2,327	38,686	5,327

Source: RHKPARs 1980–90.
[1] From 1982 this age group was re-classified as 'Juveniles'. [2] Arrests.

Table 22.2 Juvenile crime in Hong Kong over 20-year period 1976–89

Year	*No of juveniles* (7–15)		*No of young persons* (16–20)		*Total juveniles (7–15)*	*Total young persons (16–20)*
	M	*F*	*M*	*F*		
1976	1,097	121	2,605	296	1,218	2,901
1977	1,523	162	1,179	16	1,835	1,195
1978	1,461	136	3,762	470	1,597	4,232
1979	2,354	287	4,409	449	2,641	4,858
1980	3,420	433	5,704	484	3,853	6,188
1981	3,298	387	6,115	487	3,685	6,602
1982	2,570	276	6,799	535	2,846	7,334
1983	2,708	280	6,609	619	2,988	7,228
1984	2,623	286	6,743	597	2,909	7,340
1985	2,772	392	6,654	748	3,164	7,402
1986	2,364	234	5,736	715	6,117	6,451
1987	2,938	322	5,891	660	7,698	6,551
1989	6,573	864	7,545	738	7,437	8,283

Source: RHKPARs 1976–89.

Table 22.3 Youth offenders (10–14 and 15–19) arrested for shop theft 1987–91

Year	*All ages*		*10–14*		*15–19*	
	M	*F*	*M*	*F*	*M*	*F*
1987	4,219	2,839	1,918	618	587	379
1988	3,147	2,135	1,220	450	522	267
1989	2,993	1,751	991	289	599	242
1990	3,402	1,896	999	261	619	242
1991	3,407	2,055	926	381	566	219

Source: Youth Commission Survey 1991: 150.

in all cases of shoplifting reduced the opportunity for such discretion. This pushed up the numbers of juveniles arrested and prosecuted for crime in this decade.

By the mid-1980s, youth was a discrete object of social inquiry. The word 'juvenile' became synonymous with 'delinquency'. Government-funded research on juvenile crime began, and criminology blossomed as social scientists focused on ways of solving the youth crime problem. A number of studies were carried out by academics as well as organisations and agencies that came into contact with 'youth'. Writing in 1985, Mok argued that the 'upsurge in juvenile crime' over the previous decade had 'drawn tremendous attention from people from all walks of life . . . It is a major concern of not

Table 22.4 Youth offenders (10–29) males by age at arrest: ten most common crimes 1991

Crime	*Age group*				
	10–29	*10–14*	*15–19*	*20–24*	*25–29*
Shop theft	2,169	926	566	303	374
Other theft	2,657	809	804	555	489
Other robbery	2,000	602	894	312	192
Serious assault	1,706	218	675	416	397
Possession DD for trafficking	1,157	13	257	381	506
Using other's ID card	1,067	28	234	455	350
Possession of offensive weapon	1,024	122	441	280	181
Disorder/Fighting	969	41	292	301	335
Burglary/Breaking	849	214	326	173	136
Criminal damage	795	77	254	209	255

Source: RHKP statistics cited Youth Commission Survey 1991: 148.

Table 22.5 Youth offenders (10–29) females by age at arrest: ten most common crimes: 1991

Crime	*Age group*				
	10–29	*10–14*	*15–19*	*20–24*	*25–29*
Shop theft	1,019	381	219	173	246
Using other's ID card	295	14	101	123	57
Other thefts	293	56	90	88	59
Possession DD for trafficking	222	10	52	92	68
Serious assault	162	58	42	24	38
Other robberies	131	73	44	7	7
Disorder/Fighting	110	5	33	27	45
Serious immigration offences	105	0	27	46	32
Blackmail	50	25	12	7	6
Forgery	50	0	8	22	20

Source: RHKP Statistics, cited in Youth Commission 1991 Survey: 149.

only the parents, teachers and social workers but also the general public at large'.[15] Concern about rising juvenile delinquency had prompted the government, in 1973, to set up a sub-committee to study the social causes of crime 'in the hope of finding a solution to the problem' (Mok 1985: 1). The committee commissioned a study on the social causes of violent crime amongst young people, carried out by Agnes Ng of the Social Research Centre, Chinese University of Hong Kong. As Ng herself pointed out some years later, this was the point at which academic investigations into 'deviant behaviour in youth' began. But it was Mok's 1985 study that placed the study of juvenile delinquency within the context of framing social policies to eliminate it. It concluded that family relationship, peer group associations, and personal and social values:

> . . . are associated with problem behaviour. In general, problem students are found to be significantly different from promising students in the three independent variables under study. These findings are congruent with those found in previous studies on delinquency conducted both abroad and locally . . . An understanding of the factors contributing to the problem of delinquent behaviour represents the first step in dealing with the problem of delinquency. (Mok 1985: 21).

Theories of 'strain', with their concern for lack of legitimate opportunities, and demands for 'law and order' deterrence now gave way to Hirschi's control theory and Sutherland and Cressey's theory of differential association:

> Delinquency was now diagnosed as symptomatic of a behavioural abnormality caused by a weakening of the young person's interpersonal ties with family and school. Without the normalising and disciplinary constraints of these social institutions, it was felt that there was a greatly increased risk of the juvenile falling under the influence of undesirable peers and deviant subcultures . . . The solution was to lie in preventative measures which strengthened the attachment of 'vulnerable' youngsters to family, school and pro-social leisure pursuits (Gray 1997: 192).

The term 'juvenile offending' was officially preferred in Hong Kong to the phrase 'juvenile delinquency'. Juvenile offenders were classified as anyone under 16 committing an unlawful offence; young offenders were defined as persons over 14 and under 21 found guilty of committing an unlawful act by a Hong Kong court.

Table 22.6 Crime cases reported and age specific prosecutions 1985–90

Year	*Reported cases*	*Age group*					
		7–15		*16–20*		*21–30*	
		M	*F*	*M*	*F*	*M*	*F*
1985	86,944	2,772	392	6,654	748	12,980	1,642
1986	81,411	2,364	234	5,736	715	12,462	1,662
1987	81,411	2,938	322	5,891	660	11,863	1,644
1988	79,184	3,380	354	6,132	651	11,518	1,501
1989 [1]	81,808	6,573	864	7,545	738	11,518	1,463
1990 [1]	88,300	5,764	819	7,541	765	12,590	1,416

Source: RHKP statistics, cited in Youth Commission 1991: 143.
[1] Arrests.

Table 22.7 Offender rate per 100,000 by sex and age group 1987–91

Year		*1987*	*1988*	*1989*	*1990*	*1991*
Age 10–14	M	2,006	1,823	1,986	1,729	1,835
	F	401	347	294	265	358
	Both	1,238	1,117	1,175	1,027	1,127
15–19	M	2,856	3,092	3,583	3,517	3,533
	F	387	378	410	420	398
	Both	1,676	1,794	2,060	2,034	2,032
20–24	M	2,176	2,167	2,524	2,776	2,683
	F	265	256	278	287	337
	Both	1,239	1,227	1,417	1,554	1,517
24–29	M	1,833	1,830	1,799	2,053	2,016
	F	295	257	243	236	248
	Both	1,082	1,054	1,025	1,140	1,122
10–29	M	2,185	2,192	2,420	2,489	2,484
	F	329	301	299	295	327
	Both	1,285	1,272	1,384	1,416	1,423
All Ages		846	822	852	852	842

Source: Youth Commission 1991 Survey: 144 based on RHKP Statistics.

Still in its infancy, criminology took for granted the official definition of juvenile delinquency. In her earlier 1973 study, Ng had used official records to identify offenders and compare them with non-offenders to test Hirchi's control theory.[16] Published in 1975, she identified 'a number of factors of juvenile delinquency' and made some recommendations to curb what by now was thought to be the well-established 'fact' of an 'increase in juvenile crime'.[17] This was followed by a 1977 study, also conducted by Ng as part of her doctoral dissertation in the area.[18] Mok's 1985 Adolescent Mentality project was the third major study in the field.[19] Ng argued that all three studies supported Hirschi's theory.

This sudden surge of administrative criminology's interest in juvenile delinquency was facilitated by government willingness to fund research into what it identified as a 'problem' area, and by the rise of sociology and psychology as academic subjects eager to apply themselves to social issues in Hong Kong. These factors help explain the dominance of control theory and derived social work approaches to juvenile delinquency, though not the obsession with disciplining youth that drove them. Criminology (such as it was) had its roots in the 1966 and 1967 riots, after which courses began to be delivered on theories such as Le Bon's 'the psychology of the crowd' and the social and psychological aspects of crime. These were run by the University of Hong Kong's Extra Mural Department[20] as two-week courses for social workers, prison officers and, after 1967, senior police and army officers with direct experience of the riots. The courses covered social, economic, historical, legal and tactical policing issues but in the late 1960s favoured social and psychological explanations of crime – the 1967 course, for example, took as its theme 'Society and the Criminal – Treatment or Punishment?'.[21] Running alongside these psychological explanations of deviancy was a strand of thinking which favoured discipline and punishment as the remedy for juvenile offending. This influenced the establishment, in 1972, of a 'short, sharp shock' detention centre at Sha Tsui, specifically targeted at young male offenders. Originally, Hong Kong had one Detention Centre at Sha Tsui, on Lantau Island. A second centre, at Tong Fuk, was reorganised in 1975 to become a drug addiction treatment centre, whereupon Sha Tsui was divided into two sections, one for juniors (aged 14 to 16) and another for seniors (aged 17–21). An adult section (21–24) was created in 1977, and in 1979 another centre was opened at Nei Kwu Chau to alleviate overcrowding at Sha Tsui. In 1982, this closed as the numbers received into detention declined.[22] Young offenders sent to Sha Tsui had no previous penal experience and served a minimum of one month up to a maximum of six; young adults served a minimum of three months and a maximum of 12.

In the early 1970s, over 70 per cent of those admitted to Detention Centres were first offenders. Though this figure dropped in the 1980s to between 30 and 40 per cent, by 1996 it was back up to almost 79 per cent.

Sha Tsui's regime was, from the outset, disciplinary and military in character, designed to 'instil into the young male detainees a healthy respect for the law, to create self-respect and an awareness of neglected capabilities in legitimate pursuits as well as an ability to live with other people in harmony'.[23] It was founded on the belief that effective early intervention in the life of a young offender can deter him from future delinquency. The regime developed in the 1970s remains much the same today. On entry, inmates are given a uniform and have their hair shaved. The buildings are Spartan, the cells austere with few if any personal possessions. The daily schedule (which begins at 05.45 and ends at 21.00) is regimented, rigorous, and 'brisk'. Inmates are allocated a hard bed without a mattress whose blankets must be folded with military precision and presented each morning for inspection. Silence, orderliness and politeness, along with hard work and physical exercise, are characteristics of the regime. Inmates are not allowed to speak unless spoken to or given permission to interact. Foot drill is standard, as is cutting grass with shears and breaking stones into small pieces. At mealtimes, inmates receive their food through a closed hatch preventing them from seeing the canteen staff who serve them. The 'separate and silent' regime, the hard labour and the stress on religion and physical exercise are all highly reminiscent of British Victorian prison regimes.[24] The strenuous regime means that inmates must be physically and mentally capable of withstanding the stress.

In 1981, the rhetoric of youth detention altered slightly. The 'short, sharp, shock' was now to be accompanied by regimes to 'precipitate change' and 'create faith in oneself' (Law 1996: 42). This pre-figured a shift in 1982, when the entire prison system became the Correctional Services Department, with a new ethos of rehabilitation and reform.[25] As Law points out, this was followed in 1990 by the cessation of corporal punishment (ibid).

Whilst there was little change in the official rate of juvenile crime between 1974 and 1978, the two-year period 1978 to 1980 saw a doubling of the rate (from 276 per 100,000 to 561). The increases continued in the 1980s, suggesting a 'net widening'.[26] Gray's data suggest that, even while more juveniles were receiving police cautions in the 1970s, many were simultaneously being brought before the courts for minor offences without any prior cautioning. In other words, rather than diverting less serious juvenile offenders from the courts, the system was bringing more juveniles (including those who had not yet offended) into the system.[27]

From 1980, Wong observes, four kinds of youth welfare services were developed: (1) children and youth centre work, (2) outreaching social work, (3) school social work, and (4) family life education (ibid). The children and youth centres provided recreation and guidance for children and youths aged 6 to 24. They organised classes for children and structured group work services. Outreaching social work tried to establish contact with young people 'detached' from the main social institutions and thus thought to be 'vulnerable to undesirable influences' (Wong 2000).

The many youth initiatives of the 1970s produced a self-fulfilling prophecy for, with Hong Kong on the alert for signs of deviant youth, more were discovered. In 1978, recorded juvenile crime had stood at 190.3 per 100,000. In 1979, this had increased to 315.8 per 100,000, and again to 477.7 per 100,000 in 1980.[28] The 1980 official figures showed an increase of 46 per cent for juvenile crime. In his speech to LEGCO, the Governor expressed his 'deep concern' about the 'big increase' in juvenile crime, describing it as 'disturbing and bewildering'. The Working Group, under the Fight Crime Committee, reported into the causes of juvenile crime in 1981.[29] Within a year, juvenile crime was said to be showing a 'marked decrease'. Nevertheless, as Mok says, 'the problem of delinquency continued to be a hot topic of discussion in the community' (Mok 1985: 1).

The police saw juvenile delinquency as intertwined with the problem of triads. Officially described as a 'shadow of their former selves', triad gangs were now conceived as fragmented street gangs rather than the sophisticated organised crime syndicates of the 1950s. But they were still thought to attract youth, especially in high-density housing areas.[30] The fight against juvenile crime was, then, seen partly as a war against triads. This was not, however, simply depicted as a problem for the police. Countering triad influence was a responsibility that was deemed to fall to parents, who needed to provide proper guidance for, and control over, their children (ibid).

In 1986, following Mok's 1985 study, Cheung and Ng [31] used secondary school students to test an integrated model which 'incorporated the most popular theories of delinquency . . . differential association theory, control theory, strain theory and labeling theory . . . with statistical analysis performed on the data' (Ng 1992: 1). This 'gave strong indications that differential association theory made the greatest contribution in explaining adolescent deviant behaviour in Hong Kong, followed by control and labeling theory' (ibid). Another study, published in 1986, looked at youth participation in billiard rooms.[32] This was accompanied by three further studies conducted by the YWCA and various District Boards into issues such as sex knowledge, behaviour and attitudes, stealing by youths, and the effect of video game centres on youth.[33] In 1986, Law conducted research into 'problem youth' in Kwun Tong.[34] This flurry of research in everything to do with 'deviant' youth was followed by yet another study in 1987, of 'unruly youth' in Tsuen Wan, Kwai Chung and Tsing Yi by Chow, Tang and Chan.[35]

In the schools, youth indiscipline was also a focus. In 1981, the Education Department set up four-monthly surveys of unruly and delinquent behaviour in all Hong Kong secondary schools. The introduction of compulsory secondary education in the 1970s made it easier to track the behaviour of juveniles by such means (Ng 1992: 16). In government, the Census and Statistics Department started to collect specific statistics on youth crime, as did the Working Group on Juvenile Crime.

In academia, a new category of 'delinquent-prone' youth was being delineated. These were mainly young men who, Ng argued, tended to hang around places that would expose them to 'undesirable situations', such as soft drink shops, billiard rooms and recreation grounds, Kung Fu clubs, and the video game centres which had sprung up in Hong Kong in the 1980s. By the late 1980s, deviant youth (and 'potentially deviant' youth) were the subject of study, classification and systematic inquiry more intensive than at any other point in Hong Kong's history.

The studies suggested that young people in Hong Kong had a 'more open attitude towards sex and attached more value to money' (Ng 1992: 24), shared hedonistic values, and exhibited 'deviant values'. The pursuit of money was, however, far from deviant. It was a dominant social value, status and prestige being associated with conspicuous wealth, however acquired. The fact that 'problem youth' placed such a high value of getting rich quick and enjoying life thus indicated that they simply aspired to the same values as those valorised by the dominant culture. There was no analysis of the social structural obstacles they faced in achieving these aspirations in a society where life chances were distributed in a highly unequal manner.

Ng herself later suggested a connection between the territory's dominant values and Hong Kong's economic take-off during this period. In 1992, for example, Ng revisited what she termed the 'trend in delinquent behaviour' from the 1970s to the 1990s adopting a socio-economic perspective. Her 1992 study examined family, school, peer group association, free time activities and values in relation to delinquent behaviour; data for the study was sourced from official statistics and other studies based on these statistics (Ng 1992: 2).

Ng argued that Hong Kong's rapid social and economic development during this period (industrialisation, urbanisation and 'modernisation') had produced changes conducive to social disorganisation and juvenile delinquency. These changes included the building of new towns, women in the workforce, growing means of transport and communications, the commercialisation of leisure time activities, all of which had undermined 'the old forms of social control represented by the family, the neighbourhood and the local community' (Ng 1992: 4). Ng related the association between delinquency and high rates of marital and family conflict found in previous studies to the reduction of time working women spent looking after the children, and the increased financial independence of women that allowed them to leave an unhappy marriage. However, Ng went further. Adopting the tenets of modernisation theory, she argued that 'youth deviancy' existed in all societies and was an 'inevitable' aspect of modernisation and socio-economic development. Since, she argued, 'economic growth is a good sign for society', youth delinquency was simply part of the price societies had to pay for progress elsewhere (Ng 1992: 26). Hong Kong should not, she concluded, be tempted to sacrifice economic development to the goal of reducing the juvenile crime rate.

Youth in the 1980s were not, in fact very different at all from previous generations. The kinds of crime they committed were also very similar, consisting mainly of petty larceny; the main difference was the increase in shoplifting. The latter reflected the policy decision by the chain stores to routinely report shop theft to the police rather than a worsening of youth behaviour – more juveniles were simply being *reported* to the police and prosecuted as a matter of policy.[36]

The attitude of criminal justice agencies towards juvenile crime had, however, altered since the 1950s. Young people were no longer seen as victims of poverty and overcrowding but as troublemakers, especially susceptible to bad influences (criminal and political) during adolescence. Deviancy and delinquency, which in the 1950s had been seen as a reflection of prevailing economic and social conditions, were now blamed on individual characteristics and broken family bonds. The 1966 Riot Report, which had concluded that young people in Hong Kong lacked a sense of 'belonging' to society, dovetailed well with the precepts of control theory, which stressed the notion that 'delinquent behaviour occurs when one's bond to society is weakened or has broken down' (Mok 1985: 2).

Of all the available textbooks explanations of juvenile crime, Hirschi's control theory found (and still finds) greatest favour amongst academics, officials and social work professionals (see Gray 1991). Control theory is essentially conservative in that it allows deviance to be interpreted as an *atypical* phenomenon, caused when an individual with weakened ties to family, school and society fall under the influence of a deviant subculture (such as, for example, triads or subversives). 'Most young people' in Hong Kong would not, on this view, turn into delinquents unless they became involved in, or were influenced by, this deviant few (Mok 1985: 2). Thus, young offenders became the subject of a flurry of studies that found that:

> . . . the preconditions of delinquency include[d] unfavourable family relationships, undesirable peer group associations, poor choice of free time activities and inadequate moral development, while the immediate factor contributing to delinquent behaviour [were] the involvement with triad gangs and dropping out of school (Mok 1985: 3).

In classic 'net widening' fashion, Mok's 1985 study also shifted the focus on youth to include not only convicted juveniles but a new category, 'problem' youth, i.e. those not legally defined as delinquent but who were said to have demonstrated 'problem behaviour and a potential to turn to unlawful acts' (Mok 1985: 3). For Mok, prevention and cure consisted first and foremost in the strengthening of family ties to combat deviancy, followed by improved access to employment, housing, health care, education and 'liveable, safe neighbourhoods' as vital to the support of family life. Secondary strategies included outreach social work with those identified as 'detached youth', and preventative work with 'problem youngsters' who, if 'properly understood' could be 'saved from falling' into deviancy.

Writing in 1993, Cheung also sought to predict deviant behaviour amongst juveniles by widening the range of 'bad influences' to which they were exposed to include the mass media.[37]

Collectively, these studies were seen as the first truly scientific studies of delinquency in Hong Kong. Ng's early 1970s studies were characterised by simple uni-variate comparisons, whereas later studies are seen as 'more rigorous', employing more methodologically sound methods, the language of quantitative social science ('research instruments', random sampling, questionnaires, probability models) as well as the socio-psychological theories of deviance validated by academics elsewhere. But none raised fundamental questions about the relationship between the goals and values of Hong Kong society and the designation of youth as a problem. Instead, they explained juvenile delinquency within the standard parameters of administrative criminology. Though they sometimes hinted at a relationship between 'deviant youth' and Hong Kong's rapid economic development, the link was conceived in modernisation theory terms, reflecting a wider trend in Hong Kong sociology at the time (which was dominated by attempts to chart the colony's 'economic miracle'). Since economic growth was generally reckoned to be good thing, theories that located the causes of crime in capitalism or the response of official agencies enjoyed little popularity. Studies of juvenile delinquency remained essentially social-psychological and individualistic. Youth delinquency was seen principally as intentional or unintentional ('drift') deviation from consensual social values, to be neutralised by the strengthening of various social controls.

In the 1990s, some academics did critique the 'myth' that Hong Kong was an open society in which everyone who studied and worked hard could be upwardly mobile; some also attempted to bring class into their analyses of Hong Kong society. But studies of crime never adopted these more critical approaches, nor the relationship between socio-economic and political structures and delinquency, nor the relationship of the norms, goals and values of 'deviant' subcultures to those of the dominant culture. Instead, juvenile delinquency became a taken-for-granted 'fact'. Official records of it, and the volume of scholarly and official writings about it, became the evidence that Hong Kong had a 'youth problem'. The task of criminologists, social workers and law and order agencies was how to tame it.

In this, they were joined by various departments of government. New guidelines for civic education, published in August 1985, had the stated aim of fostering the capacity of young people to assume responsibility as 'full members of the adult community'.[38] At a sensitive political time, the government was concerned to keep Hong Kong stable and apolitical. Youth became part of this agenda because of its recent history of involvement in civil unrest. Fears about youth as delinquents now dovetailed with fears about youth as political activists. Thus, the new guidelines noted, there was 'a special need at this particular time in Hong Kong's social and political development for schools to renew their commitment to the preservation of social order'. Civic education would facilitate this (ibid). It stressed the development of a 'sense of belonging' to Hong Kong, respect for one's elders, politeness, harmony pride and loyalty to the school, to Hong Kong, love for China and pride in the achievements of its people, a willingness to co-operate, justice, tolerance, a sense of responsibility to the group, co-operation with others (including the government) for the common good of the group, participation in activities in support of the common good, public spiritedness, respect for other people's rights, awareness of the value of freedom, care for public property, readiness to accept compromise as a way of settling differences, appreciation of 'how democratic principles being applied in the structure and processes of the Hong Kong Government', and 'appreciation of the efforts required to ensure a prosperous and stable future for Hong Kong in accordance with the Sino–British Joint Declaration' (ibid). As in the 1970s, the government played a key part in the creation of this new discourse and, as in the 1970s, it was constituted from above as well as from below (Lam 2005).

Though the Hong Kong Education Department officially rejected political indoctrination, there is little doubt that it saw civic education as a vehicle for implanting a positive image of the Hong Kong government and the 1997 handover. The education system would help develop more 'law abiding' and 'co-operative' citizens. This 'education for depoliticization'[39] discouraged students 'from identifying with their ethnic group, indigenous culture (Chinese or local) or the political authority (the Chinese government)' (Tse 1992 in Morris and Sweeting 1997: 8). It also favoured an alien medium of instruction

(English), strove to be 'apolitical' insofar as it did not foster any particular identity with British rule or with the Chinese government in Mainland China or Taiwan, avoided 'sensitive' issues in politics and history, and was oriented towards a one-sided and distorted concept of citizenship:

> What was reflected in the formal curriculum was a kind of subject political culture concerned more with administrative output and the political system, rather than political input and one's rights and obligations . . . the curriculum carried supporting beliefs in the existing political institution and a passive image of citizenship conducive to a political culture of silence. The content of political education [was] depoliticized into 'civic education' for 'good citizens' . . . defined as passive, obedient, and complacent persons and cooperative recipients of governmental services (Tse 1997: 9).

Following the Joint Declaration in 1984, therefore, youth were captured by social work, the criminal justice system and the education system, all seeking to produce ideal citizens and discourage wayward behaviour. Hong Kong citizens were, from this point onwards, to acquire a new identity as citizens of the PRC; civic education was to encourage nationalistic, patriotic values and to 'prepare for national integration in 1997' (Tse 1997: 11). In the 1990s, shortly before and after the 1997 handover, educational institutions, in-school and after-school groups, would once again be harnessed to inculcate values favourable to Hong Kong's new sovereign power, China. The system established in the 1970s for winning the hearts and minds of Hong Kong youth thus also lent itself to recolonisation during the transition years. The strategy was, however, thwarted by the events of 4 June 1989.

Notes

1 RHKPAR 1984: 6.
2 RHKPAR 1985: 6; 1986: 6.
3 RHKPAR 1987; 1988.
4 RHKPAR 1987: 6.
5 RHKPAR 1981; 1982.
6 RHKPAR 1981: 14–5.
7 RHKPAR 182: 5.
8 RHKPAR 1983: 7.
9 RHKPAR 1983: 17.
10 RHKPAR 1983: 7.
11 RHKPAR 1980: 11.
12 RHKPAR 1984: 13.
13 RHKPAR 1985: 13.
14 RHKPAR 1988: 12.
15 Mok 1985.
16 Hirschi 1969.

17 Ng, A. 1975.
18 Ng, A 1980, first published as study in 1977.
19 Mok 1985.
20 The University had started a part-time course on law and order in 1957, after the 1956 riots, again mainly for serving police officers.
21 HKPAR 1966/7: 15.
22 Law, Yick-man 1996.
23 CSDAR 2000: 18.
24 Indeed, when in the 1990s Jones taught disciplined services students in Hong Kong about 'Victorian penality' in the UK, they immediately associated it with the regime at Sha Tsui.
25 See Vagg 1991b: 139; Law 1996: 42.
26 Gray 1997, pp 187–208.
27 Gray 1991, cited in Wong, D. 2000: 281.
28 RHKPAR 1980: 8.
29 Fight Crime Committee 1981.
30 RHKPAR 1980: 5.
31 Cheung and Ng 1988.
32 YWCA 1986a.
33 YWCA 1986b; YWCA 1986c; YWCA 1986d.
34 Law, C.K. 1986.
35 Chow et al 1987.
36 Vagg et al 1995: 359.
37 Cheung Y.W. 1993.
38 Curriculum Development Committee 1985: 1.
39 Tse 1992; Morris and Sweeting 1997: 247–64.

Chapter 23

The transition years: 1990–97

As Scott has argued, in the 1990s the colonial administration's 'right to rule' was undermined by PRC interference in the government's decisions, making it something of a 'lame duck' administration. Moreover, in anticipation of the handover, Chinese tycoons increasingly deserted the British administration to cement ties with Hong Kong's incoming masters. This, in effect, removed the core of elite support upon which the government had for so long relied.

Though both Britain and China had gone to some lengths since the 1984 Joint Declaration to calm nerves in the territory, the Communist Party's repression of the student and worker pro-democracy protests in cities around China in 1989 intensified what was already a widespread uncertainty in the territory about the 1997 retrocession. The 4 June protests prompted a huge sympathetic reaction amongst Hong Kong people, including school children, students and those in disciplined services. Throughout the preceding month of May, Hong Kong groups had sent food and supplies to the demonstrators, as well as messages of support. A number of large processions, concerts and meetings were held. When, on 4 June, the pro-democracy protests were crushed, Hong Kong witnessed its largest ever public demonstration. An estimated 1 million people marched through the streets of Central, Wanchai and Causeway Bay. Though no public order incidents were reported (the marchers were described as remarkably orderly and peaceful) rumours of possible disturbances on following days prompted the authorities to curtail the demonstrations.

In one fell swoop, 4 June 1989 exponentially increased people's anxieties about the future. Doomsday scenarios of communist oppression and the return of corruption and cronyism vied with brighter visions of a Hong Kong free of the yoke of colonialism being re-united with the motherland, of Hong Kong people running Hong Kong. The fact that people chose to emigrate in large numbers at the start of the decade suggested a lack of faith in the promise that life after 1997 would remain unaltered. In 1990 alone, the number emigrating reached 62,000; more planned to leave in the coming years.[1]

The prevailing uncertainty manifested itself in a number of ways – some suggested that the rise in bank robberies and reported corruption in the early 1990s indicated a desire to 'get rich quick' before 1997. This uncertainty intensified with the arrival, in 1992, of the new Governor, Chris Patten, whose policy speech in October 1992 provoked the wrath of the CCP leadership and marked the beginning of five years of fractious exchanges between China and the Hong Kong administration. In this atmosphere of intense political and social anxiety, all kinds of rumours were rife and all sorts of dangers seemed to threaten Hong Kong's stability.[2] In many respects, the scene was set for yet another 'moral panic' about crime.

People's fears were driven in part by perceptions of China built up during its isolation between 1949 and 1978. On the one hand, by the 1990s, Hong Kong had acquired a reputation as a cosmopolitan, free and open city. The ICAC had cleaned up corruption; the government had become more accountable to the public and to law; the territory was attractive both to those who lived there and to overseas investors. Society was orderly and the environment made more pleasant and equitable by the reforms of the MacLehose years. On the other hand, China was seen as an authoritarian, 'backward' society, riddled with crime and corruption, a place where government officials got rich by expropriating state assets and remained above the law, and where demonstrations prompted outright state repression. Such imagery fed into existing narratives of Hong Kong as a 'city of law' and China as a 'lawless land'. The contrast between the Chinese state repression of the 4 June movement, and the Hong Kong administration's tolerance of demonstrations of support, confirmed this divide.

The fear of capital flight and loss of local confidence in the territory after 1989 propelled the British and Hong Kong administrations to introduce a series of measures designed to restore confidence and assuage people's fears. These included several large infrastructure projects, such as the building of new airport at Chep Lap Kok, a high speed rail link and a six-lane highway (see Thomas 1999: 215), and a Bill of Rights (BOR) introduced in 1991. The BOR was regarded as a major effort to improve social stability. It enshrined civil liberties, entrenched the International Covenant on Civil and Political Rights, and necessitated the repeal of all legislation inconsistent with the rights laid down in the BOR (ibid). Hong Kong had a crime control system of criminal justice. The BOR had so many major implications for state agencies that they had to request a 'freeze' period in order to fillet existing laws and procedures to eliminate human rights contraventions. Probably the most significant of these was the presumption of guilt, present in a number of ordinances, and which directly contravened Article 11(1) of the BOR (presumption of innocence).[3] Once the review was completed, the system acquired a more 'due process' character, though plenty of room remained for a series of challenges to the criminal law and criminal procedure throughout the 1990s. Indeed, such cases were to form the bulk of those brought under the BOR.

The Chinese side called for the repeal of the BOR, and after 1997 it was in any case made subordinate to the Basic Law. The post–1997 administration also came under pressure from Beijing to amend it to provide a more conservative interpretation of civil liberties, and 'for the first time in Hong Kong's history, the sanctity of national security was introduced as the guiding principle in defining public order' (Thomas 1999: 251). Thomas argues that the introduction of a National Flag and Emblem Ordinance was an example of how, post–1997, law was used to restrict social and political expression (two people were convicted of defacing the SAR and national flag in 1998). For the years between 1991 and 1997, however, the BOR had a marked influence on legal culture and criminal justice, moving both in the direction of liberalism.

Crime and public order

The push for stability, caution and prudence was upset in the early part of the 1990s by continuing political demonstrations. Crime also disturbed the official picture of tranquillity in spectacular style, with a series of daring violent robberies in the first few years. These were blamed on gangsters, said to have been brought into the territory from China specifically for the purpose. Chinese gangs were also said to be using illegal immigrants to smuggle arms into Hong Kong, which were later used in the pursuit of crime. Gang leaders and triads were known to have close connections to powerful PRC officials, making organised crime a potentially politically embarrassing matter. The implication of Chinese criminals, arms and explosives in Hong Kong crime fed fears that retrocession meant moral decline and – where crime was connected to PRC officialdom – doubts about the government's capacity to enforce the law after 1997. Some of the arms (and, it was rumoured, personnel) originated from the People's Liberation Army (PLA) – large numbers of soldiers had, apparently, been demobilised in the 1980s without forfeiting their arms or uniforms; some were reckoned to be for hire to Mainland, Hong Kong and Macau-based triads.

Some of the gangsters fled Hong Kong justice for refuge in China; a few were repatriated to Hong Kong, following liaison with the Guangdong authorities and eventually stood trial in Hong Kong. Later, some would win appeals against their convictions, prompting conservatives to claim that the BOR had skewed Hong Kong's criminal justice system 'too far' away from crime control. After 1997, one of the gangsters was arrested, tried, and executed in the Mainland for other crimes committed in Hong Kong, re-awakening the old discourses of harsh Mainland justice *versus* Hong Kong's more humanitarian system. Public opinion was divided as to whether the Hong Kong authorities should have insisted on his being brought back for trial in Hong Kong where, unlike Mainland China, the death penalty did not apply (see below).[4]

As in earlier times, there were those who argued that sending offenders back to the Mainland would deter crime. Cross-border criminals were said to see Hong Kong's comparatively liberal system of justice as a haven. The comparative wealth of Hong Kong also made it attractive to mainland criminal gangs. The cross-border smuggling of luxury goods became the defining motif of the early years of the decade. Luxury vehicles, such as Mercedes Benz, Lexus, BMWs, and Toyota Crown (Hong Kong was said to have the highest number of Rolls Royce cars per head of population than anywhere else in the world) were stolen to order and smuggled by armour-plated, high powered speed boats, capable of speeds of up to 70 knots, (*da feis*) out of Hong Kong waters and into China. These exploits were often conducted in complete darkness, without radar or navigation lights, resulting in a number of fatal collisions. High speed intercepts were not, the police concluded, a viable option as they could result in death and injury. Organised crime syndicates, with criminal connections in China, were suspected. The high-speed boats were, as the police observed, equally well suited to smuggling armed criminals from and to China.[5]

As the 1990s progressed, the word 'border' was quietly replaced in official parlance by the word 'boundary', suggesting a more porous relationship between the two places in the run-up to 1997. Old issues resurfaced in different guises. Deng Xiaoping blamed China's rising crime rate on the 'flies' that flew through the 'open door' from Hong Kong and the West. In Hong Kong, on the other hand, it was argued that Mainland crime was 'infecting' the territory, bumping up its crime rate and, especially, the incidence of violent crime.

In the declining years of colonial rule, the administration had to demonstrate that British institutions could still protect the people of Hong Kong. The Chinese authorities, equally keen to ensure the territory's stability, promised that China would not become a 'typhoon shelter' for Hong Kong criminals.[6] In the mid-1990s, the Hong Kong police reported 'an excellent and increasingly important relationship with Chinese law enforcement agencies in the form of cross-border intelligence, joint operations and 'working level contacts' with the PSB. However public criticism accompanied the revelation that, in the mid-1990s (ie before the hand-over) PSB officers had crossed the border to investigate a case in Hong Kong; there were also rumours that the PLA were training alongside the PTU at Fanling. Such rumours raised the temperature in a Hong Kong already sceptical about the possibility (and desirability) of linking two criminal justice systems based on such different values.

The politicisation of the territory proceeded apace, fed partly by domestic issues, partly by China's attitude toward Hong Kong, and partly by concerns about the landscape of Hong Kong after 1997. Political reform encouraged the formation of political parties, the holding of election meetings and rallies and, of course, the holding of the elections themselves, something of a novelty for Hong Kong people (and their police). In 1991, the first of the direct elections to LEGCO were held around the territory. Demonstrations and rallies generally centred on the Central district of Hong Kong Island, which housed all the major political and financial institutions of the territory. According to the police:

> Hong Kong Island continued to record a considerable number of public processions and meetings during the year arising from both 'democratic' and local issues, such as imported labour, the Government budget, etc. which required the deployment of police resources. Victoria Park, Chater Gardens, Queen's Road East outside the New China (Xinhua) News Agency, Central Government Offices, Legislative Council Chambers and the east gate of Government House continued to be the most favoured places . . . Apart from these, the clearance of the Walled City and the issue of Human Rights also led to widespread public disquiet.[7]

The paramilitary capability of the police was deployed on a number of occasions, such as forced clearance of the pro-Nationalist village of Rennie's Mill in 1995, which provoked significant (but under-reported) public order incidents. The presence of the police at clearances was, by now, taken for granted and provoked little media attention. The PTU was also deployed on other civil duties, such as quelling minor disturbances surrounding the opening of an AIDS clinic in Richland Gardens. Nervous that any public demonstration might develop into something more serious, the authorities seemed determined to suppress relatively minor incidents by a show of force. A delicate balance had to be struck, however, as over-enthusiastic use of the PTU would harm Britain's carefully cultivated image as a benign colonial power.

Political sensitivities were running high throughout the decade. In 1997 itself, the world's media descended on Hong Kong, raising the possibility of adverse international publicity for any police action that appeared heavy-handed. A potential source of such confrontation arose when, in June 1997, student demonstrators insisted on transporting a 'Statue of Shame' from the annual Victoria Park gathering (to commemorate 4 June) to the University of Hong Kong.[8] After some pushing and shoving, and much singing of the 'Internationale' and 'We Shall Overcome', in the early hours of the morning the students finally succeeded in their objective, as the police blocking their entrance to the university campus tactfully decided not to deploy paramilitary force, and stood down.

Throughout the mid-1990s, acrimonious differences between the Hong Kong Governor and the CCP leadership in Beijing ensured continuous public debate, protests and processions. In 1995, for example, there were protests when Beijing appointed its own Provisional LEGCO to replace the existing LEGCO after 1997 – the landslide victory of the pro-democracy candidates in the 1995 elections put an end to the notion that existing LEGCO members would serve through the handover period (the so-called 'through train').

In 1997 itself, the exit of the pro-democracy party from LEGCO at midnight on 30 June, made the LEGCO building a site of great symbolic importance. A large but peaceful crowd gathered to witness the event. Simultaneously, the other major symbolic site – the Convention Centre – witnessed the formal handover ceremony, the departure of the Governor, and the installation of new office-bearers. However, the public were kept well clear of this venue partly because of fears for the security of PRC leaders during their visit to Hong Kong, as well as fears of mass protest.

It was unclear where the main threat was thought to lie – there were rumours that disaffected Mainland groups would attempt to attack the PRC leaders by bombing the Convention Centre; others thought terrorists or separatists might exploit the occasion. In any event, security was high – all police leave was cancelled and the auxiliary police, the PTU, the VIP Protection Team, the Special Duties Unit, the Explosive Ordinance Disposal Unit and the Force Escort Unit were all mobilised.[9] At midnight on 30 June, all of Hong Kong's disciplined service officers were required to replace their uniform buttons (bearing the British crown) for buttons depicting the symbol of the new regime. The evening's torrential rain continued non-stop for days afterwards. Depending on one's position, this was variously interpreted as a sign of 'the washing away of the sins of colonialism', or the 'sky weeping because the British are leaving'.

Violent crime

Certain types of offence tended in the 1990s to be taken as symbolic of wider social problems and political issues, with 1997 as a subtext. For example, spectacular violent crimes, such as armed gold shop robberies, provoked alarm in the early 1990s partly because their 'China connection' fuelled the sense that Hong Kong had already started that descent into 'lawlessness' associated in the public mind with 1997. Increasing corruption reports in 1993 reinforced fears that re-unification was already undermining law and order. Officials were anxious to reassure both the local population and overseas investors and financial institutions that Hong Kong was, and would remain, safe.

Discourse about crime in the 1990s also shifted slightly with the hollowing out of the regime's elite support in the territory. After 1992, Pattern's governorship was marked by an appeal to the grass-roots constituency of support. Issues that affected them – homelessness, crime, employment, poverty – attracted far more attention than when the government catered for elite interests alone. On his celebrated 'walkabouts' around the territory, the governor came face to face with ordinary people in a fashion not seen since the MacLehose years. The rhetoric of his term of office seemed, at least, to take account of their concerns and constantly linked their interests to the need for order, stability and the rule of law. This said, securing an environment for Hong Kong's economy remained a priority. Hong Kong's economy was far more globalised by the 1990s. This, and the territory's value as a symbol of free market capitalism, made its continuation as an international financial centre an issue for more than just the domestic police.

It was thus imperative that, in last years of the colonial regime, law and order was seen to be intact. This was equally important for Beijing, anxious to convince the world that it could maintain Hong Kong's success. The state of crime was an important indicator of the body politic. People looked for a signs of a slide into moral decay.[10] The decade began with a spate of sensational violent robberies, mostly of watch shops, gold shops and banks, and mostly involving firearms. These rose by over 24 per cent in 1990.[11] Between 1990 and 1992, there were over 100 incidents where the criminals actually opened fire (with high-powered automatic guns such as AK–47s, Polish submachine guns, pistols, or hand grenades) endangering not only the police but also the public, many of their targets being located in busy shopping and tourist areas.

However, the 1994 crime survey[12] data showed that the use of firearms was rare, the use of any weapons had declined overall and that, where weapons were used, they tended to be used in shop robberies rather than in crimes of personal violence. Few offenders carried weapons of any kind. In 1979, 47 per cent of crimes of violence and 54 per cent of robberies had been carried out by armed persons. In 1986, more than a quarter of crimes of violence involved the use of a weapon – knives or daggers – usually in robberies (45 per cent) rather than assaults (29 per cent). This was still the same in 1994 – knives and daggers were still the weapons of choice, especially in robberies (metal tools and wooden poles in assaults). Although public perceptions were that crime had become more violent, the nature of violent crime had changed little since 1979.

However, crime survey data was still poorly understood and even more poorly reported in the mass media. The official statistics retained their 'master status,' underpinning all public discourse on crime. These showed that recorded violent crime had risen. In 1990, it rose by 8.5 per cent and comprised about 21 per cent of all crime. In 1991, it rose by a further 4 per cent and comprised 22 per cent of all crime.[13] Serious assaults, woundings, robberies and rape all showed a rise. Homicide rose to its highest level in ten years by the end of 1990. The highly visible gold shop and bank robberies and shootouts made a big impression on the public mind. One incident in 1991 set the record for robbery in Hong Kong (HK$167 million); another involved police officers and robbers in a shoot-out following gold shop robberies in Kwun Tong (HK$6.15 million). Many of the targets (banks, gold shops, watch shops) were on the busy thoroughfares of Kowloon, and so were witnessed by crowds of onlookers. The NT also saw its share of violent crime. Police pursuing a prisoner who had escaped from custody became involved in a shoot-out with a gang in Kam Tin; the robbery of a Securicor van in Tin Sum ended in a double murder.[14]

The official figures for 1989 and 1990 also showed increases in recorded crime overall, up by almost 8 per cent in 1990 to 88,300. But in terms of the crime rate, things looked slightly better: In 1990, the overall crime rate had risen to 1,547.9 (per 100,000 population) but in 1991, even though crime had risen in absolute terms (to 88,659) the police were able to report a slight fall in the crime rate to 1,540.6.[15] By 1992, the force was in a position to argue that the crime rate had steadily dropped over the last ten years (to 1,446 per 100,000), and by 1993, it could claim that the crime rate was now at its lowest for ten years.[16]

Other crime

According to the crime statistics, in the early 1990s, burglary rose by 16.4 per cent (from 10,913 offences in 1989 to 12,701 in 1990 and 13,898 in 1991). Shop thefts also increased, as did snatchings. Fewer people were killed or injured but more were arrested (over 44,000). Of these, in 1990 15 per cent (6,583) were juveniles and 19 per cent young offenders (8,306); in 1991, the number of juveniles arrested rose (to 7,044). Vietnamese 'boat people' (dubbed 'VBPs') accounted for 1.8 per cent of all recorded offences in 1990 and 2 per cent in 1991, but were over-represented in categories such as wounding, serious assault, theft, public order offences and drug trafficking (ibid). The number of illegal immigrants arrested for crime (mostly ID card offences) rose by 38.7 per cent.[17]

The early 1990s also saw more bumper crops in the Golden Triangle, ensuring that narcotics enforcement once again remained a high priority. A new law in 1989 (the Drug Trafficking (Recovery of Proceeds) ordinance) enabled the confiscation of assets and property from convicted drug traffickers. The main drug entering Hong Kong was still heroin (and injecting the main form of its use) but for the first time the police reported 'ice' transiting the territory en route to markets in Japan and the Philippines.[18] Hong Kong remained a major transhipment centre for drugs from Asia to the USA, though by 1993, the police were also reporting that Taiwan seemed to have overtaken Hong Kong as the preferred transhipment centre for drugs bound for the USA. Domestically, there was also an increase in drugs such as ecstasy and ketamine, used mainly by the younger age group as part of the music, party and club scene. Despite punitive measures to deter drug taking, and the close supervision of recovering drug addicts, the official estimate of the number of drug users in the territory on the eve of the handover was around 12,000.[19]

These figures fuelled the widely held belief that crime was getting worse and fed into the discourse of a pre-1997 decline. As Broadhurst argues, the 'crime barometer' is seen as one way of measuring the state's effectiveness at crime control and suppression, indeed, of the state's capacity more generally (Broadhurst 2000: 1). In the Hong Kong of the 1990s, such measures were popularly regarded as a sign of whether the territory's administration had the capacity to withstand the challenges presented by the 1997 handover.

The authorities continued to crack down on familiar cross-border crimes such as the smuggling of cigarettes, electrical appliances, luxury goods and cars, as well as the 'people smuggling' rackets. An Anti-Smuggling Task Force (comprising police, Customs and Excise, the military and the Security Branch) was formed in 1991 to tackle the problem. New legislation was, however, said to have simply prompted the smugglers to turn to more sophisticated and clandestine methods. The institutional capacity of the police was also challenged by increasingly sophisticated commercial crimes – such as cloned phones, cheque kiting, forex frauds and advance fee frauds, as well as a new trade in bogus emigration documents and consultancies (prompted by the clamour to emigrate before 1997). Such crimes directly threatened Hong Kong's status as an international 'economic city', all the more important now that it had lost its claim to be a manufacturing centre to cities in Southern China, where plant and labour were cheaper. The authorities were quick to respond to this threat. A Computer Crime Ordinance in 1993 led to the formation of a new computer crimes section within the Commercial Crime Bureau, and new legislation was introduced in 1994 to regulate forex trading. A Hong Kong-based gang involved in credit card fraud was arrested in Miami in 1993, as a result of liaison with overseas police and private security agencies. But regulation of the financial services industry was slower, direct government intervention in such matters going against the grain for a famously *laissez-faire* administration. The result was numerous financial scams and cowboys trading within the domestic sector whilst poor regulation also made Hong Kong a haven for the irregular operation of international firms. The most spectacular commercial crime investigation of the 1990s concerned the collapse of the Bank of Credit and Commerce International (BCCI) in which – unlike elsewhere – many ordinary Hong Kong people had invested their savings. Although the failure of BCCI was an international scandal – and although commercial crimes are often seen as 'victimless' crimes – in Hong Kong its collapse affected thousands ordinary people, leading to widespread protests in the territory. This damaged the territory's reputation as a safe location for banking and investment. It was exactly the kind of thing that the Hong Kong authorities wished to avoid in the run-up to 1997.

Triads

The activities of triads also fed into the fears of the authorities and public alike concerning the break down of law and order before 1997. Because Hong Kong's triads had expanded overseas throughout the 1980s and 1990s (especially to Canada, Australia and the USA) this was interpreted by some commentators as sign that they were preparing to decant from Hong Kong after China's resumption of sovereignty. In fact, quite the opposite was the case. For Hong Kong triads, 1997 was an opportunity to join Mainland Chinese and Russian crime syndicates as one of the many forces engaged in international organised crime. In 1991, the police Security Wing prepared a report for government on the activities of triads in the territory and their expansion into Mainland China and the authorities began to detect the increased presence of Mainland crime gangs in Hong Kong. This was to become a more developed symbiosis as the decade wore on, though it also provoked inter-triad feuding, especially violent in the Portuguese colony of Macau, which derived much of its income from the tourism attached to gambling and casinos. Locally, triad involvement in the Hong Kong film business prompted an usually high-profile – and thus risky – protest by movie stars, led by Jackie Chan, calling for an end to the extortion and protection rackets run by triads. The families of local celebrities were threatened if they failed to co-operate with triad demands; contract kidnappings of the rich and famous were commonly supposed to involve triad gangsters. Triads had also expanded into more up-market nightclubs, restaurants and hotels, especially in the reclaimed area of Tsim Sha Tsui East. With 40 per cent of Hong Kong's experienced crime fighters expected to leave the territory before 1997, there were growing doubts about the capacity of the police to combat organised crime.

Triads were once again spoken of as a threat and, given their political patronage, a potential 'imperium within an imperium'. An Organised Crime Bill, introduced in 1991, accorded anti-triad work a 'much higher priority'.[20] The Organised and Serious Crimes Ordinance, which became law in 1995, allowed courts to increase ('enhance') the sentences of those convicted of organised crimes by between 25 per cent and 66 per cent.[21] The OCTB was said to be taking 'more offensive action' against triads, whilst the new law would 'destroy the power of criminal syndicates by confiscating their profits from criminal activities'.[22] In a series of operations mounted throughout the 1990s, the police continued to target major triads, such as the Sun Yee On, the 14K and the Wo Shing Wo, all of which operated substantial blackmail and loan-sharking rackets as well as extortion around vegetable markets, public light bus routes, container yard businesses, and vice establishments. The 1987 police offensive against the Sun Yee On was undone when, a few years later, the 'dragonhead' and his associates won appeals against their convictions after witnesses changed their evidence. As in the 1950s, witness intimidation was, the police argued, making it difficult to obtain convictions at trial. Unlike the 1950s, no one suggested deportation or detention without trial as a solution. Those who did seek to emigrate to Canada or Australia, however, sometimes found themselves debarred from entry due to real or suspected triad connections.

Migration

Another area that became more pressured in the run-up to 1997 was that of the presence – and ongoing arrival of – large numbers of Vietnamese 'boat people'. There was little doubt in anyone's mind that China did not wish to inherit this population at the handover, making it imperative for the authorities to resolve the situation before 1 July 1997.

After 1992, illegal immigrants from China also seemed to arrive in even larger numbers. In 1990, 27,826 illegal immigrants were arrested and these large numbers continued into the mid-1990s. Some sought employment on Hong Kong's massive infrastructure projects, also destined to be completed before the handover; some younger women were smuggled in by 'snakeheads' who promised them work in hotels and restaurants but put them to work in brothels instead; others were 'returners' who had previously been repatriated to China but returned to the territory in order to make a better living. This, the police suggested, indicated that a hard core of illegal immigrants was coming to Hong Kong regularly to work. Laws targeted at employers seemed to have little effect, despite police raids on construction sites. Hong Kong faced similar problems to other cities in China (and indeed the rest of the globalised world) as poor migrants flocked to more prosperous areas in search of work. As in China, such migrants formed a sub-strata of the informal economy, on which many of Hong Kong's infrastructure projects and booming small businesses relied. As in China, those caught working illegally ended up in detention awaiting repatriation.

This movement of population reprised the nineteenth century, when political turmoil and poverty drove migrants to Hong Kong in search of work (and often on to the USA as part of the 'coolie' trade'). A hundred and fifty years later, the authorities still struggled to manage the flow of people, the mixture of legal and administrative measures only ever partially successful. Public stereotypes of Chinese illegal immigrants as criminals were fuelled by stories of attacks on people in the country parks near the border, the murder of two elderly people in Yuen Long in the NT, robberies and thefts on the edges of urban areas and travellers' tales of Shenzhen as a crime-infested city where Hong Kong tourists were likely to be robbed, murdered – or wake up with a kidney removed. Chinese illegal immigrants thus came to be seen as folk devils carrying 'lawless China' into Hong Kong's law-abiding body.

The police force, still responsible for day-to-day crime control, now also resumed responsibility for patrolling the border from the army; it also ran three of the detention camps for Vietnamese refugees; the Anti-Illegal Immigration Bureau (founded during the 1962 wave of immigrants from China) was replaced by Crime Marine. The introduction, in 1992, of the Orderly Repatriation Scheme and Voluntary Repatriation Programme halted the large numbers of Vietnamese entering the territory (ibid). But, as 1997 drew nearer, pressure increased to clear the camps by repatriating everyone 'screened out' as an economic migrant, or resettling elsewhere those granted refugee status. The authorities were, it was said, determined to repatriate all Vietnamese migrants to Vietnam before July 1997.[23] The issue was complicated by the reluctance of partner countries to admit their quota of refugees, leaving some stranded stateless in Hong Kong.

Despite financial incentives by the European Union, not all those repatriated to Vietnam went voluntarily. The government was damaged internationally by media coverage of distraught Vietnamese in 'extraction operations' being led onto 'repatriation flights' at Kai Tak airport. The removal of others from Tai A Chau in 1996 also prompted widespread criticism of government, police and CSD tactics. In 1992, adverse publicity also surrounded a riot at Shek Kong (started by fighting between rival Southern and Northern Vietnamese) that left 24 people (including 12 children) dead and 116 wounded.[24] The use of tear gas and water cannons by the police and CSD during camp disturbances (such as that at Whitehead in 1996) prompted official enquiries and aroused public debate as to whether Hong Kong alone could manage such a difficult (and costly) issue.

A number of successful legal cases brought by Vietnamese boat people against the government also seriously damaged the administration's new image as a bastion of human rights. In 1990, for example, a group of 111 Vietnamese boat people challenged the lawfulness of their detention. The Vietnamese were not especially popular with the Hong Kong public but their spectacular victory against the government attracted huge publicity and left a lasting impression that 'little people' could win against the government in the courts. In the *Pham Van Ngo* case, for example, Mr Justice Sears strongly criticised the immigration service for detaining 111 Vietnamese boat people fleeing Vietnam for Japan, describing the fact that they had been deprived of their liberty for 18 months (on the basis on a telephone call) as 'an affront to the rule of law':

> The power to detain must be for a reasonable period of time; what that should be depends on the particular facts, on which as I have said earlier, I was being kept in the dark . . . The evidence of Mr Asprey [Secretary for Security] does not justify the conduct of the Government in depriving these persons of their liberty for such a long period of time . . . there was a clear and unequivocal promise by the Government that they would repair the boat, and the person were 'free to leave Hong Kong'; instead, the boat was destroyed and the persons found themselves in a detention centre. Any right minded democratic society should be appalled at these events . . . Fortunately, the law . . . recognises that Governments cannot behave in this manner . . . The Government, in my judgment, must have thought that . . . it was far cheaper and easier just to lock these people up, rather than help them . . . I am in no doubt that the standard of the Government's conduct fell woefully short of what would be expected in a

> civilised community . . . These 111 . . . have been treated as if they were an unwelcome nuisance rather than as human beings . . . not one word of apology has ever been offered to [them] . . . I must restrict myself to moderate language. Being as fair as I can to the Government . . . they should be ashamed at the way they have treated these 111 persons.[25]

Sears also commented that Asprey's suggestion that, whatever happened in court, the 111 would be sent back to Vietnam, appeared to be a direct challenge by the Executive to the judiciary. The judiciary was:

> . . . not only independent of the Government, it is strong enough to resist any attempt that the rule of law should be weakened because a judge's order causes embarrassment, or inconvenience, or extra financial burden on the Government. I find it disconcerting to be told by a high official that if I grant this order, these 111 persons, who have been so shamefully treated, will be deported to Vietnam . . . perhaps on more mature reflection, Mr Asprey and the other high Government officials, might like to reconsider this statement . . . I trust that the high officials of the Hong Kong Government would not wish to give the general public the impression that an order of a High Court judge can be brushed aside lightly, because if they do, they tarnish and weaken the rule of law. At this time in Hong Kong's history, it is of vital importance that the rule of law not only prevails but is seen to be supported by the Government.[26]

On the one hand, such breaches of rights reinforced the perception overseas that Hong Kong was becoming more authoritarian in the run-up to 1997. On the other hand, however, such pronouncements by the courts fuelled the belief that Hong Kong was a 'city of law', and that its institutions were capable of defending its way of life. Public confidence in these institutions was high. Indeed, the police force, despite being portrayed in pro-China rhetoric of the time as the arm of a 'colonial oppressor', had one of its most successful recruiting campaigns in 1993, reaching its establishment strength for the first time in ten years.[27] There were plans to expand its strength to 30,000 within a few years, and the visibility of uniformed officers on the streets was seen as one of the main reasons why locals and visitors felt so safe.[28]

Fight Crime!

The police force also enjoyed the goodwill and co-operation of large sections of the public through its annual 'Fight Crime' campaigns. The 1990/91 Fight Crime Campaign once more enjoined the public to 'Join Forces Against Crime', counselled parents to give their children guidance, emphasised anti-triad, anti-shop theft and anti-youth crime messages, and generally carried on where the 1989 campaigns had left off. However, the administration was not complacent about relying on its older 'hearts and minds' measures. There was a new 'fight crime' logo, a 'Fight Crime TV Special', a theme song and an altogether more polished effort at propaganda.[29] The 1992 campaign continued with the same police/community theme, but focused on the mechanics of citizen participation – with 'What to Report', How to Report', 'Safe to Report' and 'Duty to Report' sub-themes.[30]

As in the 1980s, for most of the 1990s the annual campaigns took youth crime as their main theme, together with crime prevention and crime reporting. In 1996, a commercial agency was enlisted to publicise the 'Fight Youth Crime' campaign. In 1997, female juveniles became a specific target.

Despite the sensational crimes of violence at the start of the decade, over half the crime recorded in Hong Kong in the early 1990s was in fact against

Table 23.1 Reported crime 1990–97

	1990	*1991*	*1992*	*1993*	*1994*	*1995*	*1996*	*1997*
Violent crime	18,820	19,558	18,567	17,454	17,232	17,087	15,191	13,749
Other crime	65,169	65,358	63,526	63,142	68,738	72,939	62,613	52,706
Preventive crime	4,311	3,743	1,963	1,968	1,834	1,800	1,246	912
Total	88,300	88,659	84,056	82,564	87,804	91,886	79,050	67,367

Source: RHKPARs 1990–97.

Table 23.2 Total crime and crime rate per 100,000 in HK1980–96

Year	*Total*	*Serious/key crime*	*Rate per 100,000*
1980	75,754	61,520	1,515.1
1981	79,617	64,330	1,542.0
1982	84,237	70,405	1,603.5
1983	86,000	69,157	1,612.9
1984	83,532	60,677	1,506.9
1985	86,944	66,059	1,596.7
1986	81,411	62,762	1,473.7
1987	82,914	62,204	1,485.8
1988	79,859	60,766	1,410.1
1989	81,808	60,695	1,438.7
1990	88,300	65,169	1,547.9
1991	88,659	65,359	1,540.6
1992	84,056	63,526	1,466.4
1993	82,564	63,142	1,394.9
1994	87,804	68,738	1,448.6
1995	91,886	72,939	1,484.5
1996	79,050	62,613	1,253.0

Source: Police in Figures 1979–95 (slight differences in overall crime reflect different periods of counting).

property rather than the person (53 per cent in 1991, 52 per cent in 1992) – see Tables 23.1 and 23.2. Only 22 per cent of recorded crime consisted of crimes of violence.[31] The large jump in recorded violent crime in 1990/91 was principally due to a small number of incidents of robbery with firearms. Moreover, in 1992, some big falls began to be observed in robbery, woundings and serious assaults. In both 1992 and 1993, overall recorded crime briefly fell, and the crime rate continued to decline (to 1,395 in 1993). Recorded violent crime fell in both years, mainly due to a significant fall in robbery and robbery with firearms (down by over 50 per cent) due to co-operation between the Hong Kong and Mainland authorities against the perpetrators.[32] The number of luxury cars reported stolen dropped by over 30 per cent.[33] A 'major triad extortion ring' was eliminated in 1992; narcotics seizures were up – the police seized the second largest haul of heroin in the territory's history in 1992 – and many of the armour-plated speedboats used by China-bound smugglers were either disabled or seized.[34] Successes in these areas – and against the armed Chinese gangs – remained important both to keep these 'intractable' crimes under control, but also to reassure the public that the capacity of the police to fight organised crime – even when it had Chinese links – remained undiminished.

Rises in overall crime in 1994 and 1995 were matched by increases in prosecutions for miscellaneous offences (Table 23.3). If, as research indicates, official figures tell us as much about police activity as actual crime levels, it seems that these were busy years for the Hong Kong police. Most of the rise was due to recorded crimes against property – recorded violent crimes against the person, as well as armed robberies, were still declining. Juveniles were said to account for over a third of all arrests, principally for shop theft and drug offences resulting, somewhat predictably, in a Fight Crime Committee initiative to 'steer young people away from the ruinous temptations of crime', as well as to 'take stringent measures to crack down on the criminal fraternity

Table 23.3 Miscellaneous offences prosecuted 1990–97

	1990	*1991*	*1992*	*1993*	*1994*	*1995*	*1996*	*1997*
Gambling	1,131	1,681	1,867	1,378	1,444	1,220	1,137	1,066
Hawking	8,766	6,717	7,495	11,545	12,772	14,425	11,147	7,870
Obstruction	26,237	20,999	19,086	19,680	21,212	21,196	20,356	16,692
Prostitution	283	637	622	333	457	335	497	499
Objectionable publication	344	371	216	275	435	446	581	1,082
Other	12,537	11,774	10,977	11,483	15,115	16,063	28,578	17,600
Minor narcotics	3,639	4,448	7,837	8,277	9,641	8,997	8,881	7,636
Total	**52,937**	**46,627**	**48,100**	**52,921**	**61,076**	**62,682**	**71,177**	**52,445**

Source: RHKPARs 1990–97.

[triads] who prey on them'.[35] Research by local academics was again commissioned to get at the causes of youth crime. The 1994 Fight Crime Campaign targeted the demystifying of triads 'to show them up as the cowards and leeches of society that they are' (ibid). It also boosted publicity against shop theft, and introduced a full-sized, cardboard replica of a policeman (the 'cardboard cop') into shops as a deterrent. Against triads, the police mounted several operations, which, they stated, led to the arrest of several top leaders and the elimination of syndicates engaged in extortion rackets in under-age prostitution, drug-running and blackmail (ibid). The problem of intimidation of witnesses in triad-related cases was addressed by the introduction of a witness protection scheme, already used by other agencies such as the ICAC.

The topography of crime was still an abiding interest of the authorities. As in previous decades, Kowloon retained its reputation as a crime 'hot spot' (Table 23.4). According to official figures, in 1989, 51.6 per cent all crimes of violence against the person occurred in Kowloon, which contained rather less that one-third of the population; a further 29.6 per cent occurred in the NT which had over one-third of the population; and 21.3 per cent occurred on Hong Kong Island, which had about 22 per cent of the population. In 1996, 27 per cent of all violent crime against the person occurred in Kowloon West, 14.4 per cent in Kowloon East (giving a combined total 41.4 per cent), 22.9 per cent in NT North, 17.5 in NT South (a combined total of 40.3 per cent), and 17.5 per cent occurred on Hong Kong Island.[36]

Kowloon also retained the highest concentration of police – in 1990, it had 7,433 officers, compared to 5,257 in the NT, 3,670 in Hong Kong Island, and 2,901 in Marine.[37] By 1996, Kowloon had the highest number of police of any division (4,827), followed by Hong Kong Island (4,239) and NT North (4,037). The combined forces of Kowloon East and West numbered 8,339,

Table 23.4 Crime by district 1990–97

	1990	*1991*	*1992*	*1993*	*1994*	*1995*	*1996*	*1997*
Kowloon	41,035	40,505						
Kowloon East			13,582	13,673	14,246	14,420	11,778	9,518
Kowloon West			23,144	23,476	24,552	25,885	21,232	18,355
Hong Kong Island	16,854	15,894	16,132	16,324	17,338	16,502	14,753	12,512
New Territories	29,519	31,194	30,118					
NT North				14,604	17,022	19,399	17,187	14,816
NT South				13,583	13,664	14,712	13,730	11,850
Marine	892	1,066	1,080	944	982	968	360	316
Total	**88,300**	**88,659**	**84,056**	**82,564**	**87,804**	**91,886**	**79,050**	**67,367**

Source: RHKPARs 1990–97.

almost a quarter of the police force's total strength. (In 1946, the entire Hong Kong Police Force had numbered only 2,401.)

Rises in recorded crime in 1994 threatened to tarnish celebrations marking the one hundred and fiftieth anniversary of the police force. Having briefly shown signs of decline, overall recorded crime (and the crime rate) went up again and continued to rise in 1995, when it reached a peak of 91,886 (a crime rate of 1,484, up 2.4 per cent on 1994). The only good news was that recorded violent crime fell – robberies dropped by 10 per cent in 1994 and again by 11.4 per cent in 1995 – but woundings and serious assaults (mostly triad-related) rose, by 4.5 per cent in 1994 and 9.6 per cent in 1995.[38] More people than ever were arrested (from 45,042 in 1993; 49,784 in 1994 and 53,098 in 1995). Since fewer were Vietnamese or illegal immigrants, the 'crime problem' could not be blamed quite so easily on outsiders, but police reports continued to associate crime with Chinese illegal immigrants and two-way permit holders. Trains and boats were checked; new methods of checking under vehicles were introduced at the border; the PTU was deployed in regular 'blitz' operations to arrest illegal immigrants.

Crackdowns on vice also resulted in large numbers of Chinese illegal immigrants being arrested for prostitution and/or ID card offences. When it was decided that illegal immigrants caught working in Hong Kong should face an automatic prison term, Hong Kong's prison system began to feel the consequences. A high proportion (about 90 per cent) of those arrested for prostitution were Chinese illegal immigrants. The number of young (mainly Chinese) women consequently incarcerated in Hong Kong jails now began to rise inexorably (see below).

Policing

Rapid expansion of the police in the 1970s was followed by further expansion and modernisation in the 1980s but in the 1990s, economic constraints on government spending prompted some retrenchment. China, keen to ensure that the British did not squander Hong Kong's assets before 1997, kept a close eye on the administration's expenditure. As regards criminal justice, however, this constraint was offset by counter-arguments that policing could not be allowed to suffer just at the point when Hong Kong might become 'ungovernable'. Force establishement changed only marginally (Table 23.5) but expenditure still rose, albeit less rapidly than in previous years.

Internal security aspects of policing were strengthened throughout the 1990s, though Special Branch quietly disappeared in the mid-1990s, to be replaced by a 'Security Wing'. 'Political policing' was now complicated by the fact that some of those once regarded as subversive were likely, after 1997, to be lauded as staunch communists and regime loyalists.

Concern for domestic stability and security ran alongside the increased pressure to embed the police, before 1997, more firmly in the community, in

Table 23.5 Hong Kong Police Establishment 1990–97

	1990	*1991*	*1992*	*1993*	*1994*	*1995*	*1996*	*1997*
Total	**27,578**	**27,247**	**27,206**	**27,263**	**27,319**	**27,551**	**27,716**	**28,007**
Gazetted officers	489	493	492			457	459	463
Inspectors	2,477	2,466	2,463			2,417	2,411	2,442
Junior officers	24,612	24,288	24,251			24,677	28,846	25,102

Source: RHKPARs 1990–97.

line with the government's general drift towards more concern with 'grass-roots issues'. If it were to retain public confidence, the police force had to impress upon the public that it remained free from political interference. It was helped in this by embracing the theories of New Public Management and Total Quality Management, both of which swept through the police (and all government departments) from 1989 onwards. These sparked innumerable projects designed to rationalise resources, improve 'customer service', draft performance pledges, draw-up 'mission statements' and develop 'core competencies'.[39]

Public confidence in the Hong Kong administration and its institutions was low. Performance management was part of the new repertoire of measures that helped remedy this situation. As Lee argues, the departure of the British unleashed popular demands in Hong Kong for participation and increased public spending to assuage fears about the future after 1997. The state's capacity to respond to these demands was, she argues, constrained by the Sino–British agreement and the Basic Law, which restricted reforms of Hong Kong's institutions. In these circumstances, public sector reform was the only viable alternative, launched to contain a crisis in legitimacy and 'enhance the legitimacy and capacity of the late colonial state' (Lee 2000: 123). It was able to call upon values already dominant in Hong Kong culture and ideas of good citizenship, such as economy, hard work, self-reliance, and self-improvement.

For Lee, the new managerialism was a 'micro-technology', reconstituting the normative order and the power of the state, an 'administrative ideology' and technology designed to accomplish the 'neo-liberal project' (Lee 2000: 121). Total Quality Management created an atmosphere of 'constant surveillance over individual behaviour' (ibid). Managers were given the right to manage 'utilizing managerial techniques that are powerful disciplinary tools', resulting in a managerialised dispersal of power, a shrinking of the state, and the 'enlargement of its reach into civil society' through engagement with non-state agents (ibid). In Hong Kong, this meant a consolidation of state power over subvented organisations upon which, as Lee points out, government had long depended for the delivery of welfare (and correctional) services. This ideology received a ready reception in Hong Kong, with the colonial's state's tradition of non-interventionism and valorisation of the free market.

New managerialism was applied to the Hong Kong civil and disciplined services with some speed in the early 1990s. In October, 1992, Hong Kong's new Governor, Chris Patten, announced a 'Serving the Community' Scheme, prompting the police force to adapt its culture 'from an inward looking ethos to a client based service culture'.[40] In 1997, Price Waterhouse Management Consultants were enlisted to help the police force with customer service improvements,[41] a move reminiscent of the government's deployment of McKinsey & Company in the 1970s. As in the UK, economy, efficiency and effectiveness (the 'Three Es') became the aim, although of these, economy and 'value for money' probably mattered most. In 1997, the police conducted the first of what would become routine Customer Satisfaction Surveys.

At the same time, the police force was considering a variety of ways in which it could improve its police–public relations in the run-up to 1997.[42] Police officers were to become models of decorum. In 1995, the force launched a new 'Courteous Officer' scheme aimed at 'promoting a harmonious working relationship between front-line officers and members of the public'.[43] In 1992, it had introduced mediation as a means of settling complaints against the police, and in 1994 the Police Complaints Committee was replaced by the Independent Police Complaints Council (IPCC). It too had a stated mission, which was to ensure a fair, effective and transparent police complaints system whereby every complaint was dealt with 'justly, promptly, thoroughly and without prejudice'. In line with the wider hegemonic project, it promised to be impartial, transparent, and persistent in the pursuit of truth.

The 1990s focus on 'clients' and 'customer satisfaction' prompted by the new managerialism fostered the idea that the police should be responsive to the public. The irony was that whilst this actually started as what Gray might call a more 'covert and discerning' means of governance,[44] it took on a life of its own as the police seized upon it to secure public support in the run-up to 1997. Colonial police forces have traditionally been seen as an arm of government, oppressive of, rather than answering to, the people. In Hong Kong's case, this lack of public accountability arose more by accident than design, with the elite's refusal to pay for a municipal police in the 1840s. But in any event, for 150 years, the government had been the sole 'client'. The emphasis on 'customer service' in the 1990s seemed to represent a break with this past, providing accountability to the public (albeit limited) by the 'back door'. Though the police force had, since the 1970s, stressed its partnership with the community, there had never been an effective and official mechanism that measured it success in this regard. Now, customer satisfaction surveys provided tangible evidence of police achievements. A small gap between police and government had also opened up into which public opinion could be fed, and which the police could use to argue their case for resources. Cumulatively, these small changes went some way to create the impression that, post-1997, the police force would heed the wishes of the community in its work.

The one hundred and fiftieth anniversary of the police force, in 1994, offered the police force another opportunity to boost morale and consolidate its image. By this point, the force encompassed over 39,000 staff, including 6,000 civilians and 6,000 auxiliaries. They were, in the rhetoric of the occasion, 'primed to protect a bustling metropolis of six million people against the more sophisticated villains of the modern era, and a lot more besides'.[45] The traditions of the force were described in somewhat rosy terms as:

> . . . traditions of service to the community, dedication to duty and the preservation of law and order . . . a . . . time to look back . . . to reflect on how society has changed . . . to see how Police officers coped with change in the past, and contemplate how to cope with change in the future . . . [a time] . . . to remind all in Hong Kong that Police officers have always been there – in typhoons and flood, in riots and protests, at sea, on congested roadways and on the remotest tracts of land, serving, helping and protecting.[46]

The anniversary was an opportunity for considerable hyperbole, for talk of 'Asia's Finest', of the role played by the police in helping the community, especially in times of 'typhoons and floods', and of the police's image as a force for stability and for good in these 'historic' times. A laudatory documentary was broadcast over all four local channels, accompanied by celebratory balls, commemorative books and souvenirs, full-page, colour newspaper pull-out sections and numerous public events. Nothing was said of less pleasant traditions, such as riot suppression and strong-arm squatter clearances.

In an atmosphere of political partisanship, the police adopted a line that had served them well before. Claiming the 'fair and impartial' enforcement of the law, they were generally (but not always) able to deflect complaints of political bias and heavy-handedness. This was to become even more imperative as 1997 approached, and the world's media descended on Hong Kong looking for signs of censorship and repression. One incident in 1997 itself suggested that not everyone in the police was 'on message'. A public relations blunder was committed when one officer sanctioned the playing of Beethoven at loud volume in an attempt to drown out pro-democracy protestors, prompting parallels with 1967, when loud music had also been broadcast through loudspeakers to drown out rioters near the Hilton Hotel.

Corruption

Perhaps more than any other type of crime, corruption came to symbolise the threat that the handover posed to Hong Kong society. Domestic fears of increasing corruption were linked to the symbiosis between Hong Kong and Mainland enterprises, and the widespread belief that Mainland officials were mostly corrupt. Reassuring the public that 1997 would bring no great change thus entailed keeping corruption in check.

Throughout the 1980s, as reports of private sector corruption rose, the ICAC had focused more on complex cases involving fraud, financial institutions, and banking; by 1986, these accounted for about one-third of the ICAC's caseload, rising to about a half by 1989 (Mannion 2004: 42). The international nature of some of these investigations, and their complexity, demanded greater technical expertise (such as accountancy) and more investigative time (ibid). It also required greater liaison with other bodies, such as the Hong Kong Monetary Authority, the police Commercial Crime Bureau (CCB) and private sector security bodies.

In 1994 the ICAC made public sector corruption its priority again, partly due to the re-emergence of organised corruption in the police (ibid). ICAC operations and intelligence officers took the view that corruption in government had begun to increase again around 1992, peaking in 1996, a year before Hong Kong's return to China (Mannion 2004: 55). Reports of corruption in both the public and private sectors increased markedly in 1993 by 45 per cent and remained high throughout the 1990s (Mannion 2004: 66–7). In 1995, the police and ICAC established an Anti-Corruption Steering Committee to gather information on corrupt officers, develop training in ethics, and circulate a code of ethics throughout the police force.[47]

The rise in the figures in 1993 was controversial at the time, and it was never quite clear what had produced it. One explanation was that ICAC counting procedures had altered; another that the ICAC was simply being more vigilant. Another attributed it to the rise of a 'get rich quick' mentality generated by the need to make cash quickly handover. Corruption, being widespread in both the public and private sectors in Mainland China, was also said to be contaminating Hong Kong, reinforcing deeply-held stereotypes of law-abiding, sophisticated and civilised Hong Kongers and equally deeply-rooted prejudices about 'lawless', 'uncivilised' and 'uncouth' Mainlanders. Another view was that the end of colonial rule and increasing localisation of the civil service meant that retiring civil servants were tempted to cultivate 'less scrupulous relationships with potential future employers in the private sector' (Mannion 2004: 82). A PRC-generated proposal to remove the word 'independent' from the ICAC's title briefly fuelled rumours that the 1997 'handover' was already weakening the ICAC's independence, particularly as regards the investigation of companies, officials or business people with powerful Mainland connections.

This suspicion was exacerbated in the public mind by the fact that those destined to rule Hong Kong after 1997 had already switched their support to the incoming regime. This powerful alliance of business and political elites caused much speculation about the capacity of the ICAC to investigate

Table 23.6 Reports of corruption to the ICAC, 1973–2005

Year	*All reports*	*Government*	*% Police force only*
1973	1,457	1,245	49
1974	3,189	2,745	45
1975	3,179	2,661	47
1976	2,433	1,883	46
1977	1,700	1,271	43
1978	1,234	887	39
1979	1,665	1,182	39
1980	1,772	1,159	30
1981	2,344	1,554	31
1982	2,349	1,421	29
1983	2,516	1,542	31
1984	2,365	1,406	30
1985	2,474	1,486	29
1986	2,545	1,364	25
1987	2,299	1,160	23
1988	2,162	1,046	20
1989	2,388	1,034	19
1990	2,390	1,125	20
1991	2,186	978	20
1992	2,257	1,032	20
1993	3,276	1,365	19
1994	3,312	1,381	20
1995	2,987	1,248	19
1996	3,086	1,304	19
1997	3,057	1,288	17
1998	3,555	1,456	16
1999	3,561	1,445	14
2000	4,390	1,130	19
2001	4,476	1,074	11.5
2002	4,371	1,638	12.9
2003	4,310	1,009	12.3
2004	3,746	851	11.6
2005	3,685	779	10.4

Sources: For 1974–2000: Mannion 2004: 68; for 2001–5: ICAC Annual Reviews.

corruption in any of their companies. Weakened confidence in the ICAC was therefore tied to a more general lack of confidence in the future PRC government on the Mainland, and in the incoming Hong Kong government (Mannion 2004: 66).

Even so, surveys showed that about 70 per cent of respondents still believed the ICAC to be effective or very effective and, as Mannion says, the ICAC consistently emerged in opinion polls as an institution enjoying high levels of public confidence, higher than the government, civil service and other government institutions (ibid). However, figures cited by Mannion show that in 1993, 62 per cent of the respondents surveyed said that they expected an increase in corruption due to the '1997 issue'; this rose to 73 per cent in 1994 and remained around this level until 1997 (Mannion 2004: 64). Data from the Hong Kong Transitions Project also indicated a high level of anxiety about increasing corruption in the transition years (ibid). As the post–1997 years progressed, however, confidence returned, partly because the ICAC managed to retain its independent image but also because the vigilance of the public at large resulted in a number of well-publicised incidents which, in the manner of a *conscience collective*, confirmed that Hong Kong people disapproved of corrupt behaviour and were prepared to report it.

This confidence in Hong Kong's law enforcement and legal institutions did not, however, carry over to other departments of the post-1997 government. As we shall see, when after 1997 public faith in government slumped, institutions such as the ICAC, the police and the courts were seen as the most important guarantors of Hong Kong's stability and repositories of hope that the rule of law could and would temper the post-colonial regime's growing illiberalism.

Notes

1 See Wong Siu-lun 1992: 918–33.
2 See, for example, Evans 1997.
3 Not least many of those relating to corruption, which put the onus on the suspect to prove assets and income were legitimate. One of the most significant cases was *The Queen v. Sin Yau Ming* (1992) 1 HKCLR 127. This considered presumptions under the Dangerous Drugs Ordinance, one of which was a specified weight of cannabis above which possession gave rise to the presumption that the person was engaged in trafficking drugs.
4 Chung Tze-keung ('Big Spender'). See below.
5 RHKPAR 1990: 20.
6 RHKPAR 1995: 5.
7 RHKPAR 1992: 25.
8 Also known as the 'Pillar of Shame' (see http://en.wikipedia.org/wiki/Pillar_-of_Shame and http://www.aidoh.dk/) this was created by the artist Jens Galschiøt, whose intention was to use sculptures as memorials to human rights infringements. As at 2007 there were Pillars of Shame memorialising different events in Berlin, Brazil, Mexico, Hong Kong and Rome.
9 RHKPAR 1996: 35.
10 There were however other serious events that the emergency services were called to cope with. For example, in 1992 there was a New Year's Eve tragedy at Lan Kwai Fung, when a number of people were accidentally killed in the crush surrounding the countdown to the 'Western' New Year, and in 1995 one of the territory's worst ever fires broke out at Garley Road.
11 RHKPAR 1990: 16.
12 *Crime and its Victims in Hong Kong 1989.* Hong Kong: Census and Statistics Department, Government Printer.
13 RHKPAR 1991: 17.
14 RHKPAR 1991: 27.

15 RHKPAR 1990: 16; 1991: 17.
16 RHKPAR 1992: 5; 1993: 5.
17 RHKPAR 1991: 17.
18 RHKPAR 1991: 19.
19 Central Registry of Drug Abuse in Hong Kong cited at *www.chr.asn.au*. By 2001, this figure had grown to over 18,000 though unofficial estimate put the figure at closer to 40,000 (ibid).
20 RHKPAR 1991: 5, 19.
21 RHKPAR 1996: 25.
22 Ibid.
23 RHKPAR 1996: 43.
24 RHKPAR 1992: 16.
25 *Re Pham Van Ngo* [1991] 1 HKLR 499; see also *Thang Thiueu Quyen and others* CFA No 2 of 1998 (Civil); *Long Quoc Tuong and 111 others* CFA Civil Appeal No 200/97 23 July 1998. The 111 Vietnamese were detained when their boat broke down in Hong Kong waters. They were promised repairs to the boat before being allowed to proceed to Japan. The boat was in fact destroyed and they were detained in a detention camp.
26 Ibid.
27 RHKPAR 1993: 5.
28 RHKPAR 1993: 5.
29 RHKPAR 1991: 25.
30 RHKPAR 1992: 23.
31 RHKPAR 1992: 16.
32 However, Gaylord and Lang (2006) argue that rises and falls in robbery show a remarkably close relationship with changes in real wages. They argue that declining wages are related to increased rates of 'quick cash' crimes in societies that lack a welfare 'safety net'. See Gaylord and Lang 2006.
33 RHKPAR 1992; 1993.
34 RHKPAR 1992: 18, 20.
35 RHKPAR 1994: 5.
36 Figures rounded to one decimal place.
37 RHKPAR 1990: 64.
38 RHKPAR 1994: 15.
39 New Public Management is discussed at length by the United Nations Research Institute for Social Development at http://www.unrisd.org. Total Quality Management, often abbreviated to TQM, was developed in the 1950s but became very popular in many different kinds of organisations in the 1990s. There is a reasonably useful article and list of sources at http://en.wikipedia.org/wiki/Total_Quality_Management.
40 RHKPAR 1992: 5.
41 HKPAR 1997: 95.
42 RHKPAR 1991: 37.
43 RHKPAR 1995: 41.
44 See below.
45 RHKPAR 1994: 5
46 RHKPAR 1994: 7.
47 RHKPAR 1995: 6.

Chapter 24

Images of crime and juvenile delinquency 1990–1997

Perhaps more than at any other time in the territory's history, in the years before the 1997 handover it became imperative for the British to demonstrate the superiority of their legal institutions, and their ability to provide stability, security and economic success. Maintaining Hong Kong's reputation as one of the safest cities in the world was, in these years, a task with clear political implications.

The official crime rate had been falling since 1990 – though the raw figures for actual number of reported crimes did not show any significant or sustained downward movement until the remarkable 14 per cent fall in 1996, and an equally remarkable 16 per cent fall in the crime rate (to 1,253) in 1997. Thanks mainly to this, in the year of the handover, the police could claim that overall crime was at its lowest level for 24 years.[1] Violent crime also continued its downward trend. Overall arrests fell by almost 6,000 to 47,157; police offensives against triads were credited with the reduction in armed robberies and the seizure of quantities of illegal firearms. For the police, one of the most significant events was the arrest, in 1996, of one of Hong Kong's most wanted criminals, Yip Kai-foon. His capture seemed to symbolise their success against violent crime, which threatened Hong Kong's safe and orderly reputation in the early 1990s.

Though they loomed large in the public's perception of crime, crimes of violence actually formed a much smaller proportion of the total amount of crime – property crime constituted a far bigger threat.[2] In the 1994 crime survey, 88 per cent of victimisations of personal crimes of theft and 91 per cent of household crime victimisations involved the loss of property. This figure was 28 per cent for victims of violent crime.[3]

Both the official statistics and the crime surveys indicated that crimes of violence consistently accounted for a far lower percentage of crime in Hong Kong than property crimes. They differed, however, on the level and direction of violent crime. In 1989, the rate of serious assaults reported to the police had fallen to 56.5 per cent. The official statistics therefore suggested a fall in crime. The crime surveys, however, indicated that since 1979 the level of violent victimisation had not changed – in 1994, victims were injured in 18 per cent of violent crime incidents, as compared to 14 per cent in 1979. In both 1979 and 1994, male victims were more likely to be injured than female victims. What did fall was the rate of reporting for crimes of violence. This continued to fall through the 1980s, reaching a level of 51 per cent in 1994.

Indeed, reporting rates for all crimes of violence fell significantly in 1994, as compared to previous surveys. This fall in reporting rates inevitably affected the number of crimes the police recorded. Whether or not levels of serious assault *actually* fell is therefore uncertain. What does seem clear is that, despite the panic about armed robberies, the use of weapons in crime had actually declined over the years. Where weapons were used, they did tend to be used in shop robberies rather than in crimes of personal violence, but few offenders carried weapons of any kind. In 1994, only 37 per cent of robberies and 28 per cent of assaults were carried out by offenders with weapons.[4]

In respect of other types of crime, much also remained unchanged – triads were still described as a 'menace', even though some observers argued that they functioned to provide discipline to teenager males who otherwise lacked a sense of belonging. It was also said that they functioned to maintain lower levels of crime in tourist areas, crime being bad for business. But there were rising concerns that, once Hong Kong returned to China, the territory would have more problems with less familiar Mainland triads, whilst Hong Kong-based gangs would also seek to expand their influence into the Mainland as well as hire Mainland-based gangsters to perform armed robberies in Hong Kong. The view that the triads would flee Hong Kong in anticipation of a post–1997 crackdown had no substance. For the triads, 1997 was an opportunity, not a crisis. They had already proved themselves capable of spreading to other overseas locations such as Canada, Australia and the USA. Triad-related murders and gang fights in Macau testified to Macau, Hong Kong and Mainland triads' involvement in competition over territory. Media investigations shortly before the 1997 handover also revealed the extent to which Hong Kong's triads had fostered new connections with Mainland police and officials, even to the point of establishing joint business concerns in places such as Shanghai, Shenzhen and Beijing. These alliances generated rumours locally that Mainland officials were willing to allow triads free rein in Hong Kong after 1997, in return for a share of the profits and political support. Cynics went to far as to argue that, by brokering such a deal, the Mainland authorities could, at a stroke, strip the Nationalist (Taiwanese) cause in Hong Kong of its main body of supporters. How far local people believed this depended partly upon their assessment of the government's capacity to control crime and maintain Hong Kong's way of life.

The safe city

The stories that circulated of ghosts and crime on the Mainland reinforced local beliefs that China was essentially a lawless place and that, as a place to live, Hong Kong was infinitely preferable. The claim that it was one of safest cities in the world became the *leifmotif* of the era. The 1990s also exemplified the wider point that criminal justice policy in Hong Kong has seldom been driven purely by the official crime figures. In these pre-handover years, it was politically important to ensure that Hong Kong remained one of the safest cities in the world. International investors needed to be reassured that Hong Kong would remain a safe place to do business; the international community more broadly (but Taiwan in particular) also needed to see that Hong Kong's return to China did not mean the end of life as they knew it.

But whilst the official crime figures confirmed this picture, the crime surveys suggested a different story. According to the official statistics, by the mid-1990s Hong Kong's crime rate stood at 1,448 per 100,000, a dramatic drop from the high levels of 1982, when it stood at 1,667 per 100,000. By the time the handover arrived, it had dropped again. One of the safest cities in the world had somehow just become even safer. However, the 1994 crime survey,[5] though it generally confirmed Hong Kong's status as a low-crime society, had also noted a decline in the public's reporting of crime. This suggested that a substantial 'dark figure' remained hidden beneath the story of Hong Kong's success. It also underlined the fact that the types of crime people experienced – as well as the frequency of their falling foul of it – depended on where they lived, as well as the lifestyle they led.

The crime surveys showed what the official crime figures neglected to mention: crime in Hong Kong had a distinct class as well as a gender dimension. For example, in 1994, people (especially 12 to 19 year olds) living in public permanent housing had the highest victimisation rate for crimes of violence.[6] Crimes of violence were more frequent in Housing Authority blocks than in any other type of building. There were higher *reporting* rates for private housing than for public or temporary housing, but the lowest rate of reporting for personal crime was amongst victims living in public permanent housing – only 35 per cent reported their victimisation to the police.

This differences in reporting rates skewed the official crime figures. People living in private permanent housing typically had the highest reporting rates, even though their overall victimisation rate was lowest.[7] It was their experience of crime that was reflected in the recorded crime figures. By contrast, those whose victimization was highest reported crime less. This was particularly true of youth.[8]

By 1994, the crime surveys were also revealing something about how people's lifestyles affected their propensity to fall victim to crime. Streets, lifts and stairwells were common locations of personal crime. The 1994 crime survey showed, for example, that 51 per cent of personal crimes occurred on the street and in indoor areas – 49 per cent of crimes of violence occurred indoors (48 per cent in lifts, corridors, staircases and lift lobbies). Of all personal crime incidents that happened indoors, 64 per cent occurred inside non-residential buildings. Of personal crimes of theft that happened outside,

47 per cent happened on the street and 34 per cent on public transport. These figures had a particular resonance in Hong Kong, since its vast inequalities of wealth determined that the elite were much less likely to spend time on the streets or on public transport – many were driven in luxury cars by private drivers, had their homes protected by private watchmen, and did their shopping in exclusive malls guarded by private security firms.

The crime surveys also provided a good deal of information about *when* certain types of crimes were committed. Typically, the hours of darkness are regarded as a dangerous time, though much of Hong Kong is busy and well lit much later than many modern cities. The crime surveys demonstrated, however, that it was the daylight hours that witnessed most crime: about 50 per cent of incidents in Hong Kong in 1994 took place between 6 am and 6 pm, with the majority between noon and 6 pm. Proportionately more personal crimes (65 per cent) than household crimes took place in the daytime. Burglaries were more likely to occur in the afternoon. Only car thefts and criminal damage were more likely after midnight.[9] These patterns had not changed much over time (though the proportion of household crimes that occurred at night was higher in 1994 than either 1986 and 1989).

Despite these findings, the authorities proceeded on the basis of recorded crime. This presented a blander picture, averaging out people's experience of crime and concealing the fact that some sections of the population were far more likely than others to become victims of crime. In 1995, for example, the official figures supported the 'safest city' claim by informing the public that a crime occurred in Hong Kong every 5.7 minutes, a homicide every 5 days, a rape every 3.5 days, a robbery every 1.6 hours, a burglary every 39.9 minutes, and a snatching every 5.7 hours.[10] This official 'crime clock' had been much the same for over ten years – in 1985, for example, a crime was said to occur every 6 minutes, a homicide every 5 days, a rape every 5 days, a robbery every 2 hours, a burglary every 44 minutes and a snatching every 5 hours.[11] This created the impression that crime was stable and affected everyone equally. But where people lived had a critical bearing on whether they became victims of crime. Moreover, some people were more likely to experience *multiple* victimisations.[12] Such variations between sectors of the population stood in stark contrast to the picture painted by the official statistics.

The general public had its own understanding of which were the crime blackspots. These perceptions were powerfully shaped by the media and the police and tended to label whole populations as deviant. As we have seen, in the 1840s and 1850s, the Chinese sections of Central and Western Districts were regarded by the elite as dens of iniquity, and the people who lived there were universally labelled criminals and undesirables, increasing their marginalisation. Then, as now, the official crime figures failed completely to capture the experience of crime for those living in such areas. For example, much of Hong Kong's illicit vice industry is located in Kowloon. Female sex workers here suffer crime victimisations that frequently pass unreported and unnoticed. A similar story could be told of illegal immigrants, whose status in Hong Kong deters them from any interaction with the authorities, especially the police. Thus, whilst the official statistics and the crime surveys agreed that Kowloon and the NT were crime 'black spots', neither captured the full extent of crime in the territory.[13] The picture painted by the crime surveys also lent itself less readily to the image of Hong Kong as one of the safest cities in the world. Crime was, and remains, concentrated in certain areas and within certain groups.[14] The reassuring message sent by the remarkable fall in crime in 1996/7 was also offset by a finding in 1994 that people had become much more unwilling to report crime. This reflected a wider loss of confidence in public institutions before 1997. (After the handover, however, the police force was one of the few institutions to regain public confidence.)

The crime survey also challenged prevailing stereotypes about victims and offenders. It showed, for example, that contrary to popular belief, young males were more likely to be victims of crime, and that women and the elderly were the *least* likely of any group in society to become victims of crime.[15] These findings made little impact, however, upon youth justice policy, underscoring the point that the disciplining of youth in these years was not simply the rational response of government to statistical data on crime.

Juvenile crime again

Anxieties about youth and women are often a lightning rod for wider social concerns. Attempts to control and organise them can be interpreted as an attempt to preserve existing ways of life and national purity. These are especially evident at times when the state feels under threat and during times of widespread public anxiety. In Hong Kong, fears about the possibility of a decline into disorder and ungovernability in the run-up to 1997 translated into concerns about Hong Kong's generally law-abiding young people. These concerns had little basis in reality. Indeed, Hong Kong youth were exceptionally well behaved. One in every 11 people in Hong Kong belonged to the JPC. When they did offend, young people tended to commit minor crimes, such as shoplifting of low-value goods. Nevertheless, they were deemed a special category requiring ever more intensive social control – Gray notes, for example, that large numbers of young offenders continued to be placed in residential or custodial institutions 'after very brief criminal careers and for crimes which [did] not pose a serious risk to the community' (Gray 1999: 577). As Gray concludes, in the 1990s, young offenders stood:

> . . . a good chance of being placed in residential or custodial institutions after very brief, and usually minor, periods of crime. In 1992, over two-thirds of juveniles in probation homes had had no previous convictions and only 8 per cent had offended more than once previously. The situation was similar in reformatory schools, with over a third of the

> juveniles previously having had clear records and only 20% having more than one previous conviction . . . Serious criminal careers [were] also rare in the harsher sentencing disposals, with nearly three-quarters of males under 20 admitted to a training centre in 1995 having no more than one previous conviction. Half of the young people sent to detention centres were also first offenders . . . There [was] also little evidence that the gravity of young people's crimes justifie[d] custodial sentences (Gray 1999: 581).

In 1991, an independent Commission on Youth report also suggested that Hong Kong was worrying too much about its juveniles. Concerns about rising juvenile crime were, it argued, common to societies undergoing rapid social change, and did not always stand up to scrutiny. It queried whether there really had been a dramatic change in the rates of crime committed by young people in Hong Kong over the preceding 20 years. Referring to the offender rate (gleaned from a combining the prosecution and discharge figures, rather than rates of reported crime and arrests) for youth between 1985 and 1990, the authors argued that the rate for the late 1970s and late 1980s did indeed show:

> . . . very large increases in juvenile crime. . . The rate went from 250 per 100,000 to 925 per 100,000 between 1977 and 1988. In the same period, the offender rate for adults rose from 823 to 1,613 per 100,000 . . . The prosecution rates increased greatly; in the period from 1977 to 1988 the number of juveniles prosecuted doubled while the juvenile population declined. In the same period there were dramatic increases in the number of specific crimes of particular public concern committed by juveniles. Crimes against the person rose by 300%, serious assaults by 356% and robberies by 336%.[16]

In the 1980s, the rate of admission of young male offenders below 21 to residential training or custody had almost trebled. Though the 1990s saw a slowdown, numbers continued to rise in the 1990s and by international standards, it remained high (Gray 1999: 578). In 1992, fewer juveniles and young offenders featured in the official arrest figures and Gray's research confirms a slowdown in the rate of admission of juveniles to correctional facilities. Most juveniles placed in probation homes (60 per cent) and 44 per cent of those placed in reformatory schools had been involved in property offences; this was also the case for well over half the young males below 20 admitted to training centres or detention centres (ibid).

The large increases in juvenile arrests in the 1980s were understood by the authorities as a sign that juvenile offending had reached crisis proportions. For government, police, prisons, and social workers, juvenile crime was a disturbing new phenomenon. In 1992/3, juveniles comprised almost 15 per cent of all those arrested and young offenders almost 20 per cent.[17] By 1996, the percentage of young offenders had fallen to 16.8 per cent, and juveniles stood at 13.7 per cent.[18] These fluctuations coincided with a wider fall in overall recorded crime in these years.

Whilst juveniles seemed to be more involved in property offences, they were far from the out-of-control violent youths depicted in the official accounts of crime. Vagg et al's 1995 report[19] on juvenile crime found that little violent crime was committed by juvenile and young offenders, and even where they were involved in crimes against the person, 'verbal threats and minor fist fights were the norm, with weapons rarely used' (Gray 1999: 582).

Gray suggests that Hong Kong's predisposition towards locking up its troublesome youth was driven in part by the strong belief in the idea, developed in the 1980s, that young people committed crimes because 'the normalizing bonds of family, school or work have been severed or weakened . . . greatly increase[ing] the vulnerability of youngsters to the influence

Table 24.1 Persons arrested by age group and gender 1990–97

	Juveniles		*16–20*		*21–30*		*30+*		*Total*	
	M	*F*	*M*	*F*	*M*	*F*	*M*	*F*	*M*	*F*
1990	5,764	819	7,541	765	12,590	1,416	12,791	2,327	38,685	5,327
1991	6,083	961	7,354	811	11,928	1,488	13,015	2,419	38,380	5,679
1992	5,457	1,076	6,734	922	11,111	1,728	12,218	2,574	35,520	6,260
1993	5,364	1,280	7,639	1,094	11,362	1,810	13,808	2,685	38,173	6,869
1994	5,598	1,432	7,970	1,205	12,325	1,993	16,090	3,171	41,983	7,801
1995	5,034	1,689	7,659	1,302	12,709	2,280	18,759	3,666	44,161	8,937
1996	4,889	1,590	6,743	1,198	11,050	2,155	16,182	3,350	38,864	8,293
1997	4,477	1,487	5,847	1,008	9,978	1,706	13,967	3,244	34,269	7,445

Source: RHKPAR 1990–97.

Table 24.2 Juvenile crime in Hong Kong 1990–96

Year	*No of juveniles (7–15)*		*No of young persons (16–20)*		*Total juveniles (7–15)*	*Total young persons (16–20)*
	M	*F*	*M*	*F*		
1990	5,764	819	7,541	765	6,583 (15%)	8,306
1991	6,083	961	7,354	811	7,044	8,165
1992	5,457	1,076	6,734	922	6,533	7,656
1993	5,364	1,280	7,639	1,094	6,644 (14.8%)	8,733 (19.4%)
1994	5,598	1,432	7,970	1,205	7,030 (14.1%)	9,175 (18.4%)
1995	5,034	1,689	7,659	1,302	6,723 (12.7%)	8,961 (16.9%)
1996	4,889	1,590	6,743	1,198	6,479 (13.7%)	7,941 (16.8%)

Source: RHKPARs 1990–96.

of undesirable elements and temptations' (Gray 1999: 582).[20] Noting that a relatively large proportion of arrested juveniles came from new towns of Tuen Mun and Shatin, she argues that there was a general readiness in Hong Kong to believe that delinquency resulted from the absence, in such places, of proper family, school and work ties in these areas, as well as failure of working parents to provide guidance and discipline.[21]

This goes some way to explaining why Hong Kong came to regard youth delinquency as problem requiring welfarist solutions, but not why, in the 1990s, the authorities regarded juvenile crime as such a problem. The answer to this lies outside the immediate realm of the criminal justice system, in the confluence of fresh anxieties generated by the 1997 handover. As Gray herself points out, manufacturing a moral panic about youth crime may also serve to distract public attention away from prevailing political crises, and 'justify tighter control over young people . . . seen as a threat to social order'.[22]

Gray's earlier work on the emergence of what she calls 'disciplinary welfare' in Hong Kong is helpful here. She links the emergence of more 'progressive' ways of managing juvenile crime to the wider programme of hegemonic restructuring in the 1970s.[23] The need to broaden popular support for the regime in the 1970s favoured measures designed to improve the lot of the working class, including welfarist strategies to solve juvenile crime. (Gray 1997: 190). 'Reformist' and welfarist approaches[24] were more in keeping with the administration's new image as a liberal-consultative state (Gray 1997: 191). What Gray calls disciplinary welfare was designed to 're-inforce positive links with family, school and friends and so remove the attraction of anti-social, delinquent bonds' (Gray 1997: 192). Although well intentioned, this 'progressive' approach actually provided 'a more covert and discerning way of disciplining working class delinquents' (Gray 1997: 187).

The pre-1997 regime faced a similar crisis of legitimacy and pursued similar solutions, though constraints on public spending limited its ability to deliver welfarism on the scale provided by MacLehose. In the mid-1990s, the desertion of the business elite had left Patten reliant on the grass-roots sections of society for popular legitimacy.[25] His period as Governor necessarily forced him to develop policies relevant to their concerns, including concerns about crime. The subsequent drift towards a more populist, 'soft-authoritarian' approach to law and order was also fuelled by fears that, without strong measures, society would descend into anarchy and disorder before 1997. These factors strengthened calls for a more reactionary response to juvenile delinquency. However, as the 1970s had already established a series of more 'progressive' measures to deal with problem youth, the call to clamp down on juveniles in the 1990s took the form of an expansion and intensification in disciplinary welfare, fulfilling Gray's earlier depiction of the trend in Hong Kong youth justice towards a somewhat Orwellian complex (Gray 1997: 200).

In 1992, the Fight Crime Committee announced that youth offending had become so problematic that it was to commission new research into the incidence and causes of juvenile crime.[26] Vagg et al's subsequent study broke with pre-existing thinking in Hong Kong insofar as it challenged the belief that there was 'one main pathway into delinquency and that young people are propelled into crime because of inadequate parental supervision, detachment from school and inappropriate peer associations' (Gray 1999: 584). The researchers looked instead at a variety of pathways into – and out of – deviancy, and how different socio-cultural factors might interact to reinforce one another.

In the meantime, Gray's own research underlined the fact that youth offending in Hong Kong had a strong class dimension. The majority of the youngsters who ended up in the youth justice system were from manual working-class families, with poorer levels of educational attainment, in poorly paid unskilled and unstable jobs and with few prospects of advancement (Gray 1999: 585). This meant that working class offenders had 'little to gain by conforming to conventional social ties with school or work which offer little chance of progress up the socio-economic ladder' (ibid), this being perhaps the most widely recognised route to status in Hong Kong. It came as no surprise, then, when Vagg et al found that 'persistent offenders tended to be more deeply immersed in "marginal" youth subcultures or "undesirable" leisure activities and friendship networks in which a delinquent career was likely to offer far greater rewards both in terms of material gain and in terms of status' (ibid).

These research studies provided 'a completely new way of viewing the problem of delinquency in Hong Kong' (ibid) but the prevailing ideology of youth justice, and its supporters amongst officials, youth justice professionals and criminal justice agencies proved hard to shift. The Fight Crime Committee concentrated its efforts on civic education and police school liaison teams. It paid little attention to community rehabilitation. The police continued to express concern about what they saw as the 'growing incidence of juveniles and youth involved in theft, robbery and triad offences', a combination of youth, crime and triads which brought together three of the principal bogeymen of the post-war years. With few exceptions, academics continued to suggest administrative solutions to the juvenile crime 'problem'.

The official figures for the 1980s and 1990s showed a decline in the number of these types of crimes, especially in the 10 to 14 age group, as compared to the trend in the 1970s (ibid). By the late 1980s and 1990s, however, the proportion of female juveniles arrested had risen; like the males, they were principally charged with shop theft. The great majority of offences committed by young people were in fact relatively minor, the most common being those that were easily detected, such as shoplifting.[27] The 1991 Youth Commission also pointed out that these petty crimes were more likely to be reported, and that the campaigns and police strategies focusing on youth

Table 24.3 Arrests for theft: females 1976 and 1996

	1976 *Percentage all theft (excluding burglary)*	*1996*
under 16	1.47	7.3
16–20	4.06	3.97
21–30	6.55	5.94
30–60	1.02	8.9

Source: RHKPARs 1976 and 1996.

Table 24.4 Arrests for theft: males 1976 and 1996

	1976 *Percentage all theft (excluding burglary)*	*1996*
under 16	12.9	17
16–20	15	12.6
21–30	27.3	18.3
31–60	18.84	24

Source: RHKP Statistics 1976 and 1996.

Table 24.5 Arrests for violent crime: females 1976 and 1996

	1976 *Percentage all violent crime*	*1996*
under 16	0.3	3.47
16–20	0.9	1.46
21–30	1.9	1.7
30–60	2.7	3.78

Source: RHKPARs 1976 and 1996.

Table 24.6 Arrests for violent crime: males 1976 and 1996

	1976 *Percentage all violent crime*	*1996*
under 16	6	12
16–20	22	19
21–30	40	26.7
31–60	22.5	29

Source: RHKP Statistics 1976 and 1996.

behaviour had heightened public awareness of crimes by young people, resulting in increased reporting. In 1996, almost 18 per cent of all arrests for shop theft were of boys aged under 16, whilst girls accounted for 13 per cent. For other miscellaneous thefts, boys under 16 accounted for over 18 per cent. Females accounted for 17.5 per cent of all arrests, and female juveniles made up 2.6 per cent of all criminal arrests.[28]

The recorded crime figures showed that the number of juvenile males arrested for crimes of violence had risen over the twenty-year period between 1976 and 1996. They were, however, far outnumbered by males in the 16 to 20 and 21 to 30 age groups (both also had higher arrest rates for violent crime than juvenile males). However, whereas in 1976 only 3.2 per cent of all arrests for serious assault were of juvenile males, by 1996, this figure had risen to 13.97 per cent.[29]

If official statistics tell us anything, they tell us about changes in police activity. These statistics indicate increased vigilance in the area of juvenile behaviour over this period. Presented as evidence of a real shift in juvenile behaviour, however, they fuelled popular perceptions that juveniles were getting out of hand, and that something had to be done. The crime survey findings that young people were also the most likely to become *victims* of crime made little impact.

Young people were conceived primarily as delinquents. Getting them to conform required greater supervision, discipline and control. This translated into ever-more 'reformist' measures to attach youth to society's institutions, norms and values, such as 'out-reach' youth policies, and policies to support and strengthen school and family ties. But, as Gray argues, these masked 'a covert and widened disciplinary regulation of young people's lives, increasing the numbers brought into the "net" and available for official intervention' (Gray 1997: 192). The end result was an intensive network of surveillance and control by quasi-government and non-government organisations out to capture and 'normalise' the soul, thoughts, and will of young people (Gray 1997: 194). The Hong Kong family became their primary target because of its pivotal position in the 'normalisation' of youth (Gray 1997: 198). Throughout the 1990s, patterns of consumption and popular culture (such as cantopop, 'Hello Kitty' toys, cartoons and a highly gendered dress code) also contributed significantly to the infantilisation of Hong Kong youth.

Table 24.7 Male crime as % all crime: 1976 and 1996

	1976	*1996*
under 16	2.96	8.6
16–20	9.8	20.5
21–30	18	36.5

Source: RHKPARs 1976 and 1996.

Given the economic and political tenor of Hong Kong, as well as the PRC, it is perhaps not surprising that government preferred these explanations and solutions to juvenile delinquency. Communism in the PRC rendered politically unacceptable any theory that located the causes of crime in socio-economic factors. Hong Kong's economic success made radical change equally unthinkable. In both societies, juvenile justice proceeded on the basis that delinquency was a product of individual pathology and moral shortcomings. With Hong Kong's return to China arguably driving a similarly conservative youth justice agenda, the authorities on both sides of the border therefore approached 1997 with broadly similar views on the causes of, and solutions to, juvenile crime. These remained impervious to any of the findings of crime surveys or research studies. The 1994 crime survey showed that most *victims* of violent crime were young males but the official crime statistics perpetuated the belief that they were principally *offenders*.[30] The emphasis on economic success, educational achievement and upward mobility left stranded those young people whose qualifications left them unable to find work. As Hong Kong reinvented itself as a high-tech, international financial centre, the failures of the educational system increased their economic marginalisation. All the evidence was that Hong Kong youth felt increasingly powerless, and distant from the territory's main social and political institutions. A 1991 study found, for example, that 'close to 60 per cent of boys and over 60 per cent of girls reported that they "usually" or "sometimes" felt under pressure, and felt unhappy and depressed. . . . High proportions reported loss of confidence and inability to sleep due to worry . . . 47 per cent of boys and 52 per cent of girls had potential health problems'.[31] A 1990 Survey on Civic Education as well as the Youth Commission's 1991 survey on young people's attitudes and expectations found that over 93.3 per cent of young people thought they themselves could have no impact on government policy.[32] This sense of political powerlessness was widespread. Forty-six per cent of respondents aged under 21 involved in the 1990 Survey on Civic Education gave their uncertainty about the future as the reason for not registering to vote. The 1991 Commission on Youth also found that a high number of young people lacked confidence in the stability and prosperity of Hong Kong and were concerned about their future. At the same time, a 1988 survey of social indicators in Hong Kong had found that younger and more educated people tended to be more critical of social conditions (See Howroyd and MacPherson 1992).[33]

None of this seemed to register with those charged with administering the criminal justice system. The police, CSD and social work services concentrated on making sure Hong Kong's juveniles turned into law-abiding citizens. Young offenders were to be reintegrated into the community (Wong 2000) regardless of whether the laws and the community to which they must conform were fair or just. There was also a strong belief amongst CSD professionals that custodial programmes had a negative effect on offenders and should be used as a last resort (Wong 2000: 288), making non-custodial sanctions preferable.[34] This did not, however, translate into community-based corrections. Between 1989 and 1996, the number of male young offenders below the age of twenty one sentenced to residential training or custody rose from 1,095 to 1,220 per 100,000, and in 1996 nearly 34 per cent of young males (aged 7 to 20) convicted of 'standard list' crimes received a residential or custodial sentence (Gray 1999: 578).[35] Less than 29 per cent received community-based disposals (ibid). Gray's research indicated that the existing system captured juveniles very quickly: the majority of juveniles in custody had an extremely short offending career – 66.7 per cent of those in her research who were sent to detention centre had a clean criminal record, and 70 per cent of those sent to training centre custody either had a clear record or only one prior conviction.

By the end of the 1990s, therefore, the authorities no longer depended solely or even mainly upon custodial techniques to deal with juvenile delinquency. Hong Kong's vast network of community-based social workers, youth organisations and programmes meant that non-custodial sanctions were highly effective. The state relied not so much on informal social control as an *informalised* means of state control. This expanded throughout the 1990s. A vast inter-locking mosaic of juvenile justice measures was developed, involving official and non-governmental associations loosely aligned in a comprehensive network, all concerned with disciplining juveniles.

Those performing this task – in education, social welfare, criminal justice, and voluntary sector work with juveniles – were mostly oblivious to the part they played. Like the free market, the order they helped establish seemed almost spontaneous, the work of an 'invisible hand'. In fact it required constant effort to construct and maintain. It valorised hard work, self-help, individual and family success, upward social mobility, values which, on the eve of the handover, the Governor repeatedly stressed were the foundation of Hong Kong's free, liberal and stable capitalist society. This vast mosaic of disciplinary forms and measures allowed the outgoing administration to govern from a distance, without relinquishing its claim to be a minimal state. It could also – with some justification – claim that Hong Kong was one of the safest cities in the world.

Notes

1 HKPAR 1997: 68. Note that after 1 July 1997, the Royal Hong Kong Police (RHKP) ceased to be 'Royal' and reverted to simply being the 'Hong Kong Police' (HKP).

2 Between 1956 and 1969, property crime constituted 65 per cent of all reported crime. Between 1970 and 1980, it constituted 44 per cent, and between 1980 and 1989 it levelled out at 55 per cent. See Traver 1991.

3 In most cases, the amount lost was worth less than HK$950.However, a loss of HK$950 has a more serious impact on low-income victims than on wealthy

victims. In the majority of cases (94 per cent) of personal and household theft, the property was not recovered and in the majority of cases where damage had been caused to the property, the victim had to repair the property at their own expense.

4 In the 1979 survey, 47 per cent of crimes of violence and 54 per cent of robberies were carried out by armed persons; in 1986, more than a quarter of crimes of violence involved the use of a weapon, usually in robberies (45 per cent) rather than assaults (29 per cent).

5 Department of Census and Statistics, *Crime and Its Victims in Hong Kong*. Hong Kong: Government Printer.

6 Those living in private permanent housing had the highest victimisation rate for personal crimes of theft.

7 A slightly higher percentage (42 per cent) of those living in private permanent housing reported their victimisation, whilst 40 per cent of those living in temporary housing made a report.

8 Such findings were in keeping with findings from other jurisdictions. These generally show that reporting rates are *lowest* in areas where the victimisation rate is *highest*. In Hong Kong, these were Kowloon and the NT, which consistently had higher levels of victimisation but lower rates of reporting crime. On the other hand, Hong Kong Island consistently has one of the lowest victimisation rates but one of the highest reporting rates. The finding that where and how people live affects their susceptibility to crime is also borne out by studies elsewhere. One US survey, published in 1989, showed that people living in cities and suburban areas had a greater chance of being victims of personal crime, compared to those living in rural areas. Rates of violent crime in cities were about 92 per cent higher than those in rural areas. Rural residents also experienced about 90 per cent fewer theft victimisations; household crime in the cities was about 93 per cent higher than in the rural areas. However, other types of crime are equally likely to occur in rural and urban settings. For example, domestic violence is as likely to occur in a family living in the countryside as one living in the town; it is also likely to occur in all social classes. See, for example, US Department of Justice 1989.

9 The first (1979) crime survey showed that personal crimes were more likely to take place during the day, and that more than half of all street robberies took place at night.

10 HK Police (1995) *Police in Figures*. As Muncie and McLaughlin have pointed out, the way in which crime statistics are reported depends on the intended message the user wishes to put across. For example, the Hong Kong Police 'crime clock' gives one impression of crime in Hong Kong. Another example is the statistic for burglary used in the 1982 British Crime Survey. This revealed a rate of 250 burglaries per 10,000 households in England and Wales in 1981. This could be expressed in a number of different ways, each one giving a different impression to the reader: (1) a burglary every minute throughout the country; (2) a one-in-forty likelihood of being burgled in a year; (3) the likelihood of being burgled once in every 40 years (Muncie and McLaughlin 1996b: 32). Another example from the British Crime Survey states that 'the average person can expect a robbery once every five centuries; an assault resulting in injury . . . once every century; the family car to be stolen or taken by joyriders once every sixty years; a burglary in the home once every forty years' (Lea and Young 1984: 25). Another way of describing the risks of victimisation is to say that 'The average Londoner still has to live in the city two thousand years before even having a chance of being mugged and even then the odds are three to one against a weapon being used' (ibid.). But this averaging out of crime figures fails to show that for people living in some areas the chance of becoming a victim of crime is substantially higher than elsewhere.

11 HK Police (1985) *Crime in Figures*.
12 This is especially true for women, who tend to experience repeat (or serial) victimisations of domestic violence.
13 In 1986, Kowloon had the highest rate of victimisation (54 per cent), followed by the NT (28 per cent) and Hong Kong Island (18 per cent). In 1989, however, crime victimisation in the NT began to overtake the rest – 43 per cent compared to 40 per cent for Kowloon and 16 per cent for Hong Kong Island. By 1994, a further shift had taken place: 40 per cent of all victimisations occurred in the NT, 40 per cent in Kowloon, 19 per cent on Hong Kong Island, and 1 per cent in the Marine region. A higher proportion of victimisations for personal crime occurred in Kowloon than the NT, whereas in the NT, victimisations for household crime were proportionately higher.
14 For example, crime surveys have revealed that in Britain someone is twice as likely to be burgled if s/he is an unskilled worker than if s/he is a professional, and over four times as likely if s/he is under 24 than if they are over 65. American crime surveys show that a person is more likely to be victimised if they are black rather than white, male rather than female, and aged between 24 and 34 rather than over 65.
15 The 1994 survey showed that persons aged over 65 had the lowest victimisation rate for almost all types of personal crime. However, older victims were more likely to be injured than younger victims, though the 1994 crime survey showed that most crimes of violence resulted in no injury (81.8 per cent) or only minor injury (15.8 per cent) to the victim.
16 Hong Kong Commission on Youth 1991, cited in Gray 1991: 26.
17 RHKPAR 1993: 17.
18 RHKPAR 1996: 22.
19 Vagg et al 1995.
20 Gray links both to a belief in the rehabilitative ideal amongst youth justice professionals, and to the tenets of traditional Confucianist ideas about child rearing, which emphasise proper training from an early age to instil appropriate moral standards and respect for authority.
21 This may explain why the rehabilitative ideal remains so strong in Hong Kong where it has failed elsewhere, but also why Hirschi's 'control theory' has such resonance locally. See Hirschi 1969.
22 Gray 1997: 191. Gray is here drawing on the arguments of Hall et al 1978.
23 Gray 1997.
24 Gray argues that Ng's 1975 study on the Social Causes of Violent Crimes among Young Offenders significantly affected this shift. See Gray 1991: 191.
25 Sum and Jessop.
26 This produced Vagg et al's research study.
27 Detection of such crimes became easier with the deployment within chain stores of private security in the late 1970s and 1980s. Routine activity theory also suggests that if juveniles routinely engage in unsupervised activities, such as hanging around shopping malls and stores (what some in Hong Kong call the 'Seven Eleven' phenomena), they will be more likely to engage in shop crime when the opportunity arises.
28 In 1976, female arrests amounted to just 10.4 per cent of all arrests and juvenile females accounted for an even lower percentage of arrests (0.95 per cent).
29 Whereas 45.3 per cent of arrests for serious assault in 1976 were of males aged 16 to 20 (young offenders), by 1996 this had fallen to 16.3 per cent.
30 Elsewhere, such findings prompted researchers to examine in greater depth the experience of crime amongst youth. For example, a victim study of 4,200 young

people conducted in the UK in 1992 showed that for most of the children sampled, crime was a part of everyday life. The report argued that most children will have had some experience of crime, either as a victim or as an offender. Nearly one-third of the girls in the study had been the victim of some kind of sexual offence by a male. This figure was higher for girls living in the city than in the countryside, but as they grew older and more mobile, girls from rural areas were more likely to become victims of this type of crime. Many of the girls in the study took such incidents for granted, seeing it as part of growing up. More than a quarter of all children in the study had been threatened with violence, and more than one in ten had been the victim of street theft. In the majority of cases, they did not inform the police or their parents. The survey also showed that most children, from all social backgrounds, commit some kind of offence, from shoplifting to vandalism, housebreaking and car theft.

31 Family Planning Association of Hong Kong 1991: 160.

32 Howroyd and MacPherson 1992.

33 1991 Youth Commission Survey. Young people also saw youth, pollution, transport, housing, education and old age as major social problems, and felt that public order, economic development and education policies should be given policy priority by the government

34 This echoes Vagg et al (1995) who found that (1) on release, those subject to compulsory detention acquired more deviant values than they had on arrest; and (2) an over-reaction to juvenile deviancy might intensify the problem and accidentally promote further delinquency (ibid.). The criminal justice response to juvenile crime (detention centres, training centres, drug addiction centres, rehabilitation centres and prisons) was thus regarded as less effective than the welfarist strategies developed in the late 1970s.

35 Residential training included probation home or reformatory school; custodial sentences included detention centre, training centre, drug addiction treatment centre or imprisonment. See Gray 1999: 578.

Part 3

The First Ten years of the HKSAR, 1997–2007

Chapter 25

Convergence, continuities and change: 1997–2007

On 1 July 1997, Hong Kong ceased to be a British colony and became a Special Administrative Region of the PRC (HKSAR). This brought changes but there were also continuities. The laws governing life in the SAR remained largely unaltered, but the fact that Hong Kong now had its own 'mini-constitution (the Hong Kong Basic Law) was in itself an immense change for a common law system. Whilst some of the British and Europeans departed, many lawyers, judges, police and prison officers remained. Moreover, for China as for Britain, Hong Kong's *raison d'être* was its value as an economic city, providing both a gateway into China for foreign investors and a conduit into the global economy for Mainland entrepreneurs.

Midnight 30 June did not, therefore (as some foreign observers had imagined) mean the immediate end of Hong Kong as we knew it, but it did strip away the trappings of British colonial rule. Pictures of the Queen were removed from post offices, police stations and courts; red mailboxes turned green; the Union Jack disappeared; the police ceased to be 'Royal' and reverted to simply being the 'Hong Kong Police'. In terms of political institutions, the changes were more significant and immediate. At midnight on 30 June, the elected members of the Democratic Party marched out of the LEGCO building to a crowd of cheering supporters. They were to be replaced by the Mainland-appointees of the new Provisional LEGCO. A new Chief Executive (Tung Chee hwa) replaced the Governor, and the old judiciary swore a new oath of allegiance. These formal ceremonies of transition were watched around the world. The moment was 'historic' not only because it signalled the symbolic end of the British Empire, but because it denoted the unprecedented marriage of Hong Kong, epitome of free market capitalism, to China, the last world-power committed to communism.

There was considerable hyperbole on both sides. The 'One Country, Two Systems' formula espoused by Deng Xiaoping as the rationale for the HKSAR was intended to bridge the gap between two opposites: a capitalist colony known for its liberal way of life, its common law legal system and its political freedoms, and a socialist country regarded as having an authoritarian government, a rapidly developing but still backward economy, a socialist/civil legal system and restricted socio-political freedoms. For China the handover also marked the end of a national humiliation (the loss of Hong Kong during the Opium Wars).

Hong Kongers worried about how 'retrocession' would affect their personal freedoms, human rights, and rule of law. There were already signs that the PRC, in the manner of a 're-colonising' power, wished to re-mould them as loyal patriots. The outgoing administration had started fostering 'Chinese culture study groups' in the schools, universities, and even within the disciplined services.

Because criminal law and criminal justice are pivotal to the individual's relation to the state (most notably as regards the state's power to detain, imprison and punish, as well as its right to restrict individual rights and freedoms) these areas were always likely to become sites of struggle between the old and new conceptions of Hong Kong. For the Chinese leadership, Hong Kong was a potential base for 'subversive' influences; its media and public were openly critical not only of their own administration but also the PRC leadership itself. (Hong Kong journalists were occasionally rebuked for this by Mainland leaders.) Groups suppressed on the Mainland (such as the Falun Gong) were permitted in Hong Kong; the public ignored injunctions from the new Chief Executive to leave the 'political baggage' of 4 June behind.

Beijing's task was to silence its critics without being seen as a heavy-handed oppressor. As it transpired, Beijing needed to do little: the Hong Kong administration, anxious to demonstrate its patriotism and loyalty to China, took the initiative in suppressing undesirable influences. The clarion call of the post-1997 regime was that Hong Kong people should 'love China'. Those who failed to shout it loudly enough, or with sufficient enthusiasm, became suspect. In the academy, self-censorship was being quietly counselled and practised. Although outwardly little seemed to have altered, more subtle hints and influences had a chilling effect on critics.

In 1997 itself, nearly two-thirds of Hong Kongers were optimistic about reunion with China. Initially, the continuity of the transition years was reassuring. By 2002, however, things had altered radically. A mood of pessimism had set in and only one in four remained optimistic about the reunion.[1] In 1997, Hong Kongers were 'overwhelmingly satisfied with life in Hong Kong' but, as the Tung years progressed, barely 51 per cent expressed satisfaction.[2] This partly reflected anxiety about the economy in the wake of the 1997 Asian Financial crisis, but also a deeper disquiet about the way Hong Kong was being led. Embarrassingly, the opinion polls showed that the popularity of the Chief Executive had fallen below that of the last British Governor. Tung was perceived as politically incompetent, pro-Beijing and pro-big business, his government an oligarchy of businessmen who, like the British of the 1960s, had little interest in the welfare of Hong Kong people. Poor handling of the avian flu and SARS outbreaks, corruption regarding the piling work in new housing estates, a number of scandals involving leading figures in the administration – all combined to produce high levels of public dissatisfaction.[3]

By the early 2000s, therefore, the post-1997 administration faced its own legitimacy crisis. Hong Kong society was more highly polarised; social cohesion was deteriorating; the property market had declined sharply; and the Gini-coefficient reached its highest ever point, indicating a widening gap between rich and poor. Partisanship and cronyism had also returned. The Grand Bauhinia Medal (the highest official honour) was awarded to a well-known leader of the 1967 riots, reopening 'the far from fully healed old wounds and pained memories of the 1967 leftist rampant violence . . . perhaps the single darkest age in the pro-Chinese Communist circle's historical experience in colonial Hong Kong' (Chan 2002: 16). This provoked negative public reaction and damaged the administration's legitimacy, partly because:

> Such very deliberate and obviously partisan criteria – patriotic and big business – monopolization of the communal or sectoral representation and interest articulation channels, as well as public affairs participation mechanisms under the Tung regime, can only further intensify the already worsening under-currents of political tensions and the sharpening social class schism. Is the very worst kind of the politics of exclusion and divisiveness (Chan 2002: 10).

Tung made appointments not on the basis of 'professional expertise, public service experience, administrative skills, political wisdom or developmental visions' but based on personal loyalty and ideological compatibility (ibid). Instead of being closer to the people than the British, the post-1997 government thus squandered its credit by reverting to the kind of remote oligarchy emblematic of 1960s colonialism. Many of those granted a vote under the British were also disenfranchised overnight, whilst the consultative channels established in the 1970s were dismantled.

Though the post-1997 regime took office with a mandate to depoliticise Hong Kong, numerous issues and incidents – many of them relating to crime and criminal justice – raised the political temperature. As the regime became more centralised, authoritarian and distant, mass demonstrations were organised to air disaffection and discontent. Policing became dominated by public order matters. The courts were kept fully occupied with constitutional, civil and criminal cases that tested the boundaries of liberty and rights in the new SAR. Criminal justice controversies especially arose relating to public order and to the rendition of cross-border criminals. These helped delineate the Hong Kong–China relationship by revealing more precisely the porous nature of the border between the two jurisdictions, raising entirely novel questions about what protections Hong Kong citizens could rely on when they crossed between them.

The post-1997 criminal courts

Three major institutional forces shaped the operation of criminal justice post-1997. The first was the 1991 Bill of Rights (BOR). At a stroke, this had forced criminal justice agencies to adjust their procedures so as not to contravene its human rights/due process provisions. Criminal cases questioning police powers, criminal justice procedures and court sentencing continued to outstrip any other kind of legal challenge to the authorities under the BOR. The second was the new post-1997 court structure. The Privy Council in London, once the highest court of appeal for the territory, was replaced by a new Court of Final Appeal (CFA) staffed by Hong Kong judges aided, at any sitting, by one overseas judge. Many more criminal cases went to the CFA than ever went the Privy Council. Between July 1997 and December 2005, for example, the CFA dealt with 708 criminal-related cases; between January 1989 and June 1997, the Privy Council had heard just 106 cases from Hong Kong. This represented a 567.9 per cent increase after 1997.[4]

The presence of the CFA within the territory meant that controversies once rehearsed in London now attracted much more immediate local attention. They included such fundamental issues as whether Hong Kongers had the right to burn the flag, what limits there were to freedom of expression, and what were the proper grounds for limiting the freedom to protest. In the climate of the times, it was probably inevitable that such cases would be seen as a test of the PRC's promise that Hong Kong's legal system and way of life would remain unaltered for 50 years. The CFA thus became a lightning rod for fears about the future and a fulcrum of competing visions of Hong Kong's relationship to the Mainland.

These competing visions were played out in the criminal justice system as well. Elsewhere, post-colonialism is associated with liberation from a colonial oppressor, but in Hong Kong the post-1997 regime proved more illiberal and less tolerant of dissent. The depredations of the state were partially blocked by the courts, drawing on the traditions of the common law world and the power of the BOR. However, this was now subordinate to the Basic Law whose final interpretation was, it turned out, not entirely a matter for the territory's highest court (the CFA) but for the Standing Committee of the NPC, a political body in Beijing.[5]

Court of Final Appeal
|
High Court
Court of Appeal
Court of First Instance
|
District Court
|
Magistrate's Court

Figure 25.1 Structure of domestic courts post-1997.

Considerable rhetoric was deployed in a series of high profile cases in the High Court and the CFA, setting out Hong Kong people's rights and freedoms. Gradually, however, it became clear that rights that had previously been taken for granted were now the subject of contests in the courts.

For most people, the legal system was still experienced at the level of the magistracy. Here, the vast majority of cases were conducted in Chinese (roughly between 69 and 79 per cent) or through an interpreter (if the magistrate, lawyers or defendant could not speak Chinese). By contrast, even given their high public interest, only 21 to 24 per cent of criminal cases in the CFA were conducted in Chinese; in the Court of Appeal, the percentage was about 20 per cent for criminal appeals, rising in the Court of First Instance to between 56–62 per cent for magistracy appeals (but dropping to 16 to 21 per cent for criminal trials); in the District Court, only some 11 to 12 per cent of criminal cases were conducted in Chinese. This was a poor record for a post-colonial administration and added little to the regime's legitimacy. Not until 2001 did one court (North Kowloon Magistracy – one of the seven in Hong Kong) even begin to experiment with the use of Chinese in trials and reports. Yet the Magistrates' Courts were those that dealt most directly with the Chinese population and it was on the basis of their experience here that many formed their views about the criminal justice system as a whole.

The nature of many of the cases brought before the magistracy remained familiar. In any one year between 1999 and 2005, somewhere between eight and nine thousand cases in the Magistrates' Courts involved hawking offences; another eight to nine thousand involved miscellaneous offences. In 2005, the magistracies also began to deal with infringements of public cleanliness laws. Clearly, regime change had not altered the administration's preoccupation with order, cleanliness and control.

Like the polity, the legitimacy of the post-1997 magistracy remained in the shadow of the British – 1960s' magistrates such as Miller remained inscribed on the memories of hawkers as the one man who would 'stick up for the little man against Government'. Professionalisation and new managerialism now limited the room for such 'idiosyncrasies', but Chui notes that the Association for the Promotion of Peace and Justice 'had taken on itself the task of supporting the little man in a system seen to lack accountability' (Chui 1999: 62). It is clear from her account of her experiences as a Chinese magistrate that she did not regard the system at this level (or higher up) as living up to the ideals of delivering justice 'without fear or favour'.[6]

Professionalisation did not extend quite so fully to the business of prosecution and defence. Non-legally qualified personnel were permitted to appear as Court Prosecutors in the Magistrates' Court,[7] whilst non-legally qualified legal assistants often provided the advice to legally-aided clients in the cells. Often holding a law degree but lacking the professional qualification (the PCLL) and training that allow entry to the profession, those at the 'front-line' of magistrates' justice were, therefore, on the margins of the profession; junior barristers also looked to the magistracy for a steady supply of legal aid work. Magistracy justice was 'second rate' justice, the lack of professionalism at this level reflecting a wider belief that magistrates' cases were generally 'trivial' matters.

The criminal justice system remained oriented towards crime control. The new regime was anxious to maintain levels of crime at their pre-handover low, to demonstrate its capability in maintaining Hong Kong's success and its reputation as a safe and orderly city. The eyes of the world were on it, whilst the Chinese leadership was also vigilant for signs of civil unrest. Conviction rates in all courts remained high – in 2004, for example, 77.3 per cent of cases ended in conviction (73.5 per cent in 2005). In the District Court the rates were 90.1 per cent in 2004 and 87.5 per cent in 2005; in the Court of First Instance, this rose to 89.1 per cent in 2004 and 90.4 per cent in 2005.[8] Caseloads in the lower courts reduced markedly – in the early 1990s, a professional Judiciary Administrator was appointed to reduce 'inefficiencies', since when cases had been expedited (and information filed) in a more systematic fashion. But court delay (and consequently time spent in custody on remand) remained an issue.

According to Chui, magistrates resented the fact that it was the prosecution that controlled the choice of venue for trial, enabling it to obtain extensions to the 48-hour period of detention post-charge (Chui 1999: 118). She argues that the prosecution would prevent the magistrate from dealing with the accused by not choosing the venue of trial (i.e. Magistrate's Court, District Court, or High Court) and entering a 'no plea', 'meaning that the magistrate was not to ask the defendant to plead to the charges' (ibid). Defendants would then be remanded in custody (bail only became a right shortly before the handover) allowing the prosecution more time to establish whether there was a prima facie case to be answered. For Chui, this amounted to a 'cynical manipulation of the law, but also a dangerous extension of executive power. It also blurred the distinction between executive detention and judicial remand' (ibid).

Table 25.2 Caseload of Magistrates' Courts

	1999	*2000*	*2001*	*2002*	*2003*	*2004*	*2005*
Brought forward	127,016	89,560	105,286	91,279	80,633	83,903	93,875
Filed	427,060	381,956	341,644	298,005	282,331	301,147	224,555
Disposed of	427,087	374,667	339,696	308,651	279,061	291,175	226,458
Inactive	37,429	28,992	27,044	2,336	2,349	2,144	2,687
In progress	89,560	105,286	109,162	78,298	81,554	91,731	89,285

Source: Hong Kong Judiciary Annual Reports 1999–2005.

Police

The third main influence on criminal justice after 1997 was economic constraint which, though it had begun to make itself felt in the early 1990s, was exacerbated by the Asian financial crisis of 1997. Public spending on criminal justice declined, and the terms of service of all government servants underwent radical alteration. Cutbacks included the reduction of the auxiliary police and the amalgamation of police stations in the name of cost-effectiveness and efficiency. Following a review in 1999, the auxiliary police no longer played a part in 'watch and ward' duties, but became a reserve force for use in emergencies and in crowd control during major events, such as festivals. The police force's overall share of the government budget declined; the size of the force was reduced; and a new contract system of appointment was introduced which offered less favourable terms of service and reduced security of tenure. Once deferential members of the force now vented their discontent publicly via a website. As a result, the public image of the police, so central to earlier police/public relations, became more difficult for the force hierarchy to control.

The emphasis on efficient use of resources, which began with the New Public Management in 1989, became more pronounced. This was good news for women officers, as better use was now made of their skills and experience – more women assumed senior positions, and more were sent overseas to take courses which were hitherto dominated by their male colleagues.

Despite the cutbacks, however, justice, law enforcement and peacekeeping still cost government about 12 per cent of its entire budget on the maintenance of security.[9] By 2005 the share of the budget dedicated to policing had dropped to 4.6 per cent, and plans to build a 'super-prison' had been shelved. New investment was made instead in technology, including the installation of video and audio tape recording in police interview rooms, and the remodelling of station report rooms to make them 'warmer' and more 'user-friendly' (the first one, at North Point, was widely likened to a hotel reception area). This re-shaping of the 'face' of the police was designed to reassure the public that the post-1997 force was still a servant of the community. Uncertainties remained as to what trajectory law and order post-1997 would take. Responding to this, and to fears about a post-1997 crime wave, the police force had painstakingly reiterated its commitment to traditional 'front-line' policing and maintaining 'a strong visible presence'.[10]

Just before the handover, police training embarked on a sea change. In 2006, a new police college opened, providing courses in collaboration with the Open University of Hong Kong, representing the further professionalisation of the force begun by Pennefather-Evans in the post-war period. At the same time, however, the trend towards an ever-larger police force ceased. This still left Hong Kong with one of the largest police forces (per capita) in the world, at 640 police per 100,000 people (Broadhurst 2000).

Table 25.3 Hong Kong Police Establishment 1997–2005

1997	*1998*	*1999*	*2000*	*2001*	*2002*	*2003*	*2004*	*2005*
28,007	28,759	28,495	28,695	28,665	28,389	28,150	27,754	27,404

Table 25.4 Complaints against police

2001	*2002*	*2003*	*2004*
3,241	3,822	3,383	3,222

Source: IPCCARs 2001–4.

The many years of focused police–public relations meant that, despite growing dissatisfaction with the government, public confidence in the Hong Kong Police remained high – opinion polls consistently showed satisfactions ratings of 60 to 70 per cent.[11] In October 2006, people's satisfaction with the police force reached a record high, the highest since surveys began in 1997.[12] Though some dissatisfaction remained, the police's embrace of new managerialism in the 1990s had improved the force's transparency. While the number of complaints against police barely altered, there was a felt need to reshape the complaints against the police system to bring it more in line with the public's expectation that Hong Kong institutions should be seen to be more open, fair and 'democratic'. To further improve transparency and ensure impartiality (but also to avoid having to adopt a full-blown, independent police complaints system) a lay observer scheme was introduced into the existing police complaints system in 2000, allowing observers attached to the Independent Police Complaints Commission (IPCC) to be present at interviews of both complainants and accused.[13] In many respects, it was a typical Hong Kong solution to the problem of democratic deficit, giving the appearance of autonomy and independence without actually delivering it.

By the new millennium, all parts of the criminal justice system were required to justify their output in terms of the most efficient use of resources. One side effect was the production of vast amounts of information about the administration of criminal justice (not all of it very interesting or informative). Hong Kong now had a system more documented, more audited, and more 'client conscious', than at any time in its history.

Broadhurst has observed that the Hong Kong Police Force has long acted as a quasi-independent agency, and that this has, in turn, limited the manipulation of the police and crime trends for partisan political purposes (Broadhurst 2000). New management inadvertently increased (albeit marginally) this quasi-independence. On the other hand, it also provided a brilliant solution to some presentational problems for the police and the criminal justice service more generally. Both were, inevitably, closely associated with an unpopular government. In the past, this association was tempered in the public mind by the police–public relations drive, which was itself part of the 'gigantic consultative system for feeding back to the government the views of the citizens'.[14] This system had worked well, and the problems faced by the government and the police after the 1960s riots had been largely overcome, except amongst those sections of the community that remained ardently communist and opposed to colonial rule. The 1997 handover had seen, albeit briefly, communist attacks on the police force as a tool of colonial repression, whilst others worried that it would now become the handmaiden of a new colonising power (China). The task of the police – and indeed of the dying regime more generally – was to retain the community's trust and confidence.

One way of presenting itself as a public 'service' rather than 'force' was to stress legalistic, bureaucratic, rational, politically neutral objectives though a series of performance pledges, as well as reference to economy, effectiveness, efficiency and Total Quality Management (TQM). These became the buzz-words of the police force after 1997. The new managerialism provided government and it agencies with the language it needed to convey an image of neutrality, of serving the community as a whole according to universalistic values, thus avoiding accusations of partisanship during the transition years.

Public management measures did not, however, produce real accountability. The complaints against police mechanisms remained weak – the low level of substantiated complaints continued to undermine the credibility of the system in the eyes of the public. Nor was there (as Walden observed) any real way of ensuring that the disciplined and civil services did not 'become a law unto itself'.[15] Though government appeared more open and information more freely available, there was no 'freedom of information' culture and some things remained strictly beneath a penumbra of secrecy. 'Political policing', for example, was now far less well documented in the public record than it had been. Much information remained classified and restricted. Some came to light through the efforts of the media – in 2006, for example, Hong Kongers read in their newspapers that the police and ICAC had eaves-dropped on, or used hidden surveillance devices in, 348 cases in the last three months of 2005, an average of three cases a day. Government statistics released during the controversy indicated that between February and May 2006, there were 151 cases of phone tapping and 238 other cases of covert surveillance. Moreover, the figures were for 'cases' only – the total number of *persons* subject to covert surveillance was potentially far higher as 'a crime operation may cover 30 or 40 people or a big security event like the national president coming to Hong Kong may have required monitoring 10,000 activists'.[16]

The issue came to light in two bribery cases heard in the District Court early in 2005. These related to the ICAC's use of covert surveillance in its investigations of Shum Chiu and Wong Hung-ki. In February, 2006, a High

Court judge ruled that the Chief Executive's power to authorise, by administrative fiat, the tapping of phones and covert interception of communications was inconsistent with the right to free and private communication protected by the Basic Law. However, the government was given a six-month period of grace in which to 'set its house in order'. In December 2005, the Law Reform Commission published its report on the regulation of covert surveillance. This suggested that the existing law on the interception of communications was inconsistent with Article 7 of the International Covenant on Civil and Political Rights. It recommended the introduction of safeguards against the arbitrary or unlawful intrusion into an individual's privacy by anyone, including law enforcement agencies, except under specific circumstances such as investigating serious crime.[17] In August 2006, just before the end of the grace period, LEGCO passed a new surveillance law (the Interception of Communications Ordinance) after five days of heated deliberation and despite a boycott of the vote by 25 members of the pro-democracy parties. This was widely reported in the international media as a blow to civil liberties in Hong Kong.

Hong Kong's celebrated order and stability thus still owed a good deal to the 'invisible hand' of covert political policing. Wong has also highlighted the fact that undercover police 'liaison officers' in schools were used to track and arrest triad influence. There also remained intact the network of informal state supervision comprising local organisations, mutual aid committees and voluntary bodies, all of which were still able to mobilise against crime as part of their civic duties. If anything, 1997 had seen an increase in the state's ability to mobilise at this level, since pro-communist organisations were now willing to join in a 'united front' against crime.

In addition to these non-institutional forms of 'policing' in 1999 Hong Kong had approximately 722 registered security and guarding companies employing some 160,000 people – five private police for every one official police officer, a rate higher even than Singapore, which had about 200 such companies employing fifteen to twenty thousand private police, a rate of about two to every public police officer (Broadhurst 2000). Post-1997, then, Hong Kong remained an intensively policed place.

Corruption and the maintenance of a 'level playing field'

The effectiveness of crime suppression and prevention – its detection and prosecution – is, as Broadhurst puts it, 'a fundamental measure of the capability of the State' (Broadhurst 2000). It became especially important in this regard in the early 2000s, when public confidence in the administration reached an all-time low.

Crime, and the failure to deal with it effectively, are often interpreted as threats to social order and stability. In Hong Kong's case, they were also explicitly connected to the HKSAR's chances of economic recovery and renewed prosperity. It became important for the government to reassure people that the stated foundations of the territory's success (rule of law, freedoms and liberties, an open society etc.) were still intact. The fact that the police retained such high levels of public confidence went some way to suggesting that at least *some* of these institutions had survived the general loss of legitimacy that attached to the regime as a whole.

Hong Kong is a place and a people with strong memories of corruption. In the past, its closed polity meant that an individual's life chances were highly dependent on an economy and a society open to talents. Though Hong Kong was a deeply unequal society, this inequality was seen as just because it was believed to reflect individual effort and talent. Working hard and being prudent were foundational values of Hong Kong society, with its 'bootstrap entrepreneurs' and its free market ethos. The belief that anyone could attain the Hong Kong Dream depended on keeping the playing field level by eradicating distorting factors such as corruption. The ICAC was both practically and symbolically central to this goal. It was not just a crime-fighting force. More than any other agency of criminal justice, its work was central to regime legitimacy. The belief that the Tung administration rewarded cronyism undermined its 'right to rule' and brought into question its capacity to deliver a just and impartial system of laws.

After 1997, the population became hyper-vigilant about corruption. Opinion surveys before 1997 indicated that Hong Kong people were worried about the reappearance of corruption and mainland interference in Hong Kong affairs, both of which were seen as likely to destroy that which made Hong Kong stable and prosperous.[18] These worries were so strong that up until just six months before the handover, many still rejected mainland sovereignty.

However, the worry that Mainland-type corruption was creeping into Hong Kong after 1997 was not borne out, and the proportion feeling 'very worried' about it dropped as each year passed.[19] In October 2006, the ICAC observed that there was no sign of serious corruption in the public or private sector, and that about 95 per cent of those surveyed said they had not come across corruption in the last 12 months.[20] Hong Kong was also ranked the fifteenth least corrupt place out of 159 places surveyed for the Corruption Perceptions Index compiled by Transparency International (ibid).

Other parts of the criminal justice fared less well. The Department of Justice (DOJ) was beset by accusations that those with power and influence could buy – or by-pass – justice. Its decisions not to prosecute powerful bodies such as Xinhua,[21] and influential people, such as Aw Sian (Sally Aw)[22] left the impression that there was one law for the poor and one for the rich and powerful. Adverse publicity surrounding these decisions not to prosecute prompted the DOJ to reiterate its commitment to the unbiased application of law.

These protestations were insufficient to offset the department's poor public image. The DOJ had suffered from an image problem since the early 1990s, when a number of its senior counsel became embroiled in scandal.[23] Rumours abounded of late-lunches, cronyism and a culture of 'mate-ship' amongst its staff. Though something was done to repair this image, these post-1997 incidents rekindled doubts about the DOJ's status as the bastion of legal propriety in the territory.

Chui provides some insight into how the Chinese judiciary viewed the system at the point of transition. The major problem, she argues, was the lack of an effective watchdog, giving the government 'power without accountability':

> Politics at times took control over the law. There were wrongful and unfair prosecutions. There was detention without trial. People who should not be in prison were, while people who should be in prison were not. That such things happened could not remain a secret, but those in a position to correct the injustice merely closed ranks and minds.[24]

Throughout the 1990s, the suspicion lingered that those with wealth, power or connections could escape justice. After 1997, the Prosecutions Division of the DOJ explicitly stressed its independence, freedom from interference, transparency, fairness, openness and prosecution in the public interest. Like the police before them, prosecutors recognised the need for public support if they were to escape accusations of favouritism and political interference.

The Secretary for Justice was central to the DOJ's public image. Legal adviser to the government, the Chief Executive, and the different departments of government, s/he is also a member of EXCO. S/he is supposed to act independently. However, Elsie Leung (Secretary for Justice after 1997) was widely regarded as too ready to accept Mainland interventions in Hong Kong's legal system. Her resignation, and the appointment of her successor, Wong Yan Lung, in 2005 were welcomed as a sign that the administration was, after all, open to the appointment of its critics.[25]

Some of the fiercest criticism of Ms Leung related to the DOJ's failure to seek the return ('rendition') to Hong Kong of Chung Tze-keung ('Big Spender'), a Hong Kong criminal arrested on the Mainland for crimes partly committed in Hong Kong. Cheung headed a criminal syndicate of gang members in Hong Kong, Macau and the Mainland, which committed crimes in all these jurisdictions. His crimes included the kidnap in Hong Kong of a tycoon and the son of Li Ka-shing, another Hong Kong tycoon.[26] He was arrested in Guangdong on charges of smuggling explosives and firearms, kidnapping and robbery. (He was said to have masterminded the kidnapping of Li Ka-shing's son in May 1996.)[27] Cheung and his gang had committed the kidnapping crimes in Hong Kong, but then fled to the Mainland, where they were eventually arrested by Mainland police officers. At this point, it was widely expected amongst the legal community that the Hong Kong administration would insist on Cheung's being returned to the HKSAR for trial. Instead, no objections were made to his being tried in the Mainland, according to Mainland criminal law. A public debate ensued as to whether the mainland courts had criminal jurisdiction to try Hong Kong permanent residents accused of having committed a crime in Hong Kong (Chen 2002: 74). No protest on this matter came from the DOJ, however, and Cheung was tried, sentenced to death and executed in Guangzhou in October 1999.

In another case the same year (the 'Telford Gardens' murder), Li Yuhui (a PRC citizen from Shantou, without Hong Kong residency) had allegedly murdered five Hong Kong women on the Telford Gardens Estate before he too had escaped to the Mainland. He was arrested in Shantou and the same questions were raised about whether he should be returned to Hong Kong for trial. As Chen argues, the normal procedure in such a case would be for the accused to be extradited to the jurisdiction where he is suspected of having committed the crime (Chen 2002: 74). In Li's case, however, the Shantou court sentenced him to death in March 1999. Liberal critics argued that in both cases the Secretary of Justice should have insisted upon the suspects being returned to Hong Kong for trial in the jurisdiction in which the crimes had been committed. In a familiar argument that harked back to the 1840s, however, conservative critics argued that if criminals realised they might be tried in a Mainland court, under the Chinese Criminal Code, and subject to Chinese punishments, this would deter crime.

Such cases alerted the Hong Kong press and public to signs of Mainland intervention in the administration of criminal justice and increased the sense that pre-existing freedoms and rights were under slow attack. In several cases, the government asked the Standing Committee of the NPC to intervene in decisions of the CFA, forcing a 'reinterpretation' of its decisions. The realisation that a political body (the NPC) could over-rule the CFA prompted talk of the 'end of the rule of law in Hong Kong'. The new regime, 'in its search for administrative expedience or political correctness . . . seriously undermined judicial independence and the rule of law' in two mainland-related cases (Ming Chan 2002: 7). The first of these, the *Ng Ka ling* case,[28] concerned the right of abode for Hong Kong residents' children born in Mainland China. When the CFA decided in favour of the children on 29 January 1999, the decision was hailed as victory for the rule of law in Hong Kong. Defeated, the government subsequently asked the NPC to reinterpret Articles 22 and 24 of the Basic Law to invalidate the CFA's decision. The case proved highly controversial and divided public opinion. The government argued that allowing the children into the territory would over-stretch public services and be detrimental to society. Others saw the CFA's ruling as a victory for judicial independence. The administration's invitation to the NPC was tantamount to:

> . . . opening the front gate to invite Beijing's direct judicial interference in order to save the SAR executive arm from certain defeat on purely legal

> grounds in vital matters of great consequence.' [The regime] looked to Beijing to save it from the unwelcome practical consequences of due legal process as administered by the SAR's supposedly independent judiciary system or in an anticipatory attempt with political correctness to seek Beijing's approval on controversial matters . . . [this would] . . . erode the independence of the judiciary and hamper the fair administration of justice for all, which are the key pillars supporting Hong Kong's rule of law to guarantee basic freedoms and economic air play . . . These are but two of the more alarming examples of questionable political judgment, leadership inadequacies, and legal lapses that have tarnished the SAR regime's early record and contributed to a potentially fatal constitutional crisis undermining the SAR's much cherished high degree of autonomy.[29]

There were also concerns about Mainland interference when the Chief Executive, Tung Chee hwa, told LEGCO that the Falun Gong was an 'evil cult' that should be outlawed, as it was on the Mainland. The Falun Gong remained lawful in Hong Kong and in fact, most people saw no need to take any steps at all against the group.[30] The attempt to clamp down on it provoked a legal challenge to the government. This culminated in 2005, when the CFA quashed the convictions of eight protesters on charge of wilfully obstructing and assaulting the police. The decision, seen as upholding the right to protest, also sent a message to the police that they could not arbitrarily take away this right. Having thus made the rule of law the yardstick of their legitimacy, the police were now forced to abide by it as regards the public's right to freedom of protest.

Public order

Though with each year after 1997, fears about loss of personal freedom, press freedom and freedom of speech generally diminished, worries about the rule of law intensified. The rule of law had long been strongly associated with satisfaction with life in Hong Kong.[31] Public order policing became highly contentious principally because it dealt with the intersection between personal rights and freedoms and the power of the state to circumscribe them.

Post-1997, the territory experienced an extraordinary number of public order events, including elections, demonstrations and the staging of international meetings. In 2001 alone, there were over 2,300 public order events,[32] a record number of demonstrations that led to the territory being dubbed the 'city of protests'. Political as well as livelihood issues dominated. The government's proposal, under pressure from Beijing, to introduce new anti-subversion laws (under Article 23 of the Basic Law) provoked the most contentious debate since 1997 about life in the HKSAR. A demonstration on 1 July 2003 was organised to oppose the anti-subversion law. The Hong Kong Human Rights Monitor described Article 23 as the 'gravest threat' yet to

Hong Kong's civil liberties. The march organisers counted on the support of pro-democracy groups, lawyers, students and trades unionists, but even they were astonished at the size of the turnout on the day. Some 500,000 people from all walks of life took to the streets, making this one of the largest popular demonstrations ever held in Hong Kong. It left a sense that an historic shift had occurred in the way Hong Kong people related to their government.

The march was followed by further demonstrations (on 9 and 13 July) after the government refused to back down and instead insisted on proceeding with the draft legislation. Mainland politicians were, however, becoming alarmed that media images of anti-government protests in Hong Kong could 'spill over' into China, where the PRC leadership faced its own problems with discontented workers and peasants. The pressure on the Hong Kong administration to introduce the laws thus rapidly subsided and the government eventually announced, on 5 September 2003, that it would be withdrawing (for the time being) the National Security (Legislative Provisions) Bill.

However, demonstrations continued throughout 2003, 2004 and 2005, partly generated by simmering discontent about livelihood issues, partly by the government's willingness to seek NPC interpretations of the Basic Law, partly by pressure for Beijing to announce when, exactly, Hong Kong people would be granted universal suffrage. Protests were also organised to test the constitutionality of the Public Order Ordinance provisions regarding the regulation of public processions, specifically the discretionary power of the Commissioner of Police to restrict the right of peaceful assembly for the purpose of 'public order' (*ordre public*). In a landmark case the CFA described the freedom of peaceful assembly as a:

> . . . fundamental right . . . clearly associated with the fundamental right of freedom of speech. The freedom of speech and freedom of assembly are precious and lie at the foundation of a democratic society. These freedoms are of cardinal importance for the stability and progress of society . . . A democratic society is one where the market place of ideas must thrive. These freedoms enable citizens to voice criticisms and seek redress. This is relevant not only to institutions exercising power of government but also to organisations outside the public sector which in modern times have tremendous influence over the lives of citizens. Minority views may be disagreeable, unpopular, distasteful, or even offensive to others. But tolerance is a hallmark of a pluralistic society. Through the exercise of these freedoms, minority views can be properly ventilated . . . If there is one type of law more in need than any other of being clearly and carefully circumscribed it is the type that places or permits restrictions on the exercise of fundamental rights and freedoms and criminalises exercising them beyond those restrictions.[33]

The CFA found the Commissioner of Police's power of prior restraint unconstitutional, cementing the public perception of the judiciary as defender of freedom and check on government.

Hong Kong post-1997 was thus an agitated, discontented place, a 'depressing combination' of deteriorating social cohesion, the widening gap between rich and poor as well as rulers and ruled, sharper class divisions, a frail and fragmented social fabric, threatened livelihoods, economic insecurity, and the constant threat of mainland authoritarianism and political culture coming to Hong Kong (Chan 2002: 11). The government's response was to promote Hong Kong as a 'world city' of high-tech industries, information networks, a knowledge-based, high value-added economy, an economic superhub with a Disney theme park and a Cyberport (ibid). None of these grand projects addressed the 'livelihood demands and dire poverty of the deprived grassroots and alienated middle class' (ibid). Neither did they meet any of the popular demands for social justice. Instead, they boosted the fortunes of local property tycoons and provided an ineffectual response to Hong Kong's declining economic fortunes. The preferred treatment of big business reawakened memories of the 1960s, as did allegations of special treatment for the oligarchs. Rumours circulated of cartels at government land sales, raising doubts about whether a level playing field obtained in the property market. Revelations emerged about the failure to properly scrutinise and regulate certain development schemes.[34] What Chan calls Tung's 'grand capitalist origins' inclined him towards policies that saved the economy 'for the big businesses not for the victims of the market, the unemployed, those afflicted by wage freeze, salary reduction, and negative equity' (ibid).

By 2004, the government faced a constitutional crisis. Public confidence in the Chief Executive was at an all-time low and there were calls for him to stand down.[35] In this context, a decision was taken to host the 2005 World Trade Organization (WTO) Conference, another grand project to bolster the economy, restore Hong Kong's public image and boost domestic support after the government's abysmal handling of SARs epidemic. The staging of an international event such as the WTO conference would, it was hoped, confer much-needed prestige on the administration.

However, the plan backfired. Since the 1990s, WTO meetings had attracted violent anti-globalisation protests wherever they were held. Prior to 2005, for example, there had been riots in Canada, Mexico and Korea; protests had accompanied the G8 meetings in the UK. In each place, controversy had followed the suppression by the security forces of anti-globalisation protestors. It was thus entirely predictable that such protest would attend the Hong Kong meeting and that the police would be required to provide its security. As it turned out, the role of the police in maintaining order was to prove crucial.

Coincidentally, the WTO meeting took place as several high-profile legal cases on the public's right to protest came before the courts in 2005. In May, the CFA ruled in favour of a group of Falun Gong protestors, arrested by the police for causing an obstruction in a public place (see above). The police 'had failed to pay due regard to the importance of the demonstrators' right to protest. Their arrest was therefore unlawful and they were entitled to use reasonable force in order to resist'.[36] In July, the CFA also ruled that the policing of demonstrations 'must be done in a way which fully protects . . . the precious right to protest'.[37] The fact that under the Public Order Ordinance demonstrators had to apply to the Commissioner of Police for permission to hold a march or meeting had been repeatedly criticised as giving the police an administrative power of veto over political protests. The CFA's judgment was seen as limiting the police's power to curb public protests, on the basis of 'ordre public', by emphasising the cardinal importance of the right to protest peacefully. As press commentary of the time noted, where the authorities had traditionally seen protests as a threat to stability, the CFA judges argued that free speech and demonstrations could help resolve tensions and conflicts in the community.[38]

Local newspapers were divided as to whether the courts were right to err on the side of individual rights and liberties as opposed to the interests of society as a whole but, as one journalist argued, upholding the rights set down in the Basic Law (to free speech, freedom of protest, etc.) *was* in the interests of society as a whole – the judges made their decisions:

> . . . freely, fearlessly and in strict accordance with legal principles . . . [so that] . . . the independence of the judiciary and the rule of law be preserved . . . The judges have defended not only the right to protest but also the right of people not to be arbitrarily arrested and detained. These rights contribute to Hong Kong's vibrant society and its success.[39]

In this climate, and given the fact that the WTO meeting put Hong Kong once again in the international spotlight, it was never likely that the Hong Kong police would refuse the WTO protestors permission to march. However, a moral panic now ensued amongst involved agencies concerning the containment of the anti-globalisation protestors, whom the HKSAR administration had to admit but did not especially welcome. A self-fulfilling spiral of action and reaction took shape. The meeting was billed as a massive public event, involving even more security and police personnel than the 1997 handover. The police said they had 'specific intelligence' that radical elements intended to come to Hong Kong to disrupt the meeting.[40] Police forces in other countries were sharing with them intelligence on known anti-globalisation activists, as well as tracking their movements. Hong Kong police officers were sent abroad to observe how other forces handled similar events, such as the G8 protests in the UK. LEGCO members were shown video footage by the police of violence at previous WTO meetings. Its liberal critics accused the government of demonising the demonstrators in order to justify the suppression of civil society.[41] Security preparations – such as the stockpiling of rubber bullets, running anti-riot exercises and drilling for possible chemical and biological attacks – were described as an over-reaction.[42] Conservatives opposed the entire operation, arguing that Hong Kong should bar entry into the territory of 'arch conspirators who are known to the international security services. Our police know who they are. Yet so anxious is our government to play the role of liberal Mr. Nice Guy that it is going to allow these odious hoodlums to enter Hong Kong'.[43] As a precaution, some companies hired their own private Gurkha guards and fenced off their buildings. WTO delegates had their own personal protection provided by several local and international security companies. The regional managing director of one of these (The Steel Foundation) speculated that, if it was overwhelmed by WTO protests, the government might be forced to call in PLA troops, a possibility Hong Kong's leaders would wish to avoid but an option under the Basic Law when internal security was threatened.[44] The CSD announced contingency plans to use Victoria prison to hold protestors if trouble flared up. The Immigration Department switched to 'crime control' mode and announced that it would deny entry to Hong Kong to 'miscreants' likely to cause trouble (but gave way after pressure from consular officials and some activists). [45]

Local anti-globalisation march organisers (the Hong Kong People's Alliance) joined the committee of police and government officials co-ordinating the WTO conference to work out the routes of the marches, negotiate acceptable assembly points for the crowds, and stay in 'constant communication' with each other. Two public 'protest zones' were agreed, a safe distance away from (but within sight of) the Convention Centre. The Centre itself would be a 'no-go zone' for demonstrations. The common aim of the Hong Kong organisers and the authorities was said to be making sure the demonstrations were conducted in a peaceful manner[46] but one local grassroots activist cautioned against the demonstrations becoming 'something purely academic or festive – like a carnival or an occasion where people present their papers. [That] would be such a Hong Kong way of doing protests'.[47]

Though the WTO meeting began peacefully, on Sunday 18 December 2005 Hong Kongers awoke to newspaper headlines such as 'The day Hong Kong's streets were taken over by mob rule', 'The siege of Wan Chai', 'Protest turmoil', and 'Police accused of mishandling demonstrations'. Trouble broke out at a demonstration on the Saturday night. Initially, the crowd gathered outside the WTO venue had simply engaged in a series of futile battles with the police who blocked the path to the Convention Centre.[48] The protestors faced some 2,000 police backed up by giant saltwater water canons and pepper spray. The demonstrators shouted 'Shame' and 'Fuck the Police' and engaged in minor skirmishes. These 'push and shove' battles are a well-established part of the ritual of such clashes. Whether they escalate any further depends very much on what forces come together to produce and ignite a 'flashpoint'.[49] That point seems to have been reached when about 1,000 protestors broke through the police cordon that separated them from their target, the WTO meeting in the Convention Centre. They snatched police shields and batons, threw eggs at the police, attacked them with bamboo poles, tried to overturn a police van, and pulled up metal barriers to use as weapons. They were driven back by police in riot gear using small shields, batons, pepper spray, water cannon and tear gas:

> By 7 pm and despite what looked like an impenetrable cordon of riot police, the group broke through. Police unleashed at least three canisters of tear gas into the crowd, whilst those who broke through ran to within metres of the Convention centre's main door. The police then fired another four canisters of tear gas into the first group. People fell to the floor, vomiting, tears streaming from their faces. But the Koreans in the front kept going, so another two canisters were released. 'Help me, help me', one woman screamed from the floor as retreating protestors trampled over her. Amid the choking gas, the final group continued to push on before five canisters of gas saw them turn on their heels and flee . . . The heart of Hong Kong had been turned into a battle zone and as the protestors gathered into the night on Gloucester Road, it was far from finished.[50]

An 11-hour stand-off followed, during which police tried to disperse the resisting demonstrators. One hundred and forty-one people were injured, including 61 police officers, 54 Koreans and 13 locals; 900 Korean farmers and their supporters were arrested.[51] The clashes were described as 'the worst violence Hong Kong has seen in decades'.[52] The Security Bureau issued a mass SMS text message to members of the public urging them to avoid Wanchai (ibid). The Wan Chai MTR and Cross Harbour Tunnel were closed for 12 hours; Gloucester Road was closed for 22 hours, 'paralysing traffic on the island and stranding commuters. Buildings and hotels in the areas . . . were locked down during the clashes' (ibid).

The violence was blamed on 'outsiders' who had come to Hong Kong with their own agenda. However, the mood of local people was more complex and ambivalent than this allows. Newspapers reported that many locals had shown considerable sympathy for the demonstrators, giving them food, drink and blankets, shouting words of support, and handing them towels, water and tissues when they were hit with tear gas. One newspaper claimed that Hong Kong people had 'embraced the protesting farmers of the Korean peasants' league . . . the straw-hat wearing warriors for the rights of farmers to a decent living:[53]

> They booed when protestors were sprayed with fire hoses . . . [some] yelled 'shame on you. We are all protestors here'. Some were as young as eight, others as old as 80. All were local people . . . some bore gifts, some marched, nearly all brought cameras. Florence Chi, 60, took fruit and

> water to the Korean protestors . . . 'I think they are very strong and are fighting very hard to survive. I feel so bad that they have had to come so far to have their voices heard', she said . . . Kenny Mok . . . had taken time off work to march. 'I used to be a farmer. I know how hard their lives are. I think the WTO is very unfair. I didn't tell my boss I was coming. Rich people can't understand', he said . . . Onlooker David Chan said: 'As soon as the Korean farmers rushed forward, the police sprayed them with pepper spray. Police even cracked a couple of heads with their batons. They were only protesting peacefully. The Koreans should attack them in retaliation. I have no sympathy for the police. They deserve whatever they get.[54]

Frontline police were later said to have even shared lunch boxes with their Korean charges, hours after unleashing volleys of pepper spray at them.[55] One woman from the disciplined services actually joined the protestors, teaching them to chant slogans in Cantonese.[56] The empathy that Hong Kong people expressed with the anti-globalisation protestors was also a reminder of the polarisation between classes in Hong Kong itself, which had become more acute since 1997.

For the government and law enforcement agencies, December 2005 ended with a post-mortem. The administration had underestimated the degree to which the WTO meeting would galvanise local discontent and translate it into identification with others in the world dislocated by global market forces. Hong Kongers themselves, after all, had recent first-hand experience of the power of the unrestrained free market during the Asian Financial crisis. Despite the criticisms, however, the police were said to be generally pleased that their worst fears (loss of life and damage to property) had not been realised.

The staging of such high-profile international events in Hong Kong strengthened the police's internal security and anti-terrorist capability, and secured future resources. The Hong Kong police had become part of the international co-operation between law enforcement agencies that characterised the first years of the twenty-first century. Steps were taken to promote global cooperation between prosecutors to facilitate the sharing of information, experience, training and the gathering of evidence. Global criminals – and global protestors – required, it seemed, global law enforcement. One result was increased attention to transnational crimes, such as money laundering by terrorist and drug syndicates which, as elsewhere, had assumed greater significance after the terrorist attacks on the Twin Towers in New York on 11 September 2001. There had also been terrorist attacks closer to home, in Bali in 2002, as well as separatist unrest in areas of China, the Philippines, Indonesia and Sri Lanka. With the end of the Cold War and Hong Kong's reunification with China, the territory no longer occupied a pivotal place in the 'Bamboo Curtain', but new enemies now justified the maintenance of a sophisticated internal security capability.

Prisons and punishment

The twin impulses of authoritarianism and liberalism which shaped other aspects of Hong Kong society post-1997 also influenced penal practice. Since the 1950s, the need to detain inmates securely (which once dominated the Hong Kong system) had been tempered by the need to contain them humanely, according to international standards. This became more important when, shortly before the 1997 handover, international observers decided to step up the monitoring of the conditions in Hong Kong's prisons. The Red Cross has long been mandated to visit, inspect and report on prison conditions; locals JPs could also make scheduled and unscheduled visits to any of the 24 Hong Kong penal institutions. But in 1996, following an invitation from local human rights groups, the first UK-style inspection by an Inspector of Prisons took place.

This need to be seen to abide by international standards partly stemmed from the poor reputation of Chinese prisons abroad and the desire to impress the world that Hong Kong belonged to the international community, sharing its goals and civilised standards of conduct. CSD also needed to reassure locals that the transition entailed no changes that were not also improvements. One result was a more outward-looking staff, more contact with overseas officers, and a push to gain ISO accreditation for CSD's Complaints Investigation unit.

The boast that Hong Kong had one of the lowest crime rates in the world did not translate into a lower rate of imprisonment. In fact, the HKSAR has one of the highest rates of imprisonment in Asia, backed up by a whole panoply of non-custodial sanctions and a truly extraordinary array of statutory and voluntary agencies, all keeping a watchful eye on those whom the authorities regard as offenders or potential offenders. The vigilance of this network is almost panoptical, especially in relation to youth.

Detention without trial had ceased for Hong Kong citizens but remained in place for the few Vietnamese migrants still awaiting repatriation. When the Vietnamese 'boat people' had first arrived in the late 1970s, the staff of the Prisons Department had been fully occupied guarding the camps; some male guards even married female detainees. But the sheer numbers of people arriving each year throughout the 1980s and 1990s had stretched resources and made camp life intolerable, despite the best efforts of voluntary agencies such as Caritas. By 1997, however, the numbers arriving and/or remaining had fallen dramatically. CSD might, thus, have looked forward to a period of spare capacity, better staff ratios and improvements in its estate. This was not to be the case. The penal population began to rise and by the early 2000s it had reached record levels, especially amongst the female penal population.

Like elsewhere, Hong Kong prisons had no control over how many people were sent to them or for what offences – they were simply required to receive inmates from the courts and cope as best they could. Post-1997, this meant

Table 25.5 Comparative imprisonment rates per 100,000: 2000

Singapore	345
Thailand	334
Macau	208
Hong Kong	164
Fiji	155
New Zealand	148
S. Korea	135
Canada	114
PR. China	110
Australia	108
Malaysia	104
Brunei	98
Cambodia	46
Japan	44
Indonesia	25

Source: Broadhurst SCMP 2000; original data from Asia Pacific Association of Corrections 2000.

Table 25.6 Average penal population 1996–2006

1996	*1997*	*1998*	*1999*	*2000*	*2001*	*2002*	*2003*	*2004*	*2005*
13,289	11,975	11,396	11,571	11,499	12,240	12,412	12,472	13,091	12,247

Source: CSDAR 1996–2005.

Table 25.7 Admission of adult male population

1992	*1993*	*1994*	*1995*	*1996*	*1997*	*1998*
8,631	8,054	9,342	9,791	10,013	9,182	10,084
1999	*2000*	*2001*	*2002*	*2003*	*2004*	*2005*
10,387	10,484	10,392	10,979	11,992	13,790	12,831

Source: CSDAR 1993–2005.

Table 25.8 Admission of young male population

	2000	*2001*	*2002*	*2003*	*2004*	*2005*
Prisoners	498	434	445	473	648	496
Remands	636	588	612	665	709	1,596

Source: CSDAR 2000–2005.

Table 25.9 Admission of adult female population

1992	*1993*	*1994*	*1995*	*1996*	*1997*	*1998*	*1999*	*2000*	*2001*	*2002*	*2003*	*2004*	*2005*
1,212	1,258	2,006	3,033	3,039	3,466	3,454	3,798	4,154	6,337	8,780	10,608	11,996	8,775

Source: CSDAR 1992–2005.

Table 25.10 Admission of young female population

	2000	*2001*	*2002*	*2003*	*2004*	*2005*
Prisoners	610	1,350	2,143	1,573	1,497	1,097
Remands	302	288	226	159	212	387

Source: CSDAR 2000–2005.

increased overcrowding – especially in the female institutions – despite regular attempts to expand and/or rearrange existing penal capacity.

The late 1990s and 2000s saw a rapid and ceaseless expansion of the female prison population, many of whom were Chinese legal immigrants (two-way permit and passport holders) convicted of Breach of Conditions of Stay offences and sentenced to imprisonment. Knowingly or unwittingly, most Mainland girls trafficked into Hong Kong ended up in prostitution.[57] Arrested during raids on vice establishments, they served relatively short terms of imprisonment (such as 15 months) making it difficult to provide them with a meaningful regime. The recurring presence of this section of the population in the criminal justice system in the early 2000s pushed the female imprisonment figures to new heights.

Overall female admissions for crimes against the person had not altered greatly between 1990–2000 (25 in 1991 to 23 in 2000). Male admissions for offences against property also remained stable (2,891 in 1991 to 2,859 in 2000) but the figure for women more than doubled. The biggest rise in female inmates was, however, in offences against local laws and against lawful authority. In 1991, for example, 702 women were admitted for offences against local laws. This rapidly began to increase in the mid-1990s, and in 1995 had grown to 2,524. By 2000 it had risen to 3,479, in 2001 it jumped dramatically to 6,091 and again to 8,881 in 2002, to 9,642 in 2003, to 10,676 in 2004, dropping to 7,332 in 2005. Women admitted for offences against lawful authority increased from 47 to 914 between 1995 and 2003, dropping slightly to 898 in 2004 and again to 590 in 2005.[58] Over a ten-year period, female admissions rose from 3,966 to 10,139. Male admissions also rose but less dramatically, from 13,654 in 1996 to 15,384 in 2005. Overall, admissions rose from 17,620 in 1996 to 30,070 in 2004, dropping to 25,523 in 2005.

Admissions jumped from 20,859 in 2001 to 24,366 in 2002 (ibid) and overcrowding became worse. In 2003, the average occupancy rate of Hong Kong's prison was 114 per cent, and in women's prisons 197 per cent due to a record high of 2,840 female inmates in May 2002, a 39 per cent increase in adult female prisoners and a 14 per cent rise in adult female remands in custody over 2001.[59] Further rises followed in 2003 – the female penal population hit another record high of 3,007. Overall admissions jumped by just over 9 per cent from 24,366 in 2002 to 26,659 in 2003. Hei Ling Chau, Ma Hang and part of Chi Ma Wan prisons had to be converted to accommodate female

Table 25.11 Admissions by gender 1991–2005

	M	*F*
1991	12,361	1,287
1992	11,970	1,591
1993	11,644	1,683
1994	13,226	2,727
1995	13,616	4,015
1996	13,654	3,996
1997	11,949	4,200
1998	12,692	4,052
1999	12,727	4,349
2000	12,790	4,969
2001	12,904	7,955
2002	13,168	11,198
2003	14,219	12,440
2004	16,295	13,775
2005	15,384	10,139

Source: CSDAR 1991–2005.

Table 25.12 Admissions for offences

	Against the person	*Against property*
1991	617	3,036
1992	516	3,090
1993	497	3,395
1994	523	3,912
1995	649	4,703
1996	582	4,468
1997	544	3,212
1998	489	3,010
1999	514	3,129
2000	521	3,219
2001	495	3,471
2002	544	4,356
2003	672	4,762
2004	680	5,400
2005	744	5,199

Source: CSDAR 200:83.

inmates. The number of admissions and discharges of convicted prisoners in 2002 and 2003 was 'the highest in years' (ibid). The closure of Victoria prison in 2005 added to the shortage of accommodation, male imprisonment also having undergone a less radical but still noticeable rise over the same period.

In August 2006, Hong Kong had the world's highest ratio of women in prison.[60] Per capita, the number of women imprisoned was 480 per cent higher than in Mainland China. Whereas elsewhere, women typically comprised 2 to 9 per cent of the prison population (the median percentage for Asia was 5.4 per cent and China 4.6 per cent), women in Hong Kong made up 22.1 per cent of the overall penal population (ibid). CSD blamed the figures on the high number of Mainland prostitutes coming into the HKSAR – non-locals made up 68.4 per cent of the female prison population, most convicted for prostitution, overstaying, and breach of conditions of stay offences (ibid). Many were said to be 'return offenders', giving rise to the allegation that Hong Kong's prisons were regarded by Mainland offenders as 'holiday camps' where they were provided with food, shelter, work and education:

> . . . if mainland prisoners were frugal, they could even save some money . . . By sticking together envelopes or sweeping an already-clean floor several times a day, they can make about the same amount of money they would at a full-time job back home . . . When not working, prisoners are offered an increasing number of training programmes – from beauty classes to language courses – that many mainland prisoners would not have been able to afford at home . . . When he was released [one man] told his mum he came to Hong Kong to study . . . He moved to a different region in the mainland where nobody knew about his criminal record in Hong Kong. Now fluent in English, he did not have to be a waiter any more (ibid).

Echoing the 'less eligibility' debates of nineteenth-century Hong Kong, one 'solution' that was suggested was to make the punishment of mainland prisoners harsher. Another suggestion was to build a 'Super prison' locating a variety of penal establishments in one place (and freeing up sites for private development).[61]

Overcrowding made it difficult to meet security goals. Preventing the smuggling into jail of contraband goods, especially drugs, was more difficult in overcrowded conditions, as was the enforcement of prohibitions on gambling. CSD argued that the prevention of gambling was 'a foundation stone for a peaceful and harmonious correctional environment conducive to the rehabilitation of offenders'.[62]

Overcrowding also undercut what had by this point become the *raison d'être* of punishment in Hong Kong, i.e. rehabilitation and the prevention of future offending When it changed its name in 1982 to the Correctional Services Department (CSD), the Department made these the principal justification of imprisonment. CSD's mission in the new millennium was detaining people in 'a decent and healthy environment, and provid[ing] comprehensive rehabilitative services in a secure, safe, humane and cost-effective manner, so as to enhance the physical and psychological health of prisoners, protect the public, and help reduce crime' (ibid). In line with the performance management ethos of the day, it listed its core values as humility, uprightness, honesty and personal responsibility, respect for the rule of law, orderliness and harmony, recognition that all persons have the right to correct and fair treatment with dignity, professionalism, competence and quality of service.

For reasons that Gray (above) has discussed in relation to juveniles and young offenders, CSD never resiled from the rehabilitative ideal of imprisonment even when it became discredited in the 'West'. Indeed, CSD pursued it with even greater vigour, promoting initiatives such as greater community involvement in offender rehabilitation (community education, job placement schemes, and a publicity drive) as well as a survey of the needs of discharged offenders, and a more sophisticated approach to assessing recidivism rates. Changing the public's perceptions of ex-offenders required a change in beliefs and values, in culture – exactly the kind of drive developed in the 1970s by both the ICAC and the Fight Crime campaigns. After 1999, CSD set about a similar mobilisation of the community, encouraging it to accept and support discharged prisoners, and seeking assistance from various organisations and professionals (ibid). Fight Crime campaign-style drives were adopted to foster the integration of offenders, characterised by the production of posters, essay competitions, concerts by pop bands, fashion design competitions, and a newsletter (*Rainbow*) published in 2000, for adult offenders. The emphasis on family and community relationships, seen as a more comprehensive approach to reintegration, also allowed for the more extensive reach of the state into family, culture and social life. In 2000, CSD produced a major docu-drama series (*The Road Back*), publicised initiatives through radio announcements, competitions, produced a music CD (*Dawn*), held charity dinners, erected posters and produced a video CD. Joining forces with District Fight Crime Committees as well as NGOs it pushed to drive home the messages of caring for and rehabilitation of offenders. It worked with families and with community groups, and formed a new Committee on Community Support for Re-Habilitated Offenders.[63]

Education for adult inmates was generally voluntary, but in the mid–2000s a scheme was proposed to expand education to adults in order to improve their rehabilitation and recidivism rates. Though some of the traditional vocation skills, such as carpentry and gardening, echoed an earlier ethos, reintegration now entailed training in the kinds of skills required by the restructured economy of a post-industrial Hong Kong, i.e. skills in new technologies and media. In 2000, in conjunction with the Institute of Education, a package was also announced to deliver a more modernised curriculum, and the City University of Hong Kong agreed to provide a tailor-made course on self and social development.[64]

Like the police, prison staff realised the need to present a more professional image to their 'clients', a process driven by the new public management ethos and its 'client-based' culture. Professionalisation started later in the CSD than in the police force, but by the 1990s it had reached a similar point. The need to re-create a modern prison staff free, from corruption and maladministration, sprang from problems in the 1970s and 1980s. After the 1972 riot by young offenders in Stanley, discipline within the prisons, and the integrity of prison staff, became priorities. CSD tacked such problems head on, even making television films about corrupt prison officers and their downfall. In this regard, CSD was simply another target for the ICAC and its goal of cleaning up government. But beyond this, the project entailed promoting a 'healthy lifestyle' amongst prison staff and their relatives. One way of encouraging this was to provide them with a social life free of 'bad elements' – hence the provision of sports and other recreations, fairs, outings and an extensive menu of welfare benefits. CSD also borrowed the JPOA model of staff consultation to foster good staff relations between the organisation's hierarchy and its junior staff, and prevent discontent from developing into conflict. In 2005, leadership development and management programmes were also introduced, especially for mid-career officers with leadership potential. Foundational training involved a 26-week course on subjects such as law, penology, social work techniques, criminology, self-defence, emergency response tactics, the use of weapons, scenario training, and Putonghua. Like the police and other disciplined services, and in keeping with the need to maintain integrity, morale and loyalty, CSD also provided extensive social, recreational and welfare facilities for its staff and their families.

In the new millennium, CSD reinvented itself as a 'customer' oriented' organisation, with a new corporate culture. However, fewer resources were invested in the prisons than in the police. There were, for example, few purpose-built prisons in Hong Kong and hardly any modern ones – Victoria Prison, built in the 1840s, was still in being used in 2005; Stanley maximum security prisons, built in 1937 and opened in 1938, remained the territory's main high-security jail. With a few exceptions, institutions in the more remote areas and on the outlying islands had generally served a number of purposes prior to their requisition as prisons. The more modern institutions, such as Tai Lam (maximum security female prison), the Siu Lam Psychiatric centre, and Sha Tsui Detention Centre were amongst the few built for a specific penal purpose. Plans to build one giant prison, mooted in the late 1990s, eventually foundered in 2003, partly for penological reasons, but also because of economic constraints.

Institutions and regimes also remained sparse, if not Spartan. Dormitory-style accommodation was the norm, though some institutions had single cells. Open-air exercise and productive labour remained central to their regimes. Institutions located far from the centres of population, on outlying islands, were connected via video-links to central locations, to enable inmates to keep in touch with their families.

As in the police, the argument that triads were more or less a spent force gave way in the 1990s to the claim that they were actually a major crime problem. One ongoing issue for CSD was how best to manage members of rival triad societies, inclined to continue their factional fights inside the prison walls. Separating triads on a day-to-day basis required greater knowledge of triad rituals and the tattoos marked upon the bodies of members, higher levels of vigilance, especially in workshops where allowing triads to work alongside each other entailed problems of dominance, intimidation and control within the institution. There was also the issue of how to ensure triads could be prevented from intimidating prison staff and their families outside.

In the 1990s, CSD also strengthened its capability in riot and restraint. Factional infighting between rival North and South Vietnamese in the detention camps had involved CSD staff in several incidents of mass violence in which riot formations were deployed. As a result, CSD staff began to train alongside the PTU. Even though the vast majority of Vietnamese had left by 2000, problems remained. A trivial incident at Hei Ling Chau Addiction Treatment Centre (an island institution) quickly escalated into a major incident when some 400 inmates attacked staff, ransacked premises, and set the place alight. Thirteen Vietnamese inmates, 24 CSD staff and eight police officers were injured and 54 inmates charged.[65] CSD staff deployed their riot training to deal with such incidents; indeed at Hei Ling Chau the operation to quell the disturbance was a joint CSD and PTU affair. By contrast, the day-to-day running of Hong Kong's prisons was generally a highly ordered affair, dependent upon military-style discipline amongst staff.

Hong Kong prisons mix old and new forms of discipline and welfare. Regimes have become more finely adjusted to take account of the different kinds of inmates received. Staff remain ever vigilant for signs of inmate alliances. Male inmates are held in separate institutions from female offenders, adults are separated from young offenders and juveniles, recidivists are separated from first offenders and, as far as possible, triad members are separated. When received into prison, all prisoners are given a medical examination, a short induction course, instructions on the rules, routines, regulations, rights and privileges, and are processed by a Classification and Categorisation Board, which assigns them to institutions according to their security rating:

> The Board gives due consideration to all factors including the prisoners' background, the nature of the offence, the terms and length of their sentences, the risk they pose to the community and whether or not they are first offenders.[66]

All those certified medically fit are required to engage in gainful and meaningful employment. Inmates at the Drug Addiction Centres (males are held at Hei Ling Chau, females at Chi Ma Wan) must undergo a compulsory drug treatment programme combining detoxification and psychological counselling over a period of between two and 12 months. On release, discharged inmates are subject to 12 months' supervision, during which time they can be recalled if they breach the conditions of their supervision. The regime shares the ethos of the rest of the prison system in that it stresses productive labour, the development of good work habits, and a healthy lifestyle.

Since 1999, the numbers admitted to Drug Addiction Centres have been declining steadily; the vast majority of inmates are adults. Inmates in need of psychiatric treatment are sent to Siu Lam. Adult male prisoners are accommodated at maximum security prisons (Lai Chi Kok, Shek Pik, Stanley, Siu Lam Psychiatric Unit), medium security prisons (Hei Ling Chau, Ma Po Ping, Tong Fuk, Victoria, Pak Sha Wan) or minimum security institutions (Tung Tau, Pik Uk, Ma Hang, Tai Lam, Lo Wu). Life sentence prisoners and those serving long-term sentences are housed at Stanley and Shek Pik; remands are generally housed at Lai Chi Kok.

Until 2005, Hong Kong's original prison, Victoria, still housed prisoners on remand, Mainland illegal immigrants (and persons arrested for immigration related offences awaiting repatriation or deportation), Vietnamese migrants awaiting repatriation, and foreign nationals awaiting deportation. Its outdated facilities and poor estate made it unsuitable for use as a penal institution and it was eventually closed that year, its valuable site in Central being developed for tourism and commercial purposes. Vietnamese migrants who arrived after 1997, some looking for employment, are detained tantalisingly close to Hong Kong at the Green Island Reception Centre, where they await repatriation. Since the 1980s, their numbers have decreased dramatically, reaching single figures in the 2000s.

Adult female prisoners are held at Tai Lam, which comprises a small maximum-security unit for prisoners serving longer than 12 years, a remand centre, and a mother-and-baby unit (inmates can keep their children with them up to the age of three). Elderly inmates are housed in a special section at Ma Hang. Young male inmates are sent to either Pik Uk, Lai Sun, or Shau Tsui, and those between 14 and 17 are separated, as far as possible, from those aged 18 to 21 at night.[67] Young female inmates are accommodated at Tai Tam Gap. Like young males, they receive compulsory education classes and vocational training.

In the manner of a 'total institution', CSD provides inmates with medical and social welfare support internally – it has its own educationalists, psychologists, social workers and medical staff; the occasions on which it needs to draw on outside expertise are rare. Critics of such systems have pointed out that staff undergo a kind of 'occupational socialisation' which encourages them to place their loyalty to the institution before the ethics of their profession.[68] Though numerous voluntary agencies are involved with prisoners post-release, over-arching control rests with CSD.

How CSD officers, social workers and welfare officers see their role is, therefore, extremely important, as is the overarching socio-political framework within which they all operate, and which sets the agenda for punishment and welfare.

Punishment, politics and economics

Like the police force, the prison service in any society is intricately linked to the political context in which it operates. Since the nineteenth century, all Hong Kong social institutions have been powerfully influenced by the discourse of free market capitalism. With the territory's economic take-off in the 1950s, this was accompanied by an emphasis on values and conduct suited to the production of a productive society and a disciplined workforce. This period of take-off was also one that established the popular icon of the 'bootstrap capitalist', who by dint of hard work rose from desperate poverty to become a millionaire.

The dominant ethos of Hong Kong society encompassed these values of individual responsibility, self-help, self-reliance, hard work, thrift, diligence, self-discipline, productive labour, economy, just deserts and, importantly, the belief that it was possible to overcome adverse circumstances and poor beginnings to 'make something' of oneself.

As Garland has pointed out as regards nineteenth-century England, most of these values reflected the dominant ideology of laissez-faire capitalism and the minimal state. Translated into the rationale of Victorian penality, they shaped the character of British prisons and punishments until the end of the nineteenth century, when laissez-faire capitalism gave way to monopoly capitalism, full employment gave way to extensive unemployment, and Britain began to transform into 'a society constructed around mass democracy, monopoly capitalism and an interventionist state' (Garland 1985). Penal regimes mirrored this shift and, with the drift towards interventionism and welfarism, the state extended its reach beyond the prison to intervene more directly in the social and private lives of individuals. It attempted to reengineer the circumstances that produced crime, as social work and criminology suggested, and by the application of rational means, to eliminate it and reform offenders into good citizens able, with the state's help, to overcome the obstacles to success and participate fully in society.

The trajectory of Hong Kong's economic, social, political – and hence its penal – development has been very different. In Hong Kong, the transformation of the state only began in the 1970s, and even then it only partially echoed the British experience.

For most of the colony's history, the ruling elite was content to leave the Chinese section of the population to handle its own affairs, and was aided in this by the co-operation of the Chinese elite. Where it did intervene, it did so on the basis of paternalism, to further capital accumulation, and to provide law and order. This stance, combined with its commitment to a laissez-faire philosophy, meant that the state was largely absent from the lives of most people. It did not, as a rule, intervene in social or economic affairs. Until well into the second-half of the twentieth century, government policies were 'openly biased in favour of business and the well being of the rest of the community seemed a secondary consideration' (Goodstadt 2005: 5).

This period coincides with the development of Hong Kong as a colony governed by a merchant elite generally in its own interests and restrained principally by the Colonial Office in London. Colonies were expected not to become a drain on the resources of the home government, and Hong Kong was expected to become self-sustaining within a very short period of time. Free market capitalism and capital accumulation were its *raison d'être.* This was reflected in penal institutions by the emphasis on 'less eligibility' and the productive use of convict labour – Hong Kong had no use for the treadmill imported from London; the designs for its construction lay unopened in the archives of the colonial administration. It put its convicts to work building roads and other infrastructure projects, or deported them to China or other colonial possessions. Prison regimes were more or less identical to those described by Garland as characterising Victorian penality in England but unlike England, Hong Kong's rulers felt the need to retain harsh, physical and public forms of punishment for far longer. As well as MacDonnell's brief re-introduction of branding and flogging in the 1880s, offenders were still being sentenced to the stocks, public caning and birching up to and beyond the Second World War. This persistence was mainly due to the insecurity of the colonial state, racial stereotypes of the character of the colonised population, and comparisons with the harsh nature of Mainland criminal justice.

Events between the 1880s and 1930s meant that organised labour never developed as a countervailing force capable of wresting concessions from the colonial state. In the earlier part of the twentieth century, the business elite and the state successfully subdued the labour movement, whilst after the Second World War, ideological divisions between communist and nationalist unions prevented them from developing any unity of purpose.

After 1935, Hong Kong did briefly abandon its ideological commitment to laissez-faire and non-intervention in social affairs, during which time Northcote had insisted on the expansion of social services (Goodstadt 2005: 118). This is confirmed by an examination of the forms of punishment introduced at this time, which included the development of juvenile courts, remand homes and probation. This trend was, however, reversed after the Second World War and, 'whilst the rest of the world moved in the opposite direction' Hong Kong reverted to the principle of non-intervention (ibid). Throughout the second half of the twentieth century, it acquired a reputation as the bastion of free-market capitalism, the paradigm case for free markets and limited government.

Politically, Hong Kong's geopolitical position after the Second World War stunted the development of democracy and, hence, the public's ability to influence the political and social agendas of the colonial regime. Though government did provide public housing in the 1950s, this was driven by the need to free up urban land for development rather than a shift to welfarism;

welfare was still principally provided by the voluntary sector. Access to public housing was not, for example, provided on social grounds, assistance was focussed on those who 'could become self supporting quickly', and limited to those who could be rehabilitated (ibid). This, too, was reflected in the penal sector, where voluntary organisations shouldered the costs and responsibility of supporting ex-offenders and the provision of services for youth. Until the mid-1950s, the government was able to deport those it deemed 'undesirables', such as vagrants, subversives and triads; when this option ceased to be available, it resorted to detention without trial and use of administrative sanctions. Inside the colony's prisons, Victorian penality remained largely unaltered, though with the demand for labour to supply Hong Kong's economic take-off, inmates were provided with skills relevant to the labour market. Establishments were Spartan, regimes disciplined and costs offset by the insistence that inmates engage in productive labour, either by helping maintain the prison estate or supplying manufactured goods for the government sector.

By the 1960s, the conflict between private profit and public good eventually produced polarisation and riots. In response, the 1970s forced the state to transform itself, becoming more liberal, consultative and interventionist. The fundamentals of the political structure remained, however, largely unchanged. Whilst some more popular figures were appointed to join the government, Hong Kong never became a democracy. At the same time, 'the colonial administration could not afford to let the public believe that the partnership between colonialism and capitalism would permit the business and professional classes to pillage the public sector and exploit the community unhindered' (Goodstadt 2005: 118).

Though the 1970s saw greater attention to the provision of public services and welfare issues, this was driven by the need for political legitimacy. The reformed colonial state never became a fully welfare state. The business elite managed to fight off demands for a mandatory provident fund and other forms of social insurance. As Goodstadt points out, whilst Hong Kong's financial secretary at the time, Cowperthwaite, initiated a more humane system of public assistance for the deprived and disabled in the 1970s, at the same time he helped delay the introduction of free, compulsory education to ensure that 'youngsters were not compelled to go to school instead of joining the labour force in a period when factory workers were in increasingly short supply' (Goodstadt 2005: 125). He thus picked and chose on which issues he would co-operate with the elite and assist Hong Kong's manufacturers (ibid). Hong Kong's economic success in this period meant that the territory never experienced mass unemployment, nor was the state called upon to provide mass public assistance. The subsidised public housing programme started in the 1950s also helped manufacturers by keeping wages low. The principle of 'less eligibility', self-sufficiency, and keeping public spending low still applied in the realm of punishment. With Hong Kong's economic take-off in the late

1950s, and throughout the 1960s, prison regimes were characterised by the discipline and values associated with the production of a hard-working and cheap labour force.

Hong Kong's penal philosophy only changed with the emergence in the 1970s of a more caring, consultative and socially responsive administration. Gray has argued that, whilst the business elite pushed for a more repressive regime after the 1960s riots, reformists eventually succeeded in driving through changes that resulted in a more 'correctionalist' approach to punishment, albeit this remained highly conservative and, as she describes it, amounted to 'disciplinary welfare'.

Colonial officials had not, however, relinquished the regime's basic commitment to the minimal state. Instead, the doctrine of 'positive non-interventionism' (developed by the financial secretaries of the time, John Cowperthwaite and his successor, Philip Haddon-Cave) finessed the government's laissez-faire stance:

> Positive non-interventionism involves taking the view that its is normally futile and damaging to the growth rate of an economy for the Government to attempt to plan the allocation of resources available to the private sector and frustrate the operation of market forces . . . I do qualify the term 'non-interventionism' with the adjective 'positive' . . . what this means is that the Government, when faced with an interventionist proposal, does not simply respond that such a proposal must, by definition, be incorrect. The Government weighs up carefully the arguments for and against . . . and comes to a positive decision as to where the balance of advantage lies . . . even though it is true that, more often than not, we come to the conclusion that the balance of advantage lies in not intervening . . . yet in all cases the decision is made positively, and not by default.[69]

Goodstadt argues that the government managed to generate public support for the colony's economic and political system at this time by creating a unifying ideology around the two principles of rule of law and laissez-faire. As apparently objective and impartial checks, these allayed fears that big business and property interests could exploit the public at will (Goodstadt 2005: 13). They also seemed to guarantee the operation of a level playing field, which ensured opportunities for anyone to improve themselves. The argument that 'anyone could make it' in Hong Kong's open society applied equally to delinquent youth and ex-offenders, both of whom now became the object of extensive forms of non-custodial supervision. Youth, in particular, attracted custodial sanctions after very brief offending careers and were subject to prolonged supervision upon release.

The guiding principle of the administration remained that government would stay out of the way of investors and entrepreneurs who generated wealth. It would intervene on a case-by-case basis, when industries with social obligations ran into trouble or when an institution needed regulation to prevent inequitable practices (Goodstadt 2005: 4). According to Goodstadt:

> Over time, laissez-faire took on an ethical role in Hong Kong, where it provided the rationale for restricting the claims of the privileged classes on the resources of the state. It was, in fact, the basis of a social compact made necessary by the absence of democracy. In treating laissez-faire as a matter of principle, the colonial administration created a clear distinction in Hong Kong political life between 'public' and 'private' interests. Society expected this demarcation to be observed by both the government and the business world. As a result of the commitment to laissez-faire, the government's involvement in economic affairs was much smaller than in most modern states . . . so long as the fate of business firms appeared to depend not on political connections but on market forces, non-interventionism seemed to offer a guarantee of political and economic fairness. Business fortunes were subject to the seemingly objective verdicts of the market place . . . The community came to believe that Hong Kong owed its post-war prosperity to laissez-faire (Goodstadt 2005: 121–2).

A further extension of state functions took place in the 1980s, with the gradual development of some sort of representative politics (functional constituencies) after 1985 and the formal incorporation of popular interests following geographically based direct elections in 1991.[70] This was the period in which the state intervened more directly in social life and extended the mosaic of quasi-government organisations concerned with disciplining youth in the community. Hong Kong's economic restructuring at this point also presented the state with the problem of what to do with youth whose skills and poor educational qualifications left them on the margins of society. Concerns about youth activism in the political sphere also drove state intervention in education and corrections, both of which stressed the qualities and values of good citizenship. Political and economic forces thus coalesced in the 1980s to produce a focus on youth discipline.

The events of 4 June 1989 and the desertion of the regime by the business elite in the 1990s undercut the legitimacy of the late-colonial administration. This forced it to adopt more interventionist policies that addressed grassroots social and political demands to make Hong Kong a more inclusive society. Human rights considerations – entrenched in the BOR in 1991 – also meant that those concerned with corrections had to adopt a more 'justice' or 'rights' based approach to offenders, whilst the push for popular support also produced a more 'caring' and inclusive approach towards ex-offenders, youth offenders and their families. Throughout the period, from the 1970s onwards, family and community support had become an integral part of Hong Kong's penal philosophy, driven in part by adherence to modernisation theories of crime and deviance.

By 1997, therefore, the outgoing colonial administration had moved some distance from the laissez-faire stance of previous colonial regimes. On the eve of the transfer of sovereignty, the then financial secretary, Hamish Macleod made a budget speech in which he now moved to question the usefulness of the term 'positive non-interventionism:

> . . . he said 'what we should recognise is that Hong Kong has become much more sophisticated. The government is doing more and more . . . We have to walk a tightrope. We believe in the market mechanism, but you only have to look at the way the market works in some areas . . . to realize you cannot always leave it to the market.'

Macleod later described his approach as the Hong Kong style of 'consensus capitalism' (ibid).

After 1997, Yam argues, this drift towards a more interventionist stance was also driven by the fact that the population of Hong Kong – which had expected little of the colonial regime – had higher expectations of an administration ostensibly run by and for Hong Kong people (Yam 1998). The incoming regime's lack of popular legitimacy also led it to pursue interventionist policies designed to increase its popular support. However, because China had ensured that members of the business elite were well represented on the new LEGCO, the administration was also pushed to make interventions that protected their interests. This synergy between government and big business was reminiscent of the unreformed colonial state of the 1960s, and generated considerable public disquiet as well as demands for more democracy and calls for more inclusive society. The elite was given direct and favourable access to PRC officials, whilst Hong Kong people had less access to government than before the handover. Denied political participation, they looked for a trade-off with the post-colonial administration, seeking improved material satisfaction in return for their acquiescence to its rule (Cheung, 2000). This, as we have seen, did not transpire.

The 'takeover elites', as Cheung calls them, also suffered from the 'decoloniser syndrome' of trying to surpass the achievements of the British by attempting new social and economic blueprints (ibid). Consequently, they became a good deal more interventionist than predecessor governments. Cheung adds that changes in the internal and external environments of the economy (such as the Asian financial crisis) also prompted popular demands for state intervention to assist firms and alleviate unemployment (Cheung 2000).

The end result, Cheung argues, was that, after 1997, Hong Kong acquired an active state with a strong paternalist orientation (the Singapore model) that converged with the 'state-corporatist managed market configuration' of the PRC itself. In the PRC, the state is committed to the development of the free market and the reduction of state planning. Though important differences remain, its approach to crime and deviance echoes that of Hong Kong, emphasising that the causes of crime lie in individual pathology. Reform similarly relies less on changing the individual. In the Maoist era, PRC penal thinking had, in any event, always emphasised hard work and 'reform through labour', reflecting the Marxist belief in the value of labour *per se* as well as the valorisation of the working class. It had, of course, also used 'thought reform' to reform offenders into good citizens. Such terminology is unlikely to be well received in Hong Kong, but the territory's existing system of disciplinary welfare is, Gray argues, already somewhat similar. Moreover, the type of non-custodial sanctions encompassed by disciplinary welfare cost less than imprisonment. Since it is already clear that China will demand that Hong Kong does not become a financial drain on the mother country (the Basic Law demands a balanced budget), it is likely that the Chinese leadership, like the British before them, will favour such less costly penal measures.

It is unlikely, therefore, that Hong Kong's retrocession to China will produce a radical change in the tenor of its penal thinking. Penal regimes will remain Spartan and characterised by productive labour, youth will be encouraged by an extensive array of supervisory, custodial and non-custodial organisations to become law-abiding (and patriotic) citizens, and the values of hard work, self reliance and rehabilitation are likely to remain key. It remains open to question whether the trend towards liberalism in the immediate post-colonial years will affect penality. At one level, it is now open to the regime to mobilise community support through its network of pro-communist organisations, but these represent a fraction of the Hong Kong population and are incapable of mass mobilisation on the scale organised by the colonial state in the 1970s. In addition, there are signs that the authoritarian tendencies of the post-colonial regime have been somewhat tempered by the popular demonstrations against Article 23. This episode demonstrated the degree to which authoritarianism can backfire, producing its own crisis of legitimacy. Similarly, if the calls for democracy are answered, Hong Kong future governments may be forced to respond more readily to popular opinion on law and order, though elsewhere there is evidence to suppose that this may lead not to greater liberalism but to popular authoritarianism. What is certain is that both the Hong Kong and PRC administrations wish to maintain Hong Kong's reputation as an international financial centre. In penal institutions as elsewhere, therefore, the pursuit of the 'safe city' is likely to continue to dictate priorities.

Notes

1 Hong Kong Transition Project 2002: 6.
2 Hong Kong Transition Project May 2006: 16.

3 See Chan, M.K. 2002.
4 Hong Kong Judiciary Annual Report 2005. Hong Kong: Government Printer.
5 This was to lead some to christen the Court of Final Appeal the 'Court of Semi-Final Appeal'.
6 Chui 1999. Chui's book provides numerous examples to substantiate this view and provides a welcome counter to official publications. It is one of the few accounts of judicial 'insiders' to appear in Hong Kong.
7 In 2005, there were 98 Court Prosecutors of whom 45 had legal qualifications and another 30 held law degrees.
8 HK Judiciary Annual Report 2005.
9 Broadhurst, R. (2003) 'Crime Trends in Hong Kong'. Hong Kong: Department of Sociology, Centre for Criminology, University of Hong Kong.
10 HKPAR 1999: 5.
11 hkupop.hku.hk/popexpress 15 October 2006.
12 POP Press release 3 October 2006.
13 HKPAR 2000.
14 Walden 1987.
15 Walden 1987: 23.
16 James To, Chairman of the Legco Security Panel, *South China Morning Post* 28 February 2006.
17 Law Reform Commission 24 March 2006.
18 Hong Kong Transition Project 1982–2007 (2002): 27.
19 Hong Kong Transition Project 1982–2007 (2001): 27–8.
20 Hong Kong Government Information Service (GIS) 16. October 2006.
21 Xinhua is a Chinese state information organ, colloquially known as China's unofficial embassy in Hong Kong. It failed to comply with a court order to respond to a complaint lodged by Legislative Councillor, Emily Lau, within a given time limit. Despite Ms Lau's persistence, no action was taken against it.
22 Sally Aw was chair of the Sing Tao newspaper group with close ties to Beijing and the Chief Executive. In March 1998, members of her staff were prosecuted for conspiracy with Ms Aw to defraud advertisers in the newspaper by artificially inflating its circulation figures. The case against Ms Aw was dropped; the other three were convicted in 1999. Pressed to give her reasons for not prosecuting Ms Aw, the Secretary for Justice told LEGCO that it was considered not in the public interest to do so, since it might increase the pressures on the Sing Tao newspaper group, cause its collapse and put people out of work. In the ensuing controversy, some argued that this line of reasoning meant that poor people were more likely to be prosecuted than powerful people, since they did not command such influence.
23 At one point in the 1990s, four senior Crown Counsel were questioned by the police on criminal matters. The subsequent conviction and imprisonment of 'a top crown counsel and Acting Director of Public Prosecutions on corruption charges' revealed that 'even in these times of progress in democracy and public accountability, justice in the colony could still be bought and sold'. One senior counsel was tried for attempting to procure an underage girl for sex and rape. His close friendship with the Chief Justice was well known; his marriage was 'performed by the Chief Justice by special license at the Chief Justice's official residence only a short time before his arrest' (Chui 1999). The conduct of the first Chinese Chief Justice drew criticism when he used his official residence as the campaign headquarters during his bid to become the first Chief Executive of the Hong Kong Special Administrative Region (HKSAR). The Coroner, accused of sub-letting of his government apartment to his girlfriend, was also forced to resign.
24 Chui 1999: foreword.

25 Wong had previously been associated with the Article 45 Group, critical of the government's stand on new and tighter anti-subversion laws. He had also participated in the 'silent demonstration' by the legal profession in 1999 against the government's decision to invite the NPC Standing Committee to reconsider the CFA's decision in the case of *Ng Ka ling and others v Director of Immigration* [1999] 1 HKLRD 315.
26 See Chen, Albert, H.Y. 2002: 74–5.
27 Cheung had previously been arrested in Hong Kong in 1991 (along with Yip Kai-foon, arrested and convicted in 1996) for his role in the series of sensational robberies that hit the territory that year. He had, however, won an appeal and escaped to China.
28 See note 24 above.
29 Chan, M.K. 2002: 7.
30 See Hong Kong Transition Project 2002: 32.
31 Hong Kong Transition Project May 2006: 32.
32 HKPAR 2001: 1.
33 *Leung Kwok Hung and Others v HKSAR* CFA Final Appeal Nos. 1 & 2 of 2005 (Criminal); date of judgment 8 July 2005.
34 Examples include an earlier residential housing scheme at Discovery Bay on Lantau island, and the more recent LINK REIT case, in which Lo Siu-lan petitioned the High Court for the right to have the plan judicially reviewed by the CFA. See *South China Morning Post* 19 April 2005 for summary.
35 In 2005, he was replaced by Donald Tsang.
36 *South China Morning Post* 15 May 2005.
37 *South China Morning Post* 12 July 2005.
38 *South China Morning Post* 12 July 2005.
39 Cliff Buddle, *South China Morning Post* 15 May 2005.
40 *South China Morning Post* 5 May 2005.
41 Lee Cheuk-yan, *South China Morning Post* 22 August 2005.
42 *South China Morning Post* 22 August 2005.
43 Kevin Sinclair, *South China Morning Post* 27 July 2005.
44 *South China Morning Post* 21 April 2005.
45 *South China Morning Post* 28 August 2005.
46 *South China Morning Post* 8 October 2005.
47 Guo Da-nian, *South China Morning Post* 11 March 2005.
48 *South China Morning Post* 18 December 2005.
49 See Waddington et al 1989.
50 *South China Morning Post* 18 December 2005.
51 *South China Morning Post* 19 December 2005.
52 *South China Morning Post* 18 December 2005.
53 *South China Morning Post* 17 December 2005.
54 *South China Morning Post* 18 December 2005.
55 *South China Morning Post* 17 December 2005.
56 *South China Morning Post* 19 December 2005. Such sentiments echo a longer-standing (but seldom acknowledged) ambivalence of the disciplined services towards their public order role, especially during events such as the 4 June commemorations.
57 Many young women were trafficked into the territory by 'snakeheads' and expected to work as waitresses in restaurants and bars in order to send remittances back to their families in China. Hong Kong in the 1990s was crowded with women from the Philippines who did exactly this, working long hours as private maids in order to send remittances back to their families, to pay for their children's

education, or build a house in their home village. In the 1990s, they were increasingly joined by girls from elsewhere in South East Asia, such as Indonesia. Despite a tradition of Chinese 'amahs' in earlier years, Hong Kong families no longer employed girls from China as domestic labour (though wealthy elites in Chinese cities employ them as maids and nannies).

58 CSDAR 1992–2005.

59 CSDAR 2002: 5.

60 *South China Morning Post* 13 August 2006 (World Female Imprisonment List, International Centre for Prison Studies, King's College, London).

61 Despite much lobbying, spending constraints meant that nothing came of this proposal.

62 CSDAR 2005: 65. An attempt in the 1990s to remove the horse racing pages from newspapers inside prisons was famously challenged in the courts as tantamount to censorship and an infringement of human rights, but the Commissioner and governors retain overall responsibility for enforcing regulations deemed necessary to maintain order and security in individual institutions.

63 CSDAR 2000: 5.

64 CSDAR 2000: 30.

65 CSDAR 2000: 8.

66 CSDAR 2000: 9, 13.

67 CSDAR 2000: 12.

68 Elsewhere, the existence of an independent body of doctors and social workers is regarded as a check on the closed world of the prison, bringing greater transparency and accountability.

69 Yam 1998.

70 See Cheung, A.B.L. 2000.

Chapter 26

Crime and delinquency 1997–2007

In the highly politicised climate of the post-1997 years, it was the criminal justice system, rather than crime itself, that grabbed the headlines. The official crime figures for 1997 themselves confirmed the image of Hong Kong as a tranquil, orderly low-crime place. The official statistics indicated a remarkable drop in recorded crime prior to and immediately after 1 July 1997. In 1989, reported crime had resulted in the arrest of 43,684 persons (a rate of 852 per 100,000). This dropped to 40,422 (a rate of 654 per 100,000) in 1998 (Broadhurst 2000). Why this should be so is unclear – other countries have explained such sudden drops in recorded crime in terms of wider socio-political events such as, for example, the death in August 1997 of Diana, Princess of Wales. There is a view that major events such as this lower levels of crime, though no one is quite sure why. It may also be that the Hong Kong police were distracted from their 'normal' crime control operations by hand-over duties – the force had in the past explained falls in recorded crime in these terms. In any event, it was politically useful to be able to boast that the 1997 crime rate was the lowest in 24 years.

In 1998, the police reiterated the claim that crime was considerably lower than in other metropolitan cities in the world.[1] As Broadhurst has pointed out, however, the official figures were based on a very partial picture of crime and missed completely the 'dark figure' of unreported crime indicated in the

Table 26.1 Recorded crime 1997–2005

	1997	*1998*	*1999*	*2000*	*2001*	*2002*	*2003*	*2004*	*2005*
Violent crime	13,749	14,682	15,705	14,812	13,551	14,140	14,542	13,890	13,890
Other crime	52,706	56,261	60,030	61,431	58,450	60,695	72,521	65,992	62,159
Preventive crime	912	1,019	1,036	1,002	1,007	1,042	1,314	1,433	1,388
Total	67,367	71,962	76,771	77,245	73,008	75,877	88,377	81,315	77,437

Source: HKPARs 1997–2005.

Table 26.2 Most common offences for which persons arrested 1995–2005

	1995	*1996*	*1997*	*1998*	*1999*	*2000*	*2001*	*2002*	*2003*	*2004*	*2005*
Total violent crime vs person	10,177	9,850	9,656	10,183	10,743	10,045	9,149	9,461	9,998	10,383	11,047
(Serious assault)	5,233	5,241	5,235	5,623	5,437	5,093	4,771	4,987	5,424	5,490	5,854
Total violent crime vs property	6,910	5,241	4,093	4,499	4,962	4,767	4,402	4,679	4,544	3,507	2,843
Total burglary and theft	46,479	38,907	33,132	36,415	38,384	39,650	38,253	40,367	50,080	44,662	40,873
(Burglary with breaking)	9,989	8,034	6,439	7,272	6,987	6,945	6,621	6,437	6,867	5,188	4,093
(Misc. theft)	13,324	12,055	10,968	12,275	13,418	13,969	13,318	14,751	20,015	19,409	19,266
(Shop theft)	7,568	6,950	6,011	6,032	6,227	6,973	7,470	8,122	9,304	9,186	8,750
Total all crime	**91,886**	**79,050**	**67,367**	**71,962**	**76,771**	**77,245**	**73,008**	**75,877**	**88,377**	**81,315**	**77,437**

Source: HKPARs 1997–2005.

crime surveys (Broadhurst 2000). Broadhurst also argues that if minor crimes (such as possession of narcotics, prostitution, common assault and disorderly conduct) were added into the overall crime figures, the crime rate stood at about 60 per cent greater than the selected offences used to calculate official levels of crime (Broadhurst 2000).

The official figures for the 1990s had indicated a general downward trend in overall crime, though woundings and assaults began to rise in 1991 and continued to rise into the 2000s.[2] By 2001, the police claimed that violent crime was at its lowest for 27 years.[3] That year, recorded violent crime showed an 8.5 per cent drop, regarded as 'a historical milestone not seen since the early 1970s'.[4] In 2002, another milestone was reached when the level of recorded burglaries dropped to its lowest level in 23 years.[5] The overall recorded crime rate changed little after 1997 (it remained at or just above 1,000 per 100,000) but the 1998 crime survey data were to dent this rosy picture (see below).

Despite the downward trend in violent crime, recorded woundings and serious assaults did not in fact show a marked decrease. The year 2004 saw an 8 per cent decline in overall recorded crime, whilst police offensives against robberies and burglaries were said to be responsible for drops of over 30 per cent in robbery and almost 23 per cent in burglary. The first months of 2005 saw a further decline in recorded crime (down by 4.8 per cent) with a slight drop in recorded violent crimes such as robbery, especially park robbery, which had received much publicity in 2004 and thus attracted a police reaction. The drop in crime was said to reflect both of police effectiveness in containing crime and the recovery of the economy. The economic and political problems that marked the post-1997 years were seen as challenging for law enforcement agencies. For all the government's talk of 'green shoots', the economy was slower to recover from the Asian financial crisis than other countries in the region. This not only led to unemployment but also to widespread discontent. Despite the social tensions and mass protests of these

Table 26.3 Recorded miscellaneous offences 1997–2004

	1997	*1998*	*1999*	*2000*	*2001*	*2002*	*2003*	*2004*
Gambling	1,066	1,074	1,247	900	915	855	1,026	939
Hawking	7,870	6,427	3,622	1,696	1,238	1,962	2,129	2,029
Obstruction	16,692	10,949	6,786	5,031	2,762	1,932	1,775	2,919
Prostitution	499	987	936	934	964	1,233	1,877	2,474
Objectionable publication	1,082	1,314	1,181	909	970	789	662	280
Other	17,600	17,482	17,815	17,817	18,201	17,717	18,643	20,177
Minor narcotics	7,636	6,719	5,270	6,496	6,501	5,749	5,034	4,949
Total	**52,445**	**44,952**	**36,857**	**33,783**	**31,641**	**30,237**	**31,146**	**33,767**

Source: HKPARs 1997–2004.

years, however, the police were regarded as doing a good job at containing crime to below 1996 levels, 'confirming that our anti-crime strategy of recent years has been effective'.[6]

Police reports for the new millennium charted their battles with the usual suspects. Their offensives against triads, narcotics and commercial crime continued as before, as well as against 'new' crimes such child pornography, computer hacking, money laundering, and internet-related frauds. In 2000, the police force observed that their old enemy, the triads, were involved in the lowest number of reported crimes for many years. This was important politically, since one of the major fears pre-1997 had been an increase in triad activity. However, triads were still suspected of involvement in major international organised crime, such as the smuggling of Mainlanders to the USA via Hong Kong container ships. Operations against organised crime and what were now euphemistically termed 'cross-boundary' crimes also involved more liaison with the Mainland's PSB. An undercover operation against triads (operation 'Thunderbolt'), conducted in collaboration with the Macau and Guangdong authorities, resulted in the arrest of 1,762 people in 2006, and the seizure of dangerous drugs, pirated optical discs, marked oil, and illegal cigarettes. Seizures of firearms, destined for crimes in the territory, were also put down to better liaison between the three law enforcement agencies. The shipping of girls and money into the casinos of Macau were activities for which Mainland, Macau, Hong Kong and Russian organised crime were all responsible, and which required the co-operation of international law enforcement agencies. Money laundering also attracted increased attention, as Hong Kong's financial institutions were thought to offer opportunities for money laundering to terrorist and drug syndicates.

Despite this focus on new threats to law and order, youth crime remained an obsession. Police figures noted an increase in the use of psychotropic drugs (such as ecstasy) at 'rave' parties, and the use of ketamine, cocaine, and 'ice' amongst young affluent Chinese. This shift in drug culture was said to require a different style of policing. There was a crackdown on 'quick cash' crimes and on drug abuse by youth. Police targeting of 'notorious entertainment venues' produced a 7.6 per cent surge in arrests.

Recorded crime by Mainland visitors also began an inexorable rise at this point. In an effort to boost Hong Kong's flagging economy, the government had relaxed the rules governing Mainland visitors to the HKSAR, hoping that mainland tourists would bring much-needed cash into the economy. The Mainland government concurred with this strategy, and there were also new schemes to permit skilled Mainland employees to work in Hong Kong. In 2004, Hong Kong saw the arrival of over 12 million Mainland visitors. Crime by Mainlanders was said to be taxing police and prison resources, contributing to an exponential rise in the prison population and exacerbating prison overcrowding.

By early 2006, overall crime was rising again (39,433 cases between January and June, compared to 38,117 for the same period in 2005). Serious crimes, such as bank robbery (up 120 per cent compared to 2005) and homicide increased. In the first six months of 2006 alone, there were 20 recorded bank robberies. Mainland and Hong Kong-based triads were said to be using the Mainland visitors to smuggle arms into Hong Kong on their behalf.

As these figures show, between 1997 and 2005, there was an overall drop in arrests of males, but the number of females arrested (especially in the over 21 age group) grew. This was to have a knock-on effect on Hong Kong's prisons.

The 1998 crime victimisation survey

The drop in crime in 1997 shown in the official figures was more imagined than real. The sixth (1998) crime victimisation survey (published in 1999) indicated an 8 per cent increase in crime victimisations as compared to 1994, the date of the previous survey.[7] The victimisation rate for personal crimes in 1998 was 34 per 1,000, compared to 33 per 1,000 in 1994. For household crimes the figure was 80 per 1,000 compared to 93 per 1,000 in 1994, a significant decrease. Crimes of violence accounted for 27 per cent of victimisations against the person; crimes of theft accounted for 73 per cent.

Both the official statistics and the victimisation survey indicated increases over time in wounding and assault, criminal damage and burglary, and declines in robbery (Broadhurst 2000). The crime survey also showed steep increases in sexual assaults, criminal intimidation, theft from vehicles, snatchings and pick pocketing, whereas the official figures showed only slight increases in sexual assaults, stable rates for intimidation and theft from vehicles but declines in pick pocketing (ibid). Where the police figures indicated significant declines for blackmail and fraud, the survey indicated increases (ibid).

Between 1997 and 1998, recorded crimes of violence increased by about 6.8

Table 26.4 Persons arrested by age group and gender 1997–2005

	Juveniles		*16–20*		*21–30*		*30+*		*Total*	
	M	*F*	*M*	*F*	*M*	*F*	*M*	*F*	*M*	*F*
1997	4,477	1,487	5,847	1,008	9,978	1,706	13,967	3,244	34,269	7,445
1998	4,337	1,497	5,657	956	9,808	1,696	13,153	3,318	32,955	7,467
1999	4,208	1,278	6,070	968	9,678	1,801	13,191	3,551	33,147	7,598
2000	4,765	1,464	5,303	1,162	8,978	1,999	13,212	4,047	32,258	8,672
2001	4,282	1,627	5,004	1,141	8,259	1,958	12,232	4,326	29,777	9,052
2002	3,766	1,569	5,051	976	8,605	1,906	13,430	4,362	30,852	8,813
2003	3,735	1,421	5,054	964	9,234	2,013	14,568	5,062	32,591	9,460
2004	3,648	1,249	4,834	978	9,011	2,125	15,547	5,559	33,040	9,951
2005	3,191	1,340	3,857	923	7,777	2,180	15,626	5,910	30,451	10,353

Source: HKPARs 1997–2005.

Table 26.5 Crime victimisations 1994 and 1998

	1994	*1999*
All victimisations	325,900	352,200
Rate personal crime victimisation	33 per 1,000	34 per 1,000
Rate household crime victimisation	93 per 1,000	80 per 1,000
Personal crimes as proportion all victimisations	51%	55%
Use of weapon in violent crime	19%	15%

Source: Hong Kong Crime Victimisation Survey 1999.

Table 26.6 Trends in crime HCVS and Hong Kong Police rates per 100,000

	1978	*1981*	*1986*	*1989*	*1994*	*1998*
Rape and indecent assault						
HKCVS	58	32	127	126	165	376
HKP	34	33	33	41	39	39
Wounding and assault						
HKCVS	48	83	225	121	162	181
HKP	13	99	103	123	107	129
Robbery						
HKCVS	661	633	284	229	295	200
HKP	123	160	122	114	103	48
Blackmail						
HCVS	17	17	71	33	99	25
HKP	58	22	12	10	14	7
Criminal intimidation						
HKCVS	48	35	145	102	233	251
HKP	14	10	9	10	14	15
Snatching						
HKCVS	78	146	172	111	198	129
HKP	16	39	33	26	27	14
Pick pocketing						
HKCVS	683	1,795	1,635	784	947	1,142
HKP	23	44	56	17	14	10
Deception/Fraud						
HKCVS	26	18	96	128	116	112
HKP	60	85	33	31	53	41
Burglary						
HKCVS	361	698	659	545	630	576
HKP	118	206	216	192	223	146
Theft from vehicle						
HKCVS	196	322	291	220	431	312
HKP	45	93	94	91	63	42
Criminal damage						
HKCVS	35	74	94	141	408	320
HKP	40	82	82	96	96	100

Source: Broadhurst 2000.

Table 26.7 Trends in crimes of violence

	1978	*1981*	*1986*	*1989*	*1994*	*1998*
HKCVS	36,900	40,300	43,400	31,200	52,600	58,000
Percentage reported to police	28.4	41.2	38.4	44.6	34.5	31.3
Estimated number	10,480	16,603	16,665	13,915	18,147	18,154
Actual number of reports to HKP	12,422	16,094	14,085	17,350	17,232	14,682
HKCVS rate	802.7	781.9	785.6	548.7	867.8	867.3
HKP rate	228.0	312.2	254.9	305.1	284.3	219.5

Source: Broadhurst 2000.

Table 26.8 Trends in burglary

	1978	*1981*	*1986*	*1989*	*1994*	*1998*
HKCVS	16,600	36,000	36,400	31,000	38,200	38,500
per cent reported	33.6	27.9	32.8	41.1	40.3	40.4
Estimated reports	5,578	10,044	11,939	12,741	15,395	15,600
Actual number of reports to HKP	5,412	10,592	11,942	10,913	13,509	9,765
HKCVS rate	361.1	698.5	658.9	545.2	630.2	575.7
Police rate	117.7	205.5	216.2	191.9	222.9	146.1

Source: Broadhurst 2000.

per cent.[8] Police reports indicated that overall *violent* crime rose from about 160 per 100,000 in 1970 to about 340 in 1990, peaking at about 410 in the mid-1970s and declining in 1999 to 230. The crime survey data, however, indicated that the highest rate of – and significant rises in –violent crime victimisations occurred in the 1990s (Broadhurst 2000). Both sets of figures showed that the number of violent crimes had increased in absolute terms. The survey data indicated that the rate of violent crime remained high, whereas the official rate implied a reduced risk (ibid).

Recorded figures for burglary in 1998 showed a 12 per cent increase over the previous year.[9] The crime survey data, however, showed an 'uneven decline' in burglary since 1981 (Broadhurst 2000).

The 1998 survey also revealed a continuing decline in the public's reporting of crime to the police – compared to 1994, when 31 per cent of respondents said they reported their experience to the police, in 1998 only 29 per cent made a report to the police.[10] Reporting rates for both personal crime and household had fallen, though injured victims were more likely to report the crime than uninjured victims, and reporting rates were higher where the value of property lost or damaged was higher. About two-fifths of personal crimes of theft were reported (Broadhurst 2000). The percentage of female victims reporting fell from 40 per cent in 1994 to 34 per cent in 1998 and, as in previous surveys, the reporting rate for all crimes was lowest for victims living in temporary housing areas.

Of those who did report their victimisation to the police in 1999, 26 per cent did so because it was a requirement for getting replacement documents (e.g. an ID card) or claiming insurance; 24 per cent did so because they hoped to recover the property, and only 6 per cent reported to the police because they saw it as their duty as a citizen. The Fight Crime campaigns 'report crime' message thus seems to have had a rather limited effect. Of those who did not report to the police, 49 per cent said the crime was not serious enough (they suffered no serious loss, or injury, or considered the incident unimportant); 28 per cent said they thought nothing could be done, and 8 per cent said they thought the reporting procedure too cumbersome. These findings echoed those of earlier crime surveys.

The 1998 survey showed higher number of victimisations overall than any of the previous five surveys, though the number of household victimisations had declined. The increase in victimisations in 1998 was due mainly to offences such as pick pocketing, other personal theft and indecent assault. Pick pocketing accounted for 54 per cent of personal crimes of theft; burglary accounted for 24 per cent of all household victimisations, and theft for another 48 per cent. Few (15 per cent) of all crimes of violence involved a weapon; about 20 per cent of victims of violent crime were injured (29 per cent for males, 12 per cent for females) and most injuries were minor.

Analysed by region, the crime survey found that 41 per cent of all victimisations occurred in Kowloon, 41 per cent in the NT, 18 per cent on Hong Kong Island, and 1 per cent in Marine, generally confirming the distribution of crime indicated by the official statistics. A higher proportion of personal crime victimisations occurred in Kowloon, whilst more household victimisations occurred in the NT.

Analysed by age group, the survey confirmed previous findings that persons aged 12 to 19 had the highest overall victimisation rate (65 per 1,000), as well as the highest rate of victimisation for crimes of violence (19 per 1,000) and personal theft (46 per 1,000). Their rate of victimisation for personal crimes far outstripped that of all other age groups. However, only about 22 per cent of them reported their victimisation to the police, compared to 41 per cent of victims in other age groups.[11] What is clear is that personal crime victimisation has increased for those in the youngest age group. As Broadhurst puts it, since the first survey in 1978, the risks for youth had increased (Broadhurst 2000).

As in previous surveys too, females had a higher victimisation rate for personal crimes than males (36 per 1,000 compared to 32 per 1,000) – 54 per cent of personal crimes were committed against females. In all age groups, women had a higher rate of victimisation for personal crimes than men. Young women (12 to 19) – and especially unmarried women – had the highest victimisation rate for personal crimes of theft. But as before, it was males aged 12 to 19 who had the highest overall victimisation rate (67 per 1,000) of all age/sex groups. They also had the highest victimisation rate for crimes of violence (25 per 1,000) (single males had the highest victimisation rate for crimes of violence). At the same time, however, the vast majority of violent crimes were committed by males – most of the 31,000 victimisations of violent crime by a single offender involved males over 21, though where the victim was aged between 12 and 19 the offender was also more likely to be under 21.

Most of the crime incidents reported in the survey, including burglaries and personal crimes, took place in the daytime (54 per cent); crime such as theft of or from a vehicle was more likely to occur after midnight. Almost half all incidents of personal crime occurred in the street or in outdoor areas; 46 per cent of personal crimes of theft occurred on the street and 33 per cent on public transport. These figures were on a par with the 1989 and 1994 surveys. The 1979, 1981 and 1986 surveys found a higher proportion of crimes occurring on the street or in other places outside a building. Of personal crimes that occurred inside buildings in 1998, most (77 per cent) took place inside non-residential buildings.

The topography and class-distribution of crime also remained similar over the lifetime of the 1979–99 surveys. Persons living in public permanent housing had a victimisation rate of 33 per 1,000, those in private permanent housing a rate of 35 per 1,000, and those in temporary housing a rate of 25 per 1,000. Those living in public permanent housing had the highest victimisation rate for crimes of violence; those in private permanent housing had the highest rate for personal crimes of theft. Households in temporary housing areas had a higher victimisation rate (104 per 1,000) than those in public housing estates (87 per 1,000) and permanent private housing (75 per 1,000). Overall, however, the survey found that it was young people, living in public housing, who had the highest victimisation rates for crimes of violence, whilst young people living in private permanent housing had the highest rate for personal crimes of theft.

Juvenile delinquency

Hong Kong post-1997 experienced no great shift in its discourse about youth crime. The real shift had already taken place in the 1980s, when the net thrown over youth and juveniles had become deeper, wider and more finely meshed. More were caught by the system, but not all were criminalised. This remained the situation after 1997, though with a change of emphasis in the values required for young people to become good citizens. State building and the re-colonisation of Hong Kong after 1997 required the production of new citizens, who 'loved China', respected authority and were willing to subordinate the self for the good of the nation. Education increasingly stressed a highly conservative view of Chinese culture, emphasising filial piety, civic duty and patriotism. More obliquely, the criminal justice system and welfare systems acted in tandem to finesse the ways in which disruptive youth were brought to order. Ultimately, the ideal for delinquents was not that they be labelled or punished, but that they stop offending and become good, productive citizens of a new China. This very much echoes traditions of rehabilitation and reform in the PRC since the 1950s.

In 1989, juveniles accounted for 17 per cent of all arrests in Hong Kong, but this dropped to only 14 per cent in 1998 (Broadhurst 2000). Young offenders accounted for 19 per cent in 1989, falling to 16.4 per cent in 1998 (ibid). The 'within-group' arrest rate for juveniles fell from 962 to 800 per 100,000 juveniles, and from 1915 to 1511 per 100,000 for young offenders (ibid). As Wong has pointed out, however, not all juveniles arrested in Hong Kong are prosecuted. In 1997, for example, out of 5,964 juveniles arrested by the police, only 42 per cent (2,514) were prosecuted.[12] Many others, arrested for minor offences, have been dealt with under the Police Superintendent's Discretion Scheme (PSDS).[13] The number of juveniles cautioned in this way by the police rose seven-fold between 1976 and 1997 (from 391 to 2,767 in 1997), whereas the numbers prosecuted only increased 1.6 times over the same period.[14] If those cautioned are deducted from the official figures for juvenile crime, the 'rising wave of juvenile delinquency' becomes less alarming (Wong 2000: 280).

By the new millennium, however, young people were subject to an ever more extensive network of social discipline, only some of which was directly connected to the criminal justice system. Youth organisations and welfare organisations have, however, become more closely aligned with criminal justice. Together they construct a dense network of criminal and welfare measures designed to prevent youth from re-offending. This net includes those who had not yet shown any inclination towards criminality and, with the advent of 1997, educational and cultural programmes are increasingly targeted at youth with a view to moulding them into good, patriotic citizens.

As regards custodial options for young offenders, these are also now extensive. Young offenders of either sex may be sent to a training centre, but only young males are sent to Sha Tsui Detention centre. Training Centres (at Tai Tam for females, Cape Collinson and Lai King for males) deal with young offenders sentenced under the Training Centres Ordinance to a period of training between six months to three years. How long inmates stay depends upon their 'motivation to lead a law-abiding life' and their progression through the three 'grades' (beginner, intermediate, advanced). Each inmate is assessed each month by a Board of Review, where their strengths and weaknesses are assessed. Psychological help and counselling sessions are provided. All undergo a half-day education and half-day vocational classes. The regime is orderly and regular, and echoes the ethos of the JPC and scouting and guiding movements – healthy outdoor pursuits and athletics, 'character building' activities, as well as skills, team spirit, and community service. To facilitate

Table 26.9 Juveniles: most commonly arrested offences 1996–2005

	1996	*1997*	*1998*	*1999*	*2000*	*2001*	*2002*	*2003*	*2004*	*2005*
Serious assault	783	693	1,972	647	699	626	563	596	556	577
Other robberies	339	262	325	315	574	582	468	387	362	201
Total violent crime	1,549	1,440	1,439	1,228	1,790	1,575	1,427	1,376	1,318	1,176
Burglary and theft										
Shop theft	2,157	2,040	2,060	1,690	1,802	1,773	1,897	1,623	1,454	1,367
Misc. theft	1,038	977	928	993	1,186	1,160	833	904	1,004	991
Other crime										
Criminal damage	202	192	185	202	235	220	131	172	157	133
Disorder/Fighting in public place	154	152	133	113	71	100	87	109	112	84
Public order	49	102	93	44	60	114	152	135	132	128
Unlawful society	221	208	198	234	240	199	172	145	149	135
Total for year	**6,479**	**5,964**	**5,834**	**5,786**	**6,229**	**5,909**	**5,335**	**5,156**	**4,897**	**3,531**

Source: RHKPARs and HKPARs 1990–2005.

rehabilitation, some visits are organised to local factories, youth centres and country parks. On release, the young offender is placed under supervision for three years. S/he may be recalled if caught reoffending in that time. CSD routinely claims a very high rate of success for the programme – it is claimed that over 70 per cent do not reoffend.

Like those sentenced to Training Centres, inmates of the Detention Centre are placed under supervision – for 12 months – when they leave. Like Training Centres, it claims a high success-rate, i.e. extremely low numbers reoffend within 12 months of being released.

Originally, CSD defined its success in rehabilitation in terms of an offender's completion of the three-year active aftercare supervision without reconviction. Training Centres are said to achieve a success rate of over 60 per cent for males, and over 90 per cent for females; Drug Addiction Centre inmates are said to achieve 70 to 80 per cent success rates; Detention Centres claim between a 95–100 per cent success rate for young offenders (16 to 20) and young adults (21 to 24). These high rates of success have generated some debate about the ways in which success is measured – re-conviction being at least in part a reflection of whether offenders have been caught.

Throughout the 1990s, critics expressed scepticism at the high success rates of these types of programmes. In the early 2000s, CSD began to investigate what it claimed were more sophisticated ways of measuring recidivism. In any event, the much-acclaimed success rate of the 'boot camp' regime meant that it continued in Hong Kong long after it was abandoned in the UK. Its retention may have reflected, as Gray hints, at a struggle between reformist and reactionary factions within Hong Kong's criminal justice system (Gray 1997). The reactionary faction, which in the 1970s consisted of the business and commercial elites, has once again emerged as a powerful force within the post-1997 regime, exerting considerable influence over its policies. In the 1970s, its favoured the establishment of the Sha Tsui Detention Centre, whose regime chimed with the elite's commitment to the free market, hard work, thrift and self help, values epitomised in the myth of Hong Kong's 'bootstrap capitalists'.

This aspect of the Hong Kong penal system reflected elite ideas about youth offending, the need for a disciplined workforce and the 'domestication' of troublesome youth. Politics and economics have again come together in the post-1997 regime to favour a more disciplinary approach to youth offending, both because the business elite identifies with these foundational values and is adversely disposed towards governmental intervention in social affairs, and because the regime itself faces repeated challenges by a politically-activist youth.

As Gray argues, however, the disciplinary welfare complex established in the 1970s meets the objectives of reformers and reactionaries quite well. Its success depends upon the use of custody and extensive post-release

Table 26.10 Admission of training centre inmates

	1992	*1993*	*1994*	*1995*	*1996*	*1997*	*1998*	*1999*	*2000*	*2001*	*2002*	*2003*	*2004*	*2005*
M	332	410	438	407	297	209	219	233	234	206	176	128	163	128
F	25	18	44	36	24	33	13	31	18	16	19	9	24	7

Source: CSDARs 1992–2005.

Table 26.11 Admission of detention centre inmates

	1992	*1993*	*1994*	*1995*	*1996*	*1997*	*1998*	*1999*	*2000*	*2001*	*2002*	*2003*	*2004*	*2005*
Young offenders	375	318	296	288	248	202	274	206	297	330	377	286	296	204
Young adults	46	43	56	45	58	47	37	32	50	57	57	72	54	54

Source: CSDARs 1992–2005.

Table 26.12 Admission to drug addiction treatment centres

1996	*1997*	*1998*	*1999*	*2000*	*2001*	*2002*	*2003*	*2004*	*2005*
2,650	1,916	1,776	1,369	1,414	1,737	1,291	1,283	1,337	1,698

Source: CSDARs 1996–2005.

supervision. For example, the Long-Term Prison Sentences Review Ordinance (1997) established a new statutory board to review long-term and indeterminate sentences, and to decide whether an indeterminate sentence should be turned into a determinate one. Prisoners released under the provisions of this Ordinance remain subject to aftercare supervision of between six months to two years under the Supervision After Release Scheme. The Post-Release Supervision of Prisoners Ordinance (1996) dealt with the statutory provision of supervision and help to adult discharged prisoners. In 1996, CSD also developed the kind of sentence planning approach adopted in the UK for those serving long sentences. Aftercare and post-release supervision thus loom very large in the Hong Kong system. In addition to the above supervisory regimes, there are also four gender- and age-specific 'Halfway Houses' (Phoenix House, Pelican House, New Life House and Bauhinia House) where discharged inmates reside, and from whence they go to work or school, returning each night. Here:

> The programme seeks to cultivate a sense of self-discipline and positive work-habit within a structured and supportive environment. Emphasis is placed on behavioural performance such as conduct, appearance, interpersonal relationships and strengthening of family support in monitoring the progress of residents. Individual and group counselling sessions, in-house recreation, outdoor activities and community services are organised to cultivate a spirit if civic and moral awareness among residents . . . The period of residence depends upon individual needs and progress, and is normally between one and three months . . . During their stay in half-way houses, residents are required to abide by the rules and regulations there.[15]

In 2004, CSD introduced another strand to its disciplinary welfare mosaic. The Continuing Care Project provided advice and help for supervisees thought still to require counselling after the expiry of their supervision period.[16] Hong Kong's numerous voluntary agencies also provided a myriad of 'new life' homes, villages and camps, principally for young people. CSD estimated that there were about 315 non-governmental agencies that helped it provide services to prisoners and/or helped former prisoners reintegrate into the community. Since 1993, CSD has also run a 'Personal Encounters with

Prisoners' Scheme for youths and students as part of the fight crime campaigns.[17] Like the original American schemes upon which these were based, the purpose of these encounters was to expose youths and students to prison life, let them talk to reformed inmates, with the hope that this would reduce their propensity to delinquency 'through gaining more insight into the consequences of crime' (ibid). In 2002, CSD also founded four Rehabilitation Centres, providing short-term, community-based, correctional and rehabilitative programmes between the custodial programmes of Training and Detention Centres, and the non-custodial programme run by the Social Welfare Department. In 2005, these housed 117 male and 56 female young offenders.[18]

The net of welfare-cum-control is thus ever expanding. As Wong points out, in the late 1970s, the government had sponsored a number of NGOs to run personal social services for younger people, such as school social work, outreach social work and family life education, all aimed at reducing delinquency.[19] These echoed the 'missionary movement' that organised boys' clubs and girls' clubs in the 1950s and 1960s and, like those, many of the newer NGO projects were tinged with evangelicalism, a strain that remains in evidence today.

Such agencies have not replaced the state or been replaced by it – rather they operate on a quasi-independent basis to extend the reach of the state into family life and civil society. In the 1990s, there was an explosion of social, welfare and custodial programmes relating to youth. In 1998, there were about 230 children and youth centres in different housing estates and neighbourhoods, and 32 teams of outreach social workers (220 professionals). There were also about 300 school social workers and a further 79 family life education workers, 'providing a wide range of educational and promotional programmes in 13 administrative districts of the territory' (ibid). In response to criticism that these services were fragmented, in 1994, ten integrated teams were established; by 1998, more than 28 such teams were in operation, each consisting of about ten social work professionals and five non-social work staff (ibid). This was an impressive array of professionals to combat the 'youth problem'.

In this period, probation officers serviced large numbers of juveniles and adults – Chiu points out that the number on probation almost doubled between the 1960s and the early 1970s, when a number of approved institutions (such as probation homes and reformatory schools) were established.[20] He dates the role of social workers in the rehabilitation of offenders from the 1973 White Paper (*The Way Ahead*), after which the number of probation officers attached to the courts increased. The Probation Service continued to expand throughout the 1980s and 1990s and had doubled in size by 1997. As Chiu notes, the number of probation officers was a response to the increasing number of probation sentences imposed by the courts, and the increasing number of convictions of children and young people (ibid). The probation order remains in use, one of the community-based sanctions that courts can impose on offenders:

> . . . it comes somewhere in the middle of the tariff, that is between non-supervised orders such as conditional discharge and imprisonment . . . one reason for putting minor offenders on probation is the strong belief that early intervention is effective in preventing re-offending . . . probation orders are issued after the court has considered the circumstances leading to the offence, the nature of the offence, the character of the offender and a social inquiry report . . . the term of the probation order must be specified and should be between one and three years. A number of conditions can be attached . . . The most common conditions include work and residence stipulations; abstinence from dangerous drugs; urine sampling or attendance at drug withdrawal programmes; psychological or psychiatric treatment . . .; curfews; and mid-term progress reports to the courts (ibid).

By 2000, there were 13 probation offices and three teams of CSDs consisting of more than 100 social workers serving the courts (Wong 2000: 287). Apart from probation homes, offenders could be sent to reform schools (normally for between 12 to 18 months), probation hostels, or remand homes (ibid). The aim of probation fitted well with the aim of welfare, custody, parenting and education – to prevent offending and, where necessary, to rehabilitate. This array of measures underlines Gray's point that the reformist agenda provided new, more covert and more discerning ways of disciplining youth offenders. Given the rather minor profile of Hong Kong youth in the crime statistics, the strategy worked (though the crime survey data suggests that the mainstream systems still miss much of the victimisation of young people by young people).

The effort at reintegration is not confined to those who have broken the law – potential offenders and troublesome youth are also, for example, likely to be targeted, as are their families. Government, having been nowhere in most people's lives since the 1840s, is suddenly everywhere. Disruptive (or potentially disruptive) youth with unpredictable loyalties are as much as target for the post-1997 regime as they were for the colonial government. The 'father and mother of the people' mode of the colonial state has given way to new ways of social engineering from a distance, through myriad quasi-governmental and non-governmental organisations. Despite the fact that research suggests the importance of social structural factors, delinquency is still explained in terms of individual failings, poor parental supervision and inadequate socialisation (Wong 2000: 283). The causes of crime are still seen as located within individuals and their families. Social work, counselling and support are seen as the way to re-integrate them into the community, and (re) form them into good, productive citizens. Though this welfare-oriented approach aims to help young people 'to sort out their problems at home, at school and with friends,' it actually involves the greater policing of their behaviour and lifestyle, 'to compensate for lack of parental supervision' (Gray 1996: 27).

This is disciplinary welfare at the micro-level and on a massive scale. At one level, it 'works'. Hong Kong is, apparently, a safer, more law-abiding and compliant society than many other advanced capitalist societies, though it is less exceptional within Asia, where Japan and Singapore famously enjoy similarly low levels of crime.

Though it has been popular to attribute this compliance to culture, the effect of 'soft authoritarian' governments and the strong state in Asia cannot be underestimated. Crime and criminal justice cannot be isolated from politics. In Hong Kong, the mechanisms of dispersed social control, set in place during the 1970s, were part of a massive effort at propaganda designed to make people believe in their government and feel some ownership of their society. This, too, 'worked' – just ten years after the riots, being 'made in Hong Kong' had become a badge of pride. The normative transformation which Mannion delineates in regards to corruption was actually part of a much more profound transformation in people's beliefs and expectations. The government played the lead role in this transformation. It did nothing less than create a new type of civil society from the top down.

Maintaining a level playing field was central to the colonial government's legitimacy, as were its channels of consultation. The post-1997 regime has, however, progressively dismantled these and reverted to the kind of unreconstructed regime typical of the 1960s. This may suit democratic centralism very well, but history suggests that Hong Kong's enviable levels of stability and safety owe much to the lessons learnt by the 1970's regime, and the institutions it established to remedy its democratic deficit.

The legitimacy lacking in the post-1997 regime has, paradoxically, been supplied by public faith in the ability of the institutions of law and order. As Fernandez and Keunzi point out, for Hobbes the desire for security was the main reason human beings would enter into a social contract to submit to government: 'If the government of a country in unable to perform in this area, then it is likely and understandable that people will become disillusioned with the regime with which the government is associated' (Fernandez and Kuenzi 2006: 5).

Support for any regime, therefore, depends not only upon being able to secure a strong economic performance but also upon improving the lives of citizens in respect of crime and personal safety.

Notes

1 HKPAR 1998: 3.
2 As before, the police tended to react to expressions of public concern about par-

ticular types of crime – in 1991 this had been a spate of 'head bashing' robberies. Despite (or indeed because of) a police crackdown, the number of such cases recorded increased.

3 HKPAR 2001: 1.
4 HKPAR 2001.
5 HKPAR 2002.
6 HKPAR 1999: 3.
7 *Crime and Its Victims in Hong Kong* (1999). Hong Kong: Government Printer. The 1998 survey covered 5,674,600 persons aged 12 and over and 2,000,000 households. It revealed that 175,400 persons (defined as those aged 12 and over) had experienced a total of 192,700 victimisations in 1998, and over 137,900 households had experienced 159,500 victimisations (HKCVS 1999: vii).
8 HKPAR 1998: 17.
9 HKPAR 1998: 13.
10 Over the period of the crime surveys (1979–99), 1989 was the year in which reports to the police peaked. Since then, reports overall have declined to more or less their 1981 level. This said, reporting levels are still higher than 1979, even for the age group least likely to report (12 to 19). The high point for their reporting appears to have been 1981, since which they too have been steadily dropping. The true victimisation experience of this group is, however, very hard to ascertain – young males are a notoriously difficult group for surveys to access, and their experience of crime may thus be under-estimated. Police figures may, for this reason, give a more accurate view of victimisation for this age group.
11 The elderly – those aged 65 and over – had the lowest victimisation rate for all types of personal crime, a finding which concurs with earlier victim surveys in Hong Kong, as well as surveys elsewhere.
12 Wong 2000.
13 This is now called the police cautioning scheme.
14 Wong 2000: 280; Vagg et al 1995.
15 CSDAR 2000: 35.
16 CSDAR 2003: 5.
17 CSDAR 2000: 38.
18 CSDAR 2005: 19.
19 Wong 2000: 285.
20 Chiu, W H (2003) 'The Social Work Model of Probation Supervision for Offenders in Hong Kong,' *Probation Journal* 49(4) pp 297–304.

Bibliography

Anderson, D.M. and Killingray, D. (eds) (1991a) *Policing the Empire: Government, Authority and Control, 1830–1940* (Studies in Imperialism). Manchester: Manchester University Press.

Anderson, D.M. and Killingray, D. (eds) (1991b) *Policing and Decolonisation: Politics, Nationalism and the Police, 1917–1965* (Studies in Imperialism). Manchester: Manchester University Press.

Anderson, D.M. and Killingray, D. (1991c) 'Consent, Coercion and Colonial Control: Policing the Empire Government, Authority and Control, 1830–1940', pp 1–17, in Ashworth, A. (1994) *The Criminal Process*. Oxford: Clarendon Press.

Ashworth, A. (1994) *Criminal Process*. Oxford: Clarendon.

Ball, B.L. (1856) *Rambles in East Asia*. Boston: James French.

Bard, S. (ed) (2002) *Voices from the Past: Hong Kong 1842–1918*. Hong Kong: Hong Kong University Press.

Barton, A., Corteen, K., Scott, D. and Whyte, D. (eds) (2007) *Expanding the Criminological Imagination: Critical Readings in Criminology*. Devon: Willan Publishing.

Benton, L. (2002) *Law and Colonial Cultures*. Cambridge: Cambridge University Press.

Blyth, S. and Wotherspoon, I. (1996) *Hong Kong Remembers*. Hong Kong: Oxford University Press.

Booth, M. (1991) *The Triads: The Growing Global Threat from the Chinese Criminal Societies*. London: Bantam Books.

Bottomley, A.K. (1973) *Decisions in the Penal Process*. London: Martin Robertson.

Box, S. (1983) *Power, Crime and Mystification*. London: Routledge.

Brewer, J.D. (1990) *The Royal Irish Constabulary: An Oral History*. Belfast: Institute of Irish Studies, Queen's University of Belfast.

Broadhurst, R. (2000) 'Crime Trends in Hong Kong', Hong Kong: Centre for Criminology, University of Hong Kong.

Brogden, M. (1987a) 'The Emergence of the Police – The Colonial Dimension', *British Journal of Criminology*, 27 (1) Winter, pp 4–14.

Brogden, M. (1987b) 'An Act to Colonise the Internal Lands of the Island: Empire and the Origins of the Professional Police', *International Journal of Sociology of Law*, 15 pp 179–208.

Brown, M. (2005) 'Colonial History and theories of the present' in Godfrey, B. and Dunstall, G. (eds) *Crime and Empire*. Devon: Willan Publishing.

Carrington, K. and Hogg, R. (eds) (2002) *Critical Criminology*. Devon. Willan Publishing.

Carroll, J. (1999) 'Chinese Collaboration in the making of British Hong Kong', in Ngo, Tak-wing (ed) *Hong Kong's History: State and Society under Colonial Rule*. London: Routledge.

Cartwright, J.P. (1996) 'The Evolution of the Hong Kong Police Force as a British Colonial Police Force, 1898–1941', Dissertation, MA in Public Order, University of Leicester and University of Hong Kong.

Castells, M. (1989) *The Informational City*. Oxford: Blackwell.

Castells, M. and Henderson, J. (1987) 'Introduction', in Henderson, J. and Castells, M. (eds) *Global Restructuring and Territorial Development*. London: Sage.

Cater, J. (1996) 'The 1967 Riots', in Blyth, S. and Wotherspoon, I. (eds) *Hong Kong Remembers*. Hong Kong: Oxford University Press.

Central Registry of Drug Abuse in Hong Kong, cited at *www.chr.asn.au*.

Chambliss, W. (1975). 'Toward a Political Economy of Crime', *Theory and Society*. 2

Chan, J. (2005) 'Globalisation, Reflexivity and the Practice of Criminology' in Sheptycki, J. and Wardak, A. (eds), *Transnational and Comparative Criminology*. Devon: Willan Publishing.

Chan, Lau Kit-ching (1999) *From Nothing to Nothing: The Chinese Communist Movement and Hong Kong 1921–1936*. New York: St. Martin's Press.

Chan, M.K. (1990) 'Labour vs Crown: Aspects of State–Society Interactions in the Hong Kong Labour Movement Before World War II', in Sinn, E. (ed) *Between East and West: Aspects of Social and Political Development in Hong Kong*. Hong Kong: University of Hong Kong, Centre for Asian Studies.

Chan, M.K. (ed) (1994a) *Precarious Balance: Hong Kong Becoming China*. Hong Kong: Hong Kong University Press.

Chan, M.K. (1994b) 'Hong Kong in Sino–British Conflict 1912–26', in Chan, M.K. and Postiglione, G. (eds) *Precarious Balance: Hong Kong between China and Britain 1842–1992*. Hong Kong: Hong Kong University Press.

Chan, M.K. (2002) 'The SAR in Flux', in Chan, M.K. and So, A. *Crisis and Transformation in China's Hong Kong*. New York: M.E. Sharpe.

Chan, S. (1994) 'Development of the Hong Kong Penal Policy and Programme Under the British Administration, 1841–1945', unpublished MA Dissertation, University of Leicester, Centre for the Study of Public Order.

Chan, W.K. (1991) *The Making of Hong Kong Society: Three Studies in Class Formation in Early Hong Kong*. Oxford: Clarendon Press.

Chen, Albert, H.Y. (2002) 'The Constitution and the Rule of Law', in Lau, Siu-kai (ed) *The First Tung Chee-hwa Administration*. Hong Kong: Chinese University Press.

Cheung, A.B.L. (2000) 'New Interventionism in the Making: interpreting state intervention in Hong Kong after the change in sovereignty', *Journal of Contemporary China*, 9 (24) pp 291–308.

Cheung, Bing-leung and Louie, Kin-sheun (1991) 'Social Conflicts in Hong Kong 1975–1986: Trends and Implications', Occasional Paper No 3, Hong Kong: Hong Kong Institute of Asia Pacific Studies, Chinese University of Hong Kong.

Cheung, Y.W. (1993) *Predicting Adolescent Deviant Behaviour in Hong Kong*. Hong Kong: Institute for Asia Pacific Studies, Chinese University of Hong Kong.

Cheung, Y.W. and Ng, A.M.C. (1988) 'Social Factors in Adolescent Deviant Behaviour in Hong Kong.' *International Journal of Comparative & Applied Criminal Justice*, 12, (1 & 2) Spring/Winter pp 27–43.

Chiu, W.H. (2003) 'The Social Work Model of Probation Supervision for Offenders in Hong Kong', *Probation Journal* 49 (4) pp 297–304.

Chow, N., Tang, A. and Chan, T.F. (1987) *A Comparison of Delinquent Youth and Non-delinquent Youth on the Aspect of Parental Supervision and Schooling: A Follow-up Study on Unruly Youth in Tseun Wan, Kwai Chung and Tsing Yi.* Hong Kong: Kwai Chung and Tsing Yi District Board and Tseun Wan District Board.

Chow, S. (1977) 'Economic Growth and Income Distribution in Hong Kong', unpublished Doctoral Dissertation, University of Boston, MA.

Chu, Yiu Kong (2000) *Triads as Business*. New York: Routledge Studies in the Modern History of Asia, 6.

Chui. M. (1999) *Justice Without Fear or Favour: Reflections of a Chinese Magistrate in Hong Kong*. Hong Kong: Ming Pao Publications.

Cicourel, A. (1968) *The Social Organisation of Juvenile Justice*. New York: Wiley.

Clayton, A. and Killingray, D. (1989) *Khaki and Blue: Military and Police in British Colonial Africa*. Ohio: Ohio University Center for International Studies, Monographs in International Studies Africa series number 51.

Clinard, M. and Abbott, D. (1973) *Crime in 'Developing' Countries*. New York: Wiley.

Coates, A. (1968) *Myself a Mandarin: Memoirs of a Special Magistrate*. Hong Kong: Oxford University Press.

Cohen, S. (1972) *Folk Devils and Moral Panics*. London: McGibbon and Kee.

Coleborne, C. (2005) 'Crime, the legal archive and postcolonial issues' in Godfrey, B. & Dunstall (eds) (2005) *Crime and Empire*. Devon: Willan Publishing.

Cooper, J. (1970) *Colony in Conflict*. Hong Kong: Swindon Book Company.

Crisswell, C. and Watson, M. (1982) *The Royal Hong Kong Police (1841–1945)*. Hong Kong: Macmillan.

Curriculum Development Committee (1985) *Guidelines on Civic Education in Schools*. Hong Kong: Hong Kong Government, Education Department.

Das, D.K. and Verma. A. (1998) 'The Armed Police in the British Colonial Tradition: The Indian perspective', *International Journal of Police Strategies*, 21 (2) pp 354–65.

Davies, D. (1973) 'Inherent Dangers', *Far Eastern Economic Review*, 29, 28 October.

Deflem, M. (1994) 'Law Enforcement in British Colonial Africa: A Comparative Analysis of Imperial Policing in Nyasaland, the Gold Coast and Kenya', *Police Studies: The International Review of Police Development*, 17 (1) Spring.

Department of Census and Statistics (1979) *Crime and Its Victims in Hong Kong*. Hong Kong: Government Printer.

Department of Census and Statistics (1981) *Crime and Its Victims in Hong Kong*. Hong Kong: Government Printer.

Department of Census and Statistics (1986) *Crime and its Victims in Hong Kong*. Hong Kong: Government Printer.

Department of Census and Statistics (1994) *Crime and its Victims in Hong Kong*. Hong Kong: Government Printer.

Department of Census and Statistics (1999) *Crime and Its Victims in Hong Kong*. Hong Kong: Government Printer.

Duff, P., Findlay, M., Howarth, C. and Chan, T. (1992) *Juries: A Hong Kong Perspective*. Hong Kong: Hong Kong University Press.

Dunstall, G. and Godfrey, B. (eds) (2005) *Crime and Empire*. Devon: Willan Publishing.

Eitel, E.J. (1983) *Europe in China: The History of Hong Kong from the Beginning to the Year 1882*. Hong Kong: Oxford University Press. Originally published 1895, Hong Kong: Kelly and Walsh.

Elliott, E. (1981) *Crusade for Justice*. Hong Kong: Heinemann Books.

Emsley, C. (1986) 'The thump of wood on a swede turnip: police violence in nineteenth-century England. Crime, police and the courts in British history', in Knafla, L.A. (ed) *Readings from Criminal Justice History*. London: Meckler, pp 193–217.

Emsley, C. (1991) 'The changes in policing and penal policy in nineteenth century Europe', in Godfrey and Dunstall (eds) *Crime and Empire 1840–1940: Criminal Justice in Local and Global Context*. Devon: Willan Publishing.

Emsley, C. (1998) *The English Police: a Political and Social History*. Hertfordshire: Harvester Wheatsheaf, St. Martin's Press.

Emsley, C. and Knafla, L. (eds) (1996) *Crime Histories and Histories of Crime: Studies in the Historiography of Crime and Criminal Justice in Modern History*. Westport, CT: Greenwood Press.

Endacott, G.B. (1956) 'Charles May and the Hong Kong Police Force', *Hong Kong Police Magazine*, VI (2) Summer pp 7–11.

Endacott, G.B. (1964) *Government and People of Hong Kong 1841–1962*. Hong Kong: Hong Kong University Press.

Endacott, G.B. (1978) *A History of Hong Kong*. Second Edition. Hong Kong: Oxford University Press.

Endacott, G.B. and Birch, A. (1978) *Hong Kong Eclipse*. Hong Kong: Oxford University Press.

England, J. (1989) *Industrial Relations and Law in Hong Kong*. Hong Kong: Oxford University Press.

England, J. (1990) 'Industrial Relations in Hong Kong', in Hopkins, K. (ed) *Hong Kong: The Industrial Colony*. Hong Kong: Oxford University Press.

England, J. and Rear, J. (1981) *Chinese Labour Under British Rule*. Hong Kong: Oxford University Press.

Evans, G. (1997) 'Ghosts and the New Governor', in Evans, G. and Tam Siu-mi, Maria (eds) *Hong Kong: The Anthropology of a Chinese Metropolis*. Surrey: Curzon Books.

Evans, J. (2005) 'Colonialism and the rule of law: The case of South Australia' in Godfrey, B. and Dunstall G. (eds) *Crime and Empire*.

Family Planning Association of Hong Kong (1991) *Youth Sexuality Report*. Hong Kong: FPA.

Fernandez, K.E. and Kuenzi, M. (2006) 'Crime and Support for Democracy: Revisiting Modernization Theory', Las Vegas: AfroBarometer Working Paper No 64: Department of Political Science, University of Nevada.

Fight Crime Committee (1981) *Working Group on Juvenile Crime*. Hong Kong: Government Printer.

Fletcher, C.D.St.Q. (1969) 'Riot Control in Hong Kong', *FBI Law Enforcement Bulletin*, December.

Flint, J.E. (1978) 'Frederick Lugard: The making of an autocrat (1858–1943)', in Gann, L.H. and Duignan, P. (eds) *African Proconsuls: European Governors in Africa*. New York: Free Press/Collier Macmillan Publishers and Hoover Institution.

Foucault, M. (1979) *Discipline and Punish*. New York: Vintage.
Frost, R. (1945) 'Reflections on British Colonial Policy', *Colonial Affairs*, 18 pp 309–20.
Fu, H.L. and Cullen, R. (2003) 'Political Policing in Hong Kong', *Hong Kong Law Journal*, 33 pp 199–230.
Ganapathy, N. (2005) 'Critical Reflections on Crime and Social Control in Singapore' in Sheptycki, J. and Wardak, A. (eds) *Transnational and Comparative Criminology*.
Garland, D. (1985) *Punishment and Welfare: A History of Penal Strategies*. Aldershot: Gower Publishing.
Garland, D. (1999) 'Crime control, governmentality and sovereignty', in Smandych, R. (ed) *Governable Places*. Aldershot: Ashgate.
Gatrell, V.A.C. (1980) 'The decline of theft and violence in Victorian and Edwardian England', in Gatrell, V.A.C., Lenman, B. and Parker, G. (eds) *Crime and the Law: The Social History of Crime in Western Europe since 1500*. London: Europa.
Gaylord, M. and Lang, G. (2006) 'Robbery, Recession and real wages in Hong Kong', *Crime, Law and Social Change*, 27 (1) January 1997 updated 2006, pp 49–71.
Gaylord, M. and Traver, H. (eds) (1994) *An Introduction to the Criminal Justice System of Hong Kong*, Hong Kong: Hong Kong University Press.
Girardot, N.J. (2002) *The Victorian Translation of China: James Legge's Oriental Pilgrimage*. Berkeley: University of California Press.
Godfrey, B., Emsley, C. and Dunstall, G. (2002) *Comparative Histories of Crime*. Devon: Willan Publishing
Goldstein, J. (1960) 'Police Discretion Not to Invoke the Criminal Process: Low-Visibility Decisions in the Administration of Justice' *The Yale Law Journal*, 69 (4) March, pp 543–94.
Goodstadt, L.F. (1970) 'The Fixers', *Far Eastern Economic Review*,
Goodstadt, L.F. (2005) *Uneasy Partners: The Conflict between Public Interest and Private Profit in Hong Kong*. Hong Kong: Hong Kong University Press.
Grantham, A. (1965) *Via Ports*. Hong Kong: Hong Kong University Press.
Gray, P. (1991) 'Juvenile crime and disciplinary welfare', in Traver, H. and Vagg, J. (eds) *Crime and Justice in Hong Kong*. Hong Kong: Oxford University Press.
Gray, P. (1996) 'The Struggle for Juvenile Justice in Hong Kong 1932–1995', *Hong Kong Law Journal*, 26 pp 301–20.
Gray, P. (1997) 'The Emergence of the Disciplinary Welfare Sanction in Hong Kong', *Howard Journal of Criminal Justice*, 36 (2) May pp 187–208.
Gray, P. (1999) 'Community Corrections and the Experiences of Young Male Offenders in the Hong Kong Justice System', *International Journal of Social Policy*, 28 (4) pp 577–94.
Groves, R.G. (1969) 'Militia, Market and Lineage: Chinese Resistance to the Occupation of Hong Kong's New Territories in 1899', *Journal Hong Kong Branch of the Royal Asiatic Society*, 9 pp 31–64.
Hall, C. (2002) *Civilising Subjects: Metropole and Colony in the English Imagination 1830–1867*. Cambridge: Polity Press.
Hall, S., Critcher, C., Jefferson, T., Clarke, J. and Roberts, B. (1978) *Policing the Crisis*. London: Macmillan.
Hardie-Bick, J., Sheptycki, J. and Wardak, A. (2005) 'Introduction' to *Transnational and Comparative Criminology*
Harrison, D. (1988) *The Sociology of Modernisation and Development*. London: Routledge.

Harrison, P. (1983) *Inside the Inner City*, Harmondsworth: Penguin Books.

Harvey, D. (1989) *The Condition of Postmodernity*, Oxford: Basil Blackwell.

Hawkins, R. (1991) 'The Irish Model and the Empire: A Case for Reassessment', in Anderson, D.M. and Killingray, D. (eds) *Policing the Empire: Government, Authority and Control, 1830–1940* (Studies in Imperialism). Manchester: Manchester University Press pp 18–32.

Hayes, J. (1993) *Tsuen Wan: Growth of a New Town and its People*. Hong Kong: Oxford University Press.

Hayes, J. (1996) *Friends and Teachers: Hong Kong and its People 1953–1987*. Hong Kong: Hong Kong University Press.

Hayes, J.W. (1962) 'The Pattern of Life in the New Territories in 1898', *Journal, Hong Kong Branch of the Royal Asiatic Society*, 2 pp 75–102.

Hirschi, T. (1969) *Causes of Delinquency*, Los Angeles: University of California Press.

Hong Kong Commission on Youth (1991) *Charter for Youth*. Hong Kong: Youth Commission.

Hong Kong Correctional Services Department *Annual Reports 1997–2005*. Hong Kong: Government Printer.

Hong Kong Hansard (1948), Hong Kong: Government Printer.

Hong Kong Judiciary *Annual Reports 1997–2005*. Hong Kong: Government Printer.

Hong Kong Police *Annual Reports 1997–2006*. Hong Kong: Government Printer.

Hong Kong Police (1979–95) *Police in Figures*.

Hong Kong Transition Project 1982–2007 (2002) *The First Five Years: Floundering Government, Foundering Democracy?* Hong Kong: Hong Kong Baptist University.

Hong Kong Transition *Project Reports, 2001–2006*. Hong Kong: Baptist University of Hong Kong.

Hong Kong Yearbooks: Hong Kong: Government Printer.

Howell, P. (2004) 'Race, Space and the Regulation of Prostitution in Colonial Hong Kong', *Urban History* (31) pp 229–48N.

Howell, P. and Lambert, D. (2006) 'Sir John Pope Hennessy and colonial government', in Lambert, D. and Lester, A. *Colonial Lives Across the British Empire*, Cambridge: Cambridge University Press.

Howroyd, S. and MacPherson, S. (1992) *Statistical Profile of Youth in Hong Kong*. Hong Kong: Commission on Youth.

Hunt, A. (1999) 'Anxiety and Social Explanation', *Journal of Social History*, 32 (3) pp 509–28.

Independent Commission Against Corruption, Annual Reports.

Independent Police Complaints Commission Annual Reports, Hong Kong: Government Printer.

Jarvie, I.C. (1969) 'Riots and the Future of Hong Kong', in Jarvie, I.C. and Agassi, J. (eds) *Hong Kong: a Society in Transition*. London: Routledge and Kegan Paul.

Jefferson, T. (2005) 'For a psychosocial criminology', in Carrington, K. and Hogg, R. (eds) *Critical Criminology*. Devon: Willan Publishing.

Jeffries, C. (1952) *The Colonial Police*. London: Max Parrish.

Jones, C. (1990) *Promoting Prosperity*. Hong Kong: Hong Kong University Press.

Jones, C.A.G. (1994) 'Women and the Law in Colonial Hong Kong', in Leung, B. and Pearson, V. (eds) 25 *Years of Social and Economic Development in Hong Kong*. Hong Kong: University of Hong Kong, Centre for Asian Studies Occasional Papers and Monographs, 111.

Jones, C.A.G. (2007) 'Dissolving the People', in Feeley, M., Halliday, T. and Karpik, L. (eds) *Struggles for Political Freedom*. Oxford: Hart Publishing.

Kerrigan, A. (2001) 'Policing a Colony', unpublished PhD thesis, Cardiff: University of Wales.

King, Ambrose, Y.C. (1995) 'One Country Two Systems: An Idea on Trial,' in Wang, G. and Wong, S.L. (eds) *Hong Kong's Transition: a Decade After the Deal*. Hong Kong: Oxford University Press.

Lam, W.M. (2004) *Understanding the Political Culture of Hong Kong: The Paradox of Activism and Depoliticisation*. New York: M.E. Sharpe.

Lam, W.M. (2005) 'Depoliticisation, Citizenship and the Politics of Community in Hong Kong', *Citizenship Studies*, 9 (3).

Lamont-Brown, R. (1998) *Kempeitai: Japan's Dreaded Military Police*. Stroud: Sutton Publishing.

Lau, S.K. (1982) *Society and Politics in Hong Kong*. Hong Kong: Chinese University Press.

Law, C.K. (1986) *A Study on the Behaviour and Attitudes of Youth in Kwun Tong*. Hong Kong: Working Group on Problem Youth, Kwung Tong District Board and Department of Social Work, University of Hong Kong.

Law, Yick-man (1996), 'The Origins and Developments of Detention Centre Programmes in Hong Kong', unpublished MA, University of Leicester, Centre for Public Order.

Le Bon, Gustave. (1885) *The Psychology of the Crowd*. New York: Viking (trans. 1960).

Lea, J. and Young, J. (1984) *What is to be Done About Law and Order*? London: Penguin Books.

Lee, Alice Ngor Lea (1974) 'Policing in Hong Kong 1841–1899', BA thesis, Faculty of Arts, Department of History, University of Hong Kong.

Lee, Francis Wing-Lin (2002) 'Encounters Between Police and "Unattached Youth" and The Occurrence of Juvenile Delinquency', *Police Practice and Research*, 3 (2).

Lee, Hong-nee, Connie (1995) 'Society and Policing in Hong Kong: a study of the 1956 riot', unpublished MA dissertation, University of Leicester, Centre for Public Order.

Legge, J. (1872), *The Chinese Classics*. London: Trubner, reprinted 1960, Hong Kong: Hong Kong University Press.

Lester, A. (2001) *Imperial Networks: Creating Identities in Nineteenth Century South Africa and Britain*. London: Routledge.

Lethbridge, H.J. (1969) 'Hong Kong Under Japanese Occupation', in Jarvie, I.C. and Agassi, J. (eds) *Hong Kong: A Society in Transition*. London: Routledge and Kegan Paul.

Lethbridge, H.J. (1970) 'Hong Kong Cadets, 1862–1941', *Journal of the Hong Kong Branch of the Royal Asiatic Society*, 10 (1970) 36–56.

Lethbridge, H.J. (1972a) 'Sir James Haldane Stewart Lockhart: Colonial Civil Servant and Scholar', *Hong Kong Branch of the Royal Asiatic Society*, 12 pp 55–87.

Lethbridge, H.J. (1972b) 'Penal Policy and Crime Rates: Comments on the Hong Kong Experience' *Hong Kong Law Journal*, 2 (1).

Lethbridge, H.J. (1975) 'Condition of European Working Class in Nineteenth Century Hong Kong', *Journal Hong Kong Branch Royal Asiatic Society*, 15 pp 88–112.

Lethbridge, H.J. (1978a) 'The District Watch Committee: The Chinese Executive Council of Hong Kong?' in Lethbridge, H.J. *Hong Kong: Stability and Change: A Collection of Essays*. Hong Kong: Oxford University Press.

Lethbridge, H.J. (1978b) *Hong Kong: Stability and Change: A Collection of Essays*. Hong Kong: Oxford University Press.

Lethbridge, H.J. (1985) *Hard Graft in Hong Kong: Scandal, Corruption and the ICAC*. Hong Kong: Oxford University Press.

Leung, B.K.P. (ed) (1990) *Social Issues in Hong Kong*. Hong Kong: Oxford University Press.

Leung, B.K.P. (1996) *Perspectives on Hong Kong Society*. Hong Kong: Oxford University Press.

Lo, T.W. (1993) *Corruption and Politics in Hong Kong and China*, Milton Keynes: Open University Press.

Lo, Wing-hung, Carlos and Cheuk, Chun-yin, Albert. (2003) 'Police–Public Projects in Hong Kong: An Evaluation', *Asian Journal of Public Administration*, 25 (2) pp 287–313.

Lock, Chung-sum, Andy (1993) 'To Live and Work in Peace and Contentment: The political attitudes of the Hong Kong Chinese, with special reference to the China factor, from the late 1840s to the late 1950s', unpublished MA dissertation, University of Hong Kong, Department of History.

Lomas, K.H. 'Policing in Hong Kong' unpublished paper to 18th Senior Command Course, Police Staff College, Bramshill, UK.

Lopez-Rey, M. (1970) *Crime: An Analytical Appraisal*. New York: Praeger.

Lovett, R. (1899) *The History of the London Missionary Society 1795–1895*. London: Henry Frowde.

Lowe, K. and McLaughlin, E. (1992) 'Sir John Pope Hennessy and the "native race craze": colonial government in Hong Kong 1877–1882', *Journal of Imperial and Commonwealth History*, 20 (2) pp 239–40.

Lowe, K. and McLaughlin, E. (1993) ' "An El Dorado of Riches and a Place of Unpunished Crime": The Politics of Penal Reform in Hong Kong 1877–1882', *Criminal Justice History*, 14 pp 57–89.

Lugard, Frederick D. (Lord) (1922) *The Dual Mandate in British Tropical Africa*. London: Frank Cass (reprinted 1965).

Lustgarten, L. (1986) *The Governance of Police*. London: Sweet and Maxwell.

MacKay, C.J. (2000) 'Housing Management and the comprehensive housing model in Hong Kong: A Case Study of Colonial Influence', *Journal of Contemporary China*, 9 (25): 449–66.

Mann, K. and Roberts, R. (eds) (1991) *Law in Colonial Africa*. Portsmouth, New Hampshire: Heinemann.

Mannion, M. (2004) *Corruption by Design*. Harvard: Harvard University Press.

Mark, Chi-Kwan (2000) 'A Reward for Good Behaviour in the Cold War: Bargaining over the Defence of Hong Kong 1949–1957', *The International History Review* 22 (4):837–71.

Martin, R.M. (1846) *Memorandum to Lord Stanley, November 28th 1845, Reports, Minutes and Despatches on the British Position and Prospects in China*. London: Harrison.

Mawby, R.I. (1990) *Comparative Policing Issues: The British and American System in International Perspective*. London: Unwin Hyman.

Mills, I.A. (1942) *British Rule in East Asia: A Study of Contemporary Government and Economic Development in British Malaya and Hong Kong*, London: Oxford University Press.

Milne, W.C. (1861) *Life in China*. London: Routledge.

Miners, N. (1987) *Hong Kong Under Imperial Rule, Hong Kong*. Hong Kong: Oxford University Press.

Miners, N. (1990) 'The Localisation of the Hong Kong Police Force 1842–1947', *Journal of Imperial and Commonwealth History*, 18 pp 296–315.

Miners, N. (1995) *Government and Politics of Hong Kong*. Hong Kong: Oxford University Press.

Mok, B.H. (1985) 'Problem Behaviour of Adolescents in Hong Kong: a Socio-Cultural Perspective', Hong Kong: Occasional Paper No 7, Institute of Social Studies, Chinese University of Hong Kong.

Mok, R. and Leung, I. (1996) 'Voices of the Future', in Blyth, S. and Wotherspoon, I. *Hong Kong Remembers*. Hong Kong: Oxford University Press.

Mommsen, W.J. and De Moor, J.A. (eds) (1992) *European Expansion and the Law: The Encounter of European and Indigenous Law in 19th and 20th Century Africa and Asia*. New York: Berg;

Morgan, W.P. (1960) *Triad Societies of Hong Kong*. Hong Kong: Government Printer.

Morris, P. and Sweeting, A. (1992) 'Education and Politics: The Case of Hong Kong from an Historical Perspective', in Morris, P. (ed) *Curriculum Development in Hong Kong*, Hong Kong: Hong Kong University Press.

Morris, P. and Sweeting, A. (1997) 'The Hong Kong School Curriculum and the Political Transition', *Comparative Education*, 33 (2) pp 247–64.

Muncie, J. and McLaughlin, E. (1996a) *Criminological Perspectives*. Milton Keynes: Open University Press.

Muncie, J. and McLaughlin, E. (1996b) *The Problem of Crime*. Milton Keynes: Open University Press.

Munn, C. (1995) 'Scratching with a Rattan: William Caine and the Hong Kong Magistracy 1841–44', *Hong Kong Law Journal*, 25 (2).

Munn, C. (1996) 'An Insubordinate and Semi-Barbarous People: Chinese Defendants and Criminal Justice in Early British Hong Kong, 1841–1866', Conference paper, University of Hong Kong, Centre for Asian Studies, March.

Munn, C. (2000) 'Colonialism "in a Chinese atmosphere": the Caldwell affair and the perils of collaboration in early colonial Hong Kong', in Bickers, R.A. and Henriot, C. (eds) *New Frontiers: Imperialism's New Communities in East Asia, 1842–1953*. Manchester: Manchester University Press.

Munn, C. (2001) *Anglo-China: Chinese People and British Rule in Hong Kong 1841–1880*. Richmond: Curzon Press.

Newman, G. (1990) 'Crime and the human condition', in Zvekic, U. (ed) *Essays on Crime and Development*. Rome: United Nations Interregional Crime and Justice Research Institute.

Ng, A. (1975) 'Social Causes of Violent Crime Among Young Offenders in Hong Kong', Hong Kong: Social Research Centre, Chinese University of Hong Kong.

Ng, A. (1980) *Family Relationships and Delinquent Behaviour*. New York: Columbia University Press.

Ng, A. (1992) 'Delinquent Trends in Socio-Economic Perspective', in Leung, B. and Pearson, V. (eds) *25 Years of Social and Economic Development in Hong Kong*. Hong Kong: University of Hong Kong, Centre for Asian Studies.

Ng, L.Y.Y. (1995) 'Reflections on riots in Hong Kong in the 1980s: a study in public disorder', unpublished MA Dissertation, Centre for the Study of Public Order, University of Leicester.

Norton Kyshe, J.W. (1971) *The History of the Laws and Courts of Hong Kong*. Hong Kong: Vetch and Lee, originally published 1898, T. Fisher Unwin.

Oi-Bing, D.L. (1995) 'Troubled and troublesome: young people, urbanization and the case of Hong Kong', *International Social Work*, 38: 325–39.

Old Humphrey (1844) 'Points and Pickings of Information About China', London, Grant and Griffith.

Palmer, S.H. (1975) 'The Irish police experiment: the beginnings of modern policing in the British Isles, 1785–1795', *Social Science Quarterly*, LVI.

Palmer, S. (1988) *Police and Protest in England and Ireland: 1780–1850*. Cambridge: Cambridge University Press.

Perham, Margery (1956) *Lugard. Volume 1: The Years of Adventure 1858–1898*. London: Collins.

Perham, Margery (1960) *Lugard. Volume 2: The Years of Authority 1898–1945*. London: Collins.

Penlington, V.A. (1986) *Law in Hong Kong*. Hong Kong: South China Morning Post Publications.

Petrow, S. (2005) 'The English Model?' in Godfrey, B. and Dunstall, G. (eds) *Crime and Empire*. Devon: Willan Publishing.

Pottinger, G. (1997) *Sir Henry Pottinger: First Governor of Hong Kong*. Stroud: Sutton Publishing.

Pratt, J. (2005) 'Explaining the History of Punishment' in. Godfrey, B. and Dunstall, G. (eds) *Crime and Empire* pp 25–42.

Pryor, E.G. (1975) 'The Great Plague of Hong Kong', *Journal of the Hong Kong Branch of the Royal Asiatic Society*, 15 pp 61–70.

Public Opinion Polls (POP) Express. hkupop.hku.hk/popexpress, 15 October 2006.

Quinney, R. (1970) *The Social Reality of Crime*. Boston MA: Little, Brown.

Quinney, R. (1974) *Critique of the Legal Order*. Boston MA: Little Brown.

Radzinowicz, L. and Hood, R (1990) *A History of English Criminal Law and its Administration 1750*, vol 5. London: Clarendon Press.

Riot Report (1966) *Report into the Kowloon Disturbances*. Hong Kong: Hong Kong Government Printer.

Ritchie, G. and Hermanus, M. (2004) 'Challenging Neutrality: Investigating the National Library of South Africa' paper for LIASA Conference.

Rose, N. (2000) 'Government and Control', *British Journal of Criminology*, 40.

Royal Hong Kong Police and Hong Kong Police Annual Reports.

Sayer, G.R. (1980) *Hong Kong 1841–1862: Birth, Adolescence and Coming of Age*. Hong Kong: Hong Kong University Press

Scott, I. (1989) *Political Change and the Crisis of Legitimacy in Hong Kong*. Hong Kong: Oxford University Press.

Series CO 129: Colonial Correspondence, Hong Kong 1841–1940.

Series CO 133: Annual Blue Book 1844–1940.

Shelley, L.I. (1981) *Crime and Modernization: The Impact of Industrialization and Urbanization on Crime*. Carbondale, Ill.: Southern Illinois University Press.

Sheptycki, J. (2005) 'Relativism, Transnationalisation and Comparative Criminology' in Sheptycki, J. and Wardak, A. (eds) *Transnational and Comparative Criminology*.

Silver, A. (1967) 'The demand for order in civil society: a review of some themes in the history of urban crime, police and riot', in Bordua, D. (ed) *The Police: Six Sociological Essays*. New York: John Wiley.

Simpson, A.W.B. (2004) *Human Rights and the End of Empire*, Oxford: Oxford University Press.

Sinclair, K. (1983) *Asia's Finest: An Illustrated Account of the Hong Kong Police Force*. Hong Kong: Unicorn.

Sinn, E. (1990) 'A History of Regional Associations in Pre-War Hong Kong', in Sinn, E. (ed) *Between East and West: Aspects of Social and Political Development in Hong Kong*. Hong Kong: Centre for Asian Studies, University of Hong Kong.

Sinn, Yuk-yee, E. (1982) 'The Strike and Riot of 1884 – A Hong Kong Perspective' *Journal of the Hong Kong Branch of the Royal Asiatic Society*, 22 pp 65–98.

Sinn, Yuk-yee, E. (1986) *The Tung Wah Hospital 1869–1896: A Study of a Medical, Social and Political Institution in Hong Kong*. PhD thesis, University of Hong Kong.

Sinn, Yuk-yee, E. (1989) *Power and Charity: The Early History of the Tung Wah Hospital*. Hong Kong: Oxford University Press.

Sinn, Yuk-yee, E. (1990) *Between East and West Aspects of Social and Political Development in Hong Kong*. Hong Kong: Centre of Asian Studies, University of Hong Kong.

Sinn, Yuk-yee, E. (1997) 'Xu Xi Guxiang: A Study of Regional Associations as a Bonding Mechanism in the Chinese Diaspora: The Hong Kong Experience', in *Modern Asian Studies*, 31 (2) pp 375–97.

Sirr, H.C. (1849) *China and the Chinese: Their Religion, Character, Customs and Manufactures*. London: Orr.

Skidmore, M.J. (1996) 'Promise and Peril in Combating Corruption: Hong Kong's ICAC', *Annals of the American Academy of Political and Social Science*, 547, pp 118–130.

Smart, A. (2006) *The Shek Kip Mei Myth: Squatters, Fires and Colonial Rule in Hong Kong 1950–1963*. Hong Kong: Hong Kong University Press.

Smart, C. (1995) *Law, Crime and Sexuality*. London: Sage.

Smelser, N.J. (1969) 'Mechanisms of and Adjustments to Change', in Burns, T. (ed) *Industrial Man*. Harmondsworth: Penguin

Smith, C.T. (1970) 'The Chinese settlement of British Hong Kong', *Chung Chi Bulletin*, 48 pp 26–32.

Smith, C.T. (1971) 'The Emergence of a Chinese Elite in Hong Kong', *Journal of the Hong Kong Branch of the Royal Asiatic Society*, 11.

Smith, C.T. (1985) *Chinese Christians: Elites, Middlemen and the Church in Hong Kong*. Hong Kong: Oxford University Press.

Smith, C.T (1995) *A Sense of History: Studies in the Social and Urban History of Hong Kong*. Hong Kong: Hong Kong Educational Publishing Company.

Smith, G. (1847) *A Narrative of an Exploratory Visit to the Consular Cities of China and to the Islands of Hong Kong and Chousan on behalf of the Church Missionary Society in the Years 1844, 1845 and 1846*. London: Seeley.

Spierenburg, P. (1984) *The Spectacle of Suffering: Execution and the Evolution of Repression*. Cambridge: Cambridge University Press.

Stoler, A. (2002) 'Colonial archives and the arts of governance: on the context and in the form', in Hamilton, C., Harris V., Taylor J., Pickover M., Reid G. and Saleh R. (2002) *Refiguring the Archive*. Cape Town: David Philip.

Storch, R.D. (1975) 'The Plague of Blue Locusts: Police Reform and Popular Resistance in Northern England 1840–57', *International Review of Social History*, 20 pp 61–90.

Storch, R.D. (1976) 'The Policeman as Domestic Missionary: Urban Discipline and Popular Culture in Northern England 1850–80', *Journal of Social History*, IX pp 481–509.

Sutherland, E. (1949) *White Collar Crime*. Westport, CT: Greenwood Press.

Styles, J. (1987) 'The Emergence of the Police-Explaining Police Reform in the Eighteenth and Nineteenth Century England', *British Journal of Criminology*, 27 (1) Winter.

Sumner, C. (1982) 'Crime, Justice and Underdevelopment: Beyond Modernization Theory', in Sumner, C. (ed) *Crime, Justice and Underdevelopment*. London: Heinemann.

Sum, Ngai-ling and Jessop, B. 'An Entrepreneurial City in Action: Hong Kong's Emerging Strategies in and for (Inter-)Urban Competition', Online Papers, Department of Sociology Lancaster University, Lancaster, UK, http://www.comp.lancs.ac.uk/sociology/soc045rj.html.

Sundaram, C.S. (2006) 'Seditious Letters and Steel Helmets: Disaffection amongst Indian Troops in Singapore and Hong Kong 1940–41', in Roy, K. (ed) *War and Society in Colonial India, 1807–1945*. New Delhi: Oxford University Press, pp 126–60.

Sutherland, E.H. and Cressey, D.R (1978) *Criminology*. Philadelphia: J.B. Lippincott Company.

Swaaningen, R. (1997) *Critical Criminology: Visions from Europe*. London: Sage.

Tang, J (1993) 'From Empire Defence to Imperial Retreat: Britain's Postwar China Policy and the Decolonisation of Hong Kong', *Modern Asian Studies*, 27 (1).

Thomas, N. (1999) *Democracy Denied: Identity, Civil Society and Illiberal Democracy in Hong Kong*. Aldershot: Ashgate.

Thompson, E.P. (1975). *Whigs and Hunters*. New York: Pantheon.

Ting, J. (1990) 'Native Chinese Peace Officer in British Hong Kong, 1841–1861', in Thomas, N. (1999) *Democracy Denied: Identity, Civil Society and Illiberal Democracy in Hong Kong*. Aldershot: Ashgate.

Tobias, J.J. (1977) 'The British Colonial Police: An Alternative Police Style', in Stead, P.J. (ed) *Pioneers in Policing*. Montclair, NJ: Patterson Smith pp 241–61.

Traver, H. (1991) 'Crime Trends', in Traver, H. and Vagg, J. (eds) *Crime and Justice in Hong Kong*. Hong Kong: Oxford University Press.

Traver, H. and Vagg, J (1991) *Crime and Justice in Hong Kong*. Hong Kong: Oxford University Press.

Tsai, Jung-fang (1984) 'The 1884 Hong Kong Insurrection: Anti-Imperialist Popular Protest During the Sino–French War', *Bulletin of Concerned Asian Scholars*, (March) pp 2–14.

Tsai, J.F. (1993) *Hong Kong in Chinese History: Community and Social Unrest in the British Colony 1842–1913*. New York: Columbia University Press.

Tsang, S. (1988) *Democracy Shelved*. Hong Kong: Oxford University Press.

Tsang, S. (2004) *A Modern History of Hong Kong*. Hong Kong: Hong Kong University Press.

Tsang Yok-sing (1996) 'Coming of Age in 1967', in Blyth, S. and Wotherspoon, I. (eds) *Hong Kong Remembers*. Hong Kong: Oxford University Press.

Tse, T.K.C. (1997) 'The Poverty of Political Education in Hong Kong Secondary Schools', Hong Kong: Hong Kong Institute of Asia-Pacific Studies, Chinese University of Hong Kong,

Tu, E. (2003) *Colonial Hong Kong in the Eyes of Elsie Tu*. Hong Kong: Hong Kong University Press.

US Department of Justice (1989) *Crime Victimisation in the City: Suburban and Rural Areas*. Bureau of Statistics.

Vagg, J. (1991a) 'Illegal Immigration', in H. Traver, and J. Vagg (eds) *Crime And Justice In Hong Kong*. Hong Kong: Oxford University Press.

Vagg, J. (1991b) 'The Correctional Service Department', in M. Gaylord and H. Traver (eds) *Introduction to the Hong Kong Criminal Justice System*, Hong Kong: Hong Kong University Press.

Vagg, J. (1991c) 'Policing Hong Kong', *Policing and Society*, 1 pp 235–47.

Vagg, J. (1994) 'The Correctional Services Department', in Gaylord, M.S. and Traver, H. (eds) *Introduction to the Hong Kong Criminal Justice System*. Hong Kong: Hong Kong University Press.

Vagg, J. (1998) 'Delinquency and Shame: Data from Hong Kong', *British Journal of Criminology*, 38 pp 247–64.

Vagg, J., Bacon-Shone, J, Gray, P., and Lam, D. (1995) *The Social Causes of Juvenile Crime: The Final Report*. Hong Kong: Government Printer.

Waddington, D., Jones, K. and Critcher, C. (1989) *Flashpoints*. London: Routledge.

Walden, J. (1985) *Excellency, Your Gap is Showing*. Hong Kong: Corporate Communications Ltd. Hong Kong.

Walden, J. (1987) *Excellency Your Gap is Growing*. Hong Kong: All Noble Company Limited.

Walton, J.K. (2002) 'The waters of San Sebastian' in Anderson, S. and Tabb, B.S. (eds), *Water, Leisure and Culture: European Historical Perspectives*, Oxford: Berg.

Ward, I. (1991) *The Hong Kong Marine Police 1841–1950*. Hong Kong: Hong Kong University Press.

Welsh, F. (1993) *A History of Hong Kong*. London: Harper Collins.

Wesley-Smith, P. (1983) *Unequal Treaty 1898–1997 China, Great Britain and Hong Kong's New Territories*. Hong Kong: Oxford University Press.

Wesley-Smith, P. (1994) 'Anti-Chinese Legislation in Hong Kong', in Chan, M.K. (ed) *Precarious Balance Hong Kong Between China-and Britain, 1842–1992. Hong Kong Becoming China: the Transition to 1997*. Hong Kong: Hong Kong University Press.

Williams, C. (2002) 'Being Beastly about the Germans: Police, Violence and Nationalism in mid-20th Century Britain', Paper delivered to the British Academy of Comparative Histories of Crime Conference, Keele University, July.

Wilson, D. (2005) 'Traces and Transmissions', in Godfrey, B. and Dunstall, G. (eds) *Crime and Empire*, and Devon: Willan Publishing.

Withers, C.W.J. (2002) 'Constructing the geographical archive', *Area* 34 (3).

Wong, D. (2000) 'Juvenile Crime and Responses to Delinquency in Hong Kong',

International Journal of Offender Therapy and Comparative Criminology 44 (3) pp 279–92.

Wong, E.K.W. (1996) 'An Analysis of Disorder in Hong Kong Society', unpublished MA Dissertation, Centre for the Study of Public Order, University of Leicester.

Wong, N.Y. and S. Lau (1993) 'Effects of Self-Monitoring and Perceived Approval of Delinquent Behavior Among Hong Kong Adolescents', *Journal of Youth and Adolescence*, 22 (2): 191–200.

Wong, Siu-lun (1992) 'Emigration and Stability in Hong Kong', *Asian Survey*, 32 (10) October pp 918–33.

Woodcock, G. (1969), *The British in the Far East*. London, Wiedenfield and Nicholson.

Wu, R. (1996) 'Understanding China' in S. Blyth and I. Wotherspoon (eds) *Hong Kong Remembers*. Hong Kong: Oxford University Press.

Yam, J. (1998) 'Intervention True to Guiding Policy', *South China Morning Post*, 24 August.

Young, J. (2002) 'Critical criminology in the Twenty-First Century' in Carrington, K. and Hogg, R. (eds) *Critical Criminology*. Devon. Willan Publishing.

Young, P. (2005) 'The Use of National Crime Statistics in Comparative Research' in Sheptycki, J. and Wardak, A. (eds) *Transnational and Comparative Criminology*. London: Glasshouse Press.

Youth Commission (1991) *Statistical Profile of Youth in Hong Kong*. Hong Kong.

YWCA Central and Sheung Wan District Outreach Teams (1986a) *The Pattern of Participation in Billiard Rooms of Youth in Central and Sheung Wan District*. Hong Kong: YWCA.

YWCA Ngau Tau Kok Outreaching Team (1986b) *Sex Knowledge, Behaviour and Attitudes of Outreaching Youth: A Research Report*. Hong Kong: YWCA.

YWCA Outreaching Teams (1986c) *The Stealing Behaviour of Youth in Hong Kong: A Research Report*. Hong Kong: YWCA.

YWCA Western District Outreaching Team (1986d) *The Effect of the Establishment of Video Game Centres on Youth*. Hong Kong: YWCA.

Yu Feng (1998) 'Chronicle of a City' trans. Patterson, D. in Cheung, P.Y. (ed) *Hong Kong Collage: Contemporary Stories and Writing*. Hong Kong: Oxford University Press.

Index